DRY GOODS, COTTON AND CANE:

250 YEARS OF JEWISH LIFE, BUSINESS AND AGRICULTURE IN POINTE COUPÉE PARISH, LOUISIANA

BRIAN J. COSTELLO

AND

CAROL MILLS-NICHOL

With contributions by
Teri D. Tillman

Copyright © 2022, Brian Costello and Carol Mills-Nichol

ALL RIGHTS RESERVED.
No part of this publication may be reproduced, stored in a
retrieval system or transmitted in any form or by any
means whatsoever, whether electronic, mechanical,
magnetic recording, or photocopying, without the
prior written approval of the Copyright holder
or Publisher, excepting brief quotations
for inclusion in book reviews.

Published by:

Janaway Publishing, Inc.
732 Kelsey Ct.
Santa Maria, California 93454
(805) 925-1952
www.janawaygenealogy.com

2022

Front Cover: The Weil Family: Alphonse and Rosina Dreyfus Weil and their children, Flora and Simon. Photo courtesy of the Weil-Dreyfus Family

Back Cover: Burning cane stalks at Alma Plantation. Photo by Richard Sexton © 2011

Library of Congress Control Number: 2022939764
ISBN: 978-1-59641-468-6

Made in the United States of America

In memory of all of the Jewish individuals and families who made their homes and found their livelihoods in Pointe Coupée Parish, Louisiana, sharing in the joys and sorrows of their Gentile neighbors and friends. May this work be an inspiration for strengthening the bonds of the community and promoting unity among the Abrahamic peoples.

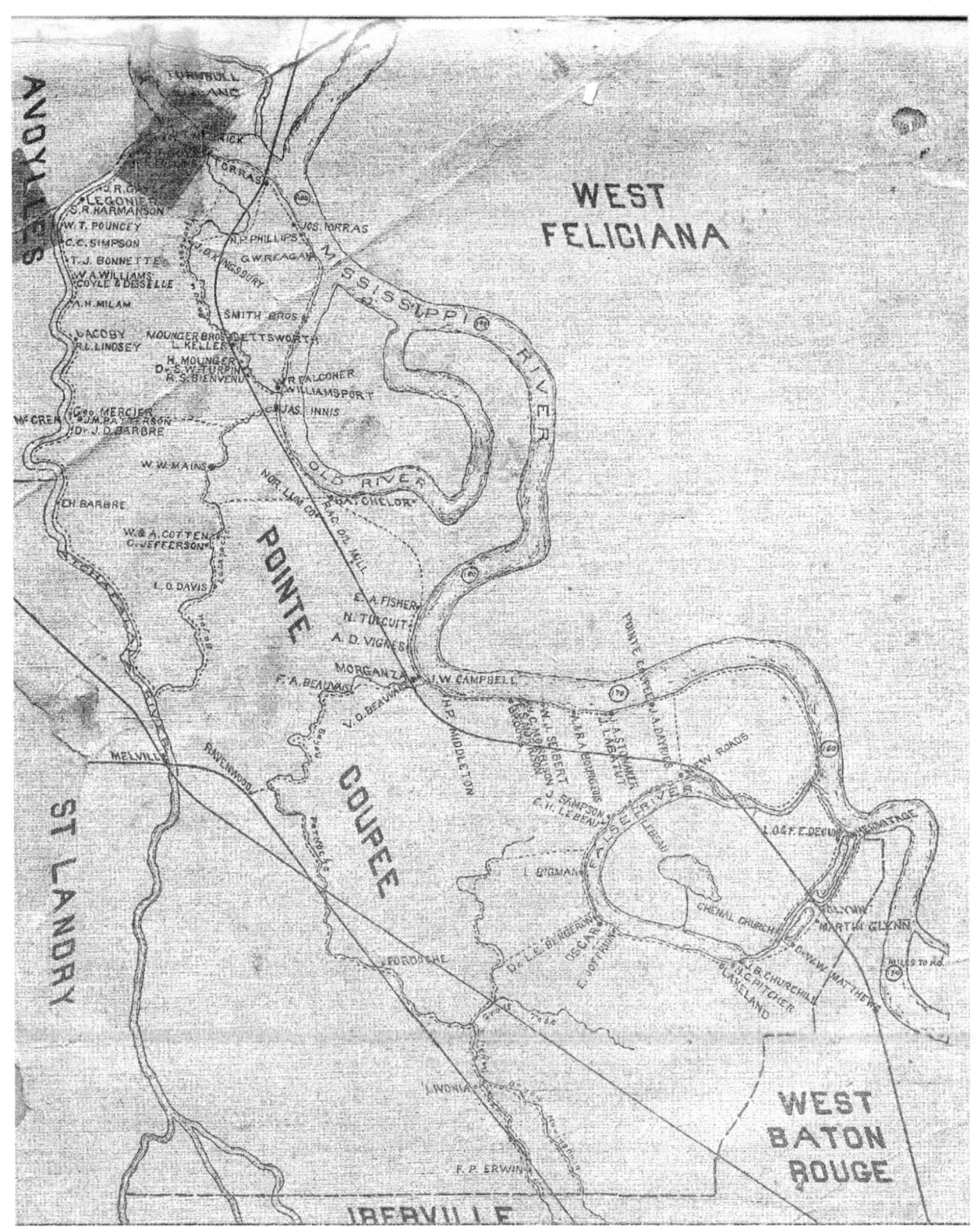

Map of Pointe Coupée Parish from *Beautiful Pointe Coupée and Her Prominent Citizens* by J.I. Sanford, 1906.

TABLE OF CONTENTS

Table of Illustrations vii

Abbreviations x

Foreword xi

Acknowledgements xv

Introduction 1

Chapter 1
       Pointe Coupée Road 21

Chapter 2
       Waterloo Area 39

Chapter 3
       New Roads 67

Chapter 4
       New Roads Branch and Chain Stores 115

Chapter 5
       False River Road and Oscar Crossing 121

Chapter 6
       Lower Chenal of False River 137

Chapter 7
       Island of False River 191

Chapter 8
       Bayou Grosse Tête 197

Chapter 9
       Bayou Fordoche and Blanks 231

Chapter 10
       Bayou Maringouin 237

Chapter 11
- Morganza 243

Chapter 12
- Raccourci – Old River 257

Chapter 13
- Bayou Latenache 295

Chapter 14
- Bayou Lettsworth 303

Chapter 15
- Red River Landing – Torras – Three Rivers 311

Chapter 16
- Atchafalaya River 329

Advertisers' Corner 337

Bibliography 345

Index 353

TABLE OF ILLUSTRATIONS

Contemporary map of Pointe Coupée Parish communities xvi

Theo Dreyfus Store at Livonia during the 1912 flood 20

Jacques Goudchaux signature in 1855 application for citizenship 30

Benjamin Weil signature in Hirschberger succession dated 1850 31

Bill from B. Teutsch's Pointe Coupée Road store dated 20 November 1900 37

1911 *Pointe Coupée Banner* Advertisement for Markle's Showboat, the Golden Rod 38

Signature of Meyer Michel in Hirschberger succession dated 1851 42

Dr. de Blainville's bill for medical treatment of Joseph Hirschberger dated 26 October 1849 45

Promissory note signed by Michel Weil to Goldsmith & Haber dated 1861 54

Tintype of 1848 Courthouse at New Roads 65

Mississippi River Landings in the 1880s 66

Signature page of marriage record of Maurice Fortlouis and Aurore Porche dated 1834 70

Simon Loeb & Co.'s Civil War era currency 73

Photo of Jacques Goudchaux - Mobile Merchant 81

Henri Cerf's $20 Confederate bank note 84

The Demouy Building 90

Jacob Moonshine Letterhead 94

Advertisement for Joe Gottlieb Insurance Agency dated 30 April 1904 98

Advertisement for Mrs. Mayer Cahen's Millinery store dated 18 October 1919 104

Anna Bondy – Mayer Cahen Tombstone 105

Kassel & Stern store at New Roads 109

Advertisement for Koenig & Brown dated 27 April 1889 112

Grossman-Weinfeld Millinery Accounting Office, New Orleans, 1917 115

Weill's Department Store, New Roads, 1960 118

Signature of Isaac Keim 122

Ben Gerson's Store at River Lake during 1890 flood 124

Isaac Bigman's check to Bernard Teutsch to pay for one mule 129

Isaac Bigman's Oscar, Louisiana, Letterhead 130

Isaac Bigman General Store and House at Oscar, Louisiana 131

Isaac Bigman's letter to Bernard Teutsch dated 26 February 1904 136

Mrs. J.S. Baum's Letterhead dated 1912 145

Signature of Amélie Weil 153

Mrs. R. Kern Letterhead 153

Mr. A. Kern Letterhead 155

Cerf Wolff's "Alma Store" Letterhead 157

Tax Payment of R. Kern to Hermann & Grossman dated 14 January 1886 165

Lazard Wolff Letterhead 181

E. Kaufman Letterhead 188

Signature of J.M. Fortlouis, the younger, in act dated 16 January 1882 193

Photo of Simon Gumbel 196

Photo of Alphonse Weil and his elder brother Félix Weil ca. 1912 196

Photo of Marie Angela Decuir 199

Trunk belonging to Mr. and Mrs. C.A. Gumble (*sic*) 200

Photos of Theodore and Blondina Wolff Dreyfus 210

Dreyfus & Wolff store Letterhead 211

Theodore Dreyfus store at Livonia, Pointe Coupée Parish 212

Theo Dreyfus store wrapping paper 212

Joseph Wolff's "Grand Leader" store at Musson, Iberville Parish 215

Photo of Alphonse Weil and Rosina Dreyfus 222

Alphonse Weil and Rosina Dreyfus Wedding Album dated 1914 224

Signature pages from Weil – Dreyfus Wedding Album dated 1914 224

Photo of Simon Dreyfus Weil and his wife, Ray Weill Weil 225

Dreyfus Sugar advertisement 229

1908 Theodore Dreyfus Letterhead 229

Weil-Dreyfus Wedding Album and Honeymoon Trip Notes 230

Signature of Isaac Levi and Hortense Dreyfuss Levi dated 17 August 1876 232

Stores at Fordoche, Louisiana, ca. 1910 236

Signature of August Keller dated 10 May 1882 on promissory note to self for $500 238

Former location of Isidore Srulovitz/Loeb store located at right during 1912 flood 248

Former Loeb's Department store, "Mr. P." Loeb proprietor, at Morganza 250

M. H. Srulovitz Letterhead 251

Detail of 1921 Sanborn Map for Morganza showing G. Srulovitz Movie House 255

Evacuation train at Morganza during 1912 flood 256

Notice in *Pointe Coupée Banner* dated 5 September 1885 from Abraham & Weil 275

Pointe Coupée Banner advertisement for Abraham & Weil "Cheap Cash Store" 275

M. J. Hochfelder Letterhead 287

Photos of Simon Bloch and Fanny Kaufman 296

Max Srulovitz general store during 1912 flood 301

1857 Pointe Coupée Parish Regulations and Fees for Merchants and Peddlers 302

Sandman-Gunst Letterhead 316

Leopold and Sylvain Sommer's "Leader Store" Letterhead 318

Interior of "The Leader" Store, L. and S. Sommer, proprietors 319

Photo of Marguérite Kahn, wife of Sylvain Sommer 319

Photo of Leopold "Lep" Sommer 320

Lep Sommer's "Leader Store" during 1912 flood 321

Thomas Goldman Letterhead 323

Photos of David S. and Daniel E. Mann 328

Signatures of Mathilde Dreyfus Benedick and Jacob Benedick 330

Mark and Brand of Olivia Benedick dated 1850 331

Tatar Bros. Letterhead 335

Advertisers' Corner 337- 343

Parish of Pointe Coupée 50 cent bill issued March 24, 1862 344

1970s photo of New Roads Hardware Store with Vee's 5 & 10 in background 344

1895 Rand-McNally Map of Pointe Coupée Parish 352

ABBREVIATIONS

Diocese of Baton Rouge – Catholic Church Records

PCP – St. Mary Church, est. 1865. Earlier St. Francis of Pointe Coupée, est. 1728
IMCL - Immaculate Conception, Lakeland, est. 1857
SJBR - St. Joseph of Baton Rouge, est. 1793
SAM – St. Anne, Morganza, est. 1872, previously, Our Lady of Seven Dolors, Raccourci

Archdiocese of New Orleans Sacramental Records

SLC – St. Louis Cathedral, New Orleans
SMNO - St. Marie, New Orleans (Chartres Street)

Southwest Louisiana Records

SWLR - Southwest Louisiana Records compiled by the Rev. Donald Hébert (CD-ROM-Database).

Abbreviations Used in our Index

PCP = Pointe Coupée Parish
EFP = East Feliciana Parish
WFP = West Feliciana Parish
EBR = East Baton Rouge Parish
WBR = West Baton Rouge Parish
h/o = husband of
w/o = wife of
s/o = son of
d/o = daughter of
Note: All family surnames included in the index are in bold print.
Also note: Unless otherwise indicated, all illustrations used in this book are housed at the Pointe Coupée Parish Library Historic Materials Collection (PCPL, HMC).

FOREWORD

By Carol Mills-Nichol

When first asked to sign on to this project, it was simply as an editor, but as the book progressed, I took more of an active part in the research. While Brian Costello had all the Civil and Church records at his fingertips, as an eleventh generation Pointe Coupéean, I had concentrated in a previous book on the study of the Jewish residents of neighboring Avoyelles, my home parish. I later expanded my study as the author of another genealogical work covering the Jews who had immigrated from the Bas-Rhin, France, to all parts of Louisiana. I was therefore, familiar with many of the French Jewish families that had passed through or lived in Pointe Coupée Parish. They were amongst the earliest to arrive in the area, attracted, to the existing Gallic culture and language, so I was able to expand on the genealogical information offered in the book.

Jews from northeastern France (aka Alsace-Lorraine), including the Bas-Rhin, Haut-Rhin, Moselle and Meurthe-et-Moselle, as well as their kinsmen and neighbors in southern Germany, often referred to as "Bavaria," but in this work as coming from the Rheinpfalz, Germany, began their trek to America in the 1830s through the beginning of the American Civil War. These Jews from Central and Eastern Europe are referred to as Ashkenazi Jews, who make up approximately 80% of the Jewish people. Ashkenazi Jews had many reasons to want to leave their homelands. They were restricted to certain occupations, such as junk and second-hand merchants, cattle and horse dealer, or itinerant peddlers and were prohibited from exercising professions such as physician, lawyer or professor. Moreover, in many small towns and villages in Europe the number of Jews allowed to live in any town was regulated by local law. In some places, only the eldest son in a family was allowed to marry and remain in his home town. His brothers were forced to travel elsewhere to marry and raise a family or wait until an elderly male Jew died in order to be able to remain. Many of those young men had no choice but to immigrate.

The final defeat of Napoleon in 1815 brought about the dissolution of the Holy Roman Empire, and the rise of the thirty-nine states of the German Confederation, and the Austrian Empire. Political unrest wracked the continent and culminated with the Revolutions of 1830 and 1848 in France, which spread throughout Central Europe. The continuous political upheaval resulted in high unemployment and failing harvests. French and German Jews, who had always been second-class citizens, even after the Declaration of Rights of Man in 1789, were especially hard hit. For many, immigration was the only way to escape the turmoil and the possibility of having to serve as cannon fodder in one of the endless wars. While gentiles were allowed to pay to provide substitutes to fight in their place, thus avoiding conscription, Jews were not afforded that privilege. For many, the arduous six-week or more sailing voyage to reach America was well worth the risk to reach a land where they could prosper without the onerous restrictions placed on their lives.

The early Ashkenazi arrivals from France and Germany had everything in common with one another, had often intermarried in Europe, and would do so also in America. The border between northern France and southern Germany, was to the inhabitants of this region, only a political invention which did not reflect the reality on the ground. Alsatians, Jews and non-Jews alike, spoke a dialect called Elsasser-Deutsch, which was an amalgam of German and Yiddish words, and easily understandable to all on both sides of the border. Yiddish, of course, was also a common language to both French and German Jews. After the institution of public education subsequent to the French Revolution in 1789, French Jews also learned to speak, read and write French to varying degrees, which naturally attracted them to Louisiana where French, German and Spanish, often took precedence over English into the twentieth century.

After the American Civil War, Prussian, Austrian and Polish Jews began to immigrate to Louisiana due to the continuing political strife in Central Europe, with its ever-shift boundaries, and continual wars of aggression which culminated in the 1870-1871 Franco-Prussian War. This second wave of mostly Eastern European Jews were less "modern," more orthodox in their religious views, many dressing in the old Eastern European way, a "shock" to the sensibilities of the now assimilated and mostly upwardly-mobile Louisiana Jews. Although Yiddish speakers, these newly-arrived Ashkenazi Jews were only slowly and sometimes reluctantly assimilated into the fabric of the established Louisiana French and Bavarian Jewry.

A third wave of Jewish immigrants, victims of the horrors of the Russian pogroms, a prelude to the coming revolution, arrived at the end of the nineteenth and beginning of the twentieth centuries. Although spread throughout America, some settled in Louisiana, where, just as in the case of the second wave, they were eventually assimilated, albeit sometimes reluctantly, into the existing community of their co-religionists.

Tracing the past lives of our Jewish brethren in their native homelands can be quite complicated. Unlike Christians, who have used fixed surnames for generations back into the Middle Ages and before, Jews historically used a different system, combining their first or given name with the given name of their father linked by "ben" in the case of a male, or "bat" in the case of a female. In the late eighteenth and early nineteenth century, European rulers decided to put a stop to that practice because it made the ability of the government to be able to properly identify its inhabitants and the family groups to which they belonged, too difficult, especially for the purposes of conscription.

Consequently, Jews living in the Austro-Hungarian Empire were obliged to take a fixed surname in 1787. Napoleon, who by 1808, had conquered most of Central Europe, issued a decree dated 20 July 1808 that by the third trimester of that year every Jew had to report to his local town hall to officially adopt a fixed surname, or to report one that had previously been in use. These 1808 name-adoption lists became the basis, and the most important tool, to be able to identify Jewish family units, back into the eighteenth centuries and before. This is not to say that certain surnames amongst the Ashkenazi Jews had not been used previously. Perhaps one-fifth of all Jews reporting had already used a surname. The "Cohen/Kahn" surname designating the priestly / rabbinical class all descending from the first high priest, Aaron, within the tribe of the Levites had long been in use, as well as the surname "Levy/Levi and its anagram Veil (Weil), used by others of the same tribe, the descendants of Levi, the son of Jacob.

Fortunately, many of the 1808 and later Jewish name adoption lists were preserved in the civil records of the towns in which they were recorded. These lists included the previous name of the individual and the new adopted name of the head of the household, the previous names of his wife and children, as well as their new given and surnames, and occasionally even their birth dates. For example: the 1808 Name Adoption list for Niederkirchen/Westpfalz, listed family #11, this co-author's maternal fourth-great-grandparents: Löb Abraham, a trader who took the name Leopold Dahlsheimer, his wife, Frommette, who became Veronique Dahlsheimer, and his children: David Löb, who became David Dahlsheimer; Zortel Löb who became Sara Dahlsheimer; Schenle Löb, who became Jeane Dahlsheimer; Olt Löb, who became Esther Dahlsheimer; and this co-authors third-great-grandmother, Mendele Löb, who became Martha Dahlsheimer. (Note: Martha Dahlsheimer, the widow of Michael Suess, became Minette Thalsheimer when she moved over the border into Lembach, Bas-Rhin, France, illustrating the difficulty we have in being able to identify Jewish relatives due to their propensity to alter their names at whim, or to have them changed by civil authorities due to differences in the prevailing spoken language in any given place.)

These name adoption lists coupled with the development of the preservation of civil records throughout Europe, became a tremendous boon to the genealogist, in search of non-Christian ancestors. Early nineteenth century civil records for Jews often recorded their pre-1808 names, as well as their post 1808 names for clarity. Other records kept by the synagogues often bring clues to the identity of family members, including the circumcision records for male members of a family, confirmation "bar mitzvah" records, as well as marriage contracts, "ketoubas," originally kept in the place of worship.

Because pre-1808 Jewish names were a combination of two first or given names, when fixed family names were adopted, some families chose to have a given name serves as their family name. Names including but not limited to Herz, Loeb, Feist, Godchot, Abraham, Isaac, Joseph, Wolf, Hirsch, Cerf, and Israël, became surnames as well as given names. Other families adopted the surnames of their non-Jewish neighbors, such as Schwartz, Weiss, Picard, or even the names of an occupation such as "Kauffman," "Schumacher," "Hoffman," or "Schneider." In one unlucky town in the Bas-Rhin, the Mayor of Kuttolsheim assigned random surnames to those who didn't already use one, including: Landerot, Longini, Frigol, Norphuro, Perinot, Pioso, Philantropos, and a name which would become familiar to Louisianians: Pompet, which was often spelled "Bombet" here.

Since Judaism is not only a religion, but an ethnicity, the only way to actually be sure if a person has Jewish ancestry is through a DNA test, not through their name, or even through an inspection of their family tree. In other words, "people are Jewish, names are not." There are, for example more Christian Schwartzes than there are Jewish ones, more Christian Kaufmans and Hoffmans than Jewish ones. This is virtually the same with almost all surnames shared by Jews and Christians alike. In early Pointe Coupée Parish a certain Friedrich Anton Weinberg was thought to be a Jew, but investigation into his family members revealed that they were, and had been Catholic. Moreover, it was rare in the early and middle nineteenth century to find a Jew with two given names, especially two non-Hebrew names.

Sephardic Jews, who make up approximately 20% of the world's Jewish population, had adopted fixed surnames as early as the tenth and eleventh centuries, especially in Spain and Portugal, where many had lived for centuries as "conversos," that is: secretly Jewish in their own homes, but Catholic in the public square. This fiction was enhanced by their adoption of common Spanish and Portuguese surnames which did not call into attention their true ethnicity, but which did not ultimately prevent their expulsion from the Iberian Peninsula during the Inquisition. These Sephardic Jews followed a different route to America from their original homes in Spain, Portugal, North Africa and the Middle East. Expelled from the Iberian Peninsula in the fifteenth century, Sephardic Jews made their first homes in England, the Netherlands, and in certain southern French cities, especially Bordeaux, where many of them were confectioners and bakers.

From Europe, they made their way in the nineteenth century to the French and Dutch islands of the Caribbean, and finally to the Carolinas in America, and to a lesser degree into Louisiana. Their surnames are often indistinguishable from other Spanish and Portuguese names used by non-Jews, many ending in a vowel such as Cardozo, Monsanto, Britto, Navarro, De Castro, but also more familiar names such as Lopez, Henriqués, Bensadon, Toledano, Cárdenas, Touro, and Joseph.

The Jews, both Ashkenazi, and to a smaller extent, Sephardic who settled in Pointe Coupée Parish, came from all three waves of immigrants who fled to America in the nineteenth century. From the earliest Sephardic Jews including the Monsantos, Isaac Fastio and Manuel de Britto from the Netherlands, via Curaçao, to the Ashkenazi Michels, Kaufmanns, Levys, and Picards from France and Germany in the 1850s, through to the Tatarskys, Herzogs and Finkelsteins who came from Poland and the Russian Empire in the 1880s and beyond, all spent time in Pointe Coupée Parish. Some stayed for a lifetime. Many, however did not. Like their co-religionists from other Louisiana parishes, they either relocated to New Orleans or Baton Rouge, or went north to the larger cities like Chicago, or New York.

Only 10 of the sixty-four parishes in Louisiana had one or more synagogues, while only 18 of the sixty-four parishes had a Jewish burial ground. Pointe Coupée Parish had neither. Yet hundreds of Jewish immigrants made their homes in the parish, until the boll weevil and consistent flooding of the Mississippi and Atchafalaya Rivers made life as they had known it, impossible. Pointe Coupée Jews travelled to Baton Rouge or to New Orleans to bury their dead. Rabbis made trips from those cities as well as from Woodville, Mississippi to perform weddings of the Jewish faithful. Jewish men and women often joined the choirs of local Christian Churches, offered their musical services for gentile weddings and other celebrations, and participated in the many fraternal organizations on equal footing with non-Jewish members. Jews even participated in Mardi Gras festivities. Anti-Semitism, which cropped up to a small degree in other parishes during the turbulent years of Reconstruction, rarely was an issue in Pointe Coupée.

While we have tried to track down and identify every Jewish person, from the many peddlers who passed through, to the plantation owners who thrived on the shores of the Mississippi, we have not, in some cases, succeeded, at least, not yet. Genealogical research is always a work in progress, so we have attempted to leave as many clues as possible, so that future researchers may finally tear down the brick walls that have prevented certain identifications. We have, however, travelled further than the basic facts, by examining all the legal traces left by these Pointe Coupéeans, their business triumphs and failures, their store inventories, their legal interactions with suppliers, and with one another. By adding these details, we hope to have presented a snapshot of what it was like to be a merchant, a farmer, even a peddler, in a rural Louisiana parish in centuries past, when the rise and fall of the Mississippi determined a person's success or failure in life. This is a tribute to the Jewish men and women who, coming from a very different world in Europe, persevered during some of the hardest times in Louisiana, to contribute to the successes of their adopted country.

Carol Mills-Nichol

1 May 2022

ACKNOWLEDGEMENTS

I owe unlimited gratitude in this specific endeavor to Carol Mills-Nichol. A kinswoman of colonial French lineage in Pointe Coupée and its daughter parish of Avoyelles, Louisiana, she, more than any other, has shared my long-standing interest in and desire to document the lives of the Jewish individuals and families who chose Pointe Coupée Parish for their home and livelihood over the course of two and a half centuries. Without Carol's generous contribution of European genealogical and historical sources, her skillful weaving of her research into mine, and her patient editing and compilation which has resulted in this work, *Dry Goods, Cotton and Cane* would not have become a reality. To her, and devoted husband, John "Jack" Nichol, and her colleague Teri Downs Tillman, a talented genealogist from Natchez, Mississippi, I owe everlasting gratitude.

My passion for "all that is old" began, literally, at the knee of my elders on False River, near New Roads, Pointe Coupée Parish, which continues to be my place of residency and work. To my paternal grandmother, Séverine Inez Aguillard Costello, who, incidentally, purchased her wedding trousseau at the iconic Theo Dreyfus store in Livonia, Louisiana, in early 1931, and to my grandfather Joseph Costello, Sr., who persuaded her to do so, I owe my love for the culture, written and oral histories of all people of Pointe Coupée. Others who have passed on and were of immense support to me and my mission as historian, genealogist and author include beloved colleagues Olinde "Toppy" Smith Haag and husband, Dr. William "Bill Haag, Glenn C. Morgan, Joyce Major Morgan, Murray G. LeBeau, Pointe Coupée Parish Clerk of Court I.G. Olinde, Capt. Mark M. Boatner III, U.S.A. (Ret.), and Ronnie Virgets. I am truly blessed to have known the late Mr. Simon Dreyfus Weil, his vivacious wife, Mrs. Ray Weill Weil, and her esteemed brother, Mr. Gus Weill, and to have been the recipient of their support, encouragement and hospitality, and their selfless sharing of wisdom, kindness and love beyond limits for me and all of our community.

I am indebted to Pointe Coupée Parish Library Director Melissa Kraemer Hymel, Library Board President Vivian Wylene Hurst, Tiffany Sneed Brue, and all members of the library staff who have patiently endured my enthusiastic outbursts regarding new "finds" in the history of Pointe Coupée through the years. Former Pointe Coupée Parish Chief Deputy Clerk of Court Jacqueline Major Saizan and colleague Julie Eshelman-Lee have my lasting thanksgiving for sharing their own vast resources and access to others. Gratitude is likewise extended to Pointe Coupée Parish Clerk of Court Lanell Swindler Landry and devoted staff who allowed me continued access to the parish's priceless archival resources, both on and off-site, during the trying years of the Covid-19 pandemic and attendant restrictions.

Certainly not least, I am most thankful for the support, generosity and friendship of Dinah Emelie Weil, Jonathan Weil, Mr. Sidney and Mrs. Ann Dreyfus, Mrs. Rachelle Dreyfus Hirsch, and Mae Blanchard Gaspard during the trying yet grace-filled year of 2022.

Merci beaucoup, and Aaron's blessing for all –

Brian J. Costello

1er mai 2022

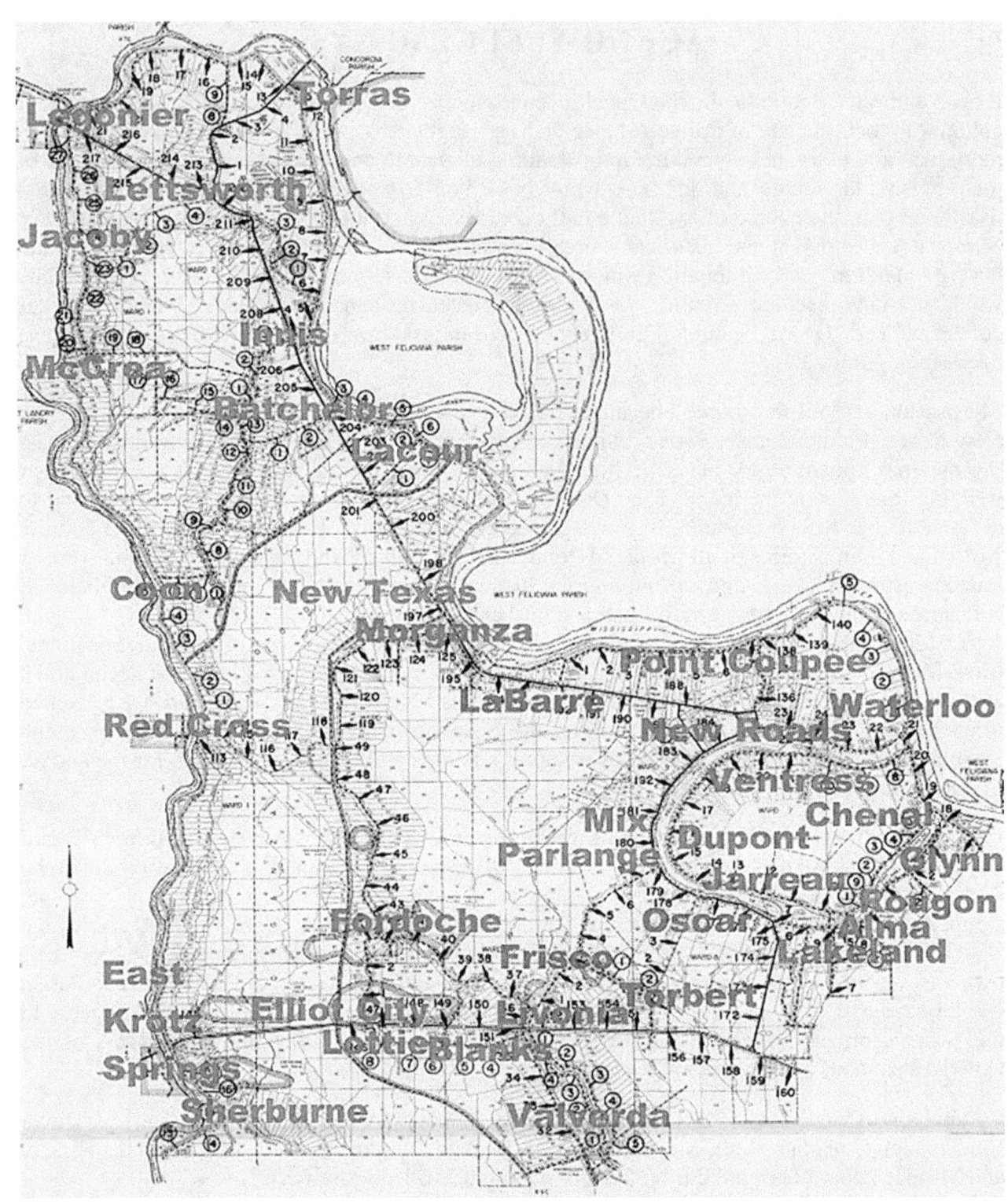

Major Towns in Pointe Coupée Parish @ www.wikipedia.com.

INTRODUCTION

CRÉOLE MESOPOTAMIA: A LAND OF PROMISE

Pointe Coupée Parish, Louisiana owes its existence to the great Mississippi River, its tributaries and distributaries which in pre-historic times, and the modern era during times of levee failure, has deposited rich alluvial soil, rendering the area ones of the most fertile on the continent. From its traditional identity as the "overlapping" point of the cultivation of cotton and sugar cane, the parish was, by the late 20th century, the producer of eight major crops.

With the Mississippi River on the east, Atchafalaya on the west, and mouth of the Red on the north, Pointe Coupée Parish may be likened to a "*Créole* Mesopotamia," a land between rivers populated primarily by French and African-Americans, but into whose genetic mix and culture the Native American, Spanish, English, German, Irish, Sicilian, mainland Italian and Oriental peoples have all made important and lasting contributions.

As early as the French Colonial period, individuals and families of the Jewish ethnicity, faith, culture and traditions made their homes in Pointe Coupée Parish as peddlers, merchants, jewelers, financiers, educators, warehouse keepers, cotton gin operators, livery stable owners, and livestock dealers. Amidst and in fellowship with their Gentile neighbors, they prospered during the "good" years of secure levees and parasite-free fields, and likewise suffered, persevered, or joined them during the bad times in the exodus from the parish to New Orleans, Baton Rouge, and other locations across the country.

Several of the most prominent businessmen and financiers in New Orleans and the nation began their careers behind wooden counters in the towns and villages of Pointe Coupée, plying the intermittently dusty or muddy streets and roads in order to provide goods to outlying residents who had little or no access to New Roads. In addition, they often oversaw the planting, cultivation and harvest of "the three Cs" – cotton, cane and corn, while sandbagging and guarding levees quivering from the stress of swollen rivers.

Pointe Coupée Parish was, in the 19th century, a microcosm of the state of Louisiana, with a densely settled, principally French and Catholic southeastern section, and a more widely populated, largely English, Irish and German Protestant northern and western sections. So clear-cut were the cultural distinctions, principally because of the predominance of the French language and local Créole dialect in the southeastern part of the parish, that residents of the south often referred to the parish as *les deux Pointe Coupée* or "the two Pointe Coupées: *Part en Bas* (the "lower" or southern part), and *Part en Haut* (the upper or northern part).

The "*Créoles de couleur*," children of white men and African-American or ethnically blended women, the latter including Franco-, Hispano-, Germanic- and Italo-African females, constituted another network of Créole settlers. Their relationships were maintained variously, before, during, or after legal marriage of one or both parties to other persons, and likewise with neither one nor both parties ever having legally married anyone.

The 1868 Louisiana Constitution lifted the ban on "interracial" marriages, and between that time and the institution of Democrat reactionary, "Jim Crow" legislation 30 years later, no fewer than a dozen marriages took place in Pointe Coupée, with court-issued licenses and in Catholic ceremonies, between white man and women of African or mixed ancestry. The husbands in the above-mentioned marriages were generally fairly recent arrivals from mainland France and Italy, but their numbers also included men of established Pointe Coupée families as well. Most of the European Jewish merchants, peddlers and clerks who settled in Pointe Coupée were bachelors, and those who eventually married were frequently well into their middle age. Some of their number, as was the case with other non-Jewish men in the area, had children out of wedlock predominantly with women of color. While the particular circumstances of such unions cannot be fully determined, it is supposed that at least some were unions in all but the law, and that the women and children were provided for by their partners.

The settlement patterns of the Jewish people mirrored that of the native population, to wit: initially along the *Cote de la Pointe Coupée* (Pointe Coupée Coast along the Mississippi River, i.e., Pointe Coupée Road), as far south as Hermitage and north to just above Morganza. It continued around the outside or western bend of *la Fausse Rivière* (False River), including the towns of Waterloo and Cook's Landing on the Mississippi, spreading along the *Chenal Supérieur* (Upper Chenal of False River, aka the *Quartier de Poulailler* or Chicken-house Neighborhood), into the parish seat and principal town of *Chemin Neuf* or *Ste. Marie* (New Road, originally in the plural, aka St. Mary's), down False River Road and continuing on the south bank of the *Chenal Inférieur* (Lower Chenal), terminating at Hermitage Landing on the Mississippi.

In the 1830s, clearing and cultivation began on Bayou Grosse Tête and spread to Bayous Fordoche and Maringouin in the next decade. Improved access to False River to the north came in the opening in 1842 of *la Manche Parlange* or Parlange Lane, built by enslaved labor through the plantation of that name, and reaching Bayou Grosse Tête at what was then the "Upper Grosse Tête Bridge" at latter-day Frisco, Louisiana. The place name Grosse Tête or "big head," in English initially applied to the area just to the west of Frisco, where a great head of waters is formed by the confluence of smaller bayous with Bayou Grosse Tête. Eventually the name was extended to the entire territory, as well as to a post office and town of the same name in neighboring Iberville Parish.

In the 1840s, the settlement of Pointe Coupée Parish advanced northward, from Raccourci-Old River on the southeast to Red River Landing, in the extreme northeastern part of the parish, and west and south along the Lower Old (before 1831, the main channel of the Mississippi) and Atchafalaya Rivers, and onto nearby Bayous Latenache and Lettsworth.

Agricultural production and commerce came almost to a complete halt in Pointe Coupée Parish during the Civil War, with the occupation of and "requisitioning" by the warring Confederate and Federal military forces. The parish was the site of continued movement and frequent skirmishes between the armies, particularly around Morganza, and along the Pointe Coupee, False River, Lower Chenal, Bayou Fordoche and Bayou Grosse Tête Roads. The proximity to the Confederate citadel of Port Hudson, across the Mississippi from Hermitage, created chaos in Lower Pointe Coupee, and many of the enslaved of the area seized the opportunity to escape to freedom in the summer of 1863.

Confederate forces cut the levees at Morganza and Hermitage in order to flood the area in a futile attempt to halt Federal movement on the west bank of the Mississippi. The neglected state of these levees resulted in years of crevasses and inland flooding in 1865, 1866, 1867, 1869 and

1874. The 1867 flood proved catastrophic to the Bayou Grosse Tête and Bayou Maringouin areas. Exacerbating matters was a severe yellow fever epidemic in 1867, which claimed victims likely in the hundreds.

Postbellum, large-scale cotton and sugar cane producers received cash advances directly from New Orleans banks and commercial houses by pledging their potential harvests, while share croppers and local small-time farmers pledged their potential crops to local merchants, in order to procure cash advances, merchandise and supplies over the course of the growing season. A majority of the merchants, peddlers, livestock dealers and other businessmen, as well as a few of the planters, who established themselves in Pointe Coupée following the Civil War were, as their predecessors had been in the decade prior the war, principally enterprising Jewish individuals and firms, originally from Alsace, France, Bavaria, and other central European countries.

Sufficient information regarding peddlers is particularly elusive, owing to their peripatetic nature and usually brief sojourns in any particular locality. Two such men, likely Jewish, were "S. Bernasky" and "J. Singer." Bernasky paid $40 for a Parish License to operate as a peddler by wagon in 1872, according to the Pointe Coupée Parish Police Jury Minutes of that year. Singer obtained a License from the Jury for $5 to operate as a peddler in 1881, which was recorded in an 1882 listing of Parish Licenses in the *Pointe Coupée Banner*. A $5 License fee had been set by the Police Jury in 1872 for the occupation of "Dealer in Cakes," likely meaning a cookie vendor.

There were probably 200 Jewish individuals and families who located in Pointe Coupée Parish over the course of about 150 years. Most maintained their residency in the parish for only a few years, before moving on to more stable economic opportunities in New Orleans or elsewhere, many of them driven out by any one or more of the eighteen major floods of the Mississippi and Atchafalaya Rivers that ravaged the parish between 1780 and 1927. Some of them remained in the area for generations, however, coping with the vicissitudes of floods, hurricanes, crop failures, epidemics and the resultant economic recessions, with and in the midst of their Gentile neighbors, employees and tenants.

Members of the Sephardic Monsanto family, including Isaac (b. ca. 1729), who died in May 1778 on the property of François Allain, and his partner and fellow merchant, Isaac Henriqués Fastio, who lived with False River area merchant Jean-Baptiste Nicollet for almost three decades, trafficked in indigo, other farm products, as well as enslaved African Americans. They were the earliest-known Jewish settlers in the area.

However, most of the Jewish immigrants of the early and mid-nineteenth century who established homes in Pointe Coupée Parish were of the Ashkenazi tradition which had its origins along the Rhine River, particularly in Rhenish Bavaria (southern Germany) and in both the Bas-Rhin and Haut-Rhin regions of France. In the later 19th and early 20th centuries, the Jewish newcomers, also Ashkenazi, were mainly from the Russian and Austrian Empires and Romania, with Russian-occupied Poland contributing the highest percentage to the Pointe Coupée population.

A concentrated search through the civil records and period correspondence of Pointe Coupée Parish from the colonial period into the 21st century yields evidence of neither a congregation nor a cemetery established among its Jewish citizens. Most Jewish marriages, funerals and interments appear to have taken place in New Orleans or Baton Rouge and, to a lesser extent, in St. Francisville across the Mississippi River. However, some Jewish marriages in Pointe Coupée were conducted at the home of the bride's parents by local justices of the peace or by visiting rabbis, such as Rabbi Simon L. Weil of Woodville, Wilkinson Co., Mississippi.

LANGUAGE

Spanish Governor Antonio de Ulloa forbade the Acadian exiles, expelled by the British from *Acadie* (Nova Scotia) in 1755, to settle in Pointe Coupée and other nearby communities, owing to his desire to have them find new homes in Bayous Lafourche and Teche in southernmost Louisiana. For that reason, the French families of Pointe Coupée Parish were almost exclusively immigrants who came directly from France and other French-speaking countries and whose descendants would be known as "Créoles," not "Cajuns," the latter a term by which the exiled "Acadians" were known in Louisiana.

The Pointe Coupée Créole dialect arose, logically, as a mutually understandable tongue among the French, who hailed from mainland France, and other Francophone areas, each having their own dialect, and the Africans, who represented many nations. Pointe Coupée Créole, in brief, consists of an archaic French vocabulary and African sentence structure, in which identifiers follow nouns in its most basilectal (further removed from standard French) form. Over the course of the nineteenth century, slight, but usually intelligible differences arose between Créole as spoken on one bank of False River versus the opposite, and between speakers having knowledge of Standard French and those who did not.

Such linguistic variation also existed amongst the languages spoken in Europe and in English as spoken by newcomers to the United States. Dinah Weil of Livonia, whose paternal grandfather was Alphonse Weil and maternal grandfather Leopold Weill, stated that despite the fact the two hailed from towns only five miles apart in Alsace, France, Leopold Weill spoke with more of a German accent than Alphonse Weil.

Standard French, often referred to as "Parisian French" by elderly informants in the late 20th century, was spoken by the educated families of Pointe Coupée Parish well into the 1900s, and its continuity was undoubtedly enhanced by the prominence of Jewish French speakers in the community. Anyone engaged in commerce or agriculture, however, needed knowledge of Créole for day-to-day communication with the larger population. Early home libraries, memoirs and letters attesting to appreciation for and use of standard French rank among 21st century residents' most treasured heirlooms.

Edward Larocque Tinker, in his 1932 work *Les écrits de langue française en Louisiane au XIXe siècle*, (*French Language Writings in 19th Century Louisiana*) devoted considerable attention to the "last" French journal in the city of New Orleans: *La Guêpe*, (*The Wasp*), founded by the Count and Countess de Baroncelli-Javon in 1902. Tinker quoted the Countess, née Gabrielle Franet de Leaumont, as stating (translated): "My newspaper goes everywhere: Romania, Baton-Rouge, Pointe Coupée, New Roads and France. President [Gaston] Doumergue receives my newspaper and reads it."

Decades of field research in and compilation and publication of Pointe Coupee Créole by Dr. Thomas A. Klinger, colleagues and students around the turn of the 20th-21st centuries was invaluable in historical and sociological documentation as well as linguistic preservation. Particularly telling of Gentile – Jewish relations and perspectives was the statement made by an elderly African American man, native of the Island of False River, in 1990 (translated from the informant's original Créole):

> If the Jew goes among [other Jews] he speaks, he has a Jewish language. Now, if he goes to live among Americans for [some] years, that fellow will speak American; you will not know he is Jewish or otherwise, unless you find that out (Klingler, Thomas A. *If I Could Turn my tongue like that: The Creole Language of Pointe Coupée Parish, Louisiana. Baton Rouge*: Louisiana State University Press, 2003).

The informant apparently defined a Jewish person not by "race," or even by "religion," but by language, and likely was referring to Yiddish. Since the early and middle 19th century Jewish settlers in Pointe Coupée Parish hailed primarily from Western Europe and, in particular from France, it is likely that their command of the French language was understandable, and appreciated, by local French and Créole speakers. By the turn of that century, however, and into the 20th century, Klinger's informant above, having been born about 1910, was referring to the Yiddish spoken by the Polish, Russian and other eastern European Jewish immigrants whose language would have been incomprehensible to the average Pointe Coupéean.

While it is obvious that Yiddish speakers in Pointe Coupée Parish would have learned enough English, French and/or Créole in order to function and transact business among their neighbors, a few of their Yiddish expressions have been preserved in the every-day language of Pointe Coupéeans, including *gelt, macher, mazel tov, schmooze, shekels, spiel,* and especially *tchotchke*. "Bric-a-brac" and "what-nots," or in Yiddish terms "tchotchkes" could be found in the stock of Lakeland retailer Ferdinand Kaufman in 1889 and the "fancy goods" offered by numerous Pointe Coupée merchants since at least the 1850s. Households increasing in disposable income and acquiring more substantial decorative items were wont to refer to the relatively inexpensive items in local stores as *tchotchkes*, and continue to do so in the 21st century.

INTERFAITH RELATIONS

While the Jewish faithful of Pointe Coupée had no synagogue, it is remembered and recorded that some of their number attended weddings, funerals, and other religious services of their non-Jewish neighbors. Several Jewish residents of late 19th and early 20th century Pointe Coupée Parish were members of Catholic church choirs. *Pointe Coupée Banner* accounts of 1899 mention Mrs. Aaron Baum, née Julia Simon, alto, and son, Simon Baum, tenor, among the Immaculate Conception Church Choir at Chenal. Continuing in this endeavor for many years, Simon Baum was in 1911 reported as offering his "splendid" and "usual melodious voice" for weddings at both St. Mary Church in New Roads and Immaculate Conception at Chenal.

The musically gifted Jean-Baptiste Alcide Bondy, who married Evelina Vignes, a granddaughter of early Jewish settler, Benjamin Jewell, and his Catholic wife, Sophie Prévost, is recorded in contemporary new articles to have attracted persons of all faiths, when he performed during Sunday Mass at the old St. Mary Church. A native of the Island of Martinique, Bondy immigrated to Louisiana circa 1840, with his commanding voice and Stradivarius violin, as a member of a French opera troupe. The Bondy children included Anna Bondy, who married

Jewish merchant Mayer Cahen, and Alcide Bondy the younger, his brother-in-law Mayer Cahen's partner in the "New Roads Fancy Grocery."

The Jews of Pointe Coupée Parish loved and respected the Christian clergymen in the area, and were often supported by the latter in times of need, irrespective of their different beliefs. Early Louisiana female journalist Martha R. Field, writing under her pseudonym "Catharine Cole" in the 22 November 1891 New Orleans *Daily Picayune*, attested to the esteem borne Fr. Pierre Berthet of the old Immaculate Conception Church at Chenal:

> Was ever a good priest so loved, I wonder? For years the Island doctor, and always priest, he is knit into the fabric of life of that quiet, unchanging neighborhood. Not long since, the little priest set out for France on a sad errand. All the people of the parish gathered in the public hall at New Roads to write for him their testimonial of regard, Jew and Gentile, Protestant and Catholic, and materialist, too, signed the paper. It was an unfading rose, gathered in the home garden they gave to the good father. When they told me of it, somehow the simple, direct loyalty, untarnished by any corrosion of selfish interest, went to the heart like a poem.

The Rev. Louis Savouré, pastor of Immaculate Conception from 1896 until 1948, served from two churches: the original on the north bank or "Island side" of the Lower Chenal, and from 1927 at the present church in Lakeland. He was a member of and served as president of the Pointe Coupée Parish Police Jury, and a director of the First National Bank in New Roads. Oscar merchant and planter Isaac Bigman, a decided Republican who opposed Fr. Savouré's staunch Democrat affiliation, officially greeted him on his arrival in the area and was among the prelate's closest friends.

FRATERNAL ORGANIZATIONS

The practice of Freemasonry was a major venue for Jewish and Gentile fraternity and charitable ministry in Pointe Coupée Parish from mid-19th into the late 20th centuries. There were lodges in several communities, the earliest known being the Livonia Lodge founded in 1851. Morganza Lodge No. 159 was organized in 1860. The De Castro Lodge, named for exiled Cuban patriot and Grand Master Dr. Antonio Vicente de Castro y Bermúdez was chartered in New Roads in 1871. Three years later, its membership merged with the former Livonia Masons as Livonia Lodge No. 220 F. & A. M. in New Roads. In 1877, the Livonia Lodge moved its headquarters to the upper floor of Cerf Wolff's "Burnt Bridge Store," near Lakeland. Wolff, a leading member, granted the lodge a nine-year lease at the nominal payment of $100 for the entire term.

While the Livonia Lodge dedicated a building of its own at Lakeland in 1890, it returned to New Roads in 1902, and in 1905 built the two-story, galleried and turreted "Masonic Temple" at the southeast corner of Poydras Avenue and West Second Street. (See Glenn Lee Greene, *Masonry in Louisiana*. Exposition Press, New York, 1962; and 14 Nov 1974 *Pointe Coupée Banner,* for further information).

The lower story of the Temple was home for many years to the New Roads Opera house, where theatricals, comedies, lectures and other community events were staged. The Opera House served as a motion picture theatre between 1914 until 1919, where Amy Paul Lesser, formerly of the firm of Stern & Lesser was the projectionist. The old Masonic Temple/Opera House was dismantled in 1951, and its soundest structural elements employed in the construction of the present building

When St. Joseph Academy, located a block west and fronting on Richy Street, was destroyed by fire in 1928, the Livonia Lodge Masons turned over the second-floor premises to the Sisters of St. Joseph so that classes could continue for the remainder of the 1928-1929 schoolyear. The students nicknamed their temporary quarters "St. Mason's" during their time there.

Notices posted in the *Pointe Coupée Banner* of upcoming meetings of the Livonia Lodge when at Lakeland in the latter 1800s, and the Fordoche and Tyrian (at Williamsport) Lodges, indicated that their office holders were both Jews and Gentiles in equal number. The Masons of Pointe Coupée Parish are recorded in contemporary issues of the *Pointe Coupée Banner* and oral tradition to have been especially solicitous to those suffering from floods and other hardships.

One of the earliest leading fraternal organizations in the United States, the Woodmen of the World, established the E. M. Weil Camp No. 517 at Fordoche, Louisiana, on 26 August 1909. It was named in honor of Jewish immigrant Ernest M. Weil, a native of Mackenheim, Bas-Rhin, France, and resident of New Orleans, Louisiana. Weil was a prominent Woodman and, at the time, Louisiana State Manager of the organization. In 1914, the Weil Camp received the donation of a 100 ft. by 100 ft. lot on the Bayou Grosse Tête Road, just above Livonia, from Humbert Major. The Woodmen had a lodge built there, but it had become inactive by 1942.

The American Legion of Honor, a national fraternal organization, counted both Gentile and Jewish members in the late 19th century, as did the local Chenal-Glynn Farmers' Association, founded in 1912, and the Pointe Coupée Parish Fair Association, established in 1914.

ENTERTAINMENT

Pointe Coupée Parish has also had a long and rich history of community-based Carnival traditions. Unlike in New Orleans, where Jews had been barred from membership in krewes and even from attending balls and other functions as guests, Pointe Coupée's celebrations were open to the general public, without prejudice to ethnic heritage or religious profession.

Way's Hotel at Williamsport, Louisiana was the site of at least two *Lundi Gras* masquerade balls hosted by the Komical Krewe in both 1898 and 1899, according to contemporary *Pointe Coupée Banner* accounts. Participation in the Komical Krewe festivities included Jewish and Gentile area residents and visitors. In both years, Isidore Blum and Achille Levy served as committee members. In 1899 they were members of the royal court: Levy as the Duke of Williamsport, and Blum as Duke of Merchon (word play on "merchandising"). In 1899, Master Clarence Blum was Page to "The Boss," as the King of the event was called. Mrs. Isidore Blum masqueraded as a "Domino" both years, and Miss Dora Mount was costumed as a "Bavarian Flower Girl" in the latter, all according to glowing *Pointe Coupée Banner* accounts.

The Community Center Carnival parade held on Mardi Gras morning in New Roads was founded in 1922 by James M. "Jimmy" Boudreaux, brother of Blanche Boudreaux, recorded as the mother of natural children by Benjamin "Ben" Stern, and is Louisiana's oldest Carnival parade after those of Rex, Proteus and Zulu in New Orleans.

New Roads' Mardi Gras annual afternoon parade, the New Roads Lions Carnival, premiered in 1941 and was the first-known Carnival parade to be staged as a charitable fundraiser. Numerous descendants of Benjamin Jewell and Sophie Prévost and of Solomon Baum and Reine Ordalie Chustz donated their time, and money toward the continued viability of the event, having reigned as royalty in the courtly retinue throughout the generations. Simone Ray Weil of Livonia was a Duchess during the 1970 Lions Carnival.

The Livonia Carnival Association parade has been an annual event since 1984, and adopted the custom of having Kings, Queens and Courts who lead the parade in the following year. The second King to rule over the festivities, in 1986, was beloved merchant, planter, cattleman and civic leader Simon Dreyfus Weil.

Baum's Hall, owned by merchant Aaron Baum, was a venue for community events at present-day Rougon on the Lower Chenal of False River. The 28 October 1899 *Pointe Coupée Banner* told of an upcoming "Gypsy Encampment" with dancing and refreshments to be held there for the benefit of the Hermitage public school. Admission was advertised at 25 cents for adults and 15 cents for children.

Home *soirées* were also a favored form of visiting and cultural exchange during the era. The Baums of Lower Chenal were at the fore. The 15 June 1889 *Banner* recounted a party of twenty-five or more Jewish and Gentile friends from New Orleans as well as Lakeland, Hermitage and vicinity at the Baum residence. The assembly was entertained by Mrs. Baum, née Julia Simon, on the zither, accompanied by her nephew Alex Cohn of Pensacola, Florida, on the violin.

The northern, or Upper Pointe Coupée, Jewish families such as the Blums, Landaus and Levys were frequently enumerated with non-Jewish friends and neighbors at Batchelor, Williamsport and Lettsworth cultural and social events and entertainments.

Jewish and Gentile motion picture fans watched silent movies and, beginning in the late 1920s, "talkies." The versatile Alcide Bondy, a descent of Benjamin Jewell and Sophie Prévost, and brother-in-law of Mayer Cahen, opened Pointe Coupée's first movie house in 1911, the Dreamland Electric Theatre, later renamed the New Bondy Theatre, at 204 East Main Street in New Roads. Other movie theatres were opened such as Conrad Langlois' "Floating Palace" theatre, built atop converted cottonseed barges, which had plied the waters of False River. The original Alamo, New Alamo, Star, and King Theatres, all subsequently opened up in New Roads.

Several rural communities had movie houses as well, including Morganza, Valverda and Jarreau. The second known operator of the Morganza Theatre was Gavriel/Gabriel Srulovitz, of an extensive Jewish commercial family from Romania.

POLITICS AND ANTI-SEMITISM

The obituaries of leading Jewish citizens, such as Alphonse Weil and his son Simon Dreyfus Weil of Livonia, included Catholic and Protestant pallbearers, a testament to strong bonds of friendship established in charitable and social fraternities as well as business connections in Pointe Coupée and adjacent parishes. While there were many times differences of opinion, conflicts resulting in violence between Christians and Jews were few and far between. The Baum-Patin affray at present-day Rougon in 1880 and the Landau-Way incident on Raccourci-Old River in 1900 were the two receiving the most public notice. In the former case, Lower

Chenal merchant Aaron Baum was ruled to have acted in self-defense, and in the latter, Maurice Landau of Raccourci-Old River was likewise exonerated. Regarding confrontations between Jewish parties, a rare example was the 1881 Meyer-Baum affair when Aaron Baum accused his neighbor, Jacob S. Meyer, of assault and battery.

A number of Jewish Pointe Coupéeans are recorded as having joined and served alongside their Gentile neighbors and friends in the Confederate Army during the Civil War. With war's end, however, there is little if any indication of bitterness regarding the Southern defeat or aggressive attempts to return to the white-only control of parish and state affairs that existed prior to the war.

Arthur Levy was the only Jew out of sixteen French Pointe-Coupéeans who chose to file as a French citizen and loyal unionist with the French and American Claims Commission. He made his claim as the tutor of his children, Thérèse and Auguste Abraham, with his late wife Marguérite Cléontine Decuir, for horses and cattle seized by Captain Hopkins, USA, at Morganza. Since all claimants to both post-Civil War Commissions had to declare that they had been loyal Unionists in order to be eligible for monetary compensation, it is difficult to ascertain just "how loyal to the union" any of them had actually been during the conflict. (See *A Guide to the French and American Claims Commission 1880-1885: Our French Immigrant Ancestors and the American Civil War,* by Carol Mills-Nichol, Janaway Publishing, Santa Maria, CA, 2017).

Significantly, names of Jewish Pointe Coupéeans appear neither among the alleged intimidators of African American voters during the controversial 1878 state political campaigns and elections nor the supposed lynchers of seven African American men behind the levee near New Texas Landing for the latter's alleged assassination attempt on Dr. William Archer that same year. Jewish citizens, who had formerly been staunch members of the Democrat party, found that their previous loyalties were severely tested during this period, not in a small part due to the violence meted out to African American men, now eligible to vote, who had flocked to the party of Lincoln. This political upheaval brought with it a smattering of anti-Semitism, unusual in the parish.

Louis Bingaman "L.B." Claiborne, veteran of the Pointe Coupée Artillery, C.S.A., founder of the *The Pelican*, *Pointe Coupée Banner*, and *The Messenger* newspapers of New Roads, had, as a rule, published complimentary accounts of Jewish families, however, he drew the line at condoning their Republican politics, and seemed especially bristled about the candidacy of Jewish former Federal Army major and staunch Republican neighbor Louis Trager.

Trager, a Russian immigrant, became, after the fall of the Confederacy, one of the largest-scale cotton planters on the Mississippi River in Concordia Parish. Trager had served under United State President Ulysses S. Grant as consul at Boulogne-Sur-Mer, France, and in 1880 acquired, in partnership with Samuel L. James, the 10,016-acre Angola and six contiguous plantations in West Feliciana Parish, opposite Red River Landing. In his 14 October 1882 issue of the *Banner*, L. B. Claiborne bristled at the thought of Trager's political ambitions:

> We have been reliably informed that several of our Jewish fellow-citizens of this parish, who have heretofore acted with the Democratic party, intend voting for Louis Trager, the Republican candidate for congress in this [Sixth] district, for the sole reason that he is a

Jew. We are surprised at this and regret very much to hear it. Certainly, these gentlemen are acting without due reflection, for they should be the very last to wish to establish a religious test of fitness for office. Do they not know that ninety-nine percent of every hundred of the citizens of this parish are Christians, and that they have always been tolerant. We hope these gentlemen will re-consider their hasty determination.

After receiving written admonishments from both Christian and Jewish readers the *Banner* owner-editor continued to his "friends of Pointe Coupée" his regret that the "complaining" readers did not make a "proper distinction between an announcement of information, and an expression of editorial opinion," and claimed than an unnamed "gentleman" informed "us" that Trager stated, "Every damn Jew in the district is obliged to vote for me." Claiborne waxed that the Democratic party "has never had a warmer support from any class of people than the Israelites," and that the party had, in return, extended its "highest honors" to J. (Judah) P. Benjamin and B. (Benjamin) F. Jonas, both former high-ranking Confederates.

Claiborne then singled out Isidore Blum, of the Williamsport, Pointe Coupée Parish commercial house of Haber & Blum, as being the "gentlemen of principle" who had contributed to the success of a recent gathering of parish Democrats. In a last flourish of self-vindication, he stated:

> This paper derives a great part of it support from the Israelites of this parish, and some of the warmest friends of its editor are of that faith, therefore they could not believe that we had any intention to cast a reflection upon their race or religion. Let them look back over the file of the BANNER from its first number.

Trager was defeated in his bid for the U.S. Congress from the Sixth District. The neighboring Bayou Sara *Feliciana Sentinel* published a mock "obituary" in its issue of 14 November 1882: "Died. On a convict plantation, of political neglect and disappointment, on Tuesday, November 7th, Louis Trager, formerly Consul at Boulogne. He was buried in West Feliciana, under a majority of 649 [votes]."

In Louis Trager's 1905 obituary the 13 October Denver, Colorado *Jewish Outlook* stated of Trager's unsuccessful bid for Sixth District Congressman: "It was then an open secret that he was legitimately elected, but through the politics of those days he was counted out. Major Trager was well known in his section of the country as always ready to assist a friend when in need, or the poor."

During the political upheaval of 1878, several African Americans testified to having fled their homes, due to activity of the local "Vigilance Committee." They took refuge in the False River area, where generations of Franco-African ties, often biological and Catholic, as well as the presence of some compassionate Jewish citizens likely was responsible for providing them safe haven. White citizens of both sexes who hid the persecuted African Americans and/or refused to tell of their whereabouts were reportedly terrorized and tortured by the pursuers as well.

EDUCATION

One of the lasting contributions to Pointe Coupéans of all ethnicities was Jewish support of public education. In Ward 10, the southernmost of the parish, at least four schools bore the name of Jewish merchants and planters. The earliest known was the Dreyfus School, opened by the Pointe Coupée Parish School Board and named to honor merchant and planter Theodore Dreyfus in 1907. It closed with other area schools upon the consolidation resulting in the establishment of Livonia High School in 1915.

That same year, the School Board renamed two Ward 10 schools for members of the Gumbel family: the one at Frisco, on upper Bayou Grosse Tête, originally the Parlange School, became the Ferdinand Gumbel School, in recognition of the namesake's donation of a two-acre lot upon which the facility stood. The Lottie School at Lottie was renamed the Simon Gumbel School, in appreciation for the gifts of $1,000 for a school library and a life-size portrait of his late father by Simon's son Henry Gumbel. In December 1915, Ferdinand Gumbel and his wife, Selma Feitel, donated a square-acre lot at another location in Ward 10 for public school purposes.

Advances in the quality of education for African American children were made in 1923, likewise through the benevolence of a Jewish businessman. The Rosenwald Schools established in New Roads, Ventress (Island of False River) and Torbert (Oscar Crossing) were among the many established by Julius Rosenwald, then president of Sears, Roebuck and Company, a national chain of department stores and catalog sales with heavy Pointe Coupée patronage. The Rosenwald school of New Roads, continues as an elementary component of the Pointe Coupée Parish Public School System in 2022.

Theodore Dreyfus, and his grandson Simon Dreyfus Weil after him, represented Ward 10 on the Pointe Coupée Parish School Board. Weil is remembered to have been, during the height of the Civil Rights movement, the sole member of the School Board to vote in favor of integrating all public schools in the parish. In 2021, his daughter Dinah Weil recalled that her father and the family withstood criticism, harassing telephone calls, and even the burning of a cross in front of their home, but remained steadfast in their commitment to quality education for all.

COMMERCE

Although some of their number specialized in certain lines such as dry goods and clothing, or groceries, the majority of 19th and early 20th century retailers in Pointe Coupée Parish were general merchants, dealing in all types of manufactured goods that the population was largely unable to produce on its own. Stores of those periods are remembered by older residents for the odors exuded, perceptible when one entered the premises, including the dyes in dry goods or fabrics, the leather of shoes and harnesses, the tempting sweetness of fruit and candy, the delectable odor of coffee, varying smells of drugs, perfumes, soaps and tobacco products, and the pungency of coal oil and kerosene.

Interior store layout was typical with dry goods, clothing, towels and blankets arranged on shelves and counters along the right-hand side, "staple" and "fancy" groceries, medicines, crockery and glassware on shelves and counters to the left, and heavier items, such as hardware and saddlery, in the rear, that section often fronted by a bar where whisky, wines and other alcoholic beverages could be purchased by the glass. In larger establishments, stools were often located along the dry goods counter, for the comfort of female shoppers. The intervening space between there and the grocery section was lined in parallel with tables bearing a variety of goods. Often there was a "side room" or warehouse, in which heavier items such as furniture and agricultural implements might be kept. Often that side room also served as a bar.

While the average family produced as much as it could for personal consumption, including vegetables, fruits, beef, swine, poultry and eggs, there were items which they definitely had to purchase from stores or peddlers. The latter included dry goods or fabrics and sewing "notions" (thread, needles, pins, buttons, etc.) for fashioning dresses, other items of clothing, bedsheets, bolster covers and mattress ticking, tableware, cookware, nails, large and small hardware, harness and tack, plows, stoves and furniture. Dry goods, later termed piece goods, but commonly referred to as "material," were sold by the "piece" or bolt, each counting approximately 35 yards of "material." Virtually every merchant or peddler offering dry goods carried calico, gingham, cotton "print," heavier "domestic" fabrics, and flannel. Many stores by the 1880s offered more luxurious textiles, including silks, satins, satinettes, taffeta and velvets, alpaca and tweeds, plus bolts of French and Spanish laces and embroidery.

Indispensable for "domestic" use was netting for fashioning mosquito *baires* or "bars" for beds, sheeting for bed linens, and ticking for making mattresses. Well into the mid-20th century, Pointe Coupée's less affluent homes, both in the town of New Roads, and rural areas featured the moss-filled ticking *matelas* (mattress), often placed atop a ticking filled with dried corn shucks called the *paillaise*.

Shoes, boots, hats, and caps were offered in several varieties and styles, although ladies' millinery invariably ended up on shelves and in boxes, because of the rapidly changing fashions, as attested to in the oral history of older merchants and consumers.

Tableware offered by merchants was usually plain "crockery," although several stocked the popular blue willow ware, and some offered queens ware, china and select pieces of porcelain. Owing to the Créole preference for coffee over all other beverages, cups and saucers were stocked by the score, and ran the gamut from huge café au lait cups / bowls to dainty demitasses for café noir.

"Staple" groceries typically purchased included flour, cornmeal, grits, rice, coffee, sugar, and salt, while "fancy groceries" became more readily available in the mid-19th century, the latter including teas and chocolate, canned fruits, vegetables, meats, and fish, bottled olives, pickles, sauces and oils, and an increasing variety of candies, cakes (i.e., cookies) crackers, dried fruits and other comestibles. Meats, either "green" (i.e., fresh) or salted, were sold by most stores, and despite the conservative Hebrew prohibition of consuming pork, most Jewish merchants and butchers stocked and sold pork to their customers.

From the earliest times, alcoholic beverages were sold by Pointe Coupée merchants. Their store inventories included French and Spanish wines, cordials, brandies, gin and above all, numerous brands of whiskey, the latter sold by the barrel and bottle.

Many 19th and 20th century stores in Pointe Coupée Parish had indoor "bars" or saloons, often at the rear of the main retail area, or in a separate room to the rear or side of the store. In the listing of Parish Licenses issued for the year 1880, the 11 October 1881 *Pointe Coupée Banner* listed the following Jewish merchants having both "retail" and "bar" licenses: Meyer Levy, Haber & Blum, Isaac Levy, H. (Henry) Picard, and A. (Alexander) Mann, all of whom figure extensively in this volume.

Most general and grocery stores stocked any of the multitude of patent medicines sold in the 19th and early 20th centuries, a staple being "Dr. Tichenor's Antiseptic Refrigerant," developed by veteran Confederate Army medic and Raccourci-Old River resident "Dr." George Tichenor. Popular for a time during the 1890s was "Mann's Cream Liniment," produced for and marketed through the firm of Mann & Weinberg, general merchants at Merrick Post Office, in northernmost Pointe Coupée Parish. Contemporary *Pointe Coupée Banner* advertisements for the Manns' product pronounced it "a certain cure" for sprains, burns, sores, toothache, headache, neuralgia, sore throat, also for colic and botts in horses and mules, as well as a "dead shot" on screw worms." Among the many pharmacists practicing in early 20th century Pointe Coupée, Murray LeBeau, son of False River Road pharmacist William LeBeau, specifically recalled two who were Jewish: Aaron Baum near present-day Rougon and Theo Dreyfus at Livonia. LeBeau recalled that:

> Patent medicines were popular but the druggists compounded prescriptions from scratch. The pharmacists would give "shotgun" prescriptions which contained a little bit of every known drug at the time in a compound. It was given to the patient in a capsule or powder to be mixed in liquids. It was bound to cure something!

Laudanum, consumed as a pain reliever, and quinine, as a fever preventative, were stocked in general stores as well as by pharmacists. However, owing to the limited economic means of most Pointe Coupéeans, the majority of residents relied, on home remedies well into the 20th century, principally teas of leaves, roots and bark of local flora and *cataplasmes* (poultices) of melted wax or mutton fat. A physician was called to a home only on rare occasions, and only in dire cases. Murray LeBeau recalled an adage attributed to Parlange Lane resident René Amar, maternal uncle of twins Charles Adalbert and Joseph Hildévert Gumbel: "When you see a doctor at a house, the priest is soon to follow."

Pointe Coupée Parish endured many epidemics during its history, including waves of cholera during the 1830s-1850s and yellow fever in 1853. The 1867 yellow fever epidemic took an unknown total number of victims. It is recorded that more than 100 were buried in St. Mary Cemetery in New Roads. Yellow fever struck again in 1878 and 1905. In the latter year, according to Murray LeBeau, New Roads Town Marshal William Morel and deputies were posted at the entrances to town with shotguns to prevent persons from either entering or leaving the town.

Typhoid epidemics occurred in 1911, following the floods of 1912 and 1913, and again in 1916 and 1925. According to 1882 issues of the *Pointe Coupée Banner*, widespread illness tended to follow floods. In the aftermath of that year's epic inundation, it was reported that a "disease of a scorpulous [nature]" had erupted on Bayous Grosse Tête and Fordoche and its spread was feared to be potentially fatal.

The number of cases during the 1918 influenza pandemic in Pointe Coupée is difficult to determine. In the Louisiana State Death Records for September-December 1918, the height of local infection, a total of 184 or 43% of the year's cumulative deaths were a result of the flu. The number of casualties may never be known owing to deaths which were not reported in official death or burial records. Murray LeBeau stated: "In the flu epidemic of 1918, it was young, healthy people who died the most. A pregnant mother was almost sure to catch it and die. During this epidemic, the bodies decomposed rapidly and no funerals were held…. The priest [or minister] went straight to the cemetery and only the pallbearers and the closest relatives were advised to go. I can remember wagons passing with the coffins in front of here, from down the river and back in Parlange Lane, for many days."

Although most merchants in 19th and early 20th century Pointe Coupée Parish conducted their operations in their own names, others did so by adopting more creative titles. Of those operated by Jewish individuals and firms, some bore the name of colors, likely that in which the stores were painted, including the "Blue Store" and "Red Store" on Pointe Coupée Road and the "White Store" just outside of New Roads. Others were operated under names such as "The Leader," "Cheap Store," and "Fancy Grocery," as well as the more exotic "Evening Star" and "Delmonico" stores. Several stores were named for the plantations upon which they stood, including "Alma," "Nina," and "El Dorado."

The financial arrangements between merchants and customers continued to be conducted well into the 20th century as it had since colonial times, according to Murray LeBeau:

> Most business was done on account. Settlement was made at the end of the year after the [customers'] crops had been sold. Some plantations used their own currency. The hired plantation workers were not paid in cash, but the landowner would back them for doctors [i.e., advance them money for medical attention].

Although some merchants made buying trips to New Orleans or even to New York City or other large cities to order their merchandise, most goods were acquired by the smaller merchants through orders taken by traveling salesman. These latter were sent out periodically by wholesale companies located in New Orleans and elsewhere with samples of their goods. Traveling salesmen or "drummers," the nickname remaining from days when they announced their arrivals by beating a drum, usually went from store to store, showing goods and taking orders, while others displayed their goods in "sample rooms" expressly built by and located inside or adjacent to hotels. The French Hotel in downtown New Roads, owned and operated by Casimir Savignol, had such a "sample room," which served for a time as the jewelry store of J. Moonshine. The drummers, the retail knights of the road, were frequently the subject of jokes. Murray LeBeau remembered:

> Traveling salesmen called "drummers" called on all the stores. They would rent a spring wagon and a driver from the livery stable and make a circuit of the river. There's a story about a drummer who arrived in town [i.e., New Roads] and got on the "hack" [horse-drawn bus] with a number of other passengers. The driver, who was a Negro [sic], let off two or three people at the hotel and the owner of the hotel asked, "John, who came in?" And the driver said, "Well, there were three gentlemen, two ladies and four drummers."
>
> Drummers were in a class of their own!

Store clerks were required to be fluent in French and/or Créole in addition to English into the beginning of the twentieth century. *Pointe Coupée Banner* advertisements for the "Nina Store," C.M. Eiseman & Co., proprietors, at Cook's Landing on the Mississippi (See "Waterloo Areas" section) in 1890, advised its readers that American (*sic*, English), French, Créole, Spanish, and German were spoken by store personnel. Nearly 20 years later, a "want ad" for the position of clerk in the Theo Dreyfus general store at Livonia in the 10 August 1918 *Banner* specified: "young man… must speak French and [be] exempt from [military] draft."

AGRICULTURE

Cotton was first successfully produced in Pointe Coupée Parish about 1800, and sugar cane approximately two decades later. Traditionally, Pointe Coupée was the northernmost area of

Louisiana where sugar cane was successfully cultivated, and the southernmost region of cotton production. An old adage ran: "Cotton is king, and Pointe Coupée is queen of the cotton-producing parishes of Louisiana." However, owing to the fecundity of the alluvial soil, deposited in pre-historic times and in repeated flood episodes, a wide variety of crops could be and have been produced in Pointe Coupée.

On the eve of the Civil War, J.W. Dorr from the New Orleans *Crescent* toured a large portion of Louisiana by horse and buggy in his capacity as business agent for the newspaper. The notes he took were compiled and presented in a series entitled "Louisiana in Slices," which appeared in the *Crescent* between 20 April and 10 September 1860. Pointe Coupée Parish harvested a sugar cane crop that autumn which set the benchmark for sugar production not equaled, let alone surpassed, for several generations. Dorr offered the following statistics for Pointe Coupée in 1860:

> The area of the parish comprises some 311,000 acres, about 28,000 of which are in cotton, 17,000 in cane and 18,000 in corn – the value of the cane considerably exceeding that of the cotton. The proportion of slaves in the parish is very large, as they number 11,000 in a total population. Of about 15,500, the whites being about 3,650 in number and the free colored about 750.

The absence of many adult white males who were away in Confederate military service, the occupation of Pointe Coupée by, and skirmishing between, the armies of North and South, the requisitioning of livestock and vehicles by both sides, and the flight of many enslaved persons seriously hampered agricultural, as well as commercial, activity during the Civil War.

Confederate authorities ordered cotton to be burned lest it fall into Federal hands, as the latter seized the same as "contraband" and profited through its sale in Northern and foreign markets. A few farmers, particularly on the Island of False River, hid their cotton in wooded areas and traded it for goods at war's end.

Following the war and the loss of much of their labor force, most planters and farmers concentrated on the less-labor-intensive cultivation of cotton and corn. Unfortunately, these crops suffered from repeated floods and parasites. Some formerly large-scale planters were able to resume sugar cane production in Pointe Coupée Parish after the Civil War, only to suffer financial reverses due to floods, and loss of their crops and real estate through judicial seizure and sale or mortgage foreclosures by New Orleans banks and financiers.

Jewish planters Rosine Michel Kern, the Levy brothers, Isaac Keim, Louis Strauss, George Gerson, Melanie Michel Landau, Simon Bloch, Jacob Grossman, August Keller, C.M. Eiseman, Adolph Seckbach, Theodore Dreyfus, Isaac Bigman and Max Rothschild were among those who engaged in "money crops" such as sugar cane and cotton. They shared in the successes and failures of their non-Jewish neighbors and counterparts, often contending with labor and tenancy issues, floods, hurricanes, insect infestations and diseases.

The rising price of cotton around 1900 resulted in all Pointe Coupée sugar cane plantations except Alma at Lakeland converting to cotton cultivation. Some 65,000 acres of Pointe Coupée were planted in cotton in 1902, producing an output of 50,000 bales. The spike in cotton production spurred the establishment of three cottonseed oil companies: Raccourci Cotton Seed

Oil Co., established in 1890, the New Roads Oil Mill (subsequently a unit of Southern Cotton Oil Co.) in 1900, which operated until 1975; and the Union Oil Mill Co., a unit of American Oil Co., opened in Torras in 1902.

For a few short years, the parish experienced great prosperity and development. In 1906, however, the boll weevil infestation, entering the American South from Mexico, via Texas, struck Pointe Coupée Parish with a severity that did not lessen for more than a decade. The first year of the infestation was relatively milder in Pointe Coupée than in other parishes, according to reports of a State-appointed Pest Commission who carefully monitored the advance of the boll weevil across Louisiana. On 19 September 1907, however, the *Daily State-Times* announced that the insect had been found on the Angola State Penitentiary Farm across the Mississippi River from Upper Pointe Coupée:

By year's end, planters in Pointe Coupée and the adjacent West Baton Rouge Parish reported that they were switching much acreage hitherto devoted to cotton back to sugar cane cultivation. The following summer, the Opelousas *St. Clarion Herald* dated 4 July 1908, informed its readers that some former cotton planters of Pointe Coupée were switching to rice cultivation, and arranging with the rice mill in Donaldsonville to process the expected harvests. There were benefits to the cultivation of rice in Pointe Coupée, West Baton Rouge and Iberville Parishes, because "river rice, or rice grown in fields near the river, is worth more per barrel than prairie rice," the latter referring to that grown in Southwest Louisiana. Moreover, just a month later, *The True Democrat* of St. Francisville devoted half of the front page of its 22 August 1908 issue to announce that the sugar cane crop had fallen victim to the "borer" insect. Southwest Louisiana was showing substantial infestation, and the spread had followed both sides of the Mississippi River, reaching Glynn Station on the west bank in Pointe Coupée. The cultivation of rice had been a safer bet.

Pointe Coupée's smaller-scale farmers, however, continued both sugar cane and rice cultivation, and grew other crops as well to minimize losses should either of the two fail. Although rice was grown mainly on False River and Mississippi River plantations, upon introduction by enterprising planters from the German Coast parishes between Baton Rouge and New Orleans, local farmers soon followed suit. In December 1909, False River farmer Benjamin Jewell, grandson of Benjamin Jewell the elder and Sophie Prévost, leased four contiguous tracts for the cultivation of rice for three years between 1910 and 1913. He paid $5.50 per acre for cleared land. The wooded portions were excepted from the lease, but Jewell was allowed to cut enough firewood to run the water pumps and rice machines.

On the eve of the 1912 Flood, it was reported that Pointe Coupée Parish was an annual producer of 64,000 bales of cotton, 3,000,000 tons of sugar, 40,000 barrels of corn, and substantial amounts of rice, onions and other vegetables.

THE GREAT FLOOD OF 1912

The region's greatest and deadliest natural disaster, the 1912 Flood, came close on the heels of the boll weevil invasion and back-to-back sugar cane freezes. Pointe Coupée and numerous parishes to the south entered a bleak period of judicial seizure and sale of properties and movables, bank and business failures, and an emigration of numerous families of all ethnicities, to New Orleans or other urban areas north and west. Although the Great Flood of 1927 is the most engrained in local and national psyche, that of 1912 was deadliest and costliest in Pointe Coupée and adjacent parishes of West Baton Rouge and Iberville, as river levels continued to rise subsequent to levee breaches on the Atchafalaya River west of Lottie and near the confluence of the Lower Old and Mississippi Rivers at Torras, pumping water inland in currents as wide and quick as those waterways.

Excessive snowmelt and record rainfall in the central Mississippi Valley spurred levee failures in that section of the nation in the spring of 1912. Floodwater advancing south through Louisiana and the steadily rising Mississippi, Red, Lower Old and Atchafalaya foreshadowed impending disaster, and thousands of citizens struggled to "top" levee crests with sandbags, check levee "slides" and landside eruptions or "sand boils." They formed levee patrols, firearms in hands, less parties from equally threatened communities opposite the swollen rivers attempted to dynamite Pointe Coupée levees.

The first levee breach to occur in South Louisiana in 1912 occurred at 2 a.m. on 6 April, on the east bank of Atchafalaya River, in Pointe Coupée Parish, just above the New Orleans & San Francisco or "Frisco" rail bridge. Seasoned flood victims, some 800 in number in the low-lying "interior" south of False River, in the Oscar Crossing, Little Italy and Cholpe sections evacuated north and took refuge in Oscar proper on and adjacent to False River Road over the next few weeks. The Atchafalaya River breach was declared incontrollable, and at nearby Lottie, two major sawmills were closed, plunging hundreds of men into unemployment. Farmers attempted small levees around their holdings, but these were to be overtopped and washed away by the subsequent torrent of the Torras breach.

Overwhelmed by the volume of water from levee breaches in North Louisiana and Arkansas and the continued rising of the rivers, the Lower Old River levee gave out at dinnertime on 1 May 1912, a half-mile east of Torras. This began the opening salvo of Pointe Coupée Parish's darkest chapter in three centuries of history.

United States Army personnel, and volunteers from Pointe Coupée manning motor launches, three railroads, and river pilots labored ceaselessly throughout the month of May in rescue and relief work. They collected flooded-out citizens and livestock in New Roads and transported them to relatively high ground in Baton Rouge and Port Hudson on the east bank of the Mississippi, and to Lafayette and other towns beyond the Atchafalaya Basin to the west.

In total, 17,000 of Pointe Coupée's population of nearly 26,000 were made homeless by the inundation. Of their number, 12,000 were housed, fed and given medical attention at evacuation centers in the surrounding cities and towns, while 5,000 fended for themselves, camped atop the levees or in the dry part of New Roads, south of the railroad. They were dependent on government assistance and the ministration of family and friends, strangers, and the Sisters of St. Joseph of New Roads, who traveled by boat to give aid to those who refused to evacuate.

By 20 May, Pointe Coupée Parish was a huge, inland sea, 90% of its surface flooded from one to 20 feet deep. The only dry ground was a one-thousand-foot-wide strip along both banks of False River, a relatively high spot "here and there" along the Mississippi levee front, and a thin "island" from above Fordoche in Pointe Coupée down into Iberville Parish, bounded on the east by the little Fordoche – Grosse Tête Levee along the bayous of that name and the main line of the Texas & Pacific Railroad on the west.

In time, the west bank of Bayou Grosse Tête was affected, the little levee breaching on 10 May at the Grimmer farm, just above the Theo Dreyfus store. The floodwaters rose to enter that landmark retail operation. Plucky residents of Fordoche saved the levee in front of their community by closing it twice, after repeated breaches.

The floodwater circling the relatively high False River riverfront, invaded the canals and bayous, raising the level of the lake by at least five feet, to within 11 feet from Main Street in New Roads. Proceeding through the *Grand Décharge* on the "Island side," floodwater filled the lakes in the Island Interior and encroached upon the cultivated farms of that densely populated area of small farmers and merchants. The section of New Roads north of the railroad, was flooded from a foot deep at the rail embankment to ten feet deep near Iron Bridge on the historic *Chemin Neuf* (New Road).

Despite the rescue and transfer of approximately 8,000 head of livestock to the highlands east of the Mississippi River, losses were heavy. Human fatalities cited by the newspapers exceeded sixty-five. There were approximately twenty in the vicinity of Torras within one day of the break. Drownings also occurred at Lettsworth, Innis, and Batchelor in the northern part of Upper Pointe Coupée, and at Erwinville in the southeastern corner of the parish. People of all ages drowned in the destruction of their homes, and in attempting to flee in government skiffs, private vessels, makeshift rafts, and on foot. Some victims succumbed while trying to rescue and relocate their livestock.

According to the United States Federal Census for 1910 the population of Pointe Coupée Parish peaked at 25,219. With the subsequent evacuation of 12,000 parish residents in 1912, the numerous individuals and families who lost homes and livelihoods in the parish sought better economic opportunities in Baton Rouge, New Orleans, and towns west of the Atchafalaya flood basin. Some even moved out of state, never to return. By the 1 July 2020 tally by the United States Postal Service, it was revealed that there were only 23,379 residents living in Pointe Coupée Parish. The part of the parish to be most affected in population loss during and in the wake of the 1912 Flood was the northern portion or Upper Pointe Coupée which had counted 6,000 residents in 1912. As of 1 July 2020, the number of residents remaining in that area according to the USPS was only 2,564 (https://louisiana.hometownlocator.com/la/pointe-coupee/, accessed 19 May 2021).

(For more and detailed information see: Costello, Brian J. *Desolation Unmeasured: The Tragic History of Floods in Pointe Coupée Parish, Louisiana*. New Roads Printing, 2017.)

RESILIENCE... UNTIL THE INEVITABLE

Among the businesses which remained solvent through the lingering distressed economy in Pointe Coupée Parish for the decade following the arrival of the boll weevil in 1906, those operated by Jewish merchants ranked among the highest in assessed value. According to the 1916 Assessment Roll, the store of Leon Levy at Blanks, had the highest of all "stock in trade" in the parish at $1,850. When many of the stores open in Pointe Coupée in 1916 had merchandise assessed as low as $25 or $50, other Jewish firms had much higher stock valuations: Tatar (formerly Tatarsky) Bros., in the rebuilt Torras community, $1,000; Sol Bernstein, Lakeland, $1,000; Theo Dreyfus, Livonia, $850; M.D. Landau, Batchelor, $800; P. Loeb, Morganza, $550; M.H. Srulovitz, Morganza, $350; Leopold Sommer, Torras, $300; Max Loeb (formerly

Srulovitz), at Lettsworth, $175; and A. Baum at Glynn, $150. It is important to note that assessed valuation was only a fraction of the merchandise's worth, with merchants' markup increasing the actual sale value to a considerable degree.

The last levee break of the Mississippi Valley Flood of 1927 occurred in Pointe Coupée Parish, at the east bank Atchafalaya River levee at McCrea. On 17 May, at 6 a.m., a breach occurred in the levee on the west side of the Atchafalaya at Melville, in St. Landry Parish. The water released by the Melville crevasse resulted in a four-foot fall in the level of the swollen Atchafalaya, but further undermined the sloughing of the levee at McCrea, in Pointe Coupée.

A span of the Texas & Pacific railroad bridge linking Red Cross and Melville collapsed at 10 a.m. on 18 May, taking with it Tony Pizzolatto and his son, residents of Maringouin. On 20 May, the Baton Rouge *State-Times* headlines blared: "Parker Orders People of Pointe Coupee to Flee as Situation Grows Critical. Vast Volume of Water Above Parish Endangering Whole Area. Suspect River is Changing Course. Engineers Report Phenomena Along Atchafalaya in Support." Maj. John Gotwals, director of the relief transport fleet in Lower Old River, had reportedly observed an incredible volume of water pouring down the Atchafalaya River. Gotwals, who considered that the flow was entirely too great for the Atchafalaya to contain within its leveed banks, suspected that the Mississippi River itself was about to shift its course into the Atchafalaya.

A slow evacuation of upper Pointe Coupée began, during which the levee at McCrea gave way at 3:15 a.m. on 24 May 1927. More than 4,000 residents fled the McCrea floodwater, some 2,000 of them being located in the Baton Rouge Red Cross camps, 1,000 in New Roads, and the balance "absorbed into private homes" of relatives in Baton Rouge and elsewhere, according to the Baton Rouge *Advocate*. Approximately 600 horses and mules were moved and 1,500 head of cattle were transported via the Gulf Coast (formerly "Frisco") Railroad from Lottie to Livingston Parish east of Baton Rouge. Cattle in the northern part of Pointe Coupée were transported by riverboats and barges.

In New Roads, the Texas & Pacific branch railroad embankment was transformed into a temporary levee by blocking the culverts beneath the tracks. The *State-Times* reported that, owing to this work, "the front of New Roads should not flood," however, the water issuing from the north reached as far south in New Roads as St. Augustine Church, on New Roads Street, just south of its intersection with Parent Street, and less than two blocks north of the railroad embankment.

By 29 May 1927, the water issuing from McCrea encompassed 330 square miles in four parishes, encompassing 75% of the surface of Pointe Coupée, 75% of Iberville, 30% of West Baton Rouge and 50% of Assumption Parishes. That portion of Pointe Coupée south of Morganza and the northern part of West Baton Rouge that did flood in 1927 did so at lower levels than in 1912. And then, what Pointe Coupéeans have deemed "a miracle" occurred:

"McCrea Flood Rush Slows Up Suddenly. Action Of Atchafalaya Waters Believed To Have Formed Sandbar At Break," ran the *New York Times* headline of a report dated May 29. The flow through the breach had decreased by 50%. New Orleans meteorologist Dr. I.M. Cline pronounced the phenomenon one of the strangest turns of events in his forty years of service with the Mississippi Valley Weather Bureau. The Sisters of St. Joseph in New Roads recalled for decades thereafter that it was the third time they had led the community successfully in prayer through the intercession of Our Lady of Prompt Succor, Patroness of Louisiana, that the parish seat be spared inundation.

"End Of Flood Is Now In Sight," stated the *New York Times* in a report datelined 30 May. On that, the sixth day after the McCrea crevasse, the Baton Rouge *State-Times* reported the inland flood to have crested.

The Great Depression followed closely on the heels of the 1927 flood, resulting in more financial distress for Pointe Coupée Parish business and industry. The State of Louisiana began to pave existing roads and open new ones in 1931, and the Town of New Roads simultaneously inaugurated a street paving program. Citizens fortunate enough to own automobiles began to shop in the parish seat as well as in Baton Rouge and New Orleans, thereby contributing to the further decline in the number of rural stores and services. By the third quarter of the 20th century, Jewish owned or operated businesses numbered three regional chain stores in New Roads as well as the Theo Dreyfus store at Livonia.

Theo Dreyfus Store at Livonia during the 1912 Flood.

CHAPTER 1

POINTE COUPÉE ROAD

Catharine Cole, the pen name of pioneer Louisiana female Martha R. Field, stated in her 29 November 1891 "Catharine's Letter's" column in the New Orleans *Daily Picayune*:

> The [Mississippi] river is found to rise higher than it used to, and all along its waters old levees are being raised, or new ones built further inland, away from the sweep of the current. In low water times the menace is from caving banks. The other day in Pointe Coupée, a bank caved in from being relieved of the pressure of the water, taking with it a warehouse in full operation.

Her observation captured much of the story, and the fate, of one of the oldest settlements in the Mississippi Valley: the *Cote* or Coast *de la Pointe Coupée* along the Mississippi River. While homes and farms still dot the land along the Pointe Coupée Road in the 21st century after three centuries of settlement, no architectural vestiges remain of the French and Spanish colonial and early American years after the systematic caving of the riverbanks and resultant levee and road setbacks.

By the 1880s, the movement of families of all ethnicities from the old Pointe Coupée Coast into the town of New Roads, to New Orleans or beyond, was reflected in the use of the term "Picayuneville," symbolizing a small place of little value, by *the Pointe Coupée Banner*. The name especially applied to the once prosperous neighborhood stretching from the "Red Store on the west to the New Road on the east."

The first-known European residents in the Pointe Coupée area, had arrived as *engagés* (contract workers) for the Ste. Reyne Concession on the east bank of the Mississippi River in 1720, but had moved to the west bank, in present-day Pointe Coupée Parish, Louisiana, by the time of the 1726 Census. Eventually, stretching for twenty-two miles from the lower mouth of *Fausse Rivière* (False River) on the south to the *Raccourci* or "short-cut" across the hairpin bend above present-day Morganza, the *Côte de la Pointe Coupée* or "Pointe Coupée Coast" along the Mississippi, developed as one of the first, permanent communities in the Mississippi Valley.

Early "cash crops" included tobacco and indigo, but by the first decade of the 19th century, large-scale planters switched to the cultivation of cotton and sugar cane. Thousands of enslaved African Americans labored to plant, cultivate, harvest and process the staples which made several local families among the wealthiest in the nation. Plantation owners usually sent their crops and received merchandise from New Orleans, but also, in many cases, did a brisk back and forth business abroad. They also traded with itinerant merchants, who traveled the Mississippi and Pointe Coupée Road to sell items which could not be produced on their plantations or farms.

The earliest knowns merchants to open stores in the area were native Frenchmen Julien Poydras, near the present-day intersection of Pointe Coupée Road and Delta Lane, the notoriously litigious Jean-Baptiste Tounoir, who operated near the site of the subsequent New Roads–Bayou Sara Ferry crossing; and Jean-Baptiste Nicollet, with whom early Jewish resident Isaac Henriqués Fastio lived, near the head of False River. Julien Poydras later opened a branch operation on False River, in what is now the city of New Roads, linking his two stores by a road whose path was roughly along present-day Major Parkway and Delta Lane. Succeeding his uncle, Benjamin Poydras de la Lande operated the two stores, as well as opening a third one on the Poydras family's Grand Bayou (later Alma) plantation at present-day Lakeland on the Lower Chenal of False River.

THE MONSANTOS AND ISAAC FASTIO

The earliest known residents and business owners of the Jewish faith in Pointe Coupée Parish, Louisiana were the Monsanto siblings, Sephardic Jews born in The Hague, Netherlands, of a family which originated in Portugal. Before coming to Louisiana, the Monsanto family had spent several years on the Dutch island of Curaçao as merchant traders.

Isaac Monsanto, said to have been the first Jewish resident of New Orleans, arrived in 1758, during the French colonial period, in the company of fellow Sephardi traders Isaac Henriqués Fastio and Manuél de Britto. All of the Monsanto siblings eventually made their way to Louisiana via Curaçao, living variously in Pensacola, British West Florida; Manchac; Natchez, Mississippi Territory; Pointe Coupée Parish, and finally New Orleans. The seven children of Pedro David Rodriques Monsanto (d. 1763), and Ester Levi (d. 1747), all born in The Hague, were Isaac (1729 - May or June 1778), Manuel (1734 - 10 July 1796), Gracia (1743 - January 1791), Angelica (1744 - 21 October 1821), Eleanora (1745 - 1796), Jacob (1746 - June 1789), and Benjamin (1747 - 1794).

The Monsantos' fluency in French, Spanish, and English made them valuable as intra- and inter-community communicators and guaranteed their personal success. By the grace of French governor Louis Billouart, Chevalier de Kérlérec, Isaac Monsanto established trade with Bordeaux, France, expanded into financing and planting, and served as a translator for the Superior Council in New Orleans. Monsanto also underwrote a British expedition up the Mississippi River to the Illinois country, which they (the British) had taken over after the French and Indian War.

Under the terms of Louisiana's *Code Noir*, foreign merchants and traders were barred from establishing in the colony, but residency and trading by the Monsantos, Fastios, and other pioneer Jewish families was tolerated by the French, although resented by some of Louisiana's native Créole population. However, when Spain finally took over the colony in 1769 with the arrival of Governor Alejandro O'Reilly from Cuba, the Jewish families were expelled from the city of New Orleans. Some of them established residency and businesses in rural communities, including the Pointe Coupée settlement.

The Monsantos exile from New Orleans precipitated the end of Isaac Monsanto's successful businesses. He was said to be staying with his sister Angelica, and her first husband, George Urquhart in Baton Rouge in 1774. By June 1775, he was in Pointe Coupée Parish where his brother Manuel, and sister Eleanor and her husband, Pierre André Tessier, a native of Saint-Domingue, were living. By the time of Isaac's death in 1778, he had settled down in a house on the François Allain plantation, near the present-day site of the Cajun II electric generating plant, northeast of New Roads, Louisiana. The inventory of his estate revealed that he had assets totaling 5,765 *piastres*, including personal effects, furniture, trunks and some merchandise, including two cases of sugar and some coffee. His customers were indebted to him for 24,995 *piastres*.

Of the three Monsanto sisters, only Eleanor had made a bad marriage. Her husband, Pierre André Tessier de Villauchamps, whom she married on 7 February 1773, at Cap-Français, Saint-Domingue, and who was described as "an abandoned man with dissipated habits," wound up in debtors' prison. His land, house and outbuildings, and slaves located in Pointe Coupée were worth less than his liabilities, so Eleanor was forced to sue for a separation of property, in order to handle her own affairs. She was a good manager, and able to provide a dowry for her daughter, Marie Eulalie, who married Pierre Roques in 1795. Her son, Charles André Tessier, born at Cap-Français, on 3 October 1775, and baptized two years later in Pointe Coupée Parish, later served as Secretary of the Spanish Colonial government. Charles and his wife, Lydia Clein/Klein, a native of Virginia, were the progenitors of the Tessier family of Upper Pointe Coupée Parish, including well-known Lettsworth centenarian David Mann Tessier (1905-2005).

While Eleanor married a Catholic, her sister, Angelica, had successful marriages to two Scottish Protestants, George Urquhart, and after his death, Dr. Robert Dow, a New Orleans physician. Eleanor's son Thomas Urquhart was born at St. Francisville, West Feliciana Parish, Louisiana, on 25 June 1773. He married Charlotte Laveau Trudeau, on 19 December 1805, at Saint Mary Church on Chartres Street, New Orleans (SMNO-M1, 14). Their daughter, Caroline married pioneer physician Dr. Isidore Labatut, of a distinguished New Orleans and Pointe Coupée Parish family, at New Orleans, on 12 November 1829 (SLC-M7, 172).

Gracia Monsanto married a Protestant Englishman, Thomas Topham, who owned land in the area of Manchac. (For a more thorough treatment of the Monsanto family in Louisiana and British West Florida see Bertrand Wallace Korn, *The Early Jews of New Orleans*, Waltham, MA: American Jewish Historical Society, 1969, pp.1-73.)

The Monsanto brothers had been, as Caribbean merchants in Curaçao, slave traders on a small scale, and, once in North America, continued to buy and sell slaves in the Louisiana territory and in Mississippi, both for their own use and for others. At one point, they individually kept a collective total of fifty-one enslaved Africans as laborers for their agricultural and trade ventures.

Isaac Henriqués Fastio, was a native of Bordeaux, Gironde, France, born there ca. 1722. He married Esther Rodrigués Henriqués, the daughter of Isaac "Le Poudrayre" Rodriqués Henriqués and Rachel de Podnonés Gomés Burguillos, on 15 May 1746, at Bordeaux. The bride was born ca. 1724 at Bordeaux, and died there on 8 February 1814. (Note: Isaac and Esther were divorced on 15 February 1798.) Fastio began working with the Monsanto brothers during their time on the Dutch island of Curaçao, in the Caribbean, and followed them to Louisiana in 1766. He is said to have been the first Jewish person in Baton Rouge.

Fastio moved to Pointe Coupée and established a trading business which continued for a half-century. By 1780, Benjamin Monsanto, Isaac Monsanto's brother, joined Fastio in partnership in Pointe Coupée. Benjamin Monsanto purchased farmland and enslaved persons, but meeting with little success, moved to Natchez, Adams Co., Mississippi, after about eight years' time, and is considered to be the first Jewish person in that state.

In 1791, several Mina slaves in the False River area planned a rebellion, from the plantation of the Widow Charles Robillard, née Marie Pourciau, which was located in what is now downtown New Roads. At the trial of the alleged perpetrators, Isaac Henriqués Fastio, as official interpreter for the Spanish government, was commissioned to sign all documentation of the interrogations of the accused, even though he did not attend any of the sessions. His comprehension of Spanish, however seems to have been limited because he needed a Spanish interpreter in order to be able to testify to authorities in New Orleans. Fastio was allowed to return to Pointe Coupée only upon city merchant Manuel Monsanto's signing a bond.

Unlike the previous, French administration, Louisiana's Spanish government forbade the enslavement of Native Americans. In 1793, an Afro-Indian enslaved woman at Pointe Coupée named Marie Jeanne sued for her and her two children's liberty. They were deemed property of merchant and planter Julien Poydras, but formerly that of Manuel Monsanto of New Orleans and held in service of his agent, Isaac Fastio, at Pointe Coupée. Marie Jeanne, then aged 60 years, stated herself to be the daughter of an African man and Native American woman. She identified her children Marie as a *griffe* (three-fourths black) and André Sarassin a *metis* (Franco-African-Indian). Marie Jeanne sued both Monsanto and Poydras. Monsanto replied that he believed her to be a mulatto (one-half European, one-half black) when he purchased her in 1782, but stated he would accept the court's judgment, either way.

Poydras' response was threefold. First, he believed her to be mulatto. Secondly, her son Antoine Sarassin's previous suit for freedom had been denied. Finally, he contended that Spain's prohibition of Native American enslavement did not apply to Louisiana. Poydras explained that French masters had been humane to enslaved Native Americans, however that Spanish aggressiveness had necessitated the prohibition. Poydras further argued that despite the transfer from French to Spanish rule, the property rights of those French who chose to remain in the colony after the change had been guaranteed. Since his enslaved Native Americans were considered property, his right as their owner could not be nullified. In the following year, 1794, Poydras was among 27 citizens who petitioned Spanish governor Hector, Baron de Carondelet, to request the Spanish king to cease the emancipation of enslaved Native Americans.

Marie Jeanne's son, Antoine Sarassin was among the leaders in the slave revolt which began on the main plantation of Julien Poydras in 1795. As one of the convicted, Sarassin was hanged, decapitated and his head placed atop a pole on the Mississippi River Road as a warning against future rebellion.

Colonial structures at Pointe Coupée with which the Monsantos and Fastios would have been familiar became history in the latter 19th century. The fort of Pointe Coupée, built in 1764 as a successor to earlier structures, was in a dilapidated state at the time of the Louisiana Purchase in 1804. An old building on the site served as the first Pointe Coupée Parish Courthouse until being destroyed by fire in 1846, upon which the seat of government was moved to New Roads on False River. A brick structure, the former powder magazine of the fort, was last mentioned as visible in 1872.

The second of three successive churches named St. Francis of Pointe Coupée was older than the fort by four years, having been built in 1760. The two structures stood on adjacent tracts on the Mississippi northeast of New Roads. The church, and its surrounding cemetery, was, for generations, the only house of worship and consecrated burial ground in the region. Systematic caving of the riverbank and the construction of a new levee behind the church and cemetery resulted in the movement of remains and markers of several pioneers buried therein between 1888 and 1892 to St. Mary Cemetery in New Roads and other places, and the dismantling of the church.

BENJAMIN JEWELL

Benjamin Jewell, believed by most descendants to be a native of Prussia, but by others to be a native of Hanover, Lower Saxony (Niedersachsen), Germany, born ca. 1750, operated a well-stocked general store at the northern terminus of the New Road, at Pointe Coupée Road, in the 1820s.

Jewell had previously been a merchant in Savannah, Chatham Co., Georgia, in the 1790s, where at some time between 1794 and 1795 he began a relationship and a family with Sophie Prévost, the daughter of Mme. Marie Prévost, a French Catholic *émigrée* from Saint-Domingue (present-day Haïti). Sophie later claimed that the wedding, said to have taken place in Savannah, was conducted by a magistrate, as neither would Jewell consent to a Catholic ceremony nor Mme. Prévost to a Jewish one. The legality of the Jewell-Prévost union was, in the wake of Jewell's death, debated in a lawsuit instituted by the widow and children of his second union, in the United States Supreme Court. In about 1804, Benjamin, Sophie and their children relocated to South Carolina, and by 1806 were living in Charleston, where he operated a clothing store. In December 1810, an act of separation was executed between Sophie and Benjamin in which she was granted custody of four of their children, and Benjamin their other five offspring.

Benjamin Jewell and the children in his care moved to Richmond, Virginia, where he married Sarah Isaacs, on 13 June 1813, in a Jewish ceremony. Benjamin and Sarah had six children of their own. They had moved to St. Francisville, Louisiana by 1818, and finally across the Mississippi River to Pointe Coupée Parish in 1819. There, Benjamin operated a store in the lower floor of their two-story residence at the northern terminus of the *Chemin Neuf*, or New Road, from which the town and parish seat on False River at the southern terminus took its name.

Benjamin Jewell died on 9 Nov 1828, aboard the vessel *Illinois*, on a return voyage from New York to New Orleans and was buried at sea. According to his succession filed in Pointe Coupée Parish (Conveyance Book 1828, No. 2737), he died intestate, following a four-day illness. His itemized inventory of movable and immovable property in Pointe Coupée Parish was valued at $30,678.97, and included a tract at the head of the New Road on the Mississippi, measuring 9 ¼ arpents front on the river, by a depth of 49 arpents; store merchandise; a four-wheel carriage, two carts; 12 horses, 10 oxen, 25 head of cattle; and a labor force of 47 enslaved persons (Old Probate Court, No. 145).

Jewell's two-story residence included a (dining) hall, cave (wine and provisions room), closet (small bedroom), and "storeroom" (his retail store) on the ground floor. Upstairs were the "upper hall" (*salon* or reception room), two bedrooms, and a closet (bathroom). Attesting to the family's wealth were a pianoforte, a secretary, sideboard and dining table, all of mahogany, a dozen gilt, rush-seated chairs, upholstered armchairs, silver flatware, a silver-plated tea urn and candlesticks, and a pair of gilt goblets.

Benjamin Jewell, like several other merchants of 19th century Pointe Coupée, had an inventory of merchandise which startles the present-day researcher and reader for its size, including 10,839 yards of fabrics, a "lot" of buttons, thread, needles, 15,000 pins, a lot of notions, 82 buckles, 24 quilts, seven coats, nine pairs of pants, 18 cravats, 1,228 pairs of suspenders, 40 muslin robes (dresses), a blue gauze robe, three gingham robes, 23 worked robes, 210 shawls, 51 veils, 117 pairs of hose, 332 pairs of gloves, 90 bandanas, 1,164 handkerchiefs, 74 hats, 486 pairs of shoes, 16 gold breast pins, 168 gilt breast pins, 24 gilt watch chains, 35 gilt watch seals, 16 gilt watch keys, 72 necklaces, 120 pearl necklaces, 24 red bead necklaces, eight pair of spectacles, 42 velvet purses, six reticules, 60 pocket books, six red pocket books, 60 combs, 188 horn side combs, 30 shaving glasses (mirrors), 576 Jew's harps, lot of flour, olives, salt herring, lot of medicines, perfume, lot soap, 11 toothbrushes, 56 metal mugs, 12 japan (i.e., ceramic) sugar dishes, 288 iron spoons, 20 tin pans, colanders, strainers, skimmers, basins, 24 candle molds, 116 pairs of scissors, six japan lamps, 24 lamps without stands, six complete lamps, 1,100 fish hooks, fishing line, twine, pails, turpentine, tar, 1,395 pounds of nails, 9,000 brass nails, latches, padlocks, pullies, 56 hoes, four saddles, lot bridles and bits, 58 pairs of trace chains; also two showcases, show glass (mirror), counter, shelves, desk, iron chest, and lot of notes receivable.

Benjamin Jewell's widow, Sarah Isaacs, and the children from their marriage, Isabella Virginia (b. 1812 in Virginia), and Jane Marie (b. 1826 in Louisiana), filed suit against Sophie Prévost, Benjamin's first wife, and their children together, in order to recover a house and lot in Charleston left by the deceased, still in possession of his first family. Sarah claimed the relationship of Benjamin and Sophie Prévost was not a legal marriage, but rather a contract of concubinage entered into by the couple in Savannah on 10 Mar 1796. The provisions of the contract were not discussed during the court proceedings, supposedly due to the "indecent" terms contained therein. Sophie, for her part, stated that she had already relinquished possession of the property in question, and repeated that the ceremony uniting her and Benjamin had been a legal civil one, adding that their children (i.e., sons) had been circumcised according to Jewish law.

The Jewell family of Pointe Coupée Parish descended, largely, through the issue of Benjamin and his first union, with Sophie Prévost. Being the children and subsequent generation descendants of a Catholic matriarch, they were principally of the Catholic, Episcopal and Methodist faiths. They were active in governmental, legal, political, mercantile, and agricultural interests, as well as in education and Christian ministry.

The eldest son of Benjamin Jewell and Sophie Prévost, Benjamin Jewell, II (1798-1879), was a cotton planter on *L'Isle de la Fausse Rivière,* (The Island of False River), known by that name since the earliest years of the settlement. The "Island" is that portion of Pointe Coupée Parish surrounded almost on three sides by the former channel of the Mississippi and on the east by the present channel. He married twice, first in Ventress ca. 1836, to Virginie Major, and second ca. 1842, to Amelina Guérin, both wives being from early French Catholic families.

Alphonse Lamartine Jewell, a son from Benjamin's second marriage, to Amelina Guérin, born on 6 August 1849 (PCP-10, 130), served as Pointe Coupée Parish Clerk of Court between 1900 and 1928. Alphonse and his wife, Philomène Adèle Major's son, Joseph Philibert Jewell, Sr. (1885-1966) succeeded his father in that office from 1928 until his death. Two sons of the latter served in state and parish offices. Joseph Thomas Jewell, Sr. was a Louisiana State Representative from 1936 through 1968 as well as Speaker of the House from 1960 until 1964. Joseph Philibert Jewell, Jr., was the Pointe Coupée Parish Assessor from 1967 until 1997. Sr. Agnes Jewell, C.S.J. daughter of Joseph Philibert Jewell, Sr. was a longtime educator. In more recent years, James Jewell Best, a great-grandson of Alphonse Lamartine Jewell, served as the 18th Judicial District Court Judge. All of the above-mentioned descendants were Catholic.

Alphonse Lamartine Jewell, Sr. is also recorded as the natural father, by Françoise Hypolite, a woman of color, of Octave Jewell, born ca. 1867. Octave was married on 4 August 1887, in New Roads, to Hélène Joséphine Fortlouis (PCP-25, 120-121). The bride was born on 10 June 1870, to Maurice Fortlouis, likely a natural son of pioneer Jewish merchant Jean Maurice Fortlouis, born to him and an unknown woman of color, ca. 1830, and Hélène Francois (PCP-27, 113). Maintaining close contact with his father's family, Octave Jewell was identified as a servant, living in the household of Widow Amélina Guérin Jewell on the Island of False River in the 1880 United States Federal Census, and as a farm laborer residing near rice planter Benjamin Jewell III (son of Joshua Joseph Jewell and grandson of Benjamin Jewell, II) and family at Mix on False River thirty years later.

In addition to Benjamin III (b. 24 October 1859, PCP-14, 93), other sons of False River sugar planter Joshua Joseph Jewell and his wife, née Marie Lodoïska Boiteux, who were married on 18 November 1858 (PCP-23, 6), included New Roads Town Marshal Joseph Emile Jewell (b. 10 January 1866 - PCP-28, 11), and Pierre Marius Jewell (b. 15 August 1871 – PCP-28, 96), proprietor of the "Three Feathers," saloon on Richy Street in New Roads.

Another son of Benjamin Jewell and Sophie Prévost, Joseph E. Jewell (c. 1805-1884), was a private tutor and publisher of one of the first newspapers of the area, the bilingual *Echo de la Pointe Coupée*, on the Pointe Coupée Road. He was married on 21 November 1835, to Jane Eliza Lewis, a native of Massachusetts, in Wilkinson Co., Mississippi. His sons, Edwin Lewis (b. ca. 1836) and Frederick Lewis Jewell (b. ca. 1840), published the popular *Jewell's Crescent City Illustrated* journal in 1873 in New Orleans. This line of the Jewell family was principally of the Episcopal faith.

Born as Juliana Jewell, ca. 1796, Hannah was the eldest child of Benjamin Jewell and Sophie Prévost. Benjamin Jewell gave his written consent to the marriage of his daughter Hannah, to Waterloo area cotton planter Delphin Vergès Vignes on 9 September 1820. The couple was married in a Catholic ceremony on 16 October 1820 (PCP-19, 182). A son, cotton planter Adolphe Vignes, married Marie Zulma Hébert, and their daughter Mary Eudora Vignes, born on 8 August 1857 (PCP-14, 33), was identified as the "wife" of Ferdinand Gumbel. According to the 1880 United States Federal Census, she was living with him, a "daughter" Leona Gumbel, a "son" Lucien Gumbel, and her brother Edward Vignes in downtown New Orleans, Louisiana. No record for their marriage has been located.

Edwin Vignes, born on 13 August 1839 (PCP-4, 227), was another of Hannah Jewell and Delphin Vergès Vignes sons. In the years following the Civil War, he owned a warehouse at Waterloo, Louisiana, where thousands of bales of cotton from Pointe Coupée Parish plantations and farms were stored prior to export via steamboat to New Orleans.

Later descendants of Hannah Jewell and Delphin Vergès Vignes included: Anna Bondy, milliner and wife of Louisiana Representative, U.S. Minter, and merchant Mayer Cahen of Assumption Parish, New Orleans, and New Roads; Alcide Bondy, Anna's brother, and partner in the "New Roads Fancy Grocery" with his brother-in-law Mayer Cahen; Mathilde Vignes, wife of Pointe Coupée Parish merchant Jules St. Germain; F.D. Vignes, co-founder with Jules Bombet, a Jewish immigrant from Brumath, Bas-Rhin, France, and Josh Kantrow, of the Vignes-Bombet wholesale grocery company in Baton Rouge; and sibling educators Bro. Cosmas Cazayoux, S.C., and Rev. Clair Cazayoux, S.J.

JULES LEVY

Jules Levy, born on 12 October 1827, at Nancy, Meurthe-et-Moselle, France, to Abraham Levy and Thérèse Weil, immigrated to Louisiana via Le Havre, France, arriving in New Orleans on 20 July 1846, aboard the *J.H. Cooper*. He filed a declaration of intention of to be naturalized and renounced his allegiance to the King of France in 1848, and allegiance to the Republic of France in 1852, in New Roads, Louisiana. He appeared in the 1850 United States Federal Census as a merchant in partnership with his brothers, Meyer and Arthur Levy, upriver of Morganza, who had total assets of $1200.

Jules Levy opened one of the first-known pharmacies in Pointe Coupée Parish, the "Pointe Coupée Drug Store," in 1859. It was located on the F.O. Bouis plantation, at Bouis Pointe (later misspelled as "Boies" Point), downriver of Grand Levee. Jules Levy advertised in an 1859 *Démocrate de la Pointe Coupée/Pointe Coupée Democrat* for his "Pointe Coupée Drug Store. It read: "Medicines, Fresh Drugs, Patent Medicines, Perfumery, &c, Depot of Hungarian Leeches. The Prescriptions of Physicians will be filled with care and dispatch, at all hours of the day or night. Drugs and Medicines for plantations in quantities to suit purchasers."

Jules was enumerated living on the plantation in the 1860 United States Federal Census with $1,200 property, along with his brother Leopold Levy.

Following the Civil War, Jules Levy returned upriver of Morganza, and, according to the 1865 IRS Report, was working as a merchant. At that time, he also acted as agent for his brother and sister-in-law, Arthur and Marguérite Cléontine Decuir Levy, and their children, who, during the Civil War, had been temporarily living in Nancy, Meurthe-et-Moselle, France. (For further information see his entry in the Raccourci-Old River Section.)

MEYER LEVY

Meyer Levy, born on 13 February 1823, at Nancy, Meurthe-et-Moselle, France, to Abraham Levy and Thérèse Weil, immigrated to America ca. 1846. He filed a declaration renouncing allegiance to the King of France in 1848 and to the Republic of France in 1852, both in New Roads, Louisiana. Meyer, who had previously lived in New Orleans, and later in Natchez, Adams Co., Mississippi, married Hevven/Henriette Müller at Natchez on 4 November 1852. Henriette was born at Dehlingen, Bas-Rhin, France, on 3 February 1826, to Jacques Müller, a merchant, and his wife, Sara Freund. Meyer and Henriette moved for a brief period to San Francisco, California, where their first child, Achille (b. 1853), was born, before returning to Pointe Coupée Parish to settle near Meyer's brothers.

One of the first-known references to Meyer Levy in Pointe Coupée was from the press of the bilingual *Démocrate de la Pointe Coupée/Pointe Coupée Democrat* of New Roads. In its 22 May 1858 issue, the paper related that Levy was injured in the previous week when leaving the store of Simon, Loeb & Co., opposite the *Democrat* office. Apparently, Levy's horse became frightened and overturned his buggy, and the unfortunate man's leg was fractured in three places above the ankle. *Democrat* staff as well as Levy's unnamed "brother," and (attorney and future judge) John Yoist, conveyed the victim into the store and sent for Dr. (Ludovic) Ladmirault to administer to him.

Levy's horse, meanwhile, had thrown off its harness and traces and ran, dragging the broken buggy shafts behind, a half-mile "below," i.e., out West Main Street before coming to a halt, "in no way injured or hurt." The journal solemnly pronounced Meyer Levy's accident "one of the most painful occurrences which it has been our task to chronicle since the first issue of the *Democrat*."

Meyer, a merchant with $300 in property, Henriette and their two sons, Achille, age six and Maurice, age three, were enumerated in the 1860 United States Federal Census living next to the Zénon Porche (later Labatut) House on Pointe Coupée Road. Meyer held a State Business License in 1867.

Meyer Levy was followed in merchandising there, in turn, by the "Young America Store" of Labatut's son Emanuel; by the "Hope Store" of pioneer retailer Roch Pedarré; then by Emanuel Labatut's younger brother, Albert, who was followed by patriarch Jules Labatut; and ultimately by the often-moving Bernard Teutsch as the "Labatut Store." Thus, this location, midway between the Blue Store and St. Maurice Landing, was the center of commerce for a heavily-populated agrarian neighborhood for more than a half-century.

The Levy family moved twice again, first near the lower end of Raccourci-Old River, and ultimately after the Civil War to Williamsport. Among Meyer Levy's last-known acquisitions were from Cerf Wolff which included four tracts in the Lakeland area and Wolff's "Burnt Bridge Store" purchased in 1882. Levy renamed the latter the "Diamond W Store," but sold it along with the four properties back to Wolff two years later.

MEYER & STRAUSS

Meyer & Strauss was the partnership of Marx (b. ca. 1822) and Edward Meyer (b. ca. 1825), and Marcus Strauss (b. ca. 1823), all natives of the Kingdom of Bavaria. Marx Meyer had immigrated in 1848. He filed a declaration in 1855 renouncing allegiance to the King of Bavaria and an oath in 1857 renouncing allegiance once again to the Bavarian King, both in New Roads, Louisiana. An attempt to write the town of his birth was transcribed as "Houlehobheim," which was probably an attempt at "Heuchelheim," Rheinpfalz, Germany.

The Meyers and Strauss were identified as peddlers, living in house of planter Charles Hagan, a native of Germany, below Grand Levee on Pointe Coupée Road in the 1850 United States Federal Census. Headed by Meyer, they were enumerated as sugar planters and merchants in the same neighborhood, with $19,000 in real estate and $60,000 in personal property in the 1860 United States Federal Census. The accompanying 1860 United States Slave Schedule showed them as the owners of fourteen enslaved persons.

Marx Meyer was subsequently a dry goods merchant near Red River Landing and was enumerated in the 1870 United States Federal Census for Pointe Coupée, Police Jury Ward 3, as a retail dry goods merchant from the "Rhein Bayern" (misspelled as "Rainbeirin") region of Germany, with a personal estate worth $1000. We believe that Marx Meyer was a brother or cousin of the three Meyer sisters from Heuchelheim, Rheinpfalz, Germany: Miriam, married to David Hirsch; Rosine, married to Isaac Dreyfus; and Caroline, married to Michel Weil, all of whom did business in Pointe Coupée Parish. We could find no further records for either Edward Meyer or Maurice Strauss.

JACQUES GOUDCHAUX

Signature of J. Goudchaux's 1855 Application for Citizenship

Jacques Goudchaux was born Jacob Lion Marx on 20 April 1808, at Kutzenhausen, Bas-Rhin, France, to Mathias Marx and his wife Michla Wolf. Although the surname Goudchaux only appears in various spellings in later records, the 1808 name adoption list for Kutzenhausen gave his parents as Mathias Marx born in 1776, Rose Michele, his wife, born in 1772, and two children: Carline Marx, born in 1802, and Jacques Marx born in 1808. Jacques Marx was married at Kutzenhausen as "Jacob Gotschot" on 14 April 1834 to Bräunle Vogel, known as "Babette", born on 23 March 1811, at Lichtenau, Baden, to Kaufman Gotchel Vogel and Louise Lazarus. Included in "Gotschot's marriage record was the fact that Jacques was born as "Marx Jacques Lion," son of Matthias Marx (later Mathieu Goetschel) and Michelè Wolf (later Michelé Rose).

Jacques and Babette had a daughter, Pauline, born as "Pauline Gaudchau", on 17 July 1834, at Kutzenhausen.

Thirty-eight-year-old Jacques Goudchaux and eighteen-year-old Benjamin Weil immigrated together, arriving at New Orleans, on the ship *Clarissa Andrews* from Le Havre, France, on 2 January 1847. With Goudchaux, but listed on another page, was his wife, Babette Vogel, age 34, and his daughter Pauline, age 9. (Note: All three had their surnames misspelled as "Goderhand" by the transcriber of the "abstract," as apparently the original record no longer exists.)

According to Pauline's marriage record at Strasbourg, Bas Rhin, France, her mother, Babette Vogel, died in New Orleans on 16 August 1847, only eight months after her arrival. Records do not permit us to know whether Pauline remained with her father in America, or was sent back to France, to be with relatives. What we do know is that Jacques Goudchaux had signed a document on 11 June 1855, applying for American citizenship at New Roads, Pointe Coupée Parish, and was present when naturalized there in 1857.

He was also present and consented to his daughter's wedding at Strasbourg, Bas-Rhin, France, on 23 February 1860. He signed the marriage certificate, and was identified as a merchant living at Strasbourg. The groom, Pauline's first cousin, Mathias Gerschel, had been born to Abraham Gerschel and Caroline Gaudschau, Jacques Goudchaux's sister, on 1 August 1830, at Niederroedern, Bas-Rhin, France.

Jacques Goudchaux returned from France in time to appear in the United States Federal Census dated 30 June 1860, declaring $100 in personal property, and living with Benjamin Weil, with whom he had originally come to Louisiana, next to planter J.H. Morrison and the latter's family on Pointe Coupée Road. Moving to the New Roads area after the Civil War, Goudchaux was a dealer in merchandise and liquor on Patin Dyke Road, just east of town.

BENJAMIN WEIL

Benjamin Weil, was born on 9 July 1830, in Rixheim, Haut-Rhin, France, to Isaac Weil, a second-hand dealer and his wife, Adelaide Levy. Benjamin filed a declaration of intention to become a United States citizen at New Roads, Louisiana, and took the oath in 1852. At that time, he declared that he was a native of the "Bas-Rhin, France," and had come to the United States at the age of sixteen in 1846. While he did leave France in late 1846, we know, from the ship's record, that he arrived with Jacques Goudchaux on 2 January 1847, aboard the *Clarissa Andrews,* a voyage, at that time, of approximately six weeks or more.

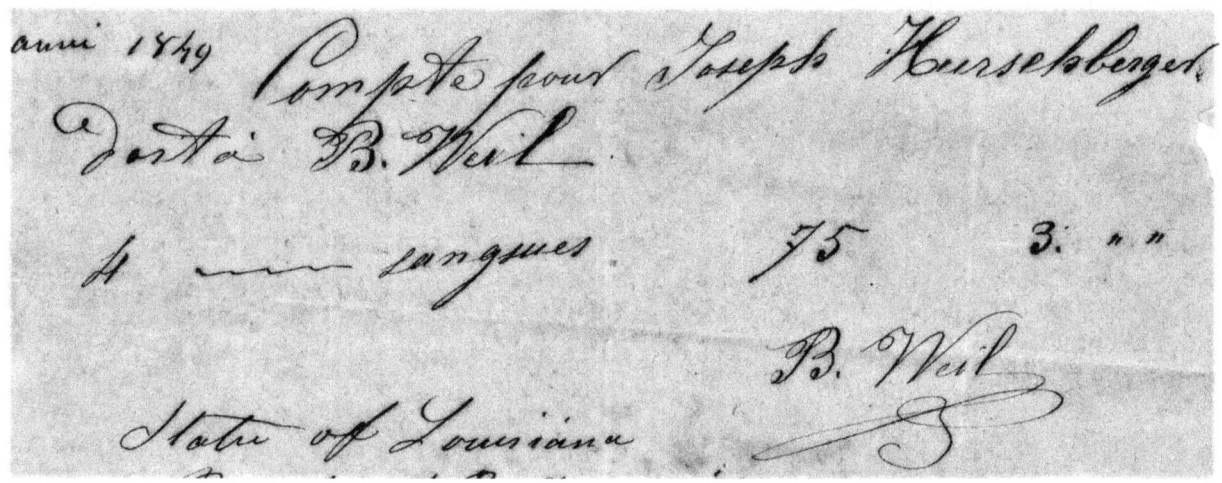

Invoice for four leeches found in succession of Joseph Hirschberger dated 1850, signed by B. Weil.

Working with his shipmate, Jacques Goudchaux, the two French peddlers shared a residence on Pointe Coupée Road, according to the 1860 United States Federal Census.

During the Civil War, Benjamin Weil served in the 1st Regiment, Louisiana Cavalry, Returning to Pointe Coupée Parish, he resumed peddling dry goods in New Roads. He married Rosine Michel, the widow of Nathan Kern, on 21 December 1870, in New Roads, but was divorced from her on 8 April 1872. Weil next clerked in New Orleans and ultimately on the Lower Chenal of False River for Aaron Loeb.

Benjamin Weil was likely the natural father of Marie Manouthe Weil, a "free woman of color," born to Cécile Lacour, a "free woman of color," ca. December 1850, according to the 1900 United States Federal Census, in or near New Roads, Louisiana. Although no father's name was listed for Marie Manouthe on either of the records for her two marriages, it is likely that it was Benjamin Weil, as her United States Federal Census listings indicate her father to be either of French or German birth.

One of the earliest known references to Marie Weil and family is found in the New Roads, Louisiana Freedmen's Bureau Field Office records at which time Cécile Lacour and her four children were issued assistance in the form of eight pounds of pork and fifty pounds of cornmeal on 6 January 1868.

Marie Manouthe Weil was married first on 19 December 1871, in old St. Mary of False River Church, New Roads, Louisiana, to Marius Vernous/Vernoux, a native of Trévous/Trévoux, Ain,

France, to Joseph Vernous/Vernoux and Marie Brun (PCP-24, 111). Theirs was one of, at least, thirteen marriages of "white" men and women "of color," with court-issued licenses that were usually followed by Catholic ceremonies in Pointe Coupée Parish between the adoption of the 1868 Louisiana Constitution, which lifted the ban on "interracial" marriage, and the 1898 legalized institution of segregation.

Marius Vernous appeared in Pointe Coupée Parish records for the first time in the 1870 United States Federal Census, when he was identified as a forty-eight-year-old retail dealer, without real estate but having $1,500 personal property, living near *Pointe Coupée Echo* editor, F.L. Jewell, on the Pointe Coupée Road. Vernous was evidently a recent arrival to the community, as he was not listed amongst the businessmen having Parish and State Licenses in 1867 or 1868.

There were at least two children born to the marriage: Catherine Léonard Vernous, born on 25 November 1872, to Marius and Marie Vignes (*sic*) (PCP-28, 120), and August Joseph Vernous, born on 15 April 1875, to Marius and Marie Veill (PCP-28, 193).

Marius Vernous died on 19 December 1877, in New Roads, and was interred there in St. Mary Cemetery (PCP-20, 85). Widowed, Marie was married again on 18 July 1881, to Francois Gabriel "Frank" Bouligny, the son of Lower Chenal sugar planter Francois Gabriel Florville Bouligny and Hélène Tounoir, the ancestor of two of Louisiana's most prominent *Créole de couleur* families (PCP-25, 16).

François Bouligny was enumerated in the 1880 United States Federal Census as a bartender for John Boudreau's "Boudreau's Retreat" saloon and billiard hall opposite the Pointe Coupée Parish Courthouse on East Main Street in New Roads. Bouligny also advertised in many 1882 issues of the *Pointe Coupée Banner* as a dog trainer "in French or English."

Three children were born to Marie Weil and François Bouligny after they moved from Pointe Coupée Parish to Baton Rouge, ca. 1883: Joseph François "Frank" born on 29 November 1884 (mother's name spelled "Wild," SJBR-20, 223); Rosa Emma (aka Ernestine), baptized (no birth date given) on 1 March 1887, to "Frank Bonligmy (*sic*) and Mary Wile (*sic*)," (SJBR 20-248); and George Claude Bouligny, born on 24 April 1893 to Frank and Mary Wiges (*sic*) (SJBR-20, 331).

According to the 1900 United States Federal Census, Marie Bouligny (b. Dec. 1850) was a widow living with her sons Frank (age 16), and George (age 7), daughter Ernestine (age 13), and Marie's mother, Cécile Lacour (age 70), in Baton Rouge, Louisiana. Ten years later Frank, Sr., a cook in a hotel, was back with the family, including Marie, his wife working as a midwife, his son George, a bellboy in a hotel, and mother-in-law, Cécile Lacour. The hotel was the landmark Istrouma Hotel at Third and Florida Streets. Frank was later, according to the 1905 *Baton Rouge City Directory*, the operator of his own restaurant at 106 Front Street (now River Road) and North Boulevard, opposite the State Capitol building. According to his World War I registration card, Frank, Jr. was working as a waiter at the Istrouma Hotel.

Marie Manouthe Weil's mother, Cécile Lacour, died on 14 February 1916, in Baton Rouge and was interred there in the St. Joseph Catholic Cemetery. Francois "Frank" Bouligny, Sr. died in Baton Rouge on 28 September 1921, although we could find no record of his burial.

Widowed a second time, Marie was enumerated in her son George Bouligny's home in Los Angeles, Los Angeles Co., California, in the 1930 United States Federal Census. Ten years later she was living alone in Los Angeles. She died there on 16 October 1945.

MOSES MANN

Moses Mann, was born on 26 April 1826, in Monsheim, Rhine-Hesse, Germany. He married Fannie Hirsch, born on 22 February 1834 in Hildesheim, Rhine-Hesse, Germany, to David Hirsch and Miriam Meyer. Moses and Fannie had one child, a daughter, Rose, born on 2 November 1861, in West Feliciana Parish, Louisiana.

Mann was prominent in merchandising in Bayou Sara and New Orleans, Louisiana, and was one of a succession of proprietors of the famous "Red Store," near the Pointe Coupée Post Office. The "Red Store" and the river landing of the same name across the levee, were Mississippi River landmarks for generations. The Red Store Plantation, on which the store and landing were located, had been the principal property of pioneer merchant, planter, statesman, poet and philanthropist Julien Poydras, and the nucleus of the epic slave rebellion of 1795.

The "Red Store," under Moses Mann's operation, was one of the earliest-known establishments to sell furniture in Pointe Coupée Parish, Louisiana. The 1876-77 Bouchereau, *Statement of the Sugar Crops*, and the 1879 *Pelican*, both had advertisements for M. Mann proprietor of the "Red Store. According to the *Pelican*, His inventory included: dry goods, trimmings, notions, clothing, ladies'; and gents' furnishing goods, hats, caps, boots, shoes, perfumery, groceries, provisions, Western produce, wines, liquors, tobacco, cigars, chinaware, crockery, glassware, cooking utensils, tinware, hardware, and furniture

Moses Mann was succeeded in the operation of "Red Store" in 1882 by Alexander "Alex" Mann, a native of Bavaria, and owner of a numerous commercial houses in West Feliciana and Pointe Coupée Parishes. We believe that Moses and Alex were probably brothers or cousins although we have not been able to verify it. Mann and his family moved to New Orleans where he engaged in the produce and commission business with Jacob Myers as Myers & Mann. Jacob Myers/Meyer, was the brother of Miriam and Caroline Meyer, the wives respectively of David Hirsch and Michel Weil. Moses Mann and his family eventually moved to Chicago, Cook, Co., Illinois, where his wife died on 17 November 1910. Moses Mann died on 27 September 1915. They were both interred in Hebrew Rest Cemetery No. 2 in New Orleans.

ALEXANDER "ALEX" MANN

Alexander "Alex" Mann, also a native of Monsheim, Rhine-Hesse, Germany, succeeded Moses Mann in the operation of the "Red Store," on Pointe Coupée Road. Many 1882 *Pointe Coupée Banner* advertisements for A. Mann, "Red Store" indicated that he carried dry goods, trimmings, notions, clothing, ladies' and gents' furnishing goods, hats, caps, boots, shoes, perfumery, provisions, family supplies and Western produce, wines, liquors, tobacco, cigars, chinaware, glassware, cooking utensils, tinware, furniture.

LOUIS STRAUSS

We believe that Louis Strauss, a partner in the L. Strauss & Co. "Blue Store," may be identified as Lazarus/Louis Strauss, a native of Prussia. According to the 1880 United States Federal

Census, "forty-year-old" "Louis" Strauss, a merchant and native of Prussia, Julius Strauss, age 27, and Gustus Hart, all clerks, were living together at Newellton, Tensas Parish, Louisiana. (Note: Many Jewish men originally born "Lazarus," had their given names anglicized to "Louis" when they came to America.) "Gustus" Hart was identified as Gus Hart, born in 1854 in Osyka, Pike Co., Mississippi, who married Bertha Lemle, a native of New Orleans.

Twenty years later, this same "Lazarus" Strauss was living in Brooklyn New York, born ca. March 1850, in Germany, with other family members, including his brother Julius, born ca. July 1852. Lazarus and Julius had immigrated ca. 1865 into the port of New York. Lazarus had married Sarah Marks, a native of Mississippi, on 8 September 1876, in Adams Co., Mississippi. They were the parents of four children: Julius, born ca. 1877 who died at Newellton on 3 July 1883, and was interred in the Natchez City Cemetery, in Natchez, Adams Co., Mississippi; Samuel, b. 1887, who died at Newellton on 6 July 1888, also buried in Natchez; Bernard, b. 1889 at Newellton, who died in New York in 1943; Bertha "Birdie," born ca. 1891 in New York, who died there in 1972. (Note: In a second marriage to Esther née Strauss in New York, on 17 April 1898, Lazarus gave his parents' names as Judas Strauss and Bertha Westheim.)

The landmark "Blue Store" or *"Magasin Bleu"* was opened prior the Civil War by Pierre Curet, a native of France, and acquired during the war years by another native Frenchman, Roch Pedarré. A clipping of an advertisement for the *"Magasin Bleu"* from an unidentified newspaper, pasted in a scrapbook entitled the *Thomas H. Hewes Civil War Scraps, Etc., February 1st 1862* housed at the Pointe Coupée Parish Library Historic Materials Collection, New Roads, Louisiana, reads: "Novelties! Cheap!" and lists the merchandise carried by the store as dry goods, shoes, boots, fancy articles, faience, pots, tinware, cutlery, hardware, groceries, wines, liquors, tobacco and cigars.

Lazarus/Louis Strauss succeeded Pedarré at the "Blue Store" in March 1882, a month marked by unprecedented levee failures and flooding. Numerous 1882-1883 *Pointe Coupée Banner* advertisements for "Blue Store," L. Strauss & Co., proprietors featured its contents including linen lawns, embroideries, trimmings, notions, gentlemen's clothing, white linen shirts, furnishing goods, and British and lisle thread hose; ladies' furnishing goods; groceries, provisions, flour, wines, liquors, perfumery, fancy articles, crockery, glassware, trunks, hardware, and saddlery.

Strauss continued in business until selling the store and the 1 x 3.5 arpent lot upon which it stood to general merchant Jean Terrabust for $1,350 in cash in 1884. The act of sale called for the northern line of the lot to be as it was in 1872, apparently at the center line of the levee in 1882 owing to the caving of the Mississippi River bank and resultant levee setbacks

Between 1882 and 1885, Lazarus/Louis Strauss owned two of the largest plantations on the Pointe Coupée "coast": St. Maurice and Sugar Land, located east and west, respectively of the "Blue Store." He purchased St. Maurice Plantation, complete with sugar mill, and the Blue Store lot in the same act, in 1882, from James Fort Muse, for $22,000. St. Maurice measured eight arpents' fronting on the Mississippi River, by a depth of 65 arpents, and was bounded above or west by the Succession of Zenon Porche (*sic*, by then Mme. Jules Labatut, née Clélie Ranson) and below or east by (the grandchildren of) Fanny Riché.

Strauss bought Sugar Land Plantation in two acts in 1883: the interest of the Green family, represented by their agent and attorney-in-fact, future United States Supreme Court Justice Edward D. White, for $5,000, and the interest of Benjamin Cooley for $500. Sugar Land measured four arpents' fronting on the Mississippi River by a depth of 80 arpents, and was bounded above or west by Judge Ebenezer Cooley and below or east by Roch Pedarré (*sic,* by then, owned by Strauss, i.e., the "Blue Store" lot), Robert Montgomery, and Mme. Jules Labatut.

According to period *Banner* accounts, Louis Strauss resided, when in Pointe Coupée, in the residence on St. Maurice: a two-story house formerly owned and occupied by the wealthy Porche and Ferrier families of Pointe Coupée and New Orleans, but replaced at the turn of the 19th-20th centuries by the Stonaker residence.

In addition to retailing and planting, Louis Strauss also ginned cotton for the public. In listing the baling charges by area ginners, the 8 September 1883 *Banner* related that Strauss's fee was $2.50 per bale, regardless of weight, and he kept the seed. Bouchereau's *Statement of the Sugar Crop Made in Louisiana* for the 1883-1884 season indicated a mere 35 hogsheads (1,000-pound barrels) of sugar produced on St. Maurice, suggesting that Strauss devoted most of his acreage to cotton cultivation. In 1885, both Sugar Land and St. Maurice were judicially seized and sold at a sheriff's sale owing to judgments rendered against Louis Strauss by Simon Gumbel & Co. and Roch Pedarré, both of New Orleans. Both plantations, passing through a succession of owners, have been top sugar producers since.

Lazarus Straus died on 22 April 1905, in Brooklyn, Kings Co., New York, and was interred there in Maimonides Cemetery, along with his first wife, Sarah Marks Strauss, who had died on 22 December 1895, and his brother Julius, who died on 5 August 1902. The family had owned a "Gents Furnishing Store" for many years in Brooklyn.

It was at St. Maurice Landing in front of the plantation, then owned by James Stonaker, that the luxury steamboat *J.M. White* exploded and burned in 1886, with a loss of at least sixty-five human lives, a prize ox which was to represent the *Boeuf Gras* in the 1887 Rex parade in New Orleans, and a substantial amount of baled cotton and cotton seed. The approximate site of the tragedy is marked by the roadside St. Maurice Oak, having one of the greatest circumferences recorded by the Louisiana Live Oak Society. Massive at present, the tree is but half of its former size. The branches on the north side were progressively removed during successive setbacks of the road and levee owing to encroachment of the Mississippi River.

DANIEL MAYER

According to the 1880 United States Federal Census for Pointe Coupée Parish, Daniel Maier/Mayer, a forty-five-year-old native of Prussia, was a clerk in "Blue Store," then owned by Roch Pedarré, and subsequently by L. Strauss & Co. Daniel married Bertha Bierman, born on 15 May 1842, at Seibersbach, Rhine-Hesse, Germany, the widow of Isaac Klein, on 21 December 1884, in New Orleans. By the time of the 1900 United States Federal Census, Mayer and his wife and nephew Moses Fraenkel born in May 1880 in Germany, had moved to Plaquemine, Iberville Parish, Louisiana, where Daniel worked as a grocer. His wife died on 3 November 1903, at Plaquemine, and was interred there in the Jewish Cemetery.

BENJAMIN "BEN" MANN

Benjamin "Ben" Mann, of the extensive Mann commercial family of West Feliciana and Pointe Coupée Parishes, was born on 13 July 1863, in New Orleans to Alexander Mann and his wife, Theresa Hausmann. He was employed as a grocer at the "Blue Store," owned in succession by Roch Pedarré and L. Strauss & Co., according to the 1880 United States Federal Census.

In subsequent years, Ben Mann was engaged as a merchant and farmer in the neighborhood. On the night of 13 December 1886, Mann, identified as a local merchant, along with James Stonaker (part owner of the "Blue Store" and St. Maurice Plantation) and J.A. Dayries (owner of the "Red Store" plantation and emporium and the father of future New Orleans Police Superintendent Provosty Dayries) were in the cabin of the luxury steamer *J.M. White* when it caught fire at St. Maurice Landing. Of the approximately 90 people aboard, Mann, Stonaker and Dayries were among the few survivors, as more than 65 men, women and children burned to death or drowned.

Ben Mann was among the first farmers in Pointe Coupée Parish to cultivate Irish potatoes. In one of his last mentions in the community, the 19 March 1887 issue of the *Pointe Coupée Banner* reported his success in planting four to five acres of the crop.

Ben Mann was married to Anna Sophia Hubertina Spitz on 23 April 1893, in West Feliciana Parish. Anna, a native of Kleinenbroich, North Rhine-Westphalia, Germany, was born there on 31 July 1869. Ben, his wife and children, Abraham Louis (b. 1895), Louis Marks (b. 1896), Lottie (b. 1899), and Mathilde (b. 1900), were enumerated as residents of St. Francisville during the United States Federal Censuses of 1900, 1910 and 1920. Ben Mann was identified successively, as a salesman, dry goods merchant, and store merchant, however we also know that he owned a barroom and a livery stable at Bayou Sara, and was President of the local Temple Sinai Jewish Congregation. Ben Mann died on 14 May 1924, at Bayou Sara, and Anna followed on 20 October 1927. They were both interred in the Jewish Cemetery at St. Francisville.

BERNARD TEUTSCH

Bernard Teutsch worked in various places in Pointe Coupée Parish during his commercial career. A native of Venningen, Rheinpfalz, Germany, he was born there on 24 July 1848. According to his naturalization record filed in West Feliciana Parish, he immigrated to Louisiana in 1867, and applied for citizenship there on 17 October 1876. Formerly a general merchant in downtown New Roads and subsequently near New Texas Landing at the turn of the 19th and 20th centuries, he simultaneously operated the "Loupe Store" and the "Labatut Store" on the plantations of those names located on Pointe Coupée Road.

Bernard Teutsch and his siblings, like many families in the 20th and 21st centuries, appear to have resided on both sides of and crossed the Mississippi River between New Roads and St. Francisville in the course of their careers. The 1900 United States Federal Census tabulation of Pointe Coupée Road, Ward 5, made on 2 June of that year identified three unmarried Teutsch siblings, Bernard, age 49, a general merchant, Herman, age 44, and Maurice, age 35, the latter two salesmen, at the "Loupe Store." On the same day, Louis/Ludwig Teutsch, age 43, misidentified as a "widower," his "daughter," Ella, age 5, and Louis's unmarried sister, Regina, age 36, were enumerated upriver at the "Labatut Store." However, the 9 June 1900 United States Federal Census for St. Francisville listed the brothers Herman, and Maurice (Mortiz) Teutsch, both unmarried, and Louis, "divorced" (*sic*), with Louis's four-year-old daughter, Lucie, all boarding with their sister, the widow Joseph Goldman, née Hannah Teutsch, born on 10 August 1845, at Venningen.

It was reported in the 1901 *Pointe Coupée Banner's* recapitulation of 1900 sales, that the "Loupe Store" had grossed $8,000 and the "Labatut Store" $4,000.

It is interesting to discover what types of merchandise Teutsch carried in his Pointe Coupée Road stores in 1900 and 1901, which may be found by reading some of the civil actions he instituted against delinquent customers. His inventory included: calico, checks, white, blue and brown cotton, flannel, lace, ribbons, thread, needles, muslin (mosquito) bars, pants, men's and boys' shirts, suspenders, stockings, men's, boys', ladies' and tomboy hats, caps, shoes; parasols, umbrellas; flour, rice, sugar, coffee, cornmeal, sardines, shrimps, baking powder, soda, milk, molasses, sausages, meat, hams, "pop," whiskey, beer; antiseptic, castor oil, pipes, soap, matches, washboards, brooms, jugs, fishing hooks and lines, garden seed, coal oil, hoes, ax handles and plow lines. In addition to being one of Pointe Coupée's first noted vendors of soda pop, Teutsch also sold (alcoholic) "drinks" by the glass.

Bill from Bernard Teutsch's Pointe Coupée Road store dated November 20, 1900

Bernard Teutsch opened a livery stable in New Roads in 1903, and ultimately a general store on Moreau Plantation at Keller, on Lower Old River, the latter in partnership with his brother Herman Teutsch. Owing to his frequent moves, Bernard Teutsch's left-over Bayou Sara letterhead was used for his Pointe Coupée Road stores, as evident in the above image.

HERMAN TEUTSCH

Herman Teutsch was born on 21 November 1854, at Venningen, Rheinpfalz, Germany, and immigrated to Louisiana the early 1870s to join his brothers. He opened a general store at Watson's Landing, on the plantation of Mme. George Watson (née Délima Parent) just west of the subsequent site of St. Francis Chapel in 1889. In numerous 1889-1890 *Pointe Coupée Banner* advertisements, H. Teutsch, operating at Watson's Landing, sold dry goods, hats, caps, boots, shoes, groceries, family supplies, wines, liquors, tobacco, cigars, valises, trunks, and general merchandise. Herman likely succeeded Mme. Watson's brother Henry Parent at that location. Parent had been listed as merchant in the immediate neighborhood in that year's July edition of Dun's *Mercantile Agency Reference Book*.

When Bernard Teutsch opened a livery stable in New Roads in 1903, Herman continued in his employ. Information recorded in the 1910 United States Federal Census, indicated that the two brothers were jointly conducting a general store on Lower Old River at Keller, Louisiana. Herman never married. He died on 12 December 1912, at St. Francisville, and was interred there in the Hebrew Rest Cemetery.

COMING.
W. R. MARKLE'S
NEW SHOW BOAT
"GOLDEN ROD"

Fordoche, September	28,
St. Maurce, September	29,
Bayou Sara, September	30,
Cook's Landing, Oct.	1,
Arbroth, October	2,

Presentig Two-Act Musical Comedy
SCHOOL DAYS
And Seven High Class Vaudeville Acts
STREET PARADE AT 10 A. M.

Mr. Markle is not interested in any other show boat than the "GOLDEN ROD" and devotes all his time to this boat.
ADMISSION   25 Cents.

23 September 1911 *Pointe Coupée Banner* Advertisement for Markle's Showboat, the Golden Rod.

CHAPTER 2

WATERLOO AREA

French settlement spread inland from the Mississippi River, along the *Chenal Supérieur de la Fausse Rivière* or Upper Chenal of False River as far as the present-day downriver part of the City of New Roads in the 1750s. Three years after Louisiana statehood in April 1812, a covered shed to hold local produce awaiting shipment downriver to New Orleans, was built on the *batture*, or land between the river and levee, immediately above the head of the Upper Chenal. The property of Constance Lacour, the widow of Vincent Claude Ternant I of present-day Parlange Plantation on False River, called the *batture* tract was subdivided into lots by local surveyor, notary and *marguillier* (church warden) Pierre L'Hermite and sold by Widow Ternant in the 1820s.

Among the earliest merchants to operate on the site was Francois Labrouche Dussin. He was followed by local French, and *Créoles de couleur* residents, and immigrant German, Italian, Polish, and Jewish settlers, who formed an increasingly diverse and prosperous community.

In the 1830s, the area figured prominently in the often-cited civil suit of Sicard vs. Chustz, when landowner Ursin Sicard sued Laurent Chustz, et al., because Chustz had been empowered by the Pointe Coupée Parish Police Jury, pursuant to a petition signed by numerous False River landowners, to break a dyke Sicard had constructed in one of the channels of the Upper Chenal. Although the Upper Chenal had not been a part of the main channel of the Mississippi River since 1822, it was the only connection between False River and the Mississippi. The *Chenal Inférieur* or Lower Chenal had become jammed with driftwood and was impassible. Sicard testified that he had had an embankment constructed to connect his property on the south side of the Upper Chenal with an island he owned between the two channels of the waterway. Despite Sicard's lawsuit, the court ruled in favor of the defendants. Ironically, the years immediately following were marked by increasingly high spring-time levels of the Mississippi, affecting the False River, and the State of Louisiana, employing convict labor, dammed the mouth of the Upper Chenal in 1842.

The residents of the *batture* community, officially named "Waterloo" when a post office opened there in 1840, were at increased risk of flooding by the Mississippi River. As a consequence, the citizens were authorized to build a community levee near river's end which connected north and south in line with the main, state-maintained levee. In 1851, this structure, called the "front levee" of Waterloo, was described as being a mere foot-and-a-half in height. However, it was repeatedly enlarged and heightened with successively higher water levels of the great river.

Waterloo was the second town in Pointe Coupée Parish to be incorporated, by an act of the State of Louisiana in 1878, three years after the incorporation of the parish seat of New Roads. It is the opinion of many researchers, that Waterloo was named not for the French military defeat near that Belgian town in 1815, but was a more refined rendition of "low water," as it was the highest riverfront area, rendering it ideal for residential and commercial development.

New Orleans *Crescent* correspondent J.W. Dorr, visiting Waterloo for his "Louisiana in Slices" series, described the town on the eve of the Civil War, on 14 May 1860:

> ...all sorts of a place, straggling along the banks of the Mississippi along a low and irregular levee... there is much business done there, though it has not the appearance of a busy place.... The place is ill built and not pleasant, and the dog population is immense. There are a number of fine places in the neighborhood, however.

During the Civil War, Waterloo merchants Meyer Levy and Nathan Kern and their families were among several Point Coupéeans who took temporary refuge in the city of New Orleans, ostensibly avoiding the prolonged struggle for and siege of the Confederate stronghold of Port Hudson across the Mississippi River from Pointe Coupée. Although some of the "expatriates" remained in the Crescent City, availing themselves of better educational and occupational opportunities, others, including the Levys and Kerns returned to Pointe Coupée.

Waterloo and its "suburbs" to the south, namely Anchor, Cook's Landing, and Nina Landing, and to the north St. Claude and Bertrand Landings, remained the region's chief export points for the cotton and sugar bound for New Orleans, and import points for merchandise from that city and Europe, as well as from river traffic for decades. The completion of the Texas & Pacific branch railroad roughly paralleling the river by several miles inland through the parish seat of New Roads in 1899, all but destroyed the prosperity of those little river communities.

During the high water of 1884, the front and back levees, the latter state-maintained, were breached. The incoming torrent claimed at least one life, overbanking the Upper Chenal, False River proper as well as the Lower Chenal. This overflow, combined with a break in the recently-closed Morganza Levee as well as at other points, submerged nearly the entirety of Pointe Coupée and several parishes to the south. In downtown New Roads, Main Street was topped by two feet of water, but many property owners built small levees around their improvements. In the Lower Chenal section of the Island of False River, water reached the eaves of smaller residences, and the Islanders were forced to feed their cattle moss and twigs lest they starve to death.

Among the agencies assisting the thousands of affected residents and livestock along the line of the Mississippi River was the American Red Cross. Clara Barton personally visited Waterloo to extend moral support and distribute material relief. The *Pointe Coupée Banner*, dated 19 April 1884 reported that she had contributed 40 sacks of corn and oats, 10 barrels meal, 12 sacks meal, 1 barrel salt, 3 kegs nails, 24 skillets, several dozen glass lamps and a small lot of clothing.

According to the New Orleans *Daily Picayune*, during the high water of Spring 1891, the approximately 279 residents of Waterloo, suffered a breach in the front levee. It was reported in the *Pointe Coupée Banner* that the flood levels in the town rose to five feet.

More disasters occurred crippling the town. The *Pointe Coupée Banner* related the collapse of the front levee and the flooding of Waterloo in 1892. Two years later, in 1894, the *Banner* reported a devastating fire. The conflagration had begun in the home of the Cyrille Pourciau family, destroying it and the adjacent St. Claude Chapel, from which latter structure only the organ was saved. The Waterloo Post Office was discontinued in 1895. According to the oral history of Eugenie Chustz Noble, by 1905 only two houses were left in what had been a thriving community of stores, hotels, saloons, livery stables, warehouses, bakeries and other businesses, as well as a public school and Catholic church. (Source: Judy Riffel, ed. *A History of Pointe Coupée Parish and its Families*. Baton Rouge: Le Comité des Archives de la Louisiane, 1982.)

Cook's (*sic*) Landing at the northeast corner of the Island of False River, and downriver from Waterloo was named for John Cooke (*sic*), a native of Ireland, the United States Surveyor for Pointe Coupée Parish and a merchant near that site. He was married to the former Dolorite Langlois of New Roads. Cooke died in 1827.

Simon Hermann was the earliest-known Jewish merchant at Cook's Landing, opening a store there during the 1860s. He relocated to New Orleans after the Civil War. Like the larger community of Waterloo upriver, Cook's Landing suffered a number of misfortunes, and was finally abandoned. Arsonists attempted to destroy the town in 1881, and the front levee broke during the high water of 1893. According to several accounts published in the *Pointe Coupée Banner*, the community was flooded to six feet deep, and one hundred acres of corn on the adjacent Nina Plantation flooded.

In 1894, the *Banner* reported that several former residents of Cook's Landing had established a new community called "Roseville" on the "protected" side of the levee (along present-day Ventress Road/Louisiana Highway 414). Cook's Landing proper continued in operation for several more years, being a site for the docking of Markle's "*Golden Rod*" and other showboats, and playing an important role during the May 1912 flood. At that time, Cook's Landing was the evacuation point for 700 head of livestock to the high land of East Baton Rouge and Livingston Parishes, and an import station for provisions, medicines and clothing for sufferers in and around New Roads. (See F*lood Sufferers in the Mississippi and Ohio Valleys* congressional report by Army officials, and contemporary Associated Press news reports.)

A number of Waterloo and Cook's Landing residents moved to Baton Rouge, New Orleans, or just a few miles inland to New Roads. The *Banner* reported through the turn of the 19th-20th centuries and oral history attests that at least three residences and a livery stable were dismantled, their elements hauled to New Roads and the structures re-erected in that town.

The village of Anchor was situated between Waterloo and Cook's landing. The smallest of the three, it survived the other two in name, as the Anchor Post Office in operation from 1888 until 1930. Joseph Duncan Major was its first postmaster, and his relatively elevated store and residence were the only structures not flooded when the levee in front of adjacent Cook's Landing gave way in 1893. However, it was surrounded by floating fences, chicken coops, chickens and the carcasses of beef animals, according to the *Pointe Coupée Banner*.

The historic names Waterloo, Cook's Landing, Anchor, St. Claude, and Robin are all preserved as street designations in 21st-century "Waterloo" and "Cook's Landing" residential subdivisions on the protected side, opposite the sites of those long-vanished places.

MEYER MICHEL

Meyer Levi Michel was born on 13 January 1826 at Struth, Bas-Rhin, France, to Abraham Michel, a native of Metz, Moselle, France, and his wife, Struth native, Jeannettte Neuburger. Meyer Michel's first marriage was before 1854 to Rosine Levi/Levy, born on 2 February 1833, at Riedseltz, Bas-Rhin, France, to Samson Levy, a native of Heuchelheim, Rheinpfalz, Germany, and his wife, Rosette Loeb, a native of Pleisweiler, also in the Rheinpfalz. Rosine was the sister of Pointe Coupée merchant, Isaac Levy, the husband of Sarah "Settie" Gumbel.

According to his declaration of intention to become a United States citizen, which was filed at New Roads in 1855, Meyer Michel arrived in New York in 1843 aboard the ship *John Harvard*, from Le Havre, France. He and Henry Lowenstein, a native of Germany, were enumerated in the 1850 United States Federal Census as peddlers, living in the house of Alexis Porche, a free man of color, and his family, just above Waterloo. However, Meyer and Rosine's first child, Henriette, had been born, according to the 1860 United States Federal Census for Pointe Coupée Parish, in the state of Tennessee in 1854.

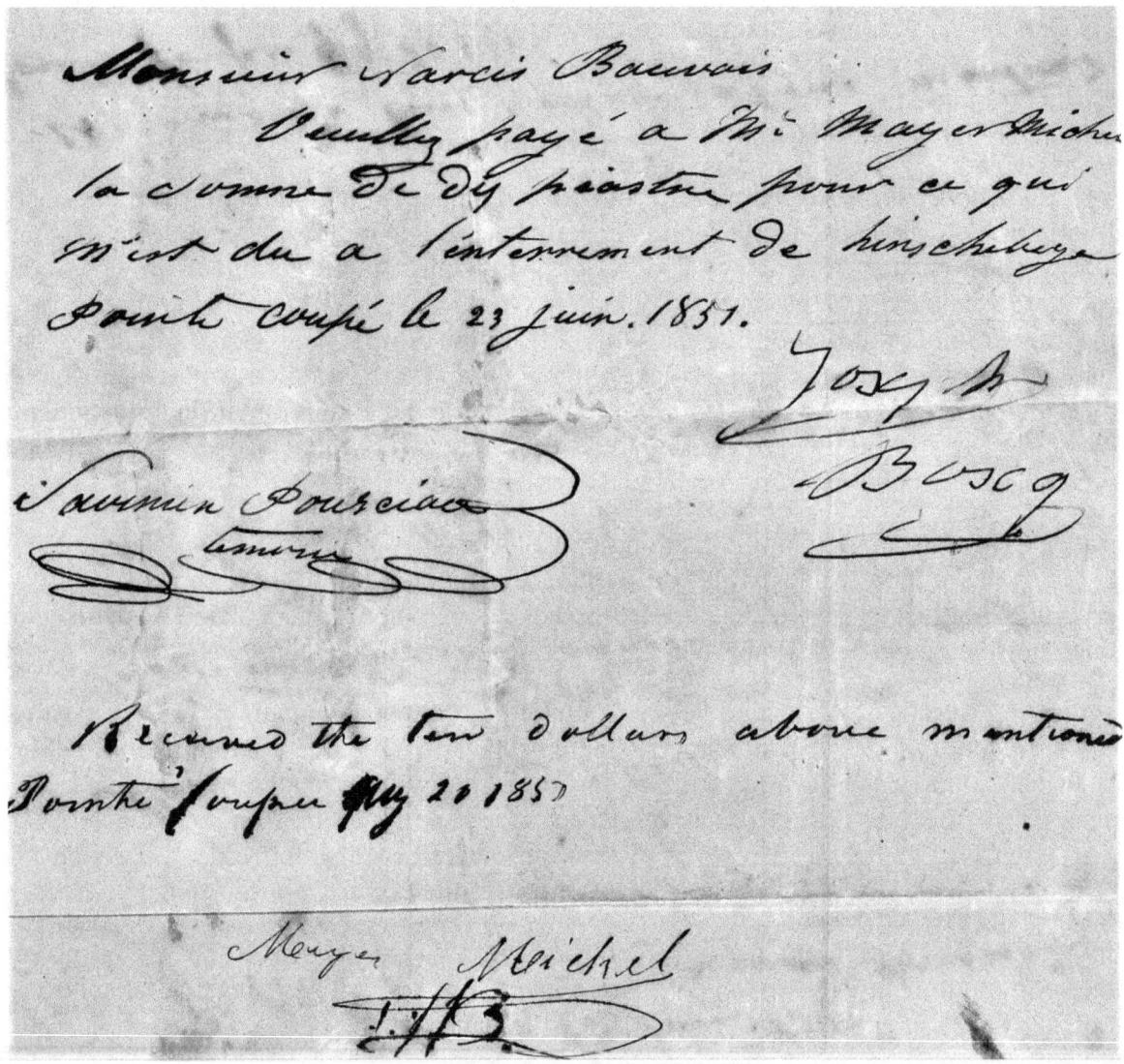

First known signature of Meyer Michel, who received $10 for the burial of Joseph Hirschberger in June 1851.

We believe that he and Rosine returned to the Waterloo area of Pointe Coupée Parish from Tennessee to be nearer to his brother, Jacob Michel, and sister Rosine Michel, the wife of Nathan Kern. In that same 1860 United States Federal Census, Meyer Michel was enumerated as a prosperous merchant with $3,000 in real estate and $2,500 in personal property. At that time peddlers Isaac Keim, and Isaac Levy, Meyer's brother-in-law, were living with him, his wife, Rosalie, and children, Henriette, Melanie (b. 1857), and Abraham (b. 1858).

In 1858, Meyer Michel's first wife, Rosine Levy, received through in act of donation from her brother Isaac Levy, an improved lot in Waterloo fronting 84 feet on the Mississippi River, extending inland 70 feet, and bounded above/north by property of the Succession of Jules St. German, below/south by a street separating said lot from the property of Mrs. Félicie Lindsly, and rear/west by property of the Succession of Louis Mougeot. This was likely the location of Meyer Michel's original, subsequently named "Evening Star" store.

In 1864, after relocating from Waterloo to New Orleans during the Civil War, Meyer Michel's wife, Rosine Levy obtained a judgment of separation of property from her husband, recouping $2,500. In lieu of a cash payment, Meyer then conveyed to her any interest he may have held in a lot of merchandise worth $1,850, and his possible interest in "a certain property situated in Waterloo" to cover the additional $650.

In 1864, Goldsmith, Haber & Co. received a monetary judgement against Meyer Michel for a balance owed. All movables found in the Michel residence at 10 Victory Street were judicially seized. Rosine Levy enjoined the proceedings, claiming that the goods were hers through the judgment of separation of property between herself and Meyer. The plaintiffs claimed the judgment was "a sham," intended to defraud them of Meyer's property. The local court ruled in Rosine's favor and condemned Goldsmith, Haber & Co. to pay her $100 in damages.

Goldsmith, Haber & Co. appealed to the Louisiana Supreme Court (No. 501), who reviewed the 1858 donation of the improved lot, store and merchandise at Waterloo to Rosine from her brother Isaac Levy. Witnesses estimated the value of the real estate at $2,500 and the inventory therein at between $1,500 and $1,800. Testimony differed as to whether the store continued in business until "1861 or 1862" in the name and for the account of Rosine or of Meyer.

The Supreme Court considered the evidence too vague to prove Rosine's ownership of the merchandise then existing in New Orleans. The lower court was reversed and Rosine was ordered to pay Goldsmith, Haber & Co. $100, as well as costs in both courts.

Two more children were born to the Michels, Estelle (b. 1862), and Henry (b. 1866), before Rosine died on 21 September 1867 of yellow fever in New Orleans, Louisiana. She was interred there in Hebrew Rest Cemetery No. 1. Widower Meyer Michel was married again on 29 June 1868, in New Orleans to Rosina Hess, the widow of A. Meyer. Rosina Hess was born on 16 March 1835, at Böchingen, Rheinpfalz, Germany. Meyer Michel and his second wife, Rosina, had four children all born in Waterloo: Lazard (b. 1869), Jacob (b. 1871), Rachel (b. 1872), and Herman (b. 1875). An 1876-1877 Bouchereau, *Statement of the Sugar Crops* advertisement for Meyer Michel indicated that he sold dry goods, clothing, hats, boots, shoes, groceries, wines, liquors, crockery, and hardware in Waterloo.

In 1878, Meyer Michel purchased three properties in quick succession. The first was a tract upriver of Waterloo fronting 132 feet on the Mississippi, and extending 40 arpents inland, bounded above/north by land of Terence Allain, and below/south by that of Heloise Riché, both people of color. The second was a tract west of Waterloo, on the Patin Dyke Road leading to New Roads, fronting six arpents on the former bank or bed of False River by a depth of approximately 30 arpents, which Michel acquired from the Succession of Mme. Marcel Samson, née Adélaïde Charras. The third, an improved tract further west, fronting 1 2/3 arpents on the

Upper Chenal of False River, with a depth of 35 arpents, was purchased from Louise Chenevert and her siblings.

Michel called the largest tract, the one nearer Waterloo on Patin Dyke Road, "Alsace Place" for his birthplace. Judging from a previous 1866 IRS tax assessment report, Meyer Michel had, by that time, transferred his mercantile business from Waterloo proper to the tract he subsequently purchased and named "Alsace," operating it as the "Alsace Store." Contained within 1879 editions of *The Pelican* and 1880-1881 and 1886 publications of the *Pointe Coupée Banner,* were advertisements for Meyer Michel's, "Alsace Store," located 1 ¼ mile west of Waterloo, Louisiana, featuring dry goods, clothing, groceries and Western produce, crockery, and tinware.

He returned to his "old stand" in Waterloo in 1881, and named it the "Evening Star Store." Levee failures and disastrous flooding at Waterloo and in most of Pointe Coupée Parish in 1884 likely spurred Michel's move to resume operations at the "Alsace Store" in 1886. Throughout his changes in location, Michel stressed his lines of "ready-made" clothing in *Pointe Coupée Banner* advertisements. In 1887, Meyer Michel announced in the *Banner* that he was selling out his Waterloo general mercantile business.

Meyer Michel died in Waterloo on 8 March 1888, and was interred in New Orleans in Hebrew Rest Cemetery No. 1. His second wife, Rosina, moved to New Orleans and died there on 21 January 1893. She was laid to rest near him. His daughter from his second marriage, Rachel Michel Baginsky, and her children after her, continued to own the Michel properties in and near Waterloo well into the second half of the 20th century.

JOSEPH HIRSCHBERGER

A contemporary of Meyer Michel at Waterloo, Joseph Hirschberger was born ca. 1826 at Gerolzhofen, Rheinpfalz, Germany. We believe he immigrated with his brother, Abraham Hirschberger, born ca, 1824 in the same town, arriving at New Orleans from Le Havre, France, on 27 November 1848 aboard the ship *Mayflower*. Abraham, misidentified as "Adam" on the ship's record, and Joseph joined two brothers Maurice and Louis Schulherr/Scooler who were living at No. 154 Old Levee Street. Abraham, like Louis Schulherr, was a jeweler, while Joseph was a dry goods salesman.

As did many immigrant merchants, Joseph Hirschberger apparently set off on horseback with his wares, ultimately setting up shop in Waterloo, Pointe Coupée Parish. Among the items in his probate file, opened in New Roads a year later, is a small journal written in old-fashioned German script. It includes tabulations of figures, likely a compilation of his purchases and sales, and his attempts at spelling local the place names Lettsworth, Latenache and Morganza. Near the front of the book is what appears to be Hirschberger's attempt at the name Alexis Porche, a *Créole de couleur*, with whom Jewish peddlers Henry Lowenstein and Meyer Michel were living at the time of the 1850 United States Federal Census enumeration.

During his brief career in Waterloo, Joseph Hirschberger sold quality ready-made clothing, furnishings, and piece goods from the New Orleans market. His probate file contains invoices from city wholesalers Goldsmith, Haber & Co.; M.L. Hellman; and Hellman & Stadeker for purchases during 1847-1849 of ladies' *robes* (dresses) of plain and embroidered muslin and calico, "Victoria" skirts, capes, shawls in silk and cashmere, fichus, scarfs, and corsets, as well as men's cottonade pantaloons, shirts, linen collars, cravats, suspenders, and cotton undershirts. Hirschberger's array of piece goods included silks, plain and printed muslins, organdy, lawn, ginghams, calico, English prints, light cambric, béarn, bobbinet, barege, alpaca, muslin de laine, flannel and domestic. He also carried hosiery for women, men and children, gloves, laces, spooled thread, pins, needles, tablecloths, merino and alpaca blankets, and parasols. Not to be undone in handkerchiefs, Hirschberger offered them in silk, linen, cambric, madras, and printed cotton.

According to a death certificate signed by a New Roads physician, Dr. Félix Eugène Ernest Edmond de Blainville, Joseph Hirschberger died in Pointe Coupée Parish on 4 October 1849, from typhoid fever. Ironically, Dr. de Blainville was one of the almost 150 victims of the explosion of the boilers of the steamboat *Louisiana* docked at the Gravier Street wharf, on 15 November 1849, according to the New Orleans *Daily Picayune*.

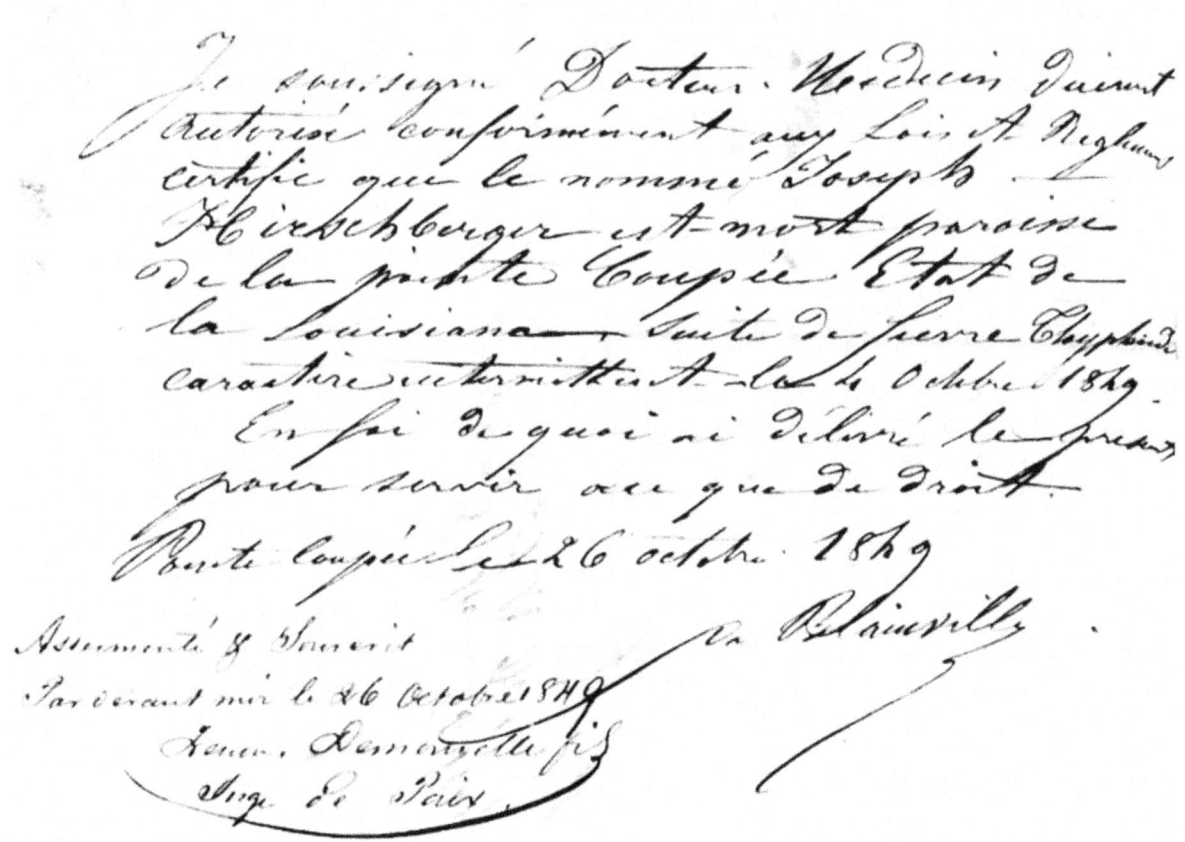

Bill of Dr. de Blainville for services to Joseph Hirschberger, deceased, dated 26 October 1849.

Louis Schulherr applied to the 2nd District Court in New Orleans, and was appointed curator of the succession of Joseph Hirschberger. The court issued an order that an inventory be made of the late merchant's effects in Pointe Coupée Parish, which was conducted at the Waterloo residence of Michel Veil/Weil on 18 December 1849. Neighboring businessmen were involved in the process, with Savinien Pourciau and Jules St. Germain as appraisers, and Joseph Grigny and Meyer Michel as witnesses. Hirschberger's estate was valued at $186.78, and consisted of merchandise, a silver watch, a Créole horse, and a note of James R. Gayle, proprietor of Belle Vue Plantation at Bayou Lettsworth, for $25, payable the previous 1 November.

Maurice Schulherr/Scooler filed the official death certificate for Joseph Hirschberger, his cousin, at New Orleans on 11 March 1850, indicating that the twenty-three-year-old decedent had succumbed on 25 September 1849 (*sic*), was a dry goods merchant and unmarried. Louis Schulherr/Scooler had filed a similar record for Joseph's brother, twenty-five-year-old jeweler, Abraham Hirschberg, who died at the Schulherr residence, No. 154 Old Levee Street, just a few weeks earlier on 17 September 1849.

Narcisse Beauvais, in his capacity as Clerk of Court of the 9th Judicial District, opened the succession of Joseph Hirschberger in Pointe Coupée Parish (Probate No. 547) through a petition of 10 January 1850, stating that the deceased merchant had left "so small a succession that no person was willing to accept the curatorship." Michel Veil petitioned the court for curatorship, on the following 3 March, describing Hirschberger's estate as "much involved in debts," and that he (Veil) was among its creditors. The court ultimately appointed Beauvais as curator, and the latter successfully moved for an inventory and public sale of the decedent's goods in order that the creditors receive the amounts owed them.

In addition to the New Orleans wholesalers' balances, Goldsmith, Haber & Co.; M.L. Hellman; and Hellman & Stadeker, Hirschberger's debts included $3.00 to local merchant Benjamin Weil for 4 leeches, $8.50 to Waterloo physician Dr. George Major for medications and bleeding, $8.35 to pharmacist A.C. Laffleur for medications, $16.00 due Laurent Moniotte for making the coffin and trimmings, $10.00 to Joseph Box to dig the grave and prepare the body.

The subsequent high water of the Mississippi River, area crevasses and flooding suspended the proceedings until two sales were finally held of Hirschberger's goods in the autumn of 1850, the first on 9 September and the second on 31 (*sic*) November, both at the Courthouse in New Roads, to which the movables were transported from Michel Veil's residence in Waterloo by Alcide Bondy. The first sale was of the decedent's merchandise, purchased by various parties, including attorney Provosty, and realizing the sum of $127.57. In the second sale, a silver watch and portfolio were sold, apparently for $7.84. The last acts included in Hirschberger's probate file were Beauvais's 10 January 1851 declaration of $167.51 received from the sales, and 9th District Court Judge Frederic Farrar's 4 April order that Beauvais, who had presented a tableau, disburse its proceeds to the creditors.

HENRY LOWENSTEIN

Henry Lowenstein, a native of Germany, born ca. 1827, was enumerated with Meyer Michel in the 1850 United States Federal Census. They were both peddlers, living in the house of Alexis Porche and his free colored family in the Waterloo area. Lowenstein did not remain in Waterloo. He relocated to Pointe à la Hâche, Plaquemines Parish, and St. John the Baptist Parish, where according to the 1864 U.S. Tax Assessment lists for Louisiana, he was a wholesale liquor dealer.

ROSINE MICHEL

Stalwart businesswoman and landowner Rosine Michel and her first husband, Nathan Kern, had grown up together in Struth, Bas-Rhin France. She was born there on 16 January 1827, to Abraham Michel and Jeannette Neuburger. (Note: While she was born "Rosine" Michel many

Pointe Coupée records identify her as "Rosina" Michel.) Nathan Kern was born there a few months later on 19 March 1827, to Léonard Kern, the younger, and his wife, Serette Emanuel Kahn.

Nathan Kern arrived in New Orleans from Le Havre France, on 3 August 1847, aboard the ship *Viola*. Rosine followed on 18 May 1849, from Le Havre aboard the ship *Charlemagne*. Nathan and Rosine were married on 14 October 1851, in New Roads, Pointe Coupée Parish. New Roads tailor Meinard Gebhart, a Catholic native of the Grand Duchy of Baden, stood as security for Kern's posting of $500 bond preparatory to his marriage to Rosine Michel.

The Kerns were early Jewish merchants in Waterloo. Their first child, Léonard Kern, was born there in 1853, followed by Abraham (b. 1855), Solomon (b. 1857- d. 1865), Meyer (b. 1860), Lazard (b. 1862), David (b. 1864), and Leopold (b. 1868). According to the 1860 United States Federal Census, Nathan Kern was already a successful merchant with $2,500 in real estate and $2,500 in personal property. Rosine's younger brother Jacob Michel, who had followed his sister and elder brother Meyer Michel to Pointe Coupée Parish, was also enumerated in the household.

Soon after the outbreak of the Civil War, Nathan Kern, his wife, Rosine, and her brother Meyer Michel and their families moved to New Orleans. There, Rosine operated a clothing store at 107 Old Levee Street. The Kerns returned to Pointe Coupée Parish at the close of the Civil War and were listed in the 1865 IRS Tax Assessment as living at False River, i.e., the parish seat of New Roads. However, *Denson and Nelson's New Orleans and Mississippi Valley Business Directory and River Guide* for 1866-1867 still listed "Mrs. R. Kern" at the 107 Old Levee Street address, and items filed by her in civil suits in which she was a party through the next few years in Pointe Coupée Parish, where she had opened her general store in 1866, included her New Orleans business letterhead.

Nathan Kern died at New Roads on 28 March 1869, and was interred at Hebrew Rest Cemetery No. 1 in New Orleans. Rosine was married a second time, on 21 December 1870, to dry goods merchant Benjamin Weil, from whom she was divorced on 8 April 1872. Details of their brief marriage are included in the "New Roads" section of this book. Rosine and her children later moved to Lakeland, Louisiana, on the Lower Chenal of False River, where she owned a plantation, leased another, and she and her eldest son Abraham "Abe" Kern, were engaged in merchandising.

JACOB MICHEL

Jacob Michel was born Jacques Michel on 23 April 1831, at Struth, Bas-Rhin, France, to Abraham Michel, a native of Metz, Moselle, France, and his wife, Jeannette Neuburger, born at Struth. Jacob followed his elder brother Meyer Michel and their sister Rosine Michel to Louisiana, arriving at New Orleans from Le Havre, France, on 13 September 1853, aboard the ship *Hope Goodwin*. Jacob filed a declaration of intention in 1858 and oath in 1860, both in New Roads, Louisiana, renouncing allegiance to the French Emperor.

According to the 1860 United States Federal Census, Jacob was unmarried, and living with his sister, Rosine, and her husband, Nathan Kern, at Waterloo. The following year, he was recorded as giving his sister Rosine an *inter vivos* donation of $2,600.

Jacob married Adèle Levy on 29 September 1863 in Woodville, Wilkinson Co., Mississippi. Adèle was born on 2 December 1833, at Belfort, Haut-Rhin, France, to Maurice Levy, a butcher, and his wife, Esther Picard/Bickart. After his marriage, Jacob Levy settled down in Bayou Sara, West Feliciana Parish, Louisiana, with Adèle where two children were born: Abraham in 1865 and David in 1867. Adèle died at Bayou Sara on 18 October 1868, and was buried in Hebrew Rest Cemetery No. 1 in New Orleans. As was the custom in many Jewish families, when a man's wife died, he often chose an unmarried sister-in-law to wed. In this case, Jacob married Adèle's younger sister, Cécile, aka Henriette Levy, on 24 June 1869, in New Orleans. Cécile had been born on 8 January 1841, at Belfort, Haut-Rhin France. Jacob and Cécile were the parents of five children all born at Bayou Sara, West Feliciana Parish: Harriet (b. 1871), Maurice Albert (b. 1873), Ralph (b. 1876), Rose (b. 1878), and Armand Simon (b. 1880).

Jacob Michel was a Bayou Sara grocer for many years. On 14 May 1888, *the Baton Rouge Daily Advocate* ran the following obituary (p. 3, col. 1): "The body of Mr. Jacob Michel, who died last week in Bayou Sara was brought to Baton Rouge and interred in the Jewish Rest, Rabbi M. Klein officiating. Mr. Michel was 56 years old, and had resided in Bayou Sara a long time, where he was respected by all who knew him." (Note: Rabbi Marx Klein was born on 2 February 1853, at Hatten, Bas-Rhin, France, to Frédéric Klein, a native of Surbourg, Bas-Rhin, and his wife, Rosine Moock.)

Cécile Levy Michel stayed in West Feliciana Parish and was enumerated there in the 1900 United States Federal Census for St. Francisville, living with her two unmarried sons, Maurice and Arnaud, who were both salesmen. She eventually moved to New Orleans to live with her daughter, Rose Michel, the wife of Edward Ries. Cécile died in New Orleans on 1 April 1920, and was interred there in Gates of Prayer Cemetery No. 2.

CERF WOLFF

One of Pointe Coupée Parish's best-known merchants, Cerf Wolff was born Isaac Wolff on 7 August 1823, at Neuwiller-lès-Saverne, Bas-Rhin, France, to Isaac Wolff, a native of the town, and his wife, Thérèse Morhange, born in Metz, Moselle, France. The given name Cerf, which he used in Louisiana, also appeared in the 1836 census for the town of Neuwiller-lès-Saverne, where he was enumerated as twelve-year-old Cerf Isaac Wolff.

According to his naturalization record filed at New Roads, Pointe Coupée Parish, he arrived in Louisiana in 1851. We believe that he was the twenty-seven-year-old, Isaac Wolff who arrived in New Orleans on 1 October 1852, from Le Havre, France, aboard the ship *Eastern Queen*. He began a lengthy career in merchandising in Pointe Coupée Parish at Waterloo, where he was enumerated with $500 in real estate and $200 in personal property in the 1860 United States Federal Census. He eventually became a partner in the Langlois & Wolff general store in New Roads, and operated the "Alma" and "Burnt Bridge Stores" at opposite ends of the Lakeland community on the Lower Chenal of False River.

The 23 June 1853 posting of Wolff's $500 bond, with New Roads tailor Meinard Gebhart as security, is the only record that was found in the Cerf Wolff – Caroline Levy marriage file in the Pointe Coupée Parish Clerk of Court's Office. There is no record of any marriage ever having taken place.

Cerf Wolff was married to Sarah Zacharias, a native of Struth, Bas-Rhin, France, on 9 December 1858, by Justice of the Peace Jules St. Germain of Waterloo. While her marriage record indicated that she had been born at Struth in 1838 to Nathan Zacharias, a native of Hoffenheim, Grand Duchy of Baden (Germany), and his wife, Mathilde Weil, a native of Haguenau, Bas-Rhin, France, we have not been able to find any record of her birth in France.

Cerf and Sarah were the parents of eight children: Helena (b. 1860), Isidore (b. 1862), Rachel (b. 1866), Cornelia (b. 1868), Thérésine (b. 1870), Lazard (b. 1982), Leopold (b. 1876), and Maurice (b. 1879). Following in their father's footsteps, both Lazard and Isidore Wolff were merchants in Pointe Coupée Parish as was their sister Rachel Wolff's husband, Maurice Levy.

UNKNOWN WEINSTEIN

Many drummers and peddlers passed through the rural parishes of Louisiana over the course of its history. One of those, an unknown man whose surname was Weinstein, left two records in Pointe Coupée Parish. He was identified as a 2nd class peddler at Cook's Landing in the 1866 IRS tax assessment report, and a peddler by cart in the 1867 Parish and State Business Licenses. He never appeared in a Pointe Coupée census, so for now the identity of peddler Weinstein remains a mystery.

ISAAC LEVY

Isaac Levi/Levy was born on 12 August 1828, at Riedseltz, Bas-Rhin, France, to Samson Levi and his wife Rosette Loeb. He likely preceded his sister, Rosine Levy, later the wife of Meyer Michel, to Louisiana. According to his obituary, he first lived in New York, and then Nebraska, before choosing Louisiana. He filed an oath renouncing allegiance to the Emperor of the French at New Roads in 1858. According to the 1860 United States Federal Census, Isaac Levy from France, having $500 in property, and fellow peddler Isaac Keim, a native of Germany, were living with the former's sister and brother-in-law, Meyer and Rosine Levy Michel, in Waterloo, Pointe Coupée Parish.

Isaac Levy served during the Civil War in the Pointe Coupée Artillery, C.S.A., as a sutler for his company. He was wounded at Vicksburg, Mississippi, but returned to his regiment and served until the end of the conflict.

Post-war, he was assessed for a watch at Waterloo in the 1865 and 1866 IRS tax assessment reports. According to an 1867 Parish Business License, Levy was a peddler on horseback. Later on, he became a landowner and merchant in the Raccourci-Old River area.

Isaac Levy was married on 11 June 1867, at New Orleans to Sarah "Settie" Gumbel, born on 29 June 1842, at Albisheim, Rheinpfalz, Germany, to Moses Hirsch Gumbel and Esther/Fanny Stern. Settie came to Louisiana with her siblings, including Ferdinand, Cornelius, Simon, Clara, and Jeannette Gumbel. Isaac and Settie were the parents of six children: Helen (b. 1868), Henry (b. 1872), Caroline (b. 1876), Samuel (b. 1878), Irma (b. 1881), and Jacob (b. 1882).

Isaac moved his family to New Orleans in 1873 where he owned a wholesale grocery business. He also founded the Levy Rice Mill which he operated until his death on 21 February 1914. He was buried in Hebrew Rest Cemetery No.1 in New Orleans. Settie died on 17 February 1937, and was interred with him.

ISAAC KEIM

We believe that there is enough evidence to conclude that Isaac Keim was born ca. 1835 at Pirmasens, Rheinpfalz, Germany, to Zacharie Keim, a native of the town, and Beyen Bloch, his wife, a native of Struth, Bas-Rhin, France, born there on 14 June 1817. The couple's two children, Isaac, and his younger brother, Aron, were born at Pirmasens, before the family moved 45 miles across the border to Struth. They were enumerated at Struth in both the 1851 and 1856 town censuses. Isaac Keim, however, did not appear in any subsequent records at Struth, either in a death record, or as a witness at his brother's wedding or in the civil recordings of his brother's children, or in the death records of his parents who both died in the town in 1876 and 1899, respectively.

In the 1900 United States Federal Census, Isaac Keim indicated that he was born in May 1836 in Germany, that he was unmarried, a butcher, had immigrated in 1858, and had never been naturalized. Other census records give approximate ages yielding a birth date from between 1834 to 1841, either in France or Germany, which makes sense because Keim was born in Germany, but spent his youth in France.

Moreover, after immigration he was recorded in the 1860 United States Federal Census living in Waterloo, Pointe Coupée Parish, with the Meyer Michel family, whose head of household was born at Struth, and for whom Keim was apparently working as a "pedler (*sic*)." According to the 1870 United States Federal Census, he was living next door to Cerf/Isaac Wolff, also a native of Struth.

Isaac Keim was subsequently a landowner, then a lessee on the Lower Chenal of False River and later lived on False River. He also clerked for merchant Isidore Lehman, a native of Ingwiller, Bas-Rhin, France, and for August Keller, both of whose stores were on Bayou Maringouin. Keim was ultimately a butcher on the north bank of the Lower Chenal on the Island of False River.

SIMON HERMANN

Simon Hermann was born ca. 1832 in Bavaria, whose origins we were unable to further identify. He filed his declaration of intention and oath in New Roads, Louisiana in 1857, at which time he renounced his allegiance to the King of Bavaria. In that document he stated that he had immigrated to America before the age of eighteen years, and had lived in Louisiana and Pointe Coupée Parish for more than five years.

Hermann obtained property at Cook's Landing, just below Waterloo, on the Mississippi River, in 1855 from Ursin Sicard, and in 1856 from Évariste Bertonière. Together, the lots formed a parcel measuring one arpent by a depth of three arpents, located at the southwest corner of the Mississippi River front and the Island Road.

That same year he was married on 3 July 1856, to Marie Angélique Bertonière, the daughter of Napoléon Bertonière and his wife Gertrude Caroline Chustz (PCP-8, 302). Marie Angélique, a Catholic, had been born in Pointe Coupée Parish on 9 November 1839.

Simon Hermann was enumerated as a merchant with $6,000 in real estate and $12,000 in personal property, suggesting a large stock of merchandise, with his wife, Marie Angélique, and children, Jacques Simon, born on 15 September 1857 (PCP-14, 45), and Louisa, born on 14

October 1859 (IMC-Lakeland-3, 6). Nicolas Barra, Simon's clerk, who lived with the Hermanns in 1860, was the godfather to Simon's infant daughter. A second son, Joseph Jefferson Hermann, was born ca. 16 July 1860 in Pointe Coupée Parish, for whom no baptismal record could be found. (Note Joseph Hermann married Bertha Cahn, the daughter of Abraham Cahn, a native of Saint-Avold, Moselle, France, and his wife, Emma Weis, a native of Ingenheim, Rheinpfalz, Germany, on 19 June 1888. The couple was interred in Hebrew Rest Cemetery in New Orleans.)

Simon Hermann enrolled in Company K, 2nd Regiment Louisiana Cavalry CSA, formerly known as Capt. Severin Porche's Company, as well as Vincent's Reg't., Mounted Partisan Rangers, as a private on 14 September 1862, at New Roads. There is no additional information about his service. During the war, Hermann's store was mentioned in the report made in March 1863 by Capt. James M. Magee of the Second Co., Massachusetts Unattached Cavalry, who ordered the burning of the "rebel" steamer *Hope*, a private vessel owned by Charles Petit, fils, anchored in the Lower Chenal of False River. The *Hope* was a fully-stocked drug store, a machine shop used for repairing "rebel" guns and other buildings near Hermitage. Anxious that no supplies be made available to the Confederate stronghold of Port Hudson across the Mississippi River, Magee also ordered the destruction of the 600 barrels of molasses aboard the *Hope* and more than 1,000 barrels of the commodity at Hermitage Landing.

Proceeding upriver to the False River or Waterloo Dyke, which sealed the head of the Upper Chenal, Magee and men located approximately 1,000 barrels of sugar and molasses at Cook's Landing, next to Simon Hermann's store, and ordered several local residents to roll them into the Mississippi. The Federals then returned to their encampment on Winter's plantation, downriver in West Baton Rouge, taking "three of the enemy" with them as prisoners, only one of whom was a Confederate soldier (from *Official Records of the War of the Rebellion*).

By 1865, Simon Hermann and his family had relocated to New Orleans, after he had sold his Cook's Landing property to Abraham Meyer, a resident of New York, for $4,000. The following year, Abraham Meyer sold the improved parcel to Meyer Weil, and the latter sold it in 1868 to Caroline Meyer, wife of Michel Weil.

Simon Hermann was enumerated as a retail furniture merchant in the 1870 United States Federal Census, living at New Orleans with his family. Simon and Angélique's last child, Louis, born ca. 1867, died in New Orleans on 30 September 1870. Simon had a presence in Pointe Coupée for several years after his and family's move to the city, as he retained a 120-arpent tract near Chenal until 1876.

Simon Hermann was ultimately a business partner of Jacob Grossman, as Hermann & Grossman, in New Orleans for six years, before he retired and sold his interest to Grossman. It was reported in the St. John the Baptist Parish newspaper, *Le Meschacébé* dated 25 February 1888, that Simon Hermann had taken his own life on 22 February 1888, in New Orleans. He was interred there in Dispersed of Judah Cemetery. Marie Angélique died in New Orleans two years later on 20 October 1890.

DAVID HIRSCH

David Hirsch, born ca. 1798, was a native of Hesse-Darmstadt, Germany. He married Miriam "Mina" Meyer, a native of Heuchelheim, Rheinpfalz, Germany, in the 1830s. She was born ca.

1803 as Martha Meyer, the daughter of Joseph Meyer and Regina Strauss. David Hirsch arrived in the Port of New Orleans on 8 December 1848, aboard the American ship *Brunswick*, with his wife, Mina (b. 1803), and his five children: Fannie (b. 1834), Sarah (b. 1837), Abraham (b 1839), Regina (b. 1842), and Amelia (b. 1846).

David Hirsch was a retail liquor dealer at Waterloo and commercial broker at nearby Cook's Landing according to the 1866 IRS tax assessment report. He was also listed as the owner of a store, warehouse, and commercial brokerage business at Cook's Landing in the 1867 list of Parish and State Licenses. However, he and his family were never enumerated in Pointe Coupée Parish. According to the 1850 United States Federal Census, he and his family were living in Lafayette, a suburb of New Orleans in Jefferson Parish. In subsequent censuses, he was enumerated in the city of New Orleans, where he was naturalized on 31 October 1854.

Through a power of attorney granted to Michel Weil, a resident of Pointe Coupée Parish, and Hirsch's brother-in-law, Hirsch sold his stock of dry goods, hats, shoes, boots, groceries, crockery "and all items usually comprising the stock of a country store," to Isaac Dreyfus, for $3,000 in 1868. David and Mina Hirsch's daughter, Fannie, married Moses Mann, a prominent businessman who worked at Bayou Sara, Pointe Coupée Parish, and New Orleans.

David Hirsch died in New Orleans on 28 March 1871, and was interred in Hebrew Rest Cemetery No. 1. Mina died on 28 April 1882, and was buried next to him.

FERDINAND GUMBEL

Ferdinand Gumbel was born on 20 February 1840, at Kirchheimbolanden, Rheinpfalz, Germany, to Moses Hirsch Gumbel and his wife, Esther "Fanny" Stern. Eighteen-year-old Ferdinand arrived in New Orleans on 17 December 1858, from Le Havre, France, aboard the ship *Bethiah Thayer*. An anonymous PDF file described the circumstances of his departure. It was alleged that in order to avoid the Bavarian draft, he "secretly disappeared." In September 1862 the royal court at Kaiserslautern sentenced him to a fine of 860 *Gulden* (equal to the value of 20 cows). His family, unable to pay, their assets were seized and auctioned off, bringing 1200 *Gulden*. The remaining 340 *Gulden* were turned over to the family. (http://www.alemannia-judaica.de/images/Images%20427/Uhrig%20The%20Jewish%20Families%20Gumbel%20from%20Albisheim.pdf)

Ferdinand joined his brothers, Simon and Cornelius Gumbel, at Pointe Coupée Parish where they were already in business. However, in March 1861, Ferdinand enlisted in the Confederate Army as a private in the Fourth Regiment, Company B, Hunter Rifles, organized at Clinton, East Feliciana Parish, Louisiana, under Captain J.T. Hilliard. He fought in the first Battle of Shiloh on 6 and 7 April 1862, and was so badly wounded that he was unfit for duty for the remainder of the war, after which he returned to work with his brothers in Pointe Coupée Parish. Ferdinand had three bales of cotton shipped from Waterloo in 1866 according to that year's IRS tax assessment report.

By 1874, Ferdinand Gumbel had relocated to New Orleans and was in partnership with Joseph Simon, Jr. and Emanuel Loeb (formerly of Simon, Loeb & Co. in New Roads), as the firm of Loeb, Gumbel & Simon, notions dealers, in New Orleans, according to that year's edition of *Soard's New Orleans City Directory*.

Ferdinand Gumbel was enumerated twice, two days apart and in different locations in the 1880 United States Federal Census. On 1 June, he was listed at 92 Constance Street, a notions merchant from Germany, with boarders Jeannette Feitel, his sister and widow of Nathan Feitel, and her children: Euphemia, Selma and Arthur Feitel. On 3 June, Ferdinand Gumbel, a forty-year-old German notions dealer was enumerated at 196 Robertson Street, together with his "wife," Mary, age 20; "daughter," Leona," age four; "son," Lucien, age two; and "brother-in-law," Edward Vignes, age 12.

Gumbel's "wife" was, in fact, Marie Eudora Vignes, born on 8 August 1857, at Waterloo, Pointe Coupée Parish, to Adolphe Vignes, a planter, and his wife, Marie Zulma Hébert (PCP-14, 33). Marie Eudora's father, Adolphe, was the son of Delphin Vergès Vignes and Hannah Jewell, and the grandson of Pointe Coupée Jewish merchant, Benjamin Jewell, and his wife Sophie Prévost. Both of Ferdinand and Mary's children had New Orleans birth certificates: Leona, born on 9 February 1876, and Lucien Joseph, born on 26 August 1878. However, we have found no marriage record for the couple. Perhaps her parents or his brothers were uncomfortable with a Jewish-Catholic marriage in the family and the couple had been compelled to marry secretly in some out-of-the-way notarial office.

However, the couple did not stay together. Marie Eudora Vignes was married on 20 December 1884, in New Orleans to Anatole E. Ker, and Ferdinand Gumbel was wed ten days later on 30 December 1884, in New York, New York, to his niece, Selma Feitel, the daughter of Ferdinand's sister Jeanette Gumbel and Nathan Feitel,

Marie Eudora Vignes' "Gumbel" children, Leona and Lucien Joseph, both used the "Ker" surname in adulthood. Leona Gumbel/Ker was married on 9 September 1897, in New Orleans, Louisiana to Joseph Glenna Grady, a native of Savannah, Chatham Co., Georgia. Leona died there on 5 February 1970. Lucien Joseph Gumbel/Ker, who achieved the rank of RADM USCG, married Rosa W. Gibbs of Savannah, where he died on 29 March 1965.

Ferdinand Gumbel had four children with his niece/wife, Selma Feitel: Herbert (b. 13 January 1886), Felicie (b. 25 May 1888), Neville (b. 29 January 1890 - died at 9 months), and Cornelius J. (b. 18 December 1895). Ferdinand spent the rest of his life in New Orleans. He gave up the notions business to become one of the most successful cotton factors in New Orleans where he made his fortune.

Ferdinand was finally naturalized in 1907 in New Orleans, Louisiana. He died on 16 March 1918, and was interred in Metairie Cemetery in New Orleans. His wife, Selma Feitel, died on 17 August 1941, and was interred with him. His brothers Simon and Cornelius, both predeceased him, as did sisters Clara Gumbel Kaufman, and Jeannette Gumbel Feitel.

Substantial acreage remains in ownership of the Gumbel family and its beneficiary Touro Infirmary in Pointe Coupée's Tenth Ward in the 21st century.

MICHEL WEIL

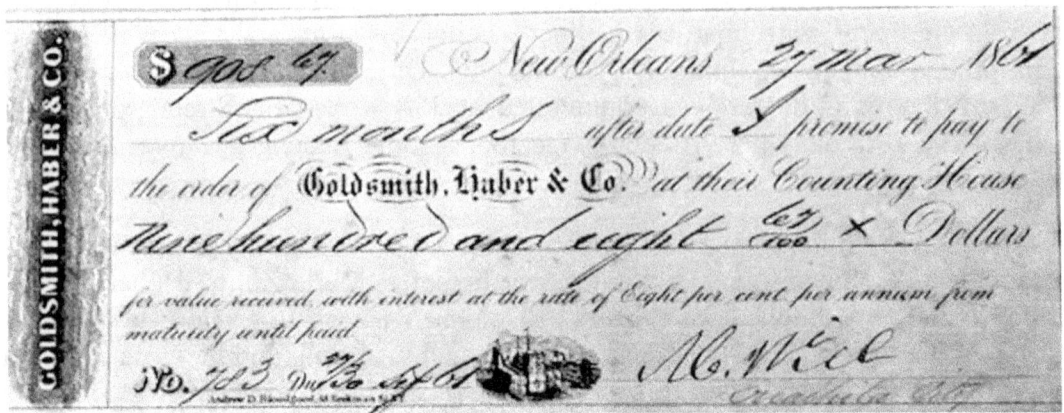

Michel Weil filed a declaration of intention to become a United States citizen in 1849 at New Roads, Pointe Coupée Parish, as "Michael Veil," a thirty-seven-year-old immigrant from the Bas-Rhin, France, who arrived in 1837 aboard the ship *Caroline*. According to available ships' records, "Michel Veil," age 25, a laborer, arrived at New Orleans from Le Havre, France, on 8 September 1837, aboard the ship *Caroline*, with Captain Legrain as Master. Unfortunately, people from that era often did not always know their birth date with any exactitude, hence the discrepancies in the ship, census, and naturalization records. In Michel's case he could have been born any year between 1811 and 1816.

The given name Michel was popular in the towns of Brumath, Struth, and Marmoutier amongst the Jewish families that lived there. We consulted *The Alsace Immigration Book, Volume 1*, compiled by Cornelia Schrader-Muggenthaler (Closson Press, Apollo, PA, 2011) and found the departure of two men named "Michel Weil," one from Struth, the other from Marmoutier. A marginal note indicated that the information about both Weils was taken from a film listing immigrants who applied for a passport between 1828 and 1838, but whose date of immigration was not listed. A check of the on-line civil records for Struth, Bas-Rhin, France, showed that Michel Weil was born on 3 January 1811 to Jacob Weil (before 1808 called "Isaac"), a native of Tieffenbach, Bas-Rhin, France, and his wife, Margarethe Neuburger. In other records, Margarethe was also known as Anne Marie or Michelet Neuburger. What is important, however, is that Margarethe and Jeannette (aka Christine) Neuburger were two sisters born to Meyer/Michel Neuburger, born in Fribourg, Switzerland, and his wife, Esther Franck. Jeannette Neuburger was the mother of Meyer, Rosine, and Jacob Michel, all three who would become longtime residents of Pointe Coupée Parish. They had apparently followed their first cousin, Michel Weil, to America. It is also worth mentioning that more than once we have found the family name spelled "Veil" instead of "Weil," including in the death record for Michel's father who died as "Isaac Veil" at Struth on 15 July 1829. (Note: "Veil" is the correct French pronunciation for "Weil." The letter "w" in the French language is always pronounced as a "v.")

While we were unable to find Michel Weil in the 1840 United States Federal Census for any town in Louisiana, we did find him ten years later, a resident of Clinton, East Feliciana Parish, Louisiana, as thirty-nine-year-old merchant, Michael Weil, living with his wife, Caroline, age 32, from Germany, and two children, Henriette and Rosalie Dreyfus, born in Germany, ages 6 and 4, respectively.

These two children have been identified as the daughters of Isaac Dreyfus, born in Herxheim, Rheinpfalz, Germany, on 15 April 1819, who died at Lafayette, Jefferson Parish, Louisiana, on 15 November 1849. He had married Rosina Meyer on 9 January 1845, at Heuchelheim, Rheinpfalz, Germany, where their first two children were born: Henrietta on 12 April 1845, and Rosalie on 16 October 1846. Rosina Meyer, was born on 15 June 1809, at Heuchelheim, Rheinpfalz, Germany, to Joseph Meyer and his wife Regina Strauss. Isaac Dreyfus, age 29, Rosalie, age 30, Henrietta, age 2 and Regina, age 1, arrived in New Orleans from Le Havre France, aboard the ship *Ferrière* on 20 May 1848. More than a year later, Isaac's death had left his widow, Rosine, and their children, Henriette and Rosalie, to seek refuge with her sister, Caroline Meyer, and her husband, Michel Weil, as reflected in that 1850 United States Federal Census. Caroline Meyer had been born at Heuchelheim, Rheinpfalz, Germany on 15 September 1805, to Joseph Meyer and Regina Strauss. The widow, Rosine Meyer Dreyfus, was misidentified in that 1850 census as the twenty-two-year-old female from France, Rosalia Myer. Missing, however, from this enumeration was baby Isaac Dreyfus, born posthumously on 26 February 1850, at New Orleans. (Note: In her 7 April 1879 last will and testament, Mrs. Caroline Weil, made many small bequests, one of which was to her nephew, Isaac Dreyfus, who was living at Barnard's Landing, Chicot Co., Arkansas.) According to Caroline's New Orleans burial record, she had been born on 18 July 1807, at Heuchelheim, Rheinpfalz, Germany, however her actual date of birth at Heuchelheim was two years earlier, not an unusual mistake for the time. Another sister, Miriam "Mina" Meyer, was the wife of Pointe Coupée merchant, David Hirsch.

Michel "Veil" was naturalized in West Feliciana Parish, Louisiana, on 4 December 1851. Returning to Pointe Coupée Parish, Weil had a judgment filed against him in the case of Goldsmith, Haber & Co. vs Michel Weil (7th Judicial District Court, No. 762). Weil had signed a promissory note in favor of the firm, composed of Louis Goldsmith, Abraham Haber and David Breddo of New Orleans, for $732.14, at 8% interest until paid. Weil accepted the judgment, which required his payment of the note and interest and costs of court, on 13 December 1866.

Michel Weil had a State Business License in 1867 and was, at that time, operating in the Waterloo area. The following year, he acted as power of attorney for the sale of his brother-in-law David Hirsch's merchandise at Cook's Landing to Isaac Dreyfus.

In 1868, Weil's wife, née Caroline Meyer, purchased a strategically located, improved three-arpent lot at the southwestern corner of the Mississippi River front and Island Road at Cook's Landing from Meyer Weil. It was formerly the site of Simon Hermann's retail operations. A year later, in 1869, Caroline sold the property to François Bernard Manuel who operated there as a general merchant for a number of years.

The couple was last enumerated in the 1870 United States Federal Census for New Orleans where fifty-five-year-old Michel Weil, a native of France, was working as a jobber, that is, a wholesale merchant. He was living with his wife, Caroline, also age 55, from Bavaria.

Michel Weil died as M. Weil, born in 1815 (*sic*) in France, on 14 February 1871, in New Orleans, in a house at the corner of Franklin and Calliope Streets, and was interred in Hebrew Rest Cemetery No. 1. His wife died as Mrs. M. Weil, born in 1811 (*sic*) in Germany, on 28 April 1879, and was interred with her husband. The couple never had children.

ISAAC DREYFUS

Isaac Dreyfus, the son of the late Isaac Dreyfus who died in 1849 at New Orleans, purchased through Michel Weil, the husband of his mother, Rosina Meyer's sister Caroline Meyer, the stock of Cook's Landing merchant David Hirsch, the husband of Mina/Martha Meyer, his maternal aunt, in 1868 for $3,000. The lot consisted of dry goods, hats, shoes, boots, groceries, crockery "and other items typically offered in country stores." The connection between Hirsch, Weil, and Dreyfus business dealings, like many in Pointe Coupée Parish, was a family matter.

In 1868, Isaac Dreyfus entered into an agreement with the brothers Stratiote M. and Alexandre Isaac, of Greek ethnicity, to provides supplies, groceries and other necessities during the year for the Isaacs to produce crops of cotton, corn, peas and other products on the plantation of Mme. Landry Landry (née Delphine Greau) and the Succession of Jean Pierre Major, both on the Island of False River. The contract called for the Isaacs to have the cotton harvest ginned, baled, and delivered to Dreyfus, who would apply its proceeds against the amount of merchandise and cash advances he had allowed them. Stratiote M. Isaac and his wife, Aglaé Colombe Chustz, were the parents of Reine Ordalie Isaac who married Solomon Baum of Chenal, on the Island of False River.

Isaac Dreyfus spent most of his adult life as a merchant, first at Barnard's Landing, Chicot Co., Arkansas, then later at Pine Bluff, Jefferson Co., Arkansas. He married Bertha Simon at New Orleans on 31 March 1875. Bertha, a native New Orleanian, was born there on 15 February 1856, to David Simon and his wife, Theresa Kaufman. Isaac and Bertha made their home in Arkansas where their children were born: Ruth (b. 1876), Hugo Clifton (b. 1882), H. Artie (b. 1885), Jerome Milford (b. 1887), and David Stanley (b. 1890).

Bertha Simon Dreyfus died at Pine Bluff on 20 October 1933, and was interred there in the Congregation Anshe Emeth Cemetery. Her husband, Isaac, followed closely on 29 March 1934, and was interred with her.

ALEXANDER "ALEX" MANN

Alexander "Alex" Mann was born on 18 April 1832, at Monsheim, Rhine-Hesse, Germany. We believe that he was the brother of Moses Mann. According to the 1910 United States Federal Census for St. Francisville, Louisiana, Alex Mann told the enumerator that he had immigrated in 1849 and had been naturalized. He took out a license to marry Theresa Hausmann in New Orleans on 23 August 1852. The bride was born ca. 1832 in Molsheim, Rheinpfalz, Germany.

Mann was enumerated as a twenty-nine-year-old merchant with $2,500 in personal property, in Baton Rouge, East Baton Rouge Parish, at the time of the 1860 United States Federal Census. He was living with his wife, Theresa Hausmann, and three children, Harriet/Henriette, age seven, Mena, age five, and Sena (aka Regina), age one. Seven more children were born to the couple: Virginia (b. 1860), Fanny (b. 1862), Benjamin (b. 1863), David S. (b. 1865), Max (b. 1867), Abraham (b. 1868), and Daniel E. (b. 1870). Mann, his wife and children, moved to Bayou Sara, West Feliciana Parish, Louisiana, in 1875. He conducted a grocery and dry goods store there for many years. During the 1870s-1880s, Alex Mann was also proprietor of the "New Orleans Cheap Store," in the Demourelle Buildings in Waterloo, with Alfred M. Weil, as manager. An 1879 advertisement in the Pointe Coupée *Pelican* read: "New Orleans Cheap Store, A. Mann, proprietor, A.M. Weil, manager: dry goods, trimmings, clothing, boots, shoes, groceries, drugs, medicines, crockery, kitchen utensils, hardware, farming implements, saddlery, ice."

Abraham J. "A.J." Michel was enumerated as a dry goods clerk living next to Alex Mann's "New Orleans Cheap Cash Store" with manager A.M. Weill (*sic*) in the 1880 United States Federal Census, He apparently succeeded Mann at the location. An advertisement for "Abe Michel's Cheap Store" at Waterloo ran in the *Pointe Coupée Banner* from 16 October 1880 through 30 April 1881.

Mann's wife, Theresa, died at Bayou Sara on 15 July 1884, and was interred in New Orleans in the Gates of Prayer Cemetery No.2.

Although retired and living near his son, Benjamin Mann, a dry goods merchant, in St. Francisville according to the 1910 United States Federal Census, Alex Mann resumed business in 1911 by assuming the store of his son-in-law C.M. (aka Maurice Cerf) Levy, his eldest daughter Harriet's husband, in Bayou Sara.

Alex Mann died on 6 November 1912, at St. Francisville, and was interred near his wife, in New Orleans at the Gates of Prayer Cemetery No. 2. Alex Mann and Theresa Hausmann's children included businessmen David, Daniel, Benjamin and Max Mann, Fannie Mann Weinberg, Mena Mann Weil, and Sena Mann Lehman, the latter three having married merchants.

ALFRED M. WEIL

Alfred M. Weil was born, Manassé Meyer, on 17 November 1848, at Nancy, Meurthe-et-Moselle, France, to Sarah Mayer/Meyer, a thirty-year-old unmarried woman working there as a dressmaker. Sarah Meyer had been born at Sarre-Union, Bas-Rhin, France, on 20 June 1817, to Manasses Meyer, a merchant, and his wife, Serin/Seurette Kahn. Sarah Meyer was married to Davit Daÿ (aka Daniel Weil) on 6 March 1849, at Sarre-Union, at which time her son, Manassé Meyer (aka Alfred M. Weil), was legitimized. Davit Daÿ had been born on 27 October 1821, at Uttenheim, Bas-Rhin, France, to Dorès Daÿ, an unmarried woman, however the birth was reported by local merchant Lion Weil, who also reported Dorès Daÿ's death on 9 November 1836. David and Sarah Daÿ arrived at New Orleans from Le Havre, France, on 15 April 1850, aboard the ship *Jersey*. There is no record of Alfred having been on board.

Three children were born to Daniel and Sarah after their arrival in New Orleans: Ariel (b. 1850), David T. (b. 1855), and Samuel "Seligmann" (b. 1860), before Daniel Weil died ca. 20 January 1864. He drowned while trying to cross Lake Clare in St. Bernard Parish, in a pirogue as reported in the New Orleans *Daily Picayune* dated 21 January 1864 (p. 2, col. 4). Weil was interred in the old Gates of Mercy Cemetery in New Orleans.

Alfred M. Weil was married to Mena Mann, the daughter of Alexander Mann and Thérèse Hausmann, on 19 June 1879, in West Feliciana Parish, Louisiana. He with enumerated with Mena at his father-in-law, Alex Mann's, "New Orleans Cheap Store" in Waterloo in the 1880 United States Federal Census. Also residing at the Waterloo store in 1880 were clerks John Goodman and Max Mann, Mena's brother. Alfred and Mena had one child, Amelia, born on 2 July 1880, at Bayou Sara. Abraham Michel, his wife, Victoria, and Victoria's brother Louis (*sic*, Meyer intended) Baginsky, who was working as a clerk, were living next door. Abraham Michel and Meyer Baginsky were likely employees of Alex Mann's "New Orleans Cheap Store."

Mena Mann Weil died on 2 August 1881, and was interred at Gates of Prayer Cemetery in New Orleans. Alfred M. Weil was married to Amelia Leopold on 13 May 1884, in New Orleans. At that time, his parents were identified as Daniel Weil and Sarah Meyer. The twenty-two-year-old bride, a native of New Orleans, was the daughter of Solomon Leopold, a native of Biedesheim, Donnersbergkreis, Rheinpfalz, Germany, and his wife, Florette Meyer, born at Kaiserslautern, Rheinpfalz, Germany. Alfred and Amelia were the parents of, Daniel Alfred (b. 1885), Benjamin Alfred (b. 1886), Cécile (b. 1887), and Leah (b. 1891).

After 1900, Alfred Weil and his family were enumerated in New Orleans where he worked as a baggage porter for a railroad. Alfred's mother, Sarah Meyer, died at New Orleans on 28 December 1915, and was interred in Gates of Prayer Cemetery No. 2. Alfred died in New Orleans on 9 December 1928, and was buried in the same cemetery. His wife, Amelia, followed on 13 September 1933, and was interred with him.

MAX MANN

Max Mann, the son of Baton Rouge, Bayou Sara and Waterloo merchant Alexander "Alex" Mann and Theresa Hausmann, was born on 3 September 1867 in Woodville, Wilkinson Co., Mississippi. He had an early start in business, being enumerated as a clerk in his father's "New Orleans Cheap Store" in Waterloo in the 1880 United States Federal Census.

Max Mann was married to Henrietta "Hattie" Schlesinger on 8 June 1892. The bride was born on 30 August 1869, at Woodville, Wilkinson Co., Mississippi. Her father, Jacob Schlesinger, a native of Stuttgart, Kingdom of Württemberg, (Germany), was a longtime merchant at Bayou Sara, West Feliciana Parish, Louisiana, where he died in 1899. His wife, Regina Loeb, a native of Gerolsheim, Rheinpfalz, Germany, died in St. Francisville, West Feliciana Parish, on 22 August 1920. Hattie's parents were both interred in Beth Israël Jewish Cemetery in Woodville.

Max and his family moved to Bayou Sara before 1900. Twenty-nine-year-old Max, a dry goods merchant, was enumerated there in the 1900 United States Federal Census with his wife, Hattie, age 27, and his three children: Theresa (b. 1895), Lawrence Isaac (b. 1897), and Vivian Claire (b. 1899). By 1910, he was enumerated as the proprietor of a well-known saloon. According to the 1920 United States Federal Census, Max and Hattie were living with their daughter and son-in-law Vivian and Albert G. Bowman in New Orleans.

Max Mann died on 18 August 1934, at Lecompte, Rapides Parish, Louisiana, and was interred in Beth Israël Cemetery in Woodville, Mississippi. Hattie Schlesinger Mann died on 7 March 1944, and was interred with her husband.

ABRAHAM "A. J." MICHEL

Abraham Michel was the son of Waterloo area merchant and landowner Meyer Michel and his first wife, Rosine Levy. He was born at Waterloo on 27 December 1858. Michel married Victoria Singer on 12 March 1879, in New Orleans. Victoria was raised in the household of Nathan Baginsky and his wife Regina Hess. We believe that Regina Hess, a native of Germany, had been previously married to Abraham Singer, a name which we found on the Abraham Michel—Victoria Singer marriage record, where Victoria's parents were recorded as being Abram and Regina Singer. There is also a record for Nathan Baginsky's marriage and bond to Regina Hess dated January 31, 1865, in New Orleans. Moreover, according to the 1870 United

States Federal Census for Mobile, Mobile Co. Alabama, where Nathan Baginsky was working as a clerk in the tax office, there was a ten-year gap in the children living in the household: twelve-year-old Victoria born in Louisiana ca. 1858, and two-year-old Meyer, born in Alabama.

Abraham Michel was enumerated as a dry goods clerk in the 1880 United States Federal Census with his wife, Victoria, and the latter's fifteen-year-old half-brother, enumerated in error as "Louis" Baginsky, who was working as a clerk. They were all living next door to Alfred M. Weil, the latter being the manager of Alex Mann's "New Orleans Cheap Cash Store" in Waterloo.

Abraham Michel apparently succeeded Mann at that location, as an advertisement for "Abe Michel's Cheap Store" at Waterloo ran in the *Pointe Coupée Banner* from 16 October 1880 through 30 April 1881. The store's offerings were highlighted as: fancy and staple dry goods; trimmings; clothing; boots, shoes; groceries, canned goods, including fruits, vegetables and fish; liquors, whiskey, beer; tobacco; queens ware, crockery, glassware, and hardware. Messages at the bottom of the ad read: "Stock Entirely New – Prices Bottom Rates – Can't be Undersold," and "Cotton, wool and moss taken in trade."

Several years later, Abraham Michel and his wife, Victoria, moved to New Orleans, where he operated a grocery store. It was reported in the 29 December 1887 edition of the New Orleans *Daily Picayune* that his store had been robbed of groceries two days previously.

The couple had no children. Victoria Baginsky Michel died in New Orleans on 27 October 1901. According to the 28 October 1901 edition of the *Daily Picayune*, her funeral was held from the residence of her half-brother Meyer Baginsky, on Pitt Street.

Widower Abraham J. "A.J." Michel was for many years the proprietor of an establishment called the Michel Hotel or simply "The Michel" at 714 Carondelet Street. He and his hotel garnered considerable media attention for several years. The 24 March 1918 edition of the *New Orleans States* reported that Michel had been released on $1,000 bond after pleading not guilty to "selling liquor to soldiers and to operating an immoral house within the prescribed limits of a military post." On 3 November 1918, the *Times-Picayune* related that Michel and Lilly Piggott were charged with operating "an immoral house" at 714 Carondelet. They both pleaded guilty in United States District Court, where Michel was sentenced to fifteen days and Piggott to three days in the Parish Prison.

In the 9 November 1929 *New Orleans States* and *New Orleans Item* obituaries of Lillian Slocum, widow of John Piggott, age 64, who died at No. 714 Carondelet Street, her relatives and friends as well as those of Abraham Michel were invited to attend her funeral. Lillian had been born on 18 April 1866 near Franklinton, Washington Parish, Louisiana, to Samuel Slocum and Melissa Ingman. She had married John A. Pigott on 21 December 1882, in Washington Parish. Her late husband had likely been a cousin to John Sebron Pigott, who with his family, had been residents of New Roads, before and after the turn of the twentieth century. It is likely that she and Abe Michel had known one another in Pointe Coupée Parish, before they opened the Michel Hotel.

The "Michel" was one of several locations where thousands of elderly Confederate veterans roomed during a mass reunion in New Orleans in the spring of 1923. Michel reported that prominent veteran Dr. S.J. Duff, a Houston, Texas dentist aged 84 years, was found dead in bed there on 11 Apr 1923. According to the same day's edition of the New Orleans *Item*, the coroner had ruled the cause of death due to "natural causes," On 2 July 1923, the *Item* reported a fire in a room at the address owned by A. and C. Denis (sons of the late Pointe Coupée heiress Antoinette Decuir, Mme. Arthur Denis), occupied by A.J. Michel, "slight damage, cause smoking in bed." Abraham J. Michel continued to live there until his death on 7 March 1933. He was interred with his wife, Victoria, in Hebrew Rest Cemetery No. 1 in New Orleans.

MEYER AND RACHEL MICHEL BAGINSKY

Meyer Baginsky was born on 12 June 1867, at Mobile, Mobile Co., Alabama, to Nathan Baginsky, an immigrant from Olesno, Silesia, Kingdom of Prussia (subsequently Rosenberg, Germany) and his wife, Regina Hess, a German national whom he had married in January 1865. According to the 1880 United States Federal Census, Meyer, living with his half-sister, Victoria, and her husband, Abraham Michel, worked as a teenage clerk in Alex Mann's "New Orleans Cheap Store," in Waterloo, Pointe Coupée Parish, Louisiana.

Meyer was married on 6 June 1895, in New Orleans, Louisiana, to Rachel Michel, the daughter of Meyer Michel, a Waterloo area merchant and landowner and the latter's second wife, Rosina Meyer Heiss/Hess, Rachel Michel was born at Waterloo on 2 April 1872. Meyer's half-sister, Victoria Singer Baginsky, had earlier been married to Abraham J. Michel, Rachel Michel's brother.

Meyer Baginsky was identified in successive United States Federal Census records for New Orleans as a salesman in 1900, a notions vendor in 1910, a salesman for importers of laces in 1930, and a merchandise salesman in 1940. Despite living in New Orleans long after the death of her parents, Rachel Michel Baginsky continued to own Michel real estate in and near Waterloo, Pointe Coupée Parish, assessed in and identified on maps in the name of "Mrs. R.M. Baginsky."

Rachel Michel Baginsky died in New Orleans on 23 December 1956, and was interred in Hebrew Rest Cemetery No. 2. In 1957, through the combined successions of Meyer and Rachel Michel Baginsky, probated in New Orleans, their children, Rose Beatrice Baginsky Love, wife of Leo Love, and Herman M. Baginsky, husband of Helene Levy, were put into possession of the Michel-Baginsky properties in Pointe Coupée Parish. A copy of the Judgment of Possession was recorded in New Roads by the Pointe Coupée Parish Clerk of Court in Conveyance Book 44, Entry 226. In 1962, the two siblings sold the Patin Dyke Road real estate, totaling 107 acres to Leo Mougeot of New Roads, who later sold it to the False River Golf & Country Club, which continues to maintain a clubhouse, greens and other improvements into the 21st century. The location is an ideal one, as the ridge-and-swale topography of the land, formed through prehistoric shifts in the course of the Mississippi River, provide natural hazards for golfing.

C.M. EISEMAN & CO., "NINA STORE"

Cassius Meyer Eiseman was born on 11 Sep 1855, at Fayette, Jefferson Co., Mississippi, to Meyer Eiseman (b. 15 May 1828, at Mehlingen, Rheinpfalz, Germany, to Abraham Eiseman and Friederika Lobred), and his wife Henriette Meyer, a native of Natchez, Adams Co., Mississippi. The Eiseman family, which included four sons and three daughters, were prosperous merchants and cotton factors in Fayette as well as in Natchez, Mississippi. They married into some of the most prominent southern Jewish families: the Joseph family, headed by Jacob Judah Joseph, born in South Carolina; the Lowenberg family, natives of Hechingen-Hohenzollern, Germany; and the storied Hyams family, whose members can be traced from Damniz, Poland, to Dublin, Ireland, London England, and finally to South Carolina and New Orleans.

Cassius Meyer Eiseman was married to Cecilia Meyer Joseph on 15 August 1876, in New Orleans. The bride was the daughter of Lisar/Elias H. Joseph (b. 19 May 1831, in Charleston, South Carolina), and granddaughter of Jacob Judah Joseph (b. 1 September 1805, in Georgetown, South Carolina). The bride's mother, Henrietta Abrams, also a native of Charleston, had been born there on 8 January 1828. Cassius and Cecilia Eiseman were the parents of three sons: Adolph (b. 1878), Harold (b. 1879), and Meyer (b. 1882), all natives of Fayette, Mississippi.

Cecilia Eiseman died on 12 June 1884, and was interred in Dispersed of Judah Cemetery in New Orleans. Cassius married Cecilia's sister, Katie Joseph, born ca. 1870 in New Orleans, on 24 April 1888, in the city. They were the parents of three children: Rita Joseph (b. 1889), Lucille Evelyn (b. 1891), and Cassius Meyer, Jr. (b. 1892).

Moving to Pointe Coupée Parish, Cassius M. Eiseman and his associates, as "C.M. Eiseman & Co.," opened the "Nina Store," at Nina Landing on the plantation of that name, just below Cook's Landing, in 1889. Formerly Pecan Grove Plantation, owned by Jean Ursin Jarreau and his wife, Marie Octavine Leblanc de Villeneuve, the property had been sold by the Jarreau heirs in 1857 to Charles W. Allen, who changed its name to Nina Plantation. The 1,080-arpent estate, its livestock and other movables were later owned by Samuel H. Snowden, at whose succession sale in 1888 it was purchased for $28,888 by the New Orleans firm of V. & A. Meyer & Co., composed of Victor and Adolph Meyer of New Orleans and Solomon Meyer of New York City.

Victor and Adolph Meyer were the twin sons of Abraham Meyer, a native of Heuchelheim, Rheinpfalz, and Helena Meyer, who was born in Essingen, Rheinpfalz. Victor was born on 13 October 1840, in the Rheinpfalz. He, his parents, twin brother Adolph, and siblings Cassius/Isaac, and Fanette, arrived at New Orleans on 10 December 1847 aboard the ship *Diana*. Victor was married on 23 December 1873, in New Orleans, Louisiana, to Sarah Eveline/Eveleen Kohn, who was born in New Orleans on 31 July 1851, to Carl Kohn and Clara White. Eveline/Eveleen's maternal grandparents were prominent New Orleanians Maunsel White and Héloise Denis de la Ronde, owners of the vast Maunsel White Plantation on Bayou Latenache, Pointe Coupée Parish. White's wife was descended from several pioneer Louisiana French families including de Pontalba, Morel de Guiramand, de Hoa and LaCoste.

Adolph Meyer, also born on 13 October 1840, in Germany, was married on 9 September 1868, in Adams Co., Illinois, to Rosalie Swift Jonas, the daughter of attorney and merchant Abraham Henry Jonas, a native of England, and his second wife, Louisa Block, born in Virginia. Rosalie was born ca. 1848 in Illinois.

The annual *Statement of the Sugar Crops made in Louisiana* by Alcée Bouchereau identified "Gen." Adolphe Meyer as the Planter/Occupant of Nina for the 1889-1890 season, and the plantation mill's output as 728 hogsheads or 918,157 pounds of sugar, including 800 tons of cane purchased from the St. Claude Plantation, immediately behind the town of Waterloo. The raw sugar produced in the Nina mill was shipped down the Mississippi River and granulated at the

Cora Mill in Iberville Parish, a forerunner of the Cora-Texas sugar mill of the 20th and 21st centuries.

In 1890, V. & A. Meyer & Co. conveyed Nina Plantation to the Farmers Land and Loan Company Limited of Jefferson Parish, Louisiana, through a "stocks and bonds exchange" valued at $150,000. The Planter/Occupant of Nina for 1890-1892 was identified in the Bouchereau *Statement of the Sugar Crops* as C. (Cassius) J. Meyer, a younger brother of Victor and Adolphe.

Cassius J. Meyer was born on 5 August 1845, in Germany, and accompanied his parents and brothers to New Orleans as "Isaac" Meyer in 1847, aboard the *Diana*. He served as a midshipman in the Confederate Navy during the Civil War. After the war, he was engaged in cotton planting in Concordia Parish, Louisiana, was married, and subsequently employed as a cotton presser in New Orleans.

Cassius Meyer chose, in turn, two wives from illustrious Louisiana French Catholic families. He was married first on 2 July 1879 in New Orleans to Emma Marie Forstall, who was born on 18 April 1858, to Henri Jean Forstall, a native of New Orleans, and Marie Ophélia Mathilde Plauché, born in Natchitoches Parish, Louisiana. Emma Forstall Meyer died in New Orleans on 17 January 1885, and Cassius was married a second time on 24 February 1886, to his dead wife's cousin, Olivia Olivier de Vézin, who was born ca. 1869 to Charles Octave Olivier de Vézin and Marie Léda Forstall.

Nina Plantation experienced peak production and output during the Meyer ownership. Cassius J. Meyer's crop for 1890-1891 set a record for the plantation, with 1,004,000 pounds of sugar produced. In the 1892-1893 season, the firm of Seckbach & Eiseman composed of Adolph Seckbach and C.M. Eiseman, leased the farmlands of Nina, and produced and milled the sugar cane, producing 656,000 pounds of sugar.

In 1893, the Farmers Land and Loan, through its vice president, Victor Meyer, sold Nina at the greatly depreciated price of $17,500 to New Orleans businessman Moses Schwartz. Only ten weeks later, Schwartz sold the place to the Pointe Coupée Planting and Manufacturing Company Limited, in which Schwartz, Seckbach and Eiseman were officers, for $27,500.

The managers of "Nina Store," while owned by C.M. Eiseman & Co., included area Catholic businessmen Franklin Louis "F.L." Howell between 1889 and1890, and Joseph James "Jimmy" Monceret in 1893. Pointe Coupée Parish's first-known soda fountain and five-cent counter outside New Roads were added to the "Nina Store" in 1890. That same year, a *Pointe Coupée Banner* advertisement informed its readers that transactions could be conducted in American (*sic*, English), French, Creole, Spanish, and German. The Nina Store purchased cotton, cotton seed, sugar cane, and other produce from its customers as did several other firms operating during that time.

Pointe Coupée Banner advertisements which appeared between 1889 and 1893 for the "Nina Store," C.M. Eiseman & Co., proprietors, highlighted: dress goods, calicoes, white and colored lawns, laces, trimmings, towels, clothing, handkerchiefs, hats, caps, ladies' hats, men's, ladies' misses' and children's shoes, fancy and staple groceries (touted the "largest and most varied assortment in the parish"), including flour, Extra sugar, Rio coffee, Bon Ton and Pickwick hams, California smoked shoulders, dry smoked shoulders and lard, liquors, "iced cold" beer, cider, pop, crockery, crystal, tinware, knives, graters, pepper boxes, woodenware, hardware, tools, faucets, saddlery, harness, curry combs, furniture (wardrobes, bureaus, washstands, bedsteads, chairs, rockers and safes), stoves, buggies, road carts, corn, oats, bran, and hay.

C.M. Eiseman was a director of the Pointe Coupée Planting and Manufacturing Company, Ltd., which purchased Nina Plantation from Moses Schwartz in 1893, Schwartz continuing his involvement as another of the five-man board. Nina Plantation changed hands several times over the next several decades, and during the ownership of Francois Ovide 'F.O." Lieux, C. M. Eiseman and A.V. Robertson contracted on 1 January 1898 to manage Nina as well as Lieux's Grand Bay Plantation immediately adjoining downriver. Lieux cancelled the agreement on 1 February 1900, citing the "financial embarrassment" of the partnership of Eiseman and Robertson.

The Eiseman family was enumerated in the 1910 United States Federal Census at 1923 State Street at which time Cassius was still identified as a planter. Cassius Meyer Eiseman died on 15 September 1914, at his "country home," Cora Plantation, in White Castle, Iberville Parish, Louisiana, where the family had business interests. He was interred in Dispersed of Judah Cemetery in New Orleans. Katie Joseph Eiseman died on 29 October 1930, and was interred with her husband.

POINTE COUPÉE PLANTING AND MANUFACTURING COMPANY, LTD.

The Pointe Coupée Planting and Manufacturing Company, Limited, chartered in 1893, was domiciled in Pointe Coupée Parish, but maintained "offices" in New Orleans for directors' meetings and the purchase and sale of produce and supplies. The original board of directors was composed of Moses Schwartz, president; Adolph Seckbach, secretary-treasurer; Cassius M. Eiseman, vice president and general manager; John Overmeyer, and M.F. Flowers.

One of Louisiana's most colorful businessmen, who often figured in litigation and celebrated court proceedings, Moses Schwartz was born on 26 April 1848, in Erlenbach, Rheinpfalz, Germany, to Simon Schwartz and Caroline Klein. He immigrated to Louisiana in 1865, and was first employed by an uncle, the well-known New Orleans merchant Abraham Schwartz, who operated the A. Schwartz & Son dry goods business in the Touro Buildings on Canal Street.

Moses Schwartz was married on 27 November 1872, in New Orleans to Ida Bernard, the daughter of Oury Bernard, a native of Lunéville, Meurthe-et-Moselle, and Julie Godchot/Godchaux, a native of Herbéviller, Meurthe-et-Moselle, France. Among the witnesses to the ceremony was the bride's cousin Louisiana's "sugar king" and upscale department store founder Leon Godchaux.

Ida had been born on 30 July 1857, at New Orleans. She lost both of her parents a year later: Julie on 11 August 1858, and Oury Bernard six weeks later on 28 September. They were interred in Hebrew Rest Cemetery No. 1. Three-year-old Ida and Jeanne Bernard, her elder sister, appeared in the 1860 United States Federal Census in New Orleans in the household of their nineteen-year-old aunt Mathilde Bernard and her husband, dry goods merchant Louis Schwartz, age 27, the latter a native of Busenberg, Rheinpfalz, Germany.

Moses Schwartz's many enterprises in New Orleans included the M. Schwartz & Co. hardware store, and his purchase of the Leeds Foundry, which he improved and expanded as the Schwartz

Foundry and Machinery works, specializing in the manufacturing and repairing of all types of sugar machinery. He and his brother, Louis Schwartz, purchased the historic Spanish Fort property near the head of Bayou St. John, and in 1878 established the popular and long-running amusement complex of that name. Moses Schwartz also purchased the Canal Street, City Park & Lake Railroad Company, subsequently known as the New Orleans, Spanish Fort & Lake Railroad Company, which connected the business district of the city with Lake Pontchartrain, via the Spanish Fort Park.

Adolph Seckbach was born on 1 February 1848, to Markus Seckbach and Dora Katz, in the Free City of Frankfurt am Main, German Confederation. According to a subsequently filed United States passport application, Adolph Seckbach, a merchant, immigrated via London in 1867, and was naturalized in New Orleans, Louisiana in 1883. He had been married, to Amelia Levy, on January 11, 1882, in New Orleans. The bride was born on 1 November 1858, in the Crescent City, to Dryades Street watchmaker Michael Levy, a native of Hanau, Hesse-Kassel, German Confederation, and his wife, Rachel Frank, born at Nordstetten Landkreis Freudenstädter, Baden-Württemberg, Germany.

The Pointe Coupée Planting and Manufacturing Co., Ltd., had purchased Nina Plantation in 1893 from Moses Schwartz for $27,500, after assuming its mortgage. The strategically located 1,080-arpent tract included a sugar mill and machinery, dwellings, cabins, stables, other outbuildings, and agricultural implements.

Plans to erect a "central sugar factory" that would process other planters' as well as Nina's cane crops failed to materialize. The company did, however, net an initial harvest producing 742,995 pounds of sugar. A 1 April 1893 letter to and published in *The Louisiana Planter and Sugar Manufacturer* indicated that a new residence and storehouse had been built, and the sugar mill and workers' quarters, currently at the mercy of the encroaching Mississippi River, were scheduled to be removed to the "safe" side of a new levee.

Riverfronts and plantations were occasionally the scenes of accidents and violence, the latter principally due to tenants' feuds and when levee "camps" were engaged in building new embankments. Nina was fraught with shootings and arrests between 1887 and 1888, according to the *Pointe Coupée Banner,* which reported on such incidents as the shooting of a tenant while in his bed in 1887. Few disturbances were noted after Cassius Eiseman and his partners took over the plantation.

The 22 September 1894 *Louisiana Planter and Sugar Manufacturer* announced that Nina and its planting company were to take the lead in that season's cane harvest, which was expected to commence two days later. However, misfortune struck in the following year, as the same periodical, in its issue dated 19 January 1895, reported the total destruction by fire of the Nina sugar mill. Arson was believed to be the cause.

On 1 April 1895, the Pointe Coupée Planting and Manufacturing Company, represented by Cassius M. Eiseman, sold Nina Plantation to its former general agent and manager, A.V. Robertson, for $15,000, with a mortgage assumption and vendor's lien. Included in the sale were all crops of cane and hay, forty-four mules, two horses, and the "machinery wreck" left from the fire (Conveyance Book 1895, No. 17232).

Moses Schwartz died after an illness of several months on 8 July 1912, in New Orleans, and was interred in Metairie Cemetery. His widow, née Ida Bernard, survived him by 40 years, dying on 2 July 1952, in Milwaukee, Milwaukee Co., Wisconsin. Her remains were returned to New Orleans for interment with him.

The Schwartz children included Walter (b. 1881), Otto (b. 1883), and Edith Jeanne (b. 1885 who married J.C. Hyman), Louis, and Elsa, the latter two of whom preceded their father in death. Moses Schwartz's uncle Abraham's son Simon J. Schwartz was a founder in 1897 of the famous Maison Blanche, one of America's largest and best-known department stores, which flourished for a century as the "Greatest Store South."

Adolph Seckback, his wife, Amelia, and their seven surviving children: Doretta (b. 1883), Arthur (b. 1884) Mathilde (b. 1887), Herbert Mervyn (b. 1888), Effie Adele (b. 1890), Ruth (b. 1891), and Myrtle (b. 1896), moved to Chicago, Cook Co., Illinois, before the 1910 United States Federal Census enumeration, where Adolph Seckbach died on 28 February 1915. He was interred there in Zion Gardens. His widow, née Amelia Levy, died in Chicago on 28 February 1915, and was buried with him.

Among the succession of owners of Nina Plantation in the early 20th century was S. Gumbel & Co. of New Orleans, who were adjudicated the property through their high bid of $21,000 at the 1918 Sheriff's Sale owing to the business failure of then-owner Joseph Villeneuve Decuir (Conveyance Book B, No. 1999, dated 1918). S. Gumbel & Co. sold Nina a year later, in 1919, for $35,000 to Alphonse J. Glynn, son of regional planter and political figure Martin Glynn. Both Nina and adjacent Grand Bay plantations remain in Glynn family ownership in the 21st century.

The site of the principal buildings of the Pecan Grove–Nina Plantation yielded archaeological finds dating from the eighteenth century, when surveyed by R. Christopher Goodwin & Associates, Inc. for the U.S. Army Corps of Engineers in 1999, preparatory to the Corps' placement of a concrete revetment to curb caving of the riverbank.

Tintype of the 1848 brick single-story courthouse at New Roads where many Jewish immigrants were naturalized.

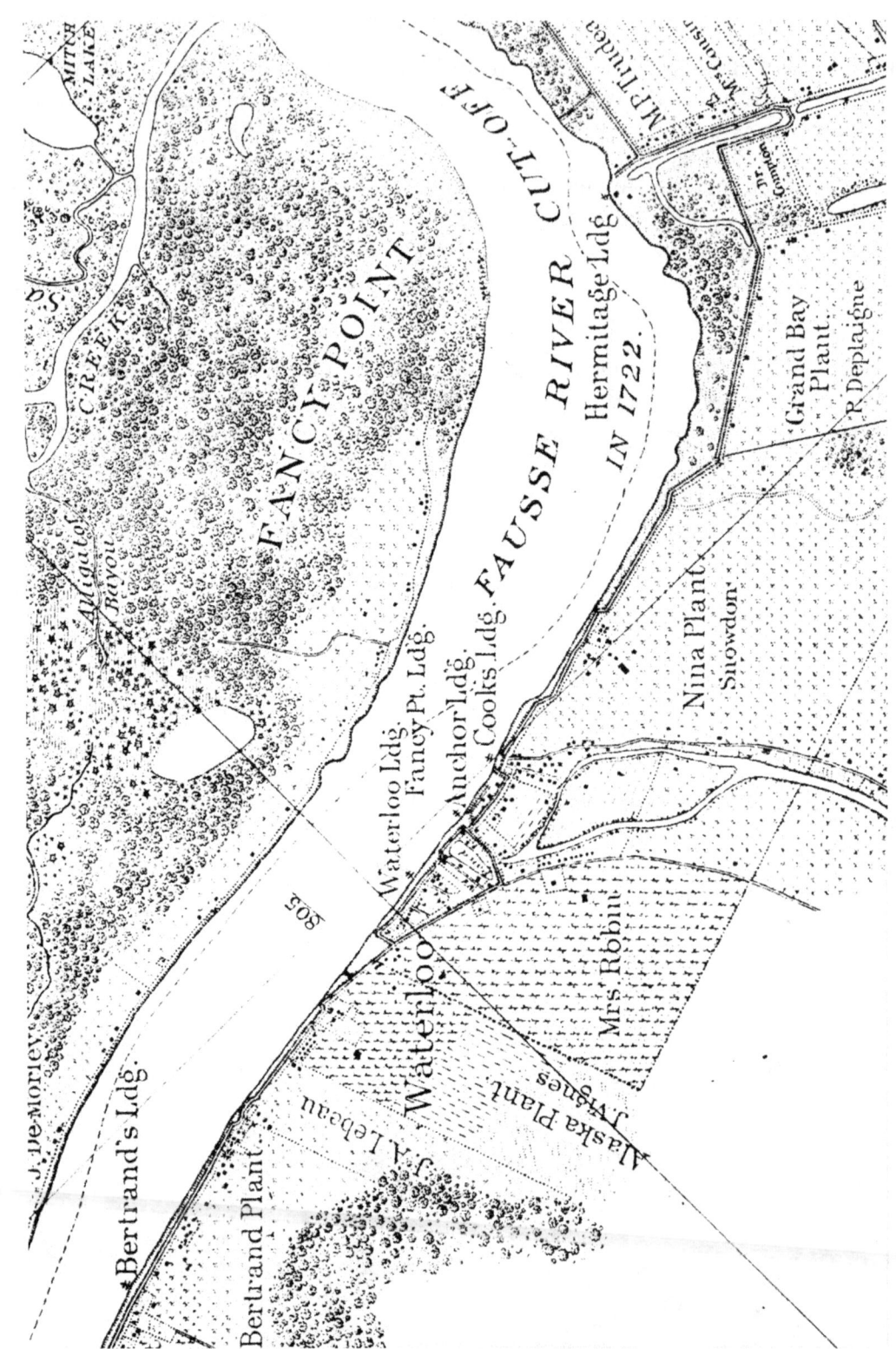

Mississippi River Landings in the 1880s.

CHAPTER 3

NEW ROADS

In "Catharine Cole's Visit to New Roads" which ran in the 22 November 1891 New Orleans *Daily Picayune*, pioneer Louisiana female journalist Martha R. Field reported:

> New Roads, the parish seat of Pointe Coupée, is an old French settlement. Before the [Civil] war, there was no one in it who could speak English, and for a long time it really had no name save that of the church, Sainte Marie. It sets out in a long row of big and little houses, along the sloping shore of False River, just as the villages of the Lake [Pontchartrain] Coast are made. The old church of Sainte Marie is at one, the big red courthouse with its deep-set porch at the other, and thus between the law and the prophets the town thrives. There are two newspapers, the *Democrat* and the *Banner*; there are two hotels, six or eight large stores and three physicians…. There are no telegraphs nor [public] telephones at New Roads. The daily mail comes overland on the haunches of a pony; life is the more serene for this.

The City of New Roads had its origin and was given its name *camino real*, or "royal road" by Spanish authorities around 1776. This road connected the growing False River area and the older Pointe Coupée settlement to the north on the Mississippi River. The French called it the *Chemin Neuf*, or New Road, and the name was henceforth linked with the community which developed at its south terminus, near the head of False River.

The New Road originally terminated at the Chemin Public or Rue du Commerce, present-day West Main Street, via St. Mary Street, but in 1805 a property exchange between Dr. Louis Gougis and the Pointe Coupée governing authorities resulted in its shift to present New Roads Street. In 1822, a "free woman of color," Marie Catherine Depau *dite* la Fille Gougis (nicknamed Dr. Gougis's daughter), apparently a natural child of Dr. Gougis, subdivided the front part of the Gougis plantation into the six-block, twenty lot development now bordered by False River to the South; Rue de la Promenade, presently West Second Street to the North; Rue du Marché, now St. Mary Street on the West; and the Rue du Pont Neuf or the New Road, today's New Roads Street, on the east. In between, and running parallel to Marché and Pont Neuf streets was the Rue de l'Indépendence, subsequently Richy Street, which ran parallel to the Chemin Public and Promenade and crossed Rue du Jackson (now First Street).

Referred to alternately as Chemin Neuf, originally in the singular, and the Village of Ste. Marie/St. Mary, for St. Mary Church established immediately west of the Gougis development in 1823, the town was named the Pointe Coupée Parish seat in 1846, after fire destroyed the courthouse at the former site of the Pointe Coupée fort directly north on the Mississippi River.

A post office was established as New Roads, Louisiana in 1858, but closed in 1861. The community was incorporated as the Town of New Roads (in the plural) in 1875. The post office reopened as "St. Mary's, Louisiana," in 1878, and changed its name to reflect the incorporation as New Roads, Louisiana in 1879. The incorporation falling into disuse, the town was incorporated again, as "New Rhodes, Louisiana" in 1894, but the name was ultimately changed back to "New Roads" in conformity with the post office in 1900.

Bridges were never built across False River, nor over the Chenals until the 1880s. The first was constructed over the Lower Chenal from Chenal proper to present-day Rougon in 1886, and the second, over the Upper Chenal, or Poulailler, in 1889. Flatboat ferries operated from, at least, the 1840s: one at the upper end of False River at the Narcisse Carmouche plantation, and the other at the Place de la Croix (Square of the Cross) opposite Old St. Mary Church in downtown New Roads. As late as the 1940s, residents of the Island of False River crossed over to the "New Roads side" by boat to work on area plantations and to shop in New Roads and False River Road stores.

The establishment of the Texas & Pacific Railroad in 1899 heralded a decade of growth for New Roads, with new streets opened to connect with and cross the railroad. Richy and New Roads Streets became a second business district for the town. North of the railroad, or "Back o' Town," African American residences, businesses, churches and schools predominated, although homes, small industries, and general and grocery stores, liquor stores and saloons belonging to native French and immigrant Jewish and Sicilian residents were located on New Roads, Richy and Claiborne (later Parent) Streets and Railroad Avenue North (now Texas Street). Private telephone lines were installed in 1890 and 1904. The False River Telephone Line and the town's waterworks system were inaugurated in 1906, and citywide electrification was introduced in 1909.

The principal business district of Main and intersecting streets bordered roughly by Poydras Academy on the west and North Carolina Avenue on the east teemed with general, dry goods, hardware, furniture and grocery stores, hotels, saloons, restaurants, bakeries, medical, legal and professional offices, newspapers and other enterprises. Richy Street was principally a commercial thoroughfare with numerous grocery stores, livery stables, and other businesses between West Main and Sixth Street, and solidly commercial as far north as Claiborne later Parent Street, two blocks north of the railroad. The two squares between the railroad and Parent were home to primarily African American businesses and residences and was referred to as "The Strip." A disastrous fire on St. Joseph's Day, 19 March 1909, destroyed most of the block of Richy Street between Sixth and the railroad.

New Roads Street, originally residential, began to develop commercially with the arrival of the automobile and, like Richy to its immediate west, was lined with wholesale grocery and lumber companies, and livery stables nearest the railroad, some of which were owned by local Jewish families.

On either side of the railroad, north and south, industries opened up including cotton gins, a cottonseed oil mill, ice and beer plants, a moss gin, and brickyard. An intricate system of freight sidings, switches, and a wye for turning the engines, connected their concerns with the main line of the railroad.

Downtown, several wharfs served commercial, industrial and recreational purposes. A steamboat landing at the foot of New Roads Street was replaced in 1902 with the New Roads Progressive League's dance, skating, and swimming pavilion. Cottonseed for area gins was transferred from stall steamers at the New Roads Oil Mill wharf to an electric tramway along Community Street, then to the cottonseed oil mill for production. A community bathing pavilion was built opposite St. Mary Church.

Three courthouses served Pointe Coupée Parish from 1847 until present times: the earliest, in James M. Bailey's Hotel and ballroom at the site of 208 West Main. The second was, a brick, single-story building strikingly similar to the contemporary Iberville Parish Courthouse in Plaquemine, and the Ascension Parish Courthouse in Donaldsonville, all three having been constructed by George Weldon. Finally in 1902, the towered and turreted Romanesque Revival courthouse was built, supplemented by the addition of a poured cement annex to the rear or north in 1940, and annexes across East Main Street to the south and Gaudin Street to the north. In each of the three courthouses, immigrants to Pointe Coupée, including numerous Jewish men signed oaths of renunciation of allegiance to their former rulers in Europe and were naturalized as United States citizens.

JEAN MAURICE FORTLOUIS

Jean Moritz Fort Louis/Jean Maurice Fortlouis, an early merchant of New Roads, was a native of Karlsruhe, Baden, Holy Roman Empire, now Germany, but his family was formerly from the fortress town of Fort-Louis, Bas-Rhin, France. According to the exhaustive research of Carol Mills-Nichol, the co-author of this book, most of the inhabitants of Fort-Louis fled after the town was besieged by Austrian, Bavarian, and Hessian forces in 1793, during the War of the First Coalition. Although some Jewish families migrated south to Haguenau, the family which adopted the Fortlouis/Fort Louis surname, crossed the Rhine River to Karlsruhe in Baden, the town just opposite their old home in France.

In 1808 Napoleon I, who had conquered much of present-day Germany and the surrounding areas, published a decree that all Jews who were not using a fixed surname, must report to the local town hall and formally chose one. No name adoption list survived for Fort-Louis because the Jews had fled the town over a decade before. It is most probable that the family known as Fort Louis, and in Pointe Coupée Parish as Fortlouis, adopted or was given the surname while in Karlsruhe, Baden. Which family they had been during the last census of Jews in Fort-Louis, taken in 1784, cannot be determined because most Jews there were not using surnames with the exception of the members of one Dreyfus, one May, and one Weyl/Weil family. What is certain about the Fortlouis family of Fort-Louis and later Karlsruhe is that they are a completely distinct family whose surname after 1808 indicates a direct bloodline.

Jean Moritz Fort Louis/Jean Maurice Fortlouis was born between 1800-1804 in Karlsruhe, Baden, to Jean Moritz Fortlouis and his wife Mina/Minette Auerbach. We have found no birth record for him, but his parents' names were given by him in his Louisiana marriage record.

On 27 March 1841, Maurice Fort Louis renounced his allegiance to King Leopold, and applied for citizenship in Avoyelles Parish, stating that he was thirty-nine-years-old, a "native of Carlsrhue? capital of Grand Duchy of Bard (Bade, Bord?)," and had arrived in America in 1819 on board the ship *Louisa* from Le Havre, France. (Jeraldine DuFour LaCour, *Avoyelleans of Yesteryear*, self-published, 1983, p. 123.) He had been previously enumerated in the 1820 United States Federal Census for East Baton Rouge Parish as an unnaturalized foreign white male merchant between the ages of sixteen and twenty-five.

Fortlouis first appeared in Pointe Coupée Parish in a conveyance record (CB 1827, Entry 2171) done in 1827 recording his purchase of land from Barthelemi Belozi, one of the earliest settlers in the parish from "Italy" (unspecified state). The Pointe Coupée Parish Clerk of Court indices available to us indicated that there was a transfer of property from Belozi to Maurice Fortlouis, However, the volume where the original record was housed was out for conservation. For that reason, a search was done for Belozi's acquisitions prior to his sale to Maurice Fortlouis. There was only one transaction recorded for Belozi: a one-half interest in a lot measuring 7 1/2 *toises* on the Mississippi River by depth of 46 *toises*, 11 *pouces*, at the head of False River, in front of the plantation of (merchant) Francois Labrouche Dussin (i.e., a *batture* lot, at riverfront, at what would become known as Waterloo), with house, cabins and other improvements, being formerly the property of the Widow Durant. (Note: 1 *toise* = 6.39436 ft.; 1 *pouce* = 1.07 inches)

We can surmise that Belozi sold this land or a part of it to Maurice Fortlouis in 1827, so we are sure that the latter was in Pointe Coupée at or even before this date. This is important because it may explain the possible identity of a young man buried on 17 March 1860, in the old St. Francis Cemetery on the Mississippi River, at the age of thirty-two years. He was interred as Jules Fortlouis (PCP-11, 181), and may have been a brother, or half-brother of Maurice Fortlouis, a free man of color, born ca. 1830 to Jean Maurice Fortlouis and an unknown woman, who has numerous descendants in the parish. No baptismal or birth records have been found for either Jules Fortlouis (b. ca. 1827) or Maurice Fortlouis (b. 1830).

In 1834 Jean Maurice purchased Lot No.3 as shown in the 1822 Pierre L'Hermite Map of the subdivision of Catherine Depau *dite la Fille* Gougis, from Herman Orth but sold it a year later in 1835 to Joseph and Washington Jewell. This was later the location of Jacob Singerman's American Department Store and the present New Roads City Hall.

In that same year, 1834, Maurice Fortlouis filed his only-known civil suit in Pointe Coupée (Early Parish Court, No. 847), successfully suing and as-yet unidentified Daniel Dreyfous, "late of this parish," for the amount of $90.18 owed by Dreyfous for merchandise purchased from Fortlouis. Dreyfous had pledged payment in a note for that amount, payable to "Monsieur Moris" (*sic*). Maurice Fortlouis posted $150 bond in prosecuting his case, with planter and political figure Pierre Porche standing security for him. Dreyfous was represented in a new trial by curator *ad hoc* F. Hayem, but the ruling rendered for Fortlouis in the first trial was upheld.

Maurice Fortlouis was married on 17 December 1834, to Julie Aurore Porche in St. Mary Church, New Roads, Louisiana (PCP-19, 233).

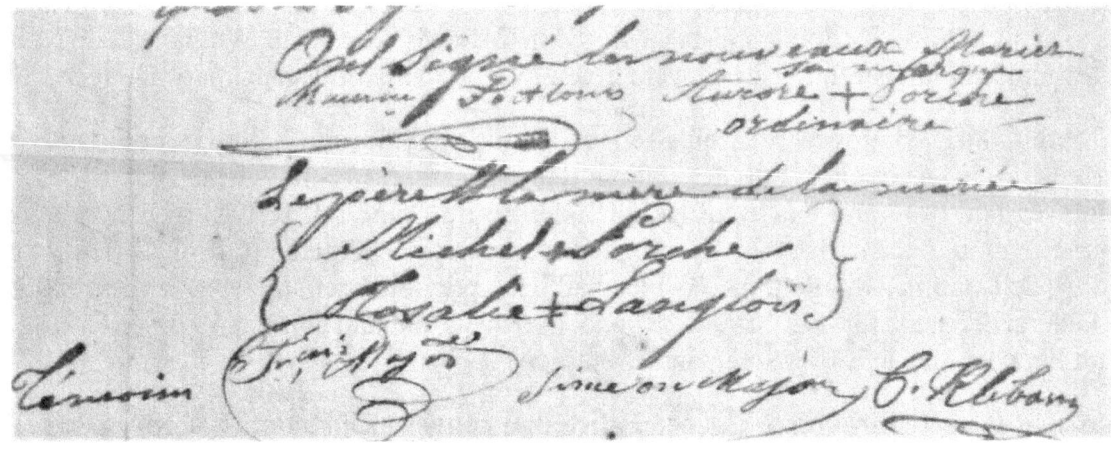

1834 Marriage record for Maurice Fortlouis, who signed and Aurore Porche, who made her mark. The brides' parents signed with an "x." The witnesses were: François Major, Simeon Major and C. [Christophe]. Kleborn.

The Porches were one of the founding families of Pointe Coupée Parish. Julie Aurore was born on 16 March 1813, at New Roads to Michel Porche, a cotton planter, and his wife, Julie Langlois (PCP-7, 258). There was no mention in the existing Catholic record that this was a mixed marriage between a Jew and a Catholic, and no dispensation from the Church exists to say that it was. However, we know that the Fortlouis family was Jewish, and to this day, all, if not religiously, are ethnically Semitic.

By 1837 the Fortlouises had moved across the Atchafalaya River to the neighboring parish of Avoyelles, where Michel Fortlouis was born on 20 July 1837. Mathilde followed on 13 December 1838. Another child, J. M. Fortlouis, who was born ca. 1836, according to an 1880 United States Federal Census, threads his way through Pointe Coupée and New Orleans records. There is no birth record for him, however, in either Avoyelles or Pointe Coupée Parishes. A fourteen-year-old "Morris Porche" (*sic*, Fortlouis intended) was enumerated with the widow Michel Porche, his grandmother in the 1850 United States Federal Census, along with other Fortlouis siblings, excluding Michel and Rosalie who were missing from the family.

Jean Maurice Fortlouis was joined by the Frank brothers, Adolph (b. Aron Frank in 1809) and Charles (b. Judah Frank in 1811), who immigrated to Avoyelles Parish, Louisiana from Nordstetten, Kingdom of Württemberg (Germany), arriving in New Orleans together on 6 July 1839. The brothers were the children of Abraham Frank and his wife Madele Fortlouis. The Franks, therefore, were likely Maurice's cousins. (Note: Similar to the mixed marriage of Maurice Fortlouis and Aurore Porche, Adolph Frank married Caroline Gaspard in a Catholic ceremony in 1842. Charles Frank married Pauline Bordelon in a Catholic ceremony in 1845.)

Charles Frank and Maurice Fortlouis went into business together as merchants in Avoyelles Parish in the town of Hydropolis, just south of present-day Marksville. Maurice and Aurore's third and fourth children were also born in Avoyelles Parish: Rosalie, born on 16 February 1841, and baptized at St. Paul the Apostle Church in Avoyelles Parish, and Leopold born ca. 1843, for which there is no existing baptismal record.

On 19 August 1843, Charles Kibbe, Bankruptcy Agent for Avoyelles Parish, filed a notice in *Le Villagéois/The Villager* newspaper in that parish, calling in accounts owed to four bankrupt individuals, including "M. Fort Louis." Subsequently the 2 November 1843 issue of the same journal announced a United States Marshal's Sale to be held on 27 November "at the residence of Maurice Fort Louis at Hydropolis" for the disposal of: a residence lot; enslaved persons, including a "negro woman" named Fanny, age 26, and her child, William, age two; 15 head of cattle, three horses, a *caleche* (four-wheel carriage), a gig (two-wheel carriage) and harness, a two-horse wagon and harness; a cart containing a small amount of merchandise and harness, household furniture, a clock, and several accounts and notes due Fort Louis; and one-half interest in a building and other improvements held in partnership between Fort Louis and Charles Frank.

After the business failure, Maurice Fortlouis took his family back to Pointe Coupée Parish to live, where two more children were born, Geneviève Stephanie, on 18 August 1845, and Théophile on 6 May 1848. Four of the seven Fortlouis children: Michel, Mathilde, Geneviève, and Théophile, were baptized at St. Mary Church in New Roads, Pointe Coupée Parish.

We know that Maurice Fortlouis died or disappeared before 9 August 1850, although there is no official record for it, because on that day the census taker, enumerated the members of the

"Mitchell Porche" family, that is Mme. Michel Porche, née Rosalie Langlois, age 74, a widow with $20,000 in assets, living on her plantation near New Roads, today located immediately east of East Main and Oak Streets in the city, her daughter, Aurore, misidentified as "Cora" Porche, and five of the seven Fortlouis children, also misidentified as Porches. Maurice Fortlouis, absent from the family, had perhaps been buried in the old St. Francis Cemetery, on Pointe Coupée Road, northeast of New Roads, the French colonial-era burial ground which systematically caved into the shifting Mississippi River between 1885 and 1892, or had left the parish not to return.

Aurore Porche was married for a second time on 14 August 1852, in a civil ceremony, to Paulin Aguillard, son of José Aguiar/Joseph Aguillard, native of Santa Cruz, Tenerife, Canary Islands, and Henriette Guérin, a native of False River, Pointe Coupée Parish. They were the parents of three children: Adèle (b. 8 June 1853), Paul Lucien (b. 27 May 1855), and Charles Swain (b. 5 July 1857). The couple was married in a Catholic ceremony on 14 November 1876 (IMCL-4, 46), three days before Paulin Aguillard died at the age of 77 years on 17 November 1876 (PCP-20, 80). Marie Aurore Porche died on 30 September 1904, at New Roads and was interred there the next day at St. Mary Cemetery.

Jean-Baptiste Abraham "Abram" Villéret (b. 11 September 1866-1912), one of Maurice Fortlouis and Aurore Porche's grandchildren, born to their daughter Rosalie Fortlouis and her husband, Charles W. Villéret, was a pharmacist at Bayou Sara, a three-term Clerk of Court of West Feliciana Parish, and a 1911 candidate for Louisiana Secretary of State.

LOUIS and ISIDORE FRANK

Louis Frank, a native of Württemberg, immigrated to Louisiana in 1844. He filed a declaration in New Roads, Louisiana in 1849 renouncing allegiance to the King of Württemberg. A "Louis Frank" was enumerated as a twenty-five-year-old laborer born in Germany in the 1850 United States Federal Census for New Orleans. After that, the record is silent. It is possible, however, that he may have been a brother to Adolph and Charles Frank, cousins of the Fortlouis family who had settled in both Pointe Coupée and the neighboring Avoyelles Parish.

Family members, and even friends from the same town tended to follow one another from place to place, a phenomenon sociologists call "chain migration." Isidore Frank had filed a similar oath in 1845 at New Roads, where he also renounced his allegiance to King William of Württemberg. No other information was given, including his age. We know that Adolph and Charles Frank, two of the eleven children of Abraham and Madele Fortlouis Frank, did not use their given birth names in America. Isidore Frank might have been their eldest brother, born in 1806 as "Isaac" Frank, and "Louis" Frank may have been their brother who was Lazarus Frank at his birth in 1824. "Isaac" and "Isidore" are two names used interchangeably by many Jews. Lazarus, which is often spelled "Leyser," in Jewish records is usually anglicized as "Louis." Louis never appeared in any other records in Pointe Coupée Parish. Isidore, however, was enumerated living in Raccourci-Old River according to the 1850 United States Federal Census.

SIMON, LOEB & CO

Simon, Loeb & Co., general merchants, all natives of the Kingdom of Bavaria (Germany), were in business from 1856 until the mid-Civil War. The firm of Joseph Simon, Jr., and the brothers Emanuel and Aaron Loeb, operated in a building leased from former merchants Seibert & Hurst, located in what is now the 400 block of West Main Street. In 1859 the *Démocrate de la Pointe Coupée/Pointe Coupée Democrat* ran advertisements for Simon, Loeb & Co. which carried dry goods, groceries, provisions, drugs, medicines, perfumery, chinaware, crockery, glassware, cutlery, and hardware. Below is an example of 1862 Civil War era currency printed by Simon Loeb & Co.

Emanuel Loeb, first of the future partnership to arrive in the United States, immigrated in 1853. He filed a declaration in 1857 and oath in 1859, both in New Roads, Louisiana, renouncing his allegiance to the King of Bavaria. According to his New York marriage record, Emanuel Loeb: was born on 14 August 1832, at Neuleiningen, Rheinpfalz, Germany, to Heinrich Loeb and Esther Kahn. (Note: His tombstone inscription reads "born on 7 October 1831.") He was married on 18 November 1876, at New York, New York, to Clara Kohlman, the daughter of Henry Kohlman and Amelia Sartorius. Clara had been born on 6 September 1853 at Vicksburg, Warren Co., Mississippi. The Sartorius brothers and sisters (Amelia, Isaac, Jacob, Philip, and Caroline) had immigrated from Germersheim, Rheinpfalz, Germany, in the 1830s and had all settled in Mississippi, primarily at Vicksburg. The Kohlmans had similarly immigrated to Mississippi, being early settlers in Brookhaven, Lincoln Co., Mississippi.

Joseph Simon, Jr. was in New Roads by 1857, where he declared that he was 29 years old and had immigrated to America in 1853. In 1859, he filed an oath renouncing his allegiance to Maximilian II, the King of Bavaria. According to his tombstone inscription, Joseph Simon, Jr. was born on 28 Oct 1828, in Sausenheim (now part of Grünstadt), Rheinpfalz, Germany. He took out a license to marry Sarah Loeb on 29 November 1859, who was born ca. 1839 at Altdorf, Rheinpfalz, Germany. They were the parents of four children: Jacob (b. 1861), Joseph (b. 1863), Samuel L. (b. 1864), and Harriett (b. 1867).

According to her cemetery inscription, Sarah Simon died from yellow fever on 3 October 1867, and was interred in Hebrew Rest Cemetery No. 1 in New Orleans. Joseph Simon, Jr. was married on 19 May 1868, to Jeanette Loeb, born ca. March 1847, in Bavaria. Simon and Jeannette were the parents of five children: Bertha (b. 1868), Henry (b. 1871), Rosa (b. 1874), Maurice (b. 1876), and Simon (b. 1880).

Aaron Loeb, Emanuel's brother, was born on 12 September 1836, at Neustadt, Rheinpfalz, Germany, to Heinrich Loeb and his wife, Esther Kahn. He was last of the trio to arrive, immigrating in 1857. He married Henrietta/Harriett Kaufman on 13 May 1873, in New Orleans. She was born on 24 December 1851, in the Rheinpfalz, Germany to Henry Kaufman, a native of Lambsheim, Rheinpfalz, Germany, and his wife Caroline Ries, a native of Herxheim bei Landau, Rheinpfalz, Germany. Aaron and Harriett were the parents of a daughter, Henrietta "Hattie" Loeb, born on 31 March 1880, in New Orleans.

The 1860 United States Federal Census enumeration at Simon, Loeb & Co. in New Roads listed Emanuel Loeb with $2,000 in real estate and $3,000 in personal property. His brother Aaron Loeb and Joseph Patin were both clerks. Joseph Simon, Jr. and his wife, Sarah, were, meanwhile, living on the Lower Chenal of False River, next to the store of Lazarus Loeb, where Simon was shown to have $100 property.

According to the *Soard's New Orleans City Directory* published in 1874, Emanuel Loeb and Joseph Simon, Jr. were partners of Ferdinand Gumbel, doing business as the firm of Loeb, Gumbel & Simon, notions dealers in New Orleans. Meanwhile, Aaron Loeb operated stores both in partnership and in sole proprietorship on the False River Road, the Lower Chenal and Raccourci-Old River.

Joseph Simon, Jr. died in New Orleans on 12 February 1901, and was buried in Hebrew Rest Cemetery No.1. His wife followed on 1 July 1926, in New Orleans and was interred with him. Emanuel Loeb died on 9 July 1895, at Richfield Springs, New York, and was buried in Salem Fields Cemetery in Brooklyn, Kings County, New York. Clara died on 10 September 1927, and was interred with her husband.

ISAAC HAYEM

Isaac Hayem, a native of France, born ca. 1839, appeared in the 1860 United States Federal Census as a peddler, living with Pierre and Clémentine Manuel, free people of color, immediately next to the Auguste Pourciau plantation, just west of New Roads (present-day area of West Main and Berthier Streets). He was possibly the same as Isaac B. Ham (*sic*) who served in the Civil War in the 4th Louisiana Cavalry C.S.A. Although details regarding Isaac Hayem's origins and later life remain elusive, he is an example of countless immigrants who attempted to establish an economic future in the United States, only, in his case, to find that his temporary residence in New Roads was a hotbed of Union activity.

There are no more records for Isaac Hayem in Louisiana after 1860, and no more clues to his identity. (Note: Hayem, also spelled Haïm, was a surname adopted by Jews mainly in the Moselle region of France.) It is conceivable that he might have returned to Europe, as did a large number of other immigrants who had left their ancestral homes due to the continuing political unrest and resulting wars, only to find themselves in the American conflict, to which they were no party, but which had cost them their livelihood, and perhaps their blood, or even the lives of loved ones.

EUGÈNE AND ADÉLAÏDE KATZENSTEIN

Who exactly is Adélaïde Katzenstein? That question is not an easy one. Her husband, Eugène Katzenstein, however, was easily traced. Eugène was the son of Nathan/Adrien Katzenstein and his wife, Nanette Hautviller, born probably at Paris, Ile-de-France, France, ca. 1830, although all records previous to 1860 were destroyed in the burning of the *Hotel De Ville* (City Hall) by the Communards in 1871. Eugène's father had been born as "Nathan" Katzenstein on 22 August 1807, at Haguenau, Bas-Rhin, France, to David Salomon Katzenstein, born on 26 December 1782, at Trimbach, Bas-Rhin, and his wife, Buna/Babette Salomon. During the 1808 Napoleonic name adoption mandate for Jews, David officially changed his son Nathan's name to "Adrien," and his wife's name from "Buna Salomon" to "Barbe Moyses." Eugène's mother, Nanette Hautviller, was born at Augny, Moselle, France, to Michel Hautviller and Frahen Cahen.

Twenty-year-old Eugène Katzenstein arrived at New Orleans on 27 December 1849, aboard the ship *Radius*. Eugène Katzenstein, a jeweler, was located at 122 Exchange Alley in New Orleans according to *City Directory* issues dated 1852 through 1880. Most records point to the fact that he was married to Adélaïde Mars, a native of France, although there is no record for it.

Among the several families from Bordeaux, Gironde, France, to settle in the New Roads area was that of Théodore Mars and his wife, Marie Duportail. The couple was married at Bordeaux, Section 1. Gironde, France, on 6 September 1832. Four children were born to them in quick succession: Pierre Gabriel on 7 January 1833, Jeanne Anne Anaïs on 17 November 1834, Jean Théophile on 29 November 1835, and Rosalie Marie on 24 July 1837. Having searched in vain, we could not confirm that the couple ever had a daughter named Adélaïde in France or elsewhere. Twenty-five-year-old Théodore, identified as a *maître d'hôtel*, applied for a passport at Bordeaux, Gironde, France, on 10 March 1836, to travel to Tampico, Mexico. His family was not with him. After a year in Tampico, he boarded the ship *Water Witch* and arrived in New Orleans on 6 September 1837. In Théodore's declaration of intention to become a U.S. citizen, filed at New Roads in 1842, he stated that he had, indeed, arrived in 1837 on the *Water Witch*. We could find no likely records for the arrival of his family. By the time of the 1850 United States Federal Census for Pointe Coupée Parish, the Mars family had settled in Sec. 78-T4S-R10E, "in the woods" west of the New Road and north of present-day Portage Canal. Théodore was confirmed in title to the 77.71 acres by United States Cash Patent No. 4435 in 1859.

Théodore's wife, Marie Duportail was enumerated in the 1860 United States Federal Census for Pointe Coupée Parish, as a widow living with her four children: Gabriel, Théophile, Marie, and Anaïs. She shared a house with the widow of Paul Friloux, née Marie Constance Lilia Dumoulin, and her four children including Julie Marceline, age 7. There is no record of Théodore's death anywhere in the United States. There is one, however, for Jeanne Anaïs Mars who died in Pointe Coupée Parish on 9 March 1869 (PCP-20, 25).

In that same year, Théophile Mars purchased a tract measuring two arpents front by 36 in depth, directly in the rear of the property of Rosine Michel Kern at New Roads where they established their residence. Théophile and his brother Gabriel Mars were successively engaged in sugar cane planting and milling, butchering and carpentry, and were married, respectively, to sisters Emma and Célina Saizan in old St. Mary Church in New Roads. In the 1870 United States Federal Census, Widow Marie Duportail Mars and her children were enumerated on Théophile's town property, sharing their home with Nathan Kern the younger, the latter a store clerk for his aunt-by-marriage next door, Rosine Michel Kern.

Adélaïde, alleged to be the first child of Théodore Mars and Marie Duportail, although never appearing with them in any census or vital record, first appeared as the wife of Eugène

Katzenstein in the 1870 United States Federal Census with a young boy, Adrien, age 5, and ten years later with the same boy, age 14, said to be a jeweler. According to that 1880 census, the household also included Marie H(arriet) Katzenstein, identified in Eugène's last will and testament as his adopted daughter, and Marie Mars, identified in his will as his adopted sister, but in the 1880 enumeration, as his sister-in-law. This Maria Mars has been identified as Rosalie Marie Mars, born in 1837 at Bordeaux, Gironde, France, to Théodore Mars and his wife, Marie Duportail, Rosalie Marie Mars married Frederick Beiner, although there is also no marriage record for this union either.

Adélaïde Katzenstein was something of a financier, and acquired, among other notes, one for $400 due Jean Pierre Corrège for the latter's salary as sexton of old St. Francis Church of Pointe Coupée in 1863. During the chaos and economic downturn of the Civil War, Corrège transferred the note to Mrs. Katzenstein, as he was likely indebted to her.

In 1867, Corrège filed suit (7th Judicial District Court, No. 1148) against New Roads attorney and sugar planter Charles Poydras, as Receiver of the Corporation of St. Francis, for payment of the note, on behalf of Mrs. Katzenstein. Corrège died shortly thereafter, and his widow, née Charlotte Fabre, was appointed administratrix of his indebted succession (7th Judicial District Court, No. 1174). Assuming his role as plaintiff, the widow Corrège received a judgment for $400, with eight percent interest from 1863, on behalf of Mrs. Katzenstein, in 1869.

As was typical of many Louisiana families who moved to the city, ties with and visits to the country were maintained by the Katzensteins. Eugène was a witness to the 1872 act of conveyance from Maria Mars to her brothers, Gabriel and Théophile Mars of New Roads, of Maria's interest in their late parents' real estate behind town and movable goods.

Eugene and Adélaïde Katzenstein moved to Hattiesburg, Forrest Co., Mississippi. Adélaïde died there in 1909. In her last will and testament, dated 1887 which she apparently never updated, Adélaïde bequeathed $5.00 to her "sister" Julie Winter, and the remainder to her "beloved" husband, Eugène Katzenstein. We have not been able to identify "Julie Winter." Eugène, however, must have been divorced from Adelaide before 1890, because he was married on 20 January 1890, to Madeleine Montiache, the widow of François Biclet. Eugène Katzenstein died on 20 June 1897, leaving his estate to his new wife, Madeleine, and to his adopted "sister" Maria Mars, and "adopted daughter," Mary H. Herndon, aka Marie Harriet Katzenstein, the widow of George Herndon, and according to her death certificate, the daughter of Louis Katzenstein, although we could find no record of any Louis Katzenstein living in the United States at that time. According to the 1900 United States Federal Census, Adélaïde and her "grandson," Prentiss Herndon, were enumerated living next door to Marie Beiner and her husband, Frederick, in Hattiesburg, Perry Co., Mississippi. Maria Mars Beiner, died at No. 1806 Mandeville Street in New Orleans on 12 April 1927. Her brother Théophile Mars's children, by then living on the Island of False River in Pointe Coupée Parish, were remembered as legatees in her will. Mary Harriet Katzenstein Herndon died from the same Mandeville Street address as Maria Mars Beiner, on 25 August 1928.

LANGLOIS & WOLFF

Langlois & Wolff, general merchants between 1865 and 1870, consisted of the partnership of Pierre Langlois and Cerf Wolff. The latter, a native of Neuwiller-lès-Saverne, Bas-Rhin, France,

Wolff was formerly a merchant at Waterloo. He entered into partnership with Pierre Langlois, a local Catholic merchant, in New Roads, and subsequently operated the "Alma" and "Burnt Bridge" stores at the eastern and western extremities, respectively, of the Lakeland community on the Lower Chenal.

Alone among the early merchants of New Roads, the location of Langlois & Wolff has yet to be confirmed in original source documentation. They are, however, likely to have occupied one or another of the West Main Street commercial locations vacated during the Civil War, these including: the former store of German national Christophe Kleborn, then owned by his partner, area financier Marguérite Villiers, *femme de couleur*, at the southwest corner of Independence (later Richy) Street; or in the former Planters' Coffee House (*sic*, euphemism for saloon, billiard parlor, and grocery store) of Guillaume Knaps, a native of Bordeaux, at the southeast corner of St. Mary Street.

A statement filed in the 1869 civil suit of Langlois & Wolff vs Jean-Baptiste Langlois, Pierre's brother (Late Parish Court, No. 42), listed some of the merchandise carried by the store: (bolts of) calico, organdy, nankeen and hickory, thread, buckles, suits, collars and cuffs, socks, handkerchiefs, felt hats, shoes, boots, rice, sugar, candy, extracts, raisins, wines, whiskies, Cocktail gin, natural and corn juice chewing tobacco, smoking tobacco, cigars, *eau de cologne*, toys, starch, wax, glue, matches, string, (fishing) lines, gun tubes and capsules.

Jean-Baptiste Langlois's charges at Langlois & Wolff over the course of the forty-five days he was a customer, are worth mentioning. He purchased whiskey and/or wine on twenty-four of those days. His most extravagant purchase, on 10 November 1866, was for a suit made of black sheeting material at $57 (2022 value: $1,017.10).

ROSINE MICHEL

In 1865, Rosine Michel, a native of Struth, Bas-Rhin, France, and previously a merchant with her husband, Nathan Kern, at Waterloo, purchased a lot from Auguste LeCoq, measuring one arpent front on the Public Road, presently West Main Street, by two arpents in depth, bounded on the east by the original St. Mary Church, and on the north and west by the remainder of LeCoq's property. The price was $2,500, and Rosine signed the act of sale with an "x." That same year, she was assessed in the 1865 IRS tax assessment list for having one carriage in New Roads.

Rosine Michel was a general merchant on her New Roads property for five years between 1866 and 1871. Rosine, widowed in 1869, and her son, Léonard Kern (b. 12 January 1853 Waterloo, Louisiana- d. 19 January 1876 Lakeland, Louisiana), were enumerated in the 1870 United States Federal Census as the owner with $3,000 in real estate and $1,500 in other property Her son, Leonard was enumerated as her store clerk. Her five other sons were also living in the household.

In 1870, the widow Rosine Michel Kern entered into a pre-nuptial contract with dry goods merchant Benjamin Weil. The prospective groom declared assets valued at $4,410, including $2,000 worth of dry goods, $2,000 due from customer accounts, two merchant's carts, a harness, a gold watch, and a silver watch. The Widow Kern declared property valued at $14,807, including a two-arpent lot with store and other improvements in New Roads, $2,500 worth of merchandise, $2,500 due from customer accounts, promissory notes, household furniture and furnishings, dishes, kitchen utensils, her clothing, linens and jewelry, $150 in United States currency and $28 in coin.

Benjamin Weil and Rosine Michel Kern were married on 12 December 1870, by Justice of the Peace Eugene Poydras. Weil moved in with Rosine and her six children from her former marriage. Three weeks into the union, however, Rosine filed suit for divorce from Benjamin (7th Judicial District Court., No 1501), stating that she had agreed to marry Weil "only if he agreed to quit his intemperate habits, and become a sober man," but Weil had lapsed into frequent "drunkenness," struck her, and "intentionally" afflicted her with syphilis.

Several neighbors testified on Rosine's behalf, including Dr. Joseph Ildévert Kleborn, a local physician, who stated he had treated her for her painful infection. George Fernandez, a general merchant and tailor operating at the current address of 101 West Main Street, said that Weil bought liquor from the Fernandez store, adding that the unfortunate man "was unfit for [business] transactions and a burden to his friends."

Nathan Kern the younger, a merchant, and Rosine's nephew-by-marriage, testified that Weil had lost $100 which was to be sent to New Orleans, and recalled that Weil was once so intoxicated that he fell out of bed, and when Rosine attempted to persuade him to change his habits, Weil tried to kick her. Rebecca Joe, identified in the 1870 United States Federal Census as age 44, a "mulatto native of Virginia," and "domestic servant" in the Kern household, stated that Weil was "always tight" (i.e., intoxicated). Prominent merchant Cerf Wolff testified that every time but once he had encountered Weil the latter was "drunk," the exception being when Weil was "dead drunk." Zénon Gebhart, a printer at the *Pointe Coupée Republican* newspaper office, across the street, stated the Weils were "almost always quarreling." Only Rosine's son, Léonard Kern, denied witnessing his mother and step-father arguing.

Merchandise inventoried in Rosine Michel Kern Weil's store in New Roads in 1871 in her suit for divorce from Benjamin Weil, (7th Judicial District Court, No. 1501), included: 163 bolts of fabric, muslin, lawn, calico, print, percale, cotton check, regular and *toile du nord* gingham, brilliantine, regular and imitation jaconet, imitation poplin, flannel, alpaca, merino, cassinette, barège veiling, buckram, delaine, molleton, tarlatan, bleached and unbleached cotton, jeans, denim, linen drill, linsey, kersey, hickory, lining, sheeting and oilcloth; towels, quilts, blankets, coverlets, mosquito *bars* (i.e., nets); fringe, braid; 30 men's coats, 12 vests, 41 pairs of pants, 43 white and colored shirts, neckties, collars, suspenders and undershirts; 3 ladies' dresses, 15 malakoffs (skirts), shawls, under-dresses, corsets and strings, mantillas, veils, and headdress combs; men's and children's socks, hosiery, gloves, 124 colored handkerchiefs and another "lot" of handkerchiefs, 57 men's and children's hats, 89 pairs of boots and shoes; coffee, salt, crackers, canned sardines, lobster and oysters, herrings, codfish, mackerels, dried apples, sweet oil, vinegar, syrup, plums, candy, cheese, meat, lard, yeast powder, red and white wines, liquors, bitters, smoking and chewing tobacco, cigars, pipes, perfumery, soap, starch, crockery, tinware, spoons, slate pencils, shoes brushes, matches, blacking, candles, lamps, lanterns, demijohns, buckets, washboards, clothes pins, gun shot and powder, coal oil, grease, water cooler, nails, padlocks, iron ties, cord, leather collars, bridles, stirrups, curry combs and brushes, and a "lot" of cow skins, for total appraisement of $2,500. The movables also included: store accounts and notes, as well as household furniture, cooking utensils, linens and bedding, jewelry and two gold watches, a horse, buggy, and peddler's wagon for a total appraisement of $2,500.

Following the judgment for divorce on 8 Apr 1872, Rosine, who was referred to thereafter as the Widow Kern, and her children moved to the Lower Chenal, where she owned considerable property. She and her son Abraham/Abram Kern engaged in merchandising.

Rosine leased the New Roads lot, store, residence and outbuildings at a rate of $35 per month to her nephew-by-marriage Nathan Kern, the younger, between 1872 and 1875. In 1873, young Kern sublet the property for the same price and sold the stock of dry goods, groceries and other merchandise therein for $300 to Pierre Courtis, formerly the clerk for the parish's *grand magasin* Coulon & Demouy, located in the Graugnard-Richy Building.

In 1874, Rosine filed suit (Late Parish Court, No. 760) and obtained a judgment against Courtis for his outstanding balance on the lease. Merchandise belonging to Courtis, at least part of which had previously belonged to Nathan Kern the younger, as well as the store fixtures, were seized and offered at public sale.

In 1880, the widow Rosine Michel Kern sold her New Roads lot with improvements, except for the store building, to merchant and mayor Joseph Richy, for which he paid $1,000 cash. The later history of the store building remains unknown at present, but it was gone by the time of the iconic photograph of the 1895 "St. Valentine's Day" snow, one of the earliest known photos of downtown New Roads. The Kern store site became the sidewalk and front lawn of the former and current St. Mary Church Rectories, located at 348 West Main Street.

At the rear of the former Kern property, the old "back yard" of Rosine and family has been since ca. 1980 the St. Mary Prayer Garden, an oasis of peace and tranquility in the center of the New Roads business district.

BENJAMIN WEIL

Benjamin Weil, a native of Rixheim, Haut-Rhin, France, and formerly a peddler living with Jacques Goudchaux, on Pointe Coupée Road was listed in the United States IRS tax assessment reports as a 3rd class peddler on False River in 1865 and a 4th class peddler in 1866. The forty-year-old Weil was enumerated in the 1870 United States Federal Census as an unmarried French peddler living at Waterloo, shortly before his brief marriage to Rosine Michel. After their divorce in 1872 he moved to New Orleans and clerked there for at least two years, initially for Frank Haas & Co. in 1874, and for the Lane Cotton Mills in 1875, according to the *Soard's New Orleans City Directory* published in those years. Weil returned to Pointe Coupée Parish and was enumerated there in the 1880 United States Federal Census as a store clerk living with general merchant, Aaron Loeb, on the Lower Chenal of False River.

NATHAN KERN, THE YOUNGER

Nathan Kern, the younger, was born on 31 December 1848, at Struth, Bas-Rhin France, to Gerschel Kern, and his wife Beijen, née Kern. The elder Nathan Kern, the first husband of Rosine Michel, was his uncle. Nathan immigrated from France in his teens and was listed as "Kern Nephew," a peddler by cart in the 1867 Pointe Coupée Parish Business License register. He may have been the "N. Kerne." age 17, who arrived in New Orleans from Le Havre, France on 23 December 1865, aboard the French ship *Jeanne Alice*.

According to the 1870 United States Federal Census, Nathan Kern the younger, age 21, a peddler, was living in the house of Widow Marie Mars and her family, immediately behind the widow Rosine Michel Kern's store and residence, in New Roads. During the Weil-Michel divorce hearing held in 1871, he stated that his first home in Louisiana had been with his aunt, Rosine Michel, and her second husband Benjamin Weil.

Nathan filed a declaration of intention to be naturalized and an oath of renunciation of allegiance to the Third Republic of France, in New Roads, Louisiana, in 1872. That same year, after Rosine and her children moved to the Lower Chenal, Nathan leased Rosine's lot, store, residence, and outbuildings in New Roads for three years at the rate of $35 per month. A year later, Nathan Kern sublet his aunt's property for the same price and sold out to Pierre Courtis for $300.

In Rosine Michel Kern's suit filed in 1874 due to delinquent rent owed by Courtis, his merchandise, some of which likely had belonged to her nephew, included: 36 bolts and remnants of dry goods, including black silk, domestic, and toweling; laces, ribbons, rickrack, trimming, and cord; thread, buttons, hooks and eyes, buckles, thimbles, tatting needles; a woolen shirt, a lot of cravats; a corset, belts, veils, and hairnets; stockings, hose, and socks; gloves; five men's hats; a pair of boots; a box of (canned) fruits, pepper, and spice; cordials; cigars, pipes; powder, brushes, combs, hairpins, a small mirror, toothbrushes, shoe brushes; spectacles, rings, fancy buttons, pearl and bead necklaces; penholders, pens, and envelopes; toy balls, fiddle strings, fishhooks; cups and saucers, plates, dishes, butter dishes, a mug, soup bowls (likely tureens), water pitchers, bowl and pitcher sets; glasses, wine and "night" glasses; spoons, teaspoons, knives, forks, boilers, pots, and covers, skillets, coffee pots and mills, tin cups and pans, sifters, strainers, graters, measures, candlesticks, lamps, a Puroline lamp, lamp chimneys, wicks, tubes and wrenches; a lot of bottles, jars, jugs, demijohns, smoothing irons, brooms, a tub, water and milk buckets, watering pots, oil cans; washing soda, starch, bluing, clothespins, wax, garden seed; nails, brads, tacks, hook staples, scissors, hair scissors, pocket knives, cooper's planes, carpenter's bits, a hole puncher, gimlets, saw files, assorted locks, sandpaper, wooden faucets, rope, well wheels; a lot of hoes, a hatchet, axe handles; harnesses and horse collars, blind bridles, a spur, trace chains, lap rings, and horse brushes; also a showcase, thread box, cheese safe, tobacco cutter, three scales and weights, and six barrel covers.

Pierre Courtis returned to France, but resumed residency in Pointe Coupée Parish in October 1884, having made the perilous journey of nearly a month on the steamship *Cumberland* that famously went aground on French Reef in the Florida Keys. Reestablished in Pointe Coupée, he began clerking for the "Blue Store," then owned by Jean Terrabust, on Pointe Coupée Road.

Nathan Kern, the younger, did not remain in the south. He moved to Chicago, Cook Co., Illinois, where he was married on 16 March 1884, to Julia Falk, who according to her death record, was a native of Sennfeld, Rheinpfalz, Germany, born there on 28 July 1855. Julia had arrived in New York, from Bremen, Germany, on 25 August 1883, aboard the steamship *Elbe*. Nathan and Julia's only child, Albert Herman, was born in Chicago on 9 February 1891, where Nathan Kern was a furniture dealer. Nathan Kern died on 2 January 1925, and was interred in Waldheim Cemetery, in Forest Park, Cook Co., Illinois. Julia Falk Kern died on 28 May 1942, in Chicago, and was interred in the Free Sons of Israel Cemetery, now part of the greater Waldheim Cemetery Co.

JACQUES GOUDCHAUX

Photo of Jacques Goudchaux, mobile merchant, courtesy of Judy Riffel, originally published in "A History of Pointe Coupée Parish and Its Families." (Le Comité des Archives de la Louisiane, 1983.) Original photo courtesy of Elsie Noble. Photo enhancement courtesy of Stella Carline Tanoos.

Jacques Goudchaux, formerly a peddler living on Pointe Coupée Road, moved to the New Roads area by the end of the Civil War. He was listed as a retail dealer, retail liquor dealer, and owner of a carriage in the 1865 and 1866 United States IRS tax assessment reports and in the 1867 Pointe Coupée Parish Business License register. In 1865, Jacques Goudchaux applied for and was granted administration of the succession of Henri Cerf, peddler and merchant, whom he said he had known back in Strasbourg, France. Cerf had died intestate and without heirs in Louisiana.

Two years later, in 1867, Goudchaux was indexed in the conveyance records of Pointe Coupée Parish, as leasing a lot on Patin Dyke Road, just east of New Roads, in what is known as the Poulailler area, from the Widow Jean Nicolas Garon, née Marguérite Bertrand.

While operating a dry goods store at Poulailler, Jacques Goudchaux, who had previously lived with Benjamin Weil, the father of a child of color with Cécile Lacour, was, himself, apparently the father of two natural children by Madeleine Olivo, a "free woman of color:" Clément and Maximilien "Max" Goudchaux. Born ca. 1826 on the Island of False River, Pointe Coupée Parish, Louisiana, Madeleine Olivo was the daughter of Henri Olivo and Eulalie Porche, both free people of color. However, in 1853, three years after the death of the family's white protectress, Madeleine Olivo, widow of Simon Porche, and the aunt of Henri Olivo, kidnappers attacked Henri Olivo and took his wife, Cecile, six of their children and 11 grandchildren, and sold them into slavery in New Orleans and Mobile, Alabama. Among the abducted were Henri and Cecile's daughter Madeleine and her four natural racially-mixed children by Hypolite Bergeron: Polite, Julie, Adélon and Eudora Bergeron.

A lengthy case prosecuted by New Roads attorney Henry Beatty in New Orleans resulted in the eventual return of at least most of the Olivo family to their homes on False River. Madeleine Olivo and her Bergeron natural children settled on Patin Dyke Road, east of New Roads near the store of Jacques Goudchaux. According to the 1860 United States Federal Census, thirty-five-year-old Madeleine Oliveau (*sic*) and her daughter Victoria, enumerated as Oliveau, but Bergeron intended, were living next door to Jacques Goudchaux and Benjamin Weil. According to the 1870 United States Federal Census, Madeleine Olivo, a forty-five-year-old farm worker, was enumerated with her children: Adélon Bergeron, age 22, also a farm worker; Victoria Bergeron, age 19, Max Goudchaux, age 6, and three-year-old Clément Goudchaux. The census taker recorded that both of the Goudchaux children had a "father of foreign birth." Maximilian was born on 3 May 1864, and baptized on 14 May 1871, with Hubert and Félicité Patin as godparents. (PCP 28, 87). Clément was born on 8 November 1867, and baptized on 22 October 1870, with godparents G. Smith and Pauline Decoux (PCP 27, 120). Both children were baptized at the old Saint Mary Church under the name of Olivo/Oliveau/Olivaut, and would only use the name Goudchaux/Godchaux in later records.

Jacques Goudchaux was found in no other Louisiana records following his 1867 lease of the Garon lot on Patin Dyke Road. Nor was he amongst the recipients of a Pointe Coupée Parish business license after that year. Moreover, J.B. Garon was recorded as having a business license for the year of 1872 for that same location on Patin Dyke Road.

Jacques Goudchaux returned to Strasbourg, Bas-Rhin, France, at some time after 1867 where he died on 15 September 1876, as Jacob Gaudchau, the sixty-eight-year-old widower of Babette Vogel. He was interred the next day at the Jewish Cemetery of Strasbourg-Koenigshoffen, where his daughter, Pauline, was also buried.

Clement Godchaux (*sic*), age 19, Jacques and Madeleine Olivo's son, died on 27 January 1884, on the Island of False River, Pointe Coupée Parish, Louisiana, and was buried in old Immaculate Conception Church Cemetery, Chenal, Louisiana, the following day (IMCL-7, 5). There is no indication that he was ever married.

Jacques and Madeleine's other son, Maximilian "Max" Goudchaux, born near New Roads, Louisiana, was married on 20 December 1889, in the old Immaculate Conception Church at Chenal, Louisiana to Marie Madeleine Joe (IMCL-4, 292). She was baptized on 10 April 1872, in New Roads, to Augustin Joe and Marie Aspasie Christophe. (PCP-27, 157). Max and Madeleine were the parents of at least four children: Ursilia, born on 20 October 1890 (PCP-29, 287), Julie, born on 12 April 1892 (PCP-29, 362), Severine, born on 28 November 1895 (PCP-30, 37), and Oralie (b. ca. 1898 – no record).

Max Goudchaux died on 19 February 1927, in East Louisiana State Hospital at, Jackson, East Feliciana Parish, Louisiana, where he had been a patient since at least the time of the 1900 United States Federal Census. Marie Madeleine Goudchaux appeared in the 1900 United States Federal Census for Pointe Coupée Parish with her children, but could not be found ten years later. According to the 1910 United States Federal Census, one of her children, twelve-year-old Oralie, was living with her godparents, Paulin and Adeline Victorin, in Ward 7. We could find no reliable death record for Madeleine Joe Goudchaux.

Madeleine Olivo died on 2 Sep 1897 in or near New Roads, Louisiana, and was buried the following day in St. Mary Cemetery, New Roads, Louisiana (PCP-22,17).

HENRI CERF

Henri Cerf was born on 7 October 1823, at Haguenau, Bas-Rhin, France, to Simon Cerf, a native of Haguenau, and his wife, Reine, née Cerf, born at Phalsbourg, Moselle, France. Henri was a merchant and peddler operating in the False River area between 1861 and 1865. He died intestate in late June or early July 1865, at the New Roads residence of building contractor and general merchant Joseph Richy after an illness during which he was attended by Drs. Ludovic Ladmirault and Ernest Robin. He was survived by siblings Salomon and Jonathan Cerf, Sophie Cerf (Mme. David) Weill, Rosalie Cerf (Mme. David) Cahen, and Julie Cerf (Mme. Edouard) Levy, all residents of Alsace, France. Also included in the succession records was his parentage back two generations. His parents, Simon and Reine had been married on 7 May 1809, in Strasbourg, Bas-Rhin. His paternal grandparents were Jonathan Cerf and Julie Lehman, and maternal grandparents were Salomon Cerf and Rosalie Levi. Details such as there were common in Louisiana successions when the decedent left heirs back in France.

The subsequent succession proceedings of the late Cerf included the presentation and payment of bills by François St. Pasteur and Villeneuve Gosserand, who lived near one another approximately four miles down False River from New Roads. St. Pasteur had hauled the late Cerf's cart, and Gosserand had provided the use of a wagon for the transport of the merchandise of the deceased into New Roads proper, suggesting that Cerf may have had temporarily set up shop in the neighborhood of Gosserand and St. Pasteur. François St. Pasteur would soon operate a store of his own, on False River Road, according to the 1866 Pointe Coupée Parish Assessment Roll.

Despite the distressed economy during and immediately following the Civil War, Henri Cerf sold many expensive items, including imported French soaps, perfumery, other toiletries, and ribbons, in addition to practical dry goods and clothing.

Area merchants Jacques Goudchaux, Benjamin Weil, and Cerf Wolff, all of whom claimed that they knew Cerf and his family back in Strasbourg, testified that Cerf neither married nor had relatives in Louisiana, his siblings all living in Alsace. Goudchaux petitioned the court on 3 July 1865, and was granted administration of the succession (7th Judicial District Court. No. 209). The court recognized Joseph Israël of New Orleans as agent for the absent heirs.

Henri Cerf's possessions, judicially inventoried and appraised, consisted of merchandise, a peddler's wagon and harness, customer accounts and notes receivable, and personal affects. The latter included a trunk containing the decedent's clothing, shoes, boots and toilette items, a valise, gold watch and chain, a "golden talisman," and smoking pipes. In coin, Cerf left 34 gold *Napoléon* 24-franc pieces, and $204 in gold, presumably American coin.

His succession file also included a $20 note of Confederate States currency, and a certificate for $3,400 in Confederate bonds dated "Confederate States Depository Office, Opelousas [Louisiana], 10 Jun 1864." These two items, being of no value, were not included in the statement of assets.

Henri Cerf's $20 Confederate Bank note from his 1865 succession papers.

Fulfilling Goudchaux's request, the movables were offered at public sale at Richy's New Roads residence in 1865, and produced the sum of $293.49. The amount allotted to the Cerf succession was $223.00, because some of the merchandise had been owned in partnership by Cerf and Richy. Merchandise in this sale included: 56 yards of planters' linen, 23 yards black muslin, four white shirts, five pair men's hose, 10 ladies' collars, five silk handkerchiefs, 23 white linen handkerchiefs, 67 Madras (handkerchiefs), 17 large combs, a lot of envelopes, pipes and (fishing) lines, and 76 pounds of nails, the majority of which was purchased by Waterloo peddler and subsequent extensive landowner and merchant Isaac Levy.

Merchandise purchased by Henri Cerf from Strasbourg which arrived in New Orleans after his death was sold in the city by Hoffmann & Marks, auctioneers, in 1865 and the proceeds submitted to the succession. It included: five pieces (i.e., bolts) of silks, 54 veils, 61 ties, 98 pieces of belting, 355 pieces of silk, satin and cotton ribbon, three pieces Scotch (plaid) velvet ribbon, 66 extracts, 12 extract and pomade sets, 60 packages of rice powder, 132 cosmetics, 120 containers *Philocome* (a French hair product), 1,392 cakes of soap, and three baskets.

The above goods were itemized in the 28 April 1865 statements of two French firms: "A la Ville de St. Etienne," Gustave Weill, proprietor, Ribbons, Silks, Silk Thread for Lacemaking, and Notions, Rue des Grands Arcades, 33, Strasbourg; and M. Weill & Cie., Perfumers and Soap Makers, Rue Montmartre, No. 103, Paris, and Rue des Sérruriers, No. 12, Strasbourg, the latter of whose letterhead featured artistic vignettes of Emperor Napoléon III in profile and medals awarded the company in trade expositions. A. M. Weill's soaps detailed in the statement included brands Guimauve, Windsor, Bouquet des Alpes, Bordelais, Modèle, and Omnibus, while others were identified as flowering rose, gents' citron, honey, and milk.

According to the list of outstanding accounts, Henri Cerf's former customers included residents of both banks of False River, the Upper and Lower Chenals and Bayou Poydras, evidence that he had made the rounds of the area to reach potential purchasers having limited or no access to New Roads.

With the collection of account balances from Cerf's customers and persons to whom he had loaned money, Goudchaux paid the creditors of the estate, and the legal and judicial expenses, variously in gold and U.S. currency.

Joseph Richy's bill included eight days' and nights' board and laundering for Cerf, 11 yards of white cotton for *la robe* (i.e., Cerf's burial garment), a "double" coffin, funeral expenses, and labor for digging the grave. Unfortunately, there was no description of the funeral or of Cerf's place of interment. Only two cemeteries, *per se*, existed in the False River area at the time: at the old St. Francis Church on the Mississippi River, and the other at Immaculate Conception on the Lower Chenal, Island of False River. St. Mary Cemetery was opened on the *Chemin Neuf* (New Road) shortly after Cerf's death and burial. Another New Roads resident, Adélard Langlois, was reimbursed $40 for medicines provided at Cerf's request during the latter's final illness.

Bayou Poydras resident Francois Nurdin had billed the succession for board provided to Cerf back in 1861. The five-year lapse between Nurdin's service and reimbursement by the Cerf succession attest to the disruption of intra-parish commerce and travel during wartime occupation and skirmishes as well as the 1865 and 1866 Mississippi River floods. The succession of Henri Cerf netted a balance of $171.07 for his siblings in Alsace.

It is interesting that a family or families described as racially mixed in postbellum census and conveyance records is spelled "Seff" or "Sept," the pronunciation of which is virtually identical with "Cerf." Any connection between them and Henri Cerf remains undetermined at present.

LAZARUS KERN

Lazarus Kern may have been born Lazare Kern on 7 April 1841, at Asswiller, Bas-Rhin France, to Daniel Kern, a native of Struth, Bas-Rhin, and his wife Fanny Grathwohl. We made this identification because he was probably the half-first cousin of Nathan Kern, the elder, who married Rosine Michel. Lazare had probably followed family members to Louisiana. He operated from New Roads as a 3rd class peddler according to the 1866 IRS tax assessment report and was a peddler by horseback according to the 1867 Pointe Coupée Parish Business License register.

ISAAC LEVIN

Isaac Levin, likely a native of the Russian Empire, was a peddler by horseback, based in New Roads, according to the 1867 Pointe Coupée Parish Business License index. Unfortunately, no other records were found for this man anywhere else in Louisiana.

AARON SCHULSINGER

Aaron Schulsinger was born on 15 June 1847, in Krakow, Austrian Empire (now Poland). According to his immigration record he arrived as a minor in 1863. and was naturalized in New Orleans in 1868. In late 1867 or early 1868, he opened the "White Store," specializing in dry goods and men's clothing, at *Les Trois Chênes* (The Three Oaks) on the property of the Widow Raymond Vignes which is now 2050 False River Drive within the city of New Roads. Aaron Schulsinger applied for a marriage license to marry Roseta Zadik on 15 September 1868, in New Orleans. Roseta, born in Prussia, ca. 1847, was the daughter of Joseph Zadik and Amelia Eudel. Roseta's brother, William, and Schulsinger both signed the marriage bond.

On 21 June 1869, Schulsinger sold his stock of merchandise, two horses, a small cart, a pair harness and a saddle to his wife's brother William Zadik, for $1,037.29 cash. In a subsequent legal document, Zadik appointed Schulsinger his agent for the operation of the retail store and peddling operations, specifying they be conducted solely for cash.

Less than three months later, on 10 September, New Orleans wholesale and retail clothier B.O. "Banny" Mesritz sued Schulsinger for $429.59, with eight percent interest from 7 May 1867. On 26 March 1867, Schulsinger had borrowed from and assigned a promissory note to Mesritz for $200, and on 7 May of the same year had bought a lot of men's clothing on credit from Mesritz which together with the costs of insurance and drayage, totaled $221.59.

The goods sold by B.O. Mesritz to Aaron Schulsinger were itemized as: 49 pairs of pants, 24 linen check shirts, 36 calico shirts, 12 white shirts, four canton flannel shirts, 24 union shirts, 24 pairs of drawers, and 48 pairs of socks. Schulsinger having failed to answer Mesritz's petition or appear as subpoenaed on 13 October 1869, the court ordered the seizure and public sale of Schulsinger's property to cover the $421.59 owed Mesritz. On 1 February 1870, William Zadik filed an injunction, stating that the property seized, including the merchandise, horse, and cart, were not Schulsinger's property but his.

In witness testimony, prominent Pointe Coupée Parish merchant, Cerf Wolff, stated that he was present in B.O. Mesritz's office when Schulsinger offered to pay Mesritz 25 cents on-the-dollar for the long-delinquent balance. According to Wolff, Schulsinger claimed he was able to get other creditors to agree to such an arrangement, but Mesritz replied that he would accept no less than 50 cents on-the-dollar. Wolff further stated that Schulsinger told Mesritz that he (Schulsinger) would not give him that much and that all Mesritz wanted was to prevent him from doing business under his own name. Schulsinger then left the office.

Wolff closed his testimony stating that he knew that the note and account due from Schulsinger to Mesritz were for more than $400, as he had seen the papers before the conversation between Schulsinger and Mesritz occurred.

P. (likely Deputy Sheriff Paul) Joffrion testified that he knew Schulsinger for about eighteen months prior to the lawsuit as a storekeeper and peddler. Joffrion stated he was also acquainted with William Zadik, and knew of him being associated with Schulsinger, but he (Joffrion) had no knowledge of Zadik owning the store at any time prior to the seizure.

Clerk of Court C.D. Hébert stated he knew Schulsinger to have kept the "White Store" on the Widow Vignes' property, but the merchant had since moved "to another place in my neighborhood," i.e., closer to downtown New Roads. On 11 September 1870, the court ruled that Zadik, having failed to sustain his injunction, dismissed it, and the sale of the seized goods could proceed.

Twenty-four-year-old Aaron Schulsinger was enumerated in the 1870 United States Federal Census for New Orleans, as a retail dry goods dealer, living with his wife Rosette, a Prussian national, age 23. By 22 December 1870, Aaron Schulsinger was in business on the Raccourci Bay or Lagoon, where he leased from brothers-in-law Emile Honoré and Jean-Baptiste Decuir the store on the plantation of Decuir's father and Honoré's father-in-law, the late Arnaud Decuir, for the year 1871, with the privilege of a further lease of three years. Schulsinger was subsequently in partnership with Pierre Félicien Bourgeois in the latter's general store at The

Village, just above Morganza. Schulsinger sold his half-interest in the merchandise to Bourgeois in 1873.

The site of Aaron Schulsinger's short-lived "White Store" in New Roads was occupied by a succession of business concerns into the 21st century, including Charles Meixner's grocery and dry goods store ca. 1880-1888, and the "Cheap John" general store and pharmacy operated by Albert Vignes and his son, John L., between 1892 and 1899. It was also the location of the first Walmart chain store at New Roads, in the latter part of the 20th century, as well as a Tractor Supply, another national chain. Les Trois Chênes, a triple growth of live oak, continues to stand near the False River Drive sidewalk at that location.

B.O. MESRITZ

Bernard Oriel "Banney" Mesritz/Van Mesritz, was born ca. 1828, in Amsterdam, the Netherlands, to Oriel Heyman/Haïm Van Mesritz and his wife, Frances Ostermann, both natives of the Netherlands. According to his New Orleans naturalization record, he arrived with his family in 1832, but was only naturalized on 16 October 1876. Mesritz applied for a license to marry Hannah Littauer in New Orleans on 3 June 1853. His wife had also immigrated as a child with her family in 1845. She was born on 9 September 1837 in Germany/Prussia to Jacob Littauer. According to the 1860 United States Federal Census, B.O. Mesritz was the proprietor of a clothing store in New Orleans. He was living with his wife "Anna," and children Rosina (age 6) Laura (age 4), Richard (age 2), and Isabella (age 7 months). Mesritz enlisted as a Private on 1 March 1862 with the Orleans Guards Infantry, Company C. That same year his second son, Jefferson Davis Mesritz was born. Bernard and Hannah were the parents of six more children: Frances (b. 1864), Henry (b. 1866), Maurice (b. 1868), Albert (b. 1869), Emma (b. 1875), and Jeannette (b. 1877).

The civil suit of B.O. Mesritz vs. New Roads merchant Aaron Schulsinger (7th Judicial District Court., No. 1458), includes testimony that Mesritz was a resident of New Orleans in 1869 and of Pointe Coupée Parish in 1870. He was back in the city by 1874, the year that he was listed in *Soard's New Orleans City Directory* at his Chartres Street clothing store.

The Mesritz family ultimately moved to St. Louis City, Missouri, where B.O. Mesritz was enumerated in the 1900 United States Federal Census as Bernard Van Mesritz, a merchant, living with his wife and seven children. Four of his sons, Jefferson, Henry, Maurice and Albert were working with their father as merchants and tailors. Mesritz Bros. Tailoring Co. was located on North 8th Street, near Olive Street, in St. Louis, Missouri.

A feature article on the occasion of the Mesritzes 50th wedding anniversary appeared in the 7 Jun 1903 *St. Louis Republic*. B.O. Mesritz died in St. Louis on 19 November 1905, and was interred at the New Mount Sinai Cemetery and Crematorium in Afton, St. Louis Co., Missouri. His wife died on 24 November 1912, and was interred with him.

WILLIAM ZADIK

William Zadik, a native of Prussia, and brother of Rosette Zadik Schulsinger, immigrated as a child with his family in 1857. From an 1870 passport application, we know that William was born ca. 18 November 1843, in Mur Goslin, Kingdom of Prussia, the son of Joseph Zadik and Amelia Eudel, and was naturalized in New Orleans in 1867. William Zadik married Rose Levy on 20 March 1866, in Mobile, Mobile Co., Alabama. Rose, the daughter of Polish immigrants Michael Levy, a merchant tailor, and his wife, Maria Lyons, was born on 13 December 1848, at Mobile.

In 1869, Zadik purchased from Rosette's husband, Aaron Schulsinger two horses, a wagon, a small cart, a pair harness, a saddle and the stock of merchandise in Schulsinger's "White Store," located at *Les Trois Chenes* (The Three Oaks) at present-day 2020 False River Drive, New Roads, for $1,037.29 in cash.

The merchandise was itemized as: 225 yards of calico, 250 yards muslin, 50 yards cotton, 45 yards blue cottonade, 60 yards denims, 10 yards checks, 20 yards jeans, and 100 yards of pants goods; three pounds of thread; three quilts, seven white tablecloths, six brown tablecloths, 12 mosquito bars; six suits, six coats, 63 pair pantaloons, 15 white shirts, 10 calico shirts, 23 other shirts, 60 (shirt) bosoms, 93 overshirts, 21 pair of linen drawers, seven pair of drill drawers, 36 jumpers; five hoopskirts, five corsets; 36 pairs of English socks, 20 pairs of woolen socks, 140 other pairs of socks; 60 pairs of stockings, 100 pairs of children's stockings; 120 handkerchiefs, 24 men's handkerchiefs, 20 madras (handkerchiefs); 65 pounds of sugar, 25 pounds of coffee, 25 pounds of crackers, 10 cans of oysters, 15 bottles of olives, 1/3 barrel of mackerel; eight gallons of anisette; lot of tobacco, three boxes of cigars; 24 combs; 10 pounds of candles; 48 knives; 11 pairs of box hinges.

That same year, New Orleans wholesale and retail clothing merchant B.O. "Banny" Mesritz sued Aaron Schulsinger for $420.59 for men's clothing sold and money loaned in 1867 (7th Judicial District Court, No. 758). The court ordered the seizure and sale of merchandise, a horse and cart supposedly belonging to Schulsinger at "White Store," but Zadik countered that the goods were his and filed an injunction. After hearing witnesses' testimony, the court ruled that Zadik failed to sustain his injunction, and it was dismissed and the sale ordered to proceed.

The 1870 United States Federal Census indicated that Zadik, a merchant, with his new wife, Rose Levy, were living with his elderly parents in New Orleans. The couple was still in the Crescent City for the birth of their first child, Aaron King in 1874, but had moved permanently to Wise Co., Texas, where their seven other children were born: Nettie (b. 1876), Isadore Louis (b. 1879), Pearl (b. 1880), Della (b. 1882), Michael Abel (b. 1884), Florence (b. 1886), and Albert York (b. 1891). The family ultimately moved to Dallas, Dallas Co., Texas, where William Zadik was enumerated in the 1900 United States Federal Census as a merchant selling (animal) hides.

Rose Levy Zadik died in Dallas on 10 May 1898, and was interred in Emanu-El Cemetery there. William Zadik died on 26 June 1923, and was interred with his wife.

EPHRAIM BLOCK

Ephraim Block was born Ephraim Bloch on 20 June 1853, at Wintzenheim, Haut-Rhin, France, to Isaac Lion Bloch, and his wife, Catherine Weil. "Bloch" is the normal spelling for the name in France which is very often anglicized as "Block" here in the United States. He filed a declaration of intention to be naturalized in Brownsville, Cameron Co., Texas, in 1873, but his oath of renunciation of allegiance to the Emperor of Germany was done in New Roads, Louisiana, in 1877. While he may have done business briefly in Pointe Coupée Parish, he settled in Texas, where he was a general merchant. He returned to Wintzenheim, Haut-Rhin, where on 22 September 1887, he married Clémence Bernheim. The bride had been born at Itterswiller, Bas-Rhin, France, on 8 January 1867, to Moïse Bernheim, a cattle dealer, and Serette Bloch. The newlyweds returned to Rio Grande City, Starr Co., Texas, where Ephraim was the owner of a general merchandise store and where their four children were born: Lucy (b. 1891), Gaston (b. 1894), Pierre (b. 1896), and Robert (b. 1898).

Clémence Bernheim Block died on 28 November 1913, in Rio Grande City, and was interred in the Hebrew Cemetery Association at Brownsville, Cameron Co., Texas. Ephraim followed on 17 August 1919, in San Antonio, Bexar Co., Texas, and was interred with his wife in Brownsville.

LENA COHN

Lena Cohn was born on 9 August 1872, in West Feliciana Parish, Louisiana, one of the seven children of Louis David Cohn, a native of Prussia, and clerk for St. Francisville, West Feliciana Parish merchant Julius Freyhan. Lena's mother was Sophia Oppenheimer, a native of Eppingen, Baden, Germany.

Lena was the wife of two New Roads businessmen and, beginning in 1904, the proprietor of the City Saloon. Her first husband, Harry Demouy, was a general merchant, pharmacist, ice depot, livery stable and omnibus proprietor, and insurance agent. He was the first Mayor of New Roads to serve under the present corporation, between 1894 and 1900. Harry, born Henry Adrien Joseph Demouy on 20 February 1867, and baptized four months later in the parish (PCP-28, 26), was the only child of Pointe Coupée merchant Henri Demouy and his wife Mary Gavin, a native of Ireland. The couple had gotten a license to marry in New Orleans on 14 September 1866.

According to his naturalization record, Henri, who had been enumerated as a resident of Pointe Coupée Parish at the time of the 1840 United States Federal Census, filed his declaration of intention to become a citizen at New Roads in 1847. He affirmed that he was a native of the department of Loire Inférieure (now Loire-Atlantique) France, and was said elsewhere to be a native of Nantes, who arrived in the United States in 1831 aboard the ship *Lindien de Nantes*. He renounced his allegiance to the French Republic in 1852. Henry and Mary were both interred in St. Mary Cemetery in New Roads. Their son, Harry, erected a Woodmen of the World monument on their behalf.

Henri's son, Harry Demouy, and his wife, Lena Cohn, were the parents of three children: Leona (b. 1890), Eugenia (b. 1893), and Harry, Jr. (b. 1896). Harry Demouy, long known as "The People's Friend – Registered Pharmacist and Merchant," organized the first parade featuring floats for Mardi Gras in Pointe Coupée Parish in 1897. While holding the office of Mayor of New Roads, the two-float parade was an advertisement for his business. He reigned as "Rex," surrounded by retainers bearing emblems symbolic of the pharmacy business. Demouy died after a long illness on 24 September 1901 in New Roads and was interred in St. Mary's Cemetery.

Following Demouy's death, Lena Cohn was married to Howard Rubin Betz, who became manager of the City Saloon located at 134 East Main Street. According to the 17 November 1900 edition of the *Pointe Coupée Banner*, this watering hole, owned by George Pourciau, had had an acetylene gas light system installed that year. Howard Betz was born on 19 February 1871, in East Feliciana Parish, to William Frederick Betz, a native of Grünstadt, Rheinpfalz, Germany, and his wife Althea Ann Jackson. Lena and Howard were the parents of four children: Alethia (b. 1906), Ferdinand (b. 1910), Louis (b. 1913), and Robert (b. 1918).

Mrs. Lena Betz obtained a business license to sell liquor in 1904, and by the following year Howard Betz was operating Betz's Saloon at 666 New Roads Street, adjacent to the Texas & Pacific Railroad, as well as the City Saloon on East Main. Howard Betz was on the False River Telephone Line in 1908. He experienced financial reverses over the next few years, as evidenced in the civil suit records of Pointe Coupée Parish, and the Betz family moved at least twice. Howard was mentioned in the drummers' notes of the 25 November 1912 New Orleans *Daily Picayune* as operating the Betz Hotel, a short-lived enterprise in the rebuilt town of Torras. The family eventually moved to Baton Rouge. There, Howard Betz was enumerated in the 1920 United States Federal Census as an employee at an oil plant.

Betz's Saloon on New Roads Street was later operated by J.R. Falconer. The City Saloon on East Main was successively occupied as Louis Pitre's barber shop and Thomas Herring's pool room and lunch house. The latter suffered three fires in four years, and the building, ultimately beyond repair, was dismantled in 1912.

The former general store and pharmacy of Lena Cohn's first husband, Harry Demouy, immediately to the east, housed, in turn, Bondy & Cahen's "New Roads Fancy Grocery Store" and Mayer Cahen alone as "fancy grocer," Purchased in 1920 by C. E. Hébert, the Demouy Building served as his Community Store grocery concern and, upon repeal of prohibition, it housed the River Side Saloon, until demolition in the early 1970s.

The Demouy Building.

Lena Cohn Betz died on 8 January 1943, at Baton Rouge, East Baton Rouge Parish, Louisiana and was interred there in the Roselawn Memorial Park and Mausoleum. Her husband, Howard Betz, followed quickly behind her on 8 June 1943, and was interred with her.

ABRAHAM & WEIL

Abraham & Weil, "New Road [*sic*] Cheap Cash Store," was the partnership of Jacob B. Abraham and Edward Weil. They operated between 1885 and 1886 in the Edward Vignes

Building, formerly the saloon of Arthur Fontaine, on the southwest corner East Main and Alamo Streets.

Jacob B. Abraham was born on 12 March 1862, at Arzheim, Rheinpfalz, Germany, to Heinrich Abraham and his wife Sarah Kahn. He immigrated to Louisiana in 1880, and was naturalized at Donaldsonville, Ascension Parish, Louisiana, in 1888. His partner, Edward Weil, was also a German national.

According to the 1880 United States Federal Census, prior to entering business with Jacob B. Abraham in New Roads, Edward Weil, a storekeeper, age 58, his wife Caroline, age 40, and their son, Adolphe Weil, age 23, also a store keeper, the latter's wife, Adele, age 21, and two children — Moise, age three, and Bertha, age eight months — were living in Napoleonville, Assumption Parish, Louisiana.

During its relatively short operation, Abraham & Weil in New Roads, despite its "Cheap" moniker, featured fine dry goods, clothing, hats and shoes. The firm stressed in the 5 September 1885 issue of the *Pointe Coupée Banner* that neither was it a branch of the Picard & Weil store in Bayou Sara, nor that it had any connection with the latter.

In its subsequent *Banner* advertisements, Abraham & Weil stated they paid cash for cotton and other country produce. An advertisement in the 17 October 1885 issue of the same newspaper featured the image of a fearsome canine surrounded by bones which read: "I WANT YOU TO PATRONIZ|E OUR FIRM!!! We are Kind to OUR CUSTOMERS, but The TERROR of our COMPETITORS! My name is LOW PRICES. Where are you?"

Merchandise advertised by Abraham & Weil's, "New Road [sic] Cheap Cash Store" as recorded in 1885 and 1886 issues of *Pointe Coupée Banner* included: (bolts of) black and colored satins, black and colored velvets, colored dress goods priced from 5 to 17 ½ cents per yard, calicoes at 5 cents per yard, dress ginghams at 10 cents per yard, black and colored cashmeres for 10 and 25 cents a yard, worsteds, white and colored flannels, jerseys, bleached and unbleached domestics, and linings; laces, embroidery, dress trimmings, ribbons, metal buttons, notions, blankets, and comforts. Ready-made clothing stocked by the firm included: men's suits, jackets, overcoats, furnishing goods and underwear; ladies' jackets, shawls, nubias, and knitted goods; children's shawls, basques, hoods, and knitted goods. Abraham and Weil also carried: kid gloves, men's derby hats, ladies' and misses' hats, men's, ladies', misses', and children's shoes, boots, ladies' slippers, staple and fancy groceries, and toys.

Despite Abraham & Weil's motto, "Quick Sales and Small Profits," the hard fact that sales were transacted on a cash basis, in the wake of 20 years of floods and during continued economic distress, is likely responsible for its brief history.

Edward Weil was deceased by the time of the July 1889 edition of Dun's *Mercantile Agency Reference Book*, at which time his widow, Caroline, had returned to Napoleonville, to run a general store. We could find no record of Edward's death. In the 1900 United States Federal Census, Caroline was enumerated as a sixty-six-year-old dressmaker, born in January 1834 in "Europe," living with her son Adolphe Weil, a salesman, and the latter's wife, Adele Klotz, and their four children: Bertha (b. 1880), Ida (b. 1883), Henry (b. 1886) and Cora (b. 1890) in Napoleonville.

Jacob B. Abraham moved to New Orleans, where he was enumerated as an unmarried clerk in the 1900 United States Federal Census. He married Blanche Kern, born ca. 1871 in New Orleans, on 30 October 1903. Blanche was the daughter of Henry Kern, born on 26 April 1826, in Essingen, Baden-Württemberg, Germany, and his wife, Frances "Fanny" Feibelman, born on 2 January 1835, in Rülzheim, Rheinpfalz, Germany. (Note: This branch of the family headed by Moyses Feibelman, a native of Rülzheim, and his wife Sarah Behr legally changed their surname to "Fellman.")

Shortly after their marriage, Jacob Abraham and his wife Blanche Kern, relocated to New York, New York where they remained. The couple was childless. Jacob Abraham died in Manhattan New York on 9 August 1935. His wife, Blanche was last enumerated in the 1940 United States Federal Census, living alone at the Hotel Dauphin in Manhattan. We could find no record of her death.

Following the closing of Abraham & Weil in New Roads, the Edwin Vignes Building was occupied by a succession of department stores: Lebeau & St. Dizier, O. St. Dizier and Co., and J.S. Lann, until the retail landmark was dismantled to make way for the New Alamo Theatre in 1935. During the flood of 1912, the temporarily-vacant building served as a ration distribution center.

ARTHUR G. WEILL

Arthur Gaston Weill was born on 1 July 1845, at Strasbourg, Bas-Rhin, France, to David Weill and his wife, Sophie Cerf, both natives of Strasbourg. Arthur Weill arrived in New York on 8 August 1864, from Liverpool, England, aboard the *City of London*. At the close of and immediately after the Civil War, the Veteran's Schedule of the 1890 United States Federal Census taken at West Feliciana Parish, Louisiana, recorded that "Arthur G. Weil" served as a private in the 15th Company, New Jersey Regiment, United States Army from January until July 1865.

Following the war, Weil apparently lived for some time in New Roads, Louisiana, moving afterwards to work, successively, in three stores in West Feliciana Parish. Arthur Gaston Weill opted for French citizenship at the end of the Franco-Prussian War at New Orleans on 1 July 1872, but was naturalized as an American citizen in West Feliciana Parish on 24 March 1876. In the 1880 United States Federal Census, Arthur Weil was enumerated as one of the clerks for Julius Freyhan's emporium in St. Francisville.

An article in the 28 June 1884 *Pointe Coupée Banner* highlighting Weil's return visit to the town stated that he was employed, successively, by the Picard & Weil store and that of Moses Mann, both in Bayou Sara, prior to working for Freyhan in St. Francisville.

The *Banner* article described Weil as: "now of West Feliciana, but in the good old time [*sic*] a resident of Pointe Coupée, where he made a host of friends who are always delighted to see him in our midst.... There will be social mirth and good humor in our little town during friend Arthur's short stay here."

Arthur Gaston Weill, who never married, died in St. Francisville on 26 January 1902, and was interred there in the Hebrew Rest Cemetery.

BERNARD TEUTSCH

The peripatetic Bernard Teutsch, a native of Venningen, Rheinpfalz, Germany, and former general merchant at New Texas Landing on the Mississippi River, above Morganza opened a general store in 1892, in Joseph Lejeune's former location, in the Clement Samson Building, on the site of what is now 313 East Main Street.

Numerous 1892 *Pointe Coupée Banner* advertisements for Bernard Teutsch, New Roads, Louisiana, listed his store stock as: dry goods, trimmings, notions, staple and fancy groceries, cakes, candies, tobacco, cigars, crockery, glassware, cutlery, and hardware. Within eight years of opening the downtown store, however, Bernard Teutsch relocated to Pointe Coupée Road and simultaneously conducted the "Loupe" and "Labatut" stores on those respective plantations.

In 1903, Bernard Teutsch was back in New Roads, with horses and mules he had purchased at the recent World's Fair. He opened a large livery and sales stable, which stretched for a block along the south side of Fourth Street, with busy Richy Street on its east or front, and Saint Mary Street on its west or rear. Directly across Richy Street, and likewise extending a block deep, to New Roads Street on its east, was the livery stable and hack depot of Auguste A. Bondy, a nephew-by-marriage and commercial and political protégé of Mayer Cahen.

A 29 October 1904 *Pointe Coupée Banner* advertisement proclaimed: "When You come to New Roads go to B. Teutsch's Stable and see The Fine Lot of Mules, Driving, Saddle and Combination Horses which he bought from the World's Fair. And he will Surely do What's Right with You. J.M. Castay and Al. Morgan, Salesmen."

Oscar, Louisiana, town merchant and planter Isaac Bigman was a regular customer of Teutsch's, until litigation ensued, with Teutsch as plaintiff and Bigman as the defendant in 1904.

Moving yet again, by 1910 Bernard Teutsch had partnered with his brother, Herman Teutsch, in a store on Lower Old River at Keller Landing.

Bernard Teutsch never married. In both the 1900 and 1910 United States Federal Census records he was enumerated as an unmarried man living with his brothers. Although the JewishGen On-Line Burial Registry, show that Regina Teutsch, born in Venningen, Rheinpfalz, Germany, on 16 March 1849, who died on 9 September 1910, was his wife, she was, in truth, his sister. She was enumerated in the 1900 United States Federal Census for Pointe Coupée Parish, Ward 5, as Louis/Ludwig Teutsch's thirty-six-year-old (*sic*) unmarried sister. Ludwig Teutsch was another one of the numerous children of Jacob Teutsch and his wife, Magdelena Kahn, who immigrated to Louisiana. Regina Teutsch died on 9 September 1910 and Bernard followed, after a long illness on 3 July 1912, in New Orleans. Bernard and Regina Teutsch were interred in the Hebrew Rest Cemetery in St. Francisville with matching headstones.

JACOB MOONSHINE

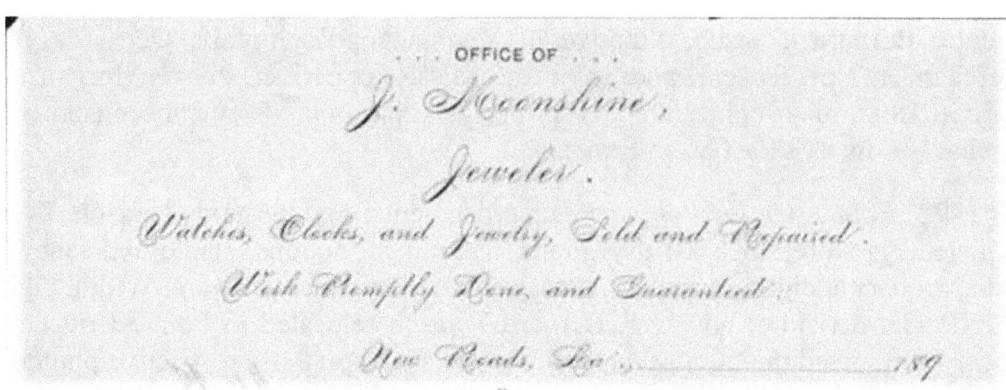

Letterhead of Jacob Moonshine (Norbert Badin Papers, Mss. 825, Louisiana and Lower Mississippi Valley Collections, LSU Libraries, Baton Rouge, LA.)

Jacob Moonshine, according to the few records we have found, was a native of Poland, Russian Empire, born ca. 1866, who immigrated in 1888, and was naturalized by 1910. His surname was likely "Monshein" in its original form. He and his wife, Sarah Dennis, were living in New Orleans by 1893, when he attested to the death of their child, Israël Moonshine, aged seven months, fourteen days, due to spinal meningitis. Another son, also named Israël Moonshine (spelled Mondshine), died at the age of four years on 4 April 1901.

Moonshine, a dealer in and repairer of jewelry, watches, and clocks, worked in New Roads between 1896 and 1898. He did business in the west half of a divided building at the southeast corner of the Beauregard Olinde – Dr. A.P. Fillastre residential lot, currently 734 West Main Street. In 1898, he transferred his operations to Lakeland. W. James McLean, jeweler and optician, succeeded him at the New Roads location.

Moonshine moved to New York in 1901, but returned to New Roads in 1908. A 5 September 1908 *Pointe Coupée Banner* article celebrating his return indicated that he had spent several years studying and working at the largest "jewelry factory" in the U.S., and could not only sell, but "manufacture" custom jewelry from customers' old gold or silver items. He resumed business at No. 217 West Main Street in a building formerly and subsequently the "sample room" of Casimir Savignol's adjacent French Hotel. Many such city and small-town hotels had a sample room, either inside or near their premises, where traveling salesmen or "drummers" could display samples of their company's merchandise for potential area retailers.

Jacob Moonshine was enumerated in the 1910 United States Federal Census for the town of Washington, St. Landry Parish, where he was operating a jewelry store. He boarded at Washington with Joseph and Olga Gatzman, former operators of the Cosmopolitan Hotel in New Roads, which burned in the Richey Street fire of 1909. By this time, Moonshine's wife, Sarah, was no longer living with him.

The brick building constructed in 1939 on the site of Moonshine's 1908 jewelry store in New Roads housed a succession of businesses, including the Auto-Lec and Western Auto chain stores, Ben Morgan's "Money Saver" department store, and The Style Shoppe, fine women's apparel (third location). We could verify no date or place of death for either Jacob or his wife Sarah.

JOSEF HERSKOVITZ, aka JOSEPH HARRIS

According to information on his headstone, Josef Herskovitz, was born on 16 April 1857, at Husi, Western Moldavia, Austrian Empire. He married Rebecca Weiser (b. 1856) in Austria where three of their four children were born: Isadore (b. 1879), Fannie (b. 1881), and Henry (b. 1884). Joseph immigrated to the United States in 1885. His wife and three children followed him to America in 1893.

Joseph Herskovitz was a general merchant in New Roads, Louisiana by 1891. In 1893 he filed a civil suit (14th Judicial District Court, No. 325) against Bienaimé Leduff, a person of color, for the latter's unpaid store accounts of 1892 and 1893. In the litigation, Herskovitz represented to the court that he had provided "goods, wares, merchandise, supplies and provisions and [cash] advances," to enable Leduff to produce crops of cotton and corn on the False River plantation of Oscar Joffrion, who opened and named the Oscar, Louisiana Post Office for himself in 1898.

Leduff's balance for 1892 was recorded as $299.71, with legal interest from 1 March of that year, and $117.82 for 1893. As Herskovitz had a lien and privilege on Leduff's potential 1893 harvest, the court authorized Pointe Coupée Parish Deputy Sheriff C. (Clairfait) Morel to seize, in preparation for public sale, Leduff's produce, animals, and agricultural implements. Nearby merchant Isaac Bigman, and Joseph Miller, appointed to appraise the property, counted approximately three bales of cotton still "in the seed," (i.e., harvested but as-yet un-ginned) about 13 acres of cotton standing in the field, a bay horse and colt, a harrow, cultivator and two plows, for which they declared a total value of $357.

Two years later, in 1895, Josef Herskovitz was recorded as making two purchases from New Roads widow Marie Rose Michel, a person of color whose 1870 marriage to Michel Olinde, a white man, had been duly licensed by the state and performed at St. Mary Church. Marriages between mixed-race couples were legal in Louisiana from 1865 until the imposition of Jim Crow laws in the 1890s.

In the first purchase record, we found that the Widow Olinde, née Marie Rosa Michel, sold six head of cattle to Herskovitz, consisting of three cows and their calves, for an unspecified price. In the next record, Rosa conveyed to Herskovitz a 186-foot-wide lot on the bank of False River, in what is presently the 600 block of West Main Street in New Roads, the bounding neighbor to the west being the St. Paul African American Episcopal Church. The price was a mere $100, suggesting that the Widow Olinde may have been unable to pay her store account with Herskovitz, and rather than going through the process of litigation, the two agreed that she would convey the property to him at a low price. A store building stood on the lot, so it is possible that Herskowitz had already been engaged in business there before acquiring the property.

Marie Rosa Olinde, who once possessed considerable property, extending from False River at the lot she sold to Herskovitz as far back as the 40-arpent line, systematically sold portions of the tract until her sole real estate was a lot in the "Red Stick" section of New Roads, on Napoleon Street. That neighborhood took its name from a red pole set up, likely at the intersection of Napoleon and Olinde Streets, by Beauregard Olinde, grandson of Marie Rosa's late husband, Michel Olinde, by his first wife, Julie Bergeron, which was employed as a signal indicating his presence at one or the other location.

While Joseph and Rebecca's fourth child, David Herskovitz was born in New York on 21 August 1896, Josef Herskovitz, a dry goods merchant, his wife, Rebecca, and children were enumerated in the 1900 United States Federal Census, living on Dryades Street in New Orleans, where the couple's last son, Solomon, was born in 1902. The family subsequently relocated to Mount Enterprise, Rusk Co., Texas, where Josef continued to deal in dry goods. Between 1900 and 1910 the family had their surname changed legally from "Herskovitz" to "Harris." Joseph Harris died on 20 September 1916, and was interred in Shreveport, Caddo Parish, Louisiana, in the Agudath Achim Cemetery. Rebecca, his wife, died on 24 May 1929, and was interred with him.

The site of Josef Herskovitz's New Roads store was successively the location of Beauregard Olinde's "Half Way Store" (forerunner of the B. Olinde wholesale grocery and beer, hardware, appliance, clothing, and furniture companies of South Louisiana), Aubin André's New Roads Garage & Auto Repair Shop, and the King Theatre and Apartments, located at 659 West Main Street. With the large, two-story apartment and former theatre building, later built on the site, the lot fetched $400,000 in a 2015 sale, according to Pointe Coupée Parish Clerk of Court Conveyance Records.

BENJAMIN RAPHAËL MAYER, AKA BEN R. MAYER

Benjamin Raphaël Mayer was born on 6 January 1855, at Natchez, Adams Co., Mississippi, the eleventh of fourteen children of John Mayer, aka Jacob Meyer Levi, and his wife, Jeannette Ries. Jacob Meyer Levi (b. 19 April 1805) had run away from his home in Landau, Rheinpfalz, Germany, at an early age at which time he changed his name for fear of being tracked down. After living in Paris for a short while, he immigrated to New Orleans, arriving on 15 January 1835, as J. Myer, age 25 (*sic*), aboard the brig *Dido* from Le Havre, France. The Ries family: Moses, his wife Eleanor Salomon and their children: Nanette, Pauline/Sibille, Minette, Jeannette, and Benjamin were also on board the ship.

Jacob Myer, aka, John Mayer was married to Jeannette Ries, born on 18 February 1818, at Obernai, Bas-Rhin, France, on 29 April 1835, at the Ries family home by her father, Moses Ries. The New Orleans *Bee* dated 5 May 1835, reported the wedding, along with two others performed that day:

> MARRIED: On Wednesday evening 29th April last by the Revd. Moses S. Reas of the Israelite Congregation. Mr. Jacob Myer to Miss Jeannette, daughter of Moses S. Reas. Also Mr. Penel [*sic*, Binell] Levy to Miss Minetta, second daughter of Moses S. Reas all of this city. On the same day by the same, Mr. Leopold Dalsheimer to Miss Adel Lam [*sic*, Lamm] of this city.

Ben Mayer's father, John Mayer, was a beloved Natchez merchant for almost fifty years.

Benjamin Raphaël Mayer married Zerlina Mendelsohn at Baton Rouge, East Baton Rouge Parish, Louisiana, on 25 May 1882. Zerlina was the second of ten children born on 9 February 1861 at Baton Rouge, to pioneer grocer Simon Mendelsohn (b. 16 August 1825), a native of Puttelange-aux-Lacs, Moselle, France, and his wife, Sophie Rosenfield (b. 16 February 1838), a native of Obernbreit, Rheinpfalz, Germany.

Ben was a Baton Rouge, Louisiana business leader for 30 years being the founder of two wholesale houses: Ben R. Mayer Grocery Co, and the Baton Rouge Grocery Co. He served on the City Council, spearheaded the capital city's electric light, streetcar and fire alarm systems and numerous other enterprises.

Prior to the arrival of the boll weevil, Ben R. Mayer Grocery Co. was one of Baton Rouge's most substantial businesses and counted many clients among the merchants of Pointe Coupée. "Ben Mayer" became more of a "household name" in Pointe Coupée in 1898, when Baton Rouge and New Roads newspapers ran nine months of articles on his plans to establish a telephone line between the two places.

The 5 March 1898 Baton Rouge *Advocate* began the hoopla by announcing Mayer's intention to construct the telephone line within 90 days. Seven days later, on 12 March, the newspaper reported that work would commence in "a few" days. A week later, the 19 March *Advocate* announced that the poles were soon to arrive in Baton Rouge, adding that no New Roads exchange would be established but that a toll line was "a certainty." The 9 April issue told of the forthcoming erection of the poles, and the issue of 23 April stated that the telephone was "coming soon."

A 7 May 1898 announcement contended that the charter of the new telephone company would be published in another city paper, the Baton Rouge *Truth*, and on 28 May the *Truth* related that the poles and wires of the "Merchants' & Planters' Telephone Co." were to arrive in Baton Rouge and the line would proceed through the length of Pointe Coupée Parish, as far as the mouth of the Red River.

The 8 October 1898 news was that New Roads would have telephone service "at once," and on the 22nd of that month the *Advocate* elaborated that the line would cover the capital city and the west bank of the Mississippi River as far north as Red River Landing. The laying of the cable across (*sic*, on the floor of) the river was to take place "soon."

There was no further mention of Mayer's proposed line, and nearly two months later, the 3 December 1898 issue of the *West Baton Rouge Parish Sugar Planter* reported the Cumberland Telephone would be the one to connect the west bank of the Mississippi River, relating, however, that its line would run only between Plaquemine, in Iberville Parish, to "Devall or Smithfield" in West Baton Rouge, with the intention of passing through New Roads and on to Red River Landing "eventually."

Neither Ben Mayer's company, the Merchants' & Planters' Telephone Co., nor the Cumberland erected lines in Pointe Coupée Parish. In 1906, a local entrepreneur, Thomas Hewes of Oscar, partner of Isaac Bigman in the Bigman & Hewes (Cotton) Ginnery inaugurated the False River Telephone Line. Within two years, the system counted 120 subscribers, 50 miles of poles, more than 100 miles of wire and continued to grow.

Jewish businesses and residences on False River and the Lower Chenal connected to the False River Telephone line by 1908 included: Mrs. Howard Betz and Mayer Cahen, both in New Roads; Isaac Bigman's store and residence, and Bigman & Hewes Ginnery, all at Oscar; Sol Bernstein, at Lakeland; A. Baum, at present-day Rougon; as well as Benjamin Jewell's descendants Raoul Vignes in New Roads, Ben Jewell, Jr. and A.L. Jewell on the Island of False River.

The *False River Telephone Directory* of 1 July 1908 stated that connections could "sometimes" be made with a private line in West Baton Rouge Parish, the subscribers of the latter including Mississippi River Road merchant A. Abramson.

Ben Mayer and his wife, Zerlina, were the parents of four children, only two of whom lived beyond infancy: Buffington Simon Mayer (b. 18 March 1887), and Benjamin Mayer, Jr. (b. 11 September 1889).

Benjamin Mayer died at Baton Rouge on 3 May 1914, and was interred in the Baton Rouge Jewish Cemetery. Zerlina Mendelsohn Mayer died at Baton Rouge on 31 December 1955, and was buried with him.

MR. and MRS. JOSEPH "JOE" GOTTLIEB

> **Joe Gottlieb Insurance Agency, Ltd.,**
> **BATON ROUGE, LA.**
> **REPRESENTING**
> American Fire Insurance Co. of Philadelphia.
> Atlanta-Birmingham Insurance Co. of Atlanta and Birmingham.
> Georgia Home Insurance Co. of Georgia.
> German-Amkrican of New York.
> German-Alliance of New York.
> Mechanics & Traders of New Orleans.
> North British & Mercantile of London.
> National of Hartford.
> Phœnix of London.
> Royal Exchange of London,
> Teutonia of New Orleans.
> Virginia Fire and Marine of Virginia.
> Western of Toronto.
>
> Gross Assets $89,914,696
> Net Surplus 18,937,036
> Losses Paid and in Process of Payment
> in Baltimore Fire 4,251,821
>
> We also represent the Eqitiple Life Assurance Society of New York and The United States Fidelity and Guaranty Company of Baltimore.
> If you need insurance of any kind (Fire, Life, Accident, Storm or any o her) call on or write us and all inquiries will be given prompt attention.
>
> **L. Bouanchaud,**   **Gottlieb Insurance Agency,**
> **New Roads, La.**   **Baton Rouge, La.**

Pointe Coupée Banner advertisement for Joe Gottlieb Insurance Agency, dated April 30, 1904.

Baton Rouge, Louisiana banker Joseph Gottlieb and his wife, Rebecca, are recorded amongst the prominent, civic-minded and charitable residents of the capital city. Joseph Gottlieb was born on 8 February 1862 at St, Louis City, Missouri, to Solomon Gottlieb (b. 1821), a native of Bavaria, and his wife Dora Streit Rosensweig (b. 1829). We believe Dora died shortly after Joseph's birth in Missouri. The Gottlieb's four older children had all been born in Baltimore City, Maryland, where Solomon had worked in the dry goods business: Moses (b. 1850), Emanuel (b. 1853), Charles (b. 1855), and Caroline (b. 1859).

Solomon, a widower, and his five children were enumerated in the 1870 United States Federal Census at Baton Rouge, East Baton Rouge Parish. Solomon worked as a grocer and dry goods merchant. His eldest son, Moses was a baker, Emanuel clerked in his father's store, and Charles was a clerk in an auction house. Caroline, age 11 and Joseph, age 8, were attending school.

By the age of eighteen years, Joseph Gottlieb was clerking for his father, Solomon. Joseph Gottlieb, familiar to Pointe Coupéeans from his association with the Ben R. Mayer Grocery Co. of Baton Rouge, had a keen interest in the development not only of the capital city but of the region. Becoming successful in affairs in several Louisiana parishes, Joe Gottlieb was among the founders of Pointe Coupée Parish's first financial institutions, the Bank of New Roads, which opened its doors in October 1899 in the Graugnard-Richy Building, later home of the American Department Store. As a director of Bank of New Roads, Gottlieb's colleagues included Pointe Coupée merchants and planters Joseph Richy, Olivier St. Dizier, Joseph Philibert Gosserand and Pervis Chérie Major.

In addition to his banking duties, Joe Gottlieb ran his own insurance agency. Former general merchant and future Mayor of New Roads, Sheriff of Pointe Coupée Parish, and President of Bank of New Roads, J. Lamartine Bouanchaud began his career in the insurance business in 1903 as the New Roads agent for Joseph Gottlieb's insurance firm. Bouanchaud eventually established his own insurance company, L. Bouanchaud Agency, which his descendants run to this day.

Joseph Gottlieb married Rebecca Hahn, ca. 1891. She was born on 18 November 1864, at Memphis, Shelby Co., Tennessee, to Emanuel Hahn and his wife, Rosa Heiman, both natives of Germany. Joseph and Rebecca were the parents of four children, all born in Baton Rouge: Ike Hahn (b. 1892), Lewis (b. 1894), Rosalie (b. 1896), and Solomon J. (b. 1900).

In memory of their son Ike Gottlieb who died in U.S. military service during the 1918 influenza pandemic, the Gottliebs established and were active in the affairs of the Ike Gottlieb Home for Working Girls. Joe Gottlieb instituted the tradition of donating shoes to underprivileged children on the Good Fellows organization's list. (Note: The Good Fellows was an inter-faith charitable fundraising committee in Baton Rouge that provided goods and services to the underprivileged in the Capital City region at Christmas beginning in the 1920s.) Mrs. Gottlieb continued this benevolent gesture as well as donating an "iron lung" for the relief of pulmonary ailments to the City of Baton Rouge.

A strong advocate for unity and charity among the faithful of the Judeo-Christian tradition in Louisiana, Mrs. Gottlieb was particularly generous with time and treasure to the Catholic and Protestant children's orphanages in Baton Rouge, the Jewish children's orphanage in New Orleans, and the Leprosarium at Carville, Iberville Parish, Louisiana.

Joseph Gottlieb died at Baton Rouge on 1 August 1936, and was buried there in the Jewish Cemetery. His wife, Rebecca Hahn, followed on 13 October 1946, and was interred with him.

JOSEPH "JOE" YATTER

Joseph Yatter, a native of the Austrian Empire, was born on 26 April 1870, to Julius Yatter and his wife, Annie, (surname unknown at present). Joseph was married on 10 October 1895, at New Orleans to Rachel Messner, born ca. 1856 in Massachusetts, the daughter of Gaspar Messner, a tailor, and his wife, Sarah Winder, both natives of Prussia. Joseph and Rachel were the parents of two daughters who survived to adulthood: Sarah (b. 1897), and Esther (b. 1900). Joseph filed his declaration of intent in 1894 to become a United States citizen and was naturalized at New Orleans on 24 May 1907. He, his wife, and two daughters were enumerated in the 1900 United

States Federal Census for New Orleans, where he operated a grocery store. Ten years later, he was enumerated as the proprietor of a grocery and bar in New Orleans. During the intervening years he conducted business in New Roads. According to advertisements in the local *Pointe Coupée Banner*, Joe Yatter was a grocer, upholsterer, mattress maker, and furniture repairer in 1903, and moved in 1904 to a new store immediately south of the Alexander (later Mrs. Olga Gatzman's Cosmopolitan) Hotel, on the west side of Richy Street, between Sixth Street and the Texas & Pacific Railroad. This was one of the few buildings on both sides of the street to survive the great "St. Joseph's Day Fire" of 19 March 1909, although the next day's *Pointe Coupée Banner* account described it as "heavily damaged."

The Yatter family had apparently moved from New Roads by 1909, as George W. Sloan opened a grocery store in Joe Yatter's former Richy Street location that year. According to the 1910 United States Federal Census, the family was living on Oak Street in New Orleans, with Joe Yatter identified as keeper of a grocery store and bar. A decade later, Joe was enumerated as a furniture dealer living on Canal Street. He also invested in 44 acres in Tangipahoa Parish, Louisiana, north of Lake Pontchartrain, which he left, along with his premises and stock of furniture in New Orleans, to his widow and surviving daughters.

Joseph Yatter died on 9 October 1923, in New Orleans, and was interred there in Gates of Prayer Cemetery. His wife, Rachel Messner, died on 3 October 1939, and was interred with him.

ISIDORE WOLFF, "THE FANCY GROCER"

Isidore Wolff, "The Fancy Grocer," son of prominent merchant Cerf Wolff and Sarah Zacharias, was born on 13 July 1862, in Pointe Coupée Parish. Isidore operated stores in Lakeland, Louisiana, on the Lowe Chenal of False River, before moving to a location in 1904-1905 that is now 155 East Main Street. His clerk in 1904 was Amilcar LeBlanc, husband of Anastasia Cazayoux. *Pointe Coupée Banner* advertisements for I. Wolff indicated in 1904 that "The Fancy Grocer," featured: canned softshell crab, *pate de foie gras*, turkey, chili con carne and sweet potatoes, dill and vinegar pickles, capers, kippered and Holland herrings, Blue Label Catsup, McIlhenny Tabasco, salad dressing, nut butter, Rolston Breakfast Food, cereals, evaporated apples, pears and apricots, creamery butter, Roquefort, Neufchatel and Munster cheese, Huyler's Candy, and meats.

During the cyclone, hail and rain storm which struck New Roads on *Pointe Coupée Banner* press day on 18 June 1904, Wolff's hand was reported as badly cut as he attempted to keep his glass doors closed.

Wolff sold his grocery business in 1905 to Alcide Bondy, a descendant of Benjamin Jewell and Sophie Prévost. Bondy transferred operations across the street into the Demouy Building, formerly the location of the general store and pharmacy of Harry Demouy, the first husband of Lena Cohn.

Isidore Wolff's former location, on the north side of East Main Street, was joined to the building on the east by merchant and restauranteur Giovanni "John" Rosso around 1921. The former Wolff store was home to a succession of business concerns, including the Cleveland Supply Co. department store between 1953 and 1961, and it, as part of the combined building, still stands in the 21st century.

Isidore Wolff moved his operations to Pensacola, Escambia Co., Florida, where he married Sidonia "Dearie" Cohen, born at Pensacola, on 15 February 1876, to Gustav M. Cohen, a native of Saxony, and his wife, Louise Simon, born on 9 July 1839, in Zweibrücken, Rheinpfalz, Germany, to Elias Simon and Philippa Amelia Schwartz. Isidore and Sidonia Cohen Wolff were the parents of five daughters: Lucille (b. 1896), Norma (b. 1898), Helen (b. 1902), Sara (b. 1904), and Lois (b. 1908).

Isidore, who worked as a wholesale broker in grains and other products, died on 4 March 1920, in Pensacola, and was interred there in Temple Beth-El Cemetery. Sidonia Cohen Wolff died in New Orleans on 2 December 1965, and was buried in Garden of Memories Cemetery in Metairie, Jefferson Parish, Louisiana. (Note: Sidonia Cohen's mother Louise Simon was the sister of Julia Simon, wife of Pointe Coupée merchant, Aaron Baum.)

MAYER CAHEN

The erudite and multi-talented Mayer Cahen immigrated to New Orleans from Le Havre, France, arriving on 9 January 1857, on board the *Mortimer Livingston*. He was listed as sixteen-year-old "Mayer Kahn," from France. He followed his parents, Israël Cahen, misidentified as Meyer Cahn, Mina Levy Cahn and his fifteen-year-old sister, Thérèse, who arrived at New York on 5 July 1856 aboard the ship *Mercury* from Le Havre. Three of the Cahen family members were first enumerated in the 1860 United States Federal Census for St. Louis City, Missouri, as Israël and Mina "Cahn," both age 50, with their son "Meyer", age 18. Israël was working there as a peddler. While we have not been able to pinpoint Mayer Cahen's exact date or place of birth, we have discovered some clues to help future researchers. We know that Mayer had an older sister, Thérèse Cahen, who married Philip Schwartz on 2 February 1864, at New Orleans, in the presence of her brother, Mayer Cahen. Philip and Thérèse had one child, Fannie Schwartz, born at New Orleans on 12 April 1865. Fannie later married Reichshoffen, Bas-Rhin, native, Simon Abraham, on 31 March 1884. Fannie is the "Mrs. Simon Abraham" listed as one of only two relatives in Mayer Cahen's 27 July 1924 obituary which appeared in that day's issue of the New Orleans *Times-Picayune*.

We were able to trace Thérèse Cahen Schwartz, who died on 16 January 1868, at Paris, 1st arrondissement, France. Her Parisian death record identified her as Thérèse Cahen, the 27-year-old wife of Philip Schwartz, and daughter of Israël Cahen and Mina Levy, born at Saint-Avold, Moselle, France. This record indicates that in 1868 Philip and Thérèse were living at Rue des Dauphins, No. 7, along with Israël Cahen and his wife Mina Lévy. Israël Cahen was one of the witnesses who signed the death certificate as "I. Cahen."

There are no complete records available on-line for Saint-Avold, however, there is on-line access to the Ten-Year Tables for that commune. A search for Israël's birth record yielded nothing despite the fact that his 1893 death record and obituary had given Saint-Avold as his birthplace. We were able, however, to verify that Thérèse had been born at Saint-Avold on 14 March 1841.

Several Louisiana records indicated that Mayer Cahen had been born at Nancy, Meurthe-et-Moselle, France, so we searched the *Archives municipals de Nancy* (City Archives for Nancy) between 1842 and 1853 which are on-line. According to the 1900 United States Federal Census, Mayer had been born in May 1847. His Louisiana State Death Certificate recorded his place and date of birth as Nancy, France, on 1 November 1847. However, we could find no record for it at Nancy.

We know that Israël and Mina Levy Cahen returned to Louisiana from France before 1872, to rejoin their son, Mayer, who had been left in charge of what remained of the family's Louisiana properties after the Civil War, because Israël was naturalized in Assumption Parish on 26 October of that year. Mina Levy Cahen died in New Orleans on 1 October 1874. Her obituary identified her as a native of Grünstadt, Rheinpfalz, Germany, and the wife of Israël Cahen. Her son, Mayer Cahen, residing at No. 113 Royal Street, signed her death certificate. It was most likely business worries and the death of their daughter in 1868, coupled with the outbreak of the Franco-Prussian War in 1871, which precipitated Israël and Mina's return to Louisiana.

Mayer Cahen had a "mammoth store," according to several 1879 editions of the *Donaldsonville Chief* newspaper. The July 1889 edition of Dun's *Mercantile Agency Reference Book*, reported that Mayer was still operating at Valenzuela in that year. According to the 23 September 1876 edition of the *Donaldsonville Chief*, Cahen had been, since early manhood, a member of Orus Lodge 190, F. & A. M.

Although we have not located a naturalization record for Mayer Cahen in Louisiana, we know that he was a member of the Republican Party. Mayer Cahen was elected Senator of Louisiana's 9th District which included Assumption, Lafourche and Terrebonne Parishes in the turbulent campaign year of 1878. Reactionary native Democrats attempting to reclaim control of local as well as state and federal offices, contested all Republican victories. Cahen's was contested by Major Silas Grisamore of Thibodaux, alleging "fraud" and voter "intimidation," according to the 16 November 1878 edition of *Le Pionnier de l'Assomption*, (*Assumption Pioneer*) published at Napoleonville, Louisiana. Cahen was confirmed in office, however, and served as a delegate to the Louisiana Constitutional Convention in 1879. The 6 May 1879 New Orleans *Daily Democrat* included vignettes of all the delegates:

> Hon. Mayer Cahen of Assumption [Parish], is a short gentleman, with a good and well-proportioned frame. He is a Republican in politics of advanced views. He has a pleasant face, with well-cut features. A good mouth, shaded with a light mustache, good natured and knowing eyes, and a square, good-shaped forehead. He is another one of the delegates who has not yet felt called upon to address the Convention, although he manifests no lack of interest in the proceedings of the body.

Mayer Cahen was identified as a dry goods merchant at Valenzuela (subsequently Belle Alliance) in Ward 1, Assumption Parish, Louisiana, living with his father, Israël Cahen, an "unmarried" retired merchant, according to the 1880 United States Federal Census. The Hon. Cahen's regular visits to New Orleans, Baton Rouge and nearby Donaldsonville were reported in all the local newspapers. The 27 October 1883 issue of the *Donaldsonville Chief* related, likely with a touch of Democrat resentment: "Senator Mayer Cahen of Assumption [Parish] has been in town [Donaldsonville] several times this week, looking as fresh and chipper as you please – in fact, chipper than a whole basket of chips."

In 1888, Cahen campaigned again for the position of Senator, but lost the election to Thomas H. Cage. Cahen contested the returns in the First Session of the state's Third General Assembly. He was backed in this petition by ten Republican voters of his former district, who were co-signees, "and others." Cahen claimed that through "bribery, corruption and other illegal devices" he was deprived of votes at several polls by "your [Democrat legislators'] friends and persons working in your interest." The reading of the petition was dispensed with, and the matter referred to a Committee on Elections and Privileges to be formed later. Cage assumed office.

Nearly a decade later, the 7 November 1896 *Le Sentinelle de Thibodaux* opined: "Assumption remains the banner Republican parish of the third congressional district. Mayer Cahen deserves a promotion and it would not surprise us a bit to see him come in for a good slice when the pie is parcelled [*sic*] out."

Cahen was among thirty-three contestants for the seat of 3rd District Presidential Elector, but received only 223 votes, according to *Le Sentinelle de Thibodaux*, dated 14 November 1896. A few months later, however, Mayer Cahen was appointed to the post of coiner for the New Orleans branch of the United States Mint. The 5 February 1899 New Orleans *Daily Picayune* related the news under the rather wry heading "Another Plum for Republican Mouths." He was described as continuing as a merchant in Assumption Parish, although he was in Washington, D. C. at the time of the appointment, but added "it is presumed he will not delay in coming back to New Orleans to take charge of his office."

According to a 22 February 1899 article in the *Baltimore* (Maryland) *Sun*, Mayer Cahen, a fifty-year-old bachelor resident of Belle Alliance, Louisiana, and forty-seven-year-old widow Anna E. Cooley, a resident of Washington D.C., applied for a marriage license in Baltimore, but upon learning that, according to Maryland law they had to be married by a minister of the gospel, the couple left without the license. Cahen had stated that he did not want to be married by a clergyman, preferring a civil ceremony. On their way back from Maryland, Mayer and Anna were married in Hancock Co., Mississippi, on 2 March 1899, by a Justice of the Peace. Mayer Cahen's bride, née Anna Bondy, had been born on 28 June 1848, and baptized as Anna Elmire Bondy in St. Mary Church, New Roads, on 1 October 1848 (PCP-10, 103). Her parents were Jean-Baptiste Alcide Bondy, a native of the island of Martinique, and his wife Evelina Vignes, born in Waterloo, Pointe Coupée Parish, to Delphin Vergès Vignes and Hannah Jewell, the daughter of Jewish merchant Benjamin Jewell and his first wife, Sophie Prévost. Mayer and Anna Bondy Cahen, having married late in life, had no children.

Mayer Cahen suffered from progressive loss of vision for many years. While U.S. Coiner, he underwent "successful" surgery for cataract removal and returned to his post after three weeks' recuperation, according to the 12 October 1902 edition of the *Daily Picayune*. A year later, however, a committee of Louisiana "Lily White" (i.e., reactionary and racist) politicians met with Republican U.S. President Theodore Roosevelt in some attempt at compromise. It was reported in the 18 July 1903 edition of the New Orleans *Daily Picayune* that as a result of the meeting, Mayer Cahen had been directed to submit his resignation as coiner of the U.S. Mint at New Orleans.

In New Roads, Mayer Cahen partnered with his brother-in-law Alcide Bondy as Bondy & Cahen, "New Roads Fancy Grocery," in the Demouy Building, located at what is now 140 East Main Street, and the former general store and pharmacy of Harry Demouy, first husband of Lena Cohn. Alcide Bondy had purchased the business in 1905 from Isidore Wolff, "The Fancy Grocer," when it was situated on the north side of East Main, and transferred operations across the street to the Demouy Building on the bank of False River. Mayer Cahen later acquired Bondy's interest and was sole proprietor of the grocery store between 1908 and 1919. He was listed on the False River Telephone Line in 1908. In 1919, about the time of Cahen's retirement, owing to his progressive loss of vision, his wife Anna assumed operation of "The Elite" millinery store immediately to the west.

> Mrs. Mayer Cahen, next door to Hebert's Grocery, has just received a line of beautiful hats and solicits the patronage of the ladies throughout the parish. She cordially invites out-of-town ladies to make her store their headquarters while in town.

Mrs. Mayer Cahen's Millinery Store advertisement in *Pointe Coupée Banner* dated October 18, 1919.

Beloved as "Uncle Cahen" to Anna's nieces and nephews, Mayer was remembered as an avid reader of several newspapers, as long as he retained a measure of vision, and to have inspired the young Bondys in their education, careers and support of the Republican Party's philosophy and agendas.

According to his Louisiana State Death Certificate, Mayer Cahen died on 5 July 1924, in New Roads, as a result of "contusions and shock from fall," contributed by his "senility, total blindness and at times abnormal depression." Anna survived him by eight years, continuing to live in their charming Pennsylvania Avenue home.

Anna Bondy Cahen died on 1 August 1932, at New Roads. Her succession inventory (18th Judicial District Court, No. 1331) revealed that the couple had possessed mahogany furniture and several artworks: marble statues portraying "The Return of Jacob" and "The Mother," and a steel engraving of "The Return of Jacob." She generously remembered several relatives and friends, naming them as heirs to her possessions. A great-niece, Patricia Bondy Lacour, resided in the Pennsylvania Avenue home in later years. In her obituary, Anna was said to have counted friends in Washington, D.C. and Baltimore, Maryland, but it remains unknown to her collateral descendants how long she might have lived away from Louisiana, since she was enumerated in the 1900, 1910, 1920 and 1930 United States Federal Census records either in New Orleans or in Pointe Coupée Parish. They were also unaware that she had been previously married to a man who used the surname "Cooley."

Mayer and Anna Bondy Cahen share the Bondy family tomb with her relatives on the second aisle of St. Mary Cemetery, Mayer's inscription being top and center, immediately below the cross. Mayer Cahen was long and affectionately stated to have been the only person of the Jewish faith laid to rest in that hallowed Catholic burial ground.

KASSEL & STERN, AND STERN BROTHERS

Kassel & Stern, "The Leader" store, owned by Moses Kassel and Benjamin Joseph Stern, was in operation from 1904 until 1905 in the two-story Delage Building, formerly occupied by the J.O. Delage and George Pourciau general stores, at the current address of 133 East Main Street.

The senior partner of "Kassel and Stern," Moses "Martin" Kassel was born on 31 December 1881, in Louisville, Jefferson Co., Kentucky, to Louis Kassel and Rachel Shmuloff/Rose Sommelwitz, natives of Siauliai, Lithuania, Russian Empire.

The partnership of Moses "Martin" Kassel and Benjamin Joseph "Ben" Stern, during its brief history, offered some of the best quality clothing, shoes, hats and millinery in early twentieth century Pointe Coupée Parish. Pronouncing itself "The Great Bargain Store," Kassel & Stern's advertisements in the *Pointe Coupée Banner* proffered, with perhaps a touch of hyperbole, "1,000 suits to choose from," "Men's Trousers. Over 600 pair to choose from," and "We carry the largest stock of Shoes to be found anywhere." The 3 December 1904 issue of the local newspaper carried the following: "We do not crow over our values. We let cold facts speak for themselves. Good honest merchandise at prices that defy competition. The secret of our success is bargains. Come price our goods and be convinced of our assertion. 'More goods for less money… Less money for more goods' than any house in the parish."

Additional 1904-1905 *Pointe Coupée Banner* advertisements for Kassel & Stern, "The Leader" store, highlighted: ladies' dress and fancy goods; men's worsted, wool, cheviot and flannel suits; beach, mackenette, ulster and raglan overcoats; Norfolk, New Brunswick, worsted, cheviot, tweed and fancy trousers; dress and flannel shirts, sweaters, neckties, socks, garters; regular, wool and fleece-lined underwear, elastic seam drawers, night robes, and overalls; boys' knickerbocker, double-breasted, and sailor suits, blouses, and neckties; ladies' and misses' shirtwaists, negligee shirts, skirts, jackets, capes, and cloaks; children's capes and cloaks; hats; and Vicci, patent leather, and velour shoes.

During the months of October and December 1904, Kassel, Stern and Nepomuck Shymanski according to several conveyance records filed in Pointe Coupée Parish, engaged in a bewildering, back-and-forth switching amongst themselves of 1/3 interest in "The Leader's" merchandise and accounts payable.

According to his marriage and death record, and cemetery inscription, Jan Nepomuck/Nathan Shymanski was born on 26 January 1859, out of wedlock, in Briesen, West Prussia, now Germany. Shymanski, a Catholic, was married at Berlin, Brandenburg, German Empire, on 12 November 1881, to Maria Auguste Helene Mötky who was born on 27 July 1859, and baptized as an Evangelical Lutheran on 6 October in Berlin. The couple's two sons: William (b. 1882), and Frederick Louis (b. 1883), were both born in Germany, before the family immigrated in 1888. Shymanski was engaged as a (clothing) cutter when he was naturalized in New York in 1891, and where his third child, Anna, was born in 1890. The couple moved to Louisville, Jefferson Co., Kentucky, where Nepomuck was in the clothing business.

In 1905, when Kassel & Stern declared bankruptcy, Nepomuck Shymanski purchased the merchandise on hand. According to the 1910 United States Federal Census, he and his wife, Helene, and youngest child, Anna were enumerated in Louisville, Kentucky, where he worked as a clothing manufacturer. The family later Anglicized their surname to "Sherman." Both he and his wife died in Louisville, and were buried in the city's Cave Hill Cemetery. She died on 21 April 1938, and was interred as "Helen Moetki Sherman," and he followed on 25 April 1948, and was buried as "John N. Sherman."

After the demise of Kassel & Stern in New Roads, the Delage Building was home to "Stern Brothers," headed by Benjamin, and heralded in the 27 July 1907 *Pointe Coupée Banner* as an "up-to-date furnishing store." The venture coincided with the height of the boll weevil infestation and resultant economic distress. In an era when exhibits of the macabre often highlighted traveling circuses, street fairs and "shows," the former Kassel & Stern location had been shuttered by 17 April 1909, when the *Banner* related: "Jack Chase [Toutant "Jack" Chase, native of Waterloo] has on exhibit for a small fee in the former Ben Stern Store a 5' tall Indian woman mummy found in California."

Successively occupied by two department stores, E.E. Flippin's "Brooklyn Mercantile Co." and J.S. Lann (second location), and J.J. Monceret's "New Roads Furniture Store," the familiar Delage Building, the second floor of which was home to Clay Camp 271 Woodmen of the World, was demolished in 1968.

After "The Leader's" closing, senior partner, Martin Kassel, moved to New Orleans and was, successively, a traveling salesman, and an employee of the nationally-recognized Elmer Candy Co. He had married first ca. 1903 to Rose Aureline Tassin, a native of Marksville, Avoyelles Parish, Louisiana, born ca. October 1883, to Joseph Alfred Tassin, II and Cecilia Grandpierre, both natives of Avoyelles Parish, and members of the Catholic faith. Martin and Rose were the parents of four children: Myrtle (b. 1904), Meyer Louis (b. 1906), Martin, Jr., (b. 1907), and Alfred (b. 1908). Rose Tassin Kassel died in New Orleans on 6 February 1914. Martin Kassel was married to Marie Viviane Breaux on 25 November 1919. Vivian, a native of Burnside, Ascension Parish, Louisiana, was born there on 14 May 1894, to James M. Breaux and Alida Bertheaux. There were no children from this marriage.

Moses Kassel died as "Martin Kassel" on 3 February 1962, at New Orleans, Louisiana, and was buried in the Garden of Memories Cemetery, at Metairie, Jefferson Parish, Louisiana. Martin's second wife, Mary Vivian Breaux, died in 1989, and was interred next to him.

Benjamin Joseph "Ben" Stern, the other Kassel & Stern partner, was born on 9 November 1890 at Bayou Sara, East Feliciana Parish, Louisiana, to Joseph Stern, a merchant and native of Bavaria, and Mary Harris, a native of Posen, Poland, Prussian Empire.

Prior to marriage, Ben Stern was said to be the father of several "natural" children with Blanche Boudreaux, a woman of color, born ca. 1868, the natural daughter of John Boudreau and Zulma George, also a woman of color. All four of the Stern children were enumerated in the 1910 United States Federal Census: Norman Stern, born 1904, and baptized that year in St. Mary Church as "John Norman Boothrex" (PCP-33, 49); Ethel Rosalie Stern, born ca. 1906; Benjamin Floyd "Bennie" Stern, born 1907, and baptized that year at St. Mary as "Ben Starn"; and Blanche Cecile Stern, born 1908, and baptized in the following year at St. Mary under the surname "Stein." At that time, they were living with their maternal grandmother, Zulma George, age 42, a cook for a private family, at New Roads. Ten years later, the 1920 Census canvassers identified a fifth child, Charles Stern, born ca. 1911, living with his mother, Blanche Boudreaux, the four older children, and their step-father, Tony Garcia, a chauffeur, in New Orleans.

Norman Stern married Marie Cecilia Jarreau on 12 February 1929, at Detroit, Wayne Co., Michigan. She was a native of Pointe Coupée Parish, born on 6 July 1902, to Léonard Jarreau and Anastasie Robillard (PCP-33,18). (Note: Léonard Jarreau was a brother of Valérien Jarreau, who married Cornélie Gumbel, natural daughter of Cornelius Gumbel and Angélique Charamel. Anastasie "Anna" Robillard was a daughter of Adele Gosserand and niece of "Tante" Louise Gosserand, the latter of whom had children with Abraham Kaufman.) Norman Stern worked in an auto factory. They had one child, John D. Stern, b. ca. December 1929. Norman was divorced from Marie Cécile on 18 March 1943, and married again on 25 December 1943, to Jenette Galloway. Norman died on 26 October 1988 at Highland Park, Wayne Co., Michigan.

Ethel Rosalie Stern married Harold Santa Cruz/Cruze, ca. 1926 in New Orleans. Harold worked originally as a fisherman and later as a clerk at an "amusement house." Their children were all born in New Orleans: Blanche (b. 1928), Olga Marguerite/Margie (b. 1930), and Harold (b. 1932). Harold, Sr. died in New Orleans on 18 December 1961. Ethel Santa Cruz later moved to San Jose, Santa Clara Co., California, and died as Ethel Rosalie Russo on 26 April 1990.

Benjamin "Bennie" Stern married Inez Lafargue on 27 May 1926, in New Orleans. The bride was born in the city on 28 December 1906, to Beauge Lafargue and Virginia Broyard. According to the 1930 United States Federal Census for Tangipahoa Parish, Louisiana, they had had three children: Lois (b. 1926), Audrey (b. 1928), and Benjamin, Jr. (b. 1930). Inez was enumerated as the head of household, divorced, who had married at age eighteen. Benjamin "Bennie" Stern died in New Orleans in May 1939.

Blanche Cécile Stern, like her brother Norman, went north to Detroit, where she married Eunice Thompson on 15 March 1926. Eunice was an auto worker. The family lived in Highland Park, Wayne Co., Michigan, where their four children were born: Dorothy (b. 1927), Earl (b. 1928), Angeline (b. 1929), and Jackie Leroy (b. 1932). The couple was divorced, although there is no record for it. Blanche married Benjamin James Havard, also an auto worker, and a native of Franklin Co., Mississippi. Blanche and Benjamin were enumerated together in the 1940 United States Federal Census for Detroit, along with Blanche's four children by Eunice Thompson, and her two children with James Havard: Leonard (b. 1937) and Margie (b. 1939). James Havard died on 7 June 1990, and Blanche followed on 17 July 2004, both in Detroit, although we could not find their place of interment.

Charles Stern, also known erroneously as Charles Stein, was married to Clovina Rey, the daughter of Octave Rey and Antoinette Gasparini, in July 1928 in New Orleans. According to the 1940 United States Federal Census, Clovina Stein/Steen/Stern was working as a maid to support her three children: Charles Joseph (b. 1929), Marie (b. 1931), and Rita Mae (b. 1929). We could find no reliable record for Charles Stern's death.

In addition to partnership in "The Leader" and "Stern Brothers" stores in New Roads, Benjamin Joseph Stern was later a partner of Amy Paul "Toot" Lesser in the Mayflower Saloon in that town, and a clerk for his brothers L. & S. Stern, two St. Francisville merchants. Leaving South Louisiana for Monroe, Ouachita Parish, Louisiana, Benjamin Joseph Stern was married there to Bessye Lieber, ca. 1919, the daughter of Leopold Lieber, proprietor of L.L. Lieber Co. in Monroe. Lieber was a German national as was his wife, Rosa Schwartz. Bessye was born on 20 October 1896 at Jackson, Hinds Co., Mississippi. Ben Stern eventually moved to Monroe with his wife to take over his father-in-law's business and where his sons, Joseph Lieber (b. 1925), Louis M. (b. 1927), and Leroy (b. 1928), were born.

Both Ben Stern, who died at Monroe on 28 November 1953, and his wife, Bessye, who died there on 5 January 1975, were interred there in the Rosena Chapel Jewish Cemetery.

Two-story Kassel & Stern Store, New Roads, located behind tree.

STERN & LESSER

Stern & Lesser operated the "Mayflower Saloon," in the Mayflower Hotel building, at the northwest corner of Katt (*sic*, likely euphemism for "sport" or "promiscuity"; present-day Plum) and St. Mary Streets, two blocks north of the Texas & Pacific Railroad. This was a partnership between Benjamin Stern, formerly of Kassel & Stern, "The Leader" store, and Amy Paul Lesser, a person of color. They leased the building from property owners Joseph and John Rosso, natives of Sicily, between 1906 and 1909.

The 1907 Sanborn Fire Insurance Map of New Roads, Louisiana, depicted the Mayflower building as divided into a "Saloon" on the eastern side and "F.B" (for "female boarding," likely a euphemism for brothel) on the western side. The 1909 Sanborn Map showed it divided into a "Pool Room" and "Dance Hall" in the front and rear of the eastern side, and "F.B." on the western side. In 1909, the Mayflower building was destroyed by fire. Stern & Lesser's merchandise, including several brands of cigars and playing cards, and their furniture and bedding were lost as well.

Amy Paul "Toot" Lesser was the son of William Lesser of Chicago, Cook Co., Illinois, and Paris-educated Amica Maria Mahoudeau, a woman of color and native of New Roads. Amica was born to attorney Amy Landry Mahoudeau and Féroline Ferrier, a New Roads native and woman of color, on 29 November 1855 (PCP-10, 245). The child's father, Amy Landry Mahoudeau, had been born on 11 June 1813, at Langeais, Indre-et-Loire, France, to Michel Gilles Mahoudeau, a baker, and his wife Marie Anne Barrier. Mahoudeau was listed as one of eight attorneys practicing in Pointe Coupée Parish according to *Livingston's Law Register* published in 1852.

Thirty-one-year-old Amica Maria Mahoudeau was married to thirty-seven-year-old William "Leser" at New Orleans on 7 December 1886, at a time when interracial marriages were still permitted. Amica and her son "Toot" Lesser lived in the former Kleborn home in downtown New Roads, immediately east of the jewelry store belonging to Jacob Moonshine. Amica and "Toot" lived with an older cousin Amélie Amar, the mother of twins Charles Adalbert and Joseph Hildévert Gumbel by prominent merchant Simon Gumbel. Oral tradition related by now-deceased local businessmen Humphrey T. Olinde Jr., of the Olinde hardware, furniture, and wholesale beer companies, contends that despite "Toot" Lesser's intelligence and abilities, he was refused a position in a New Roads bank, likely due to his mixed ethnicity. (Note: Amy Landry Mahoudeau, identified as an unmarried lawyer and resident of Waterloo, Pointe Coupée Parish, Louisiana, died at the Hôtel de l'Amirauté in Vichy, Allier, France, on 16 May 1882.)

A.P. "Toot" Lesser was identified in his 1917 World War I Draft Registration as a moving picture operator for J. Arthur Langlois (i.e., in the New Roads Opera House in the old Masonic Temple on Poydras Avenue) after which he was employed for several years by a New Orleans newspaper. For many years, "Toot" Lesser lived on Napoleon Street, in the "Red Stick" section of New Roads.

The *Pointe Coupée Banner* dated 22 December 1960 reported that the "well-known and beloved New Roads colored character," who had been reported ill, was found lifeless in his bed on the morning of 12 December, apparently of natural causes. Investigators described the small, two-room "shotgun" house of the deceased as "completely packed with the various miscellaneous items which he possessed, piled solidly four to five feet in height - with only room enough for the aged to sleep on a bed in the corner. Clothes, books, cans, newspapers and magazines and clippings, etc. were intermingled in the massive pile." The *Banner* lamented: "He was friendly and well-liked and continuously getting around despite his obviously failing health, His conversation revealed him to be quite well versed on certain subjects. He was widely known."

SAMUEL "SAM" FRANK

According to the 1900 United States Federal Census, Samuel "Sam" Frank, a tailor in Baton Rouge and New Roads, Louisiana, was born ca. January 1859, in Ohio, to Abraham Frank and his wife, Barbara Silbernagel. Abe, a native of Speyer, Rheinpfalz, Germany, and Barbara, born at Belheim, Rheinpfalz, Germany, had been married on 20 December 1853, at Cincinnati, Hamilton Co., Ohio, by Justice of the Peace, W. Chidsey. Four of their eight children were born in Ohio: Louis (b. 1856), Samuel (b. 1859), Carrie (b. 1864), and Matilda "Tillie" (b. 1867). Sophie was born ca. 1869 at Baton Rouge, Louisiana, where the family had relocated after the Civil War. The "Frank" name was a familiar one in area dry goods, clothing and furniture retailing, tailoring and dressmaking.

According to the 1880 United States Federal Census, the Franks were living on Main Street in Baton Rouge. Abraham Frank operated as "A. Frank" at 510 Main Street His son, Louis Frank, tended to the "Louis Frank & Co., Furniture Business," next door at No. 512, in the Andrew Jackson Building. Two of their children Samuel, age 21, was a tailor, and Carrie, age 16, worked as a dressmaker. Their daughter Matilda "Tillie" Frank married Abraham F. Goldman, a resident of Cincinnati, Hamilton Co., Ohio, born ca. 1863 in the Russian Empire, on 31 July 1886, at Covington, Kenton Co., Kentucky.

The "A. Frank" partnership was dissolved in 1892, with Abraham assuming all debts. Abraham discontinued his dry goods and clothing business in 1893. Father and son subsequently formed a new partnership, "A. Frank & Co.," operating at the corner of Main and St. Hypolite (later Sixth) Streets, but this, too, was dissolved, in 1897, with Abraham assuming all debts payable and receivable.

In 1893, Abraham Goldman, husband of "Tillie" Frank Goldman, established the "Ferry Row Dry Goods Store" at the corner of Main and Front Streets, opposite the Baton Rouge-Port Allen ferry landing, retailing dry goods, clothing, hats, boots and shoes. His father-in-law, Abraham Frank, purchased Goldman's inventory at a sheriff's sale in 1895. The business continued to be operated with Goldman as agent, and later in the year Goldman added a saloon next door. In 1896, he moved the inventory and consolidated with Abraham and Louis Frank in "A. Frank & Co.," at Main and St. Hypolite (later Sixth), next to "A. Frank's furniture house."

Abe's son Samuel Frank was married on 15 July 1890, in New Orleans, Louisiana to Sophie Mettler. The bride was born on 18 October 1869, at Baton Rouge to Martin Mettler, a native of Prussia, and his wife, Josephine Koehler, who had been married at Baton Rouge on 23 April 1867, at St. Joseph's Church (SJBR-19, 55). The bride's paternal grandparents were Martin Mettler and Margaret Krisier, Her maternal grandparents were Philip Koehler and Sophia Hanken, both natives of Germany, Sophie had been baptized as Anna Sophy Mettlar at St. Joseph Church on 22 November 1869 (SJBR-20, 19).

According to the 1900 United States Federal Census, Samuel, Sophie and their two daughters, Myrtle (b. 1892) and Sadie (b. 1896), were enumerated at 411 Lafayette Street in Baton Rouge. Samuel was employed as a tailor. While Myrtle Edna was baptized on 11 May 1892 at St. Joseph of Baton Rouge, there is no record for a baptism for Sadie. Myrtle's baptismal record had also indicated that her father Sam Frank was a "Jew" (SJBR-20, 318).

Several years later, Samuel Frank and his family moved to New Roads, Louisiana, where he operated the "New Roads Steam Cleaning & Dye Works" from 1907 through 1911, at 134 East Main Street, between Mayer Cahen's "New Roads Fancy Grocery" and Lena Cohn Demouy Betz's "City Saloon." Various *Pointe Coupée Banner* advertisements indicate that Sam Frank performed many services such as tailoring, clothes cleaning and dying, parasol and umbrella mending, and shoe repairing.

By the summer of 1911, Sam Frank had ceased operations in New Roads. The 30 September issue of the *Pointe Coupée Banner* announced that Mrs. Lucretia Burr Way McManus, the sister of A. Boatner Way and Blanche Way LeCoq, former manager of millinery, trimmings and notions in the Brooklyn Mercantile Co., formerly Kassel & Stern's "The Leader" store across the street, had opened her own millinery store, "The Elite," in Frank's former location.

Samuel Frank ultimately moved back to Cincinnati, Hamilton Co., Ohio, where, a widower, he was enumerated living there in a boarding house according to the 1920 United States Federal Census. He died in Cincinnati on 22 July 1929, and was buried there in Judah Touro Cemetery. His wife had died on 20 August 1912 in New Orleans, and was interred in St. Joseph's Catholic Cemetery.

A. KOENIG, "THE NATIONAL UMBRELLA MAN"

Alexander "Alex" Koenig, known to many simply as "the umbrella man" in early 20th century Baton Rouge and New Roads, was born in 1863 in Galicia, Austrian Empire, and married to Golda "Goldie" Werner, also born in 1863 in Galicia. They lived initially in New Orleans, where Alexander was listed as a clerk, residing at 86 Bienville Street, according to the 1886 *New Orleans City Directory*. He was again found in the 1910-1916 *New Orleans City Directory* editions, and the Baton Rouge City Directory in 1918. He reappeared in New Orleans again in 1919, and finally in Baton Rouge's from 1922 through 1931. Alex, his wife, Golda, and children, Joseph (*sic*, Judah Touro intended) and Dora Koenig, were enumerated in the 1910 United States Federal Census living on Louisiana Avenue in New Orleans. Alex was employed as a general merchant. Alex and Golda were enumerated in in Baton Rouge in both the 1920 and 1930 United States Federal Censuses, where he was employed as an umbrella maker and mender.

During his career in umbrellas, Alex Koenig worked out of Frank Sanchez's tailoring and cleaning location on Main Street in downtown Baton Rouge. Koenig's obituary in the Baton Rouge *State Times-Advocate* identified him as likewise plying his trade in surrounding communities. In New Roads, he set up shop in the landmark Lake View Hotel, owned and operated by Mr. and Mrs. Emile Duvernet in the former Grand Store - American Legion of Honor building at 113 West Main Street, which was destroyed by Hurricane Betsy in 1965. Advertising in the 22 February 1919 issue of the *Pointe Coupée Banner* as "A, Koenig, The National Umbrella Man," Alex informed its readers that his creations were made in high grade silks and linens, and that "Many friends in New Roads will guarantee Koenig's Work... Phone Lake View Hotel."

It is probable that Golda Werner Koenig was the "Mrs. Koenig" of Koenig & Brown millinery, which operated briefly in the downtown New Roads' Demouy Building, previously occupied by John Boudreau's dry goods and clothing store, next by Harry Demouy's pharmacy and general store, and later by Mayer Cahen's "New Roads Fancy Grocery." Koenig & Brown opened in April of 1889, the "Brown" being Miss Susan Brown, formerly of Catahoula Parish, Louisiana, who was the universal legatee in 1888 of dry goods and grocery merchant Charles Meixner. The last-named had operated in the former "White Store" of Aaron Schulsinger and William Zadik just west of New Roads. The 15 June 1889 *Pointe Coupée Banner* related that Miss Brown had recently bought out the interest of "the Koenigs" in the millinery store.

Pointe Coupée Banner dated April 27, 1889.

Golda Koenig died on 2 July 1933, at Baton Rouge. Alex followed on 17 October 1933. He succumbed at the local hospital to injuries he received after having driven off the road three nights previously while in route to Thibodaux, Lafourche Parish, Louisiana. Golda and Alex Koenig were buried together in the Baton Rouge Jewish Cemetery. The 19 October 1933 Baton Rouge *State-Times* wrote of the popular Alex Koenig: "He was a student of the Bible, and was able to repeat from memory many chapters of the Old Testament."

LEON JOSEPH

Léon Joseph was born on 28 January 1889, at Edgard, St. John the Baptist Parish, Louisiana, to Joseph Joseph, aka Joseph Jules Joseph, a native of Grosbliederstroff, Moselle, France, born there on 20 November 1855, to Isaac Joseph and his wife Zippert/Caroline Gottschott/Godchaux. Léon's mother, Bertha Feitel, a native of Eich, Rhinefalz, Germany, born there on 18 August 1851, to Daniel Feitel and Henrietta Mandler, had first been married to Moise Joseph, Joseph Jules Joseph's brother, who, born at Grosbliederstroff, Moselle on 24 April 1840, had died at Edgard on 12 February 1876.

Joseph Jules Joseph was a retail merchant at Edgard, St. John the Baptist Parish, and served as Postmaster of the community between 1891 and 1903. His daughter Beatrice Joseph, who married Pierre Rene Jacob, was Postmaster between 1914 and 1943. His brothers, Cleve and Leon Joseph, appeared in the 1910 United States Federal Census in White Castle, Iberville Parish, Louisiana, living with a half-sister, Djella Joseph Levy (b. 1873), and her family. Djella's husband, Simon Levy, and Cleve Joseph were proprietors of the large Levy & Joseph department store, where Leon Joseph was employed as a dry goods salesman. The store may have been in the block which burned in the early- to mid-1970s, which was replaced by a bank.

Leon Joseph married Louise Garrot on 27 January 1916, at Marksville, Avoyelles Parish, Louisiana. Louise had been born on 5 November 1889, to Leon Garrot, a merchant, and Marceline Florence Barbin, both natives of Avoyelles Parish. According to his World War I Draft Registration in 1917, Leon Joseph had left the White Castle store to work as a salesman at Gus Weill & Son.

Leon became an agent for New York Life Insurance Company. He, Louise and their first two children, Agnes Miriam Joyce (b. 1916), and Dorothy Ruth (b. 1917), settled in New Roads, Louisiana in 1919, where their third child, Barbara Ann, was born that September. April issues of the *Pointe Coupée Banner* that year indicated that the family was living temporarily at (Quinn's) City Hotel before moving into the Walter Bennett residence on nearby North Carolina Avenue. Immediately accepted into the community, Louise was recorded in the 28 June 1919 *Banner* as having hosted a gathering of the Matrons' Social Club: "Mrs. Joseph is quite an acquisition to the club and to society, being a charming hostess and of a pleasing personality."

In an advertisement that ran in the 20 December 1919 *Banner*, readers were advised to: "Let The New York Life Worry For You. $995,087,285 assets to back their contracts. Leon Joseph, Special Agent, Phone No. 18, New Roads, La." Two more children were born to the couple at New Roads, Leon Jules (b. 1920), and Gordon Louis (b. 1921).

The Joseph residence figured in the spectacular conflagration resulting in the destruction of the *Pointe Coupée Banner* office and plant at 2 p.m. on 15 January 1921. Located immediately south of and at the corner of East Main Street and North Carolina Avenue, the *Banner* was housed in a large, frame building, formerly the E.C. Lalande general store, and owned by Herbert Harrell. Ironically, the *Banner*'s proprietor, Conrad J. LeCoq, was Assistant Fire Marshal for the State of Louisiana and a longtime New Roads firefighter.

In a memorable oral history session in 1988, octogenarian cousins Murray G. LeBeau and Alton Gaudin discussed the April 1907 Sanborn Fire Insurance Map of New Roads, and when examining the corner of East Main and North Carolina, LeBeau stated:

> I was impressed in checking this map to see at North Carolina Avenue a printing and photography company. Behind there, looks like to me, 50 gallons of gas. That was the old *Banner* office, a big yellow store at the corner. In 1921, it was about 2 o'clock, 2:30 in the evening [sic, afternoon] when they started to print the paper. It must have been operated by gasoline or a motor. They whole thing caught on fire. [...]
> I was in town, playing with Alton's cousins, the Smith boys, at that time. All the old copies of the *Banner* and other old [news]papers were stored in that building. We didn't get closer than about a block and a half, but we could feel the heat. Across the street from there, on the riverbank, was an old fire house [Bouanchaud's Brigade No. 2].

On the evening of the fire, it was reported that firefighters had to combat flames on three sides of the *Banner* plant, flames leaping "several times" onto the residences of District Attorney Jacob H. Morrison (father of future New Orleans Mayor deLesseps S. "Chep" Morrison) to the west, Leon Joseph's to the north, and New Roads Mayor Joseph Lejeune's to the east, on the eastern, opposite corner of East Main and North Carolina. Fortunately, the three homes were saved, although the *Banner* was lost, several utility poles burned, and a portion of the town was without electricity. Both the Joseph and Lejeune homes have survived into 2022, the latter beautifully restored.

Archival issues of the *Pointe Coupée Banner* exist from a number of local attorneys who contributed their copies in order to compile as compete a set as possible, starting in 1881, which were made available to the public in a digital, online format by the Pointe Coupée Parish Library, Historic Materials Collection, in the early 21st century.

The Joseph family moved to Uptown New Orleans before the 1930 United States Federal Census where Leon was enumerated as a commercial traveler for an automobile tire factory. By 1940, he was working as a meat inspector for the City Board of Health. He died in New Orleans on 29 March 1967, and was buried there in Metairie Cemetery. There is no known record for Louise's death. However, under the heading of "Values of Estates and Inventories," published in the 23 December 1976 edition of the New Orleans *Times Picayune*, it was reported that Mrs. Louise Garrot Joseph left an estate worth $47,235.63.

CHAPTER 4
NEW ROADS BRANCH AND CHAIN STORES

GROSSMAN-WEINFELD

1917 Photo of Grossman-Weinfeld Millinery Accounting Office in New Orleans

The Grossman-Weinfeld Millinery Co., Ltd., a wholesale and retail firm founded in 1904 and headquartered in New Orleans, operated a branch store in the former New Roads Drug Store located at 155 East Main Street in 1911. Advertising as "The Largest Exclusive Millinery House in the South," the company was founded in 1904 by brothers Adolph Grossman, president, Isidore Grossman, vice president and buyer, and brother-in-law Alexander Weinfeld, secretary-treasurer, husband of their sister, Celina Grossman.

The Grossmans were children of merchant and planter Jacob Grossman, and his wife, Lena Salomon, born respectively in Lautenberg and Strassburg, Poland, Prussian Empire. Alexander Weinfeld had been born on 23 November 1871, in Wisconsin, to Appleton, Outagamie Co., Wisconsin, cattle and grain dealer Jacob Weinfeld and his wife Barbetta "Bertha" Pick, both natives of the Austrian Empire. Alexander Weinfeld was married to Celina Grossman in New Orleans on 8 July 1900.

A notice in the 10 April 1919 New Orleans *Times-Picayune* related that, effective on 8 April, 1919, Weinfeld had sold his interest in the millinery company to Adolph and Isidore Grossman. The company was re-chartered shortly thereafter, according to May and June 1919 notices in the suburban Algiers *Herald* newspaper.

Exactly when Grossman-Weinfeld or its successor corporation shuttered its New Roads store is uncertain. In 1921, the former millinery store was joined to the building to the west (i.e., the former location of Isidore Wolff, "The Fancy Grocer"), by Giovanni "John" Rosso, and the combined structure survives in the 21st century. A succession of firms occupied the former Grossman-Weinfeld Millinery location, including The Style Shoppe, fine women's apparel (second location), which was in business there from 1943 until 1958.

AMERICAN DEPARTMENT STORES

The American Department Store, New Roads, Louisiana, owned by the Singerman family of New Orleans, was one of a chain of regional junior department stores. Founder Jacob "Jake" Singerman, was born on 17 July 1873, in Poland, Russian Empire, to Herman A. Singerman and Sarah Bzurovski. According to his 1924 New Orleans naturalization record, he arrived in New York from Russia on 27 December 1904. He was married on 15 March 1908, at New Orleans, to Frieda Miller, born on 26 December 1884, in Poland, Austrian Empire, to Gatzel Miller and Rifke Klinger.

Singerman was enumerated with his wife, Frieda and son, Gustave (b. 1908), in the 1910 United States Federal Census employed as the proprietor of a tailor shop in New Orleans. Ten years later Singerman was enumerated as a manufacturer of umbrellas. Two more sons were born to the couple in the 1920s: Herman (b. 1920), and Charles (b. 1924).

Singerman's industriousness reaped its rewards. According to the 8 April 1926 edition of the New Orleans *Times Picayune,* he opened the first of a chain of one-hundred-plus American Department Stores carrying dependable merchandise at popular prices. Operating under the corporation of J. Singerman, Inc., the company motto was "We Sell as We Advertise, Always for Less," and its icon was the American Eagle. Its corporate offices were located at 209 Decatur Street, in the historic *Vieux Carré*, until moving in 1956 to larger quarters at 714 Girod Street.

One of the first branches of the American Department Store opened for business in 1930 at New Roads, in the landmark, two-story, brick 1850s-era Graugnard-Richy Building at 124 West Main Street, famed for its elaborate upper gallery ironwork. A fire caused by a defect in the building's heating apparatus three days after Christmas in 1934 resulted in thousands of dollars of damage to merchandise.

The store relocated to a newly-completed brick building, relatively narrow but deep, situated diagonally across the street at 211 West Main Street in the following year. It was familiarly, and fondly known to generations of shoppers simply as "The Chain Store." "American" offered frequent sales, and ranked third in volume and gross profits, surpassed only by locally-owned "Morgan's," founded as "The Famous" store in 1900, and the Louisiana chain of Weill's department stores.

"American," moved from downtown to a 6,000-square-foot store in New Roads Shopping Center, in the 600 block of Olinde Street in 1969. In 1972, the American Department Store, Inc. of New Roads, represented by Gustave "Gus" Singerman, Jacob's son, was among the company's branches sold to C.R. Anthony Co., the latter of which operated more than 300 stores in the nation.

Pointe Coupée Banner advertisements and company circulars for the American Department Store, New Roads, Louisiana, over the course of forty years, from 1930 through 1972, featured: men's, women's and children's dress, casual and sports clothing, denim wear, men's work clothing, swimwear, sleepwear, lingerie, foundations, underwear, neckwear, socks, hosiery, handkerchiefs, scarves, kerchiefs, men's dress and straw hats, millinery, shoes, boots and slippers; handbags, small leather goods, watches, fashion jewelry, umbrellas, luggage, school and sports satchels, piece goods (formerly termed dry goods), sewing notions, fashion patterns, table, bed and bath linens, pillows, drapery, curtains, rugs, and infant cribs.

As "Anthony's Department Store," the business continued until closing in 1984, during a period of contracting markets nationwide and a locally stressed economy. Another chain, Allied Department Store, occupied American and Anthony's former location for a few years beginning in 1985.

New Roads' original "American Department Store" location in the Graugnard-Richy Building was occupied by a succession of businesses and is currently home to "MaMama's Kitchen fine dining." The second American location, diagonally across West Main Street, likewise has housed various enterprises, including the Beauregard Square shopping center, and in is remodeled form, the municipality's City Hall.

Gus Singerman was the chief defendant in the civil suit of Harry Katz, et. al. vs Gus Singerman, et. al. (No. 45311), in which the Louisiana Supreme Court reversed the judgment appealed from, rescinded an injunction, and dismissed the plaintiffs' suit regarding a vote favoring mixed or family seating in New Orleans' Chevra Thilim Jewish Congregation.

Jacob Singerman's brother, Max, who was enumerated with Jacob, Frieda, and Gus in the 1910 United States Federal Census as a twenty-eight-year-old banana salesman, founded the "Acme Bargain Store" chain, with branches in New Orleans, Gretna, Slidell, Covington and Lutcher, Louisiana, and one location in Mississippi (*New Orleans States* 2 April 1946). Jacob Singerman died in New Orleans on 19 March 1950 and was interred there in the Gates of Prayer Cemetery. Frieda followed on 4 April 1972 and was interred with him.

WEILL'S DEPARTMENT STORES

Weill's Department Store, New Roads, Louisiana, was one of a chain of junior department stores operating in several Louisiana cities and towns during the 20th century. The company had its origins in a general store established in 1892 in White Castle, Iberville Parish, Louisiana, by Gustave "Gus Weill." Gustave Weill was born Godchaux Weill on 20 November 1864, at Schirrhoffen, Bas-Rhin, France, to Joseph Weill, a native of the town and his wife, Sara Samuel, born in nearby Trimbach, Bas-Rhin. He arrived in New York on 3 November 1882, aboard the *SS France* from Le Havre.

Although he started out his career in retailing in St. James Parish, he relocated to Donaldsonville, Ascension Parish, and then finally to White Castle, Iberville Parish, where he operated dry goods stores in both locations. He married Hermina Weil in New Orleans on 10 December 1890. Hermina, born on 8 January 1871, in Grünstadt, Prussian Empire (Germany), was the daughter of Isaac Weil and his wife, Sarah Loeb. Gus and Hermina were the parents of four children: Ray (b. 1892), Julius (b. 20 August 1893), Bernice (b. 1898), and Lester Isaac (b. 1899). Their daughter Bernice married another Weill from Schirrhoffen: Leopold Weill, born there on 24 June 1885, to Charles Weill and Emilie Kahn. Bernice and Leopold were the parents of Livonia and New Roads educator, entrepreneur and humanitarian Ray Sarah Weill (Mrs. Simon) Weil.

In 1935, Julius Weill partnered with his brother-in-law Leonard Levy and Philip Barbier, both of White Castle, to form Weill's Wholesale Dry Goods Co. (renamed Bart-Well, Inc. in 1941). The partnership opened its first two stores in 1936, in New Roads and Donaldsonville, Louisiana. The New Roads store opened in the newly-completed, two-story, brick Gosserand Building, located at 116 West Main Street, which stood on the site of The Imperial Department Store/(original) Alamo Theatre that had burned in the previous year. In 1952, Weill's was the first department store in Pointe Coupée Parish to be air-conditioned.

Weill's Department Store, New Roads, 1960. To the left, Graugnard-Richy Building, first home of American Department Store, followed by Western Auto.

When the first strip retail complex in Pointe Coupée Parish, the New Roads Shopping Center, opened in the 600 block of Olinde Street in 1963, Weill's transferred its operations there, benefitting from increased accessibility and abundant off-street parking.

Although Weill's stores in Baton Rouge (three simultaneous locations), Lafayette and Abbeville closed during the 1950s-1960s, the Bart-Well corporation maintained 13 branches for the remainder of its history. There were stores branded Weill's in: White Castle, New Roads, Donaldsonville, Plaquemine, Bunkie, Eunice, Rayne, Jeanerette, Jennings, LaPlace, Grammercy, Thibodaux, and Raymond's Department Store in Ferriday. Weill's motto through the years progressed from "Price Brings You In. Quality Brings You Back," to "Since 1892, Your Friendly Department Store," to "Where Fashion is Value."

Surpassed in volume and popularity only by locally-owned Morgan's Department Store, founded as "The Famous Store" in 1900, and which continued to operate downtown until closing in 1994, the Weill's in New Roads drew a clientele from throughout Pointe Coupée and neighboring Iberville, West Baton Rouge, West Feliciana Parishes, owing to the quality of its merchandise, its adaptation to current fashion, and frequent sales. In the mid-20th century, Weill's lines included nationally-recognized Curlee suits, Van Heusen dress and sports shirts, Campus sports shirts and Jarman shoes for men; Gay Gibson, Martha Manning, Vicky Vaughn and Toni Todd dresses for women; girls' Kate Greenway dresses; and children's Red Goose and Buster Brown shoes.

Between 1936 and 1988 *Pointe Coupée Banner* advertisements and company circulars for Weill's Department Store, New Roads, Louisiana, featured: men's, women's and children's dress, casual and sports clothing, denim wear, men's work clothing, swimwear, sleepwear, lingerie, foundations, underwear, neckwear, socks, hosiery, handkerchiefs, scarves, kerchiefs, men's dress and straw hats, millinery, shoes, boots and slippers, handbags, small leather goods, fashion jewelry, umbrellas, perfume, toiletries, luggage, piece goods, sewing notions, fashion patterns, table, bed and bath linens, pillows, drapery, curtains, rugs, lamps, crystal, glassware, cookware, cocktail shakers, small appliances, radios, electric clocks, pictures, ceramics, tie racks, clothes brushes, books, playing cards, poker chips, and toys.

Changing shopping habits by its customers favoring Baton Rouge, Lafayette, New Orleans and other markets, and an economic downturn affecting most of Louisiana in the 1980s resulted in the closing of the Weill's and Raymond stores.

The popularity of the Weill Department stores outlived both its founder and his son Julius Weill. Gus Weill died on 22 November 1925, in New Orleans. His remains were transferred to Donaldsonville, Ascension Parish, where he was interred in the Bikur Sholim Cemetery there. Hermina Weill joined him upon her death on 18 November 1933. They lie next to their son Lester Isaac, who had died on 30 December 1918.

Julius Weill died on 14 March 1956, in Baton Rouge, East Baton Rouge Parish, and was interred there in the Jewish Cemetery. His wife, the former Doris Amelia Levy, a native of Napoleonville, Assumption Parish, born there on 8 August 1900, to Morris Levy and his wife Rosa Kahn, died at Baton Rouge on 19 January 1976, and was interred with her husband.

VEE'S 5 & 10 CENT STORES

Vee's 5 and 10 Cent Store, a South Louisiana chain founded by and named for brothers Vernon, Ellis, and Eldridge Schwartzenburg of Opelousas, St. Landry Parish, opened its first New Roads location in 1942. Although the Schwartzenburg family, whose patriarch, John Schwartzenburg, a native of Switzerland, and his German-born wife, Margarethe Schneider were not Jewish, the last of their ten children, George Washington Xavier Schwartzenburg, born in Pineville, Rapides Parish, Louisiana ca. February 1860, married Rebecca Frank on 9 February 1881, at St. Paul the Apostle Catholic Church in Mansura, Avoyelles Parish, Louisiana.

Rebecca Frank was the daughter of Adolph Frank, born Jewish as Aron Frank, on 30 October 1809, in Nordstetten, Kingdom of Württemberg, (Germany), to Abraham Frank and his wife Madele Fortlouis, a native of Karlsruhe, Baden-Wurttemberg, Germany. Adolph/Aron Frank had married Caroline Gaspard, the daughter of Jean-Baptiste Gaspard, and his wife, Marie Anne Garcellier, in a Catholic ceremony at St. Paul the Apostle Church on 29 March 1842. All of their children were raised as Catholics.

George Washington Xavier Schwartzenburg and his wife Rebecca Frank had seven children, including their eldest, Ivy Schwartzenburg (b. 9 December 1882, in Marksville, Avoyelles Parish), who married Octavie Gosselin. This latter couple lived in Opelousas, St. Landry Parish, Louisiana. Three of their six children, sons Ellis (b. 6 July 1914), Vernon (b. 1916), and Eldridge John (b. 11 July 1918) were the founders of Vee's.

Ellis, Vernon, and Eldridge Schwartzenburg were also related through their great-grandfather Adolph Frank's mother, Madele Fortlouis, to one of the earliest Jewish settlers in Avoyelles and Pointe Coupée Parish, Jean Maurice Fortlouis.

Commencing operations in the Gold Drop Bakery & Mercantile building on the site of 115-117 West Main Street, Vee's was the second five-and-ten to open in Pointe Coupée Parish, preceded by locally-owned Whitney's 5 and 10 Cent Store. Whitney Lejeune, proprietor, had opened it in his and his father Joseph Lejeune's landmark New Roads Hardware building, diagonally across the street at 102 West Main in 1939.

In 1956, Vee's moved one door west, to the brick, air-conditioned Vincent Rosso Building at 119 West Main Street. When Weill's Department Store, across the street at 116 West Main, moved to New Roads Shopping Center in 1963, Vee's transferred into Weill's former location.

With the motto "You're Always Welcome," Vee's was a retail favorite for countless South Louisianans. The chain numbered 14 stores in 1971, with locations in Abbeville, Arnaudville, Breaux Bridge, Erath, Eunice (West Gate Shopping Center), Jeanerette, Kaplan, Lake Arthur, Lecompte, Marksville, New Roads, St. Francisville, St. Martinville, and Welsh. A downtown Opelousas, St. Landry Parish branch had burned in 1956.

The 26 September 1963 edition of the *Pointe Coupée Banner* carried the advertisement for "Vee's 5 and 10 Cent Store" grand opening in its new location at 116 West Main Street, formerly Weill's Department Store, which featured: men's and boys' underwear, women's lingerie, Buster Brown brand boys' and girls' clothing, babies' wear, handkerchiefs, piece good remnants, notions, kitchen and bath towels, chinaware, glassware, pots, pans, trays, ironing boards, greeting cards, stationery, school supplies, hair nets and rollers, toothbrushes, pictures and frames, party favors, holiday decorations [including ornaments, lights and artificial Christmas trees in season], artificial flowers and wreaths, dolls, toys, wheeled goods, candy.

With the opening of larger, volume-oriented discount stores in the 1970s, Vee's shifted its emphasis from small items to popular-priced women's, misses' and children's apparel, the latter including the Garanimals brand. The chain, began to shutter its stores, however, and the New Roads store, "Vee's 5 & 10 No.1" in the company, closed on 10 June 1978.

The 8 June 1978 *Pointe Coupée Banner* advertisement for Vee's 5 & 10 Store, New Roads, closing-out sale advertised jewelry, ladies' and girls' panties, bras, panty hose, children's clothing, curtains, lace and trim, ribbon, buttons, zippers, sewing, knitting and crocheting thread, sewing books, Magnolite pots, lamps, greeting cards, candy, for sale.

A succession of locally-owned businesses occupied the location, including the Al-An's Fashions, Ltd., and 2 Sisters' women's apparel stores. In the 21st century, it became the office of the City of New Roads' tourist information center.

Ellis Schwartzenburg died at Opelousas on 7 September 1982. Eldridge followed on 5 December 1991, and Vernon, on 13 April 1993. The brothers and their wives are interred in the Holy Sepulchre Mausoleum in Opelousas, St. Landry Parish.

CHAPTER 5

FALSE RIVER ROAD AND OSCAR CROSSING

Ever so many times we passed buggies and other chariots, laden with the hob-nailed trunks of drummers. There are thirty stores between New Roads and Hermitage, so no wonder the drummers are so thick on the road. ("Catharine Cole's Letter," *Daily Picayune*, New Orleans, Louisiana, 22 Nov 1891.)

Martha R. Field, aka Catharine Cole, was not exaggerating. Between the end of the Civil War and the close of the 19th century, the number of commercial establishments along the outer arc of False River proper and the Lower Chenal of False River had mushroomed from a few, widely spaced, small operations to more than two dozen mercantile houses stocked with a variety of goods. Some were affiliated with the great sugar and cotton plantations for which False River was famous, although others were independent enterprises.

Some businesses along the "Old Horseshoe" of the oxbow lake were conducted by scions of colonial French families or later arrivals from France, and the German and Italian states, however, the majority, particularly on the Lower Chenal, were the enterprises of Jewish men and women who immigrated to the area in increasing numbers beginning in the late antebellum era.

AARON LOEB

Among the earliest Jewish merchants to open on the banks of False River was Neustadt, Rheinpfalz, Germany native Aaron Loeb. Previously a member of the firm of Simon, Loeb & Co. in downtown New Roads, he was later its sole proprietor on the Lower Chenal and Raccourci-Old River.

Virginie Trahan, the widow of Charles Parlange, owner of the Parlange sugar plantation on the banks of the False River about five miles below New Roads, was enumerated with her eighteen-year-old son, Charles, Jr., in the 1870 United States Federal Census. According to this record, the plantation was worth $6,000. Charles, a future Louisiana Supreme Court Justice, was working as a retail dealer with $500 in assets. Assisting him in his commercial enterprise, was twenty-three-year-old Sévérin Labry, his clerk.

Three years later, in 1873, Virginie Trahan Parlange leased the store and the eighty-four-foot broad riverbank lot upon which it stood to Aaron Loeb. The term was for five years at $400 a year, the price of which itself was evidence of its considerable size and location. It is likely that the Parlange, later Loeb, store was near if not in the building which is now the Pointe Coupée Parish Museum and Tourist Center. This old structure is remarkable for the rare *piece-sur-piece* construction in its original, ca. 1800 section, similar to log structures but employing vertically set cypress planks, notched and dovetailed at the corners. The small, barred window on the front gallery has led some to hypothesize, without any documentation, that the building served as a place of confinement for "unruly slaves" or for a certain "demented" young lady.

The most plausible speculation is that it served for many years as a "store house," and that the open, yet barred window allowed for the safe-guarding as well as the ventilation of perishable goods. Nearby Parlange and North Bend plantation homes have barred windows as well, attesting to the "pioneer" nature of early 19th century Pointe Coupée Parish and the need for protection.

In 2007, Southeast Louisiana archaeologist Dr. Rob Mann and Louisiana State University archaeology students uncovered shards of Old Town Red, var. Rapides or Chicot Red, var. Grand Village, pottery on the upriver or north side of the Pointe Coupée Museum. Dr. Mann speculated that the site might have been an early French - Native American trading area, and that the French residents retained the pottery for other uses after the original purposes (e.g., holding bear grease) were completed.

According to the oral history of some families living on both banks of False River, including the LeBeaus and Bergerons, "the last Indians" in the area lived in the wooded "Interior" of the Island of False River, opposite Parlange. They would come out periodically to trade hand-crafted baskets for farm-raised eggs. These Native Americans reputedly continued to speak their own language, but did employ the French word *panier* (basket) when making transactions, according to the late Marie LeBeau Major. When the floods of 1882 and 1884 submerged the Island of False River, the Native Americans are believed to have moved to the highlands of nearby Mississippi, as recalled by Mrs. Major's cousin, Murray LeBeau. It is possible that the Native Americans referred to were remnants of the Tensas nation. Louis Tensas and his family lived first on the west bank, on the Charles Gremillion, later Thomas Hewes plantation, now known as Pleasant View, and subsequently on the Island of False River. His descendants, the Robert family, continue to reside in Pointe Coupée Parish and its environs.

Contemporaneous with the building of the original portion of the present Pointe Coupée Museum structure, about 1800, Bordeaux native Jacques Jarreau operated what was likely the first store established downriver of the False River branch operation of Julien Poydras. Jarreau's store was located across the road from the Museum, while the Poydras business, established in the late 18th century, was at the present intersection of False River Drive and Major Parkway in New Roads.

As a retail dealer and buyer of cotton on the Ternant-Parlange plantation, Aaron Loeb was thus one in a long line of businessmen engaged in commercial activity with Pointe Coupéeans and travelers of various ethnicities.

ISAAC KEIM

Amidst his several moves and ventures in postbellum Pointe Coupée Parish, Louisiana, Isaac Keim leased for cultivation one of the historic properties of the area, the Fabre-Britto plantation on False River, about five miles below downtown New Roads. Said to be of Cuban birth, merchant Manuel Britto was married to landowner Madeleine Fabre Both were "free people of color." Manuel operated a general store in the brick "basement" or ground floor of the Fabre residence, located close to False River Road, during the antebellum years. Although free people of color were forbidden by Parish ordinance to sell alcoholic beverages, wines and whiskies, those beverages made up a substantial part of Britto's stock according to some 1850s inventories.

Another room of the house served for about 70 years as a private school for children of color. Ribbes Léonardet, a native of France, was the resident professor at the time of the 1860 and 1870 United States Federal Census enumerations.

"Britto," a Sephardic Jewish surname originating in Portugal, is rare for Louisiana. It has led to speculation that Manuel Britto, a free man of color living in False River, was a descendant of the early Jewish settler Manuel Britto, who came to Louisiana in the 1760s with his trading partners the Monsanto brothers and Isaac Fastio. While Fastio lived for years in Pointe Coupée Parish, no trace remains of Manuel Britto, no letter, no invoice, no legal paper containing his name in the parish to suggest that he was ever a resident anywhere but in New Orleans. Since the Monsantos, Fastio and Britto, formerly residents of the Netherlands, had also spent time plying their trading vessels in the waters of the Dutch Caribbean (Aruba, Bonaire and Curaçao), as well as Cuba and Saint-Domingue (Haïti), before settling in Louisiana, it is possible, but cannot now be proven, that Madeleine Fabre's husband, Manuel Britto, was born on one of the Caribbean islands to a woman of color and to the Jewish Manuel Britto, or one of his descendants in Cuba.

Isaac Keim's lease of the plantation from Madeleine Fabre Britto, for a term of six years, commencing 1 January 1872, is illuminating as to its many terms. For the rate of $250 the first year, and $400 for each of the subsequent five years, Keim, was granted use of all but the front six arpents, demarcated by the False River and the *première bayou*," i.e., the first of the two channels across the place made by a bend of Bayou Corne au Chevreuil, the exception being the location of the Britto home and store, the latter then conducted by Alcée D. Landry as the "Bismark Store." Keim was allowed use of two cabins, a stable, a barn, and the cotton gin, with the right to install sugar-making apparatus in the latter should Keim cultivate sugar cane. Mme. Britto likewise granted him the right to cut firewood for use of sugar-making as well as for his kitchen, and gave him free passage by foot, horse, or cart for the "exploitation" of the leased property.

The contract also allowed Keim to "sub-rent" the property, subject to the agreement of Mme. Britto. It specified that in case of flooding of the leased land, which did occur owing to the Mississippi River levee crevasses of 1874, Keim's required payment would be reduced by one-half. Witnesses to the act were Manuel Britto, Professor Léonardet, and neighboring carpenter Alexis LeDuff.

Isaac Keim's lease of the Britto plantation was concluded at the end of 1877, and by 1880, he had moved on to Bayou Maringouin, in southernmost Pointe Coupée Parish.

BENJAMIN "BEN" GERSON

Benjamin "Ben" Gerson was born on 21 October 1812, in Oldenburg, Lower Saxony, Germany. He married Nancy Levy, a native of the Kingdom of Württemberg, Germany on 11 October 1847, in Memphis, Shelby Co., Tennessee. The couple moved to the Southern District of Carroll County, Mississippi, where Ben worked as a retail merchant, and where his wife gave birth to five of their seven children: George (b. 1848), Henry (b. 1849 - d. 1854), Josephine (b. 1853), Nathan (b. 1858), and Laura (b. 1861). Reuben (b. 1864 - d. 1878), and Julius (b. 1868) were born in New Orleans, Louisiana, where Ben Gerson, his wife and children settled towards the end of the Civil War. Gerson worked in the city as a cotton merchant.

Ben Gerson and his sons, George and Nathan, were active in Pointe Coupée Parish commerce and agriculture, particularly on False River and the Lower Chenal, in Waterloo, and on Raccourci-Old River. Benjamin and George operated as the firm of "Ben Gerson & Son" in Pointe Coupée and the city of New Orleans.

In 1881, Ben Gerson & Son purchased from Waterloo and False River merchant Édouard/Edward Thompson a 35' by 50' store building with attached warehouse located on the River Lake Plantation at the lower end of False River, owned by Mme. Arthur Denis, née Antoinette Decuir. The store stood on a little island, with the dual channels of the forked head of Bayou Stirling to either side. The workers on River Lake Plantation called the place "Sweet Island" because it was there that baptisms in False River were conducted by the ministers of Mt. Zion Baptist Church well into the 20th century. The tenants' "quarters" on River Lake was the birthplace and boyhood home of noted Pointe Coupée author Ernest J. Gaines

Édouard/Edward Thompson, who had opened a general store in the building in 1880, continued operations there until 1883, stocking a substantial line of dry goods, clothing, hats, shoes, musical instruments and supplies, and furniture, among other things.

Ben Gerson died in New Orleans on 12 August 1888, and was interred there in Hebrew Rest Cemetery No.1. Nancy Levy Gerson died in New Orleans on 20 January 1914, and was buried with her husband.

During the flood of 1890, the Denis Dyke, sealing the dual channels of the head of Bayou Stirling, collapsed from the pressure of the swollen False River in front of the Gerson store building. A remarkable photograph (see above) of the breach and the store was found in the

period photo album of Anna Lancaster Hewes Denis, sister of Thomas and Miguel Hewes of Pleasant View Plantation, who married Charles Denis, of River Lake. According to the *Pointe Coupée Banner*, the Denis Crevasse was one of the last breaches to be closed after the recession of floodwaters. (Note: Charles Denis was an owner of the building which was home to Abraham J. "Abe" Michel's establishment, the Michel Hotel, in New Orleans.)

Of several children born to Benjamin and Nancy Gerson, only the youngest, Julius married. He wed Bertha Livaudais in St. Bernard Parish, Louisiana on 13 July 1895. The others remained unmarried and lived with one another in New Orleans.

ISAAC BIGMAN

Isaac/Israël Bigman was born on 7 October 1862 at Kishinev, Bessarabia, Russian Empire, to Joseph Bigman, and his wife whose identity is yet to be ascertained. He immigrated ca. 1878 and settled in Chicago, Cook Co., Illinois, where he was naturalized on 3 November 1884. He came south to Pointe Coupée Parish, Louisiana, in 1886. Beginning in 1891, he began to buy and sell thousands of acres in the southern part of the parish, his earliest purchases including what became the Bayou Tommy Plantation at Oscar Crossing. He commenced the cultivation of cotton in 1894.

In 1893, Isaac Bigman opened a general store at the head of Bayou Lanquedoc (present-day Rougon aka Lighthouse Canal), in the community of Oscar, Louisiana. This location was near the demarcation line between the ecclesiastical parishes of St. Mary of False River and Immaculate Conception of Chenal. The gentle curve in False River Road there was referred to as "Wolff's Bend" for the downriver neighbor, farmer Joseph Wolff, a Catholic native of Ireland, not to be confused with the Jewish merchant Joseph Wolff of Livonia and Maringouin.

Isaac was enumerated as a thirty-eight-year-old unmarried immigrant from Romania working as a merchant in the 1900 United States Federal Census for Pointe Coupée Parish. He indicated that he was born in November 1862, had immigrated in 1878 and was naturalized. According to the *Pointe Coupée Banner*'s list of parish licenses for 1901, Isaac Bigman had had gross sales of $13,000 in 1900.

Isaac Bigman married Rosa Waldman on 22 July 1901, in Brooklyn, Kings Co., New York. Rosa Waldman was born on 3 January 1883, in Odessa, Ukraine, Russian Empire, to Daniel Waldman and Rachel Magot. According to Isaac Bigman's biography in *Beautiful Pointe Coupée and Its Prominent Citizens*, Rosa Bigman had immigrated to Louisiana "to become the bride of Mr. Bigman," which suggests a previous acquaintance in Europe between their families. Isaac and Rosa were the parents of five children: Lillian (b. 14 September 1902), Dennie/Dennis (b. 1 August 1904), Miriam Fannie (b. 9 November 1907), Joseph H. (b. 15 March 1909- d. 1919). Their last child, Clara Rosalie Bigman, was born on 12 December 1911.

In 1903, Bigman purchased the improved tract of land upon which his store and residence stood, at a sheriff's sale in the civil matter of Albert Chustz vs Paulin Pourciau, tutor, et. al., for $4,000 (21st Judicial District Court, No. 448). It was measured as one acre fronting on False River by a depth of 80 acres. This purchase brought Isaac Bigman's total holdings by 1906 to 1,300 acres, 800 being in cultivation. His store was one of the largest in the parish.

In 1910 the United States Federal census taker reported that Isaac, Rosa, his four children, and his wife's two siblings: Fannie and Joseph Waldman, both natives of Ukraine, Russian Empire, were living together in Pointe Coupée Parish, where Isaac was said to be a "farmer." Joseph Waldman was working as a clerk in Isaac's store.

During that time, Bigman was also owner in partnership with nearby landowner and attorney Thomas H. Hewes of Pleasant View Plantation as "Bigman & Hewes (cotton) Ginnery." The Bigman residence, store, and ginnery were all on the False River Telephone Line in 1908. When the New Orleans & San Francisco or "Frisco" Railroad built a branch line paralleling False River in 1910-11, a station designated "Major-Bigman" was established on a siding on the contiguous lands of Bigman and his upriver neighbor, planter, and merchant, Lubin Major.

In an era when commercial and residential fires were frequent owing to sparking fireplaces and chimneys and defective lighting and heating apparatuses, the Bigman family survived two conflagrations. The large and heavily-stocked Bigman store and all its merchandise were destroyed by 7 a.m. on 29 February 1912. According to reports in the 3 March *Pointe Coupée Banner*, the misfortune was presumed due to a defective flue.

The *New Orleans Item* carried a report on 18 March 1914 that Bigman's new store had been built, but a midnight fire consumed it. At that time, the family residence and all of its contents went up in flames as well. The $2,500 loss to his home and contents as well as the $2,000 loss of the store and contents were only partially covered by insurance.

Isaac Bigman's personality looms large in Pointe Coupée Parish records and oral history. In 1896, when Rev. Louis Savouré arrived at Arbroth Landing, West Baton Rouge Parish, on the Mississippi River to assume the pastorate of old Immaculate Conception Church at Chenal, he was famously met by "two Republicans:" Oscar Joffrion, a merchant, planter and Oscar Post Office namesake, who headed the Catholic contingent, and Isaac Bigman. The two locals are remembered to have seated the prelate, a decided Democrat, between them in a buggy and conveyed him to his presbytery at Chenal. According to oral history as well as a 17 June 1956 Baton Rouge *State-Times* feature article on Savouré, despite the prelate's party affiliation and strong opinions, and throughout his long tenure as president of the Pointe Coupée Parish Police Jury, the three became "fast friends,"

Isaac Bigman was likewise remembered for his pithy sense of political humor. Amidst reports of the horror of pogroms in the Russian Empire, the "Tobin's Tips" weekly column of items contributed by South Louisiana traveling salesmen to the *Daily Picayune* included in its 5 February 1906 installment: "Isaac Bigman, the well-known merchant of Oscar, says the Czar of Russia [Nicholas II] is a big lobster and he ought to be canned."

Isaac Bigman experienced a third fire, on 24 November 1918, which the following day's *New Orleans States* reported that a "double cottage" on Marengo Street in that city, rented by Isaac Bigman and Rufus W. Fontenot, suffered $3,000 in damages, including the occupants' furnishings valued at $300.

In the wake of the 1912 flood, Isaac Bigman divested himself of a majority of his Pointe Coupée properties, and he and his wife moved to New Orleans. He sold the False River tract where he had maintained a residence and store to farmer Sampère Achée for the price of $5,500 in 1919.

However, a 206.33-acre tract which he had bought on 13 November 1902 from Henry C. Gumbel, et.al. was still listed amongst his possessions according to his 1923 succession record.

Isaac Bigman died on 31 May 1923, in New Orleans, and was interred there in Gates of Prayer Cemetery. His widow, née Rosa Waldman, and their son Dennis/Dennie Bigman operated a dry goods and clothing store on the busy Magazine St. retail corridor in that city. A double-column advertisement in the 16 May 1926 issue of the *New Orleans States* highlighting retailers in the "Beautiful Jefferson Market Section of Magazine Street" included "Bigman's Quality Shop, Mrs. R.W. Bigman & Son, Proprietors," at 4234-36 Magazine. With the motto "Stop In And See Real Values!" mother and son advertised dry goods, notions, ladies', children's and men's furnishings, and millinery.

Within a few years, however, the firm was in bankruptcy. The *Times-Picayune* dated 28 August 1929 indicated that the R.W. Bigman and Son Dry Good Company had debts of $11,026.48, representing the store lease and open accounts in favor of jobbers, while the assets, principally merchandise, were valued at $3,202.69. Mrs. Bigman was shown to owe $26,478.48 on business obligations and property mortgages, with assets of $16,462.59. Son Dennis Bigman had liabilities of $11,276.48 and assets of $3,196.69. A majority of the creditors acquiesced to composition payments totaling 40% of the Bigman's debts, said payments to be guaranteed by Mrs. Bigman's brother Joseph W. Waldman.

Dennie Bigman died on 13 December 1935, at the age of 31 years and was interred in Gates of Prayer Cemetery. Rosa Waldman Bigman died in New Orleans on 31 December 1961. She was interred near her husband and two sons, Joseph and Dennie. Rosa's daughter, Lillian Bigman, was for 36 years associated with the upscale Goldring women's clothing chain in New Orleans. She was the vice-president and managing director of the Canal Street store at her death on 25 August 1962. Rosa Bigman's sisters, Bertha Waldman Nowak and Golda Waldman Gamburg and their spouses were also active in the mercantile history of Pointe Coupée Parish.

In the 1930s, the former Bigman residence tract on False River Road was acquired by New Orleans physician and author, Herman de Bachellé Seebold, upon which he built a Southern colonial-style country home with materials salvaged from dismantled Crescent City landmarks, including the Marigny and De LaChaise mansions. Subsequent owners included Henry P. Allendorph, of the Pitcher family of Alma Plantation at Lakeland, and for whom the house is most familiarly known as "Allendorph."

MR. BIGMAN'S HORSE TROUBLES

Considerable documentation survives regarding merchant and planter Isaac Bigman and his livestock, one being an unfortunate accident and another that culminated in a lengthy litigation. Isaac Bigman's Oscar farm, store, and residence lay within the Catholic parish of St. Mary of False River, whose pastor was the beloved Rev. Joseph Philibert Gutton from 1865 until his death in 1896. *"Père"* Gutton's demise was met with an outpouring of grief, and gratitude. Gutton was laid to rest in the burial ground he established, St. Mary Cemetery, on the historic *Chemin Neuf* (New Road). In time, Joseph Philibert Gosserand, a New Roads businessman who had been named for and raised by his godfather, *Père* Gutton, commissioned a monument to his memory. On 9 July 1901, area residents and visitors estimated in excess of 3,000 jammed old St. Mary Church and lined New Roads' streets for Reverend Father J.P. Gutton's final tribute: a requiem service for his temporarily disinterred remains, and their ceremonial return to a new tomb and impressive monument in the cemetery.

Isaac Bigman was among the visitors in New Roads that day, and witnessed the funeral procession led by the hearse and followed by carriages carrying clergy and lay officials from five parishes, as well as five benevolent societies on foot, keeping in step to the strains of the False River Brass Band. Panic ensued as a horse bolted into the crowd. The New Orleans *Daily Picayune* staff member on hand speedily telegraphed his report, which appeared in the 10 July 1901 edition:

> This morning, while the funeral carriage was passing Main and Cemetery [now New Roads] streets, a horse attached to a buggy and owned by Mr. Isaac Bigman, became frightened at the music and ran away. The animal dashed into the crowd, knocking down and injuring several people. Among the injured is Mr. Rickett [nickname of Justin] Patin [a local building contractor]. Mr. Patin was severely cut on the head and badly bruised about the body. Dr. R.M. Carruth attended the wounded man. He pronounced his injuries painful, but not dangerous.

Fast-forwarding to 1903, Isaac Bigman decided it was time to buy a new carriage horse, but was specific that it should be gentle enough to be driven by his young wife, née Rosa Waldman. The subsequent case of Bernard Teutsch vs Isaac Bigman, filed in 21st Judicial District Court, No. 493, on 14 March 1904, is rich in detail:

Bernard Teutsch, a merchant who operated at various locations in Pointe Coupée Parish for many years, was represented by his attorney, and subsequent Louisiana Lieutenant Governor, Hewitt Bouanchaud. Through Bouanchaud, Teutsch represented that Bigman was indebted to him for $165, with interest, for the purchase from Teutsch's New Roads stable of a black mule on 8 Feb 1904, and for which Bigman refused to pay.

Isaac Bigman, through his attorneys, (John) Yoist & (Miguel T.) Hewes, the latter being a brother of Bigman's partner in the Bigman & Hewes (Cotton) Ginnery at Oscar, responded that the mule in question was one which Bigman purchased from Teutsch's stable, but had not paid for it due to issues with a light bay mare he subsequently purchased from Teutsch for $100.

The testimony of Herman Teutsch and C.M. Castay, both employees of Bernard Teutsch, contended that that Bigman had purchased two animals from the Teutsch stable: on 22 December 1903, a light bay mare for $100; and on 15 March 1904, a mule for $165. Bigman purchased the mule on behalf of one of his customers, and was granted a $5 rebate by the stable, as it was Bernard Teutsch's longstanding custom to give a discount to Bigman whenever the latter bought animals on behalf of others.

While Bigman's account for the mule purchase remained unpaid, the Oscar merchant and planter visited Teutsch's, stating he preferred to try another driving mare. On Herman Teutsch's approval, Bigman left his own bay at the Richy Street stable and took a black mare on approval, which Teutsch told him would cost $175. As in the case of the previously purchased bay mare, Bigman was allowed to take the black mare on trial to Oscar, and left his light bay at the stable.

Herman Teutsch continued to testify that he met Bigman some days later "at the barber shop," where Bigman informed him that he would not pay the price for the black mare. Teutsch told

Bigman to return the animal to the stable the next day, but it was not returned. As a consequence, he sent "a boy" on horseback to return Bigman's light bay to Oscar and retrieve Teutsch's black mare. The boy returned to New Roads, but without the black mare.

Teutsch, testified that the next day, 27 February, Bigman sent by "a colored man" both of the mares and a note containing a message from Bigman and the latter's $60 draft or "check" on F. Gumbel & Co. Herman stated he read the note, replaced the check within it, wrote a message on another sheet of paper on behalf of his brother Bernard Teutsch and sent the papers back to Bigman. Teutsch, confirmed that he had penciled on the bottom of Bigman's message: "You can not take me for a God damn fool. HT." The note Herman penned for his brother read:

> Dear Sir
>
> I do not know your idea of sending me your Mare back [.] do you take me for a fool [.] I have nothing to do with your Horse so you [sic] please send me a check for my Mule for One Hundred & Sixty dollars [,] not sixty dollars & you will not delay this & oblige.
>
> B. Teutsch

Herman also stated for the record that the situation had caused him to break "*Gott*'s law," in the wording of his first message to Bigman, i.e., taking the Lord's name in vain.

In his own defense, Isaac Bigman replied that after the "fourth or fifth" time attempting to drive the light bay mare purchased from Teutsch's, the animal merely balked and jumped three times, the last time out of its harness. Bigman's tenant James Cage was similarly unable to handle the animal, so he (Bigman) was determined to "get rid" of the animal. He and Cage set out for New Roads with the mare, but stopped at the home of August Webre, the latter known as expert horse handler, but each time Webre tried to drive the animal, it headed for and scraped Bigman's buggy against a fence.

On 28 Mar 1904, L.B. Claiborne, Judge of the 21st Judicial District Court, ruled in favor of the plaintiff, Bernard Teutsch, condemning defendant, Isaac Bigman, to remit to Teutsch the sum of $160, with legal interest from 15 Mar 1904, and costs of the suit.

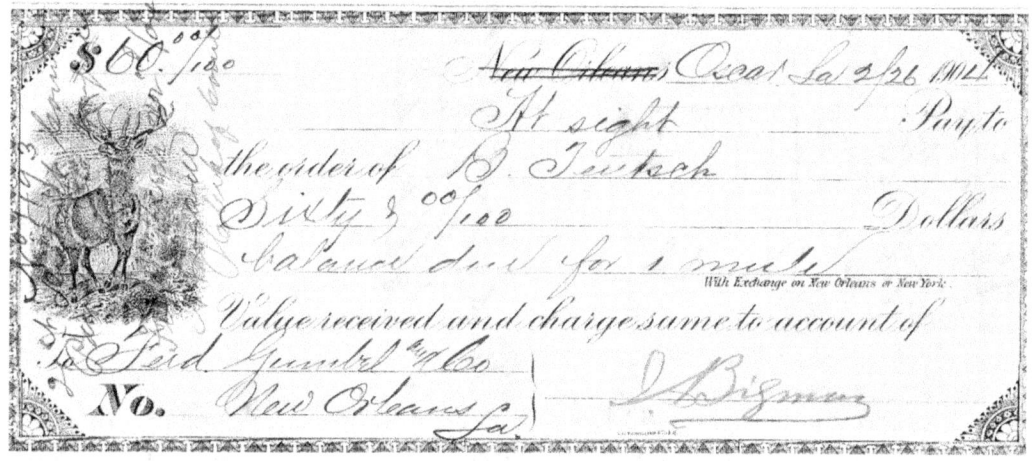

Isaac Bigman's check to Bernard Teutsch for $60, balance due for one mule.

ISAAC BIGMAN'S PLANTATION AT OSCAR CROSSING

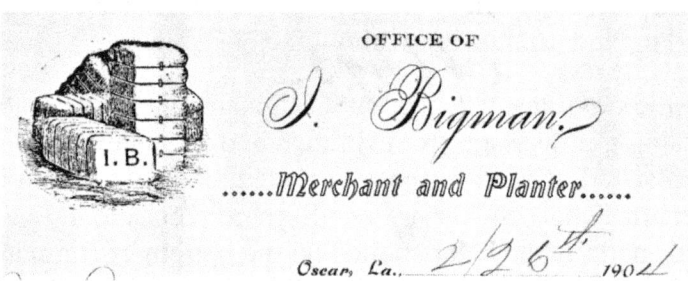

The neighborhood of southern Pointe Coupée Parish referred to alternately as Oscar Crossing and Torbert is geographically closer to Bayou Grosse Tête, but linked socially and commercially to the community of Oscar proper, several miles north, on False River Road. The earliest-known residents of the Oscar Crossing area were a branch of the Choctaw Native Americans who identified themselves as the "Tchalpte" people, the Choctaw term *akchalpi* translating as "coarse outer bark of a tree." (Lorio, Elaine C. "The Place-Names of Pointe Coupée Parish." Louisiana State University Master's Thesis, 1932.) The name appeared on maps as early as Darby's dated 1817, which indicated the bayou and swamp as "Chapte." Numerous other spellings were given by subsequent cartographers and the Public Service Commission including Chalpa, Chappe, Cholppe, and Cholpe. The Native Americans for whom the area was named remained in the area until 1865, when forced out by the floodwater issuing from the Morganza Crevasse.

The area was cleared and put into cultivation in 1890 by enterprising Sicilian farmers who settled along a thoroughfare roughly paralleling Bayou Cholpe, which continues to be known in the 21st century as Little Italy Road. Isaac Bigman began to amass and eventually disposed of thousands of acres in southernmost Pointe Coupée Parish and on False River starting in 1891. He developed the Bayou Tommy Plantation from purchases made in 1891 and 1897, to wit: in 1891, from John Yoist, 683.36 acres straddling Bayou Grosse Tête (*sic*, Tommy intended), being the S/2 of Sec. 18 and the N/2 of Sec. 19 – T6S – R10E, for the price of $683.36; and in 1891, from the Mechanics' & Traders' Insurance Company of New Orleans, the 160-acre Warren Tract, located immediately south of the first purchase, and being comprised of the S/2 of Sec. 19 – T6S – R10E, for $200.

Bayou Tommy Plantation was located just to the west of the Little Italy settlement, the latter, in turn, being west of Bayou Cholpe. The southern boundary of Bigman's property was more than six miles distant from and approximately 15 feet lower than the altitude of the Oscar community on False River Road. Despite the wooded and low-lying nature of the place, Bigman had the portion closest to and on both banks of the bayou cleared, tenanted and put into sugar cane cultivation.

Isaac Bigman had a roadway built between the False River Road at Oscar and his plantation in 1898. It was named "Bigman Lane," by Pointe Coupée Parish Police Jury in his honor and in local Créole dialect called *la Manche Beeg - mann*.

In 1906, the Colorado Southern, New Orleans & Pacific Railroad completed a major line across the southern portion of Pointe Coupée Parish, its tracks less than a half-mile from and paralleling the north line of Bayou Tommy Plantation. Ownership of the railroad passed to the New Orleans & San Francisco, nicknamed "Frisco" line, which during 1910-11 constructed a branch line, veering from the main line at Erwinville in neighboring West Baton Rouge Parish, running north to Alma Plantation at Lakeland in Pointe Coupée, then turning west and paralleling the west bank of the Lower Chenal and False River as far as the Olivo Plantation at Mix, midway between the west bank of False River. Both of Isaac Bigman's major properties were, therefore, served by the Frisco Railroad: on the main line at Oscar Crossing near Bayou Tommy Plantation, and at Major-Bigman station on the branch line at Oscar proper.

Isaac Bigman's store and house at Oscar. (*Beautiful Pointe Coupée and Her Prominent Citizens*, J.I. Sanford, 1906.)

Severe freezes in October 1910 and December 1911 ruined much of the sugar cane crops throughout Pointe Coupée Parish, sending the community into an economic depression. Due to his losses in the latter year, Isaac Bigman filed suit against Antoine Albéric Lorio (21st Judicial District Court, No. 1948), owner and operator of the Ingleside plantation and sugar factory at Lakeland, on 4 March 1912.

Bigman, through his attorneys, (Miguel Tacon) Hewes & (Allen K.) Smith, petitioned for a judgment in the amount of $3,762.38, with interest from the date of same until paid by Lorio. Bigman contended that on 19 June 1911, he and Lorio entered into a written and signed agreement whereby Bigman would plant and cultivate at least 170 acres of sugar cane on the Bayou Tommy Plantation, harvest, and ship 45 to 50 tons of cane daily, weather permitting, to the Ingleside mill in 1911 and 1912.

According to the terms of the contract, Lorio was to "influence" the Frisco Railroad to provide a sufficient number of cars for carrying the harvested cane from its main line near Bayou Tommy, and a siding, known in time as Oscar Crossing or Oscar Station, which would be financed by "all interested parties." Lorio was obliged to furnish slings for securing the cut cane in bundles, and a derrick or hoist at the Frisco siding with which to load the cane into rail cars for transport to his mill. Bigman would furnish the laborers for the construction of the derrick, but Lorio would pay their wages. For Bigman's harvested crop thus loaded, shipped and received at Ingleside, Lorio agreed to pay him "Three dollars per ton for cane" weekly. The contract also stated that in the event of a freeze or other "bud-killer," Bigman was to put his harvested cane into windrows and notify Lorio of such as soon as possible, but Lorio had the option of refusing to receive or purchase any cane which had frozen or soured.

Bigman contended he was complying with his part of the contract when on 29 December 1911 Lorio notified him that, as of the 24th (Christmas Eve), the price paid would be $2 per ton for cane sold at the factory and $1.50 for cane delivered to the rail-side derrick near Bayou Tommy Plantation. Stating that he protested to Lorio in writing, Bigman declared that Lorio refused to comply with the contracted-for price and that if he (Bigman) had consented to accepting the lower price his losses would have been great. Some 29.64 acres of cane had been left in the field owing to Lorio's act, Bigman related, estimating the harvest at 30 tons per acre.

A. Albéric Lorio, through his attorney, Albin Provosty, responded that the terms of the contract "contemplated sound cane" to be delivered to Ingleside, and paid for at the price of $3 per ton. Because of the severe cold experienced in November and December 1911, however, the cane harvested by Bigman and most other planters and farmers in the parish was, as testified by Lorio, "frozen, rotted and damaged to such an extent as to render it unfit for manufacturing and virtually worthless."

Lorio said that despite the fact that he had sent notice on or about 28 December 1911, that a maximum of $1.50 would be paid for cane delivered to the derrick or $2 for that to the mill, per ton, Bigman continued to ship several tons to the mill. Lorio credited Bigman at $1.50 per ton, applying the sum against Bigman's account with Lorio for three barrels of processed sugar purchased by Bigman for his store at Oscar.

Lorio ended by stating that he had made the same contract for $3 per ton for cane to a large number of planters, just as he did with Bigman, and all of them understood his reason for his lowering the price owing to the freeze, adding that they continued shipping their harvests to him. He closed by reiterating that the guarantee of $3 per ton did not apply to "frozen or rotten cane."

The case of Bigman vs Lorio opened as the worst flood in Mississippi Valley history to date bore down upon Pointe Coupée Parish and much of South Louisiana. Testimony was postponed until later in the year, while the parish attempted to recover from its greatest natural disaster ever. The 7 May 1912 *New Orleans Item* reported that in the first week following the breach in the Lower Old River levee at Torras in northernmost Pointe Coupée Parish on 1 May 1912, some 800 residents of the lower-lying "interior" near the Frisco Railroad main line had evacuated taking refuge in Oscar proper on False River.

By 13 May, the floodwater in the area of Bayou Tommy Plantation and Little Italy had risen to a height of 10 feet. According to various newspaper reports, approximately 350 Italian residents were rescued by boat, sent up to False River, and evacuated by Frisco trains from Major-Bigman and Knapp stations, the latter on Ingleside Plantation, to Baton Rouge, on order of the Italian Consul at New Orleans, Cavaliere Gualtiero Chilesotto.

Following the recession of the 1912 floodwater and a subsequent outbreak of typhoid fever, the case of Isaac Bigman vs A. Albéric Lorio resumed in July. Lower Chenal sugar chemist Simon Baum was excused from court attendance due to illness. Ingleside sugar mill owner and operator A. Albéric Lorio testified that as soon as he saw he was losing money he notified all parties including Bigman that he was reducing his prices.

Auguste Webre testified that he had been the manager of Isaac Bigman's Bayou Tommy Plantation for two years. Webre stated that in the previous year, about 90 acres of "good cane" grew on the plantation, of which 13,000-14,000 tons from 60 acres had been shipped to the Lorio mill. However, Bayou Tommy still had about 25 to 30 acres of good cane, "the best and heaviest" of the harvest on the ground and ready for shipment. Webre related that on or about 29 December 1911, Lorio sent instructions to have the harvesters shorten the cane stalks - normally six to seven feet high - by three to four inches from top and bottom to remove any sourness. Webre continued that he tested as many as 20 stalks in each area for sweetness, and put the cane into windrows. Webre also testified that about 40 acres of cane had been windrowed, approximately one-third of it soured, and of the cane sent to Ingleside for milling "I did find them a little water-logged."

Bigman's attorney Miguel Hewes's brother, Thomas H. Hewes, (partner with Isaac Bigman in the Bigman & Hewes Ginnery and developer of the False River Telephone Line), was also questioned. Thomas Hewes, testified that, in his additional profession of surveyor, he agreed to Bigman's request to survey the area of as-yet unshipped sugar cane on Bayou Tommy Plantation. Hewes stated that it comprised about 28 ½ acres, and much of the cane was still "eatable," i.e., not sour. When pressed by the defense, Hewes said he had tasted two or three stalks, although others were cutting and chewing pieces and declaring the juice to be sweet.

Isaac Bigman testified that that when informed by Auguste Webre that Lorio wanted the two ends of the cane stalks cut, he (Bigman) went back to Bayou Tommy and ordered it done. Bigman was emphatic that he did not send any soured cane to Ingleside. Bigman also alleged, during questioning from defense attorney Provosty, that his cane back on Bayou Tommy, when windrowed, was less exposed to damage than cane on False River, but when questioned again, said he did not know if sugar cane located more distant from False River, in general, was less likely to freeze or sour, as it was only his second year cultivating cane.

Bigman testified that when Lorio refused to receive the remaining 29.64 acres of harvested cane from Bayou Tommy, he (Bigman) attempted to have the Pitcher sugar factory on Alma Plantation at Lakeland do so. Bigman said he planned to ship two carloads of cane to Pitcher's to have it tested by a chemist (likely Simon Baum), but Lorio refused Bigman permission to use the derrick at Oscar Crossing to do so.

A judgment was rendered on 26 November 1912 in favor of Bigman, with Lorio directed to pay Bigman $305.66, at five percent interest from that day until paid. Lorio appealed to the Louisiana Supreme Court (No. 17,237), but the latter rejected Lorio's demand on 11 May 1914, and the suit dismissed at his cost in both courts.

After Isaac Bigman and his family moved on, he sold his various Pointe Coupée Parish holdings, including the 1,000.5-acre Bayou Tommy Plantation, for which Mumford Phillips paid Bigman $20,0000 in 1922. Having passed through successive owners, the area remains primarily agricultural in the 21st century.

NATHAN GAMBURG

Nechemia "Nathan" Gamburg was born on 20 May 1883, in Rovno, Ukraine, Russian Empire, to Joseph Gamburg and his wife whose name has not been discovered. He was married in the

Ukraine ca. 1907 to Golda/Goldie Waldman, the sister of Rosa Waldman Bigman and Bertha Waldman Nowak. Golda was born on 21 May 1885, in the Ukraine, to Daniel Waldman and his wife Rachel Magot. At least two, some say three, of Nathan and Golda's children were born in Rovno: Mina/Minnie (b. ca. 1907), Daniel "Gdal" Leon (b. 1908), and Gersh "Harry Joseph" (b. 1910). (Note: Social Security and other records show Gersh's date of birth as 19 December 1911 in Philadelphia, Pennsylvania.)

Census records indicate that Nathan immigrated in 1910 and was naturalized in 1914 although we could find no record for it. Nathan Gamburg, and perhaps his wife and three children, were living in Pointe Coupée Parish by 1912, probably attracted to the area because his sister-in-law, Rosa Waldman, and her husband, Isaac Bigman, were living there. In March 1912, Gamburg entered into an eight-month lease with Anthony Decuir for the latter's lot measuring 172 ft. on the Lower Chenal Road by depth of 420 ft. to the water's edge. The lot was complete with dwelling and outbuildings, and the lease was set at $5 per month. Ironically, the lease was set to commence on 1 May 1912, the day the Lower Old River levee at Torras was breached.

Twelve days later, the Baton Rouge *New Advocate* dated 13 May 1912, reported that Nathan Gamburg had been arrested on the charge of cattle speculation. Lucca Cascio had filed a complaint that Gamburg had visited him in the Italian refugee camp, located in Battle Park, in Baton Rouge, and had informed him that nineteen head of Cascio's cattle were near drowning, and that Gamburg proposed to rescue and purchase them.

The following year, Nathan Gamburg was in the news again. He was described in the 12 June 1913 New Orleans *Item* as an Oscar businessman who had discovered a method to kill the boll weevils and grasshoppers that were attacking the cotton crops. Gamburg related that he experimented on the crops on his brother-in-law, Isaac Bigman's land, and determined that the pests could be easily killed by an application of Plaster of Paris to the plants in early morning before the dew "disappears," or immediately following a light shower of rain. A Louisiana State Agricultural Department representative related that he had recommended a certain preparation to Bigman to rid his crops of the pests, but upon assessing Gamburg's method he decided the latter was more effective. The article continued that the manner in which Gamburg applied the Plaster of Paris also proved to be a valuable fertilizer, and that crops treated that way looked better and were larger than those not treated.

Gamburg explained that after witnessing the destruction of hops in his native Russia and spending several years in developing a pesticide, he determined that Plaster of Paris was the only effective treatment, and thus attempted the same method on the boll weevils and grasshoppers attacking the crops at Oscar.

Information collected by Rabbi Martin I. Hinchin, D.D., in his book *Fourscore and Eleven, A History of the Jews of Rapides Parish 1828-1919* (McCormick Graphics, 1984, pp. 162, 191), indicated that the Gamburgs had moved to Alexandria, Rapides Parish, Louisiana, as early as 1914, that Nathan and Goldie had been married in Russia, and that Gamburg was in the fur, hide and metal business. By 1918, when Nathan Gamburg registered for the World War I draft, he was using an Alexandria, Rapides Parish, Louisiana, address where he was proprietor of the

Central Louisiana Rice and Corn Meal Company. Indeed, in the 1920 United States Federal Census for Alexandria, Rapides Parish, his occupation was listed as "miller."

At some point before 1927, Gamburg had become a partner in a double-roller sugar mill several miles outside of Opelousas, St. Landry Parish, Louisiana, along with twelve acres of land and a switch to the Texas and Pacific Railroad siding. He advertised the plant for sale in the 7 August 1927 edition of the New Orleans *Times-Picayune,* at which time, he wrote that it could be used as a paper mill, or canning factory. On 11 May 1928 the Baton Rouge *State Times Advocate* announced that the "old sugar refinery" belonging to Gamburg and Richey of Alexandria, Louisiana, had burned to the ground.

Gamburg was enumerated with his family in the 1930 United States Federal Census as the proprietor of a second-hand shop at Alexandria. City Directory records for Alexandria, Louisiana, also verified that he was a dealer in furs. While living in Alexandria, two more children were born to the couple: Rosalie (b. 1915), and Dorothy Mae (b. 1922). Gamburg apparently divided his time between Alexandria and Shreveport, Caddo Parish, Louisiana, where he was enumerated in the 1940 United States Federal Census. In the 1939 *New Orleans Item* obituary of his mother-in-law, Rachel Magot, who died in New Orleans on 29 August 1939, Goldie Gamburg was mentioned as a resident of Shreveport.

According to the Social Security Death Records Index, Nathan Gamburg died in Dade County, Florida in June 1962. We have been unable to find his place of burial. His wife, Goldie Waldman Gamburg, died in Alexandria, Rapides Parish, on 23 February 1976, and was interred in the Jewish Cemetery in Pineville, Rapides Parish, Louisiana.

JOSEPH W. "JOE" WALDMAN

Joseph Waldman was born on 25 January 1891, at Odessa, Ukraine, Russian Empire, to Daniel Waldman and Rachael Magot. He was one of four siblings to settle in Oscar, Pointe Coupée Parish, Louisiana. Joseph and his sister Fannie were living with their older sister and brother-in-law Rosa, and her husband, Isaac Bigman, according to the 1900 United States Federal Census. Ten years later Joseph was enumerated as a "department store" salesman for Bigman.

The Waldman siblings and their spouses appeared frequently in *Pointe Coupée Banner* accounts between 1908 and 1910, including the news of Joe's departure for Louisiana State University in Baton Rouge in 1908. Joseph, who never married, was enumerated in the 1940 United States Federal Census as a dry goods store manager in Crystal Springs, Copiah County, Mississippi. He died in Crystal Springs on 22 August 1970, and was buried in Hebrew Rest Cemetery No. 2 in New Orleans.

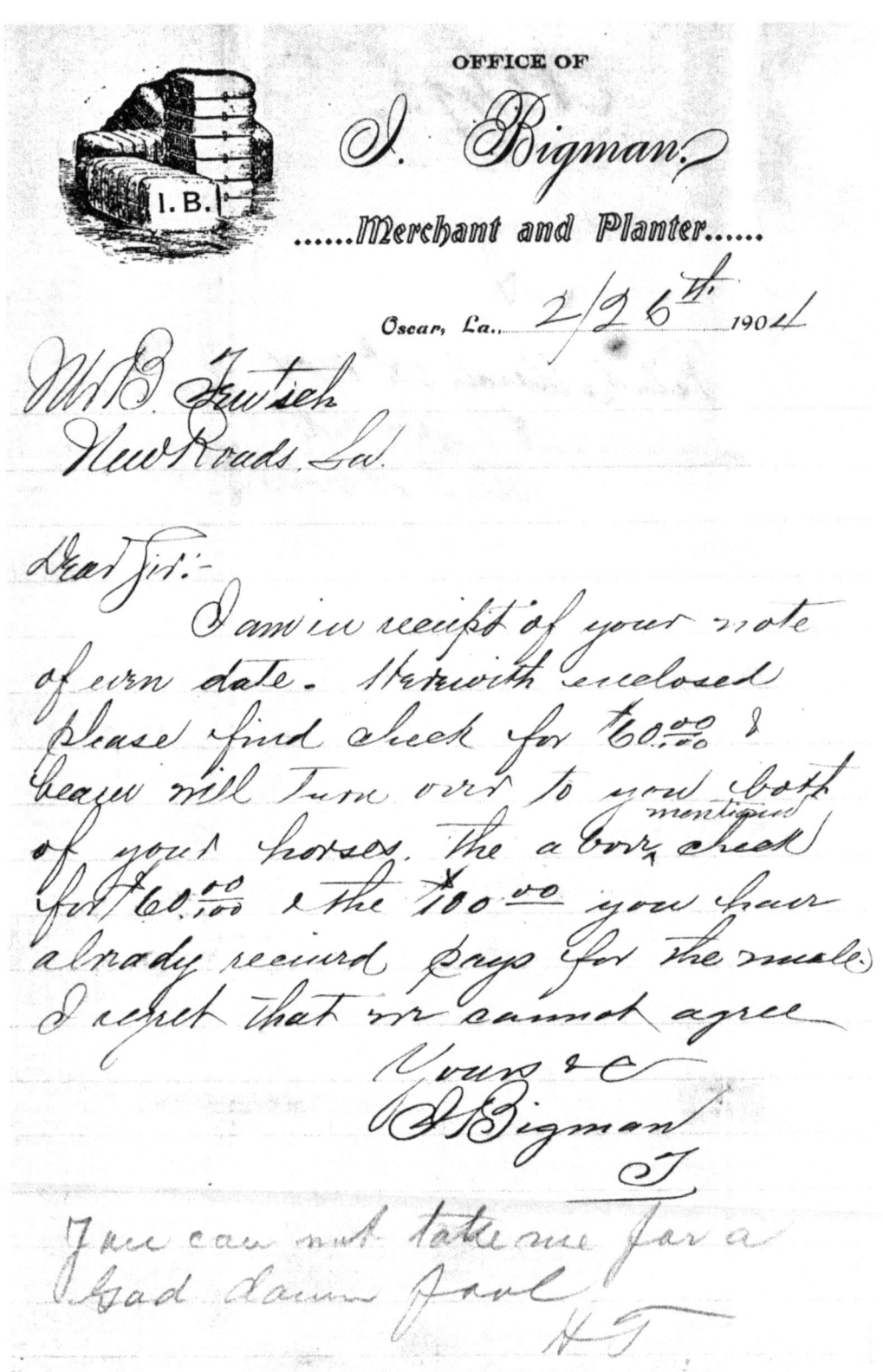

Isaac Bigman's letter to Bernard Teutsch, dated 2/26/1904, concerning payment for mule.

CHAPTER 6

LOWER CHENAL OF FALSE RIVER

The shrunken remnant of the lower stretch of a 22-mile-long horseshoe bend of the Mississippi River, the Lower Chenal of False River undulated in the former riverbed from the lower end of False River proper to the Mississippi River. Two pools of water lay within its sinuosities: *Grand Baie* (Grand Bay) on the northern shore, and *Petit Baie* (Little Bay) to the south.

During the second half of the 19th century and into the 20th, small steamboats plied the waters of False River and the Lower Chenal, pushing barges of baled cotton and barreled sugar to Hermitage and Trudeau Landings on the Mississippi, a tram over the levee, being part of the transfer, for shipment onto larger steamers to New Orleans and abroad. Imported items, including store merchandise and agricultural implements for the town of New Roads and plantations along the way, arrived by return vessels from the city and elsewhere.

The first community when heading down the Chenal from False River was Lakeland, which grew to considerable prominence. Located on and between great sugar and cotton plantations, the settlement included a post office established in 1878, and thus named because into the twentieth century the water of False River proper extended as far east as present-day Immaculate Conception Church. Parish and state drainage projects between 1904 and 1950, diverting water south from False River, lowered the level of the lake by about 10 feet, causing False River proper, in essence, to retract a few miles to the west. Thus, Gumbel, Mayer & Loeb's "False River Store" at the west end of Lakeland fronted "on False River," but since the lowering of the water level the site faces the increasingly wooded *batture* of the Lower Chenal.

Lakeland flourished as a rural trade center for southern Pointe Coupée and northern West Baton Rouge parishes. Jewish and Sicilian immigrants as well as native French and *Créole de couleur* merchants operated general stores, pharmacies, saloons and butcher shops in frame buildings, several of the latter standing until the late 20th and early 21st centuries.

One of Pointe Coupée Parish's early telephone lines was that of M.P. Phillips, established in 1886, which connected Lakeland with Arbroth Landing on the Mississippi River in West Baton Rouge Parish. In 1891, the first buildings illuminated by electricity in Pointe Coupée were at Lakeland, at J.B. Churchill's sugar mill on Alma Plantation, and at M.P. Phillips' on Oakland Plantation.

More sugar cane and cotton plantations and smaller farms belonging to descendants of Pointe Coupée's early *Créoles de couleur* were downstream from Lakeland, with post offices at Chenal (present-day Rougon), Glynn and Hermitage on the Mississippi.

Lewis Stirling Hereford established the region's earliest rail service called the False River Railroad which connected the Lower Chenal at present-day Glynn with Canaan Landing on the Mississippi in adjacent West Baton Rouge Parish. It was in operation by 1869. The Texas & Pacific opened a branch line in 1899 running between the main line at Addis in southern West Baton Rouge Parish and Ferriday in Concordia Parish. Its local station stops included Glynn and Chenal Crossing on the southern and northern banks, respectively, of the Lower Chenal, Island Crossing, New Roads, Morganza, Batchelor, Lettsworth and Torras beyond. The New Orleans &

San Francisco or "Frisco" railway established an area branch line as well, in 1910, commencing at the main line to the south at Erwinville, West Baton Rouge Parish, and running north to Alma Plantation at Lakeland. The branch line then veered west and followed the gentle curve of False River as far northwestward as Mix, Louisiana, five miles below New Roads.

In the early 1900s, the two largest sugar plantations in the area, A.A. Lorio's Ingleside and J.B. Churchill's Alma, located, respectively, at the western and eastern ends of the Lakeland community, had their own narrow-gauge railroads and rolling stock in order to expedite the movement of cane from the fields to their mills.

LAZARUS & LOEB

Lazarus & Loeb, the partnership of Leopold Lazarus and Edward Loeb, both natives of Bavaria, were the first-known Jewish merchants on the Lower Chenal of False River. They were in operation during the 1850s through the 1860s, adjacent to the plantation of Léon Decuir, a free man of color.

According to his declaration of intention to become a United States citizen filed in 1854 at New Roads, Louisiana, Leopold Lazarus immigrated in 1850 at the age of eighteen. His oath renouncing allegiance to the King of Bavaria was done in the same place in 1857. According to the United States 1860 Mortality Schedule, Leopold Lazarus, a merchant, died in Pointe Coupée Parish from consumption at the age of 28, after an illness of sixty days in March 1860.

Edward Loeb, whose name was recorded as "Édouard" Loeb, also an immigrant from the Rheinpfalz, Germany, most likely a younger brother of Emanuel Loeb, a prominent New Orleans and Pointe Coupée merchant, arrived in New Orleans on 5 December 1850, aboard the *Lemuel Dyer* from Le Havre, France, at the age of sixteen. Accompanying him was an eighteen-year-old said to be Lazarus Loeb. It is likely that this is actually the record for Leopold Lazarus, a miscommunication created when the ship's list was taken by a French crewman speaking with a German national. Edward Loeb filed a declaration renouncing his allegiance to the Maximilian, King of Bavaria on 27 April 1857, at New Roads.

Shortly after Leopold Lazarus's death, the 1860 United States Federal Census was conducted, in which Edward Loeb, a merchant, was enumerated with $4,000 in real estate and $4,000 in personal property, sharing his home with fellow native Bavarians Aaron Baum and Lazarus Simon, who were likely his store clerks. In addition, the 1860 United States Federal Slave Schedule showed that Loeb was the owner of two enslaved female "mulattos," ages 35 and 13.

Merchandise in the "Ware House" (i.e., store), inventoried in the succession of Leopold Lazarus (9th Judicial District Court, No. 2562) in 1860, included: bolts of "assorted" calicoes, ginghams, jaconets, cotton check, cassinette, flannel, white, colored and striped cotton, cottonade; embroidery "sets," thread, needles, pins; towels, white and blue blankets, tablecloths; a "lot" of clothing, men's cravats and suspenders; hoop skirts, whalebone (corset stays); men's and ladies' silk handkerchiefs, men's white linen, white and colored handkerchiefs, ladies' handkerchiefs; silk and straw hats; a lot of boots and shoes; cotton umbrellas; lot of groceries, loaf sugar, canned fruit, table mustard, pickles, Hostetter Bitters; "baskets" (i.e., wicker encased bottles) and bottles of champagne, Grigoleit, claret, port, madeira, muscat and white wines, gin, curacao, cognac, cordials, absinthe, assorted syrups and juices; chewing tobacco, snuff, pipes; a lot of medicines, colognes, essences, aromatic vinegar, soaps, Castile soap, rice powder, Lily White, powder puffs, pomature (hair dressing), powder boxes, small toilette mirrors, clothes brushes; common and fancy, white and colored crockery, china dinner and tea sets, cups, saucers, mugs, plates and bowls, teapots and pitchers, including children's sets; crystal confectionery jars, preserve dishes and madeira glasses; glass decanters, molasses pitchers, castors and sugar dishes, (drinking) glasses, tumblers; bowl and pitcher sets, china spittoons, candlesticks, flower vases, and pots; bronze figure clocks, Yankee clocks, foolscap paper, indelible ink, lead pencils, lot of fiddle string; coffee pots, sauté pots, sausage stuffers, lot cutlery, measures; candlesticks, center table lamps; washbowls, jugs, buckets; leather and wooden trunks, liquor box, water cooler; one lot hardware, nails, carpenter pencils, small rulers, compasses, shovels, cross-cut saw; one lot saddlery and harness; also a safe, scale, balances, accounts and notes receivable.

The inventory included two enslaved females, Mathilda, aged about 38, and her daughter Mary, aged about 12 years; a tract of land having one arpent front on the (Lower) Chenal by a depth of 40 arpents, bounded on one side by land belonging to Léandre (sic, Léon intended) Decuir and on the other by that of François Decuir, with the store and other buildings situated thereon.

Edward Loeb served in the Civil War in Co. F, the "Pointe Coupée Regiment" of the Louisiana Militia, achieving the rank of Second Lieutenant. He stated on his 8 June 1864 passport application done in New York, that his "certificate of citizenship was left behind there [Pointe Coupée Parish, Louisiana] at the time of my escape [*sic*] from Rebel control." The application also gave his date of birth as on or about 24 June 1833, in Germany, as well as his physical description: 5 feet 3 ½ inches tall, blue eyes, light complexion, straight nose, oval face and round chin. From this document, it is obvious that Loeb did not mention to the authorities that he had been an officer in the Confederate Army.

What we do know is that in the spring and summer of 1864 there had been intense fighting in Pointe Coupée and West Baton Rouge Parishes, as various units of the Union Army under General Nathaniel Banks retreated across the Atchafalaya River from neighboring Avoyelles Parish after the disastrous Red River Campaign. It was during this retreat that Michel Fortlouis, the son of a deceased Jewish merchant, Jean Maurice Fortlouis had been captured probably in Morganza, although there are conflicting documents which indicate Clinton, East Feliciana Parish, on 8 June 1864. At any rate, these parishes were in such disarray with Union and Confederate skirmishes practically on a daily basis that we believe Loeb either fled on his own, or was captured and escaped through the lines to New York. Michel Fortlouis was not so lucky. He, too, wound up in New York, but as a detainee in the Elmira Prison Camp, where he succumbed to pneumonia on 24 November 1864, one of the over three thousand Confederate prisoners who died there. No more records for Edward Loeb's presence in Louisiana could be found.

However, in 1866, the "firm of Edward Loeb *Frères* & Co." was apparently still active on the Lower Chenal of False River. That year, the firm, described as having "*plusieurs maisons de commerce*" (many commercial houses) in Pointe Coupée Parish, and represented by Emanuel Loeb, formerly of Simon, Loeb & Co., and Loeb, Gumbel & Simon, purportedly Edward Loeb's brother, given the title of the firm, sold to Isaac Keim, a former Waterloo peddler, two building on the firm's property, bounded by François Decuir and Léon Decuir for $4,000. The buildings were described as: a frame, two-story building on pillars, the first story composed of two rooms, and the second floor a single room, said building measuring 30 ft. by 50 ft.; and another "store or warehouse" behind, being frame, a having a single story set on pillars, and measuring 20 ft. by 30 ft.

LAZARUS SIMON

Lazarus Simon was born on 23 June 1833, at Waldhilbersheim, Rheinpfalz, Germany. He was enumerated in the household of merchant Edward Loeb, on the Lower Chenal in the 1860 United States Federal Census. It is likely that he and Aaron Baum, also enumerated there, were Loeb's store clerks.

Simon was married on 7 January 1866, to Caroline Seligman/Seeleman, the widow of Simon Schlenker. Caroline was born on 11 March 1837, at Zweibrücken, Rheinpfalz, Germany, out of wedlock, to Magdalena Gukenheim. The child was acknowledged as their daughter at Magdalena's marriage on 23 May 1837, to Baruch Seligman/Seeleman. (Note: The tombstones of Caroline Seeleman Simon and Charlotte Seeleman Schlenker both show Kaiserslautern as a place of birth. Caroline's obituary, as well as German civil records, show Zweibrücken.)

Lazarus Simon, a retail merchant, was enumerated in both the 1870 and 1880 United States Federal censuses for Durant, Holmes Co., Mississippi, living with Caroline, his step-sons, David and Moses Schlenker, and his children with Caroline: Elias (b. 1866 – d. 1867), Jacob (b. 1867), Reuben (b. 1876), and Leo (b. 1879). Caroline Simon died on 19 November 1895, and was interred in New Orleans in Hebrew Rest Cemetery No. 1. As a widower, Lazarus Simon lived with his son Leo, a bakery proprietor, in Natchez, Adams Co., Mississippi. Lazarus Simon died on 4 October 1910, at Natchez and was interred back in New Orleans in Hebrew Rest Cemetery No.1, as well.

FREDERICK MUNZESHEIMER

Frederick Munzesheimer was born on 19 April 1825, in the Kingdom Baden (Germany). According to information he gave on 22 March 1854, in his application for naturalization at New Orleans, he arrived at New York in May 1847 as a minor. He married Sarah Loeb on 15 December 1857, in New Orleans, and they settled in the port community of Hermitage, Pointe Coupée Parish, Louisiana. Sarah was born on 11 May 1831, in Bavaria, to Aaron Loeb and his wife, Fannie Eidensheim. Frederick and Sarah's first of many children, Frances, was born there on 6 October 1858.

Frederick served as the Postmaster of Hermitage, on the Mississippi River between 1857 and 1859, except for four months in 1857 when the position was held by merchant Louis H. Trudeau. During his time at Hermitage, Munzesheimer carried on a shipping, storing and freight handling business there under the name of F. Munzesheimer & Co., with co-partners L. P. Day, a native of Delaware, and James A. Landry. On 16 July 1859, he took out an ad in the *Pointe Coupée Democrat* to announce the dissolution of the partnership. The notice also indicated that the firm had on hand "a large assortment of goods of all descriptions" available for sale to the general public.

In 1860, Day & Landry sold the business to native Pointe Coupéean Louis Hermès "L.H." Trudeau, who for decades operated a general store, hotel and Trudeau's Landing, the latter the main import/export point for the Lower Chenal and Lower False River.

After closing his business, Munzesheimer moved his family to Mississippi where he resided during the Civil War, and where four more children were born: Gustave (b. 1860), Aaron (b. 1861), Emma (b. 1863), and Marcus (b. 1864). The family was back in Louisiana for the 9 August 1865 birth of their son Isidore Frederick. They settled down at Opelousas, St. Landry Parish, living there for twenty-five years or so. Frederick carried on a lucrative grocery business and in May 1869 opened up a popular ice cream and soda fountain establishment on Main Street. According to the 1870 United States Federal Census his businesses were worth $2,000.

Nine more children were born to the couple in Opelousas: Lewis (b. 1867), Alexander (b. 1868), Sidonia (b. 1870), Moses (b. 1872- d. 1872), Adolph (b. 1873), Hardy (b. 1874), Rita (b. 1875-d. 1876). Laurence (b. 1876), and Florette (b. 1877). Frederick was enumerated with his large family as a baker in the 1880 United States Federal Census for Opelousas. The Munzesheimers moved on to Dallas, Dallas Co., Texas, where Frederick died on 29 April 1893. He was interred at the Emanu-El Cemetery there. His wife, Sarah, died in Dallas on 6 June 1914, and was interred near her husband.

JOSEPH BLOCK

Joseph Block was born "Joseph Bloch" on 17 January 1830, at Altkirch, Haut-Rhin, France, to Nathan Bloch, a dealer in horses and native of Hegenheim, Haut-Rhin, France, born there on 14 September 1801, and his wife Rifke/Rebecca Brunschwig, born on 2 May 1807, in Durmenach, Haut-Rhin, France. Joseph Block immigrated ca. 1855 and was naturalized before 22 November 1862, when he applied for a passport to travel abroad.

Joseph Block took out a license to marry Frederika Meyer, the daughter of Jonathan Meyer and Charlotte Kaufman, on 9 April 1860, in New Orleans. The couple was enumerated on 13 July 1860, living on Bayou Poydras, south of the Lower Chenal. Joseph, a twenty-eight-year-old native of France was working as a peddler with his twenty-one-year-old bride, Fridirica (*sic*), born on 11 December 1836, at Ashbach bei Kusel, Rheinpfalz, Germany. Their first child, Isaac, was born ca. 1861.

Joseph Block applied for a passport for himself, his wife, and child, on 22 November 1862, at Newark, Essex Co., New Jersey, where the family had fled to escape the rigors of the Civil War. In that document Joseph Block verified his date of birth as 17 January 1830. Many immigrants from France and Germany had left their home countries in the 1840s and 1850s to escape the turmoil created when the Napoleonic Empire fell in 1815, precipitating two successive revolutions in France, one in 1830, the other in 1848. To their consternation, those same immigrants to the southern United States had found themselves caught up in a civil war, whose battlefields were in their backyard.

We cannot say whether the Block family left before or after the fall of New Orleans in late April 1862, or if they actually travelled back to France during that time. They returned, however to Clinton, East Feliciana Parish, ca. 1866, where their second child, Adolph, was probably born. The couple raised four more children all born in Clinton, where Joseph worked as a dry goods salesman: Malena (b. 1868), Leon Frank (b. 1870), Gertrude (b. 1873), and Herman/Ferdinand (b. 1875).

Frederika Meyer Block died at Clinton on 17 December 1877, and was interred in the Clinton, Jewish Cemetery. Joseph married Julia Heyman, born ca. 1855 in France, before the 1880 United States Federal Census for Clinton, East Feliciana Parish, where he was enumerated with her and his six children by his first wife. Joseph was enumerated in the 1900 United States Federal Census with his wife Julia, said to have been born in October 1855, living in the household of his son, Leon Block, at Thibodaux, Lafourche Parish, where they owned a grocery store.

Joseph Bloch died at Thibodaux on 11 July 1910. He was interred in the Jewish Cemetery at Clinton. Julia Heyman Block died on 4 May 1924, at Thibodaux, and was interred near her husband.

LOEB, GUMBEL & CO.

Among the many, mostly short-lived, partnerships established among Pointe Coupée Parish merchants and planters in the aftermath of the Civil War was that of "Loeb, Gumbel & Co." on the Lower Chenal of False River. Aaron Loeb, Cornelius Gumbel and Isaac Keim had one-third interest each in the company, which was established on 1 September 1865, and headquartered on the plantation of Edward Loeb & Co.

The purpose of Loeb, Gumbel & Co. was two-fold: to operate a store "for selling goods, buying produce, &c, and to do all business connected in the business of a country store"; and to plant cotton and other crops on the Lower Chenal plantations of Edward Loeb & Co. and J. Lafayette Matthews.

Although no contract has been located in the existing Freedmen's Bureau holdings, Isaac Keim apparently entered into an agreement with freedman Joe Paulin to cultivate and harvest crops on the Lower Chenal. Since Keim is not indicated as owning or leasing property in his own name at that time, it is logical that the arrangement would have been for Paulin to work on either the Loeb or Matthews plantations operated by Loeb, Gumbel & Co.

Joe Paulin filed a complaint at the Freedmen's Bureau office in New Roads, Louisiana, on 19 April 1866, claiming Keim had not paid him an agreed-upon salary of 75 cents per day for the preceding two and one-half months. Through the advocacy of the Bureau, a settlement was reached in which Keim paid Paulin the sum of $5 in cash (Louisiana Freedmen's Bureau, New Roads, Louisiana Field Office, Office Records, Complaints March 1866- August 1868).

PATIN & BAUM, SUBSEQUENTLY AARON BAUM

Patin & Baum, general merchants, was the partnership of Célima Patin, a free man of color, and Aaron Baum, a native of Bavaria, operating on Patin's plantation at present-day Rougon, Louisiana. They appeared as retail dealers in the 1866 IRS Tax Assessment Report.

Aaron Baum was born on 20 October 1840, at Lautersheim, Rheinpfalz, Germany, to Max Baum and his wife Johanna Fey. Seventeen-year-old Aaron Baum arrived in New Orleans from Le Havre, France, on 26 December 1857, aboard the ship *Ann Washburn*. He began his long career in Pointe Coupée Parish as a clerk in the Lazarus & Loeb general store, on the Lower Chenal. He was enumerated with the late Leopold Lazarus's partner, Edward Loeb, and Lazarus Simon in the 1860 United States Census for Pointe Coupée Parish.

On 29 June 1861, Baum enrolled as a Private in the Pointe Coupée Artillery, Company A. He was captured during the siege at Vicksburg, Mississippi on 4 July 1863, and paroled on 7 July 1863. According to available service records he returned to Pointe Coupée Parish after his release.

Patin & Baum appeared as retail dealers in the 1866 IRS Tax Assessment Report for Pointe Coupée Parish. Two years later, in 1868, Célima Patin died, and Baum purchased most of the firm's merchandise at his late partner's succession sale. Goods bought by Aaron Baum included: bolts of satinet, American and French calico, gingham, cotton checks, delaines, cambric, crepe, regular and mourning (i.e., black) jaconet, Spanish linen, veil barege, cotton, alpaca, regular and canton flannel, linsey, kersey, drilling, cottonade, sheeting, toweling, ticking, netting; serpentine, laces, ribbon, binding, tape, silk, cotton and flax thread, buttons, hooks and eyes, needles, thimbles, tablecloths, blankets; men's silk, cashmere, alpaca, linen and dress coats, wool jackets, cashmere, linen, check and cottonade pants, jean pantaloons, silk vests, white and colored fancy bosom shirts, linen check, calico and merino shirts, linen and paper collars, scarfs, neckties, suspenders and drawers; boys' linen coats; ladies' barege dresses, balmoral skirts, hoop skirts, cashmere shawls, mantilla, sontag, hair nets and pins, lace collars, belts, corsets and strings; hosiery; gloves; cotton and linen handkerchiefs; men's and boys' felt and straw hats; boots, men's, boys', ladies' misses' and children's shoes, slippers; ladies' hats; sugar, green tea, table salt, black pepper, all spice, canned lobster and sardines, pepper sauce, pickles, sweet oil, vinegar, yeast powders, lard; brandied fruit, red and white wines, claret, liquors, whiskeys, cognac; smoking and chewing tobacco, cigars, pipes; medicines, perfumery, soap, starch, candles; violin and strings; necklaces, spectacles and cases; silk parasols, fans, pocketbooks, hair, shaving and clothes brushes, combs, razors and straps; steel pens, slate pencils, ink, alphabet book, memorandum books; plates, bowls, chamber pots; French pots, boilers, skillets, frying pans, coffee mills and filters, cocoa dippers, funnels, washboards, garden seed; pistol, gun cartridges, caps, powder, shot and (gun) tubes; scissors, knives, nails, coffin nails, tacks, screws, saw files, carpenter chisels, augurs, hoes, hatchets, butt hinges, door bolts, padlocks, brass faucets, mosquito (bar) rings, bar lead, coal oil, rope; trunks; mule collar, bitts, blind bridles, stirrups, trace chains; also a silver watch, dispensatory, lot empty vials and bottles, scales, stove and pipe, 670 pounds of cotton, and 146 pounds of moss.

Later that year Baum filed an oath renouncing allegiance to the King of Bavaria and was naturalized at New Roads, Louisiana on 29 September 1868. He started a business in Fort Adams, Wilkinson Co., Mississippi, where he was enumerated in the 1870 United States Federal Census. He was listed as a retail merchant with $3,000 in assets. Aaron Baum soon returned to Pointe Coupée Parish, where he placed an advertisement in the 1876-1877 edition of Bouchereau's, *Statement of the Sugar Crops*.

Aaron Baum married Julia Simon on 5 June 1877, in New Orleans. One of the witnesses to the marriage was Simon Gumbel. Julia was born on 13 September 1849, at Zweibrücken, Rheinpfalz, Germany, to Elias Simon and Philippina Amelia Schwartz. She was the sister of Louise Simon, the wife of Gustav Cohen. Aaron and Julia were the parents of one child: Simon Baum, born ca. 1878 in Pointe Coupée Parish.

The Baum family continued in business into the early 1900s. In addition to being general merchants, Aaron Baum and Julia Simon were extensive property holders, their largest tract, upon which their store and community "hall" stood, was located on a plantation measuring seven arpents front by a depth of 40 arpents on the Lower Chenal.

In the era before sufficient law enforcement presence in Pointe Coupée Parish, criminal activity and resultant death often occurred in outlying communities. Aaron Baum's popular emporium at present-day Rougon was the scene of a fracas on the afternoon of 25 June 1880 in which the merchant resorted to self-defense. The 7 July 1880 July Baton Rouge *Capitolian-Advocate* related that Cléoville Patin, the nephew of Baum's late business partner, Célima Patin, and with whom clerk Leopold Kaufman boarded, was in the Baum store during the hours of 3 to 4 o'clock, when a certain Cadoré, likely neighboring farm laborer Jules Cadoré, came in and Patin "began to abuse and curse" the latter.

Baum reportedly "begged Patin not to curse in the store, as he [Baum] had his family there." Patin excused himself, but soon resumed his abuse and stating he intended to kill "that negro" (Cadoré), commenced firing a pistol at the latter. Other male customers succeeded in apprehending Patin and took away his pistol. Patin left the store briefly, and upon his return was given back his weapon, unloaded. The would-be assassin then demanded cartridges from Aaron and his brother Solomon Baum, which the merchants "properly refused." Patin said he would get the ammunition "if he had to kill for it."

Patin, with an open pocketknife, then pursued Aaron Baum behind a counter, despite Baum's remonstrances not to, and the latter, "believing his life in danger," produced his own pistol and fired two shots, striking Patin in the thigh and abdomen. Baum immediately surrendered to Sheriff Ernest G. Beuker, and on the following Monday was examined and "honorably discharged" by Judge (John) Yoist in New Roads.

Cléoville Patin died of his injuries the night after the incident, and was interred the following day, 27 June 1880, in the old Immaculate Conception Church Cemetery at Chenal. His burial record states he "died yesterday from an accident."

According to the 23 May 1885 *Pointe Coupée Banner*, Aaron Baum built a new home and enlarged his store that year. Despite occasional financial difficulties, the Baums managed to reclaim property conveyed to others and continued in the retail business. Aaron Baum's nephew Leopold Goldsmith, who immigrated in 1889, was enumerated with them, working as a clerk according to the 1900 United States Federal Census.

Inventories of Aaron Baum's merchandise during 1876-1897, according to Bouchereau's *Statement of the Sugar Crops* for 1876-77, civil suits, and *Pointe Coupée Banner* advertisements, included: dry goods; ribbons, thread, notions; tablecloths, blankets; men's pantaloons; ladies' balmorals, hoop skirts, chemises and corsets; men's, ladies' and boys' hats, caps; boots, men's, ladies' and boys' shoes, slippers; staple groceries, canned goods, claret, liquors; drugs, medicines, perfumery; artificial flowers, dolls, stationery; chinaware, crockery, glassware, tinware; candles, starch; pails, paints; hardware, hoe handles, bagging; coffins, caskets, metallic burial cases, and contents of two showcases; also a desk, safe, stove, two store lamps, seven mules, three horses, buggy, two wagons, corn mill, and (cotton) gin stand. The livestock and vehicles listed above were included in the inventory of goods in a civil action between brothers, Solomon Baum vs Aaron Baum.

In a 1900 *Pointe Coupée Banner* Parish Business Licenses report, Mrs. J.S. (Julia Simon) Baum reported gross sales for 1900 at $10,000. She was charged a license fee of $110.03 for 1901. The A. Baum store had a pharmacy department, and was listed on the False River Telephone Line in 1908. The couple's son, Simon Baum, was enumerated with them in the 1910 United States Federal Census for Pointe Coupée Parish. He was unmarried, age 32 years, working as a salesman in a country store. His father was employed as a "farm manager."

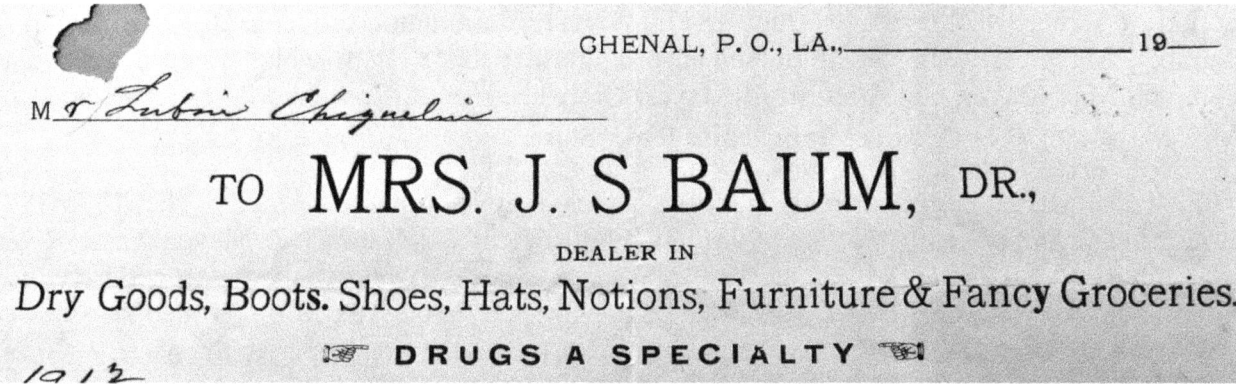

Ten years later, on 2 February 1920, the elder Baums were enumerated living in the household of their son Simon, a retail merchant, his wife Lillian, and their five-year-old daughter Dorothy Amelia, who had been born on 26 August 1914 in Fort Worth, Tarrant Co., Texas, likely her mother's home state. Simon Baum died a month later on 3 March 1920, and was interred in the Jewish Cemetery in Baton Rouge, East Baton Rouge Parish.

Simon Baum having acquired his parents' plantation on the Lower Chenal, his widow, Lillian Helen Lewis, sold it in the following year to Samuel Zink. Aaron Baum died on 3 September 1922, in Pointe Coupée Parish, was waked in the parlor of the family residence, and was interred in the Baton Rouge Jewish Cemetery. Julia Simon Baum died on 22 November 1937, and was interred with her husband and son. Simon's widow, Lillian Lewis, moved to California with their daughter, Dorothy, who was married to Nicholas Palermo on 15 April 1938, at South Gate, California. Lillian Lewis Baum married Alfred H. Bowlzer on 2 September 1954, in Los Angeles. Lillian was interred in the Memory Garden Memorial Park at Brea, Orange Co., California after her death on 12 February 1974. According to her California obituary she was born at Galveston, Texas, in 1892 (24 March 1891 according to the Social Security Death Index), and was a survivor of the devastating 1900 hurricane there.

GUMBEL, MAYER & LOEB, "FALSE RIVER STORE"

Gumbel, Mayer & Loeb's, "False River Store," was located immediately southwest of the head of Bayou Cirier. It was owned by Cornelius Gumbel, Max Mayer and Aaron Loeb, and operated by Gumbel. This three-man partnership owned three stores simultaneously in Pointe Coupee Parish, at the lower end of False River, further east on the Lower Chenal, and at Livonia on Bayou Grosse Tête.

Cornelius Jacob Gumbel was born "Carl" Gumbel on 15 May 1847, at Albisheim, Donnersbergkreis, Rheinpfalz, Germany, to Moses Hirsch Gumbel and Esther/Fanny Stern. He and his five brothers and sisters: Clara, Jeannette, Sarah, Simon and Ferdinand made their homes in Louisiana. He filed an oath in 1868 at New Roads, Louisiana, renouncing allegiance to the King of Bavaria.

Cornelius Gumbel was enumerated as a merchant with $3,000 in personal property at the "False River Store" according to the 1870 United States Federal Census. When the store building and property upon which it stood was sold by Mathilde Laurans, wife of Auguste Provosty, Jr., to Cerf Wolff in 1872, the latter leased the building to Gumbel, Mayer & Co. for $350 for the period of 1 June 1872 through 1 June 1877. A year after signing the lease, the partnership of Gumbel, Mayer & Loeb was dissolved in a single act in 1873, in which Loeb conveyed to Gumbel, Max Mayer, and the firm of Mayer, Grabenheimer & Rose, the latter represented by Max Mayer, all of Loeb's interest in "False River Store."

The "False River Store" thereafter was conducted as Gumbel & Mayer. The 1876-1877 Bouchereau, *Statement of the Sugar Crops* advertisement for Gumbel & Mayer, False River, highlighted the store's offerings as: dry goods, notions, hats, boots, shoes, groceries, wines, liquors, crockery, and hardware. The 1882 Pointe Coupée Parish Tax Roll recorded an assessed value of $3,000 for Gumbel & Mayer's merchandise, the highest in the parish that year.

In addition to retailing, Cornelius Gumbel was also active in local infrastructure improvements. In the wake of the 1874 flood, Gumbel contracted with the Pointe Coupée Parish Police Jury the following year to construct new dykes in Ward 8, and served on a committee to build a new road along the Lower Chenal there.

Like his brother Simon, Cornelius also had children in Pointe Coupée Parish before his New Orleans marriage to Rosa Dreyfus. His four children were born to Angélique/Angelina Charamel while he was directing the "False River Store" at the head of Bayou Cirier, west of Lakeland. Angélique was a descendant of an old *Créole de couleur* family. She was born on 1 April 1846 in the city of New Orleans, Louisiana, to Jean Charamel and Luce Lefebvre.

The first evidence we found for the presence of a Charamel family in Louisiana, was the 22 March 1813 marriage at St. Louis Cathedral of Joseph Charamel, a native of Jérémie, Saint-Domingue, who married Celestine Poke/Pock, born in Pointe Coupée Parish. He gave only one parent, Isavel, his mother. Celestine also gave only her mother's name, Genoveba Nadal (SLC, M3, 46). This is indicative of both the bride and groom having been born out of wedlock and/or being persons of color. We found a record of Celestine's birth on 5 January 1788, to Geneviève, a free woman, who was baptized on 27 April 1788, and whose godparents were Étienne Major and Dlle. (demoiselle = Miss) Pook (PCP-6, 11). This record is located in the *Diocese of Baton Rouge Catholic Church Records – Pointe Coupée Records 1770-1900 – Individuals without Surnames*, 2007, p. 25) We found only one recorded birth for the couple, a son, Pierre, baptized at New Orleans on 2 June 1817, at age 21 months (SLC, B-29, 139).

However, looking at the other children born to Pierre's brother, Jean Charamel and his wife, Luce Lefebvre, we made an important discovery. While Angélique was the couple's last child, her mother, Luce Lefebvre having died in New Orleans on 17 July 1846, there were three more children born previously, only one of whom we could trace. Numa Charamel, who worked as a shoemaker in New Orleans, was born to the couple on 7 August 1837. He was married to Pauline Bareigno (*sic*) and they had, at least, nine children. According to the 1860 United States Federal Census, Numa, age 23 was living with his wife, Pauline, age 23, and their first child, only identified as Marie L., age 1 year. However, Celeste Pock was also living in the household, and said to be 60 (*sic*) years old. We believe this is enough evidence to conclude that the elderly Celestine Pock, widow of Joseph Charamel was living with her grandson Numa Charamel. According to her New Orleans death certificate, Celestine died in New Orleans on 1 May 1862, at the age of 75 years. We conclude therefore that Numa's sister Angélique Charamel's paternal grandparents were also Joseph Charamel and Celestine Pock, the couple who had married on 22 March 1813 in New Orleans.

More research is certainly needed to sort out the Charamel family, many of whose male members were named "Pierre," "Jean," and "Joseph." The Charamels may have originally been from Voiron, Isère, France, via Bordeaux, and ultimately Jérémie, Saint-Domingue. There is no doubt that many of them worked as merchants in the French West Indies. They left many civil records, in both Martinique and Saint-Domingue until forced to flee during the Haitian Revolution. Some appear also to have settled in Pointe Coupée Parish, Louisiana by 1853, when "Mrs. Charlemagne" [*sic*] was listed among the *"Personnes qui sont membres de la Confrérie du Scapulaire de Marie, Pointe Coupée 5 Mai 1853* (People who are members of the Confraternity of the Scapular of Mary [,] Pointe Coupée [, as of] 5 May 1853), preserved in the Archives of the Catholic Diocese of Baton Rouge. Of the sixty members listed, two have been identified in documented records as male, at least seventeen, including Mme. Charamel, were "free people of color," and at least one was an enslaved person.

In the 1860 United States Federal Census, the "Chamois" (*sic*) family, all "mulatto" was listed next to sugar planter Paul F. Pourciau and his family, on the west bank of the False River, about four miles below downtown New Roads. The "Marie," indicated as being 13 years of age, correlates closely with Angélique Charamel's age at the time, and given that Jean Charamel had been widowed in 1846, his four children had probably been split up amongst relatives or even friends.

The four known natural children of Cornelius Gumbel and Angélique Charamel were: Joseph Cornelius "Jack" Gumbel, born on 29 June 1871, on the Lower Chenal of False River, but baptized as Joseph Cornelius Charamel (IMCL-3, 198); Eugénie Virginie Gumbel, born ca. October 1873 (according to the 1900 United States Federal Census) likely on the Lower Chenal or False River; Joseph Dunbar aka "Richard Dunbar" Gumbel, born on 29 June 1875, on False River, Pointe Coupée Parish, Louisiana, baptized as Joseph Dombart Charanelle (*sic*) (PCP-28, 204); and, Cornélie Gumbel, born on 29 June 1876, likely on the Lower Chenal or False River. Neither Virginie nor Cornélie Gumbel have any baptismal records that could be found.

Likely assisted by his father and/or paternal relations in gaining employment, Joseph Cornelius "Jack" Gumbel was identified in the 1920 and 1930 United States Federal Censuses as a cotton classer in New Orleans, Louisiana, and a cotton export salesman according to the 1940 United States Federal Census.

Jack's first child, Richard Dunbar Gumbel, was born on 4 April 1892. Richard's mother was Marie Valentine Prévost/Allen, who was born in New Orleans on 14 February 1865, to Frank Allen and Marie Sophie Prévost. They are ancestors of well-known television journalist and sportscaster Bryant Gumbel, whose lineage was outlined in a 2017 episode of the *Finding Your Roots* with Henry Louis Gates, Jr.

Jack Gumbel's second marriage was on 8 November 1893, in New Orleans, to Rosa Porche, member of a pioneer creole family that had moved to Lavaca County, Texas, from False River on the eve of the Civil War. Rosa was born in Lavaca County on 12 March 1870 (1871 on tombstone), to Pierre Porche and Rosa Collins, a woman of color. (Note: In the Pierre Porche families' last residence at Bayou Poydras, Pointe Coupée Parish, before moving to Texas, free colored descendants of Colin Lacour also lived in the neighborhood, and had assumed the surname Colin/Collins/Collie, while those in adjacent West Baton Rouge retained the surname Lacour. Rosa was probably a member of that Lacour/Collins family.)

One of Louisiana and Texas' most intriguing figures, Pierre Porche was a largescale cotton planter having a two-story residence (later the Ventress family's Lake Home Plantation) on the Island of False River, a representative to the Louisiana Constitutional Convention of 1845, and the documented father of eighteen children through his two successive wives, Célanie Gremillion and Julie Eugénie Bergeron as well as through a neighbor, Marie Bonaventure, wife of Bernard Perrault, and two women of color of the Porches' enslaved labor force, Julienne and Rosa, both of whom assumed the "Porche" surname. Moreover, during the 1850s New Orleans trial of the abductors of the Olivo family "de couleur," Pierre Porche, their neighbor, testified to having had "relations" with the young Olivo women, stating: "I have had connexion [*sic*] with most of the females, and am not ashamed to confess it, although I do not think the question pertinent. I would blush to steal, but not to answer this question. I do not know that I have children by any of them."

Anticipating the national conflict to come, Pierre Porche moved his extended family, including the issue of three of his unions, and his enslaved labor force to Lavaca County, Texas in 1860. There, they prospered in agriculture, and Pierre was instrumental in the establishment and continued in their support of a Catholic church.

One of the difficulties in sorting out Rosa Porche Gumbel's parents is the fact that both she and her brother Leon Porche both listed Rosa Collins as their mother, although Leon identified his father as "Peter" Porche, while Rose identified her father as "Alphonse" Porche at their respective marriages: Rosa Porche to Cornelius Joseph Gumbel in 1893 and Leon to Una Boyd on 6 February 1899. Moreover the 1870 United States Federal Census for Lavaca Co., Texas, shows a family headed by Rosa Porche, age 28, with her three children: Leona, age 7, Leon, age 3, and Rosa, age 3 months. This family is preceded by Julia, and her eight children. Immediately above Julia's family is the patriarch, Peter Porche, age 66, his wife and five children, including his twenty-nine-year-old son Pierre Evariste.

The question which remains now is the sixty-six-year-old Pierre Porche the father of Rosa Porche's children, or was his twenty-nine-year-old son, Pierre Evariste, the father? Taking a look at Pierre Porche's last will and testament, he appointed his legitimate son Pierre Evariste as his executor and gave him 200 acres of property in Lavaca County, Texas, adjoining acreage which was already his. He also willed 50 acres to Julienne Porche, his faithful servant, formerly enslaved, and his children by her: Cecilia, Athénaise, Adelia, Joseph, Angelle, and Julienne. Of his other legitimate children, he mentioned Josephine Porche Douglass and her daughter Marie Louise as inheriting the rest of his estate. Had he been the father of Rosa Porche's children, Leona, Léon and Rosa, he probably would have mentioned them in his will which was drawn up on 14 September 1875.

Jack Gumbel's first wife, Marie Valéntine Prévost/Allen, married John Senmanet, in 1925 and died in New Orleans in February 1941. Jack's second wife, Rosa Porche, died on 6 May 1943, in New Orleans, and was buried there in St. Louis Cemetery No. 2. Jack Gumbel moved to San Francisco, California, where he died on 22 September 1959, and was interred at Holy Cross Catholic Cemetery at Colma, San Mateo Co., California.

Cornelius Gumbel and Angélique Charamel's second child, Eugénie Virginie Gumbel, was born ca. October 1873, likely on the Lower Chenal or on False River, although we could find no record of her birth or baptism. Virginie Gumbel was married to Valérien Patin on 5 February 1894, at the Immaculate Conception Church at Lakeland, Pointe Coupée Parish (IMCL-6, 52). The groom was from another old *Créole de couleur* family of the parish. He was born on 1 November 1873, on the Lower Chenal to Paul Patin and Alida Baptiste (IMCL-4,29).

Valérien and Virginie's first six children: Marie Laurelia (b. 1894), Marie Apolina (b. 1896), Joseph Leonidas (b. 1898), Joseph Spiridonia (b. 1900), Marie Angélique (b. 1902), and Marie Cornelia (b. 1904), were baptized at the Immaculate Conception Church in Lakeland. The couple moved to Baton Rouge, East Baton Rouge Parish, Louisiana, where five more children were born: Valérien, Jr. (b. 1906), Virkison (b. 1908), Alida (b. 1910), Dauphine (b. 1914), and Elevelina (b. 1915). Valérien Patin worked in a wood yard, where by 1940 he had become its owner.

Virginie Gumbel Patin died on 25 December 1948, at Baton Rouge. We could find no record of her interment. Valerien Patin relocated to New Orleans after her death, where he worked as a carpenter. He died there on 14 September 1957. There is apparently no record of his place of burial either.

Cornelius and Angélique's third child, Joseph Dunbar, later known as Richard Dunbar Gumbel, was born on False River and baptized as Joseph Dombart Charamelle (*sic*) at old St. Mary of False River Church in New Roads. His godfather, Paulin Pourciau, was the son of False River sugar planter Paul F. Pourciau and the childhood neighbor of Angélique Charamel and her family. Richard was married on 15 August 1895, at the old Immaculate Conception Church, Chenal, to Angelina Decuir. (IMCL-6, 66) Angelina was born "Angella Decuir" on the Lower Chenal on 23 July 1873, to Léonce Decuir and Scholastie McKinney, in the extended Decuir family neighborhood (PCP-28, 148).

Richard and Angelina were enumerated in the 1900 Federal Census living in West Baton Rouge Parish with their two children: Clara (b. 25 December 1895), and Léonce (b. 11 September 1897). Joseph, enumerated as Richard, was working as a farmer. Richard and Angelina moved to New Orleans with their only surviving child, Clara, before the 1910 United States Federal Census, where he was employed as a carpenter. Angelina died on 15 May 1924, in New Orleans. Richard was married to briefly to Valentine Irène St. Amant, of yet another pioneer Chenal *Créole de couleur* family. She was born on 18 January 1884, to Joseph Charles St. Amant and Eugénie Berthe Darensbourg (IMCL-5,13). Valentine died on 28 October 1935, in New Orleans. Richard had married again, according to the 1940 United States Federal Census, to twenty-seven-year-old Eleanora, a native of Louisiana, who worked as a waitress at the Gretna High School. Richard Gumbel died in New Orleans on 18 October 1954. We were unable to locate places of burial for Joseph/Richard Gumbel or his wives.

The fourth and last child born to Cornelius Gumbel and Angélique Charamel, named for her father, was born on the Lower Chenal or on False River. Cornélie Gumbel was married on 17 February 1890, at the old Immaculate Conception Church, Chenal, to Valérien Jarreau, a descendant of one of Pointe Coupée Parishes largest families (IMCL-4, 278). The groom was born ca. 1867 on the Island of False River, to Neville Jarreau and his first wife, Joséphine Valérien Simon. Valérien Jarreau, a farmer, and his wife Cornelie's first seven known children were all born and baptized in Pointe Coupée Parish: Henriette (b. 1890), Marie Laurenza (b. 1894), Clarence (b. 1896), Joseph Neuville (b. 1897), Joseph Estelle (probably Estève, but known as "Steve," b. 1900), Rose Delia (b. 1902), and Cornelius Alphonse (b. 1904).

Like many of their generation, the family moved to New Orleans, where in the 1920 United States Federal Census, Valérien apparently stated that his parents were Mexican and spoke Spanish. This may have been an error of the census taker or one of many examples in which people of color who relocated to large cities identified themselves as Spanish, Indian or other ethnicities in order to avoid being enumerated as "negro." At least four more children were born to the couple: Carmelia (b. 1908), Lillian (b. 1910), Lawrence (b. 1915) and Joseph Monford (b. 1915).

Cornelie Gumbel Jarreau died on 25 June 1945, at Chicago, Cook Co., Illinois, and was interred at St. Mary Cemetery, Evergreen Park, Illinois. Her widower, Valérien, returned to their native Pointe Coupée Parish, where he died on 1 April 1951. We could not locate his place of burial, but it was likely in the old Jarreau family tomb in St. Mary Cemetery, in New Roads.

After leaving Pointe Coupée Parish and his four children by Angélique Charamel, Cornelius Gumbel married Rosa Dreyfus on 6 February 1877, at New Orleans. Rosa was born on 16 April 1858, at Jackson, Hinds Co., Mississippi, to Joseph Dreyfus, a native of Westhouse, Bas-Rhin, France, born there on 18 April 1826, and his wife, Babette Goudchaux, born on 8 October 1836, at Brumath, Bas-Rhin, France, to Jacques Goudchaux and his second wife, Rosette Kahn, both Brumath natives. Cornelius and Rosa were the parents of four children: Florence (b. 1878), Daisy (b. 1879), Henry C. (b. 1880), and Alice (b. 1882). The couple and their first two children were enumerated together in the 1880 United States Federal Census, living in New Orleans, Orleans Parish, Louisiana, where Cornelius was working as a wholesale merchant.

Cornelius died on 18 December 1889, and was interred in Metairie Cemetery. Rosa Dreyfus Gumbel died on 15 November 1920, at Kansas City, Jackson Co., Missouri, at the home of her daughter Florence Gumbel Batavia. She was interred in Metairie Cemetery with her husband.

GUMBEL, MAYER & LOEB, "CHENAL STORE" SUBSEQUENTLY AARON LOEB

Gumbel, Mayer & Loeb's, "Chenal Store," was one of four stores operated by the firm of that name. The "Chenal Store" on the Lower Chenal of False River, was occupied by Aaron Loeb, and situated on a tract measuring one arpent fronting on the Lower Chenal by a depth of 40 arpents, and bounded on one side by Francois Decuir and the other by Adeline Decuir.

The firm's "False River Store" near the lower end of False River and head of Bayou Cirier, was occupied by Cornelius Gumbel. Their "Store at Livonia" on the property belonging to John F. Jackson on Bayou Grosse Tête, was occupied by Max Mayer. The "Store of Mayer,

Grabenheimer & Rose." at Musson Station, Iberville Parish, Louisiana, was located on Bayou Maringouin, immediately south of the present-day town of Maringouin, Louisiana.

Aaron Loeb, a native of Neustadt, Rheinpfalz, Germany, and formerly in partnerships and sole proprietor of general stores in other parts of Pointe Coupée Parish, was enumerated in the 1870 United States Federal Census at the "Chenal Store" with $500 in real estate and $2,000 in personal property, living with his clerk, Joseph Gustave, age 30.

In a single act in 1873, the partnership of Gumbel, Mayer & Loeb was dissolved, and Gumbel and Max Mayer conveyed to Loeb all their interest in the stock of the "Chenal Store." Loeb conveyed to Gumbel, Max Mayer, and Mayer, Grabenheimer & Rose., the latter represented by Max Mayer, all of Loeb's interest in "False River Store," the "Store at Livonia," and the "Store of Mayer, Grabenheimer & Rose.

Like Aaron Baum further west on the Lower Chenal, Aaron Loeb was one of the longest-operating and most respected Jewish merchants in Pointe Coupée Parish. Advertisements in the 1876-1877 Bouchereau *Statement of the Sugar Crops Made in Louisiana,* as well as an 1879 issue of *The Pelican*, and 1880-82 issues of the *Pointe Coupée Banner* cumulatively listed the stock of A. Loeb, "Lower Chenal, near Hermitage" as: dry goods, notions, hats, caps, boots, shoes, groceries, wines, liquors, tobacco, cigars, fancy goods, crockery, tinware, trunks, and hardware.

According to the 1880 United Stated Federal Census, Benjamin Weil, the former husband of Rosine Michel, was enumerated as a clerk for and living in the household of Aaron Loeb. Within the next few years, Loeb experienced financial difficulties, and his wife, née Henrietta/Harriet Kaufman, filed suit against him (15th Judicial District Court, No. 609) in 1885 for separation of property. In her petition, Henrietta Kaufman Loeb satisfied the court through a copy of her and Aaron's marriage contract which affirmed that she brought the sum of $6,000 when they married in New Orleans in 1873. A writ of *fieri facias* was filed in Aaron Loeb's name, by which he was declared to owe Henrietta $6,000, with legal interest from 2 January 1885, less a credit of $3,627 for a payment made on 9 January.

The "credit" consisted of the value of Aaron's transfer to Henrietta and included all of his interest in two tracts on the Lower Chenal, one measuring three arpents front by a depth of 40 arpents, bounded by Numa Decuir and Adéline Decuir, together with the Loeb store and other buildings thereupon, and another tract, measuring five acres square, bounded by Paul Saizan and A. Moniotte, apparently on the north bank, or *Coteau du Chenal*, the store merchandise, valued at $500, a lot of sugar mill machinery lying in the yard of the store and residence tract, three mules, a buggy, two wagons, a cart, two cows and calves, and four monetary judgments in Aaron's favor.

The Loeb store was conducted for the next several years by Henrietta Kaufman Loeb and her brother Aaron Kaufman, as the firm of "Mrs. H. Loeb & Co." In anticipation of Aaron Kaufman's marriage to Annie Abramson of nearby West Baton Rouge Parish in 1887, Aaron Loeb built the young couple a house next door to the Loeb store. Henrietta and her brother dissolved their partnership the following year, with Henrietta assuming the business as "Mrs. H. Loeb." Aaron and Annie Abramson Kaufman subsequently moved to Baton Rouge.

Aaron Loeb apparently resumed operation of the Lower Chenal store, and was listed as a dry goods merchant there in the 1900 United States Federal Census. At that time, Leopold Kaufman, Aaron and Henrietta Kaufman's brother, was enumerated as a dry goods salesman living with his own family next door.

ISAAC KEIM

Isaac Keim, a native of Pirmasens, Rheinpfalz, Germany, and formerly a peddler at Waterloo, was a partner in the Lower Chenal mercantile and planting firm of Loeb, Gumbel & Co. in 1865 and 1866. The company's store was located on the land of Edward Loeb & Co., while their cultivation of crops took place on the Loeb & Co. plantation as well as that of J. Lafayette Matthews, located further east on the Lower Chenal, near Hermitage.

Later in 1866, Isaac Keim purchased from the firm of Edward Loeb *Frères* & Co., represented by Emanuel Loeb, two buildings on the firm's property on the Lower Chenal, said tract bounded by Francois and Léon Decuir, two descendants of color of the Decuir family, for $4,000. The buildings were described as: a frame, two-story building on pillars, the first story composed of two rooms, and the second floor a single room, the building measuring 30 feet by 50 feet; and another "store or warehouse" behind, being frame, a having a single story set on pillars, and measuring 20 feet by 30 feet.

Three years later, in 1869, James M. Ginn and Isaac Keim purchased a portion of the former Marcus McCausland Plantation at present-day Lakeland, Louisiana, for $7,372 from Rosine Michel, the widow of Nathan Kern. It was comprised of approximately 186 arpents. In 1871, Ginn & Keim were taken to court by Benjamin "Ben" Gerson, then living in New Orleans (7th Judicial District Court, No. 1478), for an unpaid balance of $1,053.83 for supplies and cash advances that Gerson had provided Ginn & Keim in 1869 and 1870. The partnership had likewise signed a crop pledge in Gerson's favor.

Gerson alleged that Ginn & Keim had shipped to "one Buford" 35 bales of cotton made from the 1870 harvest, valued at $2,000. He continued that Buford had wrongly retained the cotton, and had received it from Ginn with the "approbation" of Keim, as Ginn normally was in charge of shipping the produce. Gerson claimed that Ginn had done this in order to defraud the creditors of Ginn & Keim, including Gerson.

The court ordered the seizure and sale of James Ginn's and Isaac Keim's movable goods, which were enumerated as six mules, being the personal property of Ginn; four Hall plows, being Keim's personal property; and the property held jointly by the partnership of Ginn & Keim, consisting of four Block plows, two Hall plows, two cultivators, 90 tons of cottonseed, and four pair of doubletrees, the total appraisal of which was set at $1,000. Later in 1871, James Ginn and Isaac Keim filed an act of resiliation, by which they returned their portion of the Marcus McCausland plantation to Rosine Kern. Soon thereafter, Rosina leased the plantation to Keim for the term of 10 March - 31 December 1871, for $200, and with a lessor's privilege on his cotton crop to be produced that year. Between 1872 and 1877, Isaac Keim leased the Britto plantation on False River, and by 1880, he had moved to Bayou Maringouin, where he clerked successively, in the stores of Isidore Lehman and August Keller. Among Isaac Keim's last acts recorded in Pointe Coupée Parish was his 23 April 1876 purchase of one lot of livestock, identified as: a gray mare and colt, a dark brown horse, a roan mare and young colt, and a roan filly from, an as-yet unidentified, Amélie Weil. The gray mare, called "Miss Adolphine," was described as having been sold by Keim to Amélie Weil, on 10 January 1870, back when Keim was living on the Lower Chenal. The other animals were the gray mare's increase.

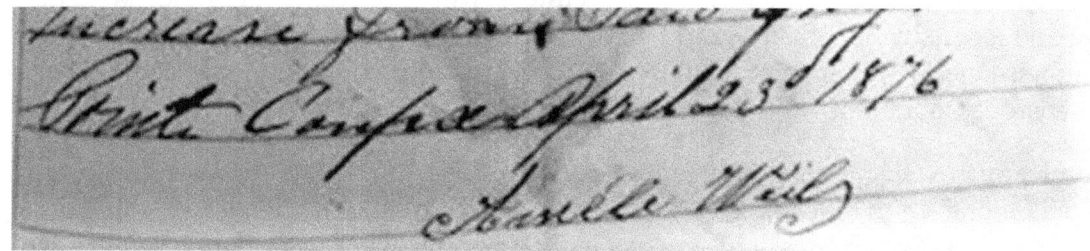

Keim's last mention in Pointe Coupée Parish was in the 1900 United States Federal Census, when he was enumerated as a butcher, living with Louis David and family, on the north bank of the Lower Chenal, on the Island of False River.

ROSINE MICHEL KERN and SON, ABRAHAM KERN

Rosine Michel, a former merchant at Waterloo and New Roads, the widow of Nathan Kern and divorced from Benjamin Weil, purchased 515 acres of the 1,100-arpent Marcus McCausland Plantation on the Lower Chenal, in 1868. In 1869, she sold the eastern portion of her share of the plantation, containing approximately 196 arpents, to the partnership of James M. Ginn and former Waterloo peddler Isaac Keim. In an act dated 1871, Ginn and Keim returned the property to Rosine.

After regaining control of the property in 1871, the widow Kern named it "Fan Plantation" and had the "Fan Store" constructed. It was conducted by her son Léonard Kern for her account. After Leonard's death on 19 January 1876, his brother Abraham "Abe" Kern, born on 3 October 1855 at Waterloo, Pointe Coupée Parish, operated the store for his mother, Rosine.

When Rosine was deposed in the case of Grossman vs. Rosina Kern and Abraham Kern, she testified that prior to his marriage, Abraham had lived in the "Fan Store," and afterward he rented a room from her at the Fan Plantation residence until he ultimately purchased the property from her in 1876 for $3,500. The plantation measured 2 ¾ x 80 arpents, with improvements. He pledged to pay her the amount in a $3,000 note at 8% interest from that year and $500 at 8% interest from 1878.

For his part, Abe Kern testified, in a subsequent court proceeding, that he had bought the store stock from his mother as well as her books and open accounts, paying her a portion of the price and giving her notes for the balance. Kern continued that facing financial difficulties, he attempted to come to an agreement with his creditors, which proved impossible, so he transferred the store and extensive merchandise to his mother, thereby giving her a privilege over certain of the creditors. Due to Abraham's inability to pay the notes, Rosine filed suit against her son (7th Judicial District Court, No. 1886) later in 1878.

Abraham Kern's extensive stock of merchandise, the largest to be recorded on the Lower Chenal, was seized, appraised in block at $4,000, and sold at public sale, including: bolts of calico, swiss, jaconet, pique, poplin, checks, alpaca, stripes, cassimere, black cassinette, veil barege, jeans, white and colored cotton, cottonade, linsey, denim, assorted flannel, twilling, vest lining and inserting; ribbons, trimming, velvet, bindings, tape, thread, cards of buttons, cards of India rubber buttons, cards of pearl buttons, buckles, hooks and eyes, needles, pins, thimbles; towels, tablecloths, quilts, mosquito bars; men's three-piece suits, coats, jacket, knitted jackets, oil cloth coats, vests, cottonade and assorted pants, white and colored shirts, overshirts, shirt bosoms, linen and paper collars, cuff and collar sets, cravats, suspenders, belts, undershirts, and drawers; ladies' scarfs, corsets and strings, and hair nets; men's and boys' socks, stockings, babies' socks; kid and other gloves; pocket handkerchiefs and head kerchiefs; men's hats, boys' straw hats, caps, women's hats, girls' straw hats; men's and boys' boots, men's, boys', women's and children's shoes; silver watches, collar buttons, shirt studs, earrings, bead necklaces; rice, popcorn, salt, tea; canned deviled ham, "assorted" fruits, tomatoes, sardines, lobster and condensed milk; mustard, coffee extract, lemon sugar, lemon extract, nutmeg cakes, jellies, sweet oil, pickles, fine and flint candy, dry cakes, pork, mackerel, yeast powder; wines, gin, beer; tobacco, cigars, pipes; a lot of medicines, cologne, rice powder, shaving soap, razor straps, shaving brushes and cups, brushes, combs, hairpins, tooth brushes, nursing nipples, mirrors; school books, pass books, writing paper, envelopes, pencils; coffee and tea cups and saucers, plates, dishes, bowls, pitchers, bowl and pitcher sets; glasses, goblets, beer glasses, jiggers, salt cellars, jars; spoons, ovens, Dutch pans, coffee mills and drippers, sifters, pie plates, tin cups, cake cutters, dipper, wash pans, chamber pots; soap, candles, matches, blacking, lye, bluing; lamps, lamp gloves and wicks, shoe flies; dolls, marbles, rubber balls, fiddle string, fishing lines and hooks; washboards, tubs, wooden and tin buckets; gun shot and caps; lot of stove pipes, nails, screws, tacks, hoes, hatchets, axe handles, pocket knives, scissors, safe locks, hinges, sandpaper, stoppers, rope, paint, whitewash brushes, axle grease; saddles, iron stirrups, horse collars, back bands, girths, blind bridles, blind (bridle) fasten nuts, trace chains, riding and buggy whips, curry combs and horse brushes; also a showcase, thread box, scale, lot of wrapping paper and bags, duster, step ladder, and chandelier.

Rosine was the highest bidder, at $500 and resumed ownership of "Fan Store." Her sons Abraham, Meyer, and Lazard Kern were enumerated there as clerks according to the 1880 United States Federal Census. An 1881 letterhead as well as account statements of Mrs. R. Kern, "Fan Store," listed the store's inventory as: (bolts of) crossbar muslin, linen, cotton, cottonade, sheeting; thread, notions; hats, shoes, breastpins; groceries, flour, grits, sugar, coffee, candy, pepper, pickles, soda, butter, meat, hams, pork; brandy, gin, cordials; tobacco, soap, hairpins, coffee pots, wash basins, brushes, gun shot, powder and caps, knives, buckets, oil; nails, hatchets, hinges; saddles, bridles; and plows. In 1882 or early 1883, Rosine sold the store and contents back to Abraham for $3,000 "cash." He resumed business, changing the name of the "Fan Store" to the "Delmonico Store."

In 1883, Rosine Michel Kern entered into a leasing agreement with her neighbor immediately to the west, Jacob Grossman, owner of the Celina Plantation, which measured four arpents on the public road by a depth of 80 arpents. Included on the property was a sugar mill, a cotton gin, a residence, and other outbuildings, livestock, wagons and agricultural implements. The ensuing suit of Jacob Grossman vs Abraham Kern and Rosina Kern (15th Judicial District Court, No. 758) relative to her breaking the contract, proved to be one of the largest cases involving Jewish litigants in Pointe Coupée Parish history.

In March 1886, by the time the suit was filed, the Widow Kern had relocated to St. John the Baptist Parish, to live with her son Meyer Kern, who testified that he had preceded her in relocating to St. John the Baptist Parish, where he was a storekeeper, and that his mother had moved "to keep house" for him.

During the short time that she leased Grossman's Celina Plantation, Rosine Michel Kern sold her Fan Plantation to her son Abe for $8,000 in 1885. The "Fan" was bounded on the west by Celina, and on the east by property of M.P. Phillips. Included in the sale of the 2 ¾ by 80-arpent tract was a dwelling house, a store (formerly "Fan," then "Delmonico Store,"), and tenants' cabins.

On 14 April 1885, Abraham Kern married Flora Goldstein at New Orleans. Flora, born on 19 August 1863, in New Orleans, was the daughter of German immigrants, Moses Goldstein, born at Billigheim, Rheinpfalz, Germany, and Bertha Lehman. Abe and Flora were the parents of five children: Sadie (b. 1886), Agathyne (b. 1887), Nathan (b. 1889), Rosebud (b. 1890), and Isaac Leonard (b. 1894).

In 1886, Abraham Kern sold the Fan Plantation, with its dwelling house, store and cabins, to Pervis Chérie Major for $5,250 in cash. Excluded from the sale by Kern were three cisterns and the plantation bell. Kern also reserved the use of the store until 15 Jan 1887 and occupancy of the house for a term of two months following the sale.

Pervis Chérie Major purchased his principal holding, River Lake Plantation, at the lower end of False River in 1892. Included on River Lake, on the little island in the forked head of Bayou Stirling, was the former store of Ben Gerson & Son. That same year, Major sold the Fan

Plantation at Lakeland to St. John the Baptist Parish native Edward Cadbert Lorio, the latter having already acquired the Celina Plantation immediately to the west from Jacob Grossman.

The Fan plantation's main house was rented by the Lorios to sugar cane farmer Albert "Soo Keen" Cline and his family. The property also included a small office occupied by Dr. James Olivier St. Dizier. Both of these structures were demolished at the turn of the 20th-21st centuries. Cline is the object of a well-known story passed down in Pointe Coupée Parish and environs oral history. It is said that Rev. Louis Savouré, then pastor of the Immaculate Conception Church, asked a young boy in Catechism class. "Who made the world? To which the child replied "Soo Keen Cline". His response was likely due to Mr. Cline's wealth and reputation as a conscientious and successful farmer. What Fr. Savouré's reaction was not recalled.

The 1910 United States Federal Census enumerated merchants to either side of E.G. Lorio and his family at Celina Planation: Frank D'Amico, native of Cefalú, Sicily, to the west, and Sol Bernstein to the east. It is therefore quite possible that Bernstein, who was in operation as early as 1900 and until 1917, could have occupied the former Fan/Delmonico Store building.

It is not known definitely what became of the "Fan Store" structure, although, a store building had been located on the adjacent Celina Plantation at the extreme northwest corner of the property since at least the first decade of the 20th century, when it was the general store and residence of Frank D'Amico. It was later the home of Eunice Bueche David, but was ultimately dismantled around the turn of the 20th-21st centuries. As no store appears on descriptions and inventories of Celina Plantation as late as 1886, it is possible that Edward C. Lorio, having acquired both properties by 1892, moved the "Fan Store" from Fan to Celina Plantation.

After an active career in merchandising and litigation, Rosine Michel Kern died in Plaquemine, Iberville Parish, Louisiana on 23 April 1888. She had been living with her sons David and Lazard who were merchants there. Rosine was buried in Hebrew Rest Cemetery No.1, in New Orleans near her first husband.

Abraham Kern spent his last years as a salesman for a dry goods store in Donaldsonville, Ascension Parish, Louisiana. He died at Donaldsonville on 3 December 1910, and was interred there in Bikur Sholim Cemetery. His widow, Flora, went to live in the household of her daughter, Agathyne and her husband, Solon Applebaum, who was a dry goods merchant at Lexington, Holmes Co., Mississippi. Flora's other daughter, Rosebud, having married Solon's brother, Nathan Applebaum, was living next door. Flora Goldstein Kern died on 4 March 1939, at Lexington, Holmes Co., Mississippi. She was interred there in the Odd Fellows Cemetery.

CERF WOLFF, "ALMA STORE"

Cerf Wolff, formerly a merchant at Waterloo and partner in the Langlois & Wolff store at New Roads, owned and operated the "Alma Store" on Pitcher & Barrow's Alma Plantation, at the corner of Bayou Poydras Road in Lakeland. In 1874, New Roads attorney John Yoist, identifying himself as a member of "the Silent firm of Wolff & Yoist," sold to Cerf Wolff all of his interest in the "Alma Store" and dwelling for $4,000. The sale included the store's stock of dry goods, groceries and hardware, the store accounts and notes, plus an unspecified number of wagons, horses, mules, and cows.

An 1871 letterhead and statement of "Alma Store" and advertisements in the 1876-1877 edition of Bouchereau's *Statement of the Sugar Crops Made in Louisiana,* 1879 issues of *The Pelican,* and 1880-1885 *Pointe Coupée Banner editions* cumulatively listed the Wolffs' wares as: dry goods; notions; ladies' and gents' furnishing goods, clothing; hats, caps; boots, shoes; groceries and provisions, Western produce; wines, liquors; medicines, perfumery, lye; tobacco, pipes; fancy articles, crockery, glassware, cutlery, tinware; hardware; and saddlery.

Among the medicines carried by Cerf Wolff in "Alma Store" was laudanum. An existing 1871 bill for customer St. Ville LeBeau, a cotton planter on the northern or "Island side" of the Lower Chenal, indicates the latter purchased a total of 148 ounces of the drug, as well as four bottles of whiskey, a box of lye, a pipe, and a pair of shoes, during an eight-month period. LeBeau's son, Confederate veteran, attorney, and professor P.O. LeBeau, was remembered in family oral history as a "laudanum fiend," and likely the consumer of that item purchased on his father's account with Wolff.

After his death in 1884, Cerf Wolff was succeeded as a general merchant in the "Alma Store" by his widow, née Sarah Zacharias. The "Alma Corner" remained a center of retail operations for generations thereafter. Joe Fiorenza, an accommodating native of Sicily, operated a popular "confectionery" (candy and fruit) store there for nearly 20 years before being murdered in his establishment, on New Year's Night 1934, by unknown parties.

CERF WOLFF, "BURNT BRIDGE STORE"

In addition to his "Alma Store" on Pitcher & Barrow's plantation of that name east of Lakeland, Louisiana, Cerf Wolff owned several tracts of land in Pointe Coupée and West Baton Rouge Parishes, and operated the "Burnt Bridge Store" on his residence at Bayou Cirier Plantation on the Lower Chenal, west of Lakeland. Wolff purchased this tract for $5,000 in 1872 from Mathilde Laurans, wife of Auguste Provosty, Jr. It measured 4 1/2 arpents wide by a depth of 80 arpents, and was bounded on the west by land belonging to the New York Warehouse & Security Co. (Ingleside Plantation) and east by that of former Confederate army colonel W.G. Vincent & Co.

Included on the property, at the southwest corner of the Bayou Cirier crossing, was the building occupied for several years previously by Gumbel, Mayer & Loeb's "False River Store." Soon after his purchase, Wolff granted the firm a continuation of their lease, for five years running from 1 January 1872 through 1 June 1877, at the rate of $350. After termination of the lease, Cerf Wolff, while continuing to own and operate the "Alma Store," 1 1/3 mile east, opened the "Burnt Bridge Store" in his building formerly occupied by Gumbel, Mayer & Co. He leased its second floor for a period of nine years, between 1877 and 1886, to Livonia Lodge No. 220, F. & A. M., for use as a lodge hall. Wolff, a stalwart member of the lodge, whose participants included Gentiles and Jews in about equal number, charged only $100 for the entire period of the lease.

According to the Antoine Albéric Lorio family, who have owned Bayou Cirier and Ingleside plantations since the early 20th century, the "Burnt Bridge" itself was a wooden bridge spanning Bayou Cirier which was destroyed by Federal troops who had encamped on its eastern side during the Civil War. The Pointe Coupée Parish Police Jury operated a toll ferry at the crossing for several years thereafter, until building a dyke to support the public road.

In 1882, Cerf Wolff sold four area properties to Williamsport merchant Meyer Levy for $7,000: the Bayou Cirier Plantation, with improvements, including the "Burnt Bridge Store"; a smaller improved tract at present-day Rougon; and two tracts east of Bayou Poydras in nearby West Baton Rouge Parish. Levy renamed the "Burnt Bridge Store" the "Diamond W Store." However, in 1884, Meyer Levy sold the four tracts of land, including the store building, back to Cerf Wolff for $8,500 cash. A succession of merchants operated the "Burnt Bridge Store and its upper floor was the venue of community balls into the 20th century, according to Lorio family oral history.

Cerf Wolff died on 4 December 1884, in Lakeland, Pointe Coupée Parish, and was interred in the Jewish Cemetery in Baton Rouge, Louisiana. His widow, Sarah Zacharias, moved to New Orleans where she died on 18 May 1904. She was interred there in Gates of Prayer Cemetery No. 2.

HENRY HYMAN

According to his burial record, Henry Hyman was born on 4 March 1836, at Poland, Russian Empire, but information given in the 1900 United States Federal Census records that he was born in August 1834. He immigrated ca. 1855 to New York where he and his wife, Francis Metz/Mertz (b. ca. August 1832 in Germany), had two children: George (b. 1858), and Flora (b. 1861).

The Hyman family probably came south after the Civil War and first appeared in Pointe Coupée Parish, Louisiana, in 1870, when he purchased an improved lot measuring 56 feet on the Mississippi River "or" on the Front Street of Waterloo, by a depth of one arpent, bounded by Jean Grouzard and Hyacinthe Pock, from False River merchant and blacksmith, Michel Michel.

Hyman and his family subsequently moved to Lakeland, where he opened a general store in 1872. The Pointe Coupée Parish Police Jury minutes for that same year indicated that Henry

Hyman paid the following amounts for his licenses: $30 to conduct a store; $25 to sell alcohol; and $40 to operate a peddling wagon. The 1876-1877 *Statement of the Sugar Crops Made in Louisiana* carried an advertisement for H. Hyman, listing the following articles in his store: dry goods, notions, hats, boots, shoes, groceries, wines, liquors, crockery, and hardware.

According to the 1880 United States Federal Census, Hyman, his wife and children were still living in the same area, but he was working as a butcher. The family was renting a room to a forty-year-old German laborer, J. Liebrech (*sic*). In 1882, Henry Hyman was succeeded as the merchant at Lakeland by Charles Gottlieb.

Henry Hyman and his family eventually moved to Vicksburg, Warren Co., Mississippi, where he was enumerated in the 1900 United States Federal Census. He was still working as a butcher as was his son, George. Henry's wife was a "boarding housekeeper. She was renting to a Polish widower, Isaac Reigler. Their daughter Flora, the first wife of Leopold Kaufman, was no longer living with the family.

Henry died at Vicksburg on 20 April 1902, from "bronchitis," and was interred there in Anshe Chesed Cemetery. Francis Hyman followed on 30 November 1909, according to the Anshe Chesed Kadisha journal, although there is no trace of her tombstone there.

CHARLES GOTTLIEB

Charles Gottlieb was born on 4 September 1855, at Baltimore, Maryland, to Solomon "Sol" Gottlieb, a native of Winnweiler, Rheinpfalz, Germany, and Doretta "Dora" Rosensweig, born in the Kingdom of Saxony. He moved as a child with his family to Baton Rouge, East Baton Rouge Parish, Louisiana, in 1863. While Sol Gottlieb was enumerated as a grocery and dry goods merchant with $1,400 in person property in the 1870 United States Federal Census, ten years later he was identified as a tailor.

Following in his father's footsteps, Charles was enumerated as a store clerk in Baton Rouge in both the 1870 and 1880 United States Federal Censuses. Moving shortly thereafter to the Lower Chenal in Pointe Coupée Parish, Gottlieb succeeded Henry Hyman as a merchant at Lakeland. He was assessed there in the 1882 Pointe Coupée Parish Tax Roll for $300 in merchandise and $25 for his ownership of a horse.

The accidental destruction by fire of the 1890 United States Federal Census records and absence of Pointe Coupée Parish business licenses between 1881 and 1900 make it difficult to determine when Charles Gottlieb returned to Baton Rouge. He was identified there in the 1900 United States Federal Census as a grocer, and in the *Baton Rouge, LA City Directory* editions of 1908-1915 as the proprietor of the Capital Billiard Hall, in the Singletary Building, near the northeast corner of Third and Convention Streets.

Charles Gottlieb died, unmarried, in Baton Rouge on 1 March 1917, and was interred in the city's Jewish Cemetery. Charles and Moses Gottlieb's brother Joseph Gottlieb was well known in Pointe Coupée Parish as the representative of the Ben Mayer wholesale company, the head of an insurance company, a founding board member of Bank of New Roads, and a welcome business visitor to New Roads according to many contemporary *Pointe Coupée Banner* articles.

JACOB S. and MRS. E. J. MEYER'S "CREOLE STORE"

Mr. and Mrs. Jacob S. Meyer operated a general store for several years on the plantation of J. Émar Juge, a person of color, on the Lower Chenal. Jacob Meyer was born on 26 March 1848, in Lautersheim, Rheinpfalz, Germany. Before arriving in Pointe Coupée Parish, Meyer had been a resident of Houston, Harris Co., Texas, where he met and married Ellen Emmich on 18 January 1872. Ellen was born on 17 November 1852, in Lafayette, Tippecanoe Co., Indiana, to Zacharias Emmich, a native of Friedenberg, Kingdom of Baden (Germany), and his wife Cecilia Margolies, born at Posen, Poland, Kingdom of Prussia. Two of Jake and Ellen's children were born at Houston: Louis (b. 1873), and Esther (b. 1875).

Jacob Meyer opened his store in Pointe Coupée Parish, Louisiana, in 1878. Two years later, he was taken to court (Late Parish Court, No. 1349) by Flash, Preston & Co. of New Orleans for $322.74 owed for merchandise in 1880. The court ruled in the wholesalers' amount, at eight percent interest, from 5 November 1879. As Jacob Meyer was unable to pay, a writ of *fieri facias* was issued, and the court ordered the seizure and public sale of his property.

Meyer's merchandise was itemized as: 19 remnants of fabrics, including dress goods, pants goods, and bed ticking; thread, buttons; eight mosquito bars; stockings, socks; 38 hats; five ladies' hats; 57 pairs of shoes; cornmeal, tea, soda cakes, candy; canned salmon, oysters, condensed milk and yeast powder; nutmeg, ginger root, cinnamon root, pickles; liquors, gin, fruit in brandy; tobacco, pipes, tobacco pouches, cigarette papers; toilet sets, combs, shaving brushes, razor straps; cakes of soap, lye, blacking, shoe brushes, stove polish; writing paper, tablets, envelopes, (fools)cap paper, ink, slate and lead pencils; china cups, other cups and saucers, mugs, plates, bowl and pitcher sets; (drinking) glass sets, large and small glasses, glass pitchers; pots, coffee mills, flasks, cheese trays; tin ware, molasses cans; candlesticks, glass lamps, burners, wicks, matches; violins; dolls, marbles; brooms, pails, washboards, washing lines, clothespins; nails, window glass, hoes, hatchets, shears, axe and saw handles, coffin screws, lap rings; riding and cart saddles, wooden stirrups, bridles, blind bridles, halters, backbands, girts, breeching. Also put up for sale were his store fixtures, consisting of a showcase, two pair of scales, a thread box, a lot of (wrapping) paper and bags, and a gray mare.

Later in 1880, Meyer's wife, née Ellen J. Emmich, petitioned for and received judgment (15th Judicial District Court, No. 6) for separation of property from her husband, citing his financially "embarrassed" state of affairs.

Following the birth of the Meyers' third child, Theodore David, in May of 1881, Ellen J. Emmich Meyer reopened the store on the Juge planation in her name. Operating as "Mrs. E. J. Meyer, Creole Store," she placed an advertisement in the 1 January 1882 *Pointe Coupée Banner* which read: "A Full Stock of General Merchandise. Family and Plantation Supplies constantly kept on hand. Sale of Horses and Mules a specialty. Liberal Advances made on all kinds of Country Produce."

At least one lawsuit filed by Mrs. Meyer against one of her customers, her landlord, J. Émar Juge (15th Judicial District Court, 199), included a small "Star" brand notebook containing a carefully written itemization of purchases by Juge and his daughter. Whether Mrs. Meyer provided such notebooks for all of her patrons or it was Juge's personal record is unknown.

Writing many years later in "The Story of My Life as Far as I Can Remember," a childhood neighbor of Jacob and Ellen Emmich Meyer, Lelia Decuir Lejeune, a younger half-sister of Angela Decuir, the latter who married Charles Adalbert Gumbel, natural son of Simon Gumbel and Amelie Amar, was obviously referring to them when she stated:

> There was a Jewish family who owned a grocery store; they always found [tailoring] customers for her [Lelia's mother, Widow Céleste Amar Decuir]. Our mother was so kind to everyone; everybody liked her and tried to help her in every way. This Jewish family had a little daughter younger than us, but we always used to play together. One day she had a birthday party. We were invited, also our niece and some other children. They served chocolate, and I did not care for mine. There was a little colored girl who was sitting on the floor behind my back. Through the pantry door between the dining room, I handed her my cup of chocolate. One of the men of the house walked in to see how we liked the party. This colored girl just dumped the cup of chocolate on the floor under the door. I was so sorry it happened with mine.

In recalling her mother's frequent and agonizing headaches, Mrs. Lejeune was likely referring to the Meyers again, stating that "…a young Jewish girl came over; seeing how she [Mme. Decuir] was suffering, she [the girl] went and asked her mother to give her a few tablets of Gesler's magnesium. So that was it. She hardly had any more headaches."

While his wife was running the "Creole Store," Jacob S. Meyer was involved in an altercation with neighboring merchant Aaron Baum, in which the latter pressed charges of assault and battery. The 25 June 1881 issue of the *Pointe Coupée Banner* reported Judge (John) Yoist as having examined Meyer and placing him under "peace bond" (i.e., restraining order). The following week, the 2 July issue of the paper related that the judge had Meyer fined $10 and jailed for contempt of court while giving his testimony. The outcome of the case remains unknown.

In the wake of the 1882 flood, Ellen Emmich Meyer had a few judgments filed against her for outstanding debts. A buggy and several head of horses were seized and sold at public sale in satisfaction of the amounts owed. In 1883, her husband, Jacob S. Meyer, declared that he had been a resident of Pointe Coupée Parish for six years, filed a homestead exemption, and further declared ownership of one bay mare, a cow and calf, and a cart, all of which were valued together at $80.

The Jacob S. Meyers moved to Baton Rouge, East Baton Rouge Parish, Louisiana, before their last child, Zacharias Emmich Meyer was born on 7 July 1889. The Meyer family, including Jacob, his wife Ellen, their sons Theodore and Zacharias, their daughter Esther and her husband, Albert Frank, with their children, Wilhelmina and Libbie, were enumerated in the 1900 United States Federal Census for Baton Rouge.

Before his death on 14 June 1906, Jacob Meyer had been working as a music dealer. His widow, Ellen Emmich, died on 13 February 1922. Both were interred in the Jewish Cemetery in Baton Rouge. (Note: Although Ellen Emmich's tombstone indicates she was born in Lafayette, Indiana, the Texas Death Certificate of her son Zacharias gives her birth as Indianapolis, Indiana.)

JACOB GROSSMAN

Jacob Grossman was born on 15 May 1848, at Lautenberg, Poland, Prussian Empire. He probably immigrated shortly after the close of the Civil War. Before immigrating, he was married to Lena Salomon, born ca. August 1845, at Strassburg, (now Brodnica), Poland, Prussian Empire. Their first child, Louis Grossman, was said to have been born in New Orleans in April 1865, although there is no record for it. The Grossmans settled in Baton Rouge, East Baton Rouge Parish, where their sons, Adolph (b. 1866), and Isidore (b. 1869), were born.

We believe that Grossman chose Baton Rouge, because his wife Lena, was either the sister or cousin of Bertha Salomon, also a native of Strassburg, who became the wife of Baton Rouge mercantile giant, Samuel Abramson. The Abramsons had met and married in Baton Rouge ca. 1860, only a few years before the Grossmans arrived.

Jacob Grossman and his family moved on to West Baton Rouge Parish, Louisiana, where he was enumerated in both the 1870 and 1880 United States Federal Censuses as a merchant. He had established a general store around which a small community grew. By 1876 he had been appointed Postmaster at the post office known as Lobdell's Store, Louisiana, on the Mississippi River. In 1879, the name of the post office was changed to Grossman's Landing, Louisiana, and he continued to serve as postmaster until succeeded by Emanuel Kaufman in 1882. Jacob and Lena's last child, Celina, was born on 29 August 1877, probably in their West Baton Rouge Parish home.

On 31 December 1879, Jacob Grossman purchased the former Robert McCoy Buford plantation at Lakeland, measuring about four arpents front on the former bed of the False River by a depth of 80 arpents, totaling 319 arpents, from Pointe Coupée Parish Sheriff, E.G. Beuker, administrator of Buford's succession, and George Pitcher, for a total price of $7,000. The property was bounded on the east by the property belonging to Rosine Michel, the widow of Nathan Kern.

The plantation was identified as Dahey in several editions of Bouchereau's *Statement of the Sugar Crops Made in Louisiana*, but, at least since the time of the Powell Map of 1848, the name Celina was attached to the site. Elaine C. Lorio, in her 1932 Louisiana State University Master's Thesis "The Place-Names of Pointe Coupée Parish," quoted Judge L.B. Claiborne as attributing the naming of the plantation "Celina" to "an Indian girl in the Choctaw Tribe, who roamed and camped on this place" in antebellum times. Claiborne, born in 1853 at the nearby Glynnwood Plantation in present-day Glynn, Louisiana, claimed that he, in his childhood, came in contact with this special branch of the [Choctaw] tribe, and traded trinkets with them."

Coincidentally, more than two years before his purchase of the plantation at Lakeland, Jacob Grossman and his wife, Lena, had a daughter, born on 29 August 1877, whom they named Celina Grossman. She was the future wife of Alexander Weinfeld, of the Grossman – Weinfeld millinery stores of New Orleans and New Roads.

Soon after acquiring Celina Plantation, Jacob Grossman filed suit against Charles A. Buford (7th Judicial District Court, No. 1957) on 9 January 1880, for the latter's continued residency on the property without his consent. Buford, a son of the former owner of the plantation, Robert McCoy Buford, was ordered by the court to vacate the premises.

Jacob Grossman leased Celina Plantation at Lakeland to Louis "Boat" David, a native of the north bank or "Island side" of the Lower Chenal in 1882-1883. David was a merchant, cotton gin, moss press, and flatboat operator in partnership with his brother-in-law, Francois Joseph "F.J." Guérin, as Louis David & Co. Their "Picayune Store," gin and press were located just east of the old Immaculate Conception Church and Cemetery at Chenal. Guérin in the contentious suit he filed against his partner, Louis David, (F.J. Guérin vs Louis David, 15th Judicial District Court, No. 559) in 1884, in order to dissolve their partnership, testified at length to David's occupation of "the Grossman place," i.e., Celina Plantation, as did witnesses for both the prosecution and defense.

Guérin stated that David had rented the Grossman plantation for David's personal account in 1883, and that the firm of Louis David & Co., of which Guérin was a partner, furnished David with corn and oats amounting to $30 and bagging and ties priced at $40. He further claimed that David had received a note for $130 as the price of sugar cane produced by the latter on the Grossman place. He contended that David had "discounted" it with neighboring merchant Abraham Kern, but David would not inform Guérin the whereabouts of said note. David also contended the note given him by Abraham Kern was for sugar cane David produced on and sold from the Grossman plantation from the crop of 1882.

F.J. Guérin also stated that Hermitage merchant F.E. Trudeau had loaned a flatboat to David (likely the reason for David's nickname, "Boat"), which was used by their company to deliver produce through the Lower Chenal to Trudeau's Landing on the Mississippi River, and to return with "merchandise," but did not specify for which store, theirs or someone else's. Guérin affirmed that he personally made the oars for the boat, and that he operated it as often as David did especially at night and when David was ill. He also alleged that David had realized three bales of cotton from his cultivation of the Grossman plantation, of which the firm received no accounting, Moreover, one of the firm's customers, Romain Harrison, continued to owe the firm a balance of $36 for goods, although Harrison had produced cotton on the Grossman plantation as well.

Louis David, denied virtually all of Guérin's claims, stating that he (David), his wife and children lived on the Grossman plantation at Lakeland for two years (1883-1883), buying their provisions from the neighboring stores of Mrs. Rosine Michel Kern, Abraham Kaufman, M.P. Phillips and (Pervis C.) Major. "While I had the Grossman place in charge, I lived on it. I gave all my time and attention to the affairs of the plantation," David stated, adding that when he went over to the "Picayune Store," his partner, F.J. Guérin, was away at Hermitage Landing, and the store had been locked. David continued that Guérin refused to let him examine the firm's books or attempt a "settlement" in order to dissolve the partnership. The partnership of Louis David & Co. was dissolved as an outcome of the suit, F.J. Guérin having paid many of its debts.

Jacob Grossman, meanwhile, had expanded his business into New Orleans in 1882, going into partnership with former Cook's Landing merchant Simon Hermann as Hermann & Grossman. After six years, Hermann retired and Grossman purchased the former's interest, and formed the new firm of J. Grossman & Sons, which had an extensive Pointe Coupée patronage.

Towards the end of 1883, Jacob Grossman, desirous of having another tenant operate his plantation at Lakeland, entered into a lease agreement with neighboring landowner Rosine Michel Kern for a period of five years beginning in 1884. Included in the lease of Celina

Plantation, was its sugar mill, cotton gin, a residence, and other outbuildings, eight mules, three oxen, two cows, a lot of wagons and farming implements. As in previous transactions, Rosine Michel Kern signed the document with an "x."

On 29 January 1886, Jacob Grossman filed suit against Abraham Kern and his mother, Rosine Michel Kern (15tth Judicial District Court, No. 758), for breach of contract. Increasingly desirous of ridding himself of his Lower Chenal property, Jacob Grossman sold the Celina sugar plantation, lock, stock and barrel to St. John the Baptist Parish native Edward Cadbert Lorio. In 1892, Lorio purchased the Fan Plantation immediately adjoining Celina to the east from Abraham Kern. Lorio descendants continue to own the combined properties to this day.

Patricia Lorio Langlois, a great-granddaughter of Mr. and Mrs. Edward C. Lorio, and her husband, Jackie, beautifully restored the Celina Plantation residence and grounds in the 1980s. It is admired by residents and tourists alike as one of the beautiful attractions of old Pointe Coupée. Mrs. Langlois, related that a deteriorating wooden cross had stood beneath the great live oak tree which continues to grace the rear of the home, and that plantation tenants avoided the area, as they feared it to be a gravesite. If so, it would likely have dated from the time of the Robert McCoy Buford family, from whose succession Jacob Grossman had purchased the plantation.

Until fairly recent years, a former store building stood at the northwest corner of the Celina tract, near the public road. In the early 1900s, it served as the combination store and residence of Cefalú, Sicily, general merchant Frank D'Amico and his family, and later as the home of Mrs. Eunice Webre David. Prior to the D'Amicos' occupancy, the store may have been the location of any of the number of Jewish mercantile businesses which operated in the thriving late 19th century Lakeland community.

Lena Salomon Grossman died in New Orleans on 5 May 1890, and was interred in Hebrew Rest Cemetery No. 1. Jacob Grossman followed her on 4 November 1899, and was interred with her. The 5 Nov 1899 New Orleans *Daily Picayune*, published an obituary and woodcut of Jacob Grossman, citing his charitable work in that city, his membership in the Jewish Widows' and Orphans' Home, and various Masonic affiliations. Jacob's eldest son, thirty-two-year-old Louis Grossman, predeceased his father having died on 20 March 1898, and is interred near his parents.

GROSSMAN VS. KERN & KERN

In 1883, Jacob Grossman, a resident of New Orleans and the partner of former Cook's Landing merchant Simon Hermann as Hermann & Grossman, wholesalers, leased to his landowning neighbor on the east, the widow Rosine Michel Kern, Grossman's Celina Plantation, at Lakeland, on the Lower Chenal of False River. The term was for 1884-1889, at a rate of $1,000 per year. Rosine Kern also agreed to insure the sugar "house" (i.e., mill) for $1,000 when not in use and $2,000 when in use, to keep the cotton gin insured for $1,000, to pay State, Parish and Levee District taxes, to take care of the livestock and their increase, not to "remove or break" any of the improvements, and to return said plantation and movables to him in sound condition at the end of the lease.

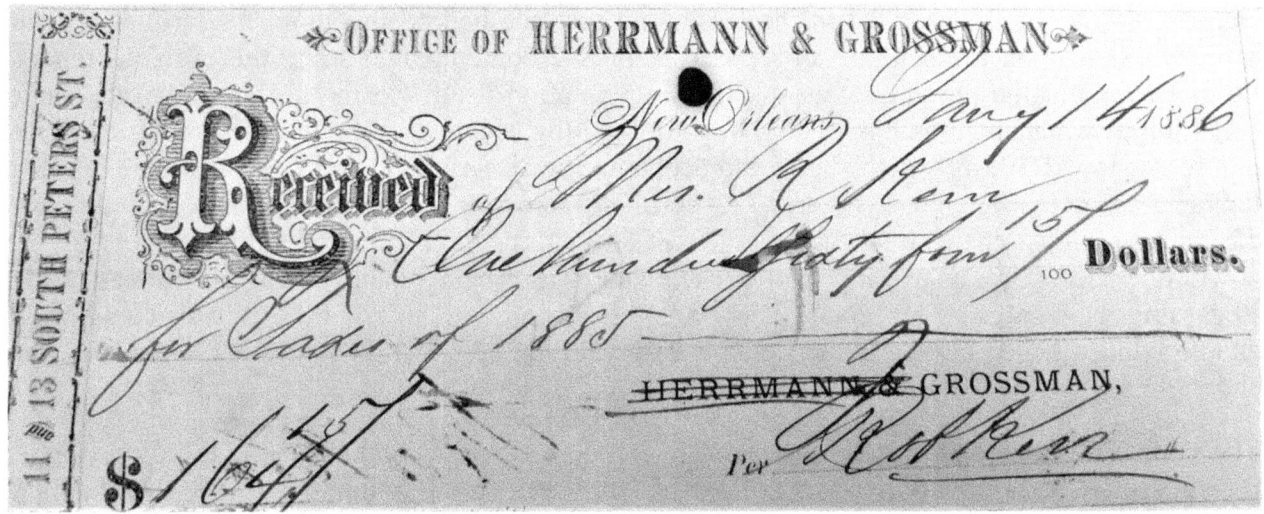

Tax Payment to Herrmann & Grossman for $164.15 paid in 1885 by Mrs. R. Kern during rental of Celina Plantation.

Three year later, in 1886, Grossman filed suit against Rosina Kern and her son, Abraham Kern (15th Judicial District Court, No. 758), for breach of contract. Grossman stated that Rosine had illegally transferred the lease to her son, and that the two "wrongfully conspired to injure Petitioner [Grossman] and deprive him of his rightful enjoyment of said property."

Grossman claimed that the despite the fact that he had deducted from the Kerns's rent the amount of $1,500, in exchange for which they agreed to construct protection levees on Celina, they failed to do so. He further claimed that they sold four of his mules and two oxen without either his knowledge or their accounting. Grossman also contended that the mother and son had sold machinery out of the sugar mill and cotton gin and had torn away flooring, bricks, and other materials from said buildings. Moreover, he alleged that they had damaged a steam boiler and removed four of Celina plantation's cisterns to their own Fan plantation next door, and had sold a valuable saddle belonging to him and kept the money.

Grossman declared the Kerns to be indebted to him in the following amounts: $1,500 for rent, four mules at $600, two oxen at $80, building materials and replacement costs at $250, damage to the boiler at $50, replacement of sugar mill engine at $150, repair or replacement of cotton gin engine at $75, four cisterns at $160, a saddle at $20, and "for unjustly denying the Petitioner of a judgement and possession of his plantation, among other injuries" the sum of $1,000."

Jacob Grossman's attorney was Thomas H. Hewes, future partner of Isaac Bigman in the Bigman & Hewes (Cotton) Ginnery at Oscar. The Kerns were defended by future Louisiana Supreme Court Justice Olivier O. Provosty, husband of Euphémie Labatut, the latter the childhood next-door-neighbor and contemporary of Alice Heine, a future Princess of Monaco.

The Kerns' response to Grossman's petition was mutual denial of "all and singular allegations." Rosine Kern admitted that she had had a contract with Grossman, but that the inventory enumerating all the movables on the Celina Plantation was erroneous, and many items listed thereon were "not found" by her, although she later testified that the inventory taken by Isaac Baum was correct and had been witnessed by Celina tenants Victorin Pourciau and William Spooner. She swore that she asked to confer with Grossman because the condition of the plantation was not as described in the lease, and that she had an inventory made of what was actually existing on it when she took possession. She contemplated suing the previous tenant, Louis David, for the missing items. As for the plantation itself, Rosine declared it in the same condition as when she took possession, but admitted that she had sold two oxen for $60 and two mattresses for $1.50, for which she would account. She also claimed that Grossman had told her to "bleed the place for all it was worth." As for the cisterns, Rosine claimed there were only three of them, and in disrepair, so she had them fixed and returned to Celina Plantation. Regarding the cows, one died, Grossman took another, and one was found in the woods six months later. Regarding the protection levee, she averred that her neighbor, Sheriff E.G. Beuker complained and convinced her to build a dyke (i.e., a dam within the bed of the bayou), and Grossman had acquiesced.

The court testimony and depositions taken in Pointe Coupée, Orleans and St. John the Baptist parishes, in the case of Grossman vs Kern and Kern are illuminating as to contemporary agricultural practices, and the state of affairs during the floods of 1882 and 1884.

Rosine's depositions were taken in St. John the Baptist Parish, where she had moved to keep house for her son, Meyer Kern. She claimed that the lease agreement between herself and Grossman had been made at the Fan Store in Lakeland, to which Abraham was not a party, nor had she transferred it to him. Rosine stated that she gave up her lease of Celina on 1 December 1885, and that her son Abraham had informed Grossman's partner, Simon Hermann, in New Orleans, since Grossman was absent from the office. She claimed that she might have continued the lease if Grossman had forgone the payments for insurance and taxes, but Grossman had refused and both her sons, Meyer and Abraham, had witnessed that conversation.

She admitted to having sold two oxen for $60, but she needed mules to cultivate the cotton crop. Four had died, and she had sold one to Cerf Wolff's wife, Sarah Zacharias, but it had drowned in Bayou Cirier. Moreover, she alleged that Grossman had given his permission to do it. As to the damage or removal of the sugar mill and cotton gin machinery, she admitted only to have moved approximately six planks from the mill to the gin in order to build a floor on which the cottonseed could be placed.

Rosine Kern accused Grossman of trying to break the lease by selling the property, first to A.A. Alford of Walls, West Baton Rouge Parish, and then to Pervis Chérie Major, but she objected each time. She ended her testimony by swearing that she had nothing to do with the crops, but only received rent from the tenants in cash, not cotton, which the previous year amounted to $900 paid on 15 August, the traditional day of the beginning of the hay harvest.

Jacob Grossman's business partner in New Orleans, Simon Hermann, testified that late in 1885, Abraham Kern visited the Hermann & Grossman office in New Orleans and claimed that his mother had "sold out everything which she owned in her name... & wanted to annul the lease." Kern continued that his mother was responsible for nothing concerning Celina and that he was ready to lease it for $800 per year, but without paying for insurance or taxes. Abraham Kern returned on 5 or 6 January 1886, at which time Grossman demanded and received cash payment for the taxes, and accepted a note for the amount of the insurance.

There were several letters from Kern to Grossman, filed as evidence in the suit, requesting the latter to either lease or sell Celina to him for $8,000. Kern also encouraged Grossman to file suit against former lessee Louis David for any rent which may have been due and for items from Celina that David had allegedly secreted in Kern's store.

Grossman testified that: the inventory of Celina Plantation had been taken by himself, Abraham Kern, and Louis David on 30 August 1883, and was correct. He also alleged that Abe Kern had told him that his mother, Rosine, had transferred the lease over to him. Grossman stated that he told Kern he had heard that Kern had sold his oxen, removed his cisterns, and damaged the sugar mill, at which time Kern became aggressive, cursed at him, and placed his hand in his back pocket as if to draw a weapon. It was because of this that Grossman said he had filed the suit against Rosine Kern, after telling Abe Kern that he would not sell Celina to him. He did consider selling the place to A.A. Alford for $8,000 just to be rid of it.

In further testimony, Grossman said he believed that Abraham Kern had removed the sugar mill engine to the cotton gin while Louis David was still in possession of Celina, and that Kern and David were in "partnership" at the time of the removal. However, he swore that he had never authorized Rosine Kern to sell anything from the plantation "and never told her to 'bleed the place."

Jacob Grossman confirmed that Rosine had paid $500 as the rent for 1884 and 1885, and that the missing livestock included the eight mules, the larger worth $200 and the smaller ones worth $100 to $150, and that the oxen which were well broken were worth $40 to $50 apiece. He also admitted to having taken one of the cows for himself.

Testifying to his business arrangement with Louis David, who rented Celina before Rosine, Grossman stated that David had a two-year lease, starting in May or June 1882, after the flood of 1882, for which David had paid him $1200 in the second year, that David had not paid tax or insurance on the plantation; that the first inventory taken had been when David was still the lessee, and that he (Grossman) had not visited the sugar mill at that time. Between the time of the first and second inventories, Grossman admitted that some things were missing, but that he had never seen the inventory dated 15 January 1884, before Rosine had assumed her lease.

Regarding the disagreement over the levee question versus a dyke, Grossman claimed that he was not involved, that he had reviewed plans for a levee with Dr. Peter Randolph, but had only learned of the dyke from Lakeland neighbor, M.P. Philips. He also stated that he thought the levee should have been built but never complained to Rosine when it wasn't constructed.

William Gross, an engineer, testified that he was employed on Celina by Abraham Kern in the fall of 1883 to take down the sugar mill engine and move it to the cotton gin, but it needed repair and a part was missing which was found at Louis David's home. Gross also said he saw a Celina cane wagon as far away as Austerlitz Plantation on False River.

Celina tenants Clément Jarreau and Victorin Pourciau claimed they had bought animals from the plantation. Jarreau purchased two oxen at $30 each, a mule, two yearlings, a heifer and some corn for around $50. Pourciau bought a mule named "Garfield" for $110, which he returned eight months later, but the mule had never left the plantation. He also bought 2 mattresses for $1.50.

Neighbor Isidore Wolff, son of Cerf and Sarah Zacharia Wolff, claimed that Grossman's mule "Claiborne" was rented to Alfred Jackson, a tenant on his mother's plantation, for $30 in 1884, but that the mule had died. Moreover, the Celina Plantation was worth about $800 annual rent in the early 1880s, but that the place had gone downhill, and it would take from $1,500 to $2,000 to rehabilitate it. The ditches, bridges, and fences would require at least $180 to repair.

Wolff stated that no levee had been built along the bayou bank on Celina in 1884, but after that year's flood a dyke near the "Fan Store" was enlarged at a cost of approximately $50, but there had been an existing levee in front of Celina (i.e., along the bank of the Lower Chenal *batture*), which was "nothing more than a large cane ridge," built in 1882, that extended to Wolff's place. He continued that a dyke had been built in 1884, across a bayou along the property line between the Phillips and Celina plantations, located on Wolff's and Grossman's land, which did not cost more than $300, although he had been willing to spend around $700 for a better one. Wolff continued that he, Abraham Kern, and Phillips had agreed to each build a portion of the work, and he thought Kern had undertaken to do some work near the Celina sugar mill as well, in a low place so as to protect it, but had abandoned the effort. It was also he who had objected to the levee between Celina and his place because it would "throw him out into the water," and would not be much protection for Celina.

Another witness, O. McHugh, testified that, when living near the sugar mill, he observed two men tear up the floor, and one of them had removed the bricks from around the boiler. Washington Spooner, living on Celina, attested to its decrepit condition, especially the fences.

A.A. Alford testified that he had, indeed, wanted to buy the plantation for $8,000, but abandoned the idea, after arriving at Kern's store with Mr. Grossman and a notary. He was prevented from seeing Rosine Kern, so he accompanied Grossman to the courthouse at New Roads where the latter initiated the lawsuit. Alford also claimed that Abraham Kern had no objection to his wanting to buy the plantation, which could realize $1,000 to $1,200 per year, as long as he was assured that Alford would guarantee the $1,200 debt that several tenants owed him at the store.

Louis David, who had rented the plantation before the Kerns took possession, was brought in to verify the 25 August 1883 inventory. He stated that there had been: eight mules, a bedstead, eight plates, six forks, a knife, a "dish soup" (*sic*, soup dish. or tureen, intended), three smoothing irons, a stove, a kettle, a lot of sugar mill lamps, two half-barrels of linseed oil, a lot of planks in the sugar mill, and another lot in the house's garret left out of the inventory. He repeated that all eight mules were on the plantation when he moved out.

Cross-examined, David went on to say there were two mattresses, three hand saws, eight plates…, and was emphatic that he saw no saucers, becoming rather agitated by the attorney's grilling. He also admitted to the possession of a pulley and wheel used in the cotton gin, but claimed that they had been lent to him and to David's former partner, F.J. Guérin by Mr. [Alexandre] Chustz in 1882, but he had returned them upon the dissolution of the David-Guérin partnership. Regarding the saddle mentioned in the complaint, David said he used it for the two years while renting Celina, but had returned it, via (his brother-in-law/first cousin), Victorin Pourciau.

For the defense, Abraham Kern, addressing the "mule" situation, stated that three mules were presently on Celina, four having died, including one which had broken its leg. The mule "Lise," bought from Isaac Keim back in 1869, and which animal Kern stated was "not worth a barrel of corn," had broken its leg and died in 1883. The mule "Claiborne," who had drowned, had once been rented out to Alfred Jackson who was Sarah Zacharias Wolff's tenant. "Garfield" was on Celina, and was leased to Victorin Pourciau for $20 or $100 in event of death; and the last mule on Celina, "Rose," was valued at $50.

Abraham Kern went on to describe a "disease" in the neighborhood, solely limited to the Celina and Phillips plantations, from which 25 to 30 mules and about as many horses died. Only two oxen were found on Celina when his mother, Rosine Kern, leased the place, and they were sold to the tenant "Jarreau the Butcher" (Clément Jarreau). Regarding the cisterns, Kern said that they had been removed so that Henry Cossey, a cooper, could make the hoops to rebuild them and have them returned to Celina. Kern claimed he sold the movables on the authority of Jacob Grossman, who told him to sell them at the best advantage and settle up with him at the end of the lease.

As for the dykes, Kern stated that E.G. Beuker "notified Rosine as a friend that if she built a levee he would cut it if necessary. Kern continued that his mother and M.P. Phillips had a dyke built at the head of the bayou which led through Celina, another on the boundary line between Celina and the Kern place (Fan Plantation) and a third in the Celina field, the latter of which was a failure that had cost him between $500 and $600. According to Kern, Jacob Grossman did not complain about the dykes. He was invited to see the Celina dyke, but within five or six acres from it, Kern had mentioned the name "Beuker" and "it was like a thunder bolt had struck him [Grossman]. Grossman reportedly gave some excuse and went back" to the store, telling Rosine Kern that he was satisfied with the dyke.

A judgement in the case of Jacob Grossman vs Rosina Kern & Abraham Kern was rendered in favor of the plaintiff, in the amount of $833. 33 ½, per month from 1 January 1884, until the property was returned to Grossman's possession.

GEORGE HYMAN

George Hyman, born, ca. January 1858, at New York, the son of Lakeland merchant and butcher Henry Hyman and his wife, Frances Metz/Mertz, was a landowner at present-day Rougon, Louisiana. In 1880, he paid Anna Decoux, the widow of Émile Bonnefoi, the sum of $400 cash for a tract measuring one arpent front on the Lower Chenal by a depth of 40 arpents, bounded by Francoise Leufroy and the widow of Émile Bonnefoi. In the 28 June 1884 edition of the *Pointe Coupée Banner*, George Hyman advertised the sale of his 40-arpent farm on the Lower Chenal, complete with new dwelling house, barn, stables, two cabins, "Buggy House," and orchard, for cash.

Soon after the sale, he married Sarah Aarons on 2 September 1885, in New Orleans. Sarah Aarons had been born there on 27 October 1865, to Moses Aarons, a cattle dealer and native of Great Britain, and his wife, Adelaide Carvalho, born in the West Indies.

George and Sarah joined his parents at Vicksburg, Warren Co., Mississippi, where he and his wife, Sarah, were enumerated there together with the elder Hymans in the 1900 United States Federal Census. Both George and his father were working as butchers. George and Sarah were childless. Sarah died on 22 June 1906, and was interred in Gates of Prayer Cemetery No. 2 in New Orleans.

George married Menorah Lobstein, the daughter of German nationals Joseph Lobstein and Fannie Engel, on 17 October 1906, at New Orleans. Menorah was born on 17 October 1878, in New Orleans. George and Menorah's first child, Henry Joseph was born in Mississippi ca. 1908. The family moved back to New Orleans before the 1910 United States Federal Census, where their other son Bernard Harold was born ca. 1910. George worked as a tailor, and eventually owned his own dry goods business. He died in New Orleans on 2 January 1923 and was interred in Gates of Prayer Cemetery No. 2. His wife, Menorah died in New Orleans on 15 January 1959 and was interred with him.

ABRAHAM and ALBERT KAUFMAN

Abraham Kaufman was born on 7 December 1854, at New Orleans, Orleans Parish, Louisiana, to Jacob Kaufman, a native of Alsace, France, and his wife, Clara Gumbel, born (ca. 1828), in Albisheim, Rheinpfalz, Germany. His brother, Albert, was born on 4 October 1860. We have a preliminary identification of Jacob Kaufman, who we believe was born Jean Kauffmann on 8 August 1816, at Gundershoffen, Bas-Rhin, France, to Abraham Kauffmann and his first wife Anne Blum (aka Minette Jacob, who died on 11 April 1819). We have concluded this because, according to the 1870 United States Federal Census, Ernest Kaufman (b.1857), another of Abraham and Albert's brothers, was living in New Orleans in the household of merchant, Isaac Raas and his wife, Sarah Kauffmann. The latter, was a daughter of Abraham Kauffmann and his second wife, Pauline Loeb. Ernest, a student, therefore, was living with his father Jacob's half-sister. Moreover, Jacob had named his first daughter Mina/Minette, and his first-born son, Abraham, after his deceased parents. (Abraham Kauffmann died at Gundershoffen on 25 September 1851.)

Active in local political affairs, Abe Kaufman, along with C.A. Gumbel, were appointed Eighth Ward Commissioners of Election by the Pointe Coupée Parish Police Jury, as recorded in the 2 September 1878 minutes of that body.

According to the 1880 United States Federal Census, twenty-five-year-old Abe was working as a merchant at Lakeland, Pointe Coupée Parish, Louisiana, along with his twenty-year-old brother, Albert Kaufman, his clerk. Gustave Finck, a German laborer, age 35, boarded with them. Abraham Kaufman purchased the property upon which his store stood from Gertrude Phillips, the wife of Alfred Hébrard, in 1883 for $1,500. The lot commenced at a distance of 138 ft. from the upper/western line of her plantation, measuring 113 ft. on the Public Road, by a depth of five acres, and bounded on all sides by her property. Witnesses to the sale were George Pitcher, of nearby Alma Plantation, and Leopold Kaufman, the New Orleans-born son of Henry Kaufman .and Caroline Ries.

Abraham Kaufman moved on to become a general merchant at Rosedale, Iberville Parish, Louisiana, as confirmed in the July 1889 edition of Dun's *Mercantile Agency Reference Book* and by the United States Federal Census records taken at ten-year intervals between 1900 and 1930. Although enumerated with his wife, Florence Haber in the 1940 United States Federal Census for New Orleans, information in that record indicated that they had been living at Rosedale, Iberville Parish, until, at least, 1 April 1935. Two other Kaufman brothers were active in the area: Ferdinand Kaufman, a merchant at Rosedale, who worked there at least from 1891 through 1900, and Otto Kaufman, who died at Rosedale on 24 October 1918, at the age of 54.

Abraham Kaufman retained his five-acre lot at Lakeland in Pointe Coupée Parish until 1897, selling it, along with the "store house" and other buildings located on it, to Isidore Wolff for $1,200.

Fifty-four-year-old Abraham Kaufman married forty-four-year-old Florence Haber, the daughter of Simon Haber and Josephine Bensadon, on 27 October 1908, at New Orleans. Josephine was the daughter of Dr. Joseph Bensadon, a Sephardic Jew born in New York but educated in Charleston, South Carolina, the first Medical Director of Touro Infirmary. Abe and Josephine had no children.

Abraham Kaufman died on 12 July 1944, in New Orleans and was interred at Gates of Prayer Cemetery No. 2. His wife, Florence Haber died on 14 June 1947, in New Orleans and was interred near her parents and sisters in Hebrew Rest Cemetery No. 1.

Albert Kaufman, similarly, did not remain in Pointe Coupée Parish. According to information contained in the 1880 and 1900 United States Federal Censuses, he was married ca. 1895, to Bertha "Birdie" Besthoff, born in Memphis, Shelby Co., Tennessee, ca. September 1869 or 1871 to Simon Besthoff, the owner of a variety store, and his wife, Clara Schloss. There is no record of the marriage either in Tennessee or Louisiana. While in New Orleans, Albert worked as the manufacturer of "fresh preserves, (?)" and later as a commercial traveler selling groceries. Albert and Birdie never had children. He died on 24 July 1916, and was interred at Gates of Prayer Cemetery No. 2. "Birdye" Besthoff Kaufman died on 3 January 1927, in New Orleans, and was interred in Temple Israël Cemetery in Memphis, Shelby Co., Tennessee, also the resting place of her parents.

The brothers, Abraham and Albert Kaufman, however, were said to be the fathers of several natural children in Louisiana. Marie Bergeron, the mother of five-year-old Abram Kaufman, was born on 4 October 1851, on the Island of False River, Pointe Coupée Parish, Louisiana, to planter and Justice of the Peace Jean-Baptiste Sosthène Bergeron and the first of his three wives, Marie Quintana (PCP-10, 169). There is no record of Marie Bergeron ever being married. Marie Bergeron, age 29, and sons Abram Kaufman, age five, and Alban Rougon, age two, were enumerated in the 1880 United States Federal Census living near merchants Abram Kaufman, age 25, and Albert Kaufman, age 20, at Lakeland, Louisiana. Marie's Kaufman son is likely the child born on 11 June 1875, and baptized "Joseph Léon Bergeron" at the old Immaculate Conception Church, Chenal, Louisiana (IMCL-4, 61). No further records for Joseph Léon Bergeron/Abram Kaufman have been located. Marie Bergeron, subsequently a resident of Oscar, Louisiana, died there on 14 April 1936, and was interred in old Immaculate Conception Cemetery in Chenal, Louisiana.

Three sons of False River resident "Tante" Louise Gosserand, a woman of color, bore the surname "Kaufman." Louise Gosserand was born ca. 1835, the natural daughter of False River cotton planter Séverin Gosserand, who never married, and Honorine des Armas, a woman of color. Louise Gosserand's sons, born at Lakeland, Louisiana, were: Albert, born 22 August 1874, and baptized under the surname "Gosserand," (PCP-28, 189), apparently the same as "Abram Kaufman" who was living with Louise in the 1880 United States Federal Census; Léon Alfred, born on 8 September 1876, and baptized under the surname "Gosserand," (PCP-28, 246), who was enumerated as "Albert Kaufman" with Louise in the same census; and Ernest "To To" Kaufman, born on 25 July 1877, who has no baptism record, but whose birth date was given by him in his 1942 World War II Draft Registration.

Ernest "To To" Kaufman, last of the surname in the False River area (pronounced *Koff – mann* in local Créole), was married on 13 Jan 1907, at Our Lady of Seven Sorrows Church, Raccourci, Louisiana, to Ernestine Pamias, who was born on 23 October 1880, at New Texas Landing, above Morganza, Louisiana, to Pierre Pamias II and Joséphine Gougis, people of color (SAM-1, 58). Her baptism took place on 13 December 1885, at the Seven Sorrows Church.

Kaufman's mother, "Tante Louise" Gosserand lived with the young couple at Mix on False River, where she died on 30 December 1937. (Note: Louise's Louisiana death certificate indicates she was born in 1846 and died at the age of 91.) Ernest and Ernestine had a daughter, Gertrude Theresa Kaufman, said to have been born on 1 January 1925, at New Roads. Ernestine Kaufman died on 21 April 1964, in New Orleans, Louisiana. Ernest "To To" Kaufman died on 7 March 1969, also in New Orleans, and was interred in St. Mary Cemetery in New Roads. He and Ernestine were survived by their daughter, Gertrude Kaufman, the wife of Ashley Joseph Leufroy of New Orleans, who sold the Kaufman farm at Mix following her father's death. Gertrude died in New Orleans on 23 April 2004, following her husband who had died on 6 July 1998.

Samuel "Sam" Kaufman, born on 15 December 1884, at Lakeland, Louisiana, was identified in his baptismal record at the old Immaculate Conception Church at Chenal, Louisiana, as the son of Al_ (rest illegible; possibly Abraham or Albert) Kaufman and Louisa (no surname given, actually "Marshall"). Joseph Hildévert Gumbel was the child's godfather (IMCL-5,30).

According to the 1880 United States Federal Census, Louisa Marshall, age 15, was living with her parents, Joe and Delphine Marshall, farmer laborers, on the Lower Chenal. Twenty years later, sixteen-year-old Samuel Kaufman was enumerated with his maternal grandparents, Doc and Delphine Marshall in the nearby Bayou Poydras area.

Samuel Kaufman was married ca. 1903, in Pointe Coupée Parish, Louisiana, to Louella LeBeau, said to have been born on 25 December 1887, according to her Social Security Death Record. We have found, as yet, no church record for her birth. Sam and Louella were enumerated in the 1910 United States Federal Census with their two sons: Ernest (b. 1906), and Melvin (b. 1909). In his 1917 World War I Draft Registration, Sam Kaufman was identified as a farm laborer at the Alma Plantation at Lakeland, Louisiana. Two more children were born to the couple while they were living in Pointe Coupée Parish: Leola (b. 1915), and Rosina (b. 1917). In the 1930 and 1940 United States Federal Censuses, Samuel and Louella were enumerated at Baton Rouge, East Baton Rouge Parish, Louisiana where Sam worked as a laborer in a refinery.

Louella LeBeau Kaufman died in June 1974, at Baton Rouge, and Sam Kaufman followed in October 1978, also at Baton Rouge. We could find no record for their place of interment.

Abraham Kaufman was also said to be the father of Ella Kaufman, born on 5 May 1891, in Maringouin, Iberville Parish, Louisiana. She was identified in the 1900 United States Federal Census as Ella "Ford," the daughter of Emiline (née Thymes) who was then the wife of William Latham. A family genealogy published online identified Ella's father as Abraham Kaufman ("Archer Family Tree," *Ancestrylibrary.com*, accessed 17 April 2021).

According to the 1910 United States Federal Census, Ella was married ca. 1909, to Henry E. Pélichet, born ca. 1888, near Maringouin, Iberville Parish, Louisiana. Henry operated a fishing camp near Ramah which was patronized by many area sportsmen. Henry and Ella were the parents of nine children: Louis, Donnie, Henry, Jr., Edward, Torris, Mattie, Doris, Leona and Annie.

Henry died on 13 November 1959, at Maringouin, and was interred in Shiloh United Methodist Church Cemetery on Bayou Maringouin. Ella died at Baton Rouge on 15 November 1987, and was interred with her husband.

BENJAMIN WEIL

Benjamin Weil, formerly a peddler on the Pointe Coupée Road, married briefly to New Roads merchant Rosine Michel in 1870 and divorced from her in 1872, worked as a clerk in New Orleans in 1874 and 1875. He returned to Pointe Coupée Parish and was enumerated in the 1880 United States Federal Census as a clerk for and living with general merchant Aaron Loeb near Hermitage on the Lower Chenal of False River.

Benjamin Weil was listed in the 1895-1897 editions of *Soard's New Orleans City Directory* as a resident of the Camp Nicholls Confederate Veterans Home. On 7 June 1900, former Raccourci Lagoon grocer and fellow veteran, Gustav Wolf, wrote from Morganza to Col. J.A. Chalaron, relating that in December 1899, he had filed a petition on behalf of Benjamin Weil, "an Inmate of the Touro Infirmary [in New Orleans], Paralized and Otherly unfit for anny Business [*sic*]," in order to obtain a Confederate veteran's pension for him. A notation on the top of the letter indicated: "Passed," and Weil presumably received a pension for the brief remainder of his life. Benjamin Weil died in New Orleans on 6 June 1901, and was believed to have been buried in New Orleans.

ISAAC "IKE" BAUM

Isaac "Ike" Baum, was born on 12 Oct 1859, at Lautersheim, Rheinpfalz, Germany, to Max Baum and Johanna Fey, He was the brother of Aaron and Solomon Baum, and similarly located on the Lower Chenal of False River in Pointe Coupée Parish. In 1884, he, was one of the witnesses to an inventory taken of the movable effects on Jacob Grossman's Celina Plantation at Lakeland when Rosine Michel Kern took possession as Grossman's lessee.

Ike Baum had relocated to Woodville (known affectionately as "Little Jerusalem, in the 19th Century), Wilkinson Co., Mississippi, by the time Grossman had filed suit against the Widow Kern and her son Abraham Kern for breach of contract in 1886. According to the trial record, Baum was not subpoenaed to appear. While in Woodville, Baum operated a store, which was robbed in 1888. The 3 November edition of the *Woodville Republican* reported the following admonition:

> On Tuesday night of last week, a burglar after an unsuccessful attempt to break in the store of I. Gunst [i.e., Israël Gunst, who appears in the "Red River Landing – Torras – Three Rivers" chapter] and the Bar Room of C.H. Neyland broke in the window of the store of Isaac Baum, and helped himself to a small amount of cash left in the drawer Keep your gun loaded with buck shot.

Well outside the realm of the Latin Gulf Coast culture, Woodville, Mississippi, got into the Carnival act in the late 19th century, as attested to in the Ash Wednesday, 15 Feb 1893 edition of the New Orleans *Daily Picayune*: [Dateline] Woodville, Miss., Feb. 14 – (Special) – "Mardi Gras was celebrated here to-day with greater success than usual. His majesty, Isaac Baum, as 'Rex,' acted his part to perfection and was ably supported."

Ike Baum later moved to Port Gibson, Claiborne Co., Mississippi, where he operated a hotel in partnership with Max Dampf. A year after Baum's death in Port Gibson on 7 July 1901, and burial in Woodville, the 5 July 1902 *Woodville Republican* reported its pleasure in meeting Max Dampf and his children. Dampf was in town to "superintend the erection of a new tombstone over the grave of his former friend and business partner, Mr. Isaac Baum, in the Jewish cemetery at this place." Max Dampf also served as administrator of the succession of Isaac Baum, of which he rendered a final accounting in 1902, according to the 6 November edition of the Port Gibson *Reveille* of that year.

JULIUS LANDAU

The 1880 Census of Ward 8, Pointe Coupée Parish, included a household on the Lower Chenal of False River consisting of two young store clerks: D.C. Hollander, age 18, a native of Louisiana, and Julius Landau, age 21, a native of Germany. While it logical that many Jewish families living in Pointe Coupée Parish, Louisiana, had relatives, whether closely related or more distant, who remained in Europe and were persecuted, suffered and died in *The Shoah*, many families interviewed in the 21st century can only surmise as much, having lost contact through the generations and/or having no word of the fates of those with whom they did keep in communication.

D.C. Hollander, the eighteen-year-old clerk enumerated in the 1880 United States Federal Census, has been identified as David Charles Hollander, born on 10 October 1862, at New Orleans to Gustavus Hollander, a tobacconist and native of Hanover, Germany, and his wife, Fannie Wolff, whose license to be married was dated 23 March 1860, at New Orleans.

Hollander's mother, Fannie was born Jeannette Wolff on 21 February 1832, at Buswiller, Bas-Rhin, France, to David Wolff, a native of Buswiller, and his wife, Josephine Welsch, born in Schirrhoffen, Bas-Rhin. Jeannette/Fannie's exact date of birth as well as a location indicated as Saverne in the 1860 United States Federal Census, has been known to researchers. While she was not born in the village of Saverne, she was born in the *arrondissement* (i.e., county) of Saverne, which includes 162 *communes* (villages), including Buswiller. On 9 August 1834, her father, David, died, leaving his widow, Josephine Welsch, in dire straits with six children, three of whom including Jeannette/Fannie Wolff immigrated to the Gulf South. Fannie's brothers, Samuel and Lazare (born Leman) Wolff were merchants in Osyka, Pike County, Mississippi.

Gustavus and Fannie Wolff Hollander were the parents of nine children, including David Charles, their first son, who was rooming with Julius Landau in 1880. Fannie Wolff Hollander died in New Orleans on 24 April 1882, and was interred in Gates of Prayer Cemetery No. 2. David Charles, who died without issue on 2 May 1898, at New Orleans, was interred in the same cemetery, as was his father who died on 23 January 1905. While the immediate Hollander family escaped the cruelty meted out in Hitler's Germany, the Landau family was not so fortunate.

Julius Landau, the clerk living with David Charles Hollander in Pointe Coupée Parish in 1880, was born on 9 Mar 1859, at Aldenhoven, Westphalia, Germany, to Jacob Landau and Caroline Herz, died on 26 September 1888 at Memphis, Shelby Co., Tennessee, and was buried in the plot of his brother, Bernhard Landau, and family in Hebrew Rest Cemetery No. 1 in New Orleans.

Julius Landau's brother, Levy Leopold Landau, the third child of Jacob and Caroline Herz Landau, was, born on 10 December 1858, but remained in his native land. He was married on 26 March 1894, in Bad Schwalbach, Hesse, German Empire, to Kathchen Wolf, who had been born in that town on 9 February 1856. Levy Leopold Landau and Kathchen Wolf perished in Theresienstadt KZ, Bohemia, previously Czechoslovakia, at that time the Nazi German "Protectorate of Bohemia and Moravia." Kathchen died on 14 October 1942, and Levy Leopold followed her less than a month later, on 12 November. One of the three known children of the couple, Ida Landau, born 14 Oct 1896, in Aldenhoven, also perished sometime after 15 May 1944, at Auschwitz KZ, in Malopolskie, formerly Poland, then the "General Government for the Occupied Polish Region." Two other children of Levy Leopold Landau and Kathchen Wolf, Martha and Kurt Landau, appear to have survived the Holocaust and lived to advanced years.

LEOPOLD KAUFMAN

Leopold Kaufman, born on 24 April 1856, at New Orleans, Orleans Parish, Louisiana, to Henry Kaufman and his wife, Caroline Ries, both natives of the Rheinpfalz, Germany, was a store clerk, living in the house of Cléoville Patin and family between the stores of Aaron Baum and Aaron Loeb according to the 1880 United States Federal Census.

Leopold was married to Flora Hyman, the twenty-one-year-old daughter of Lakeland merchant and butcher Henry Hyman and his wife Frances Metz, on 7 June 1882, at Lakeland by Rabbi Simon L. Weil of Woodville, Wilkinson Co., Mississippi. Flora died after about three weeks of marriage on 28 June 1882, and was interred in the Jewish Cemetery in Baton Rouge, Louisiana. Kaufman was married for a second time to Sarah Levy on 25 February 1891, in New Orleans. Sarah was born in New Orleans on 7 February 1868, to Moses Levy, said to be a native of "Eddendorf" (probably Ettendorf intended), Bas Rhin France, although there is no record of his birth in that town, or in any nearby French commune, and his third wife Lena/Helena Oppenheim(er), said to have been born in Burgkunstadt, Rheinpfalz, Germany.

Moïse/Moses Levy, a peddler in New Orleans, but before that a *"marchand ambulant"* in Alsace, arrived on 30 June 1854, at New York, aboard the ship *Elizabeth Kimball*, with his first wife, Sophie Samuel, and two children: Samuel, born at Herrlisheim-près-Colmar, Haut-Rhin, France, on 5 May 1851, and Julie, born on 21 February 1854, at Mertzwiller, Bas-Rhin, France. Another child, Benoît, died after eight days on 30 March 1849, at Zillisheim, Haut-Rhin. Levy was enumerated in the 1860 United States Federal Census for St. Louis City, Missouri, with a second wife, Catharina Doll, whom he had married there on 5 May 1856, Samuel and Julie, his two children by Sophie, and a son, Jacob, age two. Moses Levy married Lena/Helena Oppenheim, in New Orleans on 22 July 1863. He was the father of, at least, five more children, including Sarah, the second wife of Leopold Kaufman, and Harriet "Hattie" Levy, mother of Blanks merchant Leon "Mannie" Levy's wife Irene Esther Morais. Moses Levy died in New Orleans on 14 July 1883, and was interred there in Gates of Prayer Cemetery.

According to the 1900 United States Federal Census, Leopold Kaufman was enumerated as a salesman, born in April 1856 in Louisiana, with his wife, Sarah Levy, born in February 1874, at New Orleans, and his three daughters: Carrie (b. 1892), Miriam (b. 1893), and Ruth (b. 1894). They were living in a house next door to Leopold's sister and brother-in-law, Henrietta Kaufman Loeb, and her husband, dry goods merchant, Aaron Loeb, on the Lower Chenal near Hermitage.

Like so many small-town retailers, Kaufman moved his family permanently to New Orleans towards the end of his life and died there on 12 October 1915. He was interred in Gates of Prayer Cemetery in the city. Sarah Levy Kaufman died at New Orleans on 12 March 1944, and was interred with him.

MEYER LEVY

Williamsport merchant Meyer Levy, with a long history of merchandising and landholding on the Pointe Coupée Road and on Raccourci-Old River, purchased four tracts in the Lakeland area and Wolff's "Burnt Bridge Store" from Cerf Wolff in 1882 for $7,000. The properties conveyed were the Bayou Cirier Plantation, measuring 4 ½ arpents on the lower end of False River by a depth of 80 arpents, and upon which was located the "Burnt Bridge Store," at the western end of the Lakeland community; a smaller improved tract in Lakeland proper; and two tracts east of Bayou Poydras in nearby West Baton Rouge Parish.

Meyer Levy renamed the "Burnt Bridge Store" the "Diamond W Store," and in the following year, 1883, leased the building, complete with shelves and counters, and free-standing kitchen together with the yards in which they stood to the firm of Major & Guérin, composed of brothers-in-law Pervis Chérie Major and Emile Guerin, Jr., for 1885 through 1888 at a rate of $255 per year. In the following judicial act, Cerf Wolff's son Isidore Wolff, who owned the merchandise existing in the store conveyed it to Major & Guérin.

A year later, in 1884, Meyer Levy sold the four tracts and the store back to Cerf Wolff for $8,500. Under the Wolff's, the store resumed its former name the "Burnt Bridge Store." Meyer Levy's son Maurice, married to Cerf Wolff's daughter Rachel, operated the store, and was succeeded by Lazard Wolff, Rachel's brother.

MAURICE and RACHEL WOLFF LEVY

The marriage of Rachel Wolff, born on 10 June 1866, at New Roads, the daughter of Cerf Wolff and Sarah Zacharias, to Maurice Levy, born on 27 March 1857, in Pointe Coupée Parish, Louisiana, to Meyer Levy and Hevven Müller, united two of the great Jewish merchant families of Pointe Coupée Parish, Louisiana.

In a prenuptial contract entered into by Rachel Wolff and Maurice Levy (Conveyance Book 1883, Entry 13141), enacted at the home of her father, merchant Cerf Wolff, the future bride listed the following as her personal property, attesting to the love and affection for her by her family as well as her future in-laws: the sum of $2,500 in U.S. currency, being a donation by her parents; a pair of diamond earrings, given to her by Maurice's brother Achille Levy, valued at $185; a breast pin, the gift of her future father-in-law, valued at $125; a solitaire ring, from Maurice, valued at $175; a clock and three bronze figures, from Maurice's uncle Arthur Levy, $150; a gold watch and chain, given by her parents, $130; a pair of gold bracelets, given by her sisters and brothers, $50; a dun gray mare, gift of her parents, $150; 12 milk cows and calves, also from her parents, valued at $75; and "sundry" silver and silver-plated ware, given by friends, $250, for a total value of $3,785. Rachel was also to be in full possession of anything she might inherit from anyone, according to terms of the contract. Witnesses to the act were (Pointe Coupée Parish Sheriff) E.G. Beuker and A. (Alfred) Hébrard.

The wedding of Maurice Levy and Rachel Wolff, held on 27 March 1883, in the Livonia Lodge Hall at Burnt Bridge, was a brilliant affair, the report of which commanded 1 1/3 columns in the 31 March issue of the *Pointe Coupée Banner*. Rabbi Simon L. Weil of Woodville, Mississippi performed the ceremony, which was attended by 80 Jewish and Gentile relatives and friends from throughout Pointe Coupée as well as West Baton Rouge Parish and New Orleans. Several local guests arrived on the Lower Chenal via the steamer *Governor Wiltz*, captained by F.E. Trudeau of Hermitage. The *Banner* report told of an elegant dinner which followed and of the magnificence of the bride's costume and gifts.

After his marriage, Maurice Levy who had formerly been a general merchant at Williamsport, and then on Bayou Lettsworth, operated the store on Bayou Cirier Plantation, owned by his in-laws, the Cerf Wolff family, through the early 1890s. Maurice's father, merchant Meyer Levy, had purchased the plantation and store in 1882, but sold it back to Cerf Wolff in 1884, a year after the marriage of Levy's son Maurice to Wolff's daughter Rachel. During Meyer Levy's ownership of the store building, Isidore Wolff, brother of Rachel Wolff Levy, had conducted business there until selling his stock in 1883 to the firm of Major & Guérin.

Maurice took over the space at the end of their lease in 1888. In four years' time however, Maurice was in financial difficulty, and his wife, Rachel, took him to court (14th Judicial District Court, No. 89) for separation of property. The court ruled accordingly, and held Maurice responsible to Rachel in the amount of $3,790 (her dowry plus $5 court costs), at eight percent interest from 29 March 1883, the first full day of their marriage.

In 1895, three years after the judgment, Maurice sold his stock of merchandise to Rachel's brother Lazard Wolff for $2,000. Testifying in the case of the Widow Cerf Wolff vs (son) Lazard Wolff (14th Judicial District Court, No. 896) in 1898, Maurice Levy stated he had received the money for the transaction from Pervis Chérie Major.

Rachel and Maurice were the parents of nine children: Simon Weil (b. 1884), Cerf Wolf (b. 1885-d. 1887), Merla (b. 1887), Henrietta Muller (b. 1888), Mildred Lucy (b. 1891), Beulah (b. 1893), Meyer Arthur (b. 1894), Vivian (b. 1896), and Louise (b. 1900- d. 1901).

Rachel Levy died on 29 August 1929, and was interred in Hebrew Rest Cemetery No. 1 in New Orleans. Maurice Levy died on 12 December 1932, and was interred next to her.

ISIDORE WOLFF

Isidore Wolff, son of pioneer merchants Cerf Wolff and Sarah Zacharias, and brother of Lazard Wolff and Rachel Wolff Levy, was born on 13 July 1862, in New Roads, Louisiana. He operated three retail stores in succession, the first being the "Burnt Bridge Store" on the Wolff family's Bayou Cirier Plantation west of Lakeland.

In 1883, when Isidore Wolff sold his stock of merchandise in the store on Bayou Cirier Plantation to the firm of Major & Guérin, he (Wolff) purchased the "Alma Store" and its merchandise located on Alma Plantation, east of Lakeland, from his father, Cerf Wolff, for the then considerable price of $11,500. The transaction included three mules, two horses, three mares, two mare colts, 32 head of calves and young steers, a four-horse wagon, a jersey wagon, a buggy, and a dog cart.

Isidore Wolff offered considerable testimony in the 1886 suit of Jacob Grossman vs. Rosina Kern and Abraham Kern, because he lived between the Kerns and M.P. Phillips at Lakeland. Wolff was particular in describing neighborhood efforts in the wake of the 1884 flood to minimize subsequent inundation of the area, including the building of protection levees along bayou banks and dykes within the bayou beds.

In 1897, Isidore Wolff purchased a five-acre lot with "store house" and other improvements at Lakeland, for $1,200 from merchant Abraham Kaufman. In 1898, according to testimony filed in the case of Wolff's mother vs his brother, Widow Cerf Wolff vs Lazard Wolff (14th Judicial District Court, No. 896), Isidore Wolff was acting as business manager for their mother as well as operating his own store on his Lakeland lot. The site of Isidore Wolff's Lakeland store is now the Immaculate Conception Parish Hall and parking lot.

Wolff ultimately did business in downtown New Roads as "I. Wolff, The Fancy Grocer."

AARON KAUFMAN

Aaron Kaufman was born on 24 April 1856, in New Orleans, Louisiana, to Henry Kaufman, a native of Lambsheim, Rheinpfalz, Germany, and Caroline Ries, born at Herxheim *bei* Landau, Rheinpfalz, Germany. Aaron Kaufman, for a number of years in the 1880s was in partnership with his sister Henrietta Kaufman, the wife of Aaron Loeb, as Mrs H. Loeb & Co., in the management of the Loeb store on the Lower Chenal near Hermitage.

Just prior to Aaron Kaufman's marriage, his brother-in-law Aaron Loeb built a cottage next to the Loeb store for the engaged couple. Aaron and his fiancée, Annie "Hanchen" Abramson of nearby West Baton Rouge Parish, were married in her home parish ca. 1887. Aaron's bride was born on 26 January 1866, at Baton Rouge, to Baton Rouge and West Baton Rouge Parish merchant and tailor Samuel Abramson, a native of Zurawie, Poland, Russian Empire, and Bertha Salomon, born in Strassburg, now Brodnica, Poland, Prussian Empire. Annie's brother Abe Abramson was a well-known Baton Rouge dry goods and clothing retailer, buying the landmark "Boulevard Street Cheap Store" at the corner of present-day North Boulevard and Third St. from their uncle Hyman Abramson and operating there as "Abe Abramson" until retiring in 1912. Abe Abramson was married to Mathilde Mendelsohn, born on 2 January 1870, at Baton Rouge to pioneer Baton Rouge grocer Simon Judas Mendelsohn, born as "Simon Judas" at Puttelange-aux-lacs (now Puttelange-lès-Farcheviller), Moselle, France, on 11 August 1825, and Sophia Rosenfield, born on 16 February 1838, at Obernbreit, Rheinpfalz, Germany.

In 1888, Aaron Kaufman and his sister, Harriette Kaufman Loeb, dissolved their business partnership on the Lower Chenal. According to the New Orleans *Daily Picayune*'s 23 June 1899 obituary of Aaron Kaufman, he moved his family to Baton Rouge the following year. There, Aaron entered the dry goods business, and two children were born to them: Louis in 1892, who married Corinne Strauss, and Deborah in 1894, who became the wife of Maurice Bloomenstiel Sachse.

Aaron Kaufman died on 22 June 1899, and was interred in the Jewish Cemetery in Baton Rouge. A lengthy and moving tribute was offered in his memory by his friend Lazard Wolff of Lakeland, which was published in the 1 July *Pointe Coupée Banner*. Annie Abramson Kaufman died on 9 July 1948, and was interred with Aaron.

AUGUSTE A. LEVY

Auguste Abraham Levy was born on 20 October 1861, at Nancy, Meurthe-et-Moselle, France, to Arthur Levy, a native of Nancy, and his wife, Marguérite Cléontine Decuir, born at Raccourci, Pointe Coupée Parish, Louisiana. The couple had left Louisiana for France just before the Civil War, and did not return until 1868 well after the conflict was over. Arthur, was enumerated in the 1870 United States Federal Census for New Orleans with his wife, Cléontine who only a month later would be dead, his eleven-year-old daughter, Thérèse, and son, August, age nine. Arthur was working as a "clerk" with $10,000 in real estate and $700 in personal property.

In 1886, young Auguste Levy assumed the watchmaking business of D. Monnier in Napoleonville, Louisiana, according to an advertisement in *The Assumption Pioneer*. Moving to his mother's native Pointe Coupée Parish, Louisiana, Levy was a watchmaker and repairer at Mrs. Cerf Wolff's "Alma Store" at Lakeland, advertising in the *Pointe Coupée Banner* between 1887 and 1888. Returning to Napoleonville, he was naturalized there on 6 March 1888. By 1895, Levy had moved again and advertised in the *Weekly Iberville South* as a watchmaker and jewelry repairer at the corner of Plaquemine Street and Railroad Avenue, at Plaquemine, Iberville Parish, Louisiana.

Relocating his residence and business yet another time, to New Orleans, Louisiana, Levy was reported in the 4 August 1905 *Times-Democrat* to be up on charges brought by a former neighbor in the city, Mlle. Bertha Alpuente, of failing "to make returns or to explain his failure" to sell, an antique clock valued at $50. On the day prior to the news article, policemen allegedly found the clock in the possession of Robert S. Caillier who claimed Levy had sold it to him for $20. Auguste Levy was listed in the 1912 and 1913 *New Orleans, Louisiana City Directories* as a watchmaker and jeweler. Several more charges of accepting watches and clocks for repair but selling them off to a third party, resulted in his being sentenced to three years at hard labor for embezzlement in 1913. We could find no more mentions of him in Louisiana records.

FERDINAND KAUFMAN

Ferdinand Kaufman was born on 4 November 1861, in New Orleans, to Jacob Kaufman and Clara Gumbel. He worked as a general merchant at Lakeland, Louisiana in the 1880s, retailing quality clothing, watches, jewelry and furniture, in addition to goods typically stocked for rural consumers.

Kaufman was married first on 17 November 1887, in New Orleans to Mamie Clémence Hayem, who was born in the city on 23 August 1867. Her parents were Abraham Hayem, working as a butcher in New Orleans, born on 31 May 1842, at Montigny-lès-Metz, Moselle, France, to Lazard Hayem and Gotton Levy, and Sophie Lehman, born on 20 August 1840, at Ingwiller, Bas-Rhin, France, to Israël Lehman and Marie Baer. (Note: In her 1873 opting for French citizenship at the close of the Franco-Prussian War done at New Orleans, Sophie gave her Ingwiller date of birth in error as 15 August 1844. Her husband, Abraham Hayem, gave his date of birth in error as 15 August 1842.) Ferdinand and Clémence Kaufman had three children: Adrien (b. 1888 - d. 1889), Leslie (b. 1889), and Abe Hayem (b. 1891).

Ferdinand Kaufman's business suffered as did countless others in Pointe Coupée Parish in the wake of the floods of 1882 and 1884. As a result of insolvency, he filed suit against his creditors (15th Judicial District Court, No.1158) in 1889. His wife immediately petitioned and was granted a separation of property in order to protect her dowry. The court-ordered inventory included among the merchandise in his store at Lakeland: bolts of black silk, calico, cambric, dress goods, seersucker, gingham, linen, shirting, pique, tulle, flannel, table cloth, jeans, cottonade, Lowell, linsey, buckram; lace, ribbons, buttons, pantaloon buckles, hooks and eyes, button hooks, cotton and silk thread, tape, binding, elastic binding, cord, floss, knitting cotton, darning, needles, crochet needles; men's black and alpaca coats, overcoats, vests, pants, white and seersucker shirts, overshirts, collars, cuffs, and suspenders; ladies' sacques, balmoral skirts, bustles, cloaks, undershirts, and corset steels; socks, stockings, children's stockings; colored and white gloves; a lot of men's hats, ladies' hats, hat crepe, wreaths, artificial flowers; a lot of shoes; silver watches, watch springs, a lot of jewelry, bracelets, brass pins, spectacles, pocketbooks; grits, green tea; canned sardines, salmon and pineapple; black pepper, spice, lemon extract, mustard, cooking soda, lot of candy; whiskeys, gin, cordials; a lot of medicines, cologne, fancy soap, brushes and combs, hair oil and pins, shaving brushes, razor straps, clothes brushes, cigarette papers; pass books, receipt books, envelopes, slate pencils, slates; lot of crockery, pitchers, glassware, glass jars, coffee mills; a clock, bric-a-brac, and what-nots; violin keys and string, baseballs, fireworks, fishing corks; common and French candles, lye, clothes pins, baskets, buckets, a tub, linseed oil, coal oil, lime; a lot of hardware, nails, axe handles, hooks, coffin trimmings, chains, ties, bar iron, three beds, and a washstand; also a safe, two guns, wagon, cart, cow and calf, for a total appraised value of $564.78.

Pursuant to an 1892 suit entitled J. Vergnole, vs. Mrs C. M. Kaufman and Husband (Fifteenth Judicial District Court #1711), the contents of the store were auctioned off, after which the Kaufmans moved to Rosedale, Iberville Parish, Louisiana. Ferdinand Kaufman's wife, Clémence, died there on 4 January 1898. She was interred in Gates of Prayer Cemetery No. 2 in New Orleans. Ferdinand and his unmarried brother, Abraham Kaufman, were enumerated as merchants at Rosedale in the 1900 United States Federal Census.

Ferdinand Kaufman was married again on 2 April 1902, at New Orleans to Coralie Cohn, born on 20 December 1867, at New Orleans to Henry Cohn and his wife, Jeannette Levy. Henry Cohn was born Guillaume/William Kahn on 8 October 1833, at Schirrhoffen, Bas-Rhin, France, to Hermann Kahn and his wife Jeanne/Jeannette Bloch. Henry never used the name "Kahn" in Louisiana. His brother Joseph, born "Kahn" on 2 March 1836, to the same parents, also used the name "Cohn," as did several other families from Schirrhoffen who immigrated to Louisiana. Both Joseph Kahn/Cohn and Henry/Guillaume Kahn/Cohn were New Orleans clothing merchants. Henry Cohn's wife, Jeannette Levy, was born on 1 November 1833, at Obernai, Bas-Rhin, France, to Marx Levy and Ester Scheyen.

Ferdinand Kaufman and Coralie Cohn had one child: Hélène (b. 1903). Ferdinand spent the rest of his days as a travelling salesman for various mercantile establishments. He died at the age of 102 on 8 September 1964, and was interred in New Orleans at Gates of Prayer Cemetery No. 2, with his wife Coralie, who had previously died on 4 December 1937.

LEOPOLD GOLDSMITH

Leopold Goldsmith was born Leopold Goldschmidt on 15 February 1877, probably in or near Lautersheim, Rheinpfalz, Germany, to David Goldschmidt and his wife, Sarah Baum. Leopold was the nephew of Lower Chenal merchant Aaron Baum, who travelled back to Germany to bring him over in 1889. Aaron Baum and eleven-year-old Leopold Goldschmidt arrived at the port of New York on 29 July 1889, aboard the ship *La Bourgogne*, from Le Havre, France. (Note: His parents and several siblings immigrated in 1899 and were enumerated in Pointe Coupée Parish in the 1900 United States Federal Census.)

As a boy and young man, Leopold lived at present-day Rougon, Pointe Coupée Parish, working as a clerk in his uncle Aaron Baum's store. Upon reaching his majority, he moved to New Orleans where he became a successful Magazine Street shoe merchant. Leopold was naturalized in New Orleans on 15 December 1915.

He married Ernestine Levy in New Orleans on 19 September 1916. Ernestine was born on 18 April 1890, in Germany to Solomon Levy and his wife, Jeannette, née Levy. The Goldsmiths were the parents of two daughters, both born in New Orleans: Felice (b. 1919), and Shirley Sarah (b. 1922).

Leopold Goldsmith died on 14 February 1942, in New Orleans and was interred in Hebrew Rest Cemetery No. 1. His widow, Ernestine Levy died on 4 September 1987, at Atlanta, Fulton Co., Georgia, and was interred there in Crest Lawn Memorial Park.

LAZARD WOLFF

Lazard Wolff was born on 6 February 1872, at Lakeland, Pointe Coupée Parish, Louisiana to Cerf Wolff and Sarah Zacharias. He assumed operation of "Burnt Bridge Store," formerly one of his father's businesses, on the Wolff family's Bayou Cirier Plantation in 1895. Lazard Wolff's letterhead was similar to that used by other contemporary merchants, in that it was marked with the image of baled cotton bearing the proprietor's initials and an enumeration of the product lines he carried.

He married Mathilda Diefenthal on 18 November 1896, at New Orleans. The bride was born on 14 April 1878, at New Orleans, to Edward Diefenthal, a butcher, and his first wife, Bertha Mohr. Matilda's father had been born at 's-Hertogenbosch (Bois-le-Duc), the Netherlands, on 6 February 1848, to Adolph Diefenthal, a native of Ljubijana, Slovenia, Austrian Kingdom of

Illyria, working as an optician, and his wife, Everdina Mulder, born at Maasbommel, the Netherlands. Edward had married Bertha Mohr on 25 September 1872, at New Orleans. Bertha, was born on 2 September 1850, at Langenfeld, Rheinpfalz, Germany, to Joseph Mohr and his wife Bertina (last name unknown at present). Lazard and Mathilda were the parents of two daughters: Bertha (b. 1890), and Helen Madeleine (b. 1910)

In 1898, Wolff's wife, née Mathilda Diefenthal, filed suit (14th Judicial District Court, No. 886) against him for separation of property. She claimed that she inherited $358 from her parents, which Wolff used in his business. Her testimony was backed by that of her brother Adolph Diefenthal, Lazard Wolff's clerk, who stated Wolff used the money to pay taxes and wholesaler's accounts.

Shortly thereafter that same year, Lazard Wolff's mother, the Widow Cerf Wolff, née Sarah Zacharias, took him to court (14th Judicial District Court, No. 896) for a delinquent account of $1,846.61. She detailed the amount as $796.61 for merchandise purchased by him and wholesalers' accounts she had paid on his behalf, plus interest; and $1,000 cash she loaned him on 21 December 1895, at eight percent interest. The Widow Wolff testified that she had borrowed $2,000 from local planter and merchant, Pervis Chérie Major, placing a mortgage on her property, and loaned the money to her son Lazard Wolff to commence in business in the "Burnt Bridge Store" She continued that Lazard repaid $1,000 of the amount, with interest, to Major, but remained indebted to her for the balance.

Declaring himself their mother's business manager, Lazard's brother Isidore Wolff, stated he negotiated the $2,000 loan from P.C. Major for Lazard Wolff to buy Maurice Levy's stock of merchandise in the store. Some years previous, the store building had been acquired by Meyer Levy, father of Maurice Levy, who was married to Isidore's sister Rachel Wolff. Meyer Levy had renamed the place the "Diamond W Store." Isidore Wolff operated it, and sold his stock of merchandise in 1883 to the firm of Major & Guérin for $4,000, who, in turn, were succeeded by Maurice Levy. Isidore Wolff also stated that he had been in New Orleans during the time of Lazard's selling-out, and learned of it only upon his return.

According to merchant Aaron Baum, who operated a few miles distant on the Lower Chenal, Lazard Wolff was disposing of goods "outside of the regular business. I bought from him & I know he sold to other parties." Baum stated that Wolff owed Baum about $15, so Baum accepted some safes and bedsteads from Wolff's stock at 35 to 40 percent less than the prevailing prices in New Orleans. Another neighbor, Eugene Chustz, testified that he purchased a good, second-hand buggy for $60 as well as a "young, sound" horse from Lazard Wolff.

Adolph Diefenthal, Lazard Wolff's brother-in-law and former store clerk, stated for the record that the store had about $1,800 worth of merchandise, and Wolff instructed him to sell it at "any price." Within two to three weeks' time, all but about $500 worth of goods had been sold.

In the midst of the litigation, wholesalers Ronaldson & Puckett of Baton Rouge and J. Freyhan of St. Francisville were sustained in their interventions against the Widow Wolff, ostensibly as she was Lazard Wolff's principal creditor, and her attachment filed against them was dissolved.

The court ruled in favor of Widow Sarah Zacharias Wolff and against her son Lazard Wolff in the amounts she prayed for, to wit, $1,000, at eight percent interest from 12 December 1895, and

$796.61, with interest from 4 February 1889, as well as $50 for Lazard's rent of the Wolff store building during January-February 1898.

Lazard Wolff's remaining merchandise, judicially seized and sold in satisfaction of the judgments, was itemized as:15 pieces (bolts) of dry goods; embroidery, buttons; three pairs of stockings; 13 ladies' hats; 52 pairs of shoes; (corn)meal, coffee, cakes (cookies), crackers, candy, canned salmon and cinnamon, vinegar, pickles; toys, fireworks; cups, dishes, sifters, pots, lamp glasses (chimneys), tin buckets; garden seed, a lot of cowpeas; coal oil; two axes; double trees, plow handles; eight beds, a sofa, a chair, a wood-burning stove, a lot of stove pipe, elbows and caps; also store fixtures, consisting of three showcases, two rolls of paper, a lot of paper bags, two store lamps, and oil tanks.

Lazard stuck it out as a merchant through the turn of the twentieth century. By 1910, he, his wife and daughters, were living in New Orleans where Lazard was working as a traveling salesman for a wholesale company. Ten years later he was enumerated in the 1920 United States Federal Census with his wife and two daughters, as a clerk in a clothing store. His unmarried brother-in-law Adolph Diefenthal, age 39, a "manager in a junk business" was included in the household.

Lazard Wolff died on 3 September 1933, and was interred in Hebrew Rest Cemetery No. 1. Mathilda Diefenthal Wolff died on 17 February 1951, and was interred in Hebrew Rest Cemetery No. 2. Her daughter Helen Madeleine, who died unmarried on 19 January 1973, shares her resting place.

ADOLPH DIEFENTHAL

Adolph Diefenthal was born on 19 September 1880, in New Orleans, Louisiana, to Edward Diefenthal, a native of the Netherlands, and his second wife, Augusta Marx. Augusta, a native of Louisiana, was born ca. 1866 to Samuel Marx, a native of Landau, Rheinpfalz, Germany, and his wife, Caroline Westheimer, born in Baden-Württemberg, Germany.

Adolph Diefenthal moved to Lakeland as a young man, where he clerked in the "Burnt Bridge Store," owned and operated by his brother-in-law, Lazard Wolff, husband of Matilda "Tillie" Diefenthal. Early in the twentieth century Adolph entered the employ of Southern Scrap Material Co. in New Orleans He was vice-president of the firm by the time he filled out his World War I Draft Registration and subsequently president until his death. In three successive United States Census records done in 1910, 1920, and 1930, Diefenthal was enumerated as unmarried, living with members of the Wolff family in New Orleans.

By 1930, as president of the Southern Scrap Material Company, he had a house on Robert Street, with his sister Fannie Diefenthal, married to Aaron Levy, one of his business partners, and the Levy's three children, Sadie, Bertha, and Edward. Also living in the household was Adolph's sister, Tillie, the widow of Lazard Wolff, and their unmarried daughter, Helen. However, according to the 1940 United States Federal Census, fifty-seven-year-old Adolph Diefenthal was living with Alma Martin, age 46, Stanley Martin Diefenthal, age 21, and his mother-in-law Elizabeth Martin, age 78. All information we have found, including military service records, indicate that Stanley Martin Diefenthal was born on 27 December 1918, in New Orleans. We were unable to find a marriage record for Adolph and Alma at any time before 1940 in available New Orleans records. Moreover, Alma and her mother had been living, according to the 1920

United States Federal Census, by themselves on Dryades Street. There was no child in the household, and Alma was said to be "unmarried." However, according to the 1930 United States Federal Census, Mary Martin, Alma's mother, a sixty-seven-year-old widow was living with her thirty-eight-year-old daughter, Alma, a seamstress, said to have been married at age 25, and Alma's eleven-year-old son, Stanley A. Diefenthal.

No New Orleans birth records have been found for a Stanley A. or a Stanley Martin Diefenthal. However, after an exhaustive search we found that Stanley Adolph Martin was born on 27 December 1918, to Leonard A. Martin and Marie Stevens. We believe that this child is the same person as Stanley Martin Diefenthal. Stanley, after graduating from Tulane University in 1939, with a Bachelor of Engineering, and after serving as a marine during World War II, succeeded Adolph Diefenthal as President and Chairman of the Board of the Southern Scrap Material Company.

Adolph Diefenthal died in New Orleans on 23 July 1965, and Alma followed closely on 10 September 1965. They were laid to rest in an imposing temple-like tomb in Metairie Cemetery.

WILLIE FRIEDMAN

An article found by chance in the "Society Doings" column published in the 27 August 1893 edition of the *New Orleans Item* reprinted from the *Pointe Coupée Messenger*, identified a certain "Willie Friedman" of New Orleans who was employed "as a clerk in the large establishment of Mrs. Cerf Wolf." Willie was one of the many clerks who worked briefly for a Pointe Coupée merchant, who went on to better things. He was born William L. Friedman on 22 January 1876, at Boutté, Saint Charles Parish, Louisiana, to Joseph B. Friedman, born on 21 January 1841, at Riga, Courland, Latvia, then the Russian Empire, and his wife, Tillie Peiser, born ca. 1853, in New York. Joseph and Tillie had married on 13 March 1870, at St. Louis City, Missouri, and set up housekeeping at Holly Springs, Marshall Co., Mississippi, where they were enumerated in the 1870 United States Federal Census.

During the following decade, they moved to New Orleans, then to Boutté, Saint Charles Parish, Louisiana. They were the parents of three other children: Miriam (b. 1872), Etta (b. 1874), and Eva (b. 1877). Tillie Peiser Friedman died at Boutté on 25 October 1878, and was interred in New Orleans. Joseph married Bertha Reichenberg on 17 October 1880 in New Orleans. Their four children were all born at Boutté: Rosa (b. 1881), Leah (b. 1882), Harry (b. 1885), and Tillie (b. 1887). Joseph Friedman was the postmaster, a Southern Express agent for Morgan's Louisiana and Texas Railway, the coroner, as well as a Justice of the Peace and a general merchant at Boutté. He was referred to as Dr. Friedman.

Joseph Bernard Friedman was shot to death outside his store on 11 June 1888, at Boutté. Two men, Nick Laqué and John Alexander were later arrested. His widow, Bertha, took the children back to New Orleans to live. Willie Friedman was only twelve years old when his father was killed. By the age of seventeen, he had secured probably what was his first job at Mrs. Cerf Wolff's store. He married Lucille Barthe in New Orleans on 5 September 1899, at St. Bernard Parish, Louisiana. According to the 1900 United States Federal Census, Willie, a clerk in a store, and Lucille had settled down at Napoleonville, Assumption Parish, Louisiana, where their only child, Tillie Gertrude, was born ca. 1901. Lucille died on 13 January 1904.

A 19 June 1904 article in the New Orleans *Daily Picayune* reported that Mr. "Willie" Friedman had accepted a position with Mr. Leon Lemmel at his store in Napoleonville. Lemmel was born on 8 November 1853, at Struth, Bas-Rhin, France. He had married Blanche Kahn, born ca. 1868 in St. Mary Parish, Louisiana, to Mathias Kahn, a native of Osthoffen, Bas-Rhin, and his wife, Emma Salomon, a native of Kirrweiler, Rheinpfalz, Germany. Blanche's sister, also a Louisiana native, had married David Kling, a merchant born at Dauendorf, Bas-Rhin, France. One of their daughter's, Amelia Kling, born on 16 October 1877, at Thibodaux, Lafourche Parish, Louisiana, who, after the death of both her parents, David Kling on 7 April 1883, and Mathilde Kahn on 31 December 1892, was living in the Lemmel household of her aunt, Blanche Kahn Lemmel, married Leon Lemmel's recently hired clerk, Willie Friedman on 1 April 1906.

Willie and Amelia were the parents of a son, Lloyd Kling Friedman, born on 15 October 1907, at Lemonville, Orange Co., Texas, where the couple had settled after their marriage. William, Amelia, and Lloyd lived for many years in Texas, first at Lemonville, then at Beaumont, Jefferson Co., Texas, where William was a merchant, the secretary of the Neches Jewelry Co, and the Secretary-Treasurer of the Purity Candy Company.

Willie Friedman died on 11 October 1940, at Houston, Harris Co., Texas, and was interred there at Beth Israël Cemetery. Amelia Kling Friedman died on 4 December 1967, at Houston and was interred with her husband.

SOLOMON "SOL" BERNSTEIN

Solomon "Sol" Bernstein was born on 14 August 1867, at Neustadt-Schirwindt, Poland, Russian Empire. He immigrated ca. 1885, and was a dry goods merchant in the thriving community of Lakeland, Louisiana, where he was enumerated in both the 1900 and 1910 United States Federal Censuses. He offered quality wearing apparel, hosiery, hats, piece goods, laces and ribbons, and was on the False River Telephone Line in 1908.

According to the 1910 United States Federal Census, Sol Bernstein was located immediately east of the residence of E.G. Lorio and family, and therefore quite possibly operated in what had been the "Fan Store" of Widow Rosine Michel Kern, and later the "Delmonico Store" of her son Abraham Kern during the 1870s-1880s.

Sol Bernstein's clerks, according to various census schedules, included Meyer Prince in 1900 and Nathan Wallfisch in 1910. According to the 1900 United States Federal Census, Bernstein and Prince were sharing their home with two widowed eighty-eight-year-old African-American women: Lucy Horton, a native of Kentucky, and Rose Bashful, a native of South Carolina.

Unlike many other 18th-20th century merchants, the popular and respected Sol Bernstein does not appear to have been party to any lawsuits, whether as plaintiff or defendant, suggesting that his customers were prompt in payment, and he was likewise with his wholesalers.

The 4 February 1911 issue of the *Pointe Coupée Banner* reported Sol Bernstein's store had been robbed of several hundred dollars' worth of merchandise in the previous week. Deputy Sheriff

Jules Lieux managed to arrest one of the suspects, but three others escaped. Three weeks later, the 25 February *Banner* related that Lieux had arrested two other suspects, identified as Jim Williams and Adloe Allen in New Orleans, the pair having some of the stolen items in their possession. The paper continued that Williams and Allen were suspected of other area robberies, including that of the Texas & Pacific Railroad depot at Glynn, stating rather whimsically: "These arrests swell the boarding apartment of [the] parish [i.e., jail, in New Roads] to thirteen."

Having weathered the years marked by boll weevil, cane freezes, and the 1912 Flood, Sol Bernstein retired to New Orleans in 1917, and put his "$12,000 Well Assorted Stock of Dry Goods and Notions" at Lakeland on the auction block for cash by the Fitzpatrick Auction Co., Inc. in New Orleans, Louisiana. That day's *Times-Picayune* advertised it as: dry goods, silks, dress goods, ginghams, percales, lawns, voiles, plaids, bleached and bleached cotton and sheeting; laces, ribbons, buttons, thread, notions; men's and boys' suits, pants, dress, negligee and work shirts, men's underwear; women's dresses, waists, skirts, corsets and underwear; men's, women's and children's silk, lisle and cotton hosiery; hats, caps, and bonnets; and also, for account of the Southern Pacific [Rail] Co., groceries, rice, coffee, beans, tomatoes, 150 Yale locks and other hardware.

Solomon Bernstein, who never married, died on 15 January 1924, in New Orleans and was interred there in Gates of Prayer Cemetery. A Nathan Bernstein petitioned for administration of his succession in Orleans Parish District Court (No. 130721). He might have been the same as Samuel Nathan "Sam" Bernstein, native of Warsaw, Poland, Russian Empire, who lived briefly at Chenal, Louisiana, but his relationship to Solomon "Sol" Bernstein, if any, remains undetermined at present.

MEYER PRINCE

Meyer G. Prince, whose surname was likely Prinz in its original spelling, was born, according to his gravestone, on 7 October 1872, in Ponchatoula, Tangipahoa Parish, Louisiana, to merchant Jacob Prince and Alvina Wohl, natives of Poland, Russian Empire. He was married on 16 December 1896, in New Orleans, Louisiana, to Julia Mansberg. The bride was born on 24 February 1872, in New Orleans, Louisiana, to Dryades Street dry goods merchant Joseph Mansberg, a native of Mantfeld (*sic*), Rheinpfalz, Germany, and his wife Rebecca Mohr, a native of Langenfeld, Rheinpfalz, Germany, likely the sister of Caroline Mohr, the wife of Leopold Levy.

Meyer Prince was enumerated as an unmarried clerk, living with Lakeland, Louisiana, dry goods merchant Solomon "Sol" Bernstein in the 30 July 1900 United States Federal Census. Prince's wife, Julia, was not among the household. Neither was she located anywhere else, under the names Prince or Mansberg, in that census.

Meyer Prince apparently was affected by the slew of business and personal reverses occasioned by the boll weevil infestation and its effect on the general economy. The 11 January 1908 *Pointe Coupée Banner* carried a notice that he had filed for bankruptcy in U.S. Federal District Court. His creditors were summoned to a meeting at the Courthouse in New Roads, with attorney J.H. Morrison (father of future New Orleans Mayor de Lesseps "Chep" Morrison) as Referee.

By the time of the 1910 United States Federal Census, "N. (*sic*, M. for Meyer intended) G." Prince, employed as a wholesale merchant, his wife, Julia, their children Joe and Harold, and

Julia's mother, Rebecca Mohr Mansberg, had moved to Meyer's hometown of Ponchatoula, Tangipahoa Parish, Louisiana. According to his son Joseph Carol "Joe" Prince's 1918 World War I Draft Registration Card, the young man identified himself as a "store-keeper" with the Krauss Co. department store in New Orleans.

Relations were maintained between the extended Prince family and Sol Bernstein in Lakeland, with whom Meyer Prince had previously been a clerk. The 27 August 1910 issue of the *Pointe Coupée Banner* reported that Bernstein visited the Isaac Bigman family at Oscar, accompanied by Herbert Keritsky (*sic*) of New Orleans. Herbert Koritzky, born on 12 February 1894, in New Orleans, was the son of South Rampart Street retail shoe merchant Abram "Abe" Koritzky and Selina Prince, natives of Poland, Russian Empire. Selina Prince Koritzky, Meyer Prince's sister, had been, according to her gravestone, born on 21 January 1872.

Meyer G. Prince died on 15 June 1932, in New Orleans, and was interred there in Gates of Prayer Cemetery No. 2. His widow, née Julia Mansberg, died in New Orleans on 23 January 1956, and was buried with him.

SIMON BAUM

Simon Baum was born on 1 June 1878, at Chenal (later Rougon), Pointe Coupée Parish, Louisiana, to Aaron Baum, born in Lautersheim, Rheinpfalz, Germany, and his wife, Julia Simon, a Zweibrücken, Rheinpfalz, Germany native. He was a graduate of Louisiana State University at Baton Rouge and later was a chemist with the Louisiana Experiment Stations.

Simon Baum assisted and later succeeded his father in the general merchandise business and also established the "Chenal Poultry Farm." In 1904, *Pointe Coupée Banner* advertisements for "Chenal Poultry Farm," the following information was included: "Breeders of High Class Poultry, S. Baum, proprietor: White Wyandottes, Barred Plymouth Rocks, S.C. White Leghorns and Partridge Cochins; Eggs and Stock In Season; Agents for Cypress Incubators and Brooders."

Simon Baum also entered into partnership with J. Berthold Patin as Baum & Patin Wholesale Grocery, at nearby Glynn, Louisiana, in the early 1900s. According to the *Pointe Coupée Banner*, fire destroyed the Baum & Patin wholesale grocery as well as the Glynn Post Office on the morning of 10 August 1912, the tragedy coming only a few months after the deadly flood of 1912. The "Glynn Warehouse," listed on the False River Telephone Line in 1908, was likely the same as Baum & Patin Wholesale Grocery.

Simon Baum married Lillian Helen Lewis in Fort Worth, Tarrant Co., Texas, on 28 July 1913. Lillian was born on 13 September 1891, in Galveston, Galveston Co., Texas, to Moses Lewis, a native of Germany, and Nettie Lowenstein, born in New York. Simon and Lillian's only child, Dorothy Amelia, was born on 26 August 1914, at Fort Worth.

In his 1918 United States Passport Application for travel to Puerto Rico for employment, Simon Baum reported his occupation as "chemist." In his 1918 World Wear I Draft Registration, he indicated that he was a chemist employed by the Belle Helene (sugar) Manufacturing Co., in Belle Helene, Ascension Parish, Louisiana.

Within two years family matters compelled him to return to Pointe Coupée Parish. According to the 1920 United States Federal Census, Simon Baum, age 41, was a retail merchant living in

Pointe Coupée Parish with his wife, Lillian, age 27, and five-year-old daughter Dorothy. Also in the household were Simon's elderly parents, Aaron and Julia Baum. Simon Baum died at Chenal on 3 March 1920, one month after the census was taken. He was interred in the Jewish Cemetery in Baton Rouge, East Baton Rouge Parish, Louisiana.

The inventory in his succession proceedings (21st Judicial District Court, No. 2278) in 1920 included: his parents' former plantation, measuring seven arpent front on the Lower Chenal by a depth of 40 arpents, merchandise valued at $4,750, accounts valued at $700, forty head of cattle, two horses, a Ford sedan, and various shares of stock and bonds, for a total value of $16,130.32.

Simon Baum's widow, née Lillian Lewis, sold the plantation in 1921 to Samuel Zink for $12,500. Mrs. Zink, née Flora Guyer, was a beloved longtime teacher at Poydras High School, boarding in New Roads during the week, and offering piano lessons in the rambling Baum-Zink home at Rougon at other times. During the Zink ownership, many of those who had tenanted and farmed the plantation throughout the Baum era continued to do so, including members of the Guidroz, Bello, Pourciau, Chustz and Gremillion families.

Lillian Lewis Baum died years later on 26 June 1974, in Rockford, Winnebago Co., Illinois, but was buried in Memory Garden Memorial Park in Brea, Orange County, California.

EMANUEL KAUFMAN

Emanuel Kaufman was born on 21 August 1856, in New Orleans, to wholesale hardware merchant Marx Kaufman, a native of Gommersheim, Rheinpfalz, Germany, and his first wife, Amalie/Malche Reichenberg, a native of Marköbel (now Hammersbach), Main-Kinzig-Kreis, Hesse, Germany. Emanuel's sister, Mathilda "Tillie" Kaufman, married prominent South Louisiana planter, merchant and financier Judah Seidenbach, and was herself a partner of Gustave P. Loeffel in the Seidenbach & Loeffel plantation on upper Bayou Grosse Tête.

Emanuel served for two months in 1882 as Postmaster of Grossman's Landing, Louisiana, on the Mississippi River in West Baton Rouge Parish, succeeding Jacob Grossman in the position. Kaufman acquired considerable real estate in the Bayou Poydras section, whose waters make up the greater part of the boundary between West Baton Rouge and Pointe Coupée Parishes. He was enumerated in the United States Federal Census for 1900 as a merchant in Ward 5, West Baton Rouge Parish, Louisiana.

Emanuel Kaufman married Juliette Stern on 16 April 1902, at New Orleans. Juliette was the daughter of Henry Stern, born in Albersweiler, Rheinpfalz, Germany, on 18 February 1831, and his wife, Annette Newman, a native New Orleanian, born ca. 1845, the daughter of Carl Neumond, a native of Kaiserslautern, Rheinpfalz, Germany, and his wife Fannie Löb Shay, born in Heidenheim, Rheinpfalz, Germany.

Emanuel Kaufman's subsequent seat of business was at Lakeland Post Office, Louisiana, his letterhead reading: "E. Kaufman, Dealer In General Merchandise. Highest Market Price Paid For Cotton, Moss, Hides, Wool. Our Specialty: Hand Made Shingles, Posts, Pickets & Cross Ties." A slew of civil suits filed against Kaufman by various creditors in the 21st Judicial District Court in New Roads between 1904 and 1908 included wholesalers' bills for: knee pants, notions, blankets, men's and ladies' umbrellas, staple and fancy groceries, meat, liquors, tobacco, cigars, guns and ammunition, hardware, padlocks, hoes, axe handles, buckets, and furniture.

During the height of the boll weevil infestation and burdened by outstanding debts, Emanuel Kaufman declared bankruptcy in Federal District Court. With Jules Gremillion as trustee, Kaufman's merchandise offered at public sale on the premises consisted of: "ladies' dress goods (i.e., dry or piece goods), men's and youths' clothing, hats, caps, boots, shoes, and in fact, everything kept in a first-class country store," according to a report in the 18 April 1908 *Pointe Coupée Banner*.

Emanuel Kaufman, his wife, Juliette, and their son, Melvin (b. 1904), were living in New Orleans with Juliette's widowed father, Henry Stern, Henry's widowed son, Leonard L. Stern, a real estate broker, and several servants, according to the 1910 United States Federal Census. Emanuel's occupation was given as a commercial traveler in iron goods.

Emanuel Kaufman died on 22 October 1915, at New Orleans, and was interred in Hebrew Rest Cemetery No. 1. Juliette Stern Kaufman died on 6 July 1950, at New Orleans and was interred with her mother and father, Henry Stern and Annette Newman, in Hebrew Rest Cemetery No. 2.

HENRY NOWAK

Henry Nowak was born on 19 June 1880, at Sudlikov, Ukraine, Russian Empire. He immigrated to America in 1902, and was naturalized at New Roads, Louisiana, on 29 November 1907. Nowak had been a resident of Lakeland since at least 1909, when the *Pointe Coupée Banner* "Oscar" social column mentioned his early visits to the Isaac Bigman family.

A retail merchant, Nowak operated in a building owned by William C. McCausland, west of the intersection of the main public road along the Lower Chenal and Bayou Poydras Road. The 19 March 1910 *Banner* reported that the store had burned in the previous week. Arson was suspected, and the news account said the act had been preceded some time before by an unknown, but likely the same, person, having entered Nowak's stable and bobbed the tail of the merchant's horse.

A "heavy loser" in the fire, Nowak moved and quickly opened another store, in the Village of Maringouin, Iberville Parish, where the 1910 United States Federal Census found him on 28

April, with nineteen-year-old salesman C.E. (Chérie Eugene) Major. The latter was the son of merchant and planter Lubin Major and his wife, Evelina Moniotte, the immediate upriver neighbors of Isaac Bigman and his family on False River at Oscar.

The 17 September 1910 *Banner* reported that C.E. Major had left the employ of Henry Nowak for a job in New Orleans. A week later, on 24 September, the paper reported that Sidney Joffrion, likewise from an old and influential False River family, had been hired to fill Major's vacated position.

Nowak was married to Bertha "Bonnie" Waldman, the sister of Rosa Waldman Bigman and Golda Waldman Gamburg, on 27 October 1912, at Oscar, Pointe Coupée Parish. Many friends and relatives were in attendance, including Nathan Gamburg, the bride's brother-in-law. Bertha had been born on 6 February 1892, in the Ukraine, Russian Empire, to Daniel Waldman and Rachael Magot. Henry and Bertha were the parents of two children: Daniel (b. 1914), and Jacob (b. 1917). Henry, Bertha, and their two sons were enumerated in the 1920 United States Federal Census living on Bayou Maringouin Road where he owned a general merchandise store.

Nowak died on 11 August 1924, at Touro Infirmary in New Orleans, from kidney failure, and was interred at Gates of Prayer Cemetery in the city His estate consisted of a portion of Weems Place plantation on Bayou Maringouin, a family residence in New Orleans, Louisiana, and stock in the Bank of Maringouin and the Oriental Millinery Co. in New Orleans.

His widow, Bertha Waldman, was married a second time to Samuel Ball, also a native of Russia. Ball was a wholesale and retail merchant who operated stores in New Orleans, Hammond, Amite and Ponchatoula, Louisiana. Bertha Waldman Ball died in New Orleans on 25 March 1969, and was interred in Gates of Prayer Cemetery.

NATHAN WALLFISCH

According to a 1911 passport application filled out by Nathan Wallfisch, he was born on 15 January 1867, at Zolynia, Galicia, Austrian Empire to Mordche/Morris/Max Wallfisch and Mali/Mollie Wildenfeld. He arrived in New York on 27 March 1888, aboard the *Chateau Margaux* from Bordeaux, Gironde, France, and was naturalized in New York on 6 June 1899. He lived first in New York City, then in Orleans and Pointe Coupée Parishes in Louisiana, and finally in Brooklyn, New York.

Wallfisch was enumerated as an unmarried "department store clerk" for and living with dry goods merchant Sol Bernstein in Lakeland, Pointe Coupée Parish, in the 1910 United States Federal Census. According to a petition filed by Nathan's brother, Harry Wallfisch, a resident of Brooklyn, New York, for letters of administration of his estate, Nathan died on 4 September 1915, "in the waters off Asbury Park, New Jersey." Whether he drowned as a consequence of a swimming or boating accident was not specified.

CHAPTER 7

ISLAND OF FALSE RIVER

L'Isle de la Fausse Rivière, or The Island of False River, is the large section of Pointe Coupée Parish embraced by the present channel of the Mississippi River and its former channel of False River and the Upper and Lower Chenals. It is, in fact, the *pointe* (point) which was *coupée* (cut) as the great river adopted its present channel by 1722.

With the notable exceptions of stores, warehouses, and plantations at Cook's and Nina Landings on the Mississippi River, the thickly-settled Island of False River, had few Jewish residents or businesses. Although several large plantations were located on The Island, smaller landholdings predominated, and the farming families living and working there patronized the few small stores on The Island or, as late as the 1940s, crossed False River by boat to make purchases in New Roads and on False River Road.

The main Jewish presence on The Island of False River was through real estate, several of the farms transferring possession, usually through mortgage foreclosures, tax and creditors' sales, to New Orleans firms such as Simon Gumbel & Co. and Norman Stern. These properties were invariably held by the companies for only a brief time, the firms selling them to local residents, and often to the former owners from whom the properties had been judicially seized and sold.

In addition to ordering goods from the great New Orleans wholesale houses, some of the merchants of the Island of False River obtained their merchandise from closer suppliers. Moses Mann, who engaged in retail and wholesale sales for many years in Pointe Coupée and West Feliciana Parishes, was among the rural suppliers. His customers included Louis "Boat" David, senior member of Louis David & Co., "Picayune Store," cotton and moss ginners, east of the old Immaculate Conception Church and cemetery on the Island of False River, and lessee of Jacob Grossman's Celina Plantation at Lakeland.

David, according to his statement with Mann, had purchased $1,331.26 worth of merchandise from Mann's "Red Store" on the Pointe Coupée Road during the years 1877-1878, but made few payments, in cotton as well as cash, against his debt. Evidently a patient man, Moses Mann did not file suit against David until later in 1880 (Late Parish Court, No. 1156), by which time David's balance was $301.06.

Isaac Keim, active in retailing, farming and livestock dealing in various sections of southern Pointe Coupée Parish during the postbellum period, ended his years as a boarder in Louis David's household on the "Island side" of the Lower Chenal. The 1900 United States Federal Census enumerated Keim in the household, working as a butcher. Keim died on 25 February 1905, and was interred in the Jewish Cemetery in Baton Rouge, Louisiana.

SIMON HERMANN

Simon Hermann, heavily engaged in general merchandising and financing at Cook's Landing on the Mississippi River, was one of the first-known Jewish businessmen to invest in real estate on the Island of False River. In 1860, at the Sheriff's Sale in the suit of Ursin Sicard vs Samuel P. Day (6th Judicial District Court, No. 1678, West Baton Rouge Parish), Hermann was the high bidder for an unimproved "tract of swamp land" containing 120 arpents, bounded by lands of Lelio LeBeau and Pierre Sicard and situated behind those of Napoleon Lejeune and Desolives Lejeune. Hermann's tract was called an "interior one," as the surrounding Sicard, LeBeau and Lejeune tracts all fronted on the north bank of the Lower Chenal of False River, and the "front" of his property was about 20 arpents inland from the public road at the Chenal. Hermann remitted $280 and assumed a payment of $563 remaining on Day's mortgage due since 1856.

Samuel Day had purchased the land in 1855 from Ursin Sicard, at which time it was termed a *cyprière* (cypress swamp) having neither improvements nor fences, for $1,000. An astute businessman, Simon Hermann apparently logged the property for its valuable timber, installed improvements, built fences, and let it out to tenant farmers. A road was constructed along the line of Lelio LeBeau's property, stretching across the Island of False River, from the Lower Chenal on the south to the Upper Chenal on the north at what would later be known as Island Crossing.

The Island suffered heavily from the overbanking of the False River due to the Mississippi River floods of 1865-1874, and Hermann's neighborhood, seven feet lower than the Chenal "front," was among those in which the inundations reached the eaves of the more modest homes. Amidst plummeting property values, Hermann sold his tract to local postbellum commercial and real estate mogul Jean-Baptiste Rougon for a mere $200 in cash in 1876.

Rougon died during the 1884 Flood, and the "S. Hermann Tract" was among his 10,000-plus acres in lower Pointe Coupée and West Baton Rouge parishes inherited by his children. The Hermann property reverted to woodland in the wake of the 1882 and 1884 floods, and remained in the Rougon family until its sale by the heirs of Pierre Viléor "P.V." Rougon, son of Jean-Baptiste, at the turn of the 20th-21st centuries.

The road extending across the Island of False River, from the Lower to the Upper Chenal, which passed the S. Hermann Tract was accepted by the Pointe Coupée Parish Police Jury as a public road, but abandoned in the early 20th century owing to its being impassable in periods of heavy rainfall.

JEAN MAURICE "J.M." FORTLOUIS THE YOUNGER

Jean Maurice "J.M." Fortlouis, was born ca. 1835, to early New Roads and Avoyelles Parish merchant Jean Maurice Fortlouis the elder and Julie Aurore Porche. While no birth record exists for him in Louisiana, there are traces of his early existence. In the 1840 United States Federal Census for Avoyelles Parish, which includes no name other than that of the head of household, "M. Fortlouis," a male between the ages of 40 and 50 years, was living with two male children under age five (Michel and perhaps his namesake "Jean Maurice,") one female child under the age of five (Mathilde), his wife (Aurore) between the ages of 20 and 30 years, as well as two enslaved women. According to the 1850 United States Federal Census for Pointe Coupée Parish, which is rife with errors, two young men "Martin," age 22, and Morris, age 14, appear with Leopold, Théophile, and Stephen (*sic* Stéphanie) Porche (*sic*), their grandmother the widow "Mitchell (*sic*) Porche, and their mother, misidentified as "Cora" Porche. We believe that Martin and Morris were probably Michel and Maurice Fortlouis, although their surnames and ages are incorrect, as are the surnames of everyone with the exception of their grandmother.

Although missing from the 1860 United States Federal Census, and not a participant in the Civil War like his brothers, Michel, Leopold and Théophile, J.M. Fortlouis reappeared in records between 1874 and, 1882, as keeper of the saloon on the United States Mail and regular Saturday packet *Natchez*, commanded by Captain T.P. Leathers, according to contemporary New Orleans City Directories and regular advertisements in the New Orleans *Daily Picayune*. Living at No. 127 Rampart Street according to Soard's *New Orleans City Directory* for 1874, he was enumerated in the 1880 United States Federal Census working as a barkeeper, and living at No. 27 St. Louis Street with his wife Mary, age 42. He did, however, maintain ties with his native Pointe Coupée Parish.

On 31 July 1872, Fortlouis, described as a resident of New Orleans, bought from Pointe Coupée Parish blacksmith and merchant Marcelin Chiquelin a tract on the upper Island of False River, fronting two arpents on Upper Chenal of False River by depth of 40 arpents, bounded by Vincent Henry and Louis Mougeot, with buildings. The price was $2,250, of which Fortlouis remitted $500 in cash. He was allowed to take possession on 1 January 1873. This property was very near where his brother Leopold Fortlouis and their natural half-brother, likewise named Maurice Fortlouis, and their families lived for generations.

In 1875, Marcelin Chiquelin sued J.M. Fortlouis over the latter's unpaid promissory note of $1,200 on the Island property, less credit for $1,000 (Late Parish Court, No. 708, year 1875). The case was adjudged for the plaintiff in 1875, but Fortlouis paid the amount sued for, plus the court costs in 1876 in order to redeem the tract. Fortlouis retained the property until 1887 when, through a power of attorney granted to New Roads notary Clément E. Roy, he sold it to former Waterloo resident Cyrille Pourciau for $800, of which Pourciau remitted $300 in cash. The power of attorney from Fortlouis to Roy attached to the sale was dated 1882 and identified Fortlouis as a resident of New Orleans, but the 1887 sale itself described him as a resident of Jeanerette, Iberia Parish, Louisiana.

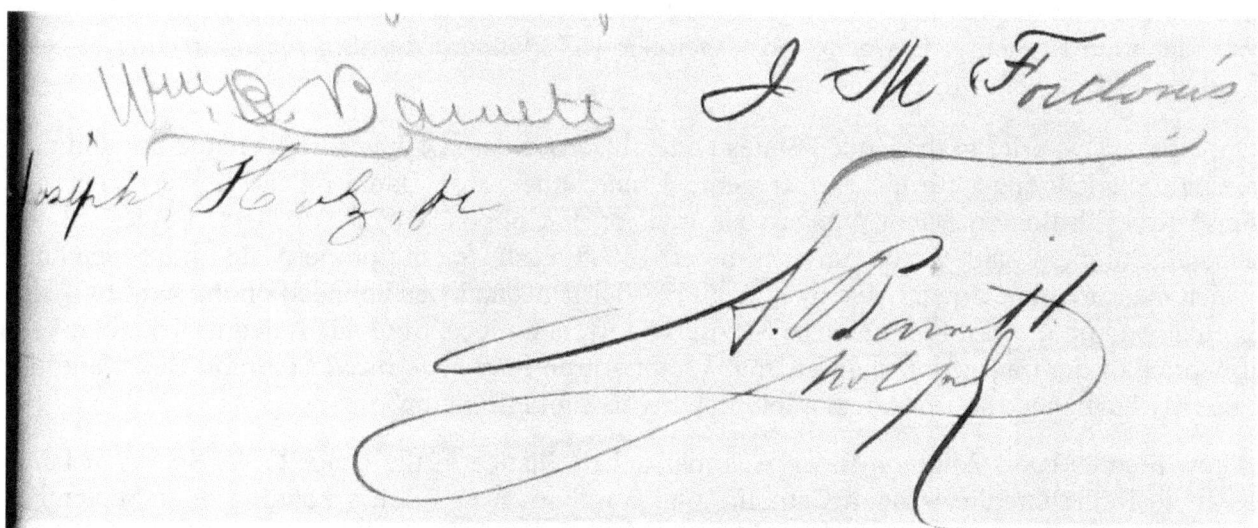

New Orleans Notarial Archives. Act dated 16 January 1882, passed before Notary Alphonse Barnett granting Clement Roy power of attorney to sell property belonging to John M. Fortlouis located on Island of False River. Volume 24, Act 105, p. 3. Courtesy Hon. Chelsey Richard Napoleon, Clerk of Civil District Court, Parish of Orleans.

Two years before the sale from Fortlouis to Pourciau, the 2 May 1885 issue of the *Pointe Coupée Banner* told of the "colony" of former Pointe Coupéeans who had relocated to the "pretty little town of Jeanerette," including Fortlouis and his half-brothers Lucien and Charles Aguillard. In addition, the 13 August 1887 *Banner* reported that Fortlouis, for so many years on the steamer *Natchez*, was spending the summer in the parish, visiting relatives and friends. He was also a witness to the marriage of his sister Geneviève Stéphanie Fortlouis to Louis Carmouche, on 27 April 1892, at St. Mary Church in New Roads.

J.M. "Maurice" Fortlouis appeared in the 1900 United States Federal Census, where he was enumerated in a household on Patin Dyke Road, just east of New Roads, headed by Theophile Fortlouis, an unmarried farmer, which included Aurore, identified as Théophile's mother, a widow, Maurice Fortlouis, age 50 (*sic*), a "taylor" (*sic*), Théophile's brother, and Philomène Fortlouis, Théophile's niece, the daughter of the late Leopold Fortlouis and his wife, Philomène Victoria Major. Despite the obvious error in age by, perhaps, 14 years, the "Maurice" listed in this record is undoubtedly the same as J.M. (John M.) Fortlouis, the former bartender on the *Natchez,* as well as the signatory of the 1882 power of attorney, pictured on the previous page. J.M. Fortlouis died on 25 December 1911, and was interred the next day in St. Mary Cemetery in New Roads. The record of his death and interment gave his age as 76 years, which suggests a birth date of ca. 1835 (PCP-22, 175). The identity of "Mary," enumerated as his wife in the 1880 United States Federal Census in New Orleans, remains undetermined, and no other record has been found to attest to Fortlouis having been married.

SOLOMON BAUM

Solomon Baum was born on 5 May 1852, at Lautersheim, Rheinpfalz, Germany, to Max Baum and his wife, Johanna Fey. He was the brother of general merchants Aaron and Isaac "Ike" Baum We believe that he was the twenty-year-old Salomon Baum, a native of Lautersheim, Bavaria, who departed Hamburg, Germany, on 9 October 1872, aboard the ship *Frisa*, arriving at New York on 29 October of the same year.

Only three days prior to the United States Federal Census dated 4 June 1880, enumerating him as a single clerk living with his brother general merchant Aaron Baum on the Lower Chenal of False River, Solomon Baum purchased a tract on the opposite bank, or "Island side," of the Chenal. Solomon paid Victor Aaron a mere $150 in cash, for the property and improvements, which measured one arpent wide by a depth of 40 arpents and was bounded on the west by Lelio LeBeau and on the east by Euphrasie Sicard, widow, and niece, of Ovide Lejeune. The relatively low price of the transaction suggests that Victor Aaron may have owed Solomon Baum and the two may have made an exchange of the property to avoid litigation.

A few months later, Solomon Baum was married by Justice of the Peace G.W. Sparks at False River to Reine Ordalie Isaac, a Catholic. She was born near Cook's Landing on 7 September 1856, to Stratiote M. Isaac, a native of Greece, and Aglaë Colombe Chustz, native of the Island of False River. Solomon and Ordalie had one child, Joseph Abraham "Abram J." Baum, born on 12 November 1881, and baptized on 3 December 1882, at St. Joseph's Church in Baton Rouge (SJBR-20, 201).

Solomon Baum died only two and a half months after his son's birth, on 26 January 1882, on the Lower Chenal, and was interred in the Jewish Cemetery in Baton Rouge, East Baton Rouge Parish. A year after his death, Solomon Baum's succession (15th Judicial District Court, No.324) was opened in Pointe Coupée Parish. His property was offered at public sale to cover his debts. His brother Aaron Baum paid $150 for the Island farm. A house on Aaron Baum's property on the opposite, southern, bank of the Lower Chenal, had also been owned by the deceased, and likely had been his home while working at Aaron's store. This house was sold by the succession to Ordalie Isaac Baum's brother J.M. Isaac for $125.

Moving to Baton Rouge, Ordalie was married a second time there on 7 July 1886, at St. Joseph Church to Leroy William Kellum (SJBR-19, 292). She died ca. 1949 in Baton Rouge. Her son by Solomon Baum, Abram J. Baum, was a farmer on the Lower Chenal and subsequently a farmer and blacksmith on Patin Dyke Road, east of New Roads. He and his descendants have always been Catholic, and well-regarded in the nursery, floral, culinary and hospitality professions and the arts in New Roads and surrounding areas.

SAMUEL "SAM" BERNSTEIN

Samuel Nathan "Sam" Bernstein was born on 2 December 1889, in Warsaw, Poland, Russian Empire, to Raphaël Bernstein and his wife, Sarah Silverman. His kinship, if any, to Solomon "Sol" Bernstein, native of Neustadt-Schirwindt, Poland, Russian Empire, and a dry goods and clothing merchant at Lakeland, remains undetermined at present.

The only known reference to "Sam" Bernstein in Pointe Coupée Parish is found in the "Oscar" social news of the 6 November 1909 *Pointe Coupée Banner*, which told of Bernstein, "of Chenal," visiting the Oscar community to bid farewell to friends preparatory to his move and new job with a "prominent firm" in New Orleans."

As his place of residence was given as "Chenal," it is probable Bernstein lived on the "Island side" or north bank of the Lower Chenal of False River, where the Chenal, Louisiana Post Office, the original Immaculate Conception Church and Cemetery, schools, and a few stores were located. Had Bernstein lived on the south bank, he likely would have been described as moving from Lakeland, Glynn or Hermitage.

After his move to the city, Sam Bernstein was married in New Orleans, Louisiana, on 6 April 1910, to Frances Levy, who was born on 13 March 1889 (1890 on gravestone), in New Orleans. Her father, David Levy had been born on 18 September 1844, at Duppigheim, Bas-Rhin, France, to Nephtali Levy and his wife, Breundel/Babette Dreyfus. David Levy had married Sophie Weill, the daughter of Moïse Weill and Julie Levy, at New Orleans on 10 November 1884. Sam and Frances Levy Bernstein were enumerated soon after their marriage in the 1910 United States Federal Census in New Orleans where he was working as a bookkeeper for a clothing store.

Sam Bernstein's World War I Draft Registration, filed in 1917, identified him as a salesman in the employ of the George H. Goodman Co., liquor wholesalers, in New Orleans. Sam and Frances never had children. He died on 18 May 1950, in New Orleans. His wife, Frances followed on 24 June 1972. They were buried together in Dispersed of Judah Cemetery in New Orleans.

Simon Gumbel.

Alphonse Weil and his elder brother Félix Weil ca. 1912.

CHAPTER 8

BAYOU GROSSE TÊTE

Having its source at present-day Frisco, Louisiana, Bayou Grosse Tête is fed by Bayous Portage, George, Black and Fordoche, and had as its chief distributary Bayou Maringouin. Bayous Grosse Tête and Maringouin were prehistoric channels of the Mississippi River, and along their banks are some of the most fertile agricultural lands, stateliest oak trees as well as a number of Native American mounds.

European settlement along Bayou Grosse Tête began about 1840. Among the earliest merchants to open up shop on the plantations and in the small communities which emerged were Jewish immigrants, several of whom rose to become among the wealthiest and most influential businessmen in New Orleans and other cities.

In 1881, Hon. H. Skipwith related in the *New Orleans Democrat*:

> The Grosse Tete, a navigable bayou, and the Baton Rouge and Grosse Tete Railroad afford ample and cheap means of shipment for the crops of sugar, molasses and cotton raised upon the Bayous [Grosse Tete,] Fordoche and Maringouin, and in the Canebrake countries [*sic*], all lying in the far western border of the [Pointe Coupée] parish (Skipwith's observations were published in Harris, Wm. H., State Commissioner of Agriculture and Immigration. *Louisiana Products, Resources and Attraction with a Sketch of the Parishes*. New Orleans: *Times Democrat,* Print, 1881.

Livonia, the second largest town in the parish, is at the hub of southern Pointe Coupée Parish and is where a number of Jewish merchants and clerks in the 19th and 20th centuries set up shop. James B. Johnson, was appointed first postmaster in the area in 1846, and named the post office "Livonia," for his birthplace, Livonia, Pennsylvania. Surrounding communities include: Frisco to the north, Fordoche to the northwest, on the bayou of that name; Valverda, to the south, at the juncture of Bayou Maringouin, and Frogmore below, both on Bayou Grosse Tête; Sparks on Bayou Maringouin at the Iberville Parish line; Blanks, Lottie and Elliot City, former lumbering centers, to the west; and Oscar Crossing (aka Torbert), Little Italy, and Cholpe to the east.

More so than any other area of Pointe Coupée Parish, the Grosse Tête and Maringouin "valley" suffered from the eighteen major floods which issued from breaks in the Mississippi and Atchafalaya River levees to the north between 1780 and 1927. Repeated washout of the bridges spanning the smaller bayous emptying into Bayou Grosse Tête on its west bank between Frisco and Bayou Fordoche led to the abandonment of the public road along that side by the second quarter of the 20th century. Exodus from southern Pointe Coupée Parish by some local families was due largely to the periodic flooding, as well as the mechanization of agriculture in the mid-20th century.

GUMBEL, MAYER & LOEB, "STORE AT LIVONIA"

One of the outstanding figures in American commerce and real estate, Simon Gumbel was born on 18 April 1832, at Kirchheimbolanden, Rheinpfalz, Germany, one of eight children of Moses Hirsch Gumbel and Esther/Fanny Stern, a native of Bavaria. His siblings Carl/Cornelius and

Ferdinand Gumbel, Clara Gumbel Kaufman, Rosa Gumbel Dreyfus, Sarah Ausette Gumbel Levy and Jeanette Gumbel Feitel immigrated to South Louisiana as well, and lived in and/or had connections with Pointe Coupée Parish. Simon arrived in New Orleans on 17 June 1848, aboard the ship *Seth Sprague* from Le Havre, France.

Simon Gumbel filed an oath renouncing his allegiance to the King of Bavaria in 1855, in New Roads, Louisiana, but was not naturalized until 24 October 1872, in New Orleans. He was one of the earliest-known merchants in southern Pointe Coupée Parish, and was listed in the 1860 United States Federal Census as having $9,000 in personal property, suggesting a substantial stock of merchandise, next to the plantation of J. Lafayette Matthews, near the confluence of Bayous Grosse Tête and Fordoche. The location of the Gumbel store was pinpointed in an article in the 4 September 1897 *Pointe Coupée Banner* as at "Portageville," i.e., where Bayou Portage drains the low-lying central "basin" of Pointe Coupée Parish between the Mississippi, False River and Bayou Fordoche into upper Bayou Grosse Tête, west of Frisco and north of Livonia.

Simon Gumbel is recorded, before marriage and during his residency on upper Bayou Grosse Tête near present-day Frisco, Louisiana, as having twin sons, Charles Adalbert "C.A." and Joseph Hildévert "J.H." Gumbel, by Amélie Amar, a Catholic "free woman of color." Amélie Amar was born ca. September 1828, in Pointe Coupée Parish, Louisiana, to Arnaud Amar, spelled variously as "Aymar," "Eymar," or "Aymard," who immigrated to America ca. 1821, from the Dauphiné region (now Isère, Drôme, and Hautes-Alpes departments) of France, and Eugénie Christopha, a "free woman of color" and local landowner. Arnaud Amar was naturalized on 9 September 1847, in Pointe Coupée Parish. The Gumbel twins were born on 10 April 1853, at Livonia, Pointe Coupée Parish, and baptized on 22 August 1853, at old St. Mary of False River Church in New Roads. In both cases, the father's and mother's names were recorded as Simon Guimbel (*sic*), and Amélie Avar (*sic*). Charles Adalbert's godparents were [New Roads tailor and Baden, Germany, native Meinard] M. Gebhart and Palmyre Amar, while Joseph Hydelverd's (*sic*) were Joseph Amar and Marie Louise Hardy (PCP-10-193). Both Joseph and Palmyre Amar were Amélie's younger siblings.

After her children grew and established their own families, Amélie Amer moved in with cousins, Amica Mahoudeau Lesser, Amica's son, Amy Paul "Toot" Lesser, and Amica's half-brother, Dr. Joseph Ildévert Kleborn on West Main Street in downtown New Roads. Jacob Moonshine conducted his jewelry and watchmaking business next door to the west in the first decade of the 20th century. The late Lottie Ophélia Jarreau Mathis recalled that she, her mother, and siblings were among the extended family hosted for coffee after Sunday Mass at St. Mary, by their Amar – Kleborn – Lesser relations back in those days of strict pre-Communion fasting.

Amélie Amar died at New Roads on 21 October 1917, at approximately 88 years of age. Her place of burial is unknown, but likely at St. Mary Cemetery in the town.

One of Simon Gumbel and Amélie Amar's twin sons, Charles Adalbert Gumbel was, as a young man, a member of the firm of I. Levi & Co., general merchants who operated the "Eliska" and "Argyle" stores on Bayou Fordoche. His partners were Isaac Levi, a native of Germany, and Joseph Aristide St. Germain of Waterloo. St. German withdrew from the partnership, but Levi and Gumbel continued to operate for at least three more years, according to the 15th Judicial District Court records. They were not, however, listed amongst the fairly-complete list of Pointe

Coupée merchants who advertised in Bouchereau's 1876-1877 edition of *Statement of the Sugar Crops Made in Louisiana*.

In 1876, and again in 1878 and 1879, C.A. Gumbel was appointed by the Pointe Coupée Parish Police Jury as a Commissioner of Elections for the Eighth Ward, according to the published minutes of that body. Gumbel was enumerated in the 1880 United States Federal Census in that same ward, employed as a store clerk and living halfway between the stores of Aaron Baum and Aaron Loeb near present-day Glynn, Louisiana, on the Lower Chenal of False River, in the heart of an historically *Créole de couleur* neighborhood.

For many years thereafter, Gumbel was a teacher in the public schools of Pointe Coupée and East Baton Rouge Parishes. The 2 February 1889 *Pointe Coupée Banner* identified him as conducting the "colored" school of the Sixth Ward, i.e., the northern bank of the Lower Chenal. Charles A. Gumbel was married on 20 July 1891, at the nearby Immaculate Conception Church to Marie Angela Decuir, of the parish's numerous Decuir *Créole de couleur* family. She was born Marie Angèle Decuir on 15 April 1860, on the south bank of the Chenal, near present-day Glynn, Louisiana, to largescale cotton planter Léon Decuir and Albertine Livie Darensbourg (PCP-14, 98).

Marie Angela Decuir, later Mrs. Charles A. Gumbel (Julie Eshelman Lee Collection, PCPL HMC).

The Gumbels relocated to Baton Rouge, East Baton Rouge Parish, Louisiana, before 1900 where they were enumerated in that year's United States Federal Census. Charles worked as a school teacher in South Baton Rouge, a historically African American section of the city. Ten years later, however, he was enumerated as a farm laborer living with his wife Angela in South Baton Rouge. Charles. Adalbert Gumbel died there, ca. 1914, but there is no known location for his interment.

Widowed and childless, Angela Decuir Gumbel moved shortly thereafter to Dayton, Montgomery Co., Ohio, where her brother Gustave Decuir and their half-sisters Miss Palmyre Decuir and Lélia Decuir, wife of Charles Lejeune, and their respective families had moved. Marie Angela Decuir Gumbel died in Dayton, Ohio on 28 June 1924, and was interred in Calvary Cemetery in that city, likewise the burial place of her Dayton siblings. Hers and her late husband Charles Adalbert Gumbel's large, stamped trunk returned "full circle" after nearly a century, and was a treasured family heirloom belonging to Julia Eshelman-Lee in 2021 in New Roads, Louisiana.

Trunk belonging to Mr. and Mrs. C. A. Gumble (*sic*) (Julie Eshelman Lee Collection, PCPL HMC).

Simon Gumbel and Amélie Amar's other child, Joseph Hildévert Gumbel, was living with his twin brother, C.A. Gumbel, in 1876, when the latter was sued as a member of the firm of I. Levi & Co., on Bayou Fordoche, west of Morganza, by New Orleans wholesale tobacco dealers King Brothers (Late Parish Court No. 878). The sacramental records of St. Mary of False River Church at New Roads record a Félicie Anastasie Gumbell (*sic*), born on 10 January 1878, to Joseph Gumbell (*sic*) and Victoria (*sic*) Morgan who lived just upriver of Morganza, or about three miles from Eliska Plantation. Félicité was baptized on 22 March 1879, at St. Mary Church. Her godparents were Eugene Tounoir (Sheriff of Pointe Coupée Parish between 1872-1873) and Elizabeth Morgan (PCP-28, 301).

In the 1880 United States Federal Census, a household upriver of Morganza, Louisiana, included Louis Bradley, age 36, Victorine (*sic*) Morgan, age 28, and Nancy, age 2, all identified as "black"; as well as Henry Clark, age 13, Eliza Morgan, age eight, Adele Morgan, age six, and Dollia Morgan, age four, all "mulatto." It is possible that two-year-old Nancy was the child born Félicie Anastasie Gumbel, living with her mother Victorine/Victoria Morgan and her little godmother, Eliza/Elizabeth Morgan, who was probably also her half-sister. The fact that Eliza/Elizabeth would have stood as the godmother at age six was not uncommon in 18th and 19th century Pointe Coupée Parish or elsewhere.

Meanwhile according to the 1880 United States Federal Census, Joseph Hildévert "J.H." Gumbel was living on the Lower Chenal of False River, residing between the stores of Aaron Baum and Aaron Loeb in the present-day Rougon-Glynn area. He was employed as a huckster. Joseph Gumbel was married ca. 1877, according to the 1900 United States Federal Census, to Charlotte Lazare/Lazard, born ca. February 1860. Research in area civil and sacramental records fails, at present, to identify Charlotte's place of birth and parentage. She is not to be confused with two other contemporary women named Charlotte Lazare/Lazard, natives of the Lower Chenal and of

False River who married, respectively, to Bernard LeBeau in 1870 and Stanislas Colas/Colar in 1885.

J.H. Gumble (*sic*), age 47, his wife Charlotte, age 40 and an adopted daughter, Mary A. Marshall, age two, were enumerated in the 1900 United States Federal Census at Baton Rouge, where Joseph was working as a farmer. Ten years later "Bull" Gumble (*sic*) was a tenant farmer, living on the property belonging to Henry Jolly and his family on Highland Road in Ward 6 of East Baton Rouge Parish. At that time neither "Bull" (apparently Joseph's nickname) nor Mary were employed, however, Charlotte, identified as "Charlotte Lazard," was working as a servant.

Charlotte Lazard Gumbel, age 57, died, according to her Louisiana State death certificate, under the name of Charlotte Lazard, in Orleans Parish, on 31 January 1918, and J. H. Gumble (*sic*) followed closely on 4 December 1918, according to his Louisiana State death certificate, at East Baton Rouge Parish. We could find no record of their interments.

According to the obituary notice of Simon Gumbel's legitimate son Joseph, with his wife, Sophie Virginia Lengsfeld, Simon had served in the Confederate Army, although there seems to be no record for it. Simon Gumbel had married Sophie Virginia Lengsfeld on 14 December 1864, at Congregation Shangarai Chassed in New Orleans. Sophie was born on 28 July 1844, in Shreveport, Caddo Parish, Louisiana, to Jacob H. Lengsfeld, a merchant, born in Illereichen, Neu-Ulm Landkreis (district), Rheinpfalz, Germany, and Henrietta Falk, born in Kirrweiler, Rheinpfalz, Germany. (Note: Sophie's sister Regina was married to Williamsport, Pointe Coupée Parish, merchant Leopold H. Levy.)

According to the 1870 United States Federal Census, Simon and Sophia Lengsfeld Gumbel and their children, Horace Simon (b. 1865), Florence (b. 1867), and Henry Elias (b. 1869), were living in New Orleans. Simon was employed as a dry goods merchant. In time, he would be the senior partner in the firm of S. Gumbel & Co., commission merchants.

Although living and working principally in New Orleans, Simon Gumbel was always heavily engaged in retail merchandising and real estate in Pointe Coupée. As the senior partner of Gumbel, Mayer & Loeb, Simon Gumbel and his colleagues operated four stores in lower Pointe Coupée and upper Iberville Parishes soon after the Civil War. The "False River Store," at the head of Bayou Cirier at the southern end of False River, was conducted by Simon's brother Cornelius Gumbel. The "Chenal Store," on the Lower Chenal of False River near present-day Glynn, Louisiana, was under the direction of Aaron Loeb. The "Store at Livonia," in the nascent community of that name on the west bank of Bayou Grosse Tête, was run by Max Mayer and later by Theodore Dreyfus. The "Store of Mayer, Grabenheimer & Rose" at Musson on Bayou Maringouin, just west of present-day Maringouin, Louisiana, was under control of Henry Grabenheimer, husband of the Gumbels' niece Euphemia Feitel.

In 1873, the firm of Gumbel, Mayer & Loeb was dissolved, and the individual stores divided amongst the former partners. The "Livonia Store" became the property of Simon Gumbel, Max Mayer, and the firm of Mayer, Grabenheimer & Rose, the latter represented by Max Mayer. The "Livonia Store" was located the plantation of John F. Jackson. In time, the firm would purchase the three-acre lot upon which the store and separate warehouse to the rear were located.

Simon and Sophie Lengsfeld Gumbel were the parents of eight more children all born in New Orleans: Cora (b. 1871), Lucille (b. 1873), Ophelia Rosalind (b. 1874), Julia (b. 1878), Beulah Louise (b. 1879), Joseph and Lester, twins (b. 1882), and Elise (b. 1884).

Simon Gumbel died after being stricken with paralysis while playing cards on vacation at Lake Harbor, Michigan, on 14 August 1909. The following day's New Orleans *Daily Picayune* headlined his career "One of the Romances of American Opportunity, Rising from Poor Immigrant Lad to Leadership in the World of Trade." His remains were conveyed to New Orleans, for burial in the city's prestigious, non-sectarian, Metairie Cemetery. Gumbel's widow, née Sophie Virginia Lengsfeld, died on 29 September 1916, in New York City, and was interred with Simon.

Simon Gumbel's membership in professional, civic, charitable and religious organizations was legion. In addition to his presidency of S. Gumbel & Co., he was president of the Orleans Cotton Press, a member of the Cotton Exchange and of the Touro Infirmary board. He was also president of Temple Sinai, treasurer of the Jewish Widows' and Orphans' Home, and of the Provident Aid Society, a member of B'Nai B'rith, the Young Men's Hebrew Society, and the Harmony Club.

Much of Gumbel's charitable work was recorded in his obituaries, however during his lifetime his giving was often anonymous. One of his most well-known bequests was a fund for the acquisition of wedding *trousseaux* for orphan brides, and his donation of the beautiful fountain at the Audubon Zoo in New Orleans.

GUMBEL & RICHY

Gumbel & Richy was the antebellum partnership of the two leading businessmen of 19th century Pointe Coupée Parish, Louisiana: Simon Gumbel, a Jew, and Joseph Richy, a Catholic. Richy, said to be a native of Heillecourt, Meurthe-et-Moselle, France, was engaged in building construction, retail merchandising, financing, planting, government, civic improvement, spiritual life and philanthropy during a long career beginning with his arrival in New Roads, Louisiana, in 1856 until his death in 1915.

In 1858, Simon Gumbel and Joseph Richy joined their talents and financial resources in establishing one of the parish's earliest industries: its first cottonseed oil mill, at Portageville, where Bayou Portage empties into upper Bayous Grosse Tête west of Frisco and north of Livonia. In a letter from neighboring planter J.L. (Lafayette) Matthews, published in that year's 12 September issue of the bilingual *Démocrate de la Pointe Coupée/Pointe Coupée Democrat*, it was described as occupying a commodious building whose cost was predicted to be $10,000. The venture was said to be Louisiana's first cottonseed oil mill outside of New Orleans.

A 4 September 1897 article in the *Pointe Coupée Banner* attributed Richy *Frères* (Brothers), consisting of Joseph and his younger brother Auguste Richy, as designers and builders of the wooden press, which had an output of two barrels of oil per day. Joseph Richy was said to be the manager of the operation, Auguste Richy the operator of the press, and Clairville Himel the machinist. The Richys' sister, Mme. François Voirin, née Hélène Richy, who would subsequently develop substantial additions to the town of New Roads, operated a "commissary" at the mill and coordinated meals for the employees. Though modest in size and scope, Gumbel

& Richy's enterprise was the precursor to several larger mills in New Roads, Raccourci, and Torras, which provided significant sources of income and employment for regional residents.

The *Banner* recalled, in the above-mentioned article, that the subsequent closure of the Gumbel & Richy mill within a few years of its establishment was due to the Civil War and resultant disruption of transportation.

MISS V. (*sic*) GUMBEL

Miss V. (*sic*) Gumbel, age 18, native of Germany, was enumerated in the 1860 United States Federal Census in the house of James K. Pickett and family on Bayou Grosse Tête near present-day Livonia, Louisiana. She was possibly the same as Sarah "Settie" Gumbel, born on 30 June 1842, at Albisheim, Rheinpfalz, Germany, who died on 17 February 1937, in New Orleans, Louisiana.

Sarah "Settie" Gumbel was one of the seven surviving children of Moses Hirsch Gumbel and Esther Fanny Stern, all of whom, after immigrating from Germany, had connections to Pointe Coupée Parish, Louisiana. No occupation was assigned her in the 1860 Census, and why she was not enumerated with her brother Simon Gumbel further up Bayou Grosse Tête at the time remains speculative.

Sarah "Settie" Gumbel married Isaac Levy on 11 June 1867, in New Orleans. Isaac, a native of Riedseltz, Bas-Rhin, France, had been enumerated as a peddler at Waterloo in the 1860 United States Federal Census, but grew to be a substantial property owner, planter and general merchant at Créole Landing on Raccourci-Old River, and a leading New Orleans businessman and miller.

EDWARD LEVY

Edward Levy, born ca. 1840 in the Grand Duchy of Baden, was enumerated as a clerk, living with John C. Lombard, also a clerk, in the house of merchant James B. Johnson and family at Livonia, Louisiana, according to the 1860 United States Federal Census. Any further identification of this "Edward Levy" is impossible due to the lack of any other verifiable records of his existence here in the United States.

MAX MAYER

Max Meyer, born on 14 April 1847, in Würzburg, Rheinpfalz, Germany, was a partner in Gumbel, Mayer & Loeb, which operated four stores in southern Pointe Coupée and northern Iberville Parishes in the wake of the Civil War. Max Mayer was in charge of the firm's "Store at Livonia." After the 1873 dissolution of the partnership of Gumbel, Mayer & Loeb, the Livonia establishment became the sole property of Simon Gumbel and Max Mayer.

On 8 January 1873, Max Mayer, was married to Josephine Feitel, born on 26 February 1855, at Vacherie, St. James Parish, Louisiana, to Nathan Feitel, a merchant, born ca. 1827, at Mettenheim, Rheinpfalz, Germany, and his wife Jeannette Gumbel, the sister of Pointe Coupée merchants Simon, Cornelius, and Ferdinand Gumbel.

The Mayers were the parents of three children: Norman Mayer (b. 1874 at Livonia), later a well-known cotton broker, and husband of Frances "Fannie" Hattie Levy, the daughter of Simon

Levy, Jr., Captain of the Confederate "Caddo Greys;" Julia Mayer (b. 1876 at Livonia), who married Albert Wachenheim, a native of Mannheim, Baden, Germany, who was the founder of the famous four-story Imperial Shoe Store at Canal and Bourbon Streets in New Orleans; and Eugene Mayer (b. 1878), who died as a child.

Active in local infrastructure and state political affairs, Max Mayer, whose motions recorded in the minutes of the Pointe Coupée Parish Police Jury in the 1870s attest to his progressive spirit, was among the subscribers to the extension of the Grosse Tête & Opelousas railway line, when work resumed on the project following the Civil War. The 15 August 1872 *Opelousas Journal* reported that trains were running as far northwest as Kenmore Plantation, on the west bank of Bayou Maringouin, and the tracks were expected to reach Lombard's plantation (subsequently a holding of Theodore Dreyfus), behind Livonia, by late September or early October. Although several sources contend the roadbed was graded as far as that latter area, the line never reached the Atchafalaya River, over which cars were to be transferred onto rails leading to Opelousas.

In the wake of the 1874 flood, the firm of Gumbel & Mayer was paid by the Pointe Coupée Parish Police Jury to build two new bridges across Bayou Grosse Tête in 1875. It is likely that these were located at or near the site of the present-day bridges at Frisco and in front of the location of the present-day Livonia High School.

Max Mayer and J. Knox Pickett were appointed by the Pointe Coupée Parish Police Jury to supervise the repair of "the road from Bayou Grosse Tête to False River [i.e., Parlange Lane]" according to the Police Jury minutes dated 3 December 1877. On 4 June 1878, Mayer and Pickett were, once again, authorized by the Police Jury to purchase lumber and supervise construction of two new bridges over Bayou Grosse Tête. Likely, these bridges supplanted those built by the firm of Gumbel & Mayer in 1875, as the Morganza Crevasse remained open from its 1874 breach until 1884, and each spring a rise of the Mississippi resulted in the overbanking of Bayou Grosse Tête and the resultant destruction of bridges and other improvements.

An important development of the 10th Ward of Pointe Coupée Parish was the building and maintenance of the Fordoche-Grosse Tête levee system, a relatively small embankment on the west side of the bayous of those names extending from above the town of Fordoche in Pointe Coupée Parish on the north, to the town of Grosse Tête in Iberville Parish on the south. Authorized by a Louisiana legislative act in 1876, the levee was built and maintained by a special tax imposed on landowners along the line, in an attempt to check the floods periodically issuing from levee breaks on the Mississippi River front between Morganza and New Roads. Unfortunately, the Fordoche-Grosse Tête levee was overtopped and/or breached in several places in the successive floods of 1882, 1884, 1890, and 1912, causing serious damage to crops and improvements and significant loss of livestock.

Max Mayer was appointed to a two-year term as commissioner of the levee district by state act of 1877, according to that year's 5 April issue of the New Orleans *Daily Democrat*.

Most of the Jewish voters in Pointe Coupée Parish were members of the Democrat political party. The New Orleans *Daily Democrat* dated 5 January 1876, reported that Max Mayer, along with merchant and planter Cerf Wolff of Lakeland, was among the parish's delegates to the Louisiana State Democratic Convention of that year.

Mayer, his wife, Josephine, and children were enumerated at the Livonia Store in the 1880 United States Federal Census. Next door to them, Solomon Loeb, Charles Kahn, and Lazare Bloch, all identified as store clerks and natives of France, shared a house.

Max Mayer died at Livonia at 10 a.m. on 21 October 1883. The following day's New Orleans *Daily Democrat* stated that friends of the deceased as well as those of C. (Cornelius) and F. (Ferdinand) Gumbel, his business partners, were invited to attend the funeral in New Orleans, with the remains due to arrive at 8 a.m. via the Mississippi River steamer *Clinton*. Mayer was interred in the Gates of Prayer Cemetery in New Orleans.

Max Mayer's succession proceedings (15th Judicial District Court, No. 466) put his widow, Josephine Feitel, into possession of one-half interest and their three children, Norman, Julia and Eugene Mayer, one-six interest each, of all of his possessions. These included his store merchandise in Livonia, judgements, and partnership interests in 13 tracts in southern Pointe Coupée Parish, the largest being Fair Oaks (formerly Chinn) Plantation, near the juncture of Bayous Fordoche and Grosse Tête. Less debts, Mayer's estate represented a total value of $74,505 for his heirs.

The inventory of Max Mayer's store, at the time of his succession in 1883, included: bolts of silks, muslin, calico, checks, linen, plaids, cottons, alpaca, cassimere, flannel, buckram, sheeting, and ticking; laces, braid, notions, silk and cotton thread, buttons, dress patterns; bedspreads, quilts, tablecloths, napkins, (mosquito) bars; a "lot of clothing" (likely men's and boys' suits, coats and pants), appraised at $300, plus itemized men's vests, white and colored shirts, collars and cuffs, scarfs, suspenders; ladies' skirts, shawls, corsets, and head kerchiefs; men's, boys', ladies', misses' and children's hosiery; handkerchiefs; men's, boys', ladies', misses' and children's shoes, boots and slippers; satchels; flour, rice, cornmeal, sugar, coffee, tea, table salt, candy, cakes, (canned) salmon, lobsters, shrimp, corned beef, mustard, and condensed milk, syrup, molasses, black pepper, yeast powder, dried apples, cabbages, pickles, mackerel, sausages, pigs' feet, lard; claret, liquors, whiskies, ales, beer, bitters; a "lot" of medicines, valued at $150; tobacco; combs, toothbrushes, blacking; school books, copy books, slates; soap, bluing, lye, wax; cups, saucers, plates, dishes, bowls, bowl and pitcher sets, chamber pots, goblets, pots, coffeepots, smoothing irons, butcher knives, pocket knives; brooms, washtubs, buckets; paint; a "lot" of hardware, appraised at $12, plus hand axes, hatchets, axe handles, hinges, clamp braces, corn mills; bagging, rope; saddles, bridles, backbands, moss collars, hames, wagon breeching; eight clocks; five beds, five armoires, seven safes, three washstands, four tables, 12 chairs, and trunks; also, store fixtures consisting of showcases, scales, and wrapping paper.

Max Mayer's widow and children continued to own a half-share in the store at Livonia, through the management of Baden-native Theodore Dreyfus. According to 21st century descendants of Dreyfus, Max Mayer and Theodore Dreyfus were "cousins," and Theodore had begun his career as a clerk in the Gumbel & Mayer store shortly after immigrating to New Orleans in 1881.

Josephine Feitel Mayer survived her husband by nearly three decades. She died in New Orleans on 25 March 1901, and was interred with Max. The Mayer and Gumbel heirs in New Orleans conveyed full interest in the three-acre Livonia store property for $3,000 cash to Theodore Dreyfus in 1902. His descendants continue to own it, as well as considerable real estate formerly belonging to Gumbel & Mayer, in the year 2022.

HENRY GRABENHEIMER

Henry/Herz Grabenheimer was born on 16 October 1849, at Diedelsheim, Grand Duchy of Baden, Germany. According to his 1892 New Orleans naturalization record he arrived at New York on 2 July 1866, aboard the ship *Bremen*, and spent some time as a partner in the firm of Mayer, Grabenheimer & Rose in southern Pointe Coupée and Iberville Parishes, and as a merchant in Crockett, Houston Co., Texas. While a partner in the Louisiana firm, his interests were managed by his partner Max Mayer.

On 29 September 1880, Henry married Euphemia Feitel, the daughter of Nathan Feitel, and Jeanette Gumbel. Euphemia was born on 20 July 1863, at Vacherie, St. James Parish, Louisiana, where her father was a general merchant. His partner, Max Mayer's wife, Josephine Feitel was Euphemia's elder sister. The nearby "Feitel" station on the Texas & Pacific Railroad, adjacent to Oak Alley Plantation, was named in Nathan Feitel's honor. Henry and Euphemia's first two children, Norman (b. 1881), and Hilda (b. 1883), were born in Crockett, Houston Co., Texas, where Henry was working. The couple and their children returned to New Orleans ca. 1885 where four more children were born: Sadie (b. 1885), Lucille Ruth (b. 1887), Edwin (b. 1892), and Sydney H. (b. 1894).

In New Orleans, Henry Grabenheimer entered into business with his wife Euphemia's uncle Ferdinand Gumbel as Ferdinand Gumbel & Co. Grabenheimer was subsequently in the wholesale grocery business, and ultimately in the wholesale liquor trade as H. Grabenheimer & Sons. Henry's petition for naturalization was done in New Orleans on 6 March 1892.

Henry Grabenheimer died suddenly on 28 July 1919, in Hendersonville, Hendersonville Co., North Carolina, while on a vacation trip with his wife and daughter. He was buried in Metairie Cemetery, in New Orleans. Local newspapers praised his personal qualities and recounted his membership in Jefferson Lodge F. & A. M., B'nai B'rith, and as a member of the Touro Infirmary board.

Euphemia Feitel Grabenheimer died on 20 May 1936, in New Orleans, and was buried in Metairie Cemetery with her husband.

AUGUST KELLER

August Keller, who served as the postmaster of Livonia, Pointe Coupée Parish from 1874 through 1879, travelled to New Orleans to wed Melanie Feitel on 7 March 1876. The marriage record indicates that his parents were Nathan and "Mary" Keller. August and Melanie's only child, Zoë Keller, was born in Pointe Coupée Parish on 22 January 1877. According to the 1880 United States Federal Census, August Keller was a native of the Prussian Empire, who indicated that he was 21 years old, as was his wife, Melanie. Their daughter, Zoë, was three years old. The couple lived in Livonia, Pointe Coupée Parish, near Max Mayer and his wife, Josephine Feitel, Melanie's sister.

Like other businessmen of the era, August Keller appears to have had simultaneous interests in different areas of the state. He was the northernmost advertiser in the epic "Country Advertisers" section of the 1876-1877 edition of Bouchereau's *Statement of the Sugar Crops Made in Louisiana*, having a store at "Cakeland" (Colfax Post Office address) in Grant Parish on the Red River above the town of Alexandria, where he retailed dry goods, boots, shoes, wines and liquors. (Note: "Cakeland" is not a town in in Louisiana. We believe his store was located near the "Kateland" plantation house in the town of the same name, later Fairmount which appears in a 1911 Rand-McNally map of Grant Parish.) In an 1877 *Colfax Chronicle* detailing the robbery of his store eight miles below Colfax, it was said that the perpetrators had entered through a hole in the roof, but had not disturbed the man sleeping in the next room, Joseph Lazarus, probably Keller's clerk who operated the store during his employer's lengthy absences. On 17 April 1880, the *Colfax Chronicle* reported that "Messrs. Grant, McKnight, and Pirtle have sold the *Kate*, to Mr. August Keller, who buys the boat for the purpose of running her in the Grosse Tête trade. She is to make one more trip to Natchitoches, and then will bid us farewell."

Focusing his interests in southernmost Pointe Coupée Parish, August Keller entered into a five-year contract on 1 January 1882 for the lease of the southeast portion of El Dorado Plantation on Bayou Maringouin, where he was briefly engaged in cotton planting and operation of the well-stocked "El Dorado Store."

J.B. NACHMAN

One of the best-known Louisiana merchants of his era, Judah/Julius Benjamin Nachman was born ca. 1830 in the port city of Riga, Latvia, Russian Empire. Nachman was married on 15 February 1866, in Baton Rouge to Amelia Stich, the widow of Jacob Michael. Born in June 1826, in Poland, Prussian Empire, Amelia had succeeded her first husband as a dry goods and clothing merchant at Main and Church Streets in Baton Rouge.

Jacob Michael, age 35, who had taken out a license to marry Amelia Stich in New Orleans on 26 March 1849, was enumerated together with Amelia S. Michael, age 22, in the 1850 United States Federal Census living at Bayou Sara, West Feliciana Parish, Louisiana, before their children were born. Jacob was a merchant owning $5,500 in personal property, including two enslaved "mulattos." Ten years later, Jacob and Amelia were enumerated together in the 1860 United States Federal Census with their three children: Michaelus (b. 1851), Victoria (b. 1855), and Pauline (b. 1859), at Baton Rouge, East Baton Rouge Parish. The last record found for Jacob Michael was his 29 June 1861 enlistment record as a private in Captain R.A. Stewart's Pointe Coupée Artillery, done at New Orleans. He was present on all rolls through October 31, 1861. There is no other record of his service. Two children were born to Amelia during the Civil War at Baton Rouge: Charles (b. 1862), and William B. (b. 1864). All five children appeared in the 1870 United States Federal Census with J.B. Nachman and his wife Amelia Stich, using the surname "Nachman." However, according to the 1880 United States Federal Census, Charles and William were enumerated as J.B. Nachman's sons, while Michael and Pauline were enumerated as step-children using the surname Michel (*sic*).

After his 15 February 1866 marriage to Amelia in Baton Rouge, Nachman assumed operation of the store, added staple and fancy groceries, corn, oats and hay to the inventory, began buying cotton from area producers, and transferred its location to Main and Fifth Streets in 1867. J.B. Nachman was naturalized in East Baton Rouge Parish on 4 April 1868.

Within a few years, J.B. Nachman opened a second store, on Bayou Grosse Tête, in Pointe Coupée Parish, near the Pointe Coupée-Iberville Parish boundary. His advertisement in the 1876-1877 edition of Bouchereau's *Statement of the Sugar Crops Made in Louisiana* indicates that he carried dry goods, notions, hats, boots, shoes, groceries, wines and liquors in this establishment.

While operating stores in Baton Rouge and southern Pointe Coupée Parish, J.B. Nachman was a witness to the wedding of Flora Hyman and Leopold Kaufman, performed by Rabbi Simon L. Weil of Woodville, Mississippi, at the home of the bride's parents, Mr. and Mrs. Henry Hyman, in Lakeland.

The 27 June 1897 edition of the Baton Rouge *Daily Advocate* announced the death of Julius B. Nachman, which took place on 23 June 1897 in Galveston, Galveston Co., Texas. We could find no record of his burial. His widow, Amelia, died on 19 November 1901 in New Orleans, and was buried there in Dispersed of Judah Cemetery.

SOLOMON LOEB

Solomon Loeb was born on 5 March 1856, at Niederbronn-les-Bains, Bas-Rhin, France, to Charles Loeb, a native of Reichshoffen, Bas-Rhin, and his wife, Julie Kauffmann, born at Bouxwiller, Bas-Rhin. According to two different passport applications, Solomon declared that he had immigrated to the United States in 1872, arriving on the *SS Helvetia* that year.

Loeb was listed as one of three store clerks living next to merchant Max Mayer and family on the west bank of Bayou Grosse Tête at Livonia, in the 1880 United States Federal Census. Loeb's companions were Charles Kahn and Lazare Bloch. Loeb was naturalized at New Roads, Pointe Coupée Parish, on 16 April 1878. He joined his brothers, Felix and Isaac Loeb, a few years later in New Orleans, as a partner in Felix Loeb & Bros, wholesale liquor merchants.

Solomon Loeb may also have been the Loeb of Cohen & Loeb, merchants, on Bayou Maringouin during the years 1883 and 1884.

Solomon travelled to California in the late 1890s, and married Dahlia Levy, ca. 1897. In California, he represented his brothers and business partners, Felix and Isaac, in their wholesale liquor business. Sol and Dahlia were the parents of two sons: Gerald Martin (b. 1899), and Sidney (b. 1904). The business partnership of Felix Loeb and Bros. was dissolved in 1907. Felix and Isaac returned to France, while Solomon stayed in California with his family, where he ran a successful wholesale liquor business and dabbled in real estate. He died, tragically in a railway accident on 4 July 1908, outside of San Francisco, California. He was interred in Cypress Lawn Cemetery, at Colma, San Mateo Co., California. His widow took her two sons to Manhattan, New York, where she died on 6 July 1962.

Solomon's brothers Felix and Isaac both lived in Paris until the Nazi occupation. They were lucky to be able to flee France. Felix and his family, and Isaac, who never married, escaped through Portugal in 1940, where they were finally reunited in Manhattan, New York, with their late brother Solomon's widow and children. Felix died in Manhattan on 19 March 1944, at the age of 92 years. Isaac followed closely on 7 June 1944, at the age of 90 years.

CHARLES KAHN

Charles Kahn was born ca. February 1857 according to information given by him or his spouse in the 1900 United States Federal Census for New Iberia, Iberia Parish, Louisiana. At that time, he was living with his wife, Emma, née Dreyfus, a Louisiana native, and their three children: Gilbert (b. 1888), Lester James (b. 1891), and Harold Abraham (b. 1897). When Charles married Emma Dreyfus at New Orleans on 26 November 1886, he indicated on two separate forms that he had been born in Paris, Ile-de-France, France, and was 29 years old at the time of his marriage. Unfortunately, Parisian civil records done before 1860 were destroyed during the fires of the May 1871 French Commune insurrection at which time the Tuileries and the City Hall were burned to the ground. Over eight million records were destroyed. An attempt has been made to reconstruct these records using other sources, but only about one-third of them have been restored. The birth records consist of the name of the child, his date of birth, but no parents are given. Only one Charles Kahn appears in these records, born on 21 July 1858, so there is no way to know if this is, indeed, the birth date of the Charles Kahn who immigrated to Louisiana in the 1870s.

Charles's wife Emma Dreyfus's parentage is, however well-known. She was born, ca. February 1861, to Jacob Dreyfus, born "Jacques" Dreyfus, on 21 September 1826, at Brumath, Bas-Rhin, France, to Daniel Dreyfus and his wife Caroline Bloch. Emma's mother, Caroline Meyer, was born Madeleine Meyer at Goersdorf, Bas-Rhin, France, to Simon Meyer and his wife Hélène Wolff. Jacob "Jack" Dryfus (*sic*) took out a license to marry Caroline Meyer at New Orleans on 18 March 1858. Emma Dreyfus Kahn was raised by her parents at New Orleans. (Note: A lack of a civil birth record for Emma was probably due to the impending Civil War and its aftermath.)

Charles Kahn was listed as one of three store clerks living next to merchant Max Mayer and family on the west bank of Bayou Grosse Tête at Livonia, Louisiana, according to the 1880 United States Federal Census. Kahn's companions were Solomon Loeb and Lazare Bloch, two other French Jewish immigrants.

Emma and Charles were living in Plaquemine, Iberville Parish, Louisiana by 1887. The family eventually moved to New Iberia, Iberia Parish, Louisiana, where Charles was identified in the 1900-1920 United States Federal Census enumerations as a dry goods and clothing merchant.

Charles died on 10 December 1928, in New Iberia, and was interred there in the Gates of Prayer Cemetery. Emma died on 5 December 1944, at Pineville, Rapides Parish, Louisiana, and was buried with her husband in New Iberia.

LAZARE BLOCH

Lazare Bloch was born on 25 February 1855, at Patterson Ville (presently Patterson), St. Mary Parish, Louisiana, to Samson Bloch, born on 28 November 1805, at Saverne, Bas-Rhin, France, to Lazare Bloch, a native of Odratzheim, Bas-Rhin, and his wife Barbe/Babette Dannheiser, a native of Saverne. Lazare's mother, Babette Israël, was born on 4 April 1821, at Romanswiller, Bas-Rhin, France, to Samuel Israël, a native of Romanswiller, and his wife, Malgy Levy, born at Duttlenheim, Bas-Rhin, France. Lazare's parents, Samson Bloch and Babette Israël, were married on 21 April 1845, at the St. Mary Parish Courthouse in Franklin, Louisiana, where several members of the family were in the dry goods and clothing trade well in the 20th century (SWLR, Franklin Courthouse, Marriages, vol 3, #366 and #367).

Lazare was listed as one of three French-born store clerks, including Solomon Loeb and Charles Kahn, living next to merchant Max Mayer and family on the west bank of Bayou Grosse Tête, Livonia, Louisiana, in the 1880 United States Federal Census.

Lazare Bloch moved to New Orleans, where the 1886 *New Orleans City Directory* listed him as working at Maas & Bloch. He and his brother Marx Bloch, a traveling agent for J. Vignes, were both living in the household of Louisa Generes Israël, the widow of Joseph Israël, at No. 92 1/2 Erato Street. The 1894 New Orleans City Directory recorded that Lazare and Marx has joined forces as Bloch Bros., liquor merchants, at No. 5 Tchoupitoulas Street.

Lazare was married in New Orleans on 26 April 1899, to Augustine Israël, his first cousin, the daughter of dry goods merchant Joseph Israël, likewise a native of Romanswiller, Bas-Rhin, born there on 21 September 1831, to Samuel Israël and Malgy Levy. Augustine's mother was Marie Louise Generes, a native of New Orleans, born there on 6 May 1842, who had the first four of her five children: Ernestine (b. 1862), Josephine (b. 1863), Augustine (b. 14 July 1865), and Samuel George (b. 1868), registered by the civil authorities at birth, and baptized in the Catholic Church.

Augustine Israël's father, Joseph, died in New Orleans on 26 October 1871. In a 1963 litigation (146 So. 2d 63 (La. Ct. App. 1963), the Appellate court overturned a lower court's ruling granting the heirs of Marie Louise Generes's last surviving child, Mamie, born in 1873, two years after Joseph Israël's death, the right of succession, due to the overwhelming evidence that she could not have been Joseph Israël's child.

Lazare Bloch and his wife, Augustine Israël, never had children. Bloch was enumerated in the 1910 United States Federal Census as a liquor merchant in New Orleans. Augustine died on 12 October 1933, and Lazare followed on 23 July 1940. They were both interred in Metairie Cemetery with the extended Bloch family, beneath a handsome monument.

THEODORE "THEO" DREYFUS

Theodore and Blondina Wolff Dreyfus.

Outstanding in Louisiana retail merchandising, planting and real estate, Theodore Dreyfus, was born Daniel Dreyfus on 2 January 1859, in Mannheim, seat of the Grand Duchy of Baden (Germany), to Meyer Dreyfus and his wife, Rosina Meyer.

Theo Dreyfus was said to have immigrated to New Orleans in 1881. According to descendants' oral history, he soon relocated to Livonia, Pointe Coupée Parish, Louisiana, and entered the employ of merchant Max Mayer, "his cousin." Dreyfus filed his declaration renouncing allegiance to the Emperor of Germany in 1887 in the parish seat of New Roads. Two years later, on 27 June 1889, he married Blondina Wolff. Blondina was born in Böchingen, Rheinpfalz,

Germany, on 16 October 1864, to Abraham Wolff and his wife Regina Kern. Merchant and livestock dealer Joseph Wolff was her brother. Theodore and Blondina Wolff Dreyfus were the parents of five children, all born at Livonia: Rosina (b. 1890), Mabel Sarah (b. 1892), Max Meyer (b. 1893), Alfred Joseph (b. 1896), and Henry Leon (b. 1899).

By 1891, Theo Dreyfus had succeeded Max Mayer in business at Livonia, forming a partnership with his brother-in-law, Joseph Wolff, as the firm of "Dreyfus & Wolff." A letterhead bearing an 1892 statement and notice of receipt of payment for 65 yards of (cotton) bagging sold in 1891 to planter John C. Burton, is seen below:

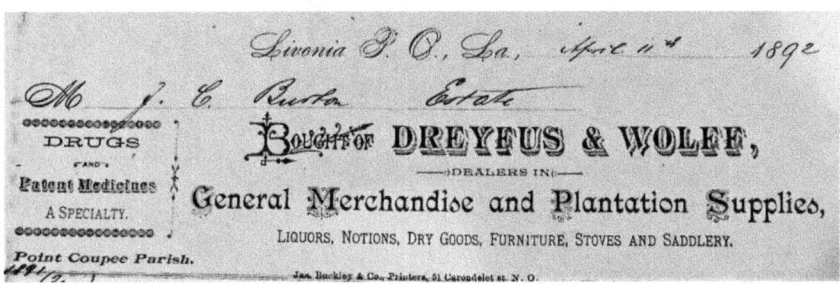

After being in partnership with Dreyfus for several years, Joseph Wolff relocated to Musson, immediately southwest of present-day Maringouin, on Bayou Maringouin in neighboring Iberville Parish. An 1899 *Daily Picayune* social item identifying him as a merchant there, told of the visit made to New Orleans by Dreyfus and Wolff.

In 1900, gross sales for the Theo Dreyfus store at Livonia were the third highest in Pointe Coupée, Parish, at $40,000 for the store and peddling cart, and surpassed only by O. Lacour Co. on Raccourci-Old River, and Lebeau & St. Dizier in New Roads.

Simon Dreyfus Weil, son of Rosina Dreyfus and her husband, Alphonse Weil, and grandson of Theo Dreyfus, related that a succession of three stores stood on the three-acre Mayer-Dreyfus lot on Bayou Grosse Tête: Max Mayer's 19th century store, which was dismantled and replaced with another building in 1922, and the latter, which burned and was replaced in 1926 with the present structure. (Source: "Standing Structure Survey, Division of Archaeology and Historic Preservation, Baton Rouge, Louisiana, Site Number 180, Dreyfus Dept. Store.") The original store was inundated by the flood of 1912, and the 1926 structure by the flood in 1927.

Theodore Dreyfus store at Livonia, Pointe Coupée Parish.

Sidney Dreyfus, another grandson of Theo Dreyfus, stated that the fire in the second store in 1925 was due to a defect in a kerosene heater. Sid Dreyfus also related that the warehouse building to the immediate rear and west of the main store building, behind the Fordoche-Grosse Tête Levee, predated the present store and was, perhaps, from the Max Mayer period.

Despite its relatively remote location and rural clientele, Dreyfus offered top-line merchandise, including men's suits, Stetson hats and Florsheim shoes, Sid Dreyfus stated. The store's wrapping paper, dating from the mid-20th century or earlier, was emblazoned with "Everything for Everybody…Livonia's Most Reliable Store," and listed Walkover and Peters shoes (for men), Peters Weatherbird shoes for boys and girls, New Era shirts and Sunset work clothes.

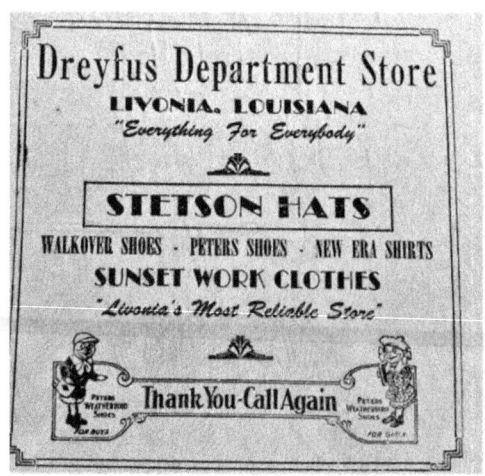

Dreyfus Department Store Wrapping Paper.

According to later oral history, Séverine Inez Aguillard, related that she was unable to purchase a certain dress in her size from Morgan's Department Store in New Roads as part of her bridal outfit in 1931. Rather than try the other ladies' apparel stores in the parish seat, she was persuaded by her future husband, Joseph Costello, he in turn likely encouraged by his relatives in Maringouin, to visit the Dreyfus store in Livonia. There, she was outfitted with a cocktail-length dress, cloche hat and hosiery for $25.

The Dreyfus store, since the 1890s, included a pharmacy department where doctor's prescriptions were filled by a licensed pharmacist, in the front, right side when one entered the store from the front gallery. It was the first-known pharmacy to open in the "interior" of Pointe Coupée i.e., beyond the Mississippi and False River. Theo Dreyfus was the first of four members of his family to work as a pharmacist in the store. He was succeeded by his son Henry Dreyfus in 1919, who was followed by Alphonse Weil, husband of Rosina Dreyfus. The fourth and last pharmacist was Alphonse and Rosina's son, Simon Dreyfus Weil.

Sidney Dreyfus recalled that on the opposite, left-hand side of the store, glass-fronted wall cases held men's suits, while other merchandise was displayed on parallel tables between the drug and clothing departments. Groceries were located toward the rear, with meats in cases paralleling the back wall. In the center of the store, a raised, railed area served as the office.

Simon Dreyfus Weil recalled that that the Dreyfus store stocked furniture as well as adult and child-sized coffins in the rear warehouse. The store also had a delivery truck, likely one of the earliest in southern Pointe Coupée Parish with the motto "Dreyfus Makes Happy Homes" on the doors. He stated that once an elderly farmer in the neighborhood made the wry remark, "Yeah, we know you make happy homes…you sell coffins!"

The truth is that the Dreyfus store, like many other rural establishments of the late 19th and early 20th centuries, whether operated by Jewish or Gentile merchants, supplied families "from cradle to coffin," with such items as wearing apparel, textiles, foodstuffs, housewares, agricultural implements and tools, and often stoves and furniture. Rachelle Dreyfus Hirsch remembered something of the incongruity of rural store's "displays" in that her grandfather's store had, atop a case, a coffin and a cattle salt block, displayed side-by-side.

Sidney Dreyfus also recalled the still-existing "closet" in the southeast corner of the warehouse which stored "out of season" winter goods' (heavy clothing). He also remembered that he and his cousin Rachelle Dreyfus, when the latter visited from Arabi, Saint Bernard Parish, playing as children in an old, unused horse-drawn "carriage" in the barn behind the warehouse. As an adult, Sid realized that the vehicle was actually an old hearse, which had been brought over by Alphonse Weil when the latter moved with his wife, Rosina Dreyfus, and children from Paincourtville in Assumption Parish to Livonia.

In addition to his mercantile interests, Theo Dreyfus acquired nearly a score of properties, totaling thousands of agricultural and forested acres, in southern Pointe Coupée Parish. Among the plantations he owned were Jackson, adjacent to the store on the west bank of Bayou Grosse Tête, Sun Island on the east bank of that waterway, Fair Oaks on the south bank of Bayou Fordoche, and the Lombard and Presley Tracts in the interior. From an initial planting of sixteen stalks of sugar cane, the agricultural operations of Theo Dreyfus grew to the production of as many as 8,000 tons of cane per season.

Theo Dreyfus served several years as a member of the Pointe Coupée Parish School Board, during which times a bond issue was passed in 1914. The Livonia, Dreyfus, and Valverda

Schools were consolidated into a single, larger Livonia School in 1915. In 1919, the Livonia School became a high school, and its building was replaced by the present, brick Livonia High School in 1936. Amongst its beloved educators were Flora Mabel Weil, granddaughter of Theo and Blondina Dreyfus and subsequently Mrs. William Katz, and Flora's sister-in-law Ray Sarah Weill Weil, wife of Simon Dreyfus Weil.

During the First World War, Theo Dreyfus served as the area registrar for the military draft between 1917 and 1918.

Theodore Dreyfus died at Livonia on 28 March 1937, and was buried in the Jewish Cemetery in Baton Rouge. His wife, née Blondina Wolff, died on 19 August 1949, and was interred with him.

Of their children who moved to New Orleans, Mabel Sarah Dreyfus was married in the city on 25 June 1915, to Edmond David Klotz. The groom, born on 3 December 1882, at Napoleonville, Assumption Parish, was the son of sugar planter, plantation store owner, and founder of the town of Klotzville, Assumption Parish, Louisiana, Abraham Klotz, and his second wife, Pauline Abraham, a native of Reichshoffen, Bas-Rhin, France. (Note: Abraham Klotz was born Abraham Glotz on 8 April 1836, at Uhrwiller, Bas-Rhin, France, to Salomon Glotz and his wife, Mertzwiller, Bas-Rhin native, Dorothée Moch.) Mabel Dreyfus Klotz died on 19 September 1954, in St. Joseph Clinic at New Roads, Louisiana, and was interred in B'Nai Israël Cemetery in Baton Rouge. Her husband, Edmond David Klotz, followed, much later, in August 1975. The couple never had children.

Max Mayer Dreyfus, the eldest son of Theodore and Blondina, owned a sewing machine company, and was married first in 1922 to Julia Buckman, and second in 1959 to Golda "Pat" Schoenbach. Max died on 4 January 1975, in New Orleans. He and his first wife, Julia, were interred there in Gates of Prayer Cemetery No. 2.

Theo Dreyfus was succeeded in his mercantile, agricultural and land management businesses by his heirs, the Weil and Katz families. The beloved Dreyfus Store continued operations until its closing in 1985.

JOSEPH "JOE" WOLFF

Joseph Wolff was born on 15 May 1861, at Böchingen, Rheinpfalz, Germany, to Abraham Wolff and his wife, Regina Kern. His sister, Blondina Wolff, was married to Theodore Dreyfus.

Joe Wolff immigrated to Louisiana ca. 1880 and was naturalized in 1892 in New Roads, Louisiana. One of the first mentions of him in Pointe Coupée Parish appeared in the 8 June 1889 *Pointe Coupée Banner* which reported that he had visited the *Banner* office in New Roads to indicate that a head of cabbage brought to the Gumbel Bros. & Mayer store at Livonia had been weighed in by him at 25 pounds.

By 1891, Joseph Wolff had formed a partnership with his brother-in-law, Theo Dreyfus, as the firm of "Dreyfus & Wolff" in the former Gumbel & Mayer store. After being in partnership with Dreyfus for a few years, Joseph Wolff relocated to Musson, immediately southwest of the present-day town of Maringouin, on Bayou Maringouin in neighboring Iberville Parish.

Wolff's store at Musson was called the "Grand Leader." Exceptionally broad, it was the size of two ordinary country stores, and boasted a "general merchandise" department on the right side when facing the front gallery and a "millinery and fancy goods" department to the left. According to the 1920 United States Federal Census, Wolff was no longer engaged as a general merchant at Musson, but was, instead, a livestock dealer in Maringouin. It is likely that the 1912 flood which reached the Texas & Pacific Railroad embankment to the east of Wolff's store, had seriously damaged it and caused his business to collapse.

Joseph Wolff's "Grand Leader" store, Musson, Iberville Parish.

Although residing in Iberville Parish, Joseph Wolff continued to have interests in Pointe Coupée. In 1905, he purchased a tract of 20 acres on the west bank of Bayou Grosse Tête, designated as Lot 10 of the Subdivision of Frogmore Plantation. His heirs continued to own the property into the mid-20th century before selling it as individual lots.

An active Mason, Joseph Wolff also retained membership in Fordoche Lodge 292 F. & A.M. He was elected Tyler (guardian of the door) of the lodge for 1905, according to that year's 8 April 1905 edition of the *Pointe Coupée Banner*. Joseph Wolff died, unmarried, in Livonia on 12 August 1924, and was interred in the Jewish Cemetery in Baton Rouge.

He should not be confused with the Joseph Wolff, a resident at Wolff Bend, Oscar, Louisiana, on the False River. The latter was Catholic, a native of Ireland, and the downriver neighbor of merchant and planter Isaac Bigman.

SOLOMON "SOL" ADLER

Solomon "Sol" Adler was born illegitimate, but recognized by his father, on 4 September 1858 at Schirrhoffen, Bas-Rhin, France, to Abraham Adler, a native of Berlichingen, Baden-Württemberg, Germany, living at Schirrhoffen, and working as a book binder, and Josephine Levy. In his declaration of intention to become a United States citizen filed at New Roads in 1887, Solomon Adler declared that he had immigrated in 1880, was a native of Alsace, then part of Germany, and renounced his allegiance to Emperor William, the ruler of the German Empire.

Within two years, Adler was conducting a general store at Livonia, according to the July 1889 edition of *The Mercantile Agency Reference Book* by R.G. Dun & Co. Unfortunately, the record number of failures in the Mississippi River levees due to the May 1890 flood halted all activity in and around Livonia for months.

Adler was married on 12 December 1894, at New Orleans, to Clara Feibelman, a native of Rülzheim, Rheinpfalz, Germany, born there on 9 March 1868, to Moses Feibelman and his wife, Clara Arent. Sol and Clara's only child, Leonard Emil Adler, was born at New Iberia, Iberia Parish, Louisiana, on 24 December 1895, where the family had moved following the devastating floods in Pointe Coupée Parish. He, his wife, and son were enumerated there in the 1900 United States Federal Census at which time he was working as a grocer.

The Adlers ultimately relocated to New Orleans, where Sol worked first, according to the 1910 United States Federal Census, as a travelling salesman for a whiskey distributor. In both the 1920 and 1930 Federal Censuses, he was enumerated as a salesman in a dry goods department store. His son, Leonard, worked for the Marconi Wireless Telegraph Company, as a wireless operator on steamers.

Adler died on 11 July 1936, in New Orleans, and was buried in Hebrew Rest Cemetery No.2. Clara survived him by more than two decades, dying in New Orleans on 6 June 1958. She was interred with her husband.

DREYFUS & VALLET, "LIVONIA SAW MILL"

Dreyfus & Vallet's "Livonia Saw Mill" opened in 1897 as the partnership of planter and merchant Theodore Dreyfus, and Louis Vallet/Vallette. Also engaged in commercial logging and the operator of a general merchandise "emporium" just above Livonia, Louis Vallet was the son of Désiré Vallet/Vallette and Marie Celestine Lanclos, who were married on 8 September 1853, at the Opelousas, St. Landry Parish Courthouse (SWLR, Opelousas Courthouse, Marriage #1107). Louis Désiré Valette was born on 24 December 1858, and baptized at St. Anne's Catholic Church at Youngsville, Lafayette Parish, Louisiana (SWLR, Youngsville Church v. 1, p. 4).

Louis's father, Désiré Vallet, was a native of Bordeaux, Gironde, France, and a circus performer who went under the name of "*Désiré L'Hercule*." Immediately after the Civil War, the elder Désiré opened a coffee house (euphemism for saloon) and restaurant in New Roads. In addition to his legitimate children, Désiré Vallet was the father of two natural children, Désiré "Dé Dé" and Eulalie "Lalie" Vallet, by Claire Olivo, a free woman of color and sister of Madeleine Olivo, who was the mother of natural children by Pointe Coupée Road and New Roads merchant Jacques Goudchaux. Claire Olivo and her elder child, "Dé Dé" Vallet, baptized as Désiré Oliveau on 7 November 1852, at age 4 months (PCP-9, 195), were among the Olivo family members kidnapped and sold into slavery in the 1850s. Fifty-seven-year-old Désiré Vallet died on 27 January 1880, in the parish and was interred the following day (PCP-11, 257).

Dreyfus & Vallet turned out virgin Pointe Coupée Parish cypress and cottonwood lumber, with deliveries made to all points on False River and the Mississippi River, "at the lowest possible prices." Edward Joffrion was the manager of the operation, according to a 16 April 1897 advertisement in the *Pointe Coupée Banner*. After the dissolution of the Dreyfus & Vallet partnership, Louis Vallet continued to be occupied in commercial logging in the area.

ARTHUR WEIL

Arthur Weil was born on 14 December 1879, at Weil Plantation, Bayou Rapides, near Alexandria, Rapides Parish, Louisiana, to Simon Weil, a native of Ingenheim, Rheinpfalz, Germany, and Josephine Levy, born at Marco, Natchitoches Parish, Louisiana. Josephine was the daughter of Edouard Levy, a native of Frankfurt-am-Main, Germany, and his wife, Adilie Hernandez, born ca. 1833, in Natchitoches Parish, Louisiana, to Jerome Emmanuel Hernandez and Marie Agathe Nolasco de Porcuna.

By 1903, Arthur Weil was a resident of Livonia, and appeared in various social items published by the *Pointe Coupée Banner*. The 25 July 1903 issue reported that he and fellow Livonian Hyman Myers had made a "flying trip" to Alexandria and Weil, Louisiana. It is uncertain when Arthur Weil entered the employ of the Theo Dreyfus general store at Livonia, but the 1 February 1908 *Banner* mentions him as formerly of that firm when he went into business for himself, opening a saloon near Livonia.

After his time in Livonia, Weil appeared in the 1910 United States Federal Census as a dry goods salesman, living with his widowed mother and other family members in Alexandria, Rapides Parish, Louisiana. About a year later, he moved to the Panama Canal Zone, where he worked as a pipefitter and car repairman at the Canal Zone, until his resignation on 31 March 1915. He remained in Panama where he owned a saloon. He married Ida Isabel Icaza at Panama City on 30 October 1915. The bride had been born in Panama on 12 April 1893. They were the parents of three children: Edward Simon (b. 1919), Arthur, Jr. (b. 1920), and Josephine (b. 1928 - d.1940). He had briefly returned to Alexandria, Rapides Parish, Louisiana, for a short stay, but applied for a passport to return to Panama on 1 July 1919, in time for the birth of his first child.

Arthur Weil died on 29 July 1941, in Ancon, Panama City, Panama, and was buried in the Corozal American Cemetery in Corozal, Panama. Ida Isabel Icaza Weil died on 11 October 1970, at Inglewood, Los Angeles Co., California. We could find no record of her burial.

ABRAHAM "ABE" FRISHMAN

Abraham "Abe" Frishman was born on 26 November 1867, at Natchez, Adams Co., Mississippi, to Samuel Frishman, a native of the Russian Empire and Rosa Blumenthal, a native of Prussia. Sam and Rosa had been married at Natchez on 17 February 1866. Samuel Frishman served as a Private in the 59th Illinois Infantry, U.S.A., in the Civil War. Abe Frishman was listed as a dry goods salesman, living with his cousin Moses Marks, a merchant tailor, and the latter's family in Natchez, according to the 1900 United States Federal Census.

The 25 July 1903 edition of the *Pointe Coupée Banner* mentioned that Frishman was returning to Livonia from a two weeks' trip to his "home in Natchez." It is probable that he was one of the many clerks who worked for the Theo Dreyfus general store in Livonia.

Abe Frishman died on 9 October 1909, in Port Gibson, Claiborne Co., Mississippi, and was buried there in the Port Gibson Jewish Cemetery. He never married.

HYMAN MYERS

Hyman Myers was described in the 25 July 1903 *Pointe Coupée Banner* as a resident of Livonia, who accompanied fellow Livonian Arthur Weil on a trip to Alexandria and Weil, Louisiana. He is probably the same as Hyman Myers, born on 27 or 29 August 1878, or 29 August 1879, as the dates vary according to the several records, in Mississippi, or in Louisiana, depending upon the source. Hyman was the son of Louis Myers, a native of Kujawsko-Pomorskie, Poland and his wife, Bertha Hart. Hyman was a one-year-old boy, born in Mississippi, according to information in the 1880 United States Federal Census for New Orleans, where he was living on Camp Street with his father, Louis, a merchant, his mother, Bertha, and siblings, Alfred (b. 1866), Joseph (b. 1868), Mary (b. 1873), and Robert (b. 1876).

Hyman Myers was an active Mason, being elected Junior Warden of Fordoche Lodge No. 292 F. &A.M., according to the 8 April 1905 issue of the *Pointe Coupée Banner*. Because Arthur Weil, his 1903 travel partner, was identified in the 1 February 1908 *Banner* as being a former employee of the Theo Dreyfus general store in Livonia, it is possible that Hyman Myers worked for Dreyfus as well.

Neither Hyman Myers nor his elder brother, Joseph Myers, could be located in the 1900 United States Federal Census, but they eventually relocated to Texas. Hyman was enumerated in the 1910 United States Federal Census as a dry goods clerk, living in Gonzales, Gonzales Co., Texas. In his 1918 World War I Draft Registration document he indicated that he was a salesman in the employ of Harry Gusinsky in that city.

Hyman Myers died unmarried on 27 February 1929, in Gonzales, and was interred in the Gonzales Jewish Cemetery.

LEHMAN KAHN

Lehmann Kahn was born on 1 July 1879, at Schirrhoffen, Bas-Rhin, France, at that time under the control of Germany, to Daniel Kahn and his wife, Fanny Hirsch, both natives of the town. Lehman immigrated with his elder brother Lucien Kahn (b. 20 March 1877, at Schirrhoffen) to New York, where they arrived on 11 May 1895, aboard the *SS La Touraine*. Lehman was naturalized in New York on 3 August 1901. Lehman and Lucien Kahn were the nephews of Joseph Cohn, Jr. who had settled in Convent, St. James Parish, Louisiana, so after six years in New York, the brothers headed south.

Lehman, a store clerk during most of his career, made his way to Livonia, Pointe Coupée Parish, Louisiana, and was mentioned as resident there in the 6 January 1907 *Daily Picayune* "Society" section. It is possible that he, as did several other young Jewish men of the area, worked in the Theo Dreyfus general store.

When he signed his 1918 World War I Draft Registration card, Lehman Kahn was working as a clerk at Houma, Terrebonne Parish, in the "Leader Store," owned by Julien and Maurice Joseph, both natives of Bouxwiller, Bas-Rhin, France. Lehman Kahn relocated ca. 1922, to Baton Rouge, Louisiana, where another cousin from Schirrhoffen, Daniel Kahn, was working at the Farrnbacher Dry Goods Company, and where Lehman presumably worked until moving with his brother, Lucien, to Fort Smith, Sebastian Co., Arkansas.

Lehman Kahn died unmarried on 2 February 1927, at Fort Smith, and was in interred there in the Jewish Cemetery.

SEIDENBACH & LOEFFEL

The partnership of Seidenbach & Loeffel, composed of Mrs. Judah Seidenbach, née Mathilda Kaufman, and Gustave P. Loeffel, the second husband of Ray Munster, step-sister of Judah Seidenbach, was among the many Jewish landholders in Ward Ten, Pointe Coupée Parish, Louisiana.

Mathilda "Tillie" Kaufman was born on 22 October 1862, in New Orleans to wholesale hardware merchant Marx Kaufman, a native of Gommersheim, Rheinpfalz, Germany, and Amalia Reichenberg, born in Marköbel (now Hammersbach), Main-Kinzig-Kreis, Hesse, Germany. Mathilda was married on 4 January 1882, in New Orleans to Judah Seidenbach, born in Portsmouth, Scioto County, Ohio, on 7 April 1850, to Lehmann Seidenbach and his first wife, Caroline Siegel, natives of the Kingdom of Bavaria. Lehmann Seidenbach was enumerated in the 1850 United States Federal Census as a jeweler and in the 1860 Census as a dealer in rugs.

Judah Seidenbach was the owner of general stores simultaneously at Devall and Chamberlin in West Baton Rouge Parish, and sugar plantations at Chamberlin and elsewhere in Louisiana. He was, for thirty years, the "finance man" of A. Lehman & Co., wholesale dry goods merchants of New Orleans. Seidenbach, and his heirs after his demise, also sold handmade shingles, "21 inches long, of all heart cypress," according to advertisements placed jointly with the Bertha Lumber Company of New Roads in the *Pointe Coupée Banner*. Judah Seidenbach was Vice President of the Southern Scrap Material Company and a director of the Barataria Canning Company. Despite a heavy workload and less-than-robust health, Judah Seidenbach was an active member of Temple Sinai, and his civic and charitable works were legion.

Judah Seidenbach died on 7 October 1903, at the Jackson Sanitarium in Dansville, Livingston County, New York, where he was seeking treatment for an unspecified illness. Jackson was an early alternative health care facility which popularized the hydrotherapy cure for various diseases, as well a diet of unprocessed grains, fruits and vegetables. The Seidenbachs were buried under a handsome, domed monument in Hebrew Rest Cemetery No. 1 in New Orleans.

Henrietta "Yetta" Stern, born on 9 February 1836, in Germany, was the second wife of Judah Seidenbach's father, Lehmann Seidenbach. After Lehmann Seidenbach's death in December 1862 in Portsmouth, Ohio, Yetta headed the large household, first in Portsmouth and subsequently in New Orleans, Louisiana. Yetta Stern Seidenbach was enumerated in the 1870 United States Federal Census as the owner of a shoe store and was living with three of the children born to her late husband Lehman Seidenbach and his first wife, Caroline Siegel: Judah (b. 1850), Joseph (b. 1851), and Cecilia (b. 1853); two born to Lehman and Yetta in Ohio: Meyer (b. 1860), and Samuel (b. 1861), and Rachel "Seidenbach," age two, born in New York, as well as Yetta's mother, Esther Stern, age 68.

When Rachel/Ray married her first husband, Nathan Childs, on 5 March 1890, she used the name Ray Seidenbach. The couple had one child: Solomon Ned Childs (b. 1891). After Nathan Childs died in New Orleans on 11 April 1896, Ray married Gustave Peter Loeffel, on 6 June 1900, at New Orleans.

Loeffel was born on 30 November 1863, in New Orleans, Louisiana, to Eduard Ernst "Edward" Löffel and Louisa Frederick, Evangelical Lutheran natives of Teningen, Grand Duchy of Baden. Edward Löffel was a cooper, first in New Orleans and later at Bayou Goula, Iberville Parish. In her marriage record to Gustave Peter Loeffel, Ray, born ca. 1869 in New York, used the surname "Munster" and indicated that her parents were Gottschalk Munster and Henrietta Stern.

In 1906, Mrs. Mathilda Kaufman, the widow of Judah Seidenbach, and Gustave Loeffel, husband of Ray Munster, purchased the former Paul Bergeron Plantation on upper Bayou Grosse Tête, for $6,000 from Nicholas Schwab, husband of Henrietta Sicard. The property, comprising Sec. or Lot 6 and part of 7-T6S-R9E, contained 240 acres, and was located on the south bank of the bayou, midway between Parlange Lane to the west and Bigman Lane to the east. Schwab had purchased the rich, cotton-producing land in 1901 from Leon Paul, Josephine, and Olivia Bergeron, the children of Confederate Army casualty Paul Bergeron. Subsequently, and during the Seidenbach & Loeffel ownership, the bayou tract was worked by tenant farmers.

In 1921, Loeffel sold his one-half interest to Mathilda. As payment, Loeffel was returned his four promissory notes: one in the amount of $500, and three for $1,000 each, that he had made out with a mortgage on the tract. In 1924, Mathilda Kaufman Seidenbach sold the place for $6,000 to The Bomer-Blanks Lumber Company of Blanks, Louisiana. Subsequent owners included the Humble Oil Company and Exxon Corporation. In her sale to Bomer-Blanks, the Widow Seidenbach retained all rights to oil, gas and minerals, and through the grant of leases, her name and those of her heirs continued as familiar ones in the legal records of Pointe Coupée Parish for decades. The area has produced oil and gas since Christmas Day, 25 December 1948.

Mathilda "Tillie" Kaufman Seidenbach died in New Orleans, Louisiana on 27 August 1942. She was interred with her husband, Judah Seidenbach, in Hebrew Rest Cemetery No. 1. Mathilda Kaufman Seidenbach's descendants continued to own considerable real estate in West Baton Rouge Parish, Louisiana in the year 2022.

Gustave Peter Loeffel died in his native New Orleans on 22 September 1922, and was buried there in the Masonic Cemetery No. 1. His widow, Ray, was married a third time, in 1939, to Solomon "Sol" Reinach, the widower of Florence Mendelsohn. Sol died in 1953. The Munster name appears only one other time, in Ray Munster Reinach's burial record at Hope Mausoleum, although in her lengthy obituary published in the *Times Picayune* on 5 March 1972, she was referred to as Ray Seidenbach, the thrice married, one-hundred-three-year-old widow of Nathan/Ned Childs, Peter Loeffel, and Sol Reinach, Efforts to find her father, Gottschalk Munster, in other records have been fruitless.

ALFRED JOSEPH "JOE" DREYFUS

Alfred Joseph Dreyfus, son of Theodore and Blondina Wolff Dreyfus, was born on 15 March 1896, at Livonia, Pointe Coupée Parish, Louisiana. He served in the United States Navy during World War I. After returning from the service, Joe and his brother, Max Dreyfus, were enumerated in the 1920 United States Federal Census as farm managers for their father.

Continuing the family tradition, Joe Dreyfus had a long career in retail merchandising. His son Sid Dreyfus related that Joe operated a succession of commissaries adjacent to major bridge construction projects, including those at the rebuilt town of Torras in Pointe Coupée Parish, and Coushatta, in Red River Parish. Joe Dreyfus was later the proprietor of a general store in

Melville, St. Landry Parish, in the 1920s, specializing in ready-made clothing. He ultimately operated a general store at Krotz Springs, St. Landry Parish, which encompassed several thousand square feet of retail and warehouse space as well as living quarters above.

A Mason, Alfred Joseph Dreyfus, through his changes in residency, remained a member of Fordoche Lodge 292 F. & A.M. During his membership, the lodge moved its headquarters from Fordoche in Pointe Coupée Parish to Maringouin in Iberville Parish.

Alfred Joseph Dreyfus was married on 21 March 1922, in Norfolk, Norfolk Co., Virginia, to Doris Van Os, the daughter of Joseph Van Os and Rosa Schloss. Doris was born on 15 June 1902, in Norfolk. She and Joe had met several years earlier when he was in that city in the navy. They made their home in Krotz Springs. They were the parents of three children: Marian Rose (b. 1923), Theodore (b. 1932), and Sidney (b. 1936).

The couple died just months apart in 1988: Doris on 10 May in Opelousas, and Joe on 21 December in Krotz Springs. They were interred in the Menachim Aveilim Cemetery in Lafayette, Lafayette Parish, Louisiana.

HENRY LEON DREYFUS

Henry Leon Dreyfus, another son of Theodore and Blondina Wolff Dreyfus, was born in Livonia, Pointe Coupée Parish, on 25 June 1899. He attended Loyola University in New Orleans, Louisiana. According to the 25 May 1919 edition of the *New Orleans Item* he received his certificate as a pharmacist on 23 May 1919. Henry served as a pharmacist in his father's store at Livonia, and as Livonia Postmaster between 1926 and 1931. As was the case in may small towns in the early twentieth century, and attested to by Henry's nephew, Sidney Dreyfus, the Livonia Post Office was located inside the Dreyfus store.

On 22 May 1931, Henry Dreyfus was married in New Orleans to Janet Jacobs, daughter of dry goods merchant Wolf Jacobs, a native of Bialystok, Poland, Russian Empire, and his wife, Hannah/Ann Abramson. Janet was born on 26 November 1899, in New Orleans. Henry, Janet and daughter, Rachelle, lived in Arabi, Saint Bernard Parish, Louisiana, then a developing suburb of New Orleans, where Henry was a pioneer business leader. His Dreyfus General Store specialized in "Dry Goods and Fine Foods," and occupied two successive buildings: a two-story, frame, galleried structure, and a two-story, masonry Spanish mission style building, the latter having family living quarters above.

Their only child, Rachelle Dreyfus (b. 1937), subsequently Mrs. Marcus Hirsch, was a dedicated supporter in the relocation of The Museum of the Southern Jewish Experience from Utica, Mississippi, to New Orleans which took place in June 2019.

Visits were exchanged between the various children and grandchildren of Theo and Blondina Wolff Dreyfus in the various communities in which they had located. Jonathan Weil of Livonia recalled a festive Sunday chicken dinner hosted by Uncle Henry, Aunt Janet and Rachelle during his youth.

Janet Jacobs Dreyfus died on 21 July 1993, and Henry Leon Dreyfus followed on 9 November 1994, both in New Orleans. They were interred there in Hebrew Rest Cemetery No.3.

ALPHONSE WEIL

Alphonse Weil and Rosina Dreyfus.

Widely-regarded in American finance and retailing, Alphonse Weil was born on 11 April 1874, at Reichshoffen, Bas-Rhin, France, to Simon Weil, a native of the town, and his wife, Friederika Sichel, born at La Walck, Bas-Rhin. He immigrated to New York, arriving there on 13 July 1891, from Le Havre, France, on board the *SS La Champagne*.

Alphonse's first employment was for Abraham Klotz, a native of Uhrwiller, Bas-Rhin, France, around whose planting and mercantile company grew the small community of Klotzville, located just north of Napoleonville, Assumption Parish, Louisiana. Alphonse Weil most likely came into Klotz's employ through one of the two sisters, Julia and Pauline Abraham, both natives of Reichshoffen, who were successively Abraham Klotz's wives.

Alphonse Weil was naturalized in Napoleonville, Assumption Parish, Louisiana, in 1900. He was a clerk, then bookkeeper for Klotz, and when the latter incorporated his business in 1907 shortly before his death, Weil became secretary of the Abraham Klotz Planting and Mercantile Co., Ltd., where he remained for twelve years.

Weil lived for a time with his brother Felix, a retail clothier in Orange, Orange County, Texas, prior to marrying Rosina, daughter of merchant and planter Theodore and Blondina Wolff Dreyfus of Livonia, Louisiana. The ceremony uniting Alphonse and Rosina was conducted at her parents' home by Rabbi Max Heller of New Orleans on 5 March 1914. The couple's lovely

Wedding Book included photos of their gifts, signatures of attending guests, among whom were leading Jewish and Gentile citizens from near and far, as well as relatives whom they visited on their wedding trip to Paris, Alsace, Baden and New Orleans.

The chronology of their trip, rendered likely in Rosina's hand, in the album, notes successively during their time in Alphonse's native Reichshoffen: "Alphonse began to remember the town"; on 4 April, "Was at temple in Reichshoffen"; on the 10th, "1st day of Passover"; on the 11th, "Alph's Birthday"; and, as a foreboding to the coming conflict which would rend their ancestral Europe asunder, the 13 April entry is: "Saw many soldiers," as well as the more prosaic "Easter Holidays, cherry trees in bloom."

Settling in Paincourtville, Assumption Parish, Louisiana, the Weils had two children: Flora Mabel (b. 1916) and Simon Dreyfus (b. 1917). Alphonse Weil managed and eventually purchased Levy Bros. department store in the town, and served as a director of Bank of Paincourtville.

In 1930, the Weils moved to Livonia to assist his wife's parents in the Dreyfus retail and agricultural enterprises. Rosina served as president of the company, and Alphonse the secretary-treasurer and general manager of Dreyfus's, as well as the third family pharmacist to practice in the store. Alphonse Weil was appointed a director of Bank of Maringouin, in adjacent Iberville Parish, in 1938. He was elected president of that institution in 1961, and served until 1970, reputedly the oldest bank president in the United States.

One of the most familiar and respected figures in Louisiana, Alphonse Weil was also one of its most remarkable, being fluent in English, French, German, Spanish and Hebrew. He was particular that Dreyfus store employees be conversant in French and/or Creole, in those years before English took precedence over French in South Louisiana.

Amidst the anxiety and concern for loved ones back in France during the Second World War, Alphonse Weil and his family at Livonia received a photo with handwritten greetings from his nephew, Robert Simon Weil, son of Alphonse's brother Jacques Weil and his wife Alice David, who was fighting for the liberation of France in 1944.

Alphonse Weil died three days after his 98th birthday at the Medicenter in Baton Rouge. On his birthday, 11 April 1972, family members had visited him in his hospital room to offer congratulations. According to the *Pointe Coupée Banner* dated 20 April 1972: "He was coherent, and most appreciate of their presence, though his condition had steadily weakened during the recent week." He was buried in the Jewish Cemetery in Baton Rouge, and his pallbearers and mourners, like those of his late father-in-law, Theo Dreyfus, included influential Jewish and Gentile regional leaders. Rosina Dreyfus Weil died on 9 July 1974, also in Baton Rouge, and was buried with her husband.

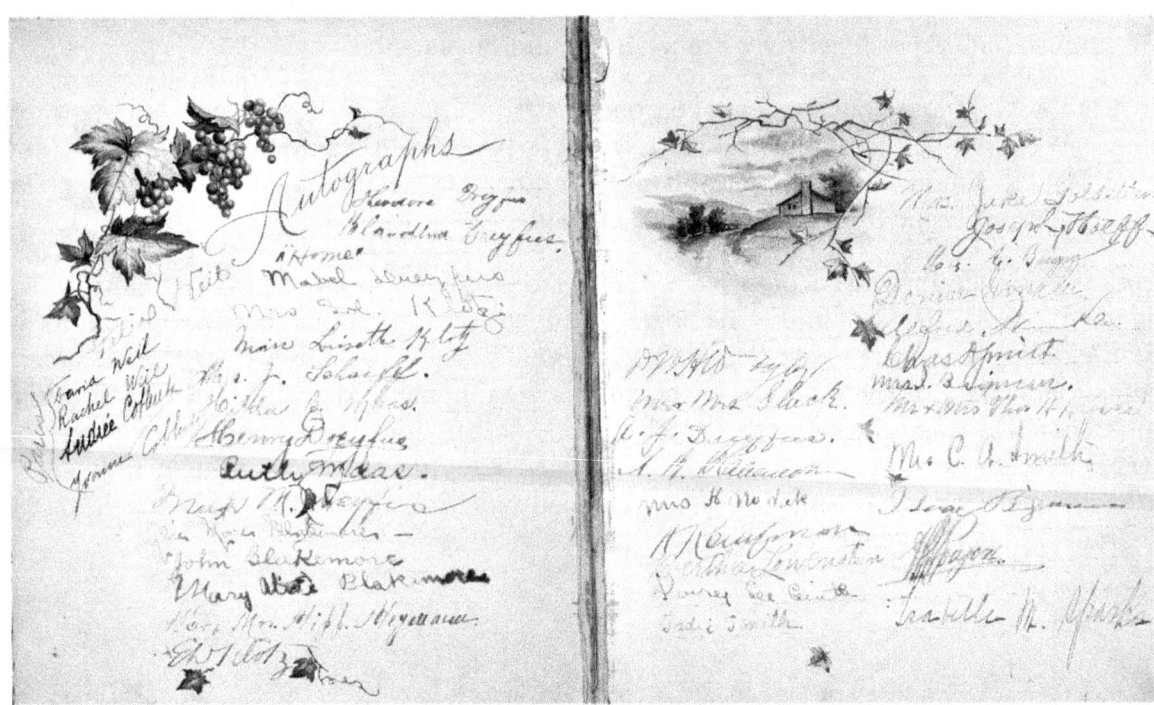

1914 Wedding Book of Alphonse Weil and Rosina Dreyfus, Livonia, Pointe Coupée Parish (Courtesy of the Weil & Dreyfus families).

SIMON DREYFUS WEIL

Simon Dreyfus Weil was born on 1 November 1917, at Paincourtville, Assumption Parish, Louisiana to Reichshoffen native Alphonse Weil, and his wife, Rosina Dreyfus, born at Livonia, Pointe Coupée Parish, Louisiana. Simon was educated at Mount Carmel Convent in Paincourtville and Belle Rose High School, both in Assumption Parish.

The Weil family moved to Livonia in 1930, where his parents assisted in the operation of his maternal grandfather Theo Dreyfus's general store and agricultural enterprises. Simon attended Louisiana State University in at Baton Rouge, graduating in 1938 with a B.S. in Commerce. First cousin Sidney Dreyfus recalled the energy and dedication of young Simon Weil during his college years, hauling sugar cane by tractor and cart to Poplar Grove sugar mill near Port Allen in West Baton Rouge parish, to the amazement of mill owner Horace Wilkinson.

Commissioned as a Second Lieutenant in the United States Army, Weil served in the 24th Infantry during World War II in the South Pacific. He was separated from active service in 1946, retaining the rank of Major in the U.S. Army Reserve.

Simon Weil was married to Ray Sarah Weill at Lafayette, Lafayette Parish, Louisiana, on 24 February 1946. Ray was the daughter of Leopold Weill, born on 24 June 1885, at Schirrhoffen, Bas-Rhin, France, and his wife, Bernice Weill, born in White Castle, Iberville Parish, Louisiana on 1 March 1898. Simon and Ray were the parents of three children: Simon Jonathan (b. 1948), Dinah Emilie (b. 1951), and Simone Ray (b.1953).

Simon Dreyfus Weil and his wife, Ray Weill Weil.

After resuming civilian life, Simon Weil was involved in the day-to-day operation of the Dreyfus Department Store as well as the Estate of Theo Dreyfus, which involved the cultivation of sugar cane, cotton and corn, the raising of commercial beef cattle, the maintenance of timberlands, and the development of oil production, across thousands of acres in Pointe Coupée and Iberville Parishes.

As a civic leader, Weil was active in 4-H, member and president of the Pointe Coupée Parish Farm Bureau; board member and subsequent advisor of the Pointe Coupée Parish Fair Association, member of the Upper Delta Soil Conservation District, the Pointe Coupée

Cattlemen's Association, the Pointe Coupée Sportsman's League, and the Louisiana Wild Life and Fisheries Association.

In 1956, Simon Weil was amongst a number of influential citizens who organized the Guaranty Bank and Trust Company of New Roads, which opened for business in the following year. He served for many years on the bank's board of directors. Weil also served on the board of directors of B'nai Israël Temple in Baton Rouge, where he and his family were members. He belonged to the Hunter-Fabre Post 248 American Legion in New Roads, and was active in state-level American Legion affairs, and as a Louisiana Agricultural Advisor. In his "spare" time Simon Weil enjoyed 4-H activities, boating, fishing, and time with family and friends at his home, "Golden Grass," adjacent to the three-acre Dreyfus store tract.

Simon Weil, his sister and brother-in-law, Flora Mabel and William "Bill" Katz continued to operate Dreyfus Department Store at Livonia, long after most rural stores had been crushed by giant city retailers in a rapidly changing retail market. The closing sale held in 1985 proved a bittersweet event for family and customers, many of whom came from near and far to relive fond memories of shopping in days past and to purchase merchandise as "souvenirs" of a quickly vanishing mode of commerce. Sidney Dreyfus related that the remaining merchandise was shipped to and sold from his and his father's retail store in Krotz Springs, St. Landry Parish. He marveled that one customer had even bought a box of white cotton stockings, long since *passé* as a fashion item.

Simon Weil died on 12 December 2000, at Livonia, and was interred in the Jewish Cemetery at Baton Rouge. His wife, Ray Sarah Weill died on 9 June 2020, at Livonia and was interred with him.

Simon Weil was recalled by persons from near and far, even beyond Pointe Coupée and Iberville Parishes, as an intelligent but humble man, rich in wisdom and prudence. "He was everyone's 'favorite first cousin'," first cousin Sid Dreyfus, stated in 2021 upon encountering another one of Weil's admirers, former Livonia Chief of Police, John Sparks.

WILLIAM RUPRECHT "BILL" KATZ

William Ruprecht Katz, a native of Dahn, Rheinpfalz, Germany, was born Wilhelm Ruprecht Katz on 8 October 1914, to Joseph Katz and Thekla Teutsch, He immigrated to the United States, arriving at New York on 22 July 1938, aboard the *SS Washington*, as Nazi terror and persecution gripped his native country. Katz joined the Pennsylvania National Guard and was sent to train in Louisiana, where he met his future wife, Flora Weil of Livonia. Bill Katz served as a U.S. Army language specialist in North Africa, Sicily and mainland Italy during World War II.

Upon his return to Louisiana, he married Flora on 20 January 1946, and entered into a partnership the same year with his brother-in-law, Simon Dreyfus Weil, at the "Dreyfus Department Store, Inc." in Livonia. Flora Weil Katz assisted her brother and husband in the daily activity of the store. Former customers fondly recall the "jokes" shared between the brothers-in-law, regarding who was the more industrious of the two. Meanwhile, Bill Katz also served as master sergeant in the U.S. Army Reserve until 1952. Bill and Flora were the parents of three children: Doris Rose (b. 1948), Joseph Alphonse (b.1952), and Daniel Simon (b. 1953)

Katz kept in touch with relatives, who lived overseas following the nightmare of the holocaust and destruction of the Second World War. He was an active member of Beth Shalom Synagogue in Baton Rouge and Temple Shalom in Lafayette.

Bill Katz died on 11 February 2003, in Baton Rouge, Baton Rouge Parish, Louisiana, and was interred in the Liberal Synagogue Cemetery there. Flora Weil Katz followed on 9 July 2007, and was interred with her husband.

RAY SARAH WEILL WEIL

Vivacious and accomplished Ray Sarah Weill was born on 22 August 1923, at Lafayette, Lafayette Parish, Louisiana, to Leopold Weill, and his wife, Bernice née Weill. Ray's father, Leopold Weill, was born at Schirrhoffen, Bas-Rhin, France, on 24 June 1885, to Charles Weill, and his wife, Emilie Kahn, both natives of the town. Leopold Weill immigrated to New York, arriving there on 13 August 1905, with his brother, Jacob, aboard the *SS Etruria* from Liverpool, England. Leopold began his employment upon his arrival in the United States with the Jasmin Tobias department store in Donaldsonville, Ascension Parish, Louisiana. Leopold Weill and Jasmin Tobias, the son of Maas Tobias and Marie Anne Weill (b. 3 February 1831, at Schirrhoffen, Bas-Rhin to Abraham Weill and his wife Barbe Levy), were second cousins. After a few years in Donaldsonville, he became a livestock dealer in Abbeville, Vermillion Parish, then in Donaldsonville, Ascension Parish, and finally in Lafayette, Lafayette Parish.

Leopold Weill married Bernice Weill, his second cousin once removed, on 25 June 1919, at the Hotel Gruenwald (now Hotel Roosevelt), in New Orleans. Bernice had been born on 1 March 1898, at White Castle, Iberville Parish, Louisiana, to Godchaux "Gus" Weill (b. 20 November 1864, at Schirrhoffen, Bas-Rhin, France) and his wife, Hermina Weil (b. 8 January 1871, at Grünstadt, Rheinpfalz, Germany). After the destruction of his massive Lafayette stable by fire, Leopold turned to real estate development. One of his projects was the luxury Bendel Gardens subdivision in Lafayette, which honors former Lafayette resident, and New York City fashion retailer, Henri Willis Bendel (b. 22 January 1868, at Lafayette to William Louis Bendel and Mary Plonsky). Leopold and Bernice Weill were the parents of four children: Emelie Leslie (b. 1920), Ray Sarah (b. 1923), Leopold, Jr. (b. 1925), and Gus Solomon (b. 1933).

Ray Sarah Weill, Leopold and Bernice's second child, attended Southwestern Louisiana Institute (subsequently renamed University of Louisiana at Lafayette) and Louisiana State University at Baton Rouge. In her hometown, she was city editor of the *Daily Advertiser* newspaper.

Ray Sarah Weill was married on 24 February 1946, at Lafayette to Simon Dreyfus Weil of Livonia. She and her husband established their home and reared their family near the Dreyfus Store. Ray was employed as a teacher at nearby Livonia High School to instruct gifted children. She is remembered fondly for the loving care she extended to all of her charges, including at least one child who was a monolingual Créole speaker. Above and beyond her educational duties with the Pointe Coupée Parish School System, Mrs. Weil helped prepare her students for their First Communion which she coordinated with Rev. Francis L. Lamendola at nearby St. Frances Cabrini Church.

Continuing her love of journalism, Ray Weil and Sylvia Roberts of New Roads were the founding publishers of the New Roads *False River Reporter*, a newspaper which appeared for a short time in 1976 and 1977. Mrs. Weil was a stalwart figure in local and national work for the American Cancer Society and other humanitarian and charitable efforts. Her sparkling personality, hospitality and innate care for others of all walks of life will long be remembered in and far beyond her native Louisiana.

Ray and Simon Weil's three children, Simon Jonathan "Jon," Dinah Emilie, and Simone Ray, excelled both in youth and maturity in livestock breeding and exhibition, as well as sports. Dinah was Pointe Coupée Parish Sugar Queen in 1968, and gained renown globally in Brahman cattle breeding. The three siblings are the fourth-generation who are actively involved in the continued viability and productivity of the Estate of Theodore Dreyfus.

One of Ray Weill Weil's brothers, Gus Solomon Weill, born on 12 March 1933, at Lafayette, was a well-known advertising and public relations specialist, an author of poetry, plays and novels, a member of the Council for the Development of French in Louisiana (CODOFIL) and noted political analyst. A frequent visitor to Livonia and New Roads, particularly to the Pointe Coupée Parish Library, Gus spent several of his final years at the home of his sister Ray Weill Weil and renewed friendships in the area.

Remarkably active and proverbially dressed in style, Ray Sarah Weill lived to an advanced age. She died on 9 June 2020, at her beloved "Golden Grass" home in Livonia.

ESTATE OF THEODORE DREYFUS, INC.

The Estate of Theodore Dreyfus, Inc., was chartered in 1965, its act of incorporation recorded in Corporation Book 2, Page 366, at the Pointe Coupée Parish Clerk of Court. The company's stated purposes are to engage in farming, to own farm equipment, raise crops, buy and sell lumber, grow timber, operate wholesale and retail stores, sell, exchange, and deal with property of all kinds, borrow and lend money, invest in stocks, bonds and securities, engage in oil and gas leases, drill for oil, buy and sell royalties and minerals, engage in mineral leases, and participate in the development of minerals.

The corporation was to be in effect for 99 years from 12 March 1965, with its location and post office address on Louisiana Highway 77, at Livonia, Louisiana, the address of the Dreyfus Department Store, Inc. The capital stock was set at 10,000 shares, and the paid-in-cash amount was $40,000. The registering agents were Simon Weil and Mrs. Flora Weil Katz, both of Livonia. The directors were Henry Leon Dreyfus of New Orleans, Max Meyer Dreyfus of New Orleans, Mrs. Rosina Dreyfus Weil of Livonia, Alfred Joseph Dreyfus of Krotz Springs, and Simon Dreyfus Weil of Livonia.

The corporation's first officers were Mrs. Rosina Dreyfus Weil, president; Max M. Dreyfus, vice president; Alfred J. Dreyfus, secretary; and Henry L. Dreyfus, treasurer. The incorporators were Mrs. Rosina Dreyfus Weil, Alfred J. Dreyfus, Henry L. Dreyfus, Max M. Dreyfus, Simon Dreyfus Weil, and Mrs. Flora Mabel Weil Katz.

The office of the Estate of Theodore Dreyfus, Inc. is located in the former Dreyfus Store warehouse, which retains much of its antique character while serving the needs of an active, 21st century corporation.

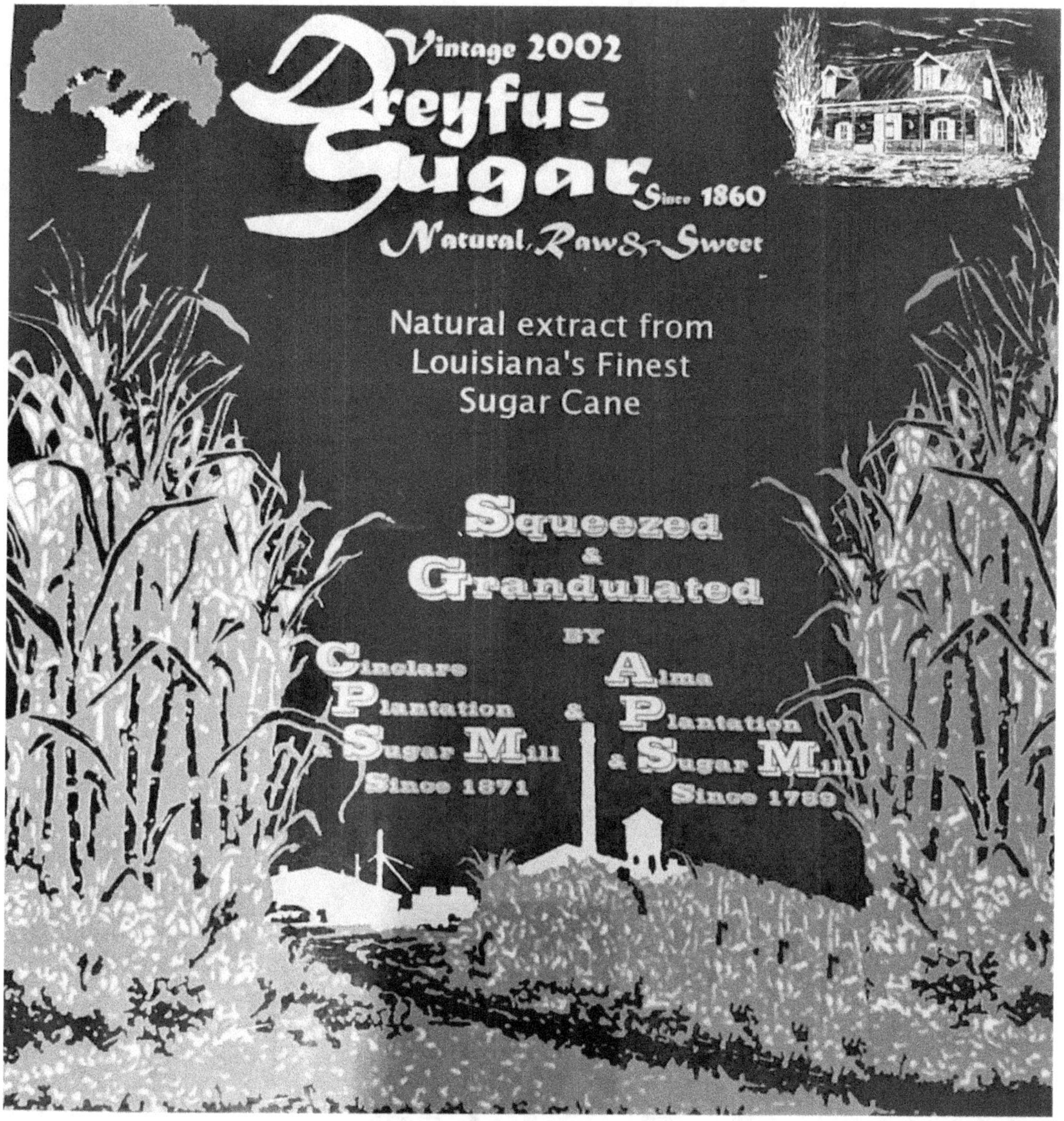

Livonia, La., March 25th 1908

DRUGS
—AND—
Patent Medecines,
—A—
SPECIALTY.

Bought of THEO. DREYFUS,
—DEALER IN—
Dry Goods, Notions, Hats, Shoes, Liquors,
FURNITURE, STOVES,
Saddlery and Full Line of Groceries,

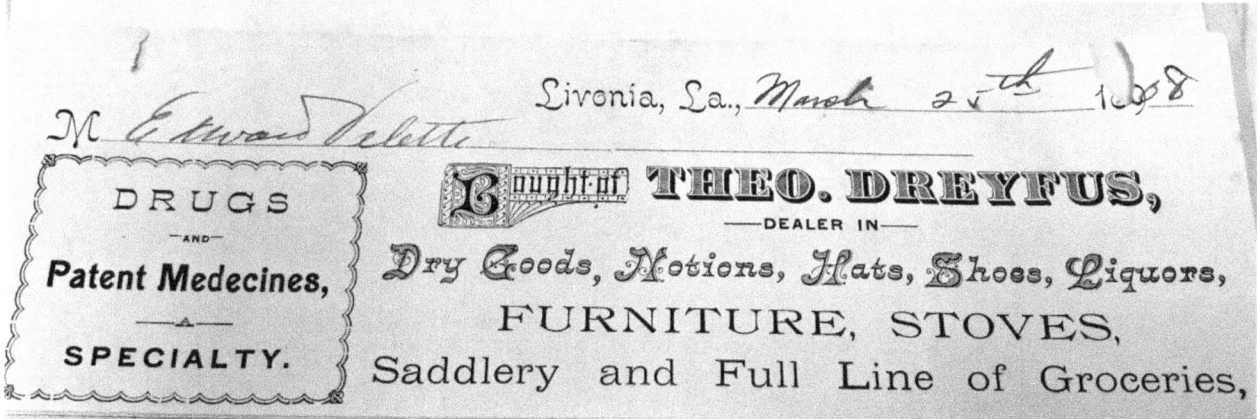

1908 Theodore Dreyfus Letterhead

1914 Weil - Dreyfus Wedding Book – Notes on the Honeymoon trip.

CHAPTER 9

BAYOU FORDOCHE AND BLANKS

Winding from its head at the Mississippi River at Morganza to its confluence with Bayou Grosse Tête just above Livonia, Bayou Fordoche has historically been a region of large plantations. The name of the bayou, and incorporated town along its southwestern stretch, is derived from a Native American word translated variously as "underbrush… briars …wild animals' lair."

West of Morganza, Bayou Fordoche makes a gradual turn from east to south, between Eliska and Crescent Park plantations. A post office called Viva, Louisiana operated briefly near Eliska, but the general area continues to be known by some as Tiger Bend, notorious as a "rough neighborhood in the old days" by local Civil War and oral historian Brian Gabor.

The Battle of Stirling Plantation or Fordoche Bridge, fought between Crescent Park and Argyle plantations on 29 September 1863, was the largest and deadliest engagement of the Civil War in Pointe Coupée Parish. A 3,000-man Confederate force under Texas General Thomas Green won a tactical victory over a greatly-outnumbered Federal contingent of 650 soldiers under Maj. Gen. Napoleon J.T. Dana and Lt. Col. Joseph B. Leake. The Federals lost 16 killed, 45 wounded, and 454 captured, while Confederate losses amounted to 26 killed, 85 wounded and 10 missing.

In 1864, the Battle of Fordoche Road was a rolling conflict fought from Morganza in Pointe Coupée Parish to Rosedale in Iberville Parish during which the Union cavalry pursued Confederate forces who retaliated with a succession of rearguard defensive volleys.

Between the cultivated lands of Bayou Fordoche and the Atchafalaya River to the west, are dense woodlands, most now encompassed within the confines of the Morganza Floodway. Intense logging of the region and processing of native hardwoods took place in the late 19th and first half of the 20th centuries. Communities which developed around the mills included Fordoche, Blanks, Canebrake (present-day Lottie), Elliot City and Ravenswood.

Blanks is located two miles south of Bayou Fordoche via the False River Station Road, and two and one-half miles west of Livonia via State Road (Louisiana Highway 81). Named for the Blanks family, who were part-owners in the Bomer-Blanks lumber company, a Post Office of that name was opened in 1913 with Wilkins Brown as its first postmaster. False River Station Road, now River Station Road, was named for the Texas & Pacific railway station of that name located midway between the bayou and Blanks.

I. LEVI & CO.

I. Levi & Co., was a partnership of three young men, the senior partner Jewish and the junior partners Catholic, that operated the "Eliska Store" on the plantation of the Widow Auguste Provosty, née Eliska Labry, as well as the "Argyle Store" on the Downing Plantation, both on the east bank of Bayou Fordoche, in the early 1870s.

The partnership of Isaac Levi, J. A. St. Germain, and C.A. Gumbel was apparently formed shortly after the 1870 United States Federal Census, as no merchants or store clerks were indicated as living along the bayou at the time. Records, however, show that St. Germain withdrew from the partnership in 1873.

We have not been able to identify Isaac Levi/Levy as we have not found him in any census records. We do know, according to his marriage record, that he was born in Germany and that his parents were Aaron Levi and Fanny Levi. Whether Fanny was born a "Levi" or Isaac was unaware of his mother's maiden name is not known.

Joseph Aristide St. Germain, a native of Waterloo, Pointe Coupée Parish, was a son of Waterloo grocer and Postmaster Jules St. Germain and Dorothée Boudreau. After withdrawing from the firm, J.A. St. Germain moved to New Orleans, where he married Waterloo native Anna Mathilda Vignes, on 13 August 1880. The bride was the daughter of planter James Vignes and Joséphine LeBeau, and a great-granddaughter of Benjamin Jewell and Sophie Prévost.

Charles Adalbert Gumbel, born on upper Bayou Grosse Tête, was a twin, the natural son of pioneer merchant Simon Gumbel and Amélie Amar, a free woman of color. His twin brother, Joseph Hildévert Gumbel, was recorded as living with him on Bayou Fordoche in 1876, and receiving notice on Charles Adalbert's behalf of the civil suit of New Orleans tobacco wholesalers King Brothers vs I. Levi & Co. in 1876 (Late Parish Court, No. 878).

Because of its location in the "interior" of Pointe Coupée Parish, merchandise for the "Eliska" and "Argyle" stores was transported by wagon from Morganza Landing, more than twelve miles distant, and beyond Tiger Bend, in the case of the "Argyle." Following St. Germain's withdrawal, Levi and Gumbel continued to operate the "Eliska Store" as late as 1876, according to 15th Judicial District Court records.

In 1875, Isaac Levi entered into a prenuptial contract with Hortense Dreyfus of New Orleans, in which she declared she was bringing personal property of $3,000 to the union. Hortense Dreyfuss was born on 20 May 1851, at Sélestat, Bas-Rhin, France, to Raphaël Dreyfuss, a native of Westhouse, Bas-Rhin, and his wife Nanette/Jeannette Levy, born at Weiterswiller, Bas-Rhin, France. Isaac and Hortense were married in New Orleans on 20 December 1875. (Note: Hortense's elder sister, Palmyre Dreyfuss, born on 27 February 1849, at Sélestat, was the wife of Félix Fraenckel, a native of Rothbach, Bas-Rhin, France, who was a merchant in Baton Rouge, East Baton Rouge Parish.)

On 17 August 1876, Isaac conveyed the contents of the "Argyle Store" on Bayou Fordoche to Hortense, the entire interest of which he apparently had come into possession. The contents were identified as a stock of dry goods, groceries, medicines, hardware, saddlery, and furniture, as well as the store fixtures and accounts, representing a total value of $1,425. The transfer between spouses was made in partial satisfaction of Hortense's cash brought into the marriage.

Signatures on Conveyance record dated 17 August 1876

Both the "Eliska" and "Argyle" stores appear to have been short-lived enterprises, as neither was listed in the relatively complete business advertisers' section for Pointe Coupée Parish in the 1876-1877 issue of Bouchereau's *Statement of the Sugar Crops Made in Louisiana* or in contemporary newspapers. Isaac and Hortense vanished after this from Louisiana records and we have not been able to trace them further either in America or France.

ISIDORE LEHMAN

Isidore Lehman was born on 7 July 1844, at Ingwiller, Bas-Rhin, France, to Israël Lehmann, a native of Schwenheim, Bas-Rhin, France, and his wife, Marie Baer, a native of Ingwiller, Bas-Rhin. His father died in 1854 leaving nine children ranging in age from three to twenty-four years. Isidore, along with his brother Leon Lehman, and two sisters, Adele and Sophie Lehman, immigrated to Louisiana ca. 1872.

After working a few years in New Orleans, Isidore Lehman opened a mercantile establishment near the Wiley Barrow plantation on Bayou Maringouin. He was enumerated there in the 1880 United States Federal Census living with his clerk, Isaac Keim, who had been previously engaged in retailing, farming and livestock trading on the Lower Chenal. After his employment with Lehman, Keim clerked for August Keller in the latter's nearby "El Dorado Store."

Isidore Lehman was married to Regina/Sena Mann on 2 January 1887, at Bayou Sara, West Feliciana Parish, Louisiana. Sena was born on 1 March 1858 at New Orleans to Alexander Mann and his wife, Theresa Hausmann, both German nationals. Alex Mann was the operator of numerous stores in West Feliciana and Pointe Coupée parishes. Sena was the sister of merchants Benjamin, David, Max, and Dan Mann, and Fannie Mann, wife of merchant Harry Weinberg.

Eight years later, Isidore was listed in the July 1889 edition of Dun's *Mercantile Agency Reference Book* at Ravenswood Station, Louisiana, the center of the Pointe Coupée lumber industry, located midway between Bayou Fordoche and the Atchafalaya River on the Texas and Pacific Railway.

JOHN Z. SOLOMON

John Z. Solomon was born on 25 March 1864, in New York, to clothing store operator Jacob Solomon and his wife, Freida "Fanny" Lauferti, natives of Kaiserslautern, Rheinpfalz, Germany. John Solomon was married to Gussie Peyser in Macon, Bibb County, Georgia by Rabbi Jacob P. Jacobson on 9 November 1887. Gussie was born in Alabama, to Maurice "Morris" Peyser and Marla "Mollie" Butoslovsky, natives of Posen, Poland, Prussian Empire. Gussie's sister Celia Peyser was married to Raccourci-Old River businessman Isidor B. Mount.

John Solomon, a merchant, and his wife, Gussie, were enumerated in Ozark, Dale County, Alabama, in the 1900 United States Federal Census, boarding in the house of Thomas and Augusta Mason. Apparently soon afterward, the Solomons relocated to Fordoche, in southern Pointe Coupée Parish, where he opened a general store.

A dedicated Mason, "J.Z." Solomon was elected Treasurer of Fordoche Lodge 292 F. & A.M., according to the 8 April 1905 issue of the *Pointe Coupée Banner*. Two other Jewish merchants were elected to office that year: Hyman Myers of Livonia and Joseph Wolff of Maringouin.

John Z. Solomon died on 29 November 1905, in New Orleans, Louisiana, and was buried in Rosehill Cemetery in Macon, Georgia. He was survived by his widow, née Gussie Peyser, and "absent heirs," apparently his siblings, M. Solomon, H. Solomon, and Lena Solomon Levi (21st JDC, No. 856, filed 1906).

John Solomon left an estate consisting of store merchandise, open store accounts, a horse, a cow, a buggy, a wagon, and the sum of $150 in cash. The merchandise was sold on the premises for $606.20 to Harry D. Mount, Gussie's nephew, and his partner, Hubert G. Landau. The stock included: dry goods, notions, clothing, hats, boots, shoes, groceries, tobacco, cigars, and hardware. The sale of the other movables brought the gross value of John Z. Solomon's estate to $1,716.66. Debts amounted to $1,715.82, leaving for Solomon's heirs a balance of 84 cents, of which 42 cents was remitted to his widow, Gussie Peyser Solomon. His siblings, M. Solomon, H. Solomon and Mrs. Lena Solomon Levi, received the other 42 cents, or 14 cents each.

Gussie Peyser Solomon moved back to Macon, Bibb Co., Georgia, and died there on 23 June 1932, where she was interred with her late husband in Rosehill Cemetery.

MOUNT & LANDAU

The short-lived firm of "Mount & Landau" at Fordoche, Louisiana, was the successor to the general mercantile business of John Z. Solomon, after Gussie's nephew Harry D. Mount and his partner, Hubert G. Landau, acquired the store's merchandise at Solomon's succession sale in 1906. Only a year later, in 1907, Mount & Landau were successfully sued by Hubert G. Landau's brother, Maurice D. Landau (21st Judicial District Court, No. 1012) in the amount of $606.60, which included charges for 12 silk umbrellas, a trunk, other unspecified merchandise, and for cash advances. No final judgment could be found in the file.

According to his 1918 WWI Draft Registration, Harry David Mount, was born on 4 November 1886, in the state of Georgia. At that time, he stated he was a merchant at Batchelor, Pointe Coupée Parish, on Raccourci-Old River, where his father, Isidor B. Mount, who had since moved to Montgomery, Alabama, had been an enterprising businessman. Harry later joined his family in Montgomery, where he died on 2 December 1926, and was interred with his parents in Oakwood Cemetery.

Harry D. Mount's onetime business partner at Fordoche, Hubert G. Landau, was born on 1 January 1889, at Créole Landing, on Raccourci-Old River, to Marcus and Melanie Michel Landau. Following the dissolution of Mount & Landau at Fordoche, Hubert Landau relocated to New Orleans, where according to the 1910 United States Federal census he was living with his brother Julius Meyer, their widowed mother, Melanie Michel Landau, and sister-in-law Rose Landau. Both men were working there as dry goods clerks.

Hubert Landau died from chronic pulmonary tuberculosis in Asheville, Buncombe Co., North Carolina on 18 April 1921, and his remains were returned to New Orleans for burial in Hebrew Rest Cemetery No. 1.

ISAAC DREYFUS

Who is the Isaac Dreyfus that appears in the 1910 United States Federal Census in the area of Bayou Fordoche? This record is the only one anywhere in Louisiana, or elsewhere for that matter, that mentions any Isaac Dreyfus with a wife and children using these names. According to the census, Isaac Dreyfus, born about 1880 in Louisiana, a laborer in a "stave mill," perhaps an iron worker employed by a cooper, lived with his wife "Rosa" born about 1882 also in Louisiana. Married ca. 1898 they had three children, with only two living: Denny (b. 1900), and Lillian (b. 1904).

One cannot help but notice the resemblance to the Isaac Bigman family, enumerated on False River Road. Granted Bigman was twenty years older than Isaac Dreyfus, but his wife Rosa Waldman was the same age as the "Rosa" married to Dreyfus. What is really peculiar is that Bigman and Dreyfus both had children named Lillian and Dennie/Denny who were close in age. The name "Denny" is particularly troubling as it is an unusual name for a Jewish child, even in Louisiana. We could find no other information about this family unit anywhere in the United States. Was this a census taker's mistake?

LEON "MANNIE" LEVY

Leon Levy, a leading general merchant, the son of Achille Levy and his second wife, Julia Rosa Levy, and grandson of Pointe Coupée merchant Meyer Levy and his wife Hevven Müller, was born on 27 February 1892, at Williamsport, Louisiana, at the upper end of Raccourci-Old River. He hailed from a family that had been extensively engaged in retail merchandising, planting and real estate since the mid-19th century.

"Mannie" Levy opened a general store at Blanks, Louisiana, which in the 1915 Pointe Coupée Parish Tax Roll had merchandise assessed at $1,000. In 1916, Levy's "stock in trade" was assessed at $1,850, the highest valuation in the parish.

On 24 October 1916, Leon Levy was married in New Orleans to Irene Esther Morais, the daughter of Adrian Joshua Morais and Hattie/Harriet Levy. Irene was born on 8 March 1895, in New Orleans. The Morais family were Sephardic Jews who had settled at the end of the eighteenth century in Kingston, Jamaica. Adrian Morais' wife, Hattie/Harriet Levy, was the daughter of New Orleans peddler Moses Levy and his third wife Lena/Helena Oppenheim. Leon and Irene were the parents of a daughter, Beryl Estelle, born on 4 February 1918.

Cyprien Léonce "Leon C." Kern, a native of Napoleonville, Louisiana, served as Blanks postmaster from 1915 through 1918. He was, according to his 1917 World War I draft registration, an employee of Leon Levy. This is evidence that the Blanks Post Office was located in Levy's store, a typical arrangement in rural Pointe Coupée as late as the third quarter of the 20th century.

A month after Kern appeared before the draft registrar, Theodore Dreyfus, for Ward 10, Pointe Coupée Parish, Leon Levy registered in New Orleans, as a resident of that city. He was employed as a salesman with the Leon Fellman department store (later Feibleman's), at No. 800 Canal Street. Leon Levy was identified in the 1920-1940 Censuses in New Orleans, respectively, as salesman "City" (*sic*), dry goods retailer, and department store salesman.

Leon Levy died in New Orleans on 12 May 1979, and was interred in Hebrew Rest Cemetery. No. 1. His widow, Irene, died in the city on 3 March 1997, and was interred with him.

Though demolished around the turn of the 20th-21st centuries, the site of "Mr. Leon's Store" is still pointed out by Blanks area residents.

Stores at Fordoche, Louisiana, ca. 1910.

CHAPTER 10

BAYOU MARINGOUIN

Having its origin at, and roughly paralleling Bayou Grosse Tête to the west, Bayou Maringouin and the town of the same name in neighboring Iberville Parish, owe their name to an insect. According to an oral tradition, Créole-speaking laborers who were engaged in the laying of the Baton Rouge, Grosse Tête & Opelousas Railroad were attacked by swarms of mosquitos, *maringouins* in the Créole dialect, in the area. The name was applied to the waterway as well as to the neighborhood.

The railroad reached as far northwest as Livonia Station by 1857 and was graded further toward the Atchafalaya River, but was never completed as planned. One of its stations in Iberville Parish was Musson, located immediately southwest of the present-day town of Maringouin. The latter community is located in Iberville Parish, its northern limit being the Pointe Coupée – Iberville parish line, and was incorporated in 1907. Maringouin and much of northern Iberville Parish have had strong genealogical and commercial ties to New Roads and southern Pointe Coupée Parish throughout history.

ISIDORE LEHMAN

Isidore Lehman, a native of Ingwiller. Bas-Rhin, France, started his career in Louisiana in partnership with his brother, Leon, in New Orleans, until the latter's death in 1873. He then moved to Pointe Coupée Parish and opened up a retail store near the home of the Wiley Barrow family on the west bank of Bayou Maringouin, where he was enumerated in the 1880 United States Federal Census. He was one of the earliest-known Jewish merchants at that location.

After his 1887 marriage to Regina/Sena Mann, Lehman relocated briefly to an area midway between Bayou Fordoche and the Atchafalaya River, at Ravenswood Station on the Texas and Pacific Railway which serviced the burgeoning Pointe Coupée lumber business.

Ravenswood being a rather isolated place, the couple moved to Rayne, Acadia Parish, Louisiana, ca. 1892, where Lehman became one of the town's founding dry goods merchants. He was enumerated with his wife and five children: Theresa (b. 1889), Mabel (b. 1892), Leona (b. 1894), Maude (b. 1896), and Alphonse (b. 1898), on Texas Avenue in Rayne, along with his two salesmen and boarders, Rufus Hoffpauer, and Cemar (*sic?*) Bernard, on 8 June 1900, at the time of that year's United States Federal Census.

After over twenty years at Rayne, Regina Mann Lehman died there on 28 November 1920. She was interred in the Menachim Aveilim Cemetery, at Lafayette, Louisiana. Isidore Lehman died on 22 August 1927, at Austin, Travis Co., Texas, and was interred in Lafayette with his wife.

AUGUST KELLER

August Keller, formerly the Postmaster of Livonia, Louisiana from 1874 until 1879, leased the southeastern portion of El Dorado Plantation on the west bank of Bayou Maringouin, bounded on the south by Kenmore Plantation from Wiley Barrow on 1 January 1882. The term was for five years, at a rate of $75 per year. Keller commenced a large-scale retailing operation as the "El Dorado Store," and began the cultivation of cotton. However, tragedy struck soon afterward with the great flood of 1882, when crevasses in the Mississippi River levee at Morganza and Scott Plantation northeast of New Roads and in the Patin Dyke area submerged the Maringouin and Grosse Tête region and numerous parishes to the south.

In February 1883, five of Keller's creditors filed suit against him, in the 15th Judicial District Court, for balances due: New Orleans commission merchants Simon Gumbel & Co., Simon being Keller's wife's uncle; New Orleans wholesale grocers and produce dealers Simon, Loeb & Co. (formerly of New Roads); Livonia merchant Max Mayer; Keller's former store clerk Isaac Keim; and New Orleans wholesale wine and liquor merchant, Joseph Dreyfus.

Depositions were taken in Orleans and Pointe Coupée Parishes. In New Orleans, Simon Gumbel declared that early in May 1882, he and his company advanced Keller $2,500 for the latter's merchandising and planting operations in Pointe Coupée, and Keller ran up additional charges with Gumbel & Co. for cash advances and goods in the amount of $4,574.10, against which the latter remitted nine bales of cotton. Keller requested a further loan of $4,000, but the company refused. The firm did advance Keller another $2,500, when Keller stated that he had some mules worth about $1,000 which he rented out to "negroes" on credit.

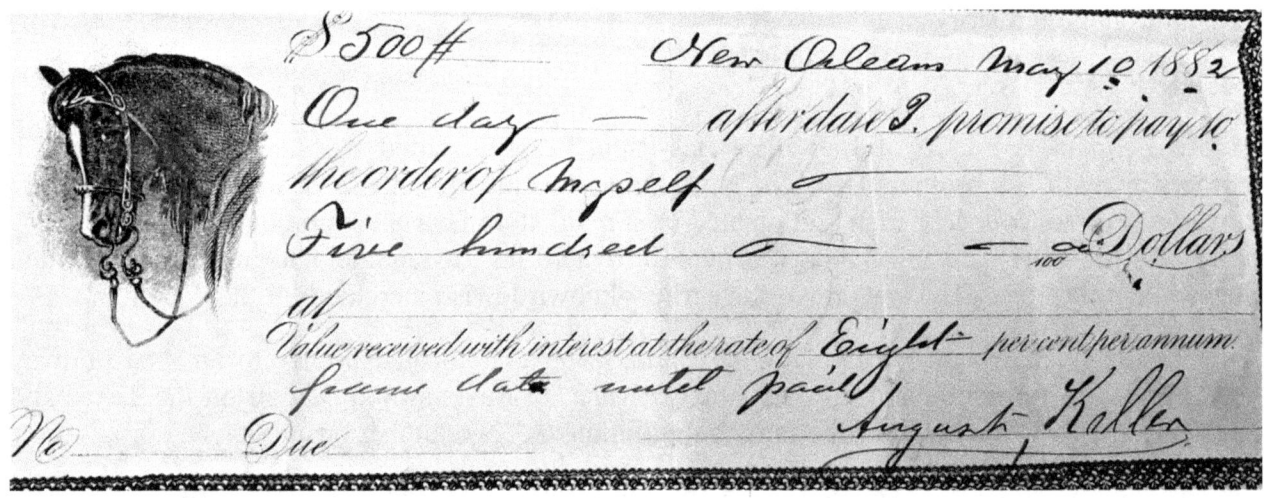

Signature of August Keller dated 10 May 1882 on promissory note to self for $500 during bankruptcy hearings.

Shortly thereafter, Livonia merchant Max Mayer informed Gumbel & Co. that Keller had seized the mules from the "negroes," shipped the animals to Plaquemine, Louisiana, for sale, and was converting his other property into cash. The mules were then sold to George W. Leonard in New Orleans, according to Gumbel. Other members of the firm of Simon Gumbel & Co. verified the senior partner's deposition, including Isidore Hechinger, who stated he went to El Dorado Plantation, and found Keller's mules gone and the latter's store merchandise "reduced." Simon Gumbel's brother-in-law, William H. Lengsfeld, also of Gumbel & Co., added that Keller had told him he (Keller) had a credit of about $1,000 with the New Orleans Cotton Seed Association, with which Keller said he intended to pay off debts.

George W. Leonard, keeper of a livery and sales stable in New Orleans, testified that Keller sold him six mules for $650 and a pony for $50. Leonard related that Keller told him he (Keller) could have gotten a higher price for his animals "in the country… but not for cash," and that he was getting out of the planting and retail business.

Isaac Keim stated that he was a store clerk for August Keller, and that the latter was removing "groceries and goods" from the store and trying to sell as much as he could for cash. Keim related that he gave Keller cash for the items he (Keim) sold on behalf of the business.

J.K. (James Knox) Pickett, stated that he had lived near Keller, and that the merchant was "selling merchandise lower for cash than any other merchant," and it was being said that Keller was going to leave the area.

Max Mayer related that Keller owed him two notes of $500 each, and that Keller was selling his own merchandise and sending away other goods. Mayer stated: "He [Keller] came from New Orleans, had the mules driven to the [Texas & Pacific] Rail Road Depot & went off with them. I informed the creditors of what was going on."

The court ruled in favor of the plaintiffs in all four suits, in the following amounts: $4,285.30, with interest, to Simon Gumbel & Co., representing cash advances and merchandise forwarded to Keller; $1,000 with eight percent interest from 10 May 1882 to Max Mayer, for notes owed him by the defendant; $701.58 to Simon, Loeb & Co. for balance owed on wholesale liquor and wine sales to Keller; $210 to Isaac Keim, the amount he had deposited for safekeeping with Keller, but which the latter refused to give him; $700 with interest from 20 February 1883 to Joseph Dreyfus for wholesale wines and liquors sold to Keller on credit.

Deputy Sheriff C. (Clairfait) Morel was empowered by the court to seize August Keller's property in order for it to be judicially appraised and offered at public sale in satisfaction of the monetary judgments. Keller's property, spread across three area plantations, El Dorado and Kenmore on Bayou Maringouin and Frogmore on Bayou Grosse Tête, included: a "store house," double cabin, "corn house," the "El Dorado (railroad) Station House," $3,700 worth of store merchandise, 30 sacks of cotton seed, a buggy and harness, a two-horse wagon, a skiff, and a lot of harness, all on El Dorado; an old (cotton) gin stand, a platform scale, a lot of moss, a (cotton) gin house, press, machinery, gin stand, and all apparatus appertaining, 50 sacks of cotton seed, and an old two-horse wagon, all on Kenmore; and about 20 sacks of cotton seed, a lot of household furniture, a stove, a trunk, two "dry" (animal) hides, a lot of plows and harrows, and about 30 head of cattle "at large," all on Frogmore Plantation.

Despite testimony that August Keller's store merchandise had been "reduced" at sacrifice prices in his hasty attempt to leave the area, court-appointed appraisers F.A. Erwin (subsequent owner of El Dorado Plantation) and A. Kaufman (Abraham Kaufman, a Lakeland general merchant) took charge of the itemization. Along with the firm of Landau & Hess on Raccourci-Old River, August Keller's inventory appeared to be the largest in the parish after Joseph Richy's (formerly Coulon & Demouy, originally Graugnard *Freres*) "grand magasin" in New Roads.

The "El Dorado Store" merchandise seized for sale included: bolts and remnants of dress goods, calico, piqué, checks, Carolina plaid, cotton, stripes, veil stuff (*sic*, veiling), alpaca, duck, jeans, linsey, flannel, sheeting, bed ticking, (mosquito) bar cloth; ruffing, embroidery, ribbons, fringe, trimming, binding, thread, buttons, buckles, thimbles, pins; quilts, blankets, bedspreads, towels, mosquito bars; men's dress, sack and woolen coats, cardigan jackets, men's and boys' pants, white and colored shirts, drawers, collars and cuffs, cravats, suspenders; ladies' Balmoral skirts, shawls, corsets and corset laces; men's, boys', ladies', misses' and children's hosiery, socks; gloves; handkerchiefs; men's, boys', ladies', misses' and children's shoes, boots and slippers;

men's and boys' hats and caps; ladies' "fine" hats; watches, necklaces, bracelets, pocket books, umbrellas, fans and (artificial) flowers.

Keller's grocery lines included flour, cornmeal, oatmeal, rice, grits, sugar, coffee, salt, beans, candy; canned oysters, sardines, mustard, and fruits; jellies, sweet oil, pepper, assorted extracts, bitters, pickles, dried apples, molasses, cooking soda, (beef) meat, pork, sugar-cured hams, sides, salted fish and herring. Alcoholic products included wines, liquors, whiskies, gin, cordials, cherry bounce, syrups, and beer, and tobacco was also sold

His large supply of drugs, medicines and chemicals included: laudanum, paregoric, calomel, vermifuge, castor oil, Dover powders, condition powder, Mustang liniment, Simmons' liver regulator, cod liver oil, McLane liver pills, Blue Mass, St. Jacob's oil, R.A. Relief, extract of celery, extract of vermicella (bandy-bandy snake), elixir of arnica, essence of peppermint, spirits of niter, spirits of turpentine, s(illegible) of ether, carbolic acid and Epsom salts. Toiletries and toilet goods included cologne and cakes of Lily White, brushes, fine combs, hairpins, razors and razor straps, blacking and shoe polish. Books and stationery included school, copy and time books, writing paper, foolscap, ink and pencils.

China and crockery items stocked by Keller included cups, saucers, plates, deep dishes, steak dishes, covered dishes, bowls, pitchers, teapots, sugar bowls and dishes, butter dishes, fruit stands, bowl and pitcher sets, soap and toothbrush stands, toothbrush mugs, jugs, demijohns and covered chamber pots. Other housewares and housekeeping goods included coffee mills, coffee pots and drippers, ovens and lids, flasks, teaspoons, forks and knives, waiters, caddies, smoothing irons, tin plates and pans, milk pans, coal oil cans, market baskets, brooms, washboards, tin buckets, water buckets, clothes lines; glass lamps, chimneys, burners and wicks; soap, starch, candles and matches.

Household fixtures included clocks and trunks, while musical instruments included violins, accordions and harmonicas. Keller's stock of games and playthings included: playing cards, dolls, miniature horse-and-buggies, tops, toy horses, drums, bugles, flutes, guns and pistols. Sportsmen's items included revolvers, pistols, gun cartridges and shot, pistol wipers, fishing lines and hooks.

Keller's stock of hardware and related items included nails, screws, rivets, thumbtacks, mosquito bar rings, hinges, caps, coffin caps, axes, hatchets, handsaws, pincers, shears, braces and bits, weeding hoes, horse brushes, curry combs, rope, twine, coal oil, lard oil, turpentine and axle grease. Saddlery and harness included riding saddles, bridles, reins, halters, girts, and trace chains.

The "El Dorado Store" fixtures included: a (floor) showcase, a jewelry showcase, a thread cabinet, six bracket and three hand lamps, a lot of weights, measures and scoops, a tobacco cutter, a meat axe and knife, a tin cash box, show cards, a feather duster, two twine holders, a "fine" desk and a "common" desk, a shoe punch, a step ladder, a pair of a pair of counter scales, a balance scale, and a coal oil tank.

Public sales were held on 10 March and 1 December of 1883. The store merchandise and fixtures were offered in the first sale, with $1,654.53 realized through the purchases of various bidders. In the 1 December 1883 auction, the five-year lease of the section of El Dorado Plantation and the store and kitchen thereon were sold to the firm of Cohen & Loeb for $1,100, $235, and $25, respectively. Simon Gumbel & Co. purchased the "gin house" for $200, the El Dorado (railroad) Station House for $28, and the old gin stand for $2.50. Total sales for 1 December 1883 yielded $2,173,30, which less Sheriff's, Clerk of Court's and printers' costs of $42.07, netted $2,123.23 for Simon Gumbel & Co., which was acknowledged as received by its attorney, Thomas H. Hewes of the New Roads law firm of Hewes & Parlange.

After the loss of his store and plantation, the record fell silent on August Keller, or so we thought. When his daughter Zoë married Joseph Mendes Meyer, a native of Beauregard, Copiah Co., Mississippi, on 2 March 1900, the festivities were held in New Orleans, at the home of the bride's uncle, Ferdinand Gumbel. There was no mention of August at the ceremony. That same year, Melanie Keller, a "widow," was living alone in a boarding house in New Orleans. At that time, she gave her date of birth as September 1859. There was, however, more to discover.

According to an entry at *Findagrave.com*, August Keller died on 4 December 1903, at Fort Worth, Tarrant Co., Texas. Information given by the local Jewish congregation indicated that Keller was born in Cologne, Nordrhein-Westfalen, Germany, in 1854. An obituary from the *Fort Worth Star-Telegram* revealed that Keller had been a resident of the city for only about nine years. He had been the proprietor of a news stand and book stall at the corner of 6th and Main and was survived by his wife, Jennie Mann Minville whose record was attached to his *findagrave* entry. A search of New Orleans marriage records revealed that twenty-year-old Jennie Mann, born on 13 October 1871, at New Orleans to Joseph Mann, a native of Hesse-Darmstadt, and his wife Mathilde Beer/Baer, born at Harskirchen, Bas-Rhin, France, had been married to thirty-nine-year-old August Keller, a native of Cologne, Germany, the son of Leib Keller and Jeannette Frank, on 6 January 1892. From this information we concluded that Keller and his first wife, Melanie Feitel must have been divorced. But was the August Keller, a resident of Texas, the same as August Keller who had been a merchant at Livonia, Pointe Coupée Parish?

Further investigation turned up another obituary for Keller, written in the Alexandria *Daily Town Talk* dated 5 December 1903, which announced the death of August Keller at Fort Worth the previous day, and continued that: "He was well-known in this [Rapides] and Grant parish, having at one time been in the lumber business with Mr. J.M. Nugent." We know that from the advertisement in Bouchereau's 1876-1877 edition of *Statement of the Sugar Crops Made in Louisiana*, that Keller had had a store at "Cakeland" (likely "Kateland," Colfax Post Office address) in Grant Parish on the Red River above the town of Alexandria. A further search of old newspapers revealed that Keller had been listed as a juror for the 1878 January term of the Ninth Judicial District Court at Grant Parish. Also, in the year 1878, according to the local *Colfax Chronicle*, Keller had been amongst the delinquent taxpayers in Grant Parish for both state and local taxes. In March 1886, Keller had been one of the participants in the annual Purim Masquerade Ball, at Alexandria, Rapides Parish, sponsored by the local Jewish Congregation. Keller masqueraded as a "grey domino." His acquaintances, Auger Siess and Jacob Levin, both active in the long leaf yellow pine lumber industry, as partners with the Nugent and Ball families in the area, also participated: Siess as a "pine woods oxen driver," and Levin as a "pine woods old woman." Moreover, it was reported in the *Daily Town Talk* dated 10 April 1886, that August Keller had been a guest at the wedding of Jacob Levin and Pearl Weinberg at Alexandria, and had gifted them a "large silver caster."

We believe that this is sufficient evidence to conclude that the August Keller who died in Texas was the same August Keller who had also been a merchant in Pointe Coupée Parish, and a merchant and investor in the lumber business in Grant Parish. After his 1892 marriage to Jennie Mann, the couple had evidently made their home in Fort Worth, Texas. The widow Jennie Mann Keller married Jacob Minville on 30 April 1909, in New Orleans. They had no children. Jennie died on 4 February 1954, at Asheville, Buncombe Co., North Carolina, and was interred there in Riverside Cemetery. Melanie Feitel Keller died on 29 December 1916, and was interred in Metairie Cemetery. When August Keller's only child Zoë Keller's uncle Ferdinand Gumbel died in 1918, she was left a specific bequest of $10,000.

COHEN & LOEB

The identity of the senior partner of Cohen & Loeb is still a mystery. The partnership kept an exceptionally well-stocked general store on Bayou Maringouin in the 1880s. The junior partner was likely Solomon Loeb, formerly Max Mayer's clerk at Livonia, who has appeared elsewhere in this book.

The first-known mention of the firm of Cohen & Loeb is found in the lawsuit demanding the seizure and public sale of goods of Bayou Maringouin merchant August Keller a few miles south on El Dorado Plantation on Bayou Maringouin. On 1 December 1883, the partnership purchased the remaining term of the five-year lease of the bayou bank property upon which the store stood for $1,000 and the store and kitchen buildings for $25.

In the 1884 Pointe Coupée Parish Tax Roll, Cohen & Loeb were assessed with $700 worth of merchandise and $100 worth of animals, however its location was given as on Kenmore (*sic*) Plantation, the property bordering El Dorado to the south. Whether the firm was located in the former Keller store on El Dorado or had moved the store building onto adjacent Kenmore and did business there is undetermined at present. Moreover, no other references to the firm of Cohen & Loeb have been located in either legal documents, newspaper accounts, or advertisements.

CHAPTER 11

MORGANZA

> In this section are "Grand Levee" and "Raccourci Levee," great works both, but it is within a space of miles below the mouth of Red River that the [Mississippi River] current exerts it most disastrous violence, and the most extraordinary exertions are necessary to successfully combat it. (Dorr, J.W. "Louisiana in Slices," New Orleans *Crescent*, 17 May 1860.)

For nearly two centuries, the place names "Morganza" and "Grand Levee" have been synonymous with the might of the Mississippi River, ever seeking to shorten its path to the Gulf of Mexico, and man's often futile attempt to restrain it. Situated at what was the upper reach of the original Côte de la Pointe Coupée (Pointe Coupée Coast, along the Mississippi River), the area of present-day Morganza, Louisiana, was, at the dawn of the 19th century, the vast plantation belonging to Bordeaux, Gironde, France, native, Jean Jarreau. Subsequently acquired by the surveyor, Charles Morgan, born in New Jersey, it became one of the leading sugar producers in Pointe Coupée. Morgan's transport of enslaved African Americans across the American South to Pointe Coupée, has been the continued subject of scholarly research.

Morgan's plantation was at the juncture of the Mississippi and Bayou Fordoche, along which latter stream the Opelousas Road followed, then veered to the west and onto a ferry crossing at the Atchafalaya River. Morgan's plantation and the village that grew around it was important as a point of east to west access as well as an entry point for cattle driven to the Mississippi from Texas.

One of the earliest known mixed marriages between a Christian and Jew in Pointe Coupée Parish was that of Charles Morgan, Jr., son of plantation owner and community founder Charles Morgan and his wife Hyacinthe Allain, and Virginia Raphaël, which was celebrated on 8 July 1839, in New Orleans. Virginia was descended from several of the pioneer Sephardic Jewish families who came to the Thirteen Colonies from England before the American Revolution.

A post office was established as "Morganzia [*sic*], Louisiana" in 1848, but discontinued in 1851. It was reopened in 1854, had its names changed to "Fordoche, Louisiana," after the nearby head of Bayou Fordoche. It was changed back to "Morganzia," in 1855. In 1873, the name was changed again, this time to "New Texas," for the river landing of the same name just around the curve of the mighty Morgan's Bend in the river. "Morganza [note spelling]" post office was established in 1885, but discontinued a year later. "Morganza" post office was reopened in 1899 and continues to operate into the 21st century.

Morganza was the scene of almost constant skirmishes between Federal and Confederate forces between 1863 and 1865, and the location of a major Union encampment established in 1864. As many as 4,000 troops were housed at a time, in quarters ranging from tents to frame structures built from parts taken from area citizens' homes, outbuildings and fences requisitioned for the purpose.

Fannie Riché, a *Créole de couleur* cotton planter and avowed loyalist, filed for and received judgment in her favor for materials and livestock requisitioned by the Federal army from her property downriver near Red Store Landing. Unfortunately, she died shortly before she was to receive the money in 1879.

The establishment and discontinuance of postal service, as well as the loss of a hotel, stores, and a Presbyterian church at antebellum Morganza were the result of the caving of the Mississippi River bank. Moreover, more than forty percent of the nation's floodwaters were funneled to a point immediately in front of Morganza and Grand Levee which caused frequent levee failures. Eighteen major floods were responsible for levee breaks or crevasses between 1780 and 1927, and in all but a few years, the most serious of the breaches occurred at Morganza and/or Grand Levee.

Particularly serious breaks and the resultant floods included those of 1850 and 1863, when Confederate forces deliberately cut the levee in an attempt to halt Federal troop movement in the parish. The flood in 1865 was caused by the neglected state of the levees during the Civil War which provided little resistance against the usual spring flooding. In 1867, the waters of the Mississippi and False River met resulting in the destruction and loss of livestock in the low-lying Bayou Grosse Tête valley. In 1869, with damage mainly in the immediate area and in 1874, with several breaches causing water to pour over the levee from Waterloo to Hermitage, the break at Morganza ultimately prevented the Island of False River from being inundated.

In 1882, floodwater issued from the as-yet unclosed Morganza breach as well as the breaking of the Scott Levee immediately north of New Roads and resultant breach of the Patin Dyke east of town. Nearly the entirety of the parish was inundated. The Main Street of New Roads was flooded with four feet of water at the height of the crisis, and at least one death by drowning was reported. Losses were estimated at $2 million, including 2/3 of the parish's livestock. Through the efforts of Louisiana Senator Charles Parlange, a native of False River, supplies including meat, flour and cornmeal, as well as oats and hay for livestock were sent to the parish.

The newly-repaired Morganza Levee broke again within weeks in 1884, and combined with the breach of the front and rear, main levees downriver at Waterloo, the parish was flooded almost as severely as in 1882. New Roads had two feet of water and at least two casualties were recorded. Government rations were provided to thousands of Pointe Coupéeans in 1884, including 1,780 people on the Island of False River.

Repaired once again, the Morganza Levee broke in two places along the Mississippi and Atchafalaya Rivers in 1890. Pierre Félicien Bourgeois and J.A. Oubre were reported by the New York Times as having saved the levee from breaking in the New Texas area. They sank in mud up to their knees in an effort to sandbag the wave wash, while "ladies of culture and refinement" filled and passed them the sacks of earth.

Some 4,500 destitute were counted in Pointe Coupée Parish due to the 1890 flood, the first local disaster in which large-scale evacuations were undertaken. Steamboats and Texas & Pacific trains removed people and livestock to the high land east of the Mississippi River. At least eight deaths by drowning were reported: six at Erwinville, including five members of the Watson family, as well as two others attempting to close a levee breach on Preston Plantation northeast of New Roads.

In a letter to Morganza businessman Thomas Heard Campbell dated October 23, 1945, ninety-year-old Marie Philomène Elida Vignes, widow of Bouis Léonard Bergeron, and a great-niece of Delphin Vergès Vignes, related memories of the April 22, 1890 Morganza levee crevasse. She stated that the breach remained open for "two or three years," during which time the famous steamboat *Natchez* was stuck in the crevasse but later pulled out. Research into the series of vessels named *Natchez* suggests that this was the sternwheeler *Natchez VIII*, which was launched in 1891 and was destroyed in 1918 or 1919. (Source: Louisiana State Archives, Baton Rouge, Louisiana, "T.H. Campbell Collection.")

The year 1900 signaled a new beginning for Morganza, when the Texas & Pacific Railroad was completed connecting Addis to the south in West Baton Rouge Parish, with Ferriday upriver in Concordia Parish. New businesses were built facing the railroad, not the levee and river as in the past. The Village of Morganza, the third community in Pointe Coupée Parish to be incorporated, received its charter in 1908. Despite damage wrought by the flood of 1912, the town grew, mainly due to investments by the Citizens' Bank of New Orleans which financed the expansion of the town immediately to the southeast of the 1900 development in 1913. Morganza grew to have a number of businesses, including several general stores and a theatre owned by members of the Srulovitz/Loeb/Hart family.

The area continued to thrive from 1939 through 1955 with the building of the Morganza Spillway, control gates, and Floodway north and west of the town. Designed to carry off a percentage of Mississippi River floodwater to the Gulf of Mexico between guide levees, in the event that the river's flow registered 1.5 million cubic feet per second upriver at Red River Landing, the flood gates were opened in 1973 and again in 2016.

After the death of Virginia Raphaël, the widow of Charles Morgan, Jr., in 1858, the next-known Jewish resident of Morganza was Confederate Army veteran Gustav Wolf, a native of the Principality of Hohenzollern-Hechingen (present-day Baden-Wurttemberg, Germany), who was formerly a grocer and the agent of merchant Henry Picard on Raccourci-Old River.

The Jewish presence in Morganza, however, was largely that of the extended Srulovitz family, natives of the Kingdom of Romania, some of whose members assumed the surname Loeb, while another chose the name Hart.

CHARLES MORGAN, JR. AND VIRGINIA RAPHAËL

Charles Morgan, Jr. and Virginia Raphaël were married on 8 July 1839, by Associate Judge of the City Court of New Orleans, O.P. Jackson. The groom was born ca. 1815 on the plantation of his parents, Charles and Hyacinthe Allain Morgan, at present-day Morganza, Louisiana. Although there is no baptismal record for Charles, as was done for his sisters, Agustina, Marguerite and Marie Françoise, there is a marriage record for his father, "Carlos Morgan of New Jersey, the son of James Morgan and Maria Everston" on 28 February 1807, to "Jacintha Allain," the daughter of "Francisco Allain and "Maria Francisca Richard" (SJO-7,8). Charles, Jr.'s bride, Virginia Raphaël, was born in Virginia ca. 1820, to Isaac Raphaël (1795-1857), a native of Philadelphia, Pennsylvania, according to the 1850 United States Federal Census for Louisville, Jefferson Co., Kentucky, and his wife, Clarissa Ann Wolfe (1800-1872), born in Richmond, Henrico Co., Virginia. Virginia Raphaël's grandfather, Solomon Raphaël, a

Sephardic Jew said also to have been born in Philadelphia ca. 1740, had married Charlotte Jacobs on 15 October 1788, at Philadelphia.

Charles and Virginia Raphaël Morgan's seven children were all born at Morganza: Julia Hyacinthe (b. 1841- d. 1901), later Mrs. Maurice Abrams; Medora (b. 27 February 1843-d. 1937), later Mrs. John Shook; Adele (b. 12 July 1845-d. 1930), later Mrs. Harry L. Zebal; Corinne (b. ca. 1846-d. 1857 at Morganza); Charles "III," (b. 27 April 1849-d. 1902); Raphaël Clifton (b. 11 July 1852-d. 1931), who married Dora R. Hamilton; and Blanche Mertel (b. 22 February 1855-d. 1947), later Mrs. John George Washington Peters.

Charles Morgan, Jr., a half-owner, with James Clark of the Mississippi River steamboat *Natchez No. 2*, died at Morganza on 1 September 1855. His place of burial remains uncertain, but might have been in the old St. Francis Catholic Church Cemetery downriver, northeast of New Roads, or perhaps in the "plantation cemetery" at Morganza, mentioned as having recently caved into the Mississippi River, according to J.W. Dorr's "Louisiana in Slices" installment dated 14 May 1860, published in the New Orleans *Crescent*.

Charles Morgan, Jr.'s succession (9th Judicial District Court, No. 1425), administered by his widow, Virginia Raphaël, indicated that his estate was appraised at $22,640, including: the Morgan sugar plantation of his late parents, measuring 24 arpents front on the Mississippi River by a depth of 80 arpents, with improvements; a plantation, upriver, measuring 14 arpents front by a depth of 40 arpents; a tract measuring four arpents front by a depth of 30 arpents, farther upriver; fractional Sec. 62_T4S-R8E, containing 248 acres; a 1,000 arpent plantation on the east bank of Bayou Grosse Tête (at Livonia); and an enslaved labor force of 163 persons.

In 1856, a public sale made of other property belonging to the late Charles Morgan, Jr. grossed $8,015, and included: a mule, two horses, two mares, two colts, a rifle, a buggy and harness, several items of household furniture, and real estate consisting of Lots or Sections 60 and 61-T4S-R8E, containing 861.3 acres, fronting on Bayou Fordoche. Attorney Auguste Provosty purchased the real estate. Morgan's widow was the high bidder for a mahogany secretary at $15 and a sopha (*sic*) at $8. Morgan's debts totaled $5,785.42, including accounts to local Jewish firms Simon & Loeb of New Roads and Meyer & Strauss of Pointe Coupée Rd., as well as expenses of the steamer *Natchez No. 2*, including $150 in accounts and Morgan's half-interest in amounts due its builder and former owner Capt. Thomas P. Leathers, S.M. Bayley & Co., and J.B. White.

Virginia Raphaël Morgan died on 16 November 1858, at Carrollton, Jefferson Parish, Louisiana, and was interred in the Sephardic Dispersed of Judah Cemetery in New Orleans. The unmarried Morgan children, Madora (sic), Adele, Charles (III), Raphaël, and Blanche, were enumerated in the household of their paternal grandmother, the Widow Hyacinthe Allain Morgan, in the 1860 United States Federal Census. At that time, Hyacinthe was identified as a planter with $300,000 worth of real estate and $12,000 in personal property.

The memory of Charles and Virginia Raphaël Morgan's children who relocated to New Orleans after the death of their grandmother Hyacinthe Allain Morgan, was largely forgotten in Pointe Coupée Parish by the mid-1900s. Virginia Raphaël was identified in family genealogies simply as "a Jewish lady." (e.g., Thomas, LaVerne III, *LeDoux*, 1982.) Oral and written history of St. Mary Episcopal Church of Morganza, built in 1910, however, relates that the altar candlesticks of that charming house of worship were donated by Morgan descendants then Sunday school students of Christ Church (now Cathedral) in New Orleans. It is likely that Charles, Jr. and Virginia Raphaël Morgan's descendants were among their number.

ISIDORE SRULOVITZ/LOEB

Isidore Srulovitz/Loeb, a native of the Kingdom of Romania, who immigrated to America in 1899, was born on 15 January 1869, to Lazar Srulovitz and his wife, Rebecca Herskovitz. Any relationship between Rebecca Herskovitz and New Roads merchant Josef Herskovitz is unknown at present. Isidore's brothers, Max and Pincus also immigrated to America.

Isidore and Pincus Srulovitz were partners in a general store in Morganza which was opened in 1906 in the former E.A Fisher & Son store, on a lot purchased by Pincus that year from Eliska Tircuit Muse. In 1908 they moved into the former location of "The Gum," one of James E. Alexander's several enterprises, situated a block north near the southeast corner of Railroad Avenue East and Elk (later Fordoche) Road. Likely due to Isidore Srulovitz/Loeb's subsequent insolvency a few years later, Pincus withdrew from the partnership and opened his own store in their former location.

Isidore Srulovitz filed a petition at New Roads to have his name legally changed to Isidore Loeb, which he announced in the 3 April 1909 edition of the *Pointe Coupée Banner*. On 15 April 1910, Isidore Srulovitz was enumerated as "Isadore Loeb," a thirty-nine-year-old native of Romania, who had arrived in America on Thanksgiving Day 1899. Also living in the Morganza household was his brother Pincus/Philip Srulovitz/Loeb, his niece and nephew, Fannie Srulovitz, age 16, and Gabriel Srulovitz, age 15. Isidore was a dry goods and grocery merchant, and was assisted by Gabriel, a store clerk.

Isidore (Loeb) Srulovitz (*sic*), age 40, married Esther Grasioni/Grasiany, age 26, on 24 July 1910, in New Orleans, Louisiana. The bride was born 10 January 1881, in the Kingdom of Romania, to Sabetay Grasioni and his wife Ermoza (surname not indicated). Esther had been previously married to Leon Feder. Their child, Moses/Morris Feder, was born on 5 August 1903, in New Orleans.

Later in 1910, Isidore Loeb filed suit for insolvency (21st Judicial District Court, No. 1654). His assets included: dress goods, embroidery, laces, ribbons, notions, clothing, ladies' cloaks, hosiery, hats, shoes, groceries, drugs, stationery, crockery, sporting goods, hardware, and stoves; also, a lot of open accounts and notes, and the improved lot at the southeast corner of Railroad Avenue East and (Bayou) Fordoche Road in Morganza, for a total appraised value of $4,930. Isidore Loeb was succeeded as a general merchant in the former "Gum" store by The LeBlanc Co., Gesner and Louis LeBlanc, proprietors.

Former location of Isidore Srulovitz/Loeb store at right during 1912 flood.

Isidore and his wife, Esther, moved first to Montgomery, Montgomery Co., Alabama, where they were enumerated together in the 1920 United States Federal Census. Isidore was working as a retail grocer. Living with them was Isidore's sixteen-year-old stepson Morris Loeb, born Morris Feder to Esther and her first husband Leon Feder.

Isidore Loeb, his wife, Esther, and Morris subsequently relocated to Mobile, Mobile Co., Alabama, where Morris was married to Amelia Morningstar, the daughter of Alexander Morningstar and Leila Olensky, on 4 March 1923. Isidore and Esther were enumerated living together in the 1940 United States Federal Census for Mobile where they were owners of a grocery store.

Esther died on 10 March 1952, at Mobile. Eighty-three -year-old Isidore Loeb died on 20 November 1952, five hours after being beaten with a baseball bat in the fourth attempt in eight months to rob his store. (*The Huntsville* [Alabama] *Times* dated 21 November 1952, page 12, col. 6.) Esther and Isidore were both interred in Ahavas Chesed Cemetery in Mobile.

PINCUS/ PHILIP SRULOVITZ/LOEB

According to his tombstone inscription, Pincus Srulovitz was born on 9 October 1877, in the city of Galatz/Galati, Kingdom of Romania, the son of Lazar Srulovitz and Rebecca Herskovitz. Pincus came to America in 1899 with his elder brother, Isidore.

Pincus Srulovitz had his name changed legally to Pincus Loeb in 1912, in New Roads, Louisiana. Loeb later anglicized his given name from Pincus to Phillip. Pincus/Philip Loeb was commonly referred to by generations of fellow Pointe Coupéeans as "Mr. P. Loeb."

Pincus Loeb acquired a number of lots in Morganza as well as the former William Berthelot property, just above town on the Mississippi River. Indicative of the encroachment of the great river through the 19th and late 20th centuries, deeds for this tract continued to state its acreage as being 52, but only 27 acres were determined through survey as having escaped the caving of the bank, resultant levee, railroad and highway, and the digging of "borrow pits" for the Morganza Floodway levee construction system.

In 1906, Pincus Srulovitz purchased from Eliska Tircuit, widow of Capt. James Fort Muse, an improved lot fronting 60' on Railroad Avenue East by a depth of 150' for a mere $140. Bounding on the north was the "Hotel Lot" of Pierre Félicien "P.F." Bourgeois on which stood the two-story hostelry ultimately operated by Mrs. Félix Arnaud Beauvais, née Minnie Shaw.

A large frame building stood on the newly purchased lot. It had formerly been the general store of Edward August Fisher, the husband of Regina Bourgeois and son-in-law of P.F. Bourgeois. Fisher was the son of Alsace native Auguste Fisher and the oft-married, four-times-widowed, former Morganza Freedmen's Bureau School teacher, Julia Eulalie St. Vrain Bourgeat Fisher Higgins See. Edward Fisher's step-father, Jacob See, had clerked for Picard & Weil's store at Bayou Sara, West Feliciana Parish, Louisiana, before operating a general store of his own between 1871 and 1873 on the former A.B. Thompson, later J.M. Bailey plantation at Livonia.

A story and a half in height, the Fisher-Srulovitz/Loeb Building in Morganza had a balcony inset in the facade gable, and was strikingly similar in appearance to Casimir Savignol's "French Hotel" and Mrs. Noel Major's "New Roads Hotel," both in the parish seat, and likely built by the same contractor. Pincus and his brother Isidore Srulovitz operated a general store there, until moving a block north, near the intersection of Railroad Avenue East and Elk (subsequently Fordoche) Road.

Pincus Srulovitz was married on 4 February 1908, in New York City to Rebecca "Becky" Kaufmann. A Romanian by birth, she was the daughter of Lazer Kaufmann, a native of Satoraljaujhely, Kingdom of Hungary, and Dora Bucholtz, born in Dragusenii, Bessarabia, Russian Empire.

Likely owing to the insolvency of Isidore in 1910, Pincus/Philip went into business for himself, opening the landmark Loeb's Department Store in the former E.A. Fisher building owned by him. Encompassing 3,000 square feet, the building was divided into a store in front and the Loebs' family quarters in the rear. In time, its front gallery was enclosed to form display windows. The upper-level gable and inset balcony was covered by a stepped and arched false front. Similar in layout to other general stores of the period, Loeb's had a relatively large, main retail area for clothing, piece goods and sewing notions, groceries and household merchandise, and a narrow "side room." The latter, in Loeb's case, was along the right/southern side of the building. It was designated as a hardware and furniture warehouse on the 1921 Sanborn Fire Insurance Map of Morganza.

Former Loeb's Department Store, Pincus/Phillip Srulovitz/Loeb, proprietor, pictured in 1977, dismantled a few years later.

In addition to retailing and real estate, Philip Loeb was, according to several issues of the 1917 *Pointe Coupée Banner*, an alderman for the village of Morganza. He was also among the initial stockholders of the Bank of Morganza, chartered in 1918, purchasing $500 in stock at the time of incorporation. A financial casualty of the Great Depression, the Bank of Morganza was liquidated in 1931 and its plot and charming masonry building on the southwest corner of West Railroad Avenue and Ryan Street was sold to Charles Serio for $1,000. N. A. "Ted" Melancon, Jr. subsequently operated a feed and seed store there, followed by the Bank of New Roads, who established their first Morganza branch in the building. In the year 2022, it was home to The Red Apron Café and catering business.

Loeb died on 27 October 1943, in Morganza, and was buried as "Pincus Loeb" in the Ahavas Chesed Cemetery in Mobile, Mobile Co., Alabama. His widow died on 7 August 1955, in New Roads, and was interred with her husband.

The Loebs were succeeded in the business by their daughters: Tillie Loeb, the wife of Jack Blum, and Misses Rachel and Sarah Loeb. Jack and Tillie Blum, who had no children, later moved to Baton Rouge, Louisiana, where they operated Blum's Food Store at 2401 Huron Street and lived in the Istrouma suburb. With the Blums in the capital city, and Tillie's sisters, Rachel and Sarah Loeb, hospitalized at the East Louisiana State Hospital in Jackson, East Feliciana Parish, Loeb's Department Store held a closing sale advertised in the local *Pointe Coupée Banner*, offering groceries, clothing, dry goods and hardware, and finally passed into area retail history in 1965.

Loeb's was the second-to-last locally-owned Jewish business to operate in Pointe Coupée Parish, Louisiana, being survived only by Dreyfus Department Store in Livonia. The Loeb Building, later used for the storage of livestock feed, and the lot upon which it stood were acquired by neighboring grocer Clarence J. "Woots" Wells, and was demolished in the 1980s. The former

Berthelot property owned by Philip Loeb, upriver, was donated by his heirs to Beth Shalom Synagogue of Baton Rouge, Louisiana, from whom it passed into private ownership.

Tillie Loeb, the eldest daughter of Philip Loeb and Rebecca Kaufmann, was born on 8 December 1908, in Morganza. According to the 12 April 1934 *Pointe Coupée Banner*, Tillie was married in 1934, at Mobile, Mobile Co., Alabama, to Jack Blum, a native of Bacau, Kingdom of Romania, born there on 2 July 1907, to Bernard Blum and Sarah Clara Silberman. Jack is remembered in Pointe Coupée Parish as being an adept spoons musician, spoons music having been familiar in Eastern Europe since at least the 18th century. Jack Blum died on 30 November 1973, and Tillie on 6 May 1997, in Baton Rouge, Louisiana. They were both interred in the Liberal Synagogue Cemetery in Baton Rouge.

Rachel Loeb was born on 29 December 1909, in Morganza, and died on 22 June 1968, at the East Louisiana State Mental Hospital at Jackson, East Feliciana Parish, Louisiana. Sarah Loeb was born in Morganza on 17 March 1911, and died on 7 January 1991, in Baton Rouge. Neither Rachel nor Sarah had ever been married. They were both interred in Baton Rouge's Liberal Synagogue Cemetery.

MAX SRULOVITZ THE YOUNGER/MAX H. HART

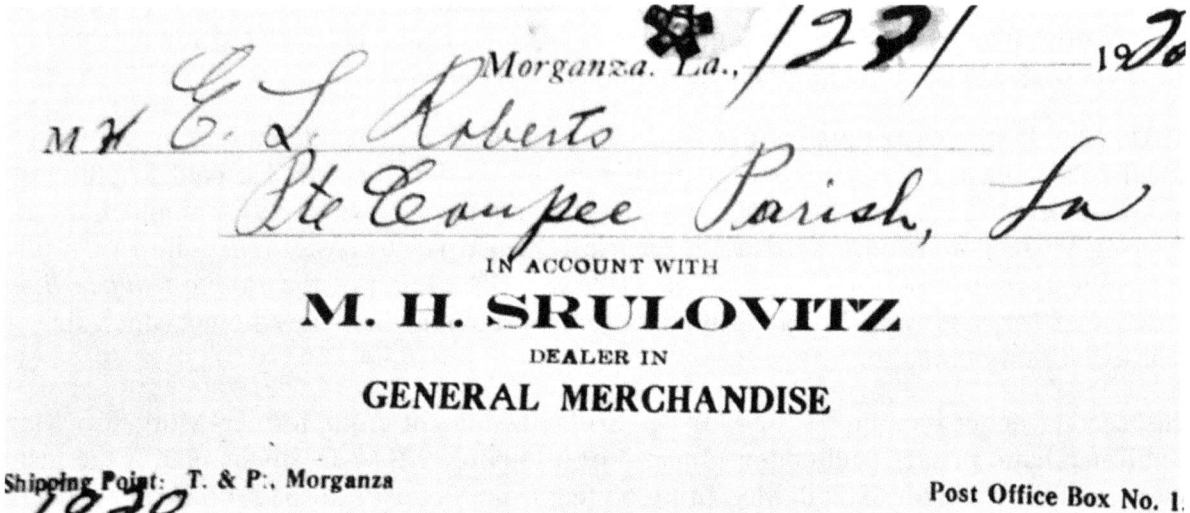

Max Srulovitz the younger, was born on 12 November 1887 (23 November 1887, according to his passport), in Oancea, Kingdom of Romania, He was a nephew of Pointe Coupée Parish general merchants Isidore, Pincus and Max Srulovitz the elder.

Max left ca. 14 November 1907 from Antwerp, Belgium, aboard the *Red Star Line* for New York. According to the 1910 United States Federal Census, he was enumerated as a salesman for his uncle Max Srulovitz at Mains, Louisiana, on Bayou Latenache.

On 16 June 1911, twenty-three-year-old Max H. Srulovitz was married at Washington, Washington Co., Pennsylvania, near Pittsburg, to twenty-one-year-old M. Della Slosower. The marriage record indicated that he was from Mains, Louisiana, and she, from Pittsburg, Allegheny Co., Pennsylvania, although these towns were their residences and not their places of birth.

M. Della Slosower, identified in subsequent documents as Dora or Marie Slosower, may have been Mariem Zloczower, age 16, who with Bruine (sic) Zloczower, age 14, both tailoresses, arrived at Ellis Island, New York in 1907, destined for Pittsburgh. They were designated on the ship manifest as natives of Mold. Banila, Bucovina, then in the Austrian Empire, and presently the city of Banyliv, Ukraine, where their grandfather Motel Zloczower resided.

In the 1910 United States Federal Census, "Mary" Slosower, who arrived in America in 1908 (*sic*) was described as a shirt maker, living with her cousin Minnie Slosower Snyder in Pittsburgh. Minnie was the daughter of Yudel "Earl" Slosower and his wife, Rebecca Midonik, immigrants from Radautz, Bucovina, Austrian Empire (now Rădăuți, Romania), who had arrived in America in 1904 with their five daughters, including Minnie (b. 1880), and one son, all born in the Austrian Empire.

As a petitioner for naturalization, Max Srulovitz the younger filed a request in 1914 in New Roads, Louisiana, for a change of name from Max Srulovitz to Max H. Srulovitz, but no order authorizing such is located in the file.

According to the 8 February 1916 *New Orleans Item*, and the 21 August 1917 *New Orleans States,* "M.H. Srulovitz," a Morganza merchant, was listed among the "country buyers" at the New Orleans Association of Commerce's merchandise markets in those years. When he filled out his World War I Draft Registration in 1917, Max H. Srulovitz declared his dependents to include his wife, Della, their children, and his father, L. Srulovitz.

In 1918, Max H. Srulovitz purchased two parcels in Morganza: a residential lot on the west side of the Texas & Pacific Railroad, and a commercial lot on the east side. He paid $1,000 cash to longtime Morganza general merchant, postmaster and farmer James W. Campbell for a lot measuring 95 feet front on the Texas & Pacific Railroad right-of-way (*sic*, Third or Railroad Avenue West) by a depth of 420 feet. The 11 May 1918 edition of the *Pointe Coupée Banner* reported that Mr. and Mrs. M. H. Srulovitz were occupying their new home which they had purchased at Morganza.

In his second acquisition in 1918, Max H. Srulovitz bought from former Morganza Mayor, general merchant, planter, and cotton ginner Virgil Olivier "V.O." Beauvais one of the historic properties of the town for $2,250. Measuring 65 feet front on East Railroad Avenue by a depth of 160 feet, the lot was bounded on the north by land formerly belonging to Max's uncle, Isidore Srulovitz, and on which Isidore and Pincus Srulovitz/Loeb had operated a general store in the former location of Rush Alexander's "The Gum" store from 1908 until 1910. Two commercial buildings occupied the Beauvais-Srulovitz lot, the larger one, to the south, having been the V.O. Beauvais General Merchandise Store, with its familiar "star and crescent" motif on the stepped gable façade.

Excavations in the rear or east of the Beauvais-Srulovitz store site for sewerage work in the mid-20th century uncovered human remains. They were thought to be those of Federal soldiers from the Civil War fort at Morganza that stood immediately east between 1864 and 1865.

Max H. Srulovitz continued working as a merchant in Morganza for several years. On 1 February 1920, he applied for a passport to travel to Romania and Algeria to visit relatives. There was no mention of his wife or children accompanying him. Once in Paris, on 12 March

1920, he applied to amend his passport to include travel to Algiers, Tunis, Morocco, in addition to Italy, France and Switzerland, in order to visit relatives.

At as yet an undetermined time, but between the 7 January 1920 and the 5 April 1930 United States Federal Census enumerations, Max H. Srulovitz assumed the name "Max H. Hart." It is possible that the "H" middle initial was for "Herz," a common Jewish given name, which translates from the German as "heart."

Max H. Srulovitz sold his East Railroad Avenue commercial property in two transactions: in 1922, the northern portion to Miss Mary Glorioso, a native of Cefalu, Sicily, and the southern portion in 1933 to Norris Amédée Melançon, who had become Miss Glorioso's husband in the interim. The couple operated the Melançon's Café there for decades, first in the former V.O. Beauvais Store and, beginning in the 1940s, its brick replacement. The "café scene" in the 1969 independent film *Easy Rider* was filmed at Melançon's, then owned by the Joseph family, with an internationally-renowned Hollywood cast being joined by Pointe Coupée Parish "extras."

Before selling the southern part of his East Railroad Avenue lot, complete with the former V.O. Beauvais Store in 1933 to N.A. Melançon, Max Hart had rented the building to other general merchants, first to J.S. Landry, then to Robert C. Dawson. In 1932, Hart filed suit against Dawson (18th Judicial District Court., No. 1359) for $75 in outstanding rent due, plus five percent from date of judgment. A writ of *fieri facias* was entered, as a number of Dawson's other creditors, including E. Morgan & Bro. of New Roads, proprietors of Morgan's Department Store and New Roads Wholesale Grocery Co., had already received judgments against him in their favor, and Dawson's extensive inventory had been seized and sold at public auction. The sale netted $6.30 less than the court costs, and none of the creditors were shown to have received anything.

Max and Marie Hart and their three children moved to Eudora, Chicot County, Arkansas, before the 1930 United States Federal Census enumeration, where Max bought the M. Schwartz store and founded "The New M.H. Hart Store, The Bargain Center of Eudora." According to the 1940 United States Federal Census, Marie assisted as a saleswoman. As Nazi German terrorism gripped Europe, Max and Marie Hart were able to provide refuge in their Eudora, Arkansas, home to her niece and nephews Erika, Otto and Herbert Zloczower. Sixteen-year-old twins Erika and Otto, students in Nazi-occupied Vienna, were identified as the children of Leo Zloczower of Vienna, natives of Wolkendorf (near Brasov, in Transylvania; present-day Vulcan, Romania). Holding passports dated 21 August 1939, the children departed on 1 October from Genoa, Italy, bound for the United States and the care of uncle M.H. Hart.

Erika, Otto and Herbert "Sloss" were enumerated in the 1940 United States Federal Census living in the Hart home in Eudora, Arkansas. According to an on-line genealogy, their parents, Leo Zloczower and Regina Druckman, died in Kovno, Lithuania, during the terrible "Ninth Fort Massacres of November 1941" which resulted in the deaths of 4,934 men, women and children. The killings took place near Kovno on 21 and 29 November and are notorious as the first, systematic, mass murder of "German Jews" during the Holocaust. Regina Druckman perished on 23 November 1941, and her husband followed on 29 November 1941.

Max H. Srulovitz/Hart died on 14 February 1957, in Eudora, Chicot Co., Arkansas, and was buried in Greenville Jewish Cemetery in Greenville, Washington Co., Mississippi. Marie D.

Sloss Hart died on 26 March 1971, and was interred with her husband. Her date of birth incised on her tombstone reads 29 September 1893.

The Srulovitz/Harts were survived by their children, all of whom had been born in Morganza, Louisiana: Anna Ruth Hart (b. 1913), who married Carneal Warfield; Dr. Noah Leon Hart, M.D., of New Orleans (b. 1915), and Harold Irwin Hart (b. 1919).

GAVRIEL/GABRIEL SRULOVITZ

Gavriel/Gabriel Srulovitz, the nephew of Pointe Coupée Parish general merchants Isidore Srulovitz/Loeb, Pincus Srulovitz/Philip Loeb, and Max Srulovitz/Loeb, was born on 21 February 1894, in Galatz, Kingdom of Romania. Fourteen-year-old Gabriel arrived at New York from Trieste, Italy, on board the *SS Laura*, on 2 July 1908. His Ellis Island record indicates that he was born at Galatz, Romania, to Ersky Srulovitz, a resident of Galatz. Gabriel was accompanied by his sister Fany Clara Srulovitz, age 18. Their destination was New Orleans, Louisiana, which was crossed out and "Morganza, La" substituted.

Gabriel, working as a dry goods and grocery salesman, and his sister Fannie, were enumerated living with their uncle Isidore Srulovitz, a dry goods and grocery merchant, in Morganza, Louisiana, in the 1910 United States Federal Census. In his registration for the World War One Draft in 1917, Gabriel described himself as unmarried, a clerk for his uncle M. (Max) H. Srulovitz in Morganza, Louisiana, and the support of his parents.

In 1920, Gabriel Srulovitz purchased a 60 ft. x 150 ft. parcel on Second Avenue (i.e., Railroad Avenue East), known as the "Alexander Store Lot" for $1,050 from Earl L. Parmalee, agent of Mary Smith, the wife of Hebert S. Jackson. The large frame structure on the lot had been the location of the Golden Rule Department Store, opened by Rush Alexander subsequent to his closing of "The Gum" in 1908. The lot was bounded on the north by his uncle Pincus/Philip Loeb's lot, the location of Loeb's Department Store.

Gabriel Srulovitz was the second-known movie theatre operator in Morganza, being preceded by the Morganza Theatre Company, which was founded in 1914 and produced its own electricity. Gabriel's picture palace, likewise called the Morganza Theatre, was located in the former Golden Rule Store. The 1921 Sanborn Fire Insurance Map of Morganza described the theatre as being sheathed in metal siding, its apparatus worked by means of a Fairbanks Morse gasoline engine, with heating provided by stoves.

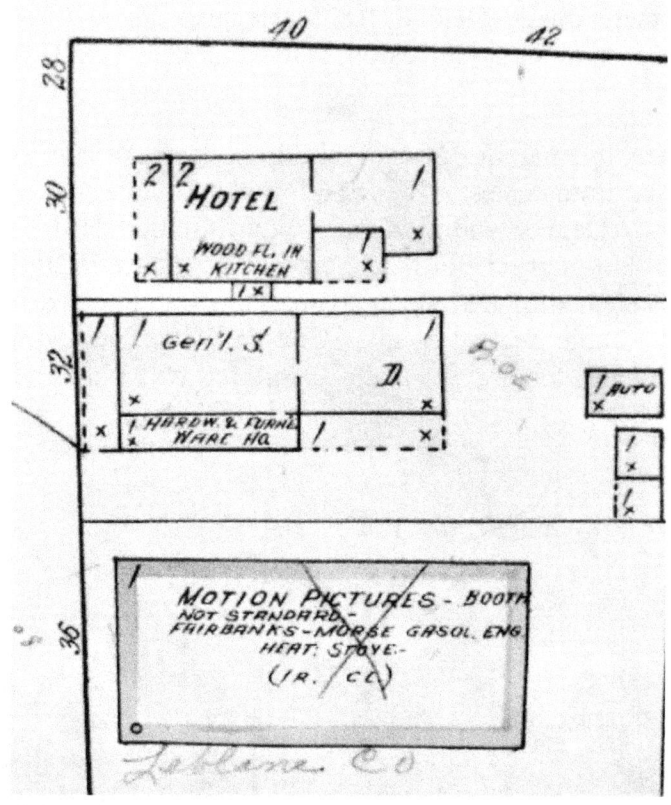

Portion of 1921 Sanborn Map for Morganza showing Srulovitz Movie House at bottom.

In 1922, Gabriel Srulovitz sold the Alexander lot to Morganza general merchant Gesner LeBlanc for $825. Srulovitz excepted from the sale and reserved for his ownership "his picture show outfit and benches in said building." LeBlanc was among several local residents who were chartered in Pointe Coupée Parish, Louisiana, in 1923, as the "Columbia Theatre Incorporated." The theatre was destroyed by fire, and succeeded by the "Century Theatre," built in 1934, across the railroad tracks at the northwest corner of West Railroad Avenue and Sansone Street. The site of the Golden Rule Department Store-Columbia Theatre has been vacant since then.

On 26 October 1925, "Gavriel" Srulovitz applied for American citizenship in New Orleans, Louisiana; however, he had been married on 4 January 1925, as "Gabriel Hart" to Miriam Rebecca Kamil, at Mobile, Mobile Co., Alabama. The couple was divorced two years later in Arkansas. Gabriel Hart worked the rest of his life as a dry goods merchant at Eudora, Chicot Co., Arkansas. He was married again on 15 May 1958, at Greenville, Washington Co., Mississippi, to Mrs. Sylvia Reed Lauchly, both residents of Eudora. Gabriel died on 7 January 1973 at Lake Village, Chicot Co., Arkansas, and was interred there at Mt. Carmel Cemetery. His wife followed on 20 April 1974 and was interred with him.

Gabriel's sister, Fanny Srulovitz, a resident of Ferriday, Concordia Parish, Louisiana, was married to Norman/Nathan Pechersky, a baker employed by the Natchez Baking Company, on 16 June 1913, at the residence of Rabbi Seymour G. Bottigheimer at Natchez, Adams Co., Mississippi, according to the 17 June 1913 edition of the *Natchez* [Mississippi] *Democrat*. The couple eventually moved to Denver, Denver Co., Colorado, where Nathan Pechersky, a baker, aka "Nathan Chester," applied for citizenship on 14 April 1920, as a former native of Odessa,

Russian Empire, born there on 20 October 1886. He also stated that he had immigrated to America ca. January 1905, landing at Galveston, Galveston Co., Texas, from Bremen, Germany, aboard the *SS Chemnitz*.

Nathan and Fannie were the parents of two children, Herman/Hyman Chester (b. 1915 in Natchez, Mississippi), and Louis Chester (b. 1916 in Lake Village, Arkansas). His wife, Fannie, died on 31 May 1920 at Denver and was interred in Golden Hill Cemetery, at Lakewood Jefferson Co., Colorado. He married Bertha Seren on 22 August 1920, but divorced her on 30 June 1937. Nathan Chester died on 26 January 1982, and was interred near Fannie in the same cemetery. His third wife, Annie Leavett Susman Chester, whom he had married on 4 September 1953, at Denver, died on 19 October 1990, and was interred with Nathan.

Evacuation Train at Morganza during 1912 flood.

CHAPTER 12

RACCOURCI-OLD RIVER

Settlement of northern or "Upper" Pointe Coupée proceeded steadily along the Mississippi River, upriver of present-day Morganza between the 1770s and the 1830s. This area encompassed *L'Anse* or "the outer shore" of the subsequently-named Morgan's Bend, through "The Indian Village," more commonly known as "The Village" for the Ofogoula Native American settlement existing there in the 1770s and across the *Raccourci*, or shortcut, through a long and narrow hairpin bend of the Mississippi, to the lower end of what was before 1847 the main channel of the Mississippi.

The Raccourci Cutoff, across the next horseshoe-shaped bend, undertaken as a State of Louisiana project as a means of expediting river traffic through a shorter channel, left behind an oxbow lake, first dubbed Lake Lafayette. Then, as now, it received water from the Mississippi during flood stages. Originally named for the Marquis de Lafayette, who was deeded thousands of acres of land in the area by the United States government in recognition of his assistance during the American Revolution, it was subsequently known as Raccourci-Old River. Because the Raccourci Cutoff was formed after the building of levees, Raccourci-Old River is lined by a levee, whereas False River, which was created by a natural shortening action of the Mississippi by 1722, and prior to settlement on the west bank, remains un-leveed.

The area along the Mississippi River and Raccourci Levees from Morganza to Créole Landing on Raccourci-Old River presented a particularly diverse ethnic representation. In addition to colonial French, African American, and *Créole de couleur* families heavily engaged in cotton and sugar cane cultivation, retail merchandising, and providing firewood for passing steamboats, the residents included German Protestant merchants and engineers, Cuban fruit vendors, and Irish levee contractors and "ditchers" (i.e., drainage laborers).

Settlements on Raccourci-Old River and its lower branch, the Raccourci Lagoon or Bay, included Planchette, later renamed LaCour, Créole Landing, Batchelor, Williamsport, and Smithland, where the main channel of the Mississippi is again reached. Continuing upriver were Phillipston and Red River Landing. Veering westward along Lower Old River, part of the main channel of the Mississippi before the Shreve Cutoff in 1831, were the ill-fated towns of Torras, Keller and Merrick, the latter being at "Three Rivers," or the confluence of the Lower Old, Red and Atchafalaya areas. Continuing westward from Three Rivers, and down the east bank of the Atchafalaya River, were the China Grove, Legonier, Jacoby, McCrea, Coon and Red Cross communities. Legonier has been, since 1928, the site of a combination rail and traffic connection with Simmesport, across the Atchafalaya River to Avoyelles Parish.

Along all of the above-mentioned waterways, as well as the inland Bayous Latenache and Lettsworth, were to be found in the later 19th and early 20th centuries the stores and landholdings of some of the Jewish inhabitants of Pointe Coupée Parish. Upper Pointe Coupée was primarily a section of large landholdings, including sugar cane and cotton plantations worked by enslaved labor prior to the Civil War, and sharecroppers or tenant farmers for a century thereafter.

For decades, the only house of worship in the vast territory was St. Stephen's Episcopal Church at Williamsport, consecrated in the decade prior to the Civil War by Bishop Leonidas Polk, "the

Fighting Bishop of the Confederacy." A monument to Confederate Soldiers which is ordinarily to be found on courthouse squares and in other public areas of countless cities and towns of the American South, is not located at the Courthouse in New Roads, but in St. Stephen's Cemetery.

Following the Civil War, Catholic churches were established at New Texas Landing, just upriver from Morganza, at Red River Landing, and at Jacoby on the Atchafalaya River. White Baptist congregations were established later, on the Atchafalaya and at Bayou Latenache. Unlike the southern part of Pointe Coupée Parish, where virtually all *Créoles de couleur* and a large percentage of African-Americans have continued to practice the Catholic faith, Upper Pointe Coupée manifested the opposite, with African American congregants being overwhelming Baptist. Churches and cemeteries of that faith were established in communities and on plantations in remarkable number and proximity.

The reactionary period following the Civil War was marked by intimidation of and violence toward African Americans by a locally organized "Vigilance Committee." An alleged conspiracy to assassinate several Raccourci-Old River white residents by aggrieved African Americans, who were, it was said, conspiring to exterminate all the whites and seize their land, resulted in the rounding up of five or six "blacks" who were arrested, tried by a jury, sentenced and executed on the same day the trial had taken place. After the lynching, a congressional hearing was held by federal authorities in New Orleans to investigate voter intimidation suffered by African Americans in the Upper Pointe Coupée and Bayou Fordoche sections. Among the several names of intimidators alleged by African American witnesses, it appears that no Jews had taken part.

After the end of Reconstruction in Louisiana, Upper Pointe Coupée led the parish in adopting 19th century innovations. In the 3 May 1884 edition of the *Pointe Coupée Banner,* John W. Tenny, a "practical engineer and gas fitter" at Merrick, Louisiana, advertised as the agent for Sunlight Gas Machines, at Merrick.

Carefully following the establishment and extension of telephone service in Pointe Coupée Parish, the *Banner* related that "telephonic communication" was first established in the parish by the firm of Blanks & Cornwell, that constructed a line extending for a mile between their store at Smithland and Miles' Landing on the Mississippi River in 1885. Only a year later, in 1886, N.P. Phillips installed a five-mile-long telephone line, connecting his house on Old Hickory Plantation on the Raccourci Lagoon with his store at New Texas on the Mississippi River. Phillips's line was followed shortly by a third system in Upper Pointe Coupée: that of J. Foster Collins, connecting the latter's store on Elmwood Plantation on the Atchafalaya River with the Mortimer store at Red River Landing on the Mississippi.

MEYER LEVY

Meyer Levy, born on 13 February 1823, to Abraham Levy and Thérèse Weil at Nancy, Meurthe-et Moselle, France, was one of the first and most prosperous Jewish merchants and landowners in Pointe Coupée Parish. After years working at Pointe Coupée Road, near the Zénon Porche, later the Labatut house, he moved his family further upriver after the Civil War.

In 1868, he purchased twelve mules, two horses, and two sugar cane wagons which were located on his brother Jules Levy's plantation on the Raccourci Lagoon for $1,500. Meyer Levy was enumerated in the United States Federal Census for 1870 near the lower end of Raccourci-Old

River as a dry goods merchant, with $4,000 worth of property. Living with him and his family was John Christy (*sic*), age 45, a native of Russia, identified as a laborer.

Meyer Levy amassed one of the largest landholdings in Upper Pointe Coupée, and by the time of the 1884 Assessment Roll owned nine tracts, totaling 2,364 acres. The family residence and store were at Williamsport, where, in 1872, Levy leased land and buildings to his son, Achille Levy, and the latter's business partner, Isaac Feist. The latter two operated as "Levy & Feist, general country store merchants," for a term of three years. In his next judicial act, Meyer Levy sold all the merchandise in his "store house" in Williamsport to Levy & Feist for $524.63. Achille Levy was subsequently the sole proprietor.

Eight years later, Meyer Levy purchased the contents of a store occupied by his son, Maurice Levy, at Williamsport, consisting of dry goods, "assorted" groceries, medicines, and hardware, plus store accounts, notes receivable, and "a lot" of horses, for $1,500 cash, and resumed working as a merchant.

Meyer and his wife, Hevven Müller, were enumerated in the 1880 United States Federal Census sharing their home with Arthur Fontaine, age 28, a native of Belgium, who was employed as a laborer. Fontaine subsequently operated a saloon in the Edwin Vignes Building in New Roads. He was followed in that location by Abraham & Weil's "New Road [*sic*] Cheap Cash Store." Fontaine was ultimately the partner of Maurice Levy in a store on Bayou Lettsworth.

A report in the 5 May 1885 *Pointe Coupée Banner* related that one of the owners of the journal had visited the store of Meyer Levy's son, Achille, at Williamsport, where they were pleased to find their "old friend Mayer [sic] Levy, Esq., as talkative and pleasant as usual."

Hevven "Henriette" Muller Levy died on 23 March 1888, at Williamsport. Meyer Levy, followed her in death, likewise at Williamsport, on 22 May 1891. The couple was interred in Hebrew Rest Cemetery in New Orleans. Levy's Williamsport business was carried on by his eldest son, Achille.

JULES LEVY

Jules Levy, an immigrant from Nancy, Meurthe-et-Moselle, France, along with his brothers Meyer, Isaac and Arthur Levy, settled after the Civil War farther up the river, in the Raccourci area. The 1865 and 1866 IRS reports identified Jules as a merchant and assessed him for a carriage and a gold watch there. During this time, Jules also acted as the agent for his brother and sister-in-law, Arthur and Marguérite Decuir Levy, and their children, who were temporarily living in the Levy's native France.

In 1865, Jules Levy purchased from his sister-in-law, Marguérite Decuir Levy, the following properties in the Raccourci area for $40,000: a 1,300-arpent plantation (apparently Hope Plantation on the Raccourci Lagoon), complete with residence, sugar mill, steam engine, corn cribs, stables, outhouses, cabins, and all horses, mules, cattle, wagons, carts and farming "utensils" located on the plantation; a tract to the rear of the one above mentioned, containing 13 arpents; and a tract at The Village (upriver of Morganza, Louisiana), fronting 8 ½ arpents on the Mississippi River, which she had inherited upon the deaths of her father in 1846 and mother in 1848 as their sole heir.

Two years later, in 1867, Jules Levy leased the plantation on Raccourci Lagoon, identified as "Hope," to Émile Honoré and Louis Dupéron. Honoré, one of several *Créoles de couleur* to serve in local, parish and state offices in the wake of the Civil War, was Sheriff of Pointe Coupée Parish from 1870 through 1872.

The 1870 United States Federal Census identified Jules Levy as a merchant with $10,000 in real estate and $2,000 in personal property in the Raccourci area. He was living with his brother, Leopold Levy, as well as his "housekeeper," Josephine Charlot, and two children, Alfred, age 17, and Sarah Levy, age 13, all three identified as "mulatto." It is possible that Alfred and Sarah were the natural children of Jules Levy and Josephine Charlot, although there are no birth or baptism records for the children, perhaps because the father was Jewish.

Sarah Levy had a brief marriage to Auguste Landry, born ca. 1841, which produced two children both born in New Orleans: Auguste Jr., born on 3 August 1876, and Achille George, born on 12 May 1880. Sarah and Auguste were no longer living together at the time of the 1880 United States Federal Census. Auguste was enumerated living alone, two doors from Ferdinand Gumbel. Both Auguste and Achille and their mother, Sarah Levy moved north, where Sarah died on 30 September 1938, in Benton Harbor, Berrien Co., Michigan. It is interesting that her son, Achille, indicated that his mother, Sarah Levy, had been born in Nancy, Lorraine, France.

Auguste Landry Jr. married Stephanie Glapion, of an old *Créole de couleur* family, the daughter of Télésphore Glapion and Amélie Balitz, on 19 March 1897, in New Orleans. According to his 1917 World War I draft registration card, he was living in Chicago, Cook Co., Illinois, and was working as a milkman. He listed his next of kin as his mother, Sarah Levy, a resident of Michigan.

Alfred A. Levy, married Emma Moran/Maurin on 22 August 1887, in New Orleans. In one marriage record which includes his parents, Alfred stated that his father was Arthur Levy and his mother, Mary Fontaine. His New Orleans Death Certificate also gave his father as Arthur Levy. Alfred and Emma had several children including: Leona (b. 1894), Oswald Jules (b. 1896), and Ethel Mary (b.1900). Whether Alfred Levy was Jules' son or his brother Arthur's is a question that cannot now be answered.

In 1874, Jules Levy donated to his niece and nephew Thérèse and Auguste Levy, children of his brother, Arthur Levy, and the latter's deceased wife, Marguérite Decuir, his plantation on the Mississippi River which Jules had purchased in 1865 from Marguérite. The property was valued at $4,000, and subject to the lifetime usufruct of Babet Decuir, Marguérite Decuir Levy's first cousin of color, on account of whose relationship with Marguérite's first husband, Ovide Lejeune, Marguérite had sued for and was awarded a judgment of divorce. Jules Levy stated in his conveyance to young Thérèse and Auguste Levy that the value of the property would increase upon the marriage or death of Babet Decuir, thereby ending her hold on the property.

Jules Levy died on 9 January 1876, in New Orleans from "congestion of the brain." He was buried there in Hebrew Rest Cemetery No.1. His brother, Arthur Levy, testified in Jules Levy's succession proceedings in New Orleans that Jules died "intestate, unmarried, without any posterity or forced heirs." It is still possible that either Alfred and/or Sarah Levy listed in his home in the 1870 United States Federal Census were his natural children by Josephine Charlot.

According to Louisiana law, illegitimate children were not allowed to inherit unless legally recognized by their father, which was apparently not the case here.

ARTHUR LEVY

Arthur Levy was born on 22 September 1830, in Nancy, Meurthe-et-Moselle, France, to Abraham Levy, a native of Ingenheim, Bas-Rhin, France, and Thérese Weil, born at Nancy. Fifteen-year-old Arthur Levy, accompanied by his brother Jules, arrived in New Orleans from Le Havre France, on 20 July 1846, aboard the *J.H. Cooper* He was not naturalized until 1874, in New Orleans, Louisiana.

On 11 October 1856, Arthur Levy was married in Wilkinson County, Mississippi, to Raccourci, Louisiana heiress and divorcée Marguérite Cléontine Decuir, a Catholic. Marguérite was born ca. 1827, the daughter of prominent Raccourci planter Jean-Baptiste Dorsin Decuir II and Marguérite Lacour, two descendants of the parish's first settlers.

Prior to marrying Arthur Levy, Marguérite Decuir had obtained a much-cited divorce from Ovide Lejeune on account of his long-term relationship with Babet Decuir, a "free woman of color," and Marguérite's first cousin. The court's judgment in Marguérite's favor regarding her rights to her separate property was thereafter cited in a number of similar cases. After the divorce, Ovide Lejeune was married to Laura Archer Turpin. They were the parents of Lt. Gen. John Archer Lejeune of U.S. Marine Corps fame.

Arthur and Marguérite lived in Nancy, Meurthe-et-Moselle, France, off and on, between 1859 and 1868. While there is no birth record for their daughter, Thérèse, at Nancy born ca. 20 June 1859, there is one for their son, Auguste Abraham, who was born at Nancy on 20 October 1861. In the Levy's absence, Arthur's brother, Jules Levy, acted as their agent. As such, in 1861, Jules issued a promissory note for $500 to merchant Jacques Goudchaux for a balance owed Goudchaux by Arthur and Marguérite, secured by a mortgage on Marguérite's Hope Plantation on the Raccourci Lagoon. While living in France, Arthur Levy was assessed, according to IRS tax reports in 1865 and 1866, for a gold watch at Raccourci, likely to have been in the custody of his brother Jules.

After Marguérite Decuir Levy's sale of her inherited properties in the Raccourci area to her brother-in-law, Jules Levy, in 1865, she and her husband moved to New Orleans, where according to the 1870 United States Federal Census, Arthur Levy was enumerated there as a store clerk with $10,000 in real estate and $700 in personal property. Marguérite Decuir Levy died on 11 August of that year in New Orleans. It is not known if she converted to Judaism, but she was buried in Hebrew Rest Cemetery No. 1 in New Orleans.

Arthur Levy became a representative for Berkson Bros., New Orleans wholesale grocers and dealers in Western produce, wines, liquors, tobacco and cigars. He advertised in several 1879 issues of *The Pelican* newspaper in New Roads as well as its successor journal, the *Pointe Coupée Banner*, beginning in 1880. Levy was later employed as a traveling representative of the H.R. Gogreve wholesale grocery company of New Orleans. While visiting Waterloo in that capacity during the high water of 1890, Levy fell overboard from a skiff. He nearly drowned but was rescued by local resident Joseph Grouzard, owner of the Waterloo Hotel, according to the 31 May 1890 report in the *Pointe Coupée Banner*.

In 1880, Arthur Levy sued before the French and American Claims Commission, as the tutor of his children, Thérèse and Auguste Abraham, for $13,345 plus 6% interest for horses and cattle taken near Morganza as a result of the Union occupation of Pointe Coupée Parish during the Civil War, by Captain Hopkins of the Kansas Cavalry. Because all claimants had still to be French citizens as of 15 January 1880, Levy, himself was ineligible because he had become a naturalized American on 19 October 1874. Therefore, the resolution of the case revolved around the citizenship of Arthur's children. It was decided that since they both had been minors in 1874, when their father had become a citizen, that they too were citizens of America, unless, upon reaching their majority, they had made a declaration of their intention to become French citizens. Because they had not done that, the claim was disallowed. The Arthur Levy claim was one of sixteen filed in the parish, eleven of which were denied.

In 1895, Arthur Levy filed suit in Pointe Coupée Parish (14th Judicial District Court, No.574) against his nephew, Achille Levy, for three promissory notes, totaling $3,871.84, at eight percent interest, made by Achille to Arthur and secured by mortgages on Achille's property. As Achille was unable to pay, the court ordered the seizure and sale of the property, which consisted of an improved 22-acre tract fronting on Raccourci-Old River at present-day Innis, with the exception of the small building called the "Exchange," likely a saloon, located thereon and owned jointly by Achille Levy and Isidore Blum, as well as a 56-acre tract on Bayou Lettsworth. Arthur was awarded the two tracts for $1,950, being the highest bidder at the auction sale. Also seized in the suit, but apparently not sold, were: two horses, two mares and two colts, a mule, 25 cows and calves, 11 hogs, an old buggy, and three wagons. The Notice of Seizure likewise listed a barouche (a stylish two-seat carriage), but this item was crossed out.

Within a few years, Arthur Levy resumed his affiliation with Berkson Bros., another New Orleans wholesale grocery and commission house, and was their agent for New Roads, according to the *Banner* dated 19 December 1896.

Arthur Levy died on 8 August 1901, at his residence, No. 627 Ursulines Street in New Orleans, and was buried in Hebrew Rest Cemetery No.1 with his wife.

ISIDORE FRANK

Isidore Frank, who renounced his allegiance to King William of Württemberg in 1845, at New Roads, Louisiana, was identified as a thirty-five-year-old grocer, with $250 property, living near planter John Watson and Dr. John G. Archer at the lower end of Raccourci-Old River, according to the 1850 United States Federal Census. Laborer John Ragan, age 35, a native of Ireland, was living in Frank's household.

Isidore Frank did not appear in any other records in Louisiana. However, in the list of Parish Licenses paid for in 1880, published in the 1 January 1881 *Pointe Coupée Banner*, "I. Frank" paid the $5 fee for a peddler's license. As previously mentioned, Isidore and another brief resident of Pointe Coupée Parish, Louis Frank, may have been the brothers of Charles and Adolphe Frank, also immigrants from Württemberg, who were longtime residents of Avoyelles Parish.

DANIEL LEVY

Daniel Levi/Levy was born on 12 November 1826, at Klingenmünster, Rheinpfalz, Germany, to Emanuel Levi and Schoenel Bach. Daniel came to America ca. 1853, and was married in New Orleans, Louisiana, on 14 March 1855, to Eliza Haas. According to her tombstone, Eliza was born on 28 April 1835 in the Kingdom of Bavaria.

Daniel Levy soon became a landowner at Williamsport, Pointe Coupée Parish, Louisiana, with property extending from Raccourci-Old River on the front or east to Bayou Lettsworth on the rear or west. In 1858, he sold a lot at the front of the tract to W.D. Smith and John Boyd, as trustees of the short-lived congregation of the Presbyterian Church at Williamsport. This parcel, containing approximately 12 acres, fronted one arpent on the levee, and was bounded on the south by the property of St. Stephen's Episcopal Church.

Serving as Postmaster of Williamsport in 1858 and 1859, Daniel Levy's tenure ended with his death in New Orleans on 20 September 1859. He was buried there in Gates of Mercy Cemetery, which was demolished in the 1950s.

Levy's widow, Eliza, was appointed natural tutrix of her and David's minor children: Sarah/Sallie, Emanuel, and David Levy, by the 7th Judicial District Court in Pointe Coupée Parish in 1860. At that time the succession was characterized as being large and "consisting of lands, slaves and personal property."

Eliza Haas, identified as "Ellis" (later correctly, Elise) Haas, the widow of Daniel Levy, was married again on 4 March 1863, in New Orleans to Louis Casper Michael, born on 27 December 1832, at Filehne, Posen, Kingdom of Prussia (now Poland). Elise and Louis were the parents of three children: Maurice M. (b. 1865), Julia (b. 1866, later Mrs. Emanuel Untermeyer), and Pierre Louis (b. 1867- d. 1889).

In 1867, Eliza opened the succession of her late first husband, Daniel Levy, in New Orleans, Louisiana (Orleans Parish Succession 28737). She identified herself as the natural tutrix of her children Sallie/Sarah (b. 1856, later Mrs. Jacob Sonnentheil), Emmanuel (b. 1858), and David, no age given, but deceased as an infant. She declared the Pointe Coupée Parish property, which had been appraised at $300, as "unproductive," that "the taxes and other annual expenses are gradually absorbing the property." The enslaved persons, which had constituted the most valuable part of the succession, had fled during the Civil War, or had subsequently been freed. She considered it in the best interest of the children, therefore, to have the land sold at public auction.

Louis and Elise Michael and their children moved to Galveston, Galveston, Co., Texas, ca. 1868, where Louis was a successful business man with the firm of Greenleve, Black & Co. Louis Michael died on 19 March 1883, at Galveston, and was interred in the Hebrew Benevolent Society Cemetery there. Elise Michael died on 27 November 1915, in Manhattan, New York, and was interred in Beth El Cemetery in Ridgewood, Queens Co., New York.

Siblings of Daniel Levy who also immigrated to Louisiana included: Samuel Levy, who died in 1855 at Bayou Sara, West Feliciana Parish; Abraham Levy, who died in Jackson, East Feliciana Parish, in 1899; and Hannah Levy, who married Jacob Wolf, and died in New Orleans in 1899.

MARCUS LEVY

Marcus Levy was born ca. 1837 in Germany, and filed an oath in 1859 at New Roads, Louisiana, renouncing his allegiance to the Emperor of Germany. He was identified in the 1860 United States Federal Census as a merchant with $3,500 real estate and $1,000 personal property. Leopold Levy, age twenty, possibly his brother, was living with him, near Williamsport.

Marcus enlisted as a private in Company B of the Pointe Coupée Artillery, C.S.A. on 29 June 1861 at New Orleans. He fought with his regiment to defend Island No.10, a chain of islands below Cairo, Illinois, which was considered "the gateway to the Confederacy." The Confederate Army was routed on 7 April 1862, and despite the efforts of Gen. Leonidas Polk to save his 7,000-man army, over 6,000 men were captured, including, Marcus Levy, on 8 April 1862, near Tiptonville, Lake Co., Tennessee. The prisoners were taken to Camp Douglas, near Chicago, Cook Co., Illinois. Marcus was admitted to the U.S.A. Prison Hospital at Camp Douglas. He died there on 1 May 1862, from, according to his record, typhoid pneumonia.

He was probably first interred on prison grounds or in the old Chicago City Cemetery on Lake Shore Drive in Chicago. However, in 1866 the government's lease on Camp Douglas expired and the camp demolished. That same year, the old Chicago City Cemetery was closed due to constant flooding. More than four thousand Confederate soldiers who died at Camp Douglas were reinterred at the Confederate Mound, a mass grave, in Oak Woods Cemetery in Chicago, Illinois.

"Marcus Levy" was listed as a retail (merchandise) dealer and retail liquor dealer at Williamsport in the 1865 IRS Tax assessment report. It is likely, however, that the "Estate of Marcus Levy" was intended in the assessment.

LEOPOLD H. LEVY

Leopold Levy (aka Leopold H. Levy) was born ca. 18 July 1841, in Germany, according to information on his tombstone. According to his marriage record, his parents were only identified as F. Levy and Caroline Levy. However, Leopold H. Levy's death certificate gave his parents as Feistel Levy and Caroline Langfeld. His date of birth was given as 15 July 1839. Leopold was enumerated in the 1860 United States Federal Census with Marcus Levy, a merchant near Williamsport, who may have been his brother (See above entry).

In 1871, Leopold Levy signed a marriage contract with Regina Eugenia Lengsfeld, who was born on 6 July 1848, in Shreveport, Caddo Parish, Louisiana, to Jacob H. Lengsfeld, a native of Illereichen, Landkreis Neu-Ulm, Rheinpfalz, Germany, and Henrietta Falk, born at Kirrweiler, Rheinpfalz, Germany. Regina's sister, Sophie Virginia Lengsfeld, was married to Simon Gumbel, also a Pointe Coupée merchant. In the marriage contract, Regina Lengsfeld declared the princely sum of $10,000, received as a gift from her father. She and Leopold Levy were married on 8 November 1871 in New Orleans. The original records show a marriage between L.H. Levy and E. Regina Langsfield. (Note: Langfeld/Langsfeld is a common misspelling for Lengsfeld/Lengsfield in Louisiana records. Given that Leopold's mother was Caroline "Langfeld," he may have been marrying a cousin.) A copy of the contract was filed in the Pointe

Coupée Parish Clerk of Court's office in New Roads in 1872. They were the parents of two children: Charles Frank (b. 1872 in New Orleans), and Nellie (b. 1887 in St. Louis).

In all subsequent records, Levy was identified as L.H. Levy. He, Regina, and his two children were longtime residents of St. Louis City, Missouri, where he owned the Hub Furniture Company. Regina died on 16 February 1902, from cancer. She was interred in the New Mount Sinai Cemetery and Mausoleum in Afton, St. Louis County, Missouri. Leopold H. Levy died in St. Louis City, Missouri, on 4 January 1920, and was interred with his wife. His son, Charles Frank Levy, became the President of his late father's furniture company. Leopold Levy's *St. Louis Post Dispatch* obituary indicated that he had been the captain of a steamboat before and after the Civil War and that he had served in the Confederate Army during the Civil War, where he was promoted to Captain. His sister, Caroline, was the wife of Léon Moyse, briefly a merchant at Red River Landing, Pointe Coupée Parish.

LEOPOLD LEVY

Leopold Levy was born on 11 July 1825, at Nancy, Meurthe-et-Moselle, France, to Abraham Levy and Thérèse Weil. He may have been the twenty-year-old (*sic*) Leopold Levy, a French national, who arrived at New Orleans from Le Havre, France, on 14 January 1850, aboard the ship *Buena Vista*. He was one of the five children out of the nine born to Abraham and Thérèse who came to Louisiana, including Arthur, Jules, Meyer, and a sister Caroline, who married David Dalsheimer.

Leopold was first enumerated in Louisiana, as a resident of Pointe Coupée Parish in the 1860 United States Federal Census with his brother, Jules, living on the F.O. Bouis plantation, at Bouis (later misspelled as Boies) Point, downriver of Grand Levee, with $1,200 property.

On 13 June 1861, Leopold Levy enlisted in Captain R.A. Stewart's Pointe Coupée Artillery, in Pointe Coupée Parish. He served until 23 September 1861 and was stationed at Columbus, Hickman Co., Kentucky, working as their commissary clerk. His commanding officer, R.A. Stewart, wrote a letter bearing that date indicating that Leopold Levy, a native of Nancy, Meurthe, France, age 35, about 5' 5" tall, with blue eyes, a light complexion and sandy (?) hair, was entitled to be discharged "by reason of a surgeon's certificate." Because he had not been paid since his enlistment, he was due $74.06 for his service.

In the midst of the Civil War, on 2 August 1863, Leopold Levy was married in Woodville, Wilkinson Co., Mississippi, to Caroline Mohr. She had been born ca. 1851 at Langenfeld, Neustadt an der Aish, Bad Windsheim, in the Rheinpfalz, Germany, to Joseph Mohr, and his wife, Bertina (last name not given).

Leopold Levy was enumerated twice in the 1870 United States Federal Census: on 5 June with his brother, Jules Levy and household, upriver of Morganza in Pointe Coupée Parish; and on 22 June as a wholesale dry goods merchant with $1,200 in personal property, living with his wife, Caroline, and their three daughters, Thérèse Albertine (b. 1864), Julia Rose (b. 1866), and Mathilde "Tillie B." (b. 1868) in New Orleans. It is likely that Leopold was visiting and/or doing business with his brother Jules near Morganza, and had returned home to his wife and children in New Orleans within the 17 days' time that had elapsed between the two census enumerations.

At least three more children were born to Leopold and Caroline Levy at New Orleans: Abraham Gaston (b. 1870), Samuel B. "French" (b. 1872- d. 1874), and Bella (b. 1876). Both Leopold and Caroline Mohr Levy died in 1876: she on 3 May in New Orleans, and he on 8 July, also in the city. They were both interred there in Hebrew Rest Cemetery No.1.

Two of their children had further Pointe Coupée connections. Julia Rose Levy became the second wife of Achille Levy of Waterloo, Raccourci-Old River and New Orleans. Mathilde "Tillie B." Levy married Isidore Blum of Williamsport. Moreover, Caroline Mohr's sister Bertha was the wife of Edward Diefenthal, and her sister, Rebecca, was the wife of Joseph Mansberg.

ISIDORE BLUM

Isidore Blum was born on 1 April 1850, at Bayou Goula, Iberville Parish, to Aron Blum and his wife, Mina "Minette" née Blum. Aron Blum had been born on 10 July 1819, at Rothbach, Bas-Rhin, France, to Lazare Blum, a native of Mulhausen, Bas-Rhin, and his wife, Judith Fraenckel, born at Rothbach. Aron's wife, Minette Blum, was born on 28 July 1820, at Gundershoffen, Bas-Rhin, France, to Isaac Blum, a native of the town, and his wife, Rosine Vogel, born in Gunstett, Bas-Rhin. Aron and Minette Blum immigrated to Louisiana, arriving in New Orleans on 4 October 1847, aboard the ship *Oxnard*. They were married in New Orleans on 25 February 1849. (Note: Isidore Blum's grandmother, Judith Fraenckel, was the aunt of Felix Fraenckel, whose wife, Palmyre Dreyfuss's sister, Hortense Dreyfuss was married to Fordoche merchant, Isaac Levi.)

Aron became a dry good merchant at Bayou Goula, Iberville Parish, Louisiana, where four of his five children were born: Isidore (b. 1850), Rosalie (b. 1852), Philip (b. 1856), and Abraham (b. 1857). The family relocated to Baton Rouge, Louisiana, where their last child, Henriette, was born in 1860. Aron was enumerated as a coffeehouse keeper along with his wife and five children in the 1860 United States Federal Census. Aron's wife, Minette, died in Baton Rouge on 25 October 1864, and was interred in the local Jewish cemetery. Aron married Caroline Haber on 21 June 1865, in New Orleans. Caroline was born on 19 November 1841, as "Kindle" Haber to Abraham Haber and his wife Miriam Junger at Oberlustadt, Rheinpfalz, Germany. Aron and Caroline were the parents of Isidore Blum's six half-siblings all born in Baton Rouge: Thérèse (b. 1866), Samuel (b. 1868), Lena (b. 1871) Lazare (b. 1872), Joseph (b. 1875), and Henry M. (b. 1877).

Aron's twenty-year-old son, Isidore Blum, was enumerated in the 1870 United States Federal Census for Pointe Coupée Parish as a dry goods merchant living with twenty-year-old Joseph Haber, a native of Bavaria, as his clerk, near the lower end of Raccourci-Old River. Blum reported $15,000 in "personal estate," likely the value of the contents of his store. Joseph Haber, born ca. 1850 in Oberlustadt, Rheinpfalz, Germany, was the brother (or half-brother) of Caroline Haber, Aron Blum's second wife. Joseph had arrived on 19 November 1869, from Hamburg at New Orleans, aboard the *SS Bavaria* to join his siblings Caroline Haber and Valentin Haber, the latter who had wed Rosalie Blum, Isidore Blum's sister, on 6 May 1868, at Baton Rouge.

In the 1876-1877 edition of Bouchereau's *Statement of the Sugar Crops Made in Louisiana*, the two men, Isidore Blum and Joseph Haber, advertised as "Haber & Blum, Williamsport, Louisiana," dealers in dry goods, notions, hats, boots, shoes, groceries, wines, liquors, crockery, hardware, and saddlery. An official contract of partnership was filed in the Pointe Coupée Parish

Clerk of Court records in New Roads in 1880, stipulating a five-year term. Immediately thereafter, Rosalie Blum Haber, the widow of Joseph's brother Valentin Haber, conveyed to the two men for the price of $2,500 all of her interest in the former partnership of Haber & Blum, her late husband apparently having been a member, including merchandise and fixtures in the Williamsport store, and an unspecified number of horses, mules, cows, and wagons. According to the 1880 United States Federal Census, the widow, Rosalie Blum Haber, was living in the household with Joseph Haber and Isidore Blum, her brother, at Williamsport.

In 1882, landowner James Innis, for whom Innis, Louisiana, would be named, leased for the period of five years, at the rate of $225 per year, to the firm of Haber & Blum the building known as the "Haber & Blum Store," together with outhouses, yards and gardens. It was located on the northeast corner of Innis Plantation, also known as the Lafayette Grant for having been part of the property granted to the Marquis de Lafayette by the U.S. government.

Isidore Blum was married at Williamsport by Rabbi Simon L. Weil of Woodville, Wilkinson Co., Mississippi, on 1 June 1885, to Mathilda "Tillie B." Levy, the daughter of Leopold Levy, born in Nancy, Meurthe-et-Moselle, France, and Caroline Mohr, a native of Bavaria. Mathilda was born on 4 August 1868, in New Orleans. She was a sister of Julia Rose Levy, the second wife of Achille Levy of Waterloo, Raccourci-Old River and New Orleans.

Isidore and Mathilde Levy Blum were the parents of five children, all born in Pointe Coupée Parish: Leopold Jacob (b. 1886), Minette (b. 1888), Clarence (b. 1890), Callie (b. 1892), and Aaron (b. 1894).

According to the 1900 United States Federal Census, Isidore Blum was sole proprietor of the store. He also served as the Postmaster of Williamsport, Louisiana, from 1898 until 1902. The Blum family subsequently relocated to Macon, Bibb Co., Georgia, where Isidore was enumerated as proprietor of a shoe store in both the 1910 and 1920 United States Federal Censuses.

Mathilda "Tillie B." Levy Blum died on 12 January 1905, in Macon. Isidore Blum died there on 24 February 1924. They were interred in Macon's Rose Hill Cemetery.

Joseph Haber died, unmarried, on 11 February 1911, at Baton Rouge, East Baton Rouge Parish, Louisiana, and was interred there in the Jewish Cemetery.

ISAAC LEVY

Isaac Levy, a native of Riedseltz, Bas-Rhin, France, who began his meteoric career as a peddler at Waterloo, Louisiana, ranks among the most prosperous Jewish businessmen, planters and land owners of 19th and early 20th century Louisiana. In 1870, he leased a lot measuring 1 ½ arpents on the public road by depth of three arpents, bounded by Alfred Morgan and the remainder of the Lejeune plantation from Jean-Baptiste Lejeune, (Jr.) of New Roads, for three years at $100 per year. The location was Créole Landing, on Raccourci-Old River, the center of a rich agricultural section of Pointe Coupée Parish, as well as a busy import/export point connecting with the Mississippi River.

Isaac Levy and his wife, née Sarah "Settie" Gumbel, were enumerated at Créole Landing in the 1870 United States Federal Census, where he was working as a merchant with $2,000 worth of personal property. The family moved to New Orleans, in 1874 according to his obituary in the April 1914 issue of the New York City periodical, *Simmons' Spice Mill*. He established a wholesale grocery business and subsequently the Levy Rice Mill in the Crescent City.

Despite his commercial and industrial work and residency in New Orleans, Isaac Levy continued his retail operations at Créole Landing. He amassed considerable real estate to become a dealer in livestock and a prosperous farmer. Levy's store was one of the most well-stocked in Upper Pointe Coupée. Advertisements carried in Bouchereau's *Statement of the Sugar Crops* as well as in the local *Pelican* and *Pointe Coupée Banner* newspapers dating between 1876 and 1879 listed the following items: dry goods, laces, ribbons, trimmings, notions, clothing, hats, caps, boots, shoes, groceries, wines, liquors, tobacco, medicines, perfumery, queens ware, crockery, tinware, hardware, saddlery, and plantation supplies.

Among his first real estate transactions, Isaac Levy purchased an 80-acre tract in the New Texas "interior" settlement, in 1876, located midway between New Texas Landing on the Mississippi above Morganza and Bayou Latenache, from Marguérite Amanda Lacour for $500 in cash. Two years later, he sold the property back to Marguérite Lacour, for the reduced price of $296.36 in cash.

In 1877, Isaac Levy made his two major purchases in Pointe Coupée, at Créole Landing. First, at the sheriff's sale resulting from the judgment of the Citizens Bank of Louisiana vs. George O. Hall, he purchased lots 4, 5, 6, and 11 of Normandy Plantation, formerly part of the vast antebellum sugar plantation of Amaron Ledoux, Alphonse Miltenberger and Hall. Lots 4, 5, and 6 fronted on Raccourci-Old River. Levy's purchase totaled $2,480, for which the Citizens Bank issued a mortgage which he had paid in full by 1881.

Later in 1877, Isaac Levy paid Jean-Baptiste Cazayoux and his wife, née Marie Virginie LeBeau, of New Roads, $7,500 cash for the plantation immediately to the east, and upon which the Levy store was located. The tract fronted five arpents on the Raccourci Lagoon and had a depth of 70 arpents, bounded on the west by Levy's portion of Normandy Plantation, and on the east by Dr. William Archer's land, complete with dwelling house, sugar mill, boiler, steam engine, cabins, barns and stables, as well as six mules, three cows, a wagon, and all of the agricultural implements. Cazayoux had acquired the property the previous year from Félicie Lacour, the wife of Jean-Baptiste Lejeune, Jr. noted above. Levy called this property "Unique Plantation," which was cultivated by tenant farmers, but initially under Levy directly.

By 1880, Levy had entered into a partnership with Melanie Michel Landau so they could run the store at Créole Landing, as well as the cotton planting operation on Unique Plantation. Melanie and her family were listed in the United States Federal Census of that year, with her husband, Marcus Landau, identified as a store clerk. When Isaac Levy and Melanie Landau's partnership ended in 1884, she and Jacob Hess assumed operation of the store and cotton planting as "Landau & Hess." After Hess's death, Melanie became the sole operator. Following her insolvency in the 1890s, her husband, Marcus Landau, assumed the operation.

On his portion of Normandy Plantation, Isaac Levy entered into annual agreements for 1881 and 1882 in which Francis Gomez, Jr., a native of Assumption Parish, would manage the place and cultivate sugar cane and corn. Gomez was to receive one-third of all sugar, molasses, and corn produced, and would assume one-third of all the losses which might occur. Gomez subsequently filed suit against Levy in the Orleans Parish Civil District Court, claiming he (Gomez) was due the sum of $5,770.10, being his one-third share of the net proceeds of sugar, cotton, corn, and hay produced and sold.

Levy countered, offering a statement of the gross proceeds of the crops and of the expenses of production, storage and shipping, for which Gomez's net share amounted to $276.21. Levy asked that the Court have Gomez reimburse him for his open store account, two promissory notes, and the sum of $5,000 as compensation for Gomez' supposed mismanagement during 1882. The Orleans Parish Civil District Court ruled for Gomez in the amount of $471.34, with costs, and in favor of Levy for the $114.40 store account and $513.14 for the promissory notes due him. Gomez vs Levy was dismissed, with the costs assigned to Levy.

Gomez appealed to the Louisiana Supreme Court, which stated that the cultivation of cotton and production of hay were not part of the contract, but it was satisfied that Levy had rendered Gomez the latter's net share of the cotton. As for the hay, the record indicated that it was used as forage for the farm animals, and the Supreme Court ruled that Gomez had no share in it. While Gomez's chief protest was his payment of insurance for the sugar mill and property taxes, although he apparently had made no objection to these charges when examining the statement of expenses ending September 1882, he had objected to being charged $250 for the death of oxen and a mule which had died under his charge. The court agreed with him that he should not have been held responsible for their deaths from natural causes.

As to Levy's claims of mismanagement by Gomez, the court saw no cause. Balancing the accounts of proceeds and expenses, the court ruled Gomez's one-third share in the profit to be $959.68, subject to his aggregate store account and promissory notes totaling $627.24. Levy's claims for damages, dismissed in the lower court, was affirmed by the Supreme Court, which likewise assigned the court costs to Levy.

Among his last recorded acts in Pointe Coupée Parish, Isaac Levy sold a lot in the right-angle bend of the Raccourci-Old River levee at the front of Unique Plantation, measuring 2 ½ acres front on the public road by a depth of three acres in 1907, for $300 cash to the Mount Zion Religious Society. An African American Baptist congregation, formed in 1887, Mount Zion's church and burial ground still occupy the site.

Isaac Levy died on 21 February 1914, and was buried in Hebrew Rest Cemetery No. 1 in New Orleans. In 1922, Isaac Levy's widow and children sold the Unique Plantation and his portion of Normandy Plantation to neighboring sugar cane and cotton planter and merchant, Ovide B. Lacour, for $20,000. Lacour consolidated these properties with several contiguous ones to the east along the Raccourci Lagoon, thereby creating one of the largest landholdings in Pointe Coupée Parish. Créole Landing is now called Old River Landing, and is the location of a lakeside dock, restaurant and recreational camps.

Isaac Levy's widow, Sarah "Settie" Gumbel, died on 17 February 1937, in New Orleans and was interred with her husband.

AARON SCHULSINGER

Aaron Schulsinger, a dry goods and clothing merchant at the "White Store" at *Les Trois Chênes* (The Three Oaks), present-day 2050 False River Drive, New Roads, closed his business and moved to the Raccourci-Old River area in late 1870. On 22 December, he took out a one-year lease beginning on 1 January 1871, with the privilege of a three-year renewal, on a store building and half-acre lot at the upper (northwestern) line of the plantation of the late Arnaud Decuir from Émile Honoré and Jean-Baptiste Decuir.

This plantation, one of the historic holdings of the prominent Decuir *famille de couleur*, now within the Morganza Floodway, fronted on the Raccourci Bay or Lagoon. The store was likely the one mentioned in Decuir's 1865 proceedings (7th Judicial District Court, No. 398) as holding "one Lot of dry goods which belong to his son & himself, in equal shares. His half was valued at the sum of two hundred & twenty-five dollars." Decuir's "son" and partner was likely Jean-Baptiste Decuir, who was listed as a watchmaker on the place, according to the 1870 United States Federal Census. According to the same census, Émile Honoré, a planter, the husband of Adoréa Decuir, lived next door. Adoréa was Arnaud Decuir's daughter, and Jean-Baptiste Decuir's sister. A leader in the Reconstruction-era government, Émile Honoré served as Pointe Coupée Parish Sheriff from 1870 until 1872.

The 12 October 1872 *Pointe Coupée Echo* listed four business licenses in the name of Aaron Schulsinger: two in the amount of $30 and two in the amount of $25. He was obviously operating in two locations, selling merchandise and liquor at both. Pointe Coupée Parish conveyance records also show Aaron Schulsinger in partnership with Pierre Félicien "P.F." Bourgeois in the latter's general store at The Village, just upriver of Morganza. In 1873, Schulsinger sold his half-interest in the merchandise, including dry goods, shoes, groceries, liquors, etc., to Bourgeois for $1,600.

A leading sugar cane and cotton planter and philanthropist, P.F. Bourgeois accumulated three plantations on the Mississippi River: Fleta, the location of his residence and store and Sugar Land and St. Maurice, the latter two formerly owned by Louis Strauss. Bourgeois also owned Silver Mount Plantation on the east bank of Bayou Fordoche, midway between Morganza and Argyle, a property which was subsequently owned by Simon Gumbel & Co. of New Orleans.

The 1874 edition of *Soard's New Orleans City Directory* listed Aaron Schulsinger as a clothing dealer at 64 Chartres Street, in the city, but the 1880 United States Federal Census enumerated him as a merchant in Ward 1, Tensas Parish, without his wife, Roseta, from whom he may have been divorced.

Ever the rolling stone, we caught up with forty-five-year-old Aaron Schulsinger in Muscatine, Muscatine Co, Iowa, where on 23 May 1893, he married thirty-two-year-old Sarah Spiro, a native of the city of Prague, Bohemia (now the Czech Republic). His 29 June 1900 application for a United States passport to travel abroad with his wife, gave us the following details about his life. He had immigrated from Hamburg, Germany, on or about the 23rd day of June 1863, aboard the ship *Golden State*. He had lived for thirty-seven years in the United States, in Louisiana, where he was naturalized, and then in New York, and later at Seattle, King Co., Washington State. He also stated that he intended to live abroad for several years, but would return.

Aaron Schulsinger died in Los Angeles County, California, on 28 January 1919, and was interred there in Home of Peace Memorial Park. His widow, Sarah Spiro died on 9 November 1928, in Seattle, King Co., Washington, and her cremated remains were placed in Queen Ann Columbarium in that city. We believe that there were no children from either marriage.

AARON LOEB

Pioneer merchant Aaron Loeb, extensively engaged in retailing in New Roads, on Parlange Plantation on False River, and on the Lower Chenal, also operated a general store on Innis Plantation, just below Williamsport, Louisiana, in the 1870s-1880s. The most remote of Loeb's enterprises, the Innis Plantation store was located 25 miles or so northwest of New Roads.

Advertisements for A. Loeb, Innis Plantation, in the 1879 issues of *The Pelican* newspaper published at New Roads were identical to those of his Lower Chenal store, and advertised the stock carried as: dry goods, embroideries, laces, ribbons, trimmings, notions, hats, caps, boots, shoes, perfumery, fancy goods, staple groceries and provisions, liquors, crockery, glassware, hardware. At the bottom of the Innis store ad in the 30 August 1879 issue was the statement: "Polite and attendant clerks are always in attendance, and prepared to satisfy the wishes on those who call on him [*sic*]."

According to the 1910 United States Federal Census, Aaron Loeb was retired, and living on his own income. Within a few years, he and his wife Henrietta/Harriett Kaufman moved to Rayne, Acadia Parish, Louisiana. Aaron Loeb died on 17 July 1915 at Rayne. Harriett Kaufman Loeb died there as well, on 26 February 1929, a year after the couple's daughter, Hattie Loeb, the wife of Charles Kahn, had passed away in the same town. Aaron Loeb and his wife Harriett Kaufman were interred in the Jewish Cemetery in Baton Rouge, East Baton Rouge Parish, Louisiana.

ACHILLE LEVY

Achille Levy, the son of Meyer Levy and Hevven Müller, was born on 10 September 1853, during his parents' brief residence in California. He moved with his family to Pointe Coupée Road, where his father was a merchant near the Zénon Porche, later Jules Labatut House.

In 1872, nineteen-year-old Achille Levy and Isaac Feist formed a partnership and leased land and buildings at Williamsport from Levy's father, Meyer Levy. They also purchased all of Meyer Levy's merchandise in the "store house" in Williamsport. In 1874, the firm of Levy & Feist paid Thomas D. Black $750 in cash for a lot of movables, consisting of: a bay mare, a two-year-old colt, a milk cow and calf, a mule, a yearling, a yoke of oxen, a buggy, two bedsteads, an armoire, and a bureau. Subsequently, Achille Levy operated the store alone, and his advertisement in the 1876-1877 edition of Bouchereau's *Statement of the Sugar Crops Made in Louisiana* listed his merchandise as: dry goods, notions, hats, boots, shoes, groceries, wines, liquors, medicines, crockery, and hardware.

Achille Levy was married on 7 February 1877, in New Orleans to Lisette Wolf, the daughter of Aaron Wolf, a native of Speyer, Rheinpfalz, Germany, born there on 22 January 1826, and Sarah Weil, born at Ingwiller, Bas-Rhin, France on 22 February 1832. Lisette was born on 18 July 1856, in New Orleans, where she died on 25 October 1881, and was buried in Hebrew Rest Cemetery. Achille was married again on 7 June 1883, to his first cousin Julia Rose Levy, the daughter of Achille's uncle Leopold Levy and Caroline Mohr. Julia was born on 7 November 1866, in New Orleans, and was the sister of Mathilda "Tillie B" Levy, the wife of Isidore Blum.

Apparently having discontinued retailing for his own account and having moved to New Orleans, Achille Levy advertised in several 1879 issues of *The Pelican* newspaper as being "connected with A. Wolf & Co., a New Orleans importers and retailers of china, silver, glassware, cutlery, lamps, and "general house furnishing goods." "A. Wolf" was most likely his father-in-law.

After a few years, Achille Levy returned to Williamsport as a merchant, according to an article in the 2 May 1885 issue of the *Pointe Coupée Banner*, which reported that he and his father were visited at the store by "one of the proprietors" of the newspaper. In the wake of the 1890 flood however, Achille and other merchants and planters of Pointe Coupée Parish suffered substantial financial losses. In 1895, his wife, Julia Rosa Levy, petitioned for and received a judgment (14th Judicial District Court, No. 569) against Achille for separation of property. Although no contract of marriage had been entered into by the couple, Julia successfully represented that she had brought into the marriage the sum of $387, which was used by Achille for "his own benefit and management." Her petition was supported by Achille's uncle Arthur Levy, who testified that Julia had inherited that amount from her late father, and that Achille's affairs were "in great disorder" and his assets insufficient to cover his debts.

Achille and Julia Levy were the parents of nine children: Sarah (b. 1885), Carrie Leah (b. 1886), Henry Muller (b. 1888), Henrietta (b. 1890), Leon "Mannie" (b. 1892), Ruth E. (b. 1894), Ada (b. 1896), Mayer (b. 1899), and Tilden Arthur (b. 1906).

The Levys appeared frequently in social items in the *Pointe Coupée Banner* at the turn of 19th-20th centuries, including references to them in the "Williamsport Dots," a *Banner* column, in 1898 and 1899 and in the "Batchelor News" column in 1904. The 14 January 1899 *Banner* "Komical Krewe Krumbs" reported that Achille Levy was named Duke of Williamsport and Isidore Blum the Duke of Merchon for the krewe's upcoming Carnival masquerade ball.

Achille Levy served as Postmaster of Innis, Louisiana, in 1904 and 1905. Five years later, the 1910 United States Federal Census found him employed as a commissary clerk for a camp of levee laborers, living upriver on the Black Hawk – Vidalia Road in Ward 3, Concordia Parish.

Moving ultimately to New Orleans, Achille Levy died there on 9 April 1926, and was buried in Hebrew Rest Cemetery No. 1. His widow, Julia Rose Levy, died in New Orleans on 26 September 1946, and was interred with him.

ISAAC FEIST and MARCUS ISAAC FEIST

Isaac Feist was born "Marc" Feist on 7 September 1837, at Trimbach, Bas-Rhin, France, to Moÿse Feist, a native of the town, and his wife, Bezel/Babette Moock, born at Oberseebach, Bas-Rhin. Marc/Isaac was also known as "Félix" Feist in the 1841 town census for Trimbach and "Meyer" Feist in the 1851 census for the town. Marc/Isaac had a half-brother, Isaac Feist, born on 5 May 1851, in Trimbach to Moyse Feist and his second wife, Judithe "Jetta" Lehmann. Marc/Isaac immigrated to Louisiana probably as "Félix" Feist on 16 January 1854, aboard the Bark *John Curtis*. M. Feist was enumerated in the 1860 United States Federal Census at Harrisburg, Poinsett Co., Arkansas, working as a clerk for his uncle Zadock Moock. He served as a private, enlisting as "I. Feiss" in the Confederate Army in Smith's Company F, 5th Arkansas Army, on 10 June 1861, and was mustered out as a "musician" at the end of the war.

Marcus's half-brother, Isaac Feist, immigrated to New Orleans, ca. 1866, just after the 1866 Trimbach town census where he was enumerated as Isaac Feist with his widowed mother, Judith Lehmann.

Marc/Isaac, known most often as Marcus Feist in America, was married to Henriette "Harriet" Kahn in July, 1867, at Magnolia, Pike Co., Mississippi, the record for which burned with all the county records in the Pike County Courthouse fire of 1882. Henriette was born on 7 October 1844 at Brumath, Bas-Rhin, France, to Théodore Kahn, a native of the town, and Sophie Levy, born at Wingersheim, Bas-Rhin. Isaac, Harriett, and their first child, Mose (b. 1869 in Mississippi), were enumerated in the 1870 United States Federal Census living in New Orleans, where Feist was working as a dry goods merchant with $1,000 in personal property.

By 1872 Isaac Feist (b. 1851) was working as a clerk for Lehman, Godchaux & Co., and in 1873 was a clerk for Émile Benjamin, possibly his mother Judith Lehmann's relative. Isaac's half-brother, Marcus/Isaac Feist, was already a merchant living in Millikin's Bend, Madison Parish, Louisiana, where his daughter Bettie was born in that year according to her later death announcement, and Lazarus was born in 1873. Three more children were born to them at Millikin's Bend: Samuel (b. 1877), Julia (b. 1880), and Marcus (b. 1882, after his father's death.)

We believe that it was probably the younger Isaac Feist (b. 1851), a resident of New Orleans, who was in partnership with Achille Levy as "Levy & Feist," operators of a "general country store" on property leased from Levy's father, Meyer Levy, at Williamsport, Louisiana, between the years 1872 and 1875. Isaac, born in 1851 in Trimbach, had opted for French citizenship at New Orleans on 11 July, 1873, but was naturalized in New Orleans on 5 May 1878.

Following the news of the silver strikes in Colorado in late 1876, the town of Leadville was founded the next year by resident miners. Isaac Feist sought his fortune out west and his name first appeared in Leadville in an article in the *Leadville Weekly Herald*, dated 15 November 1879, which indicated that he was a founding member of the B'nai B'rith lodge there. Isaac Feist died at Leadville on 29 March 1881. An article in the *Leadville Daily Herald* indicated that "Isaac Feist, age 28, died at his rooms on Harrison Avenue [...] The remains will lie at Rogers' until friends in New Orleans are heard from." Isaac Feist was interred on 1 April 1881 in Leadville's Evergreen Cemetery, after relatives responded that he should be buried out west.

Marcus/Isaac Feist died at Milliken's Bend on 8 November 1882, and was buried in Anshe Chesed Cemetery across the Mississippi River in Vicksburg, Warren Co., Mississippi. His widow, Henriette "Harriet" Kahn, survived him by many years. She died on 19 February 1934 at Vicksburg, and was interred in the same cemetery.

HENRY PICARD

Henry Picard was born Isaac Bickart on 26 August 1824, at Horbourg-Wihr, Haut-Rhin, France, to Adam Bickart, and his wife, Esther née Bickart, both natives of Horbourg, a village just two miles outside of the picturesque town of Colmar, known as the "Venice of France." "Bickart," "Bigart," and "Bigert" are the original spellings for a name which some French Jews transformed into "Picard," because of the similarity of the pronunciation. Other early Picard inhabitants of Pointe Coupée Parish, however, whose ancestors arrived from the Detroit Post circa. 1760, were Catholic. Henry/Isaac's father, Adam Bickart, had been born at Horbourg on 16 nivôse, an IV (6 January 1796), to Raphaël Bickart, le vieux (the elder), and his wife, Sara Dreyfus. Adam's wife, Esther, had been born on 13 messidor, an IX (2 July 1801), at Horbourg, to Hirtz Bickart and his wife, Jeannette Weil(ler). Adam and Esther were married at Horbourg on 13 February 1818.

Isaac immigrated ca. 1849, and was first enumerated in the 1850 United States Federal Census as "I. Pickard," a twenty-five-year-old peddler from France, who had stopped at the home of a local farmer at Lexington, Dallas Co., Alabama. He made his way down to Mobile, Mobile Co., Alabama, where he married Henrietta "Yetta" Markstein, née Prag, on 9 November 1855. "Yetta" Prag, whose first husband, Nathan Markstein, had died on 13 July 1854, at Mobile, was the mother of a daughter, Jane Markstein, born on 21 June 1848, in Mississippi Co., Missouri. Henrietta Prag had been born on 3 August 1823, at Halle, District of Gütersloh, North Rhine-Westphalia, Germany, to Isaac Prag and his wife, Jette Weinberg.

Isaac was naturalized in Mobile in 1859, using the name "Isaac Pecard." In the 1860 United States Federal Census, and in all subsequent records, Isaac would be known as "Henry Picard." Perhaps Isaac decided to adopt the name of his long-since deceased maternal grandfather, Hirtz Bickart, who had died in 1806, leaving his wife, Jeannette Weiller, a widow with five children. "Hirtz" is usually anglicized to "Henry." Henry Picard was enumerated in 1860 as a grocer in Mobile, with $1,000 in assets, living with his wife, Henrietta, his twelve-year-old daughter, Jane Picard (*sic* Markstein), and his brother, Samuel Picard, a twenty-year old immigrant from France. Samuel had been born Samuel Bickart at Horbourg-Wihr, France, on 12 November 1839, to Adam Bickart and his wife, Esther née Bickart.

During the turbulent years of the Civil War, the Picards moved from Alabama, stopping first in New Orleans, where another French immigrant, Simon Weil, met his future wife, Jane Markstein, who regularly used the surname "Picard." Simon Weil was born on 23 March 1838, at Bischheim, Bas-Rhin, France, to Leopold Weill, a native of the town, and his wife, Sara Hausser, born in Strasbourg, Bas-Rhin. A license to marry was issued to Simon Weil and Jane M. Picard at New Orleans on 13 June 1864. The couple's only child, Caroline "Carrie" Weil, was born in New Orleans on 8 June 1865.

The following year, Simon, his wife and child, along with his father-in-law, Henry Picard, and the latter's wife, Henrietta Markstein, moved to Bayou Sara, West Feliciana Parish, where Henry Picard entered into partnership with Simon Weil as the firm of "Picard & Weil." They were enumerated as merchants in Bayou Sara in the 1870 United States Federal Census, and in neighboring St. Francisville ten years later.

Picard & Weil advertised extensively in *The Pelican*, a New Roads journal published between 1879 and 1880, and its successor paper, the *Pointe Coupée Banner* from 1880 through 1885. With the opening of the un-affiliated Abraham & Weil's "New Road [sic] Cheap Cash Store" in the latter year, Picard & Weil emphasized in the 5 September *Banner* (p. 3) that they were not opening a branch in that town, and insisted that they were continuing to operate in Bayou Sara. (See notice on following page) In the same issue Abraham and Weil gave notice that their new store was not a branch of Picard and Weil.

SPECIAL NOTICE.

UNDERSTANDING that it is rumored that the new Store which we have just opened in New Road is a branch of the house of Picard & Weil of Bayou Sara, we respectfully beg to notify the public that our Store is not a branch nor have we any connection with the above named firm. We are dealing solely on our own account and hope by fair dealing and **Low Prices** to give full satisfaction to all who favor us with their custom.

Very Respectfully,
ABRAHAM & WEIL.
New Road, Sept 5, '85.

JUST OPENED!
CHEAP CASH STORE.
— AT —
NEW ROAD, LA.
(Next door to Quinn's Hotel.)

Motto: "Quick Sales and Small Profits."

The undersigned respectfully notify the public that we have just opened a

CHEAP CASH STORE.

And having bought a new and complete stock of Fine Goods, will sell the best in the market at the Lowest Prices possible.

We have a large assortment of Staple and Fancy Groceries, Dry Goods, Clothing, Hats, Boots and Shoes, Furnishing Goods, Notions, and everything belonging to a First-class Store.

All we ask the public, is to call and examine, and we feel sure that they will save

TIME, MONEY AND TROUBLE

by buying from us. You will be convinced that the name "CHEAP CASH STORE" is deserved.

Very Repectfully,
sept 5 85. ABRAHAM & WEIL.

Pointe Coupée Banner dated 3 October 1885

Henry Picard, however, had opened a general store on Dr. John G. Archer's plantation on the Raccourci Bay or Lagoon in Upper Pointe Coupée in 1879. He was still in business there at the time of publication of the July 1889 issue of *Dun's Mercantile Agency Reference Book*. According to that source, he was a member of the firm of "Picard & Picard" in Bayou Sara. His original partner and son-in-law, Simon Weil, had died at Bayou Sara on 26 April 1884, and was replaced by Julius Picard, born in New York, on 5 March 1848, to August Picard and his wife, Fanny Levy.

Some on-line genealogies indicate that Julius Picard's father, August, born ca. 1812, was Isaac/Henry Bickart's half-brother. We believe, however that August might actually have been born Isaac Jacques Bickart on 24 April 1812, to Raphaël Bickart and his wife Sara Dreyfus at Horbourg. Therefore, Henry/Isaac's father Adam Bickart was August/Isaac Jacques's brother, which made Henry/Isaac and August's son Julius, first cousins. Julius became the second husband of Henry's adopted daughter, Jane Markstein, the widow of Simon Weil, on 11 May 1886, at Bayou Sara, West Feliciana Parish, Louisiana. Julius and Jane never had children.

Advertisements for "H. Picard, New Store," on Dr. Archer's Plantation, Raccourci, appearing in 1879 issues of *The Pelican*, highlighted the merchandise carried as: dry goods, trimmings, notions, hats, caps, boots, shoes, perfumery, groceries and Western produce, wines, liquors, crockery, glassware, hardware, and saddlery. As Henry Picard resided in and conducted business in West Feliciana Parish, he was represented in Pointe Coupée by an agent, Gustav "Gus" Wolf. A grocer as well, Wolf acted for Picard at least twice in 1880: in the purchase of two black mares from William Hunt for $125 cash, and the lease of an improved three-acre lot on Longwood Plantation from Ovide Lacour for $200 payable at the end of the term 1 January-31 December 1880.

Henrietta/Yetta Prag Markstein died 25 March 1897, in New Orleans, and was buried there in Hebrew Rest Cemetery No. 1. Henry Picard followed her in death on 23 June 1902, also in New Orleans, and was interred with her. Julius Picard died on 11 April 1903, in New Orleans and was interred there as well. The three Picards, Yetta, Julius and Henry, share one headstone. Jane Markstein Picard died in Manhattan, New York, on 22 March 1918. She was cremated at the Fresh Pond Crematory, in Queens, New York. There is no record for the disposition of her remains.

GUSTAV "GUS" WOLF

According to his gravestone, Gustav Wolf was born on 9 May 1837, in the Principality of Hohenzollern-Hechingen (present-day Baden-Wurttemberg, Germany). Immigrating to Louisiana, he enlisted at Bayou Sara, West Feliciana Parish, and served in Company B, 4th Regiment, 3rd Brigade, 1st Division of the Louisiana Militia, C.S.A. during the Civil War.

Post-war, Wolf appeared in the 1870 United States Federal Census as a thirty-three-year-old retail merchant in Fort Adams, Wilkinson Co., Mississippi, the only Caucasian in a household headed by eighty-year-old Andrew Palmer. Also in the household were Celeste Montgomery (age 37), a cook, and her two children: Anna (age 14), and Ben (age 12).

By the time of the 1880 Census, Gustav Wolf and C. (Celeste) Montgomery had moved to the Raccourci Lagoon in Pointe Coupée Parish, Louisiana. Living midway between the plantations of Pierre Francois Pecquet du Bellet and John C. Burton, Wolf was enumerated as a retail grocer, whose parents were natives of Poland, with Celeste who was a "servant." When Gustav Wolf departed from the Raccourci Lagoon area is uncertain. He does not appear in any extant, contemporary issues of local newspapers. Wolf was identified as a resident of the Camp Nicholls (Confederate) Soldiers' Home in *Soard's New Orleans City Directory* in 1897 and 1898.

In a letter from him dated 7 June 1900, Morganza P.O., La., and written in support of Benjamin Weil's application for a Confederate Pension, Gustav Wolf stated that he (Wolf) had left New Orleans the preceding December. It is not known how long Wolf remained in Morganza. He died in the Soldiers' Home in New Orleans on 1 April 1910, according to the following day's New Orleans *Times-Democrat*. He was interred there in Hebrew Rest Cemetery No. 1. According to his obituary, he left no relatives in the United States.

GUSTAV SPIRO

According to his 1906 United States Consular Registration Certificate, Gustav Spiro was born on 26 January 1839, in Ostrowo, Poland, Prussian Empire. He immigrated from the Free City of

Hamburg, Germany, on the ship *Borussia* on 6 April 1867, and arrived in New York on 24 April of the same year. Having made his way South, Spiro was identified in the 1870 *New Orleans City Directory* as a salesman for Cohen & Hadersold, dealers in "fancy goods" at 54-56 Royal Street, and living at 155 Customhouse (now Iberville) Street in that city.

According to the 1880 United States Federal Census, Gustave Spiro was employed as a clerk, living in the home of Léon O. Lacour near the head of Raccourci-Old River at Hog Point in Pointe Coupée Parish, Louisiana. Although that census modestly listed Lacour as a "retail grocer," he was, in fact, a leading general merchant of Upper Pointe Coupée, and his "Enterprise Store" on John B. Stewart's plantation was one of the parish's largest. "Enterprise Store" advertisements in 1879 issues of *The Pelican* featured: "Staple, Dress and Fancy Dry Goods in Great Variety," men's and boys' clothing, hats, caps, boots, shoes, "Choice Family Groceries," provisions, crockery, tinware, hardware, and general plantation supplies. "In fact, the Enterprise stocked everything usually kept in a first-class country store."

After his employment with L.O. Lacour on Raccourci-Old River, Gustav Spiro moved again. He appeared in St. Paul, Ramsey Co., Minnesota, in the 1886 *City Directory* as a partner in Hubert & Spiro, having "rooms" (i.e., renting office space) at 272 Rice Street in that city. Spiro was naturalized in St. Paul on 26 October 1897, and in the 1900 United States Federal Census, still unmarried, was identified as a cigar dealer there. According to the 1906 St. Paul City Directory, he was still a tobacconist.

He registered with the American Consulate in Berlin, Germany, on 17 August 1907, and declared that he had returned to Europe because of poor health. Gustav Spiro is recorded as having died on 22 January 1922, in Berlin.

BENJAMIN, GEORGE, and NATHAN GERSON

George Gerson was born on 21 July 1848, in Carroll County, Mississippi. His brother Nathan was born in New Orleans on 27 November 1858. They were the sons of cotton merchant Benjamin "Ben" Gerson, a native of Oldenburg, Lower Saxony, Germany, and Nancy Levy, born according to her tombstone in Hebrew Rest Cemetery No.1, in Nuremberg, Rheinpfalz, Germany.

Ben and George Gerson were active as "Ben Gerson & Son" in real estate and financing in various areas of Pointe Coupée Parish, including lower False River, the Lower Chenal, Waterloo, and Raccourci-Old River, beginning in the mid-1870s. George often represented his father in transactions involving the firm. Simultaneously, George Gerson served as a member of the Pointe Coupée Police Jury, the Minutes of which suggest him to have been a progressive and civic-minded man of influence.

In 1879, after to his term on the Police Jury, George Gerson bought a 1,300-arpent portion of Old Hickory Plantation fronting nine arpents on the Raccourci Bay or Lagoon; the adjoining 130-arpent Mérile Lacour Tract; and Section 83-T3S-R8E, containing 600 acres. Old Hickory was complete with a dwelling house, sugar mill, livestock and farming implements. He acquired possession through two sheriff's sales: one for the ½ interest owned by the Succession of H.C. Sheppard, and the other for the ½ interest seized in the suit of Rosine Grandeury vs Mathias

Sauter, et al. Gerson then mortgaged all of the above for $30,000 to the Mechanics and Traders Insurance Company of New Orleans, payable in nine promissory notes.

The portion of Old Hickory not purchased by George Gerson belonged to the Poydras Funds, the educational bequest of Julien Poydras administered by the Pointe Coupée Parish Police Jury. Upon Gerson's offer to the Police Jury to lease or purchase that part of Old Hickory, the Commissioners of the Poydras Funds leased the property for $300 for 20 years to Ben Gerson & Son, according to their 4 December 1879 official minutes. The lease was recorded in 1880, with John Boudreau representing the Police Jury and as Commissioner of the Poydras Funds. The property was described as having approximately 365 acres, fronting on the Raccourci Bay or Lagoon, and having been acquired by the Police Jury in a judicial agreement with former owner Dr. James A. Turpin.

In 1879, Ben's son, Nathan Gerson, opened the "Old Hickory Store" on his father and brother George's plantation. The Parish business license was issued in the name of George Gerson, and the 1882 Pointe Coupée Parish Tax Roll recorded an assessed value of $2,500 for the store merchandise. The Old Hickory Plantation was the main customer of Nathan's store. Among the items charged by the plantation between 1884 and 1885 were: Lowell fabric, salt, soap, candles, coal oil, lamp wicks, nails, screws, tacks, padlocks, hinges, (note) books, ink, cups, buckets, moss collars, muzzles, seed, feed, and oats. The various medicines carried by the store for mule and human use, included "Tichenor's," the famous "antiseptic refrigerant" developed and marketed by nearby Williamsport veteran of the Confederate Army, "Dr." George Tichenor. Credits on behalf of the plantation included six months' rent of the store building, at $200.

George Gerson was enumerated in the 1880 United States Federal Census as a planter at Old Hickory, his neighbors to either side being clerk M. (Mérile, Jr.) Lacour and merchant A. (Antoine) Landenwetsch. A year later, in 1881, George Gerson purchased the property of Lucien A. Ledoux at a state tax sale. It included 356 acres of *batture* land between the Raccourci Lagoon and Raccourci-Old River, bounded on the east by his own property and on the west by land belonging to Mme. Ursin Soniat du Fossat née Célestine Allain. She was amongst a number of Pointe Coupéeans who relocated to France during the Civil War, and an acquaintance of many of the Parisian *literati* of the era. Gerson sold this last-described property two years later, in 1883, to nearby planter Ovide Lejeune.

The crevasses in the Mississippi and Atchafalaya River levees and disastrous floods of 1882 and 1884 were unprecedented in damage to Pointe Coupée and numerous parishes to the south. Owing to George Gerson's inability to pay his mortgage on Old Hickory and adjacent properties, the Mechanics and Traders Insurance Company successfully took him to court (15th Judicial District Court, No. 619), in the amount of $35,000, with legal interest. The court ordered the seizure and public sale of Gerson's real estate and movable property. George's brother, Nathan, was sustained in his opposition to the seizure of $470 worth of items that were actually his, all of which were ordered returned to him, including: a portable engine, a draining carrier, a riding disc cultivator, a disc harrow, six iron coolers, three stacks of pea vine hay, and 40 barrels of corn.

At the public sale of George Gerson's real estate, livestock, and farming implements, the Mechanics and Traders was adjudicated the property through its high bid of $20,067. After a deduction of $233.18, the company was left with a credit in its favor of $19,833.82. Soon afterward, Gerson filed suit for respite against his creditors (15th Judicial District Court, No.

652), "owing to losses from overflow and failure of crops, as well as heavy losses in the mercantile business sustained by the firm of Ben Gerson & Son, of New Orleans."

George Gerson's assets consisted of a ½ interest in the firm of Ben Gerson & Son, amounting to $125,963.19. His liabilities were given as $75,309.56 as a member of the firm, and $104,905.59 in personal debts. The latter amount included notes and a mortgage due on Old Hickory Plantation for $35,000, interest and costs, less the net proceeds of the sale of said plantation on 21 March 1885 for $19,833.32.

After the 1885 bankruptcy, the Gerson brothers returned to New Orleans where they lived with their elderly mother and several siblings. George was employed as a wholesale liquor merchant, and finally, according to the 1920 United States Federal Census, the manager of an alcohol distillery.

Nathan Gerson was employed as a traveling salesman for the W.G. Wheeler clothing company of New Orleans. He represented and solicited business for the firm in the New Roads area, according to an article in the *Pointe Coupée Banner* dated 5 September 1885.

Nathan Gerson died on 26 September 1919, in New Orleans, and was interred there in Hebrew Rest Cemetery No. 1. George Gerson followed on 28 March 1926, in New Orleans, and was buried there in Hebrew Rest Cemetery No. 2. Neither brother had ever married.

MAURICE LEVY

Maurice Levy, the son of Meyer Levy and Hevven Müller, operated a general store in the 1870s at Williamsport, Louisiana. He advertised his goods in the 1876-1877 edition of Bouchereau's *Statement of the Sugar Crops Made in Louisiana* as: dry goods, notions, hats, boots, shoes, groceries, wines, liquors, medicines, crockery, and hardware. Three year later, in 1880, Maurice sold the contents of his store, the store accounts, notes receivable, and a "lot" of horses to his father, Meyer Levy, for $1,500 cash. The merchandise conveyed included dry goods, "assorted" groceries, medicines, and hardware.

Subsequently, Maurice Levy entered into partnership with his father's former employee Arthur Fontaine as "Levy & Fontaine," general merchants, on Bayou Lettsworth, and was sole proprietor by 1889. In 1888, Maurice entered into a five-year lease with the family of his wife, née Rachel Wolff, of the "Burnt Bridge Store" near Lakeland, and operated that store until 1895, after which he and his family moved to New Orleans.

MARCUS and MELANIE MICHEL LANDAU

Marcus Landau and wife, Melanie Michel, were longtime residents of, and engaged in retailing and cotton planting on Isaac Levy's Unique Plantation at Créole Landing on Raccourci-Old River. Marcus Landau was born on 28 April 1844, in Pölland, (Sankt Pölten, Lower Austria, west of Vienna, likely intended). He was married, ca. 1877, to Melanie Michel, born at Waterloo on 7 October 1856, to Meyer Michel and his first wife, Rosine Levy.

According to the 1880 United States Federal Census, Marcus, Melanie and their sons, Morris/Maurice (b. 1878) and Arthur (b. 1880), were sharing their home at Créole Landing with an unidentified H. Levy, age 15. Marcus and young Levy were identified as store clerks. The store and the cotton cultivation on Unique were then being operated in a partnership between Isaac Levy (b. 1828) and Melanie Michel Landau. In the 1882 Pointe Coupée Parish Assessment Roll, this store had the highest appraised value of merchandise in the parish, at $3,000.

When the partnership of Isaac Levy and Melanie Landau ended, Melanie entered into a similar one with Jacob Hess, as "Landau & Hess," on 21 March 1884. According to his tombstone inscription, Jacob Hess was born on 28 July 1864, at Böchingen, Rheinpfalz, Germany. He was probably a nephew or a brother of Melanie's father Meyer Michel's second wife, Rosine Hess, also from Böchingen. Melanie Landau held a two-thirds interest and Jacob Hess a one-third interest in the firm of Landau & Hess. For his interest, Hess borrowed $1,187.50 from Melanie, payable to her in two notes at five percent interest. After only a year and a half in business, Jacob Hess died on 5 August 1885, at Créole Landing, and was buried at the Jewish Cemetery in Baton Rouge.

In the absence of a curatorship being established, Melanie Landau successfully petitioned the court on 9 September that an inventory of the firm's property be taken (15th Judicial District Court, No. 709). Landau & Hess' stock, one of the largest in contemporary Pointe Coupée Parish, and store fixtures were appraised at $4,029.03 and included: dress goods, plaids, tarlatan, checks, prints, cambric, Lonsdale cotton, damask, veiling, osnaburg, buckram, cassimere, alpaca, flannel, jeans, shirting, sheeting, lining, mattress ticking, and mosquito netting, laces, embroidery, braid, small and sash ribbons, serpentine, elastic, and tape; comforts and blankets; men's suits, coats, pants, vests, overcoats, knitted jackets, "jeans pants," white shirts, flannel and wool shirts, knit, merino and flannel undershirts and drawers, overshirts, neckties, collars, and scarfs; boys' coats and pants; ladies' shawls, scarfs, corsets and corset ribs; hose, stockings, socks, and garters; dress and riding gloves, gauntlets; handkerchiefs; 70 men's hats and two caps; two boys' hats; 77 pairs of men's boots, gaiters, brogans, low-quarter and lace shoes; 18 pairs of boys' boots and brogans; 20 pairs of ladies' gaiters, polka and button shoes and low-quarter slippers; 37 pairs of children's polka, pegged and cap-toe shoes; silver rings, breastpins, spectacles; and (artificial) flowers.

Staple and fancy groceries on hand included: Alaska brand flour, (corn) meal, grits, white sugar, coffee, green tea, salt, white beans, red beans, "fine" crackers, spice, cinnamon bark, nutmegs, jellies, pickles, chowchow, syrups, vinegar, and soda, while canned goods included sardines, mackerels, salmon, lobsters, beef, peaches, pineapples, banana preserves, cayenne pepper, mustard, lemon sugar, condensed milk, baking powder, and yeast powder, while fresh meats included pork and shoulders. Bottled alcoholic beverages included port wine, sherry, Rock & Rye whiskey, anisette, cherry bounce, brandied peaches, brandies cherries, beer, and Fletcher's, Owen and Hop bitters.

Landau & Hess also carried medicines, castor oil, worm cure and trusses, as well as chewing and smoking tobacco, briar pipes; cologne, face powder, soaps, carbolic soap, combs, brushes, toothbrushes, razors, shaving "glasses" (small mirrors), and tweezers; spelling books, readers, copying books, letter and note paper, ink, penholders. Housewares included cups and saucers, shallow and deep dishes, teapots, pitchers, bowl and pitcher sets; (drinking) glass sets, goblets, glass pitchers; tablespoons, teaspoons, table knives and forks, sardine cutters, butcher knives, coffee mills, sifters, skillet lids, tin cups, pie plates, tin pans, smoothing irons, carding cards, water basins, milk strainers, watering pots, tin buckets, oil cans; tin lamps, glass lamps, burners, chimneys. and wicks; as well as candles, matches; shoe dressing, blacking, beeswax, stove polish, bluing, lye, scrubbing (wash) boards, scrub brushes, and brooms.

The store also stocked: Smith & Wesson and British Bull Dog pistols, gun caps, cartridges, powder and shot, and fishing hooks and lines; shovels, hatchets, coopers' drawing knives, axe helves (handles), monkey wrenches, shoe punches, silver screws, coffin screws and tacks, rivets, shoe scrapers, French locks, padlocks, hinges, faucets, saw files, and corn mills; rope, bagging; axle grease, turpentine, coal oil, "gasoline oil," Paris Green, and lime.

Men's and ladies' saddles were inventoried, as well as wooden stirrups, spurs, saddle girts, bridles and reins, and curry combs; double trees, muzzles, halters, backbands, trace chains; four plows, colters and bands; and furniture consisting of two tester beds, a third bed, 21 straw-seat chairs, six wood-seat chairs, a wire safe, and a trunk.

The store fixtures included: a showcase, 12 candy jars, counter, meat and medicine scales, measures, a mortar, a (meat) slab and knives, a tobacco cutter, a center lamp, a desk lamp, wrapping paper and paper bags, a Hall "money safe," coal oil tanks and barrels, and cotton scales.

Landau & Hess' customer accounts amounted to $12,544.08 and notes receivable to $3,455.30. Other assets of the partnership including the standing crops of cotton and corn on Unique Plantation, 14,637 pounds of moss, 123 ½ sacks of cotton seed, three wagons, 13 mules, six horses, a mare, two colts, five head of cattle and an ox, appraised in total at $7,301.65. One of the wagons and the most of livestock were listed as being "in the hands of" individual tenant farmers.

Among the customer accounts owed Landau & Hess were those of the river steamers *Hamilton* and *Maria A.*, evidence of the continued viability of Raccourci-Old River as a commercial and transportation route decades after the shortening of the main channel of the Mississippi River. Another account receivable was that of the Raccourci Benevolent Association, one of many medical and burial benefit societies formed by African Americans in the wake of the Civil War.

Landau & Hess's gross value amounted to $27,330.06. Liabilities were listed as $9,370.42, including $777.50 to Isaac Levy for rent of the plantation, and various wholesalers' accounts, netting a balance of $17,959.64 for the firm. Jacob Hess's 1/3 interest therein, amounted to $5,986.54, and combined with the trunk and clothing of the decedent valued together at $35, grossed $6,021.43 for his estate.

A year later, on 10 December 1886, Melanie Landau filed suit (15th Judicial District Court, No. 890) against the Heirs of Jacob Hess for a settlement of the late partnership of Landau & Hess. Mrs. Landau represented that she had used "every endeavor" to induce Isaac Levy, agent of Hess's parents in Germany, to affect a settlement, but he had yet to do so. She stated that, according to Levy's request, she had continued the business "as if said Hess had not died," until the end of the business year, 27 February 1886.

The court appointed New Roads attorney Albin Provosty as curator *ad hoc* for Hess's heirs. Mrs. Landau presented the firm's end-of-year statement, as prepared by her bookkeeper, Jules Ledoux. Based on the statement, which included Hess's debts to Melanie as well as to the firm, and the naturally-diminished amount of merchandise and livestock, the court ruled on 1 February

1887, that Mrs. Landau pay to Hess's heirs his $111.95 net interest remaining therein, with legal interest from 27 February 1886. The court further ruled that the Hess heirs pay Provosty a $20 fee for his services, and declared the firm of Landau & Hess dissolved.

While continuing to operate Landau & Hess in the wake of Jacob Hess's death, Melanie Landau and her husband, Marcus, sustained the loss of two children. The 8 August 1885 *Pointe Coupée Banner,* sympathizing with the family, stated the two boys, one aged about five years, likely Arthur, and the other an infant, had succumbed to "pernicious fever," probably malaria or yellow fever. Three other sons would live on: Maurice David (b. 1878 – d. 1923), Julius Meyer (b. 1886 - d. 1919), and Herbert (b. 1888 - d. 1921 from tuberculosis).

In 1894, Melanie Michel Landau, citing financial "embarrassment" due to "the great depreciation in the price of the cotton crops of 1891 and 1893, the low yield of the crops of 1890, 1892 and 1893, the losses of crops of her customers by overflow during the past four years," petitioned the court (14th Judicial District Court, No. 389) for a respite from her creditors. The court appointed her husband, Marcus Landau, syndic of the proceedings.

Melanie Landau's assets were listed as store merchandise, appraised at $950; two mules, at $250; three Créole horses, a mare and two colts, $190; eight other mules, $800; a draft in the amount of $40; a mortgage note of Mrs. M.A. Dietrich of Raccourci, Louisiana, $600; and hundreds of dollars in judgements, notes and store accounts. She owed several hundred dollars for wholesalers' bills and legal charges, as well as $5,475 payable in three notes to Isaac Levy for rent.

The store merchandise, less than one-quarter of the inventory she had co-owned in Landau & Hess a decade earlier, consisted of: bolts of silk, calico, gingham, jeans, linsey, flannel, bleached domestic, Lowell, buckram, ticking, coffin trimming; trimmings, notions; bedspreads, towels; men's and boys' coats, vests and pants, jackets, overshirts, undershirts, drawers, overalls, rubber leggings; ladies' knitted jackets, jerseys, shawls; a lot socks; 32 men's and boys' hats, 11 caps; one lady's hat; 14 pairs men's shoes and boots; 51 pairs ladies' shoes; two pairs misses' shoes; 26 pairs children's and babies' shoes; four pairs slippers; canned salmons, sardines, corn, potted ham and baking powder; stick candy, allspice, salt, black pepper, tomato catsup; drugs, medicines; cigarette papers; looking glasses (mirrors); ink, mucilage; crockery, glasses; coffee mills, (coffee) drippers, skillets, sifters, knives, smoothing irons; candles, soap, starch, concentrated lye, stove polish, clothespins; lamps, lamp globes and wicks, lanterns; shoe brushes; an accordion; pistols, (gun) cartridges, Bowie knives, fishing hooks; a lot of hardware, including screws and locks, lap rings, saws, hoes, cultivator points, froes, and cow bells; saddles, saddlebags, leather and wood stirrups, double trees, leather collars, hames, leather bridles, muzzles, trace chains, and horse brushes; a plow; three bedsteads, a bed tester, three wardrobes, six washstands, three safes, a rocker, a mattress, five bedsprings, four baby chairs, cradles, six looking glasses (mirrors); stove pipes and elbow, washing pots; also, two showcases, a cheese safe, nine candy jars, two counter scales, a tobacco cutter, two hanging lamps, wrapping paper and paper bags, a stepladder, an iron safe, a coal oil tank, cotton scales; and about 100 barrels of corn.

Through Sheriff E.G. Beuker, the court offered Melanie Landau's property at public auction on her premises at Créole Landing on 28 March 1894. Melanie's husband, Marcus Landau, was adjudicated all of the property through his high bid of $675 in cash, from which were deducted legal charges and taxes, leaving a balance of $32.97. Another privileged debt, that of Jules Ledoux for his salary as store clerk, more than exceeded that amount, thereby leaving nothing for Melanie Landau's creditors.

In addition to assuming operations of the store at Créole Landing, Marcus Landau was also a director of one of the earliest-known industries in Upper Pointe Coupée: the Lakeside Cotton Oil Co., Limited. He was identified as such in a meeting notice posted in the 11 January 1896 *Pointe Coupée Banner*.

The Landau family figured prominently around the turn of the 19th and 20th centuries in the civic life of the community as well. Several *Banner* issues of 1898 report Melanie Landau as a member of the Ladies' Social Club of Batchelor, and her as hosting as well as attending functions of that early organization.

According to the 1900 United States Federal Census, the Landau family continued to reside on Isaac Levy's Unique Plantation at Créole Landing, with Marcus enumerated as a general merchant and farmer and son Maurice Landau as bookkeeper for the establishment. Sons Julius and Herbert Landau were also enumerated in the household, as well as Young E. Davidson, age 30, a native of Kentucky, employed as a store salesman, a boarder, Robert Bowmaker, age 82, a native of Scotland, and Hannah Harrison, age 26, their African American cook.

Marcus Landau died at Créole Landing on 12 October 1904, and was buried in Hebrew Rest Cemetery No. 1 in New Orleans. The 11 December 1904 *Pointe Coupée Banner* included an expression of sympathy for Marcus's demise by his fellow members of Livonia Lodge 220, F. & A. M. in New Roads. Meanwhile, the 26 November *Banner* reported that Mrs. Landau's cotton gin had burned, along with a large amount of cotton seed.

Marcus Landau's succession proceedings (21st Judicial District Court, No. 590) were opened in 1908. He and his widow were separate in property, and Marcus's movable and immovable goods were appraised together at $14,890.07. He also left a life insurance policy in the amount of $5,000. His estate included: store merchandise and fixtures, valued at $1,250, 76 open store accounts, 12 mules, four horses, an old buggy, four wagons, a lot of plows, harrows, cultivators, "working implements" and gears (plow harness). Most valuable amongst the movables was a cotton ginning and pressing outfit, listed at $350, as well as 75 open store accounts. All of the above were advertised in the 17 June 1905 *Banner* to be offered at public sale on 22 June, but Landau's succession file contains no indication of the sale taking place.

Marcus Landau also died in possession of five tracts of land in the "interior" section, west of Raccourci-Old River, totaling 588.21 acres. No transfer was made of this real estate for years. In the meantime, Melanie Michel Landau moved to New Orleans. She died in that city on 17 March 1914, and was buried with Marcus in Hebrew Rest Cemetery No. 1. In 1918, their three surviving sons were put into possession of the five tracts of land left by their father.

A.B. MITCHELL, "NEW ORLEANS CHEAP STORE"

Among the several Jewish merchants to operate at Williamsport, at the upper end of Raccourci-Old River during the 19th century, was Abraham B. Mitchell, proprietor of the "New Orleans Cheap Store," not to be confused with the earlier store of that name operated by Alex Mann at Waterloo. A native of Poland, Russian Empire, Mitchell, whose surname was likely Anglicized from a Jewish original, was born ca. November 1860, and according to the 1900 United States Federal Census, he immigrated in 1882.

The store received its goods from Mississippi River steamboats which landed at Smithland, near the head of Raccourci-Old River. It was originally operated by A. B. Mitchell & Co., and was assessed for $800 worth of merchandise in the 1884 Pointe Coupée Parish Tax Roll. Mitchell became sole proprietor with the withdrawal of his partners, L. Shaffer and L. Nathan, effective 1 January 1885, according to the notice in the subsequent 10 January issue of the *Point Coupée. Banner*.

On 1 April 1885, Abraham B. Mitchell was married in New Orleans to Estelle Block. She was born Esther Bloch on 8 November 1860, at Duttlenheim, Bas-Rhin, France, to Samuel *dit* (called) Simon Bloch and his second wife, Jeanne Judas. We have made this determination due to the naturalization record of Estelle/Esther's sister, Sarah Bloch, who immigrated to America in 1895 and was enumerated with her sister in the 1900 United States Federal Census for New Iberia, Iberia Parish. Sarah applied for American citizenship in 1937, in Houston, Harris Co., Texas. She swore that she had been born in Duttlenheim, on 8 August 1872. This date is erroneous because Sarah Bloch was born at Duttlenheim on 18 August 1863, to the same parents. Additionally, the Bloch sisters' half-brother, Ernest Bloch, born on 17 January 1877, to Samuel, *dit* Simon Bloch and his third wife, Johanna Falk/Falck, immigrated in 1895, and lived both in Crowley, Acadia Parish, and Alexandria, Rapides Parish, where he died from typhoid fever on 7 January 1902.

Auguste Bloch and his wife, Sara Falk/Falck, another Bloch - Falk family immigrated to Louisiana. Sarah Falk Bloch and Jeannette Falk Bloch were half-sisters born to Heymann Falk: Sarah, to his first wife, Hannah/Jeannette Levy, and Jeannette to his second wife, Jeannette Dreyfuss. (See: Carol Mills-Nichol, *Louisiana's Jewish Immigrants from the Bas-Rhin, Alsace, France*, Santa Maria, CA: Janaway Publishing, Inc., 2014, pp. 56-59, 62, 65, 70). The Falk/Falck, formerly Fälkel, family, originally from Duppigheim, less than three miles from Duttlenheim, had lived in the former place, using the surname Falk/Falck since before the French Revolution.

The 2 May 1885 *Pointe Coupée Banner* account of its reporter's visit to Williamsport described A. B. Mitchell as "an industrious and energetic merchant... amiable and prosperous," and referred to Estelle as "one of the fair Alsatian daughters transplanted to this country."

A. B. Mitchell suffered financial difficulties in the wake of the 1884 flood, and was taken to court by three major creditors in 1886. St. Louis, Missouri wholesalers Marx & Haas filed suit against Mitchell (15th Judicial District Court, No. 775) for a balance of $115.85 due on merchandise purchased in the preceding year. A judgment was rendered in the plaintiff's favor in 1887. A writ of *fieri facias* was entered, as Mitchell's property was shown to consist only of a note in his favor, dated May of 1885, in which Willie E. Doherty pledged three bales of cotton to Mitchell.

Mitchell's merchandise and store fixtures had been judicially seized and sold in the suit simultaneously filed against him by New York clothing wholesalers August, Bernheim & Baer (15th Judicial District Court, No. 776). The court ruled in favor of the plaintiffs in the amount of $257.75 for merchandise sold to Mitchell in 1885, plus eight percent interest. Oppositions had been filed by Mitchell's landlord, Ezra F. McKee, for $20 monthly rent of the store building for the term 1 September 1886-1 January 1887; by Mitchell's former clerk, Ernest F. Platt, for $307 salary due; and by B. Rosenberg, boot and shoe wholesaler, for $262.35 due on purchases.

Merchandise seized from A. B. Mitchell consisted of: bolts of worsted dress goods, calico, plaids, flannel, sheeting, and domestic; thread, notions; men's white and colored shirts, and undershirts; corsets; hosiery; hats; shoes; a lot of salt, crackers; canned oysters, salmon and lobsters, mustard, and soda; whiskey; a lot of drugs; tobacco, cigars; matches; glassware, tinware, lamps and brackets, mirrors; brooms, water buckets; saddlebags; and hoes; also, two showcases and other store fixtures.

Also seized were the following, recently received at Smithland Landing and awaiting transport to the store: a half-barrel of whiskey, a half-barrel of anisette, a case "said to contain cigars," five boxes of soap, and an iron safe. A dark sorrel horse was likewise seized as the property of A.B. Mitchell.

The public sale of the above, to various parties and over several days, brought in $901.65 cash, which less $87.04 court costs and legal charges, netted $813.71. The court had ordered the net proceeds to be allotted to A.B. Mitchell's creditors in the following order: first to landlord McKee, second to former clerk Platt, third to August, Bernheim & Baer, and fourth to B. Rosenberg. Plaintiff August, Bernheim & Baer appealed to Fourth District Civil Court (Suit No. 68), protesting that the payments to the other three parties would unjustly reduce the amount due them from Mitchell. The higher court, respecting, as did the lower court, McKee's and Platt's claims against Mitchell as privileged, and B. Rosenberg's settlement for only part of what was due them, rejected the appeal and affirmed the ruling of the local court.

A.B. Mitchell was sued again in 1886, by cotton and sugar factor and wholesale merchant Simon Bloch (15th Judicial District Court, No. 864), for the amount of $155.38 due on merchandise purchased by Mitchell, with eight percent until paid. Bloch filed a supplemental petition in the case, against local warehouser Benjamin G. Cornwell, alleging that in order to evade his creditors, Mitchell had sold notes and accounts receivable to Cornwell for $300 cash.

Mitchell denied the allegations, and responded that he owed wholesalers H. & C. Newman a note in the amount of $1,700, less a credit of the value of four bales of cotton, and that Cornwell paid the debt, for which Mitchell conveyed his (Mitchell's) notes and accounts receivable to Cornwell. The $300 that Mitchell received from Cornwell, was for the balance of the value of the conveyance.

The court ruled in favor of Bloch and against Cornwell in the amount of $155.38, with five percent interest until paid. Cornwell appealed to the Fourth District Circuit Court, which in 1887 rejected the appeal and confirmed the ruling of the local court.

A.B. and Estelle Mitchell relocated to New Iberia, Louisiana, where they were enumerated in the 1900 United States Federal Census. Mitchell was employed as a grocer. He, Estelle, and their children, Hannah (b. 1886), Julia (b. 1890), Willard (b. 1893), and Beulah (b. 1897), shared their home with Mitchell's brothers Lazard and Dave Mitchell, the former a barroom manager and the latter a barroom clerk, as well as Estelle's sister Sarah Block.

The extended Mitchell family eventually moved to Houston, Harris Co., Texas, where A.B. Mitchell was enumerated in the 1910 United States Federal Census as a saloon salesman along with his wife, his brother Lazard Mitchell, and his son-in-law Joe Levy, a dry goods salesman, who was married to Hannah Mitchell.

Abraham B. Mitchell died in Houston, on 2 October 1912, and was interred in Beth Israël Cemetery in that city. According to his 6 October 1912 obituary in the New Orleans *Times Democrat*, he had also been a merchant at Crowley, Acadia Parish, Louisiana where another brother David resided. Estelle Bloch Mitchell, whose date of birth on her tombstone reads 10 November 1865, survived him by decades, and died on 6 December 1940, also in Houston. She was buried with her husband. Estelle's sister, Sarah Bloch, died in Houston on 31 May 1945, and was also interred in Beth Israël Cemetery.

HARRY FINKELSTEIN

One of several members of a Jewish family to engage in commerce in Upper Pointe Coupée, Harry Finkelstein (originally Finkielsztejn) was born in Suwalki, Poland, Russian Empire, on 3 July 1870. He was one of several children of Josiel Tavia Finkielsztejn and his first wife, Fejga Rudsztejn.

Harry Finkelstein first appeared in the *Pointe Coupée Banner* in its issue dated 28 September 1895, which mentioned him as a merchant from Williamsport on a visit to the parish seat of New Roads. Unlike most businessmen of his day, Finkelstein does not appear to have been involved in litigation, either as a plaintiff or defendant, in the local court. This suggests that his customers paid promptly and he paid his wholesalers in return.

On 27 February 1901, Harry Finkelstein was married by Rabbi T. Shaufarber in Mobile, Mobile Co., Alabama, to Charlotte "Lotta" Kosminsky. She was born in 1867 in Chicago, Cook Co., Illinois, to clothier Abraham Kosminsky, a native of Poland, Russian Empire, and Catherine "Kate" Stein, born in Bohemia, Austrian Empire. Harry and Lotta Finkelstein's only child, Eli, was born on 29 April 1902, and died at the age of three days on 2 May 1902, in New Orleans.

Harry Finkelstein died in New Orleans on 26 July 1905, and was interred in Gates of Prayer Cemetery in that city. His succession (Orleans Parish Civil District Court, No. 76862) was opened and administered by his brother Nathan Finkelstein, a merchant on Bayou Latenache, near Innis, Pointe Coupée Parish, as well as in New Orleans.

The estate of Harry Finkelstein consisted of interests in two New Orleans firms with heavy patronage in Pointe Coupée: a 1/3 interest in Finkelstein Bros. & Friedberg, and a ½ interest in Finkelstein & Friedberg. The first company consisted of Harry and Nathan Finkelstein and Louis W. Friedberg, the latter a recent owner of White Hall Plantation, near Legonier on the Atchafalaya River in northwestern Pointe Coupée. The first-named company had been worth $12,644.12, but owing to merchandise loss by fire, and even taking into account anticipated insurance reimbursement, the decedent's share was estimated at a mere $100. The second company, composed of the late Harry Finkelstein and Louis W. Friedberg, had also suffered a loss of merchandise and sundries due to fire, and Finkelstein's interest in what remained was estimated at $1,000.

Nathan Finkelstein represented himself, three sisters, two brothers, a half-sister, two half-brothers, and their father, Josiel Tavia Finkelstein, as Harry's heirs. Four of the absent heirs, Lena Finkelstein Levenson, Rose Finkelstein Harrick, and Israël (likely the same as I.H.) and Sam Finkelstein, were represented by Louis Amazon Hubert, a New Orleans attorney. Hubert was a musician and photographer and had been named for his grandfather, who was the first owner of Pleasant View Plantation at Oscar on the False River, later owned by Thomas Hewes.

Harry Finkelstein's widow, Charlotte "Lotta" Kosminsky, filed opposition to the proceedings, claiming her share of community property in his estate. Nathan Finkelstein satisfied the court that Lotta's share amounted to $400, which she was awarded.

Nathan and his siblings, Lena, the wife of Sam Levenson, of New York; Julia, the wife of Julius Harrick, also of New York; Lily, the wife of Herman Friedman; Israël Finkelstein; and Sam Finkelstein, of Wilkes Barre, Pennsylvania, were each allotted $113.16. Half-siblings Fanny, Shepsel, and Reuben Finkelstein, the latter two both minors, each received $52.76. Family patriarch Josiel Tavia Finkelstein, as father of the deceased, received $333.47 from Harry's estate.

Widowed, Charlotte "Lotta" Kosminsky Finkelstein returned to Mobile, Alabama, and lived with her widowed mother and siblings. She died there on 23 July 1953, and was interred in the city's Springhill Avenue Temple Cemetery with her family.

MAX HOCHFELDER

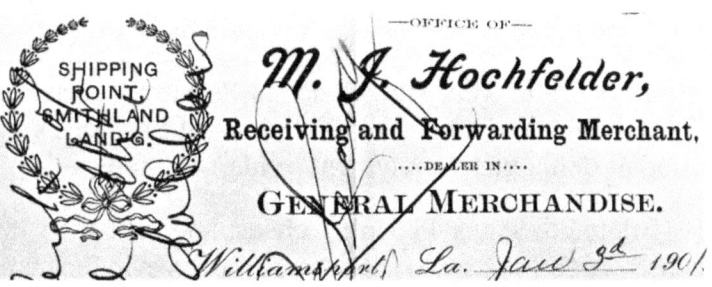

Max J. Hochfelder, a native of the Kingdom of Hungary, was born on 16 March 1871, to Berthold Hochfelder and Julia Glasser. He was married on 10 April 1899, in New Orleans, Louisiana, to Jennie Katz, a native of Brooklyn, Kings Co., New York. She was born there on 15 May 1873, to Alexander Katz and Rosalie Deusterwaldt, both natives of Germany. Max and Jennie were the parents of three children: Julia (b. 1901), Bernard (b. 1903), and Joseph K. (b. 1906).

Max and Jennie settled in Williamsport, Pointe Coupée Parish, Louisiana, where he did business as "M.J. Hochfelder, Receiving and Forwarding Merchant, and Dealer in General Merchandise." His letterhead identified the store's shipping point as Smithland Landing, on the Mississippi. According to the 1900 United States Federal Census, the Hochfelders shared their home with Jennie's sister Nellie Katz. Isidore Blum, another Williamsport merchant, lived two doors down from the Hochfelders. According to that same record, Max had immigrated in 1890 and had been naturalized, although we found nothing to verify it.

While at Williamsport, Max Hochfelder was involved at least twice in litigation: once as a plaintiff and the second time as a defendant. In 1899, he filed suit against Bayou Lettsworth merchant Thomas Goldman over the matter of an iron safe. Hochfelder claimed in the local, 2nd District Magistral Court, that as part of a settlement with Louis W. Friedberg, owner and resident of White Hall Plantation, at Legonier, on the Atchafalaya River, Hochfelder came into possession of a number of items, including an iron safe. The safe was, at that time, in Goldman's store, who refused to give it to him. The local court ruled that Goldman turn the safe over to Hochfelder, but when the latter went to retrieve it, he was denied the combination by Goldman. Hochfelder, deeming the safe "useless," sued Goldman for $30, and was awarded $25. Goldman appealed to the 14th District Court in New Roads (Case No. 1255). The higher court reversed the judgment of the lower court, and assigned the costs to Hochfelder.

In 1900, Max Hochfelder leased the front 18 3/2 acres of the "Achille Levy Pasture" at Williamsport at the rate of $5 per acre and a horse at $25 for the same period to H.W. Jones, for a period of one year. The animal was to be used by Jones in the cultivation of cotton and corn on the property. Before the year elapsed, Jones filed suit against Hochfelder in the local 3rd Magistral Court for breach of contract, claiming that Hochfelder initially rented him a roan mare, but later took it back leaving Jones a black horse in its place, only to return a second time and take that animal away as well.

Hochfelder's defense, apparently, was that Jones used the animals for purposes other than cultivating crops. Jones countered that the contract did not specifically deny his use of the animals "to drive to church or otherwise." A judgment in Jones's favor in the amount of $25 was granted by the local court, and affirmed by the 21st Judicial District Court (Case No. 179).

One of the last-known references to Max Hochfelder in Pointe Coupée was in the list of Parish Licenses for the year 1901, published in the 23 March issue of that year's *Pointe Coupée Banner*, in which he was identified as delinquent in payment of his $210 fee.

By the time of the 1910 United States Federal Census, the extended Hochfelder family had relocated to New Orleans, where Max was a furniture store owner for many years. At that time, his sister-in-law Nellie, divorced from Robert Steiner (m. 23 February 1903, in New Orleans), and her two children, Edgar and Arthur, were living with the Hochfelders. Nellie Katz Steiner worked as a salesperson in Max's store until her death on 12 December 1915. She was interred at Gates of Prayer Cemetery in New Orleans.

Max J. Hochfelder died on 23 August 1945, in New Orleans, and was interred there in Gates of Prayer Cemetery. His widow, Jennie, died within a year, on 21 August 1946, and was buried with him.

ISIDOR B. MOUNT

Upper Pointe Coupée entrepreneur Isidor Berg Mount, born on 20 May 1852, in Greisen, Kingdom of Saxony (Germany), immigrated to America in 1872, and was naturalized in 1875. He was married to Celia Peyser on 2 December 1877, in Monroe Co., Georgia. (Note: This marriage shows a license date of 30 November 1878, and a marriage date of 2 December 1877. The documentation is located between licenses and marriages that occurred in January 1878.) The bride was born on 10 June 1860 (1861 on gravestone) in Macon, Bibb Co., Georgia, to retailer Maurice "Morris" Peyser and Marla "Mollie" Butoslovsky, both natives of Posen, Poland, Prussian Empire. Celia Peyser Mount's sister Gussie Peyser was the wife of Fordoche, Louisiana, general merchant John Z. Solomon.

Isidor and Celia Mount and their children, Bernard (b. 1880), Bertha (b. 1882), Dora (ca. 1884) Harry D. (b. 1886), and Alfred Isaac (b. 1887), settled at the turn of the 19th-20th centuries at Smithland, Louisiana, above Williamsport, where Isidor operated a dry goods and grocery store. He also served as Postmaster of Smithland between 1901 and 1904. On 3 June 1905 it was reported in the *Daily Signal*, published at Crowley, Acadia Parish, Louisiana, that the general merchandise store of Isidore Mount located at Smithland Landing had been completely destroyed by fire, with little or no insurance. Also in 1905, Isidor Mount partnered with Alex Barrow to open one of the first-known drug stores north of Morganza. *The New Era Druggists' Directory, Vol. 11*, of that year indicated that the Barrow & Mount pharmacy at Batchelor carried drugs, sundries, paints, tobacco, cigars, books, and stationery.

In later life, Isidor and Celia Peyser Mount lived with their son Bernard and his family in Montgomery, Montgomery Co., Alabama. Isidor died there on 29 February 1924, and was buried in Oakwood Cemetery. Celia died on 1 August 1941, also in Montgomery, and was interred with her husband.

ALFRED I. MOUNT

Alfred Isaac Mount, one of Pointe Coupée Parish's civic leaders, was born on 4 March 1887, at Montezuma, Macon Co., Georgia, to Isidor B. and Celia Peyser Mount. Moving with his parents to Raccourci-Old River in Pointe Coupée Parish, Louisiana, his 1917 World War I Draft Registration card indicated that Alfred was engaged as a dry goods and grocery merchant at the town of Batchelor. Alfred was married on 1 December 1922, in Baton Rouge, Louisiana, to Annis Cotton. The bride was born on 15 January 1888, at Innis, Louisiana, to Bayou Latenache cotton planter Jere Brown Cotton and Martha "Mattie" Buchanan.

Engaged in the retail dry goods and grocery business for 44 years, Alfred Mount also served as a member of the Pointe Coupée Parish Police Jury, representing the Third Ward, between 1940 through 1950. He, wife, Annis, and daughters, Martha (b. 1924) and Celia (b. 1927), were members of St. Stephen's Episcopal Church.

Celia Mount, born on 6 November 1927, reigned as Pointe Coupée Parish Sugar Queen and was chosen Louisiana Sugar Queen VI from amongst other Parish Sugar Queens at the 1947 Louisiana Sugar Festival in New Iberia. She was married on 7 August 1948, at St. Stephen's Church to Bob McAlister. She was for many years prominent in Episcopalian ministry.

Alfred Isaac Mount died on 14 March 1960, in New Roads, Louisiana, and was interred in St. Stephen's Episcopal Cemetery. His widow, née Annis Cotton, died on 1 May 1976, also in New Roads, and was interred with him. Their daughter Celia Mount McAlister died on 16 November 2020, in Cleburne, Johnson Co., Texas, and was interred there in Cleburne Memorial Cemetery.

MAURICE D. LANDAU

Maurice David Landau, son of Marcus and Melanie Michel Landau, was born on 22 July 1878, in the port city of Greenville, Washington Co., Mississippi. He spent his childhood at Créole

Landing on Raccourci-Old River, Pointe Coupée Parish, Louisiana, where his parents were engaged in retail merchandising and cotton planting on Isaac Levy's Unique Plantation. According to the 1900 United States Federal Census, Maurice D. Landau was the bookkeeper at his father's store.

On 7 July 1900, Maurice was involved in an incident on Raccourci-Old River that was reported in the 11 August 1900 issue of the Lucy, Louisiana, newspaper *Le Meschacébé*. It was termed "A most deplorable shooting affray." They named the principals as Landau, "a prominent young merchant of that place," and A. Boatner Way, son of Judge and Mrs. A.J. Way of Williamsport:

> As to the cause which led up to the difficulty, little is known. Young Way was instantly killed. Landau surrendered to the authorities, and at the hearing was exonerated. The affair is deplored by the entire community. Both men occupied prominent places in business and social circles. A. Boatner Way, at the time of his death, was occupied in raising cotton and [sugar] cane. He leaves a widow and two small children.

Augustus Boatner Way was the brother of Mrs. Conrad J. LeCoq, née Blanche Amanda Way. She and her husband were the longtime owners and publishers of the New Roads and Pointe Coupée Parish official journal, the *Pointe Coupée Banner*.

Maurice Landau was married on 16 April 1901, at Innis to Bertha Mount, the daughter of neighboring general merchant Isidor B. Mount and Celia Peyser. Bertha was born on 14 September 1882 in Forsyth, Monroe Co., Georgia. Maurice and Bertha were the parents of four children: Arthur Peyser (b. 1903), Dora "Babs" (b. 1905), Rosa (b. 1907, and Marie (b. 1909).

Following in the tradition of his parents and maternal grandfather, Meyer Michel, Maurice Landau was engaged as a dry goods and grocery merchant. He was identified as such, at Batchelor, in both the 1910 and 1920 United States Federal Censuses. He also held the office of Postmaster of Batchelor, Louisiana, from 1909 until 1917, and was succeeded in the position by his wife, Bertha, from 1917 until 1929.

In the wake of the devastating 1912 Flood, Maurice D. Landau as an individual and as M. D. Landau & Co. declared bankruptcy. His assets consisted of a 1/3 interest in five tracts of land in Pointe Coupée Parish, inherited from his father, totaling 839.20 acres. The real estate was put up for public auction at the Courthouse in New Roads on 4 April 1914, by Deputy Sheriff Joseph Desormes, trustee, according to the 16 March 1914 *New Orleans Item*.

Maurice D. Landau died in Montgomery, Montgomery Co., Alabama, on 5 December 1923, and was buried there in Oakwood Cemetery. His widow, née Bertha Mount, died in New Orleans, Louisiana, on 4 February 1963, and was interred with her husband.

ISAAC LEVY

Isaac Levy, not to be confused with the Isaac Levi/Levy born in Riedseltz, Bas-Rhin, France, who married Sarah "Settie" Gumbel, or the Isaac Levi, a native of Germany, who married Hortense Dreyfuss, was a resident of the Williamsport, Louisiana area in the late 19th century.

Despite research in vital, conveyance, and civil suit records of Pointe Coupée Parish, this Isaac Levy is known of only through his probate file (14th Judicial District Court, No. 948), in which

Ramsey A. Falconer, of a Williamsport merchant family, applied on 30 March 1898, for an inventory and administration of the deceased Levy's estate. The court acquiesced on 4 April, and Falconer posted administrator's bond on 15 April. Ramsey Falconer subsequently died, and on 28 February 1900, his brother William R. Falconer, declaring himself a creditor of the late Isaac Levy, successfully petitioned the court to succeed Ramsey in administering the succession and calling for an inventory of the estate of Levy, "late a resident of Pointe Coupée Parish."

Isaac Levy left substantial property, appraised at a total of $2,139 and itemized as: 73 bales of cotton, "in the hands of" neighbor J.C. Cole and the Williamsport firm of Haber & Blum, a black horse, five mules, and ten head of cattle. The sale of the above, to various parties, minus Levy's debts, netted a balance of $267.20.

Isaac Levy's probate file has evidence of neither dates or places of death and burial nor of family and/or other heirs.

LUCIUS P. LEVEE

Lucius Place Levee (pronounced *Lev-vee*), a widely-known Texas & Pacific Railroad conductor, was born on 6 November 1875, in Waco, McLennan Co., Texas, to Edward Boudinot Levee and Alice Landis Place, and his ancestry can be traced back to his paternal great-great-grandfather, Lion Levy, a Sephardic Jew, born in 1764, in Woolrich, England, who died in Charleston, Charleston Co., South Carolina in 1835.

Lion Levy's wife, Sara Nunez Cardoza, born in 1780, was the daughter of David Nunez Cardoza, born in 1763 in New York, who fought in the American Revolutionary War of 1776, and his wife, Leah Benjamin. Lion and Sara Cardoza Levy's son David Cardoza Levy, born in 1805, in Charleston, married Anna Maria Moses, born in 1805, also in Charleston. Their son Lionel Cardoza Levy, born in 1827, in Charleston, married Eleanor Moïse, the daughter of Aaron Moïse (b. 1783 in Saint-Domingue) and Sarah Cohen, a native of Charleston. (Note: Eleanor Moïse's lineage can be traced back to her grandfather Abraham Moïse, said to have been born in 1736, in Strasbourg, Bas-Rhin, France. After immigrating to Saint-Domingue, Abraham Moïse married Sara Sen on the island of St. Eustache. The couple and their three children fled Saint-Domingue in 1791, and settled in Charleston.) Eleanor and Lionel Cardoza Levy's second son Edward Boudinot Levy (b. 1849) married New Orleans native, Alice Landis Place, on 25 April 1872, at New Orleans in a civil ceremony. The bride had been born in New Orleans on 10 July 1847, to Lucius Holmes Place, said to be a merchant from Ohio, and Elizabeth Landis, born in Louisiana.

Edward Boudinot Levy was enumerated in the 1880 United States Federal Census for Waco, McLennan Co., Texas, as Edward Levy, along with his wife, Alice, and his first four children: Edward Boudinot (b. 1873), Lucius Place (b. 1875), Frederick Ransom (b. 1878), and Lionel Cardoza (b. May 1880). Two more sons, Frank Landis (b. 1882), and William Aubrey (b. 1884) were born to the couple, before Alice Levy died on 5 August 1885, in Muskogee Co., Georgia. She was interred in the private Levy-Moses Cemetery on Esquiline Hill, Columbus, Georgia.

It is not known when Edward Boudinot Levy, Sr. changed the spelling of his surname to "Levee," although his children all adopted the new orthography. Edward B. Levy was still using "Levy" as were his children according to the 1900 United States Federal Census taken in Leon

Co., Texas. His New Orleans Death Certificate, issued on 16 May 1923, was in the name of Edward B. Levee. His son, Lucius, was using the spelling as early as 12 September 1918, when he registered for the draft at Thibodaux, Lafourche Parish, Louisiana, where he was employed on the "Lafourche Branch" of the Texas and Pacific Railway as a conductor.

Lucius Place Levee was married to Lillian Sarah Shepherd on 17 February 1909, at the bride's home in Napoleonville, Assumption Parish, Louisiana, by the Rev. Father L. H. L'Anglais, pastor of St. Anne Catholic Church. Lillian, a native of Napoleonville, was born there on 8 June 1885. Lucius and Lillian were the parents of two children: Lucius Place Jr. (b. 1910) and Lillian (b. 1912).

In 1925, Lucius P. Levee acquired a large tract fronting on the upper end of Raccourci-Old River, between Williamsport and Smithland, Louisiana, from Natchez, Mississippi, businessman and real estate developer Louis Fry. Comprised of two contiguous properties, the northern portion was Henrietta Plantation, containing 935.38 acres, while the southern part was called Motley Place, measuring 65 acres. Fry, a native of the Austrian Empire and husband of Regina Goldberger, had purchased the two properties in 1918 from Mrs. Elizabeth Montfort Bienvenu. Included in Fry's sale to Lucius Levee were a large number of plows, harrows, cultivators and sweeps, tools, a wagon, eight mules, and an existing oil, gas and mineral lease. The total price was a mere $600 cash.

Lucius and Lillian Levee were active in community affairs in Upper Pointe Coupée, although they had been enumerated with their two children in the 1930 United States Federal Census at their residence in New Orleans on Nashville Street.

Lucius Place Levee died on 28 November 1943, at Bunkie, Avoyelles Parish, Louisiana. His wife, née Lillian Sarah Shepherd, died on 22 July 1968, in New Orleans, and her funeral took place at St. Vincent de Paul Catholic Chapel at Innis, Pointe Coupée Parish. Both Lucius and Lillian Levee were buried in St. Stephen's Episcopal Church Cemetery near Innis.

MARIE ALICE HEINE, PRINCESS CONSORT OF MONACO

Marie Alice Heine, the first American Princess Consort of Monaco, had extensive connections with New Orleans, the city of her birth, and Raccourci-Old River. At the latter place, her maternal grandfather, Alphonse Miltenberger, was in partnership in one of Louisiana's largest sugar cane operations.

Louis Joseph Alphonse Miltenberger was born on 8 September 1808, at Santiago de Cuba, to Dr. Louis Christian Miltenberger, a native of Erstein, Bas-Rhin France, born there on 11 October 1765, to Francisci Josephi Miltenberger and Maria Ursula Angst, and his wife, Marie Aimée Mersier, born at Saint-Domingue on 14 November 1780, to Antoine Mercier and Julienne Elizabeth Fongravier

After Louis Christian Miltenberger's death, Marie Aimée Miltenberger, née Mercier, built the stately "Miltenberger Buildings" on the downtown, river corner of Royal and Dumaine Streets in the *Vieux Carré* in New Orleans. Her son, Alphonse, and his family lived in the downriver unit and brothers Aristide and Gustave Miltenberger and their families inhabited the central and upriver units, respectively.

New Orleans commission merchant Jules Labatut, a native of Pointe Coupée Parish, his wife, Clélie, and children were the next-door downriver neighbors of Alphonse Miltenberger. Bankrupt by cessation of business due to the Civil War, the Labatuts permanently relocated to the former Zénon Porche plantation on Pointe Coupée Road. Their architecturally significant home, the "Labatut House," ranks as one of the most admired antebellum homes of the South.

Alphonse Miltenberger was a commission merchant in New Orleans, and in 1839 he formed a partnership with Pointe Coupée Parish native Amaron Ledoux. The two were joined by a Ledoux in-law, George Otis Hall, and the trio operated as "A. Ledoux" a brokerage firm in New Orleans.

The partnership of A. Ledoux, Miltenberger & Hall expanded into sugar cultivation, owning a plantation from 1839 until 1860 which measured 40 arpents on what was then the main channel of the Mississippi River, but subsequently Raccourci-Old River, by a depth of 80 arpents. According to the 1850 United States Federal Census, the plantation of Ledoux, Miltenberger & Hall was valued at $130,000. The highest yield from the plantation was 704 hogsheads (1,000-pound barrels) of sugar, produced from the 1858 harvest.

Alphonse Miltenberger married Marie Céleste Léda Dorfeuille (b. 1814) on 16 June 1831, and they had one child, Marie Céleste Amélie Miltenberger, born on 25 May 1832, in New Orleans. After his first wife's death in 1849, Alphonse married Marie Odile de Marigny (b. 1828). The couple had two children: Georges Prosper (b. 1854), and Odile (b. 1862).

The Ledoux family traveled to Europe yearly throughout the 1850s, and finally decided to relocate there permanently. Providentially, in 1860, Ledoux, Miltenberger and Hall sold their Raccourci-Old River plantation, for $280,000. The Civil War soon ensued, and was followed by repeated levee failures and flooding in Pointe Coupée and numerous parishes to the south from 1865 through 1927. In a 20 May 1868 letter to his New Orleans attorney Edward Phillips, Amaron Ledoux, residing in Paris, stated: "I can assure you, dear sir, that I would not accept [a river plantation] and all that Grand Levee Country besides, as a gift, if I were obliged to hold it and keep the levees in repair." The Miltenberger and Hall families similarly moved and made their homes in France, with several of the offspring marrying into the French nobility. One of those matches produced a future princess of Monaco.

On 5 April 1853, Alphonse Miltenberger's eldest child, Marie Céleste Amélie, married Michel Heine, one of two Jewish brothers born to Isaac Heine, a native of Germany and later a merchant at Bordeaux, Gironde, France, and his French wife, Judith Michel. Armand Heine was born on 19 August 1817, at Bordeaux, Section 1, under the name of Heyman Heine. Michel Heine followed on 19 April 1819. In the 1830s the two brothers travelled to Germany to stay with their uncle Salomon Heine, a wealthy banker, and father of the German poet, Heinrich Heine. Salomon gave Armand and Michel 100,000 *marks* and sent them to America to make their fortune. Arriving at New Orleans in the 1840s they worked as commission merchants and bankers at an office on Common and Carondelet Streets.

Michel and Amélie Miltenberger Heine were the parents of three children: Marie Alice (b. 1857), Paul Henri (b. 1860 - d. 1862), and Isaac Georges (b. 1861). While Marie Alice was born in New Orleans, her two brothers were born in Paris. When in Louisiana, they resided with Amélie's family in the Miltenberger Buildings. Marie Alice Heine was the same age as next-door neighbor Euphémie Labatut, the daughter of Jules Labatut and Clélie Ranson, the future wife of Louisiana

Court Justice Olivier Otis Provosty, a native of Pointe Coupée Road. Ultimately, the Miltenbergers and Heines remained in France, as had the Amaron Ledoux and George Hall families.

Michel Heine's brother Armand was married in New Orleans to Marie Amélie Kohn on 31 October 1859. While Michel and his family returned to France, Armand remained to look after the Heine cotton press which was seized in 1862 by Union General Benjamin F. Butler. (See: Carol Mills-Nichol, *A Guide to the French and American Claims Commission 1880-1885: Our French Immigrant Ancestors and the American Civil War*, Santa Maria, CA: Janaway Publishing, 2017, p. 342). Their claim for just under $70,000 for rent of and damage to the cotton press by the Union Army was disallowed.

Armand and his family returned to France where he and Michel became partners in the French Bank, Fould & Co. After the death of the last Fould partner, the brothers took over the bank under the name of A. & M. Heine. The "*Bankhaus* Armand & Michel Heine," along with Rothschild *Freres et Cie.*, operated banks in Paris and New Orleans. Michel Heine also invested in cotton and real estate.

Moving in society with similarly monied families, the Heines were often at the court of Emperor Napoléon III and Empress Eugénie. The imperial couple stood as godparents when Marie Alice Heine was baptized into the Catholic faith preparatory to her first marriage, in Paris in 1875, to Marie Odet Armand Aimable Chapelle de Jumilhac, Marquis de Jumilhac, later the 7th Duc de Aiguillon. They were the parents of two children: Armand de Jumilhac, who became the 8th and last Duc de Richelieu, as well as the Duc d'Aiguillon and Marquis de Jumilhac; and Odile de Jumilhac, the latter marrying Gabriel de La Rochefoucauld and becoming Comtesse de La Rochefoucauld, and later Princesse de La Rochefoucauld-Montel (Bavarian title).

In what historian Thomas Fuilléron, director of the Monaco Palace Archives, termed "one of the very first love marriages of the Principality," Marie Alice Heine, after the death of the Marquis de Jumilhac, was wed on 30 August 1889, at Paris, Île-de-France, France, to Albert Honoré Charles Grimaldi, aka Albert I, Sovereign Prince of Monaco. Having a strong business knowledge, Marie Alice helped to make Monaco financially sound and developed the principality as a cultural center with opera, theatre and ballet, the latter under the direction of Sergei Diaghilev.

Both Marie Alice and Albert are said to have engaged in extramarital affairs, and for Marie Alice's supposed relationship with composer-singer Isidore de Lara, the Prince famously slapped her in view of the audience in the Salle Garnier. The Prince and Princess were judicially separated in 1902, but remained married. She survived Albert by two decades, having never remarried, and died at the age of 67 on 22 December 1925, in Paris. She was interred there in the fashionable Cimetière Père-Lachaise.

CHAPTER 13

BAYOU LATENACHE

Undulating from what was then the main channel of the Mississippi River (now Raccourci-Old River) on a southwestwardly path to the Atchafalaya River, picturesque Bayou Latenache is the most densely populated part of northern or Upper Pointe Coupée. It drains the great "bowl' of Upper Pointe Coupée, completely ringed by levees since the construction of the northern guide levee of the Morganza Spillway/Floodway in the 1940s, through a gate in the guide levee and into the floodway.

"Latanache" is believed to be a Créole form of a Native American word for "palmetto" or "fan-palm," which were abundant in the low-lying interior of Pointe Coupée before parish-wide drainage improvement projects of the late 1940s. Satellite villages of the Tunica people were located in the northeastern part of Pointe Coupée Parish, across from their principal settlements on the Mississippi River, in present-day West Feliciana Parish. In 1764, the Tunica were accused of attacking a British party on the river, and the French, undertaking an investigation, noted among the three chiefs one named "Latanache." Whether the bayou in Upper Pointe Coupée was named for him, he for the bayou, or both for the native flora is not known.

Settlers from elsewhere in the United States began to inhabit Bayou Latenache in number during the 1840s because the area was one of the chief cotton-producing regions in Pointe Coupée. Made up of large land holdings and agricultural operations, the area was populated by African Americans in a much higher proportion than whites.

The Latenache region was subject to flooding from both the Mississippi and Atchafalaya rivers time and again, particularly in 1912, when scores of deaths by drowning were reported after the levee breach near the juncture of the Lower Old and Mississippi Rivers at Torras.

As in all but a few areas of 19th and early 20th century Pointe Coupée Parish, Jewish merchants predominated in local commerce and owned several of the largest plantations.

SIMON BLOCH, "TAYLOR PLANTATION"

Simon Bloch, a prominent merchant, planter, and owner of thousands of acres in Louisiana, was born "Sigismond" Bloch on 22 May 1831, at Riedseltz, Bas-Rhin, France, to Henry Bloch, a native of the town and Julie Strauss, born in Gundershoffen, Bas-Rhin. Eighteen-year-old Simon Bloch arrived in New Orleans from Le Havre, France, on 14 January 1850, aboard the ship *Buena Vista*. He was married on 13 June 1854, at New Orleans, to Fanny Kaufman. The bride had immigrated with her parents, arriving in New Orleans from Le Havre on 24 October 1848, aboard the ship *Jacques Lafitte*. Fanny was born at Ingenheim, Rheinpfalz, Germany, on 8 February 1836, to Jonathan Kaufman, a native of Ingenheim, and his wife Helena Firnberg, born in Mannheim, Grand Duchy of Baden (Germany).

Locating in Opelousas, St. Landry Parish, Louisiana prior to the Civil War, Simon Bloch was a general merchant there as a partner in Bloch, Dupré & Co., which was liquidated and reestablished in 1873 as J. Bloch & Co., composed of Simon and his younger brother, Joseph Bloch, born at Riedseltz on 13 May 1833. Joseph Bloch was originally associated with Solomon

Firnberg, also a merchant at Opelousas, the youngest brother of Helena Firnberg who was Joseph's brother Simon's mother-in-law. The northwest corner of Main and Bellevue streets in downtown Opelousas, where the Bloch Store was located, continues to be referred to in the 21st century as "Bloch Corner." Four squares north is Bloch Street, opened through the land of and named for Joseph Bloch in 1878.

Although "Joseph" Bloch had his name crossed out, with "Simon" written in its place, in the 1860 United States Federal Census enumeration for Opelousas, where one of them was said to be living alone, working as a merchant with $4,000 in assets, we believe Simon's residence was probably at New Orleans. His brother, Joseph Bloch, newly arrived at New Orleans from Le Havre, France, on 31 May 1858, aboard the ship *Zenobia,* had most likely been sent to St. Landry Parish to take charge of Simon's Opelousas general store.

In New Orleans, Simon Bloch was, for a quarter-century, the head of S. Bloch & Co., a leading cotton and sugar factor and commission merchant, with a large patronage from Pointe Coupée Parish. By 1880, he had entered agriculture as well, and was identified as a planter according to that year's United States Federal Census. At that time, Simon, his wife, Fanny, his "son" Charles, age 24, working as a sugar planter, daughter, Cécile Julia, age 12, and two servants were living at No. 204 Esplanade Avenue in New Orleans.

Sigismond "Simon" Bloch and Wife Fanny Kaufman. Photo courtesy of Linda Stewart.

While Charles is listed as his son in this census, a 1904 codicil in Simon's will indicated that Charles Block, residing in Dallas, Texas, was "no relation of his." Simon bequeathed him $100 because he claimed that he had spent a lot of money raising and educating him.

Charles Block, the twenty-five-year-old "son" of S. Block and F. Block, was married on 29 June 1882, at New Orleans, to Lillie B. Cochran, a native of Opelousas, St. Landry Parish, born to John Cochran and Eliza Perrault. Charles Bloch, was enumerated with his wife, Lillie Cochran, in the 1900 United States Federal Census for Dallas, Texas, working as a bookkeeper.

If not Simon's son, who was Charles Bloch? Additional research has revealed what we believe to be the truth. Fortunately, Charles Bloch's Texas death certificate gave his date of birth as 24 March 1856. A search of on-line French records revealed that Charles Bloch was the twelfth child born on that date at Struth, Bas-Rhin, France, to Joseph Bloch, a cattle dealer, and his wife, Jeannette/Henriette née Bloch, both natives of the town.

Joseph Bloch's sister, Beyen Bloch, was married to Zacharie Keim, a native of Pirmasens, Rheinpfalz, Germany. Their son Isaac Keim, born about 1835 at Pirmasens, had immigrated to Louisiana in the 1850s. He was a merchant in Waterloo, where he lived with the Meyer Michel family, also immigrants from Struth, and was later a landowner in the Lower Chenal. We believe that Charles Bloch, was probably sent by his parents to join his first cousin, Isaac Keim, in Louisiana. Because Keim never married, we also believe that Simon Bloch, a native of Riedseltz, who was a man of greater means than Keim, and whose marriage had been childless until the birth of his daughter, Cécile, born in New Orleans on 26 November 1867, took over Charles' education and apprenticeship as a sugar planter and raised him as his own into early adulthood. It is also possible that Simon's warm and paternal feelings towards Charles had soured after Charles married out of the faith in 1882.

Simon and Fanny Bloch's only child, Cecile Bloch, was married at Temple Sinai in New Orleans by recently-arrived Rabbi Max Heller on 22 March 1887, to Nathanial A. Mayer, a Chicago, Illinois banker. A lavish reception followed at the home of her parents, at 522 St. Charles Avenue. The wedding gifts on view included silver, bronze and gilt artworks and other pieces. The reporter covering the event noted among the twenty-one guests who sat down to dinner at gold and silver place settings: Mr. and Mrs. Isaac Levy, who owned Unique and part of Normandy Plantations at Créole Landing on Raccourci-Old River, as well as representatives of the illustrious Godchaux, Schwartz, Newman, Kaufman, Isaacs, and Dreyfous mercantile families of New Orleans. Charles Augustus Kaufman, founder of the department store which bore his name on the Dryades Street retail corridor of Uptown New Orleans for generations, was a maternal uncle of the bride. Charles Bloch did not appear on the extensive list of invitees at the reception for the bride and groom published in the New Orleans *Daily Picayune* the following day.

Cécile's husband, Nathanial A. Mayer, was born on 30 October 1856 at Chicago, Cook Co., Illinois, to Leopold Mayer and his wife, Regine Schultz, both German immigrants. He and Cécile made their home in Chicago, where Simon and Fanny Bloch eventually relocated.

Throughout the decades, Simon Bloch acquired considerable real estate in Louisiana. Two of his largest properties were in Pointe Coupée Parish: Taylor Plantation on Bayou Latenache and the Richards Tract on the Atchafalaya River. Encompassing 1,581.06 acres on both banks of Bayou Latenache, between the communities of Innis and Mains, Taylor Plantation was an antebellum holding of William and Lucy Lewis Taylor. William was said to be a relative of United States President Zachary Taylor. The main residence, located on the west bank of the bayou, was from its earliest years a showplace in the parish.

In successive transactions in 1881, the heirs of the late Mrs. Taylor, headed by Cameron E. Thom, sold the plantation to Upper Pointe Coupée farmer and 2nd Louisiana Cavalry, C.S.A. veteran Robert H.F. Sewall for $5,000, and Sewall sold a quarter interest to Simon Bloch for $3,000 and a half interest to George H. Smith of Pointe Coupée for $3,000. Smith died soon afterward, and Bloch and Sewall bought Smith's remaining quarter interest in the plantation for $2,500.

The 1882 Pointe Coupée Parish Tax Roll recorded that the partnership of "Bloch & Sewall" had real estate assessed as $20,500, livestock at $1,980, vehicles at $320, and store merchandise at $600. Two years later, following the ravages of the 1882 and 1884 floods, the plantation was assessed at a depreciated $5,000 and the livestock at $800, an indication that neither vehicles nor store merchandise remained. Simon Bloch became full owner of Taylor Plantation through the purchase of Sewall's interest in 1887, for $3,500.

Bloch retained the Taylor place as an operating plantation through the flood of 1890, during which time temporary levees built to protect the Latenache area were "shattered," under assault from crevasses in the Mississippi River levee to the east and the Atchafalaya to the west according to contemporaneous *Pointe Coupée Banner* accounts. Restoring the plantation to a state of productivity after the flood, Bloch held Taylor until 1898, when he sold it to Raccourci-Old River merchant and major landholder Ovide Lacour for $20,000. The conveyance from Bloch to Lacour included 31 mules, three four-horse wagons, all farming implements, and crops of corn, hay and moss.

Simon Bloch subsequently acquired, as sole proprietor, the Stephens property, an 893-acre tract on the Atchafalaya River and the corresponding 150-acre *batture* between the levee and river bank, south of McCrea, which he held until his death.

At some time before 1900, Simon and Fanny Bloch moved to Chicago, Cook Co., Illinois, to be near their daughter, Cecile Bloch Mayer, and their grandchildren, Edwin (b. 1888) and Helen (b. 1892) Mayer. According to the 1900 United States Federal Census, the Blochs lived on Drexel Avenue, with Simon's occupation recorded as a "planter." He and Fanny made annual, extended visits to New Orleans, where Simon maintained his membership on the Touro Infirmary and Jewish Orphans Home boards.

Fanny Kaufman Bloch died in Chicago on 6 January 1905, and was interred in Rosehill Cemetery. Her widower, Simon, moved into the stately Lexington Hotel on Michigan Avenue, and ultimately to the home of his daughter, Cecile Bloch Mayer. After suffering three months from a cerebral thrombosis and six days from bronchopneumonia, Simon Bloch died on 3 April 1908, in the Belden Avenue Hospital in Chicago, and was buried with Fanny in Rosehill Cemetery.

Cecile Bloch Mayer was sole heir of Simon and Fanny Kaufman Bloch's estate.

Charles Bloch's wife, Lillie Cochran, died on 19 November 1928, and Charles followed on 17 May 1935, in Dallas, Harris Co., Texas. They were interred in Grove Hill Memorial Park. They never had children.

NATHAN FINKELSTEIN

Nochim Finkielsztejn/Nathan Finkelstein, a native of Suwalki, Poland, then part of the Russian Empire, was born there on 15 January 1861, to Josiel Tavia Finkielsztejn and Fejga Rotsztejn. Nathan immigrated to America with his wife, Anna/Annie Borowsky, and their first four children in 1892. Chaia Feije Borowsky, known as Anna or Annie Borowsky in America, had been born in March of 1865 in Poland, and she and Nathan Finkelstein married there ca. 1883. She may have been related to Stanislas Borowski (*sic*), born ca. 1877 in "Germany," who immigrated in 1899, and was enumerated as a hostler in the 1900 United States Federal Census, living next door to general merchant Marcus Landau and his family at Créole Landing on Raccourci-Old River.

Nathan and Annie Finkelstein were the parents of seven children, four born in Poland: Reuben (b. 1884), Gussie (b. 1886), Marx (b. 1887) and Esther (b. 1891). Their daughter, Ida (b. 1895), and two sons, Solomon (b. 1897) and Abraham (b. 1899), were born after the family's arrival in Louisiana ca. 1895.

Nathan's brother, Harry Finkelstein, was a merchant at nearby Williamsport, having worked there since at least 1895. Nathan administered Harry's succession in New Orleans following his death in 1905. I.H. Finkelstein, a merchant at Mains on Bayou Latenache and subsequently a resident of LaCour on the Raccourci Lagoon, was likely their brother, Israël, mentioned as a co-heir to Harry's estate.

Nathan Finkelstein was enumerated in the 1900 United States Federal Census as a general merchant, living with his wife and children on upper Bayou Latenache in Pointe Coupée, between the homes of the Leslie L. Humphries and John D. Goode families. Their son, Reuben, age 15, was working as a store clerk.

On 12 March 1910, the *Pointe Coupée Banner* reported that Nathan Finkelstein and Louis W. Friedberg, "both of Torras," had been arrested four nights previously by Deputy Sheriff Joseph Desormes on the charge of selling liquor without a license. The two were said to have purchased the stock of liquor at a bankruptcy sale. The matter was rectified, the *Banner* stated, by Finkelstein and Friedberg who paid for a license to sell liquor as well as all court costs.

Finkelstein and Friedberg filed suit against Pointe Coupée Parish Sheriff Ernest G. Beuker (21st Judicial District Court, No. 1820), claiming they were not, as the sheriff contended, liquor wholesalers in Pointe Coupée and the two men petitioned for the return of the license fee and court costs they paid, plus current court costs. The court ruled in the sheriff's favor, and Finkelstein and Friedberg appealed, but the higher circuit court ruled against them in 1911. Meanwhile, Louisiana State Rep. Joseph Octave LeBeau of Chenal, a former Josephite seminarian who was remembered in the 21st century as a man of great piety, introduced House Bill 177 at the 1910 session of the Louisiana House of Representatives to reimburse the $100 that Finkelstein and Friedberg had been ordered to pay for a state liquor license, but the bill failed.

In little more than a month's time after their arrest in Torras, Louis Friedberg and Nathan Finkelstein were both enumerated with their families in the 1910 United States Federal Census in New Orleans. Nathan Finkelstein was also a partner in a New Orleans dry goods and notions company with his brother Harry Finkelstein and Louis Friedberg as Finkelstein Bros. & Friedberg. The company suffered great losses due to fire which destroyed much of the merchandise and sundries in 1905. When Louis Friedberg withdrew to concentrate on his men's clothing stores in the city, Nathan Finkelstein continued as Finkelstein Dry Goods & Notions Co.

Sometime before the 1920 United States Federal Census enumeration, Nathan Finkelstein and his family had moved to Second Street in Uptown New Orleans. Nathan was still a dry goods merchant working with his sons, Solomon and Abe, employed, respectively, as a dry goods clerk and a salesman.

Nathan Finkelstein died on 19 August 1921, in New Orleans, and was interred there in Gates of Prayer Cemetery. His widow, Anna "Annie" Borowsky, died in New Orleans on 15 August 1930, and was interred with him.

I.H. FINKELSTEIN

Izraël Hercko "I.H." Finkelstein was a merchant at Mains, Louisiana, on the west bank of Bayou Latenache in the early 20th century. He was the brother of Nathan and Harry Finkelstein who were all merchants in Pointe Coupée Parish and New Orleans. Izrael Hercko Finkielstejn was born in Suwalki, Poland, Russian Empire, on 20 January 1854, to Josiel Tavia Finkielstejn and Fejga Rotsztejn. Israël was married at Suwalki in 1875 to Chaja Rachel Jaworkowski, the daughter of Girsz Jaworkowski and Rejza Bialostowki.

Israël Finkelstein inherited $131.91 from his brother Harry, whose succession was administered in New Orleans by their brother Nathan in 1905.

Back at Mains on Bayou Latenache in Pointe Coupée Parish, I.H. Finkelstein granted power of attorney to future Morganza merchant Isidore Srulovitz to manage the store and transact business in his (Finkelstein's) name for the period 6 April 1905 until 1 January 1906.

In one of his last-known references in Pointe Coupée Parish, I.H. Finkelstein was mentioned as a "business visitor" to New Roads from LaCour on the Raccourci Lagoon in a 25 March 1911 article published in the *Pointe Coupée Banner*.

Israël H. Finkelstein died on 4 May 1913, in Brooklyn, New York, and was survived by his wife, Chaja Rachel, and children, Rashe Ethel Sandofsky, Kate Loeb, Ida Sandofsky, as well as Fannie, Nathan, Solomon, and Abe Finkelstein. His widow was appointed administrator of his succession in the Kings County, New York, Surrogate Court.

MAX SRULOVITZ THE ELDER/MAX LOEB

Max Srulovitz the elder was born on 15 April 1880, in the Kingdom of Romania, to Lazar Srulovitz and his wife, Rebecca Herskovitz. Max, as well as his brothers Isidore, Pincus and L. Srulovitz, all immigrated to Louisiana. Max Srulovitz arrived in America in 1900, and was naturalized at New Roads, Louisiana, in 1912.

He operated a general store and was a retailer of the popular Peters brand shoes in an old and, even then, decrepit commercial building on the Batchelor property at Mains, Louisiana, on the west bank of Bayou Latenache. His location was a strategic one in upper Pointe Coupée, being just below the road which led west, past Mount Mariah Church and School and through the New California community, to the Atchafalaya River at McCrea. To the south of Srulovitz's store was the bridge over the Latenache and the road connecting to the Texas & Pacific Railroad and Batchelor on Raccourci-Old River.

Max Srulovitz, the Elder's store at Bayou Latenache during 1912 flood.

In 1909, Max Srulovitz filed suit against Pointe Coupée Parish Sheriff Ernest G. Beuker for having fined Srulovitz for not having a liquor license. A neighboring tenant farmer, testifying for the defense, stated that he drank wine by the glass in Srulovitz's store and identified a bottle of liquid held up in court as the type of beverage sold by Srulovitz. The court ruled in favor of the Sheriff, and ordered that Max Srulovitz pay $200 for a State License and $1,000 for a Parish License for the sale of alcoholic beverages for the year 1909.

According to the 1910 United States Federal Census, Max Srulovitz had been joined by a nephew, Max or Max H. Srulovitz, who was identified as a store clerk. Max the uncle, or elder, was married on 28 August 1911, in New Orleans, Louisiana, to Helena Kahn, a native of that city. Helena was born on 12 December 1892, to Joseph Kahn, said to be a native of Alsace, France, and Bertha Goldenberg, born on 14 March 1854, in New Orleans, to Charles Goldenberg and his wife, Rosine Leopold, both German immigrants.

With floodwater rising as high as ten feet in the Latenache neighborhood during the harrowing Mississippi River flood of 1912, Max Srulovitz's store building was severely undermined according to reports in the *Pointe Coupée Banner*. An iconic photograph of the time, seen above, likely taken the morning after the 1 May 1912 crevasse at Torras, shows two men, one white and one African American, sitting on the gallery roof of the rickety Srulovitz store.

In 1913, Max submitted a petition and note of evidence to change his name from "Max Srulovitz" to "Max Loeb" in 1913 in Pointe Coupée Parish, Louisiana, but no order authorizing such is located in the file.

Following the flood and some return to normalcy, Max relocated his business to the Lettsworth community. As "Max Loeb," he filed a notice in the 16 January 1915 *Pointe Coupee Banner* to notify the public that he had filed a notice with the Police Jury to secure licenses to sell retail wines, beer and liquor in the building formerly occupied by Alfred Platt at Lettsworth. The 1916 Pointe Coupée Parish Tax Roll Loeb as a merchant there, with merchandise assessed at $175.

While in the store at Lettsworth, Max Loeb, in 1914, was belatedly taken to court by B. Dreyfus & Son, Natchez, Mississippi wholesalers (21st Judicial District Court, No. 2334), for merchandise he had bought from them as Max Srulovitz during 1911-1912 for his Bayou Latenache store. The goods attest to the incongruity of Max's quality merchandise offered in such a dilapidated building, being itemized as: bolts of silks, gingham, bleached (cotton), ticking and oilcloth, Willimantic brand thread, bedsheets, men's pants and suspenders, ladies' vests and corset strings, hosiery, handkerchiefs, Hoyt's colognes, combs, razors, and pencils.

Police of Trade.

TAVERNS, GROG SHOPS, &c.

§ 1.

ART. 361.—Any person wishing to hauk or peddle, to keep a billiard table, store or grog shop, or generally to vend, traffic or deal in any goods, wares, merchandize of any kind, within the limits of this parish, shall be bound to pay into the hands of the parish collector, in advance, the amount due by him according to the tariff hereafter established, and receive from the Collector a license therefor, signed by the President of the Police Jury and Auditor, as herein provided, authorizing him to carry on his trade or occupation for the space of one year.

ART. 362.—The following tariff of licenses is hereby established:

For each public billiard-table, fifty dollars.

For each grog shop, fifty dollars.

For each store, twenty-five dollars.

For each cart merchant, fifty dollars.

For each box or pack merchant, on horseback, twenty-five dollars.

For each box or pack merchant, on foot, ten dollars.

For selling bread, for each cart, twenty-five dollars.

For selling meat, for each cart, ten dollars.

For each trading boat on the Mississippi river, one hundred dollars.

1857 Pointe Coupée Parish Regulations and Fees for Merchants and Peddlers.

CHAPTER 14

BAYOU LETTSWORTH

The origin of the name "Lettsworth" which was given to the bayou and to the community in Pointe Coupée Parish is still unknown. In the late nineteenth and early twentieth centuries cotton plantations and farms as well as the commercial enterprises of a number of Jewish residents were located along its banks. The waterway, originally called Bayou Depassau, meanders across the northeast corner of Pointe Coupée Parish, from its origin near Torras and Red River Landing on the north to its sealed mouth at Williamsport at the upper end of Raccourci-Old River on the south. Between the bayou and the Mississippi River is a low marshy area, formerly known as Lac Depassau, and now consisting of Lake Moreau and smaller bodies of water.

The community of Lettsworth, where the Texas & Pacific branch railroad nearly touched the bayou, became a center of some importance, with a depot and several stores. Like Torras to the northeast, the Lettsworth area had hundreds of residents owing to the large number of plantations in the vicinity. Also, like Torras, Lettsworth met its demise in the flood of 1912 which caused many small-scale farmers and plantation tenants to relocate beyond Pointe Coupée Parish. New Orleans newspapers reported the drowning of 12 evacuees in the accidental capsizing of a government rescue launch on the seventh day of the flood "near Lettsworth…in the Battle Axe district." No longtime area resident interviewed in the 21st century recalls such a place, and it is possible that the site of the tragedy was actually the area of Bayou Ballahack which is, in fact, near Ravenswood, and about 15 miles due south of Lettsworth.

DAVID and WILLIAM WEIL

Brothers David Leopold Weil and William Leopold "Willie" Weil were two of the nine children of Leopold Weil and his wife, Bena Maier. Leopold had been born on 12 July 1836, at Ingwiller, Bas-Rhin, France, to Samuel Weil, a native of the town, and his wife, Caroline Oppenheim, born in Haguenau, Bas-Rhin. Leopold immigrated to Louisiana, arriving on 23 January 1854, aboard the ship *Württemberg*. He married Bena Maier in New Orleans on 31 July 1856. David, their fourth child, was born on 23 December 1863, in New Orleans. William Leopold "Willie" Weil followed on 6 November 1865.

According to the 1880 United States Federal Census, the teenaged Weil Brothers were living in the household of Margaret Ross and her family on Bayou Lettsworth. David Weil and John Kelly were enumerated as "sewing machine agents." This appears to be the Weil brothers' only verified appearance in the parish. Their father, Leopold, and his brothers, Jacob and Marx, who all immigrated to Louisiana, had, themselves, started out as peddlers. It was not unusual for French and German immigrants to apprentice their own teenage sons as traveling merchants in order to give them a start in the retail business.

David was married on 16 October 1894, in Chicago, Cook Co., Illinois, to Bena Wolf, born there on 16 November 1876. He and his bride lived in New Orleans where their four children were born: Clara (b. 1897), Emile Wolf (b. 1899), Amalie (b. 1900), and Leopold (b. 1906). David made his living as a shoe merchant, and later sold dry goods and hats. He died on 29 January 1936, and was interred in Hebrew Rest Cemetery No. 1 in New Orleans. Bena Wolf Weil died on 25 May 1967, and was interred with him.

William L. Weil worked as a clothing merchant in New Orleans. He was also a director of the Leopold Weil Building and Improvement Co., a member of Woodmen of the World, and active in many Jewish charities. William was married on 13 October 1913, at Chattanooga, Hamilton Co., Tennessee, to Stella Wassman. The bride was born at Chattanooga on 12 June 1877, to Isaac Wassman, a native of Bavaria, and Lena Rose. William and Stella lived in New Orleans, where he died on 11 February 1918, from Bright's disease. He was interred in Hebrew Rest Cemetery No. 2. Stella survived him by several decades, and died on 3 March 1956, in Augusta, Richmond Co., Georgia. She was buried there in Westover Memorial Park. They were married only four years and never had children. Stella never remarried.

LEVY & FONTAINE

Arthur Fontaine, born ca. 1852 in Belgium, was listed as a laborer, living in the household of Williamsport, Louisiana merchant Meyer Levy and his wife, Henriette Müller, in the 1880 United States Federal Census. Fontaine relocated to New Roads, where he leased Vignes's "café" (*sic*) building on the bank of False River, opposite the southeast corner of the Courthouse square between 1883 and 1884, from Edwin Vignes, a descendant of Benjamin Jewell and Sophie Prévost. From a decade prior, the spacious frame structure had housed the saloon of another native of France, Jules J. Buzzetti. The lease from Vignes to Fontaine included a billiard table and decanters.

After the expiration of the lease, Arthur Fontaine returned to Upper Pointe Coupée, and Edwin Vignes leased the building to the firm of Abraham & Weil, who opened the "New Road [sic] Cheap Cash Store," in September 1885, which, in contrast to its sobriquet, offered fine dry goods and clothing.

Fontaine entered into partnership with Maurice Levy, son of his former employer, Meyer Levy, as "Levy & Fontaine," general merchants on Bayou Lettsworth. Maurice Levy had operated a store at Williamsport, Louisiana, in the 1870s, but sold his inventory to his father in 1880. Maurice remained in partnership with Fontaine on Bayou Lettsworth for a few years before acquiring the latter's interest. Maurice Levy was identified as sole proprietor of the Bayou Lettsworth store in the July 1889 edition of Dun's *Mercantile Agency Reference Book,* but in late 1888, had entered into a five-year lease with the family of his wife, née Rachel Wolff, of the "Burnt Bridge Store" near Lakeland. Levy conducted a general store there until selling his stock of merchandise to Rachel's brother Lazard Wolff in 1895.

L. FISHMAN & CO.

L. Fishman & Co., at Lettsworth Station on the Texas & Pacific branch railroad, was the early 1900s partnership of Louis Fishman and Abraham Herzog. Lazar "Louis" Fishman was born ca. 1862, possibly at Kiev, Ukraine, Russian Empire. He immigrated before the turn of the twentieth century, and was naturalized in New Roads, Louisiana, on 29 April 1902.

Abraham Joel Herzog was born, ca. 1862, in Vilna, Lithuania, Russian Empire, and immigrated ca. 1893. He filed a declaration of intention for naturalization in Washington, D. C., on 4 August 1893. The oath of witnesses as well as his final oath renouncing allegiance to Tsar Nicholas II of Russia were filed in New Roads on 31 October 1904.

Herzog had first been married to Sarah Yetta Goldman, who was born ca. 1864, also in Vilna. She was a sister of Thomas Goldman, a merchant at Bayou Lettsworth and Torras. Three children were born to the couple before they immigrated: Samuel (b. 1887), Charles Eli (b. 1888), and Mattie (b. 1889). Two more sons were born in Washington D.C.: Harry (b. 1895), and Louis (b. 1901). Sarah Yetta Goldman's surname appeared as "Katz" in the marriage records of her children, Harry, Samuel and Mattie, which might indicate that she had been previously wed to a "Katz" before her marriage to Herzog.

Sarah died on 14 June 1902, in New Orleans, Louisiana, and was interred there in Ahavas Sholem Cemetery. Abraham was married to Mary Sneike, who had been born on 25 April 1879, in Lithuania, Russian Empire, to Moishe Leib Sneike and Chia Smeade-Kling. Abraham and Mary were the parents of Celia Herzog, born on 3 June 1915.

In 1903, Smith Bros. Co., Ltd. filed suit against L. Fishman & Co. (21st Judicial District Court, No. 407). Merchandise seized and offered for public sale in satisfaction of the judgment included: dry goods, notions, overshirts, undershirts, shoes, hats; staple groceries, canned goods, soda, lard, wines, whiskeys; drugs, tobacco; chinaware, crockery, glassware, bottles, lamps, slates, garden seed, brooms, washboards, buckets, coal oil barrels; nails, axe handles, rope, coal oil; and four large cooking stoves and six small cooking stoves (the stoves being at Texas & Pacific railroad depot); plus three showcases and contents, store fixtures, lamps, a safe, and a number of open accounts.

After dissolution of the partnership, Abraham Herzog and his family moved to Torras, Pointe Coupée Parish, where they were engaged in merchandising for the next several years. That same year, Fishman was one of the signatories on a charter that was filed in June 1903 to form the New Roads Electric Light and Power Co., Ltd.

Louis Fishman eventually relocated to Athlone, Concordia Parish, Louisiana, where he did business as a plantation supply merchant and financier. He also served as Postmaster at Athlone from 10 September 1921, until his untimely death on 28 March 1922. He was murdered in his store in what was believed to be a robbery. The only suspect, Henry Laughlin, was apprehended in June 1922, and housed in the County Jail in Natchez, Adams Co., Mississippi, from where he escaped in September of the same year.

Louis Fishman was buried in the Natchez City Cemetery in Natchez, Adams Co., Mississippi. His sister, Rebecca Fishman, was the wife of well-known Natchez wholesale dry goods merchant Jonathan Seiferth, both of whom upon their deaths were interred near Louis.

THOMAS GOLDMAN

Thomas Goldman, a native of Vilna, Lithuania, Russian Empire, was born there on 2 August 1865. According to the 1900 United States Federal Census, Goldman immigrated in 1882, and had been naturalized. His sister, Sarah Yetta Goldman, was the first wife of Bayou Lettsworth and Torras merchant Abraham Joel Herzog. Thomas Goldman was married on 2 June 1889, in the Washington, D.C., to Celia Friedberg, who had been born in April 1867, in Linow, Poland, Russian Empire, to Samuel Friedberg and Sarah Yawitz. Celia's brother, Louis W. Friedberg, was an owner of White Hall Plantation on the Atchafalaya River in Pointe Coupée Parish and later a well-known men's clothing retailer in New Orleans.

Thomas and Celia Goldman settled on Bayou Lettsworth in Pointe Coupée Parish in the late 1890s, where he opened a store. According to the 1900 United States Federal Census, Thomas Goldman's nephew Samuel Herzog, son of Abraham Herzog and Goldman's sister, Sarah, was living with Thomas and his wife, Celia Friedberg, and their first three children: Mattie (b. 1892), Samuel (b. 1895) and Esther (b. 1896). Young Herzog, born ca. August 1887, was attending school and may have also been employed as Goldman's store clerk. Two more children were born to Thomas and Celia at Bayou Lettsworth: Solomon (b. 1901), and Hannah (b. 1902).

By 1904, the extended Goldman family transferred their business and residence to the growing town of Torras where Thomas opened another general store.

REUBEN FINKELSTEIN

Reuben Finkelstein, the son of Bayou Latenache general merchant Nathan Finkelstein and Anna "Annie" Borowsky, was born on 15 October 1884, in Poland, Russian Empire. Reuben immigrated to America in 1892, with his parents and three other children: Gussie, Marx and Esther. Three more siblings were born in Louisiana: Ida, Sol and Abraham.

Fifteen-year-old Reuben Finkelstein was enumerated in the 1900 United States Federal Census as a clerk in his father's store. In a few years' time, the still-minor Reuben established a retail store and saloon of his own, in a building owned by largescale landowner George Keller at Lettsworth. In 1905, Finkelstein sold all of the merchandise, the store safe, and store and bar fixtures to Walter S. Chambliss for $154.36.

Reuben Finkelstein did not appear with his parents and siblings in New Orleans in either the 1910 or 1920 United States Federal Censuses. On 21 January 1912, indicating that he was a resident of Orleans Parish, Louisiana, he was married by Rabbi W. Wellman in Houston, Harris Co., Texas, to Chana/Anna Hartstein, who was born on 16 March 1892, in Boryslav, Lviv, Ukraine. She was the daughter of Houston merchant Israël Hartstein, a native of Vienna, and Rizha/Rosa Weidinger, born in Sambir, Lviv, Ukraine.

According to the 1930 United States Federal Census, Reuben, Anna and their five children: Ruby (b. 1914), Florence (b. 1916), Joseph (b. 1917), Dorothy (b. 1919), and Betty (b. 1921), were living in New Orleans. Reuben was the manager of a ladies' clothing store. The Finkelsteins eventually returned to Houston, where Reuben died on 3 March 1941. He was interred there in Beth Yeshurun Cemetery. Anna died in Houston on 8 January 1966, and was interred with him.

THE OAK GROVE PLANTING COMPANY

"The Oak Grove Planting Company" was one of several agricultural corporations formed following the flood of 1912. Chartered on 31 December of that year for a period of 99 years, the company was headquartered on Oak Grove Plantation on Bayou Lettsworth, which had historically been a top producer of cotton. The founding directors of the company included Robert S. Bienvenu, Sim H. Lowenburg, Emanuel Samuels, and G. H. Bienvenu. The Bienvenus were longtime Upper Pointe Coupée landowners and planters, while Lowenburg and Samuels were businessmen from Natchez, Adams County, Mississippi.

Simon Hill "Sim H." Lowenburg was born at Natchez on 27 October 1867, to Isaac Lowenburg, a native of the Principality of Hohenzollern-Hechingen, and Ophelia Mayer, born at Natchez, on

21 July 1843, to Jacob Meyer Levi (aka John Mayer), a native of Landau, Rheinpfalz, Germany, and Jeannette Ries, born at Obernai, Bas-Rhin, France. Isaac Lowenburg was one among many Jewish merchants to operate on Commerce Street in Natchez, and served two consecutive terms as mayor of the city.

Sim H. Lowenburg was married on 31 March 1891, at St. Louis, Missouri, to Medea Eiseman. She had been born on 24 March 1870, at Fayette, Jefferson County, Mississippi, to general merchant and farmer Meyer Eiseman, a native of Mehlingen, Rheinpfalz, Germany, and Henrietta Meyer. One of Medea Eiseman's brothers, Cassius Meyer "C.M." Eiseman, was the owner of Nina Plantation, Store, and Landing near Cook's Landing, Pointe Coupée Parish, Louisiana. Sim and Medea lived on Commerce Street in Natchez with their three children, Isaac (b. 1892), Henrietta Ophelia (b. 1898), and Dorothy (b. 1901- d. 1901), where he was a wholesale grocer.

Emanuel Samuels had been born in Sulzdorf, Rheinpfalz, Germany, on 14 August 1866, to Gerson Samuels and Johanna Schmidt Frank, both natives of the Rheinpfalz. Emanuel Samuels immigrated from the port of Bremen, aboard the steamer *Fulda*, and arrived in New York City on 4 August 1883. Settling in Natchez, Adams Co., Mississippi, he was married there on 11 March 1890, to Helen Lowenburg. A Natchez native, born there on 13 July 1869, Helen was the daughter of merchant Isaac Lowenburg and his wife, Ophelia Mayer, and the sister of Sim H. Lowenburg, Emanuel Samuels' occasional business partner. Samuels was also a wholesale grocer who lived in Natchez with his wife and two children: Frank Lowenburg (b. 1890), and Marguerite (b. 1894).

In 1913, a year after the charter of Oak Grove Planting Company in Pointe Coupée Parish, the firm purchased substantial properties on Bayou Lettsworth from Susie Hamilton, wife of Robert S. Bienvenu, including: the well-known Oak Grove Plantation, comprising 1,359.52 acres on the west side of the bayou at Bienvenu Station; McPhaul Plantation, in a bend on the east side of the bayou, containing 120 acres; a one-third interest in the 392-acre Hamilton Tract, on the west bank of Bayou Lettsworth; 30 mules, and all "implements and utensils" appertaining, including plows, harrows, cultivators, gear, harness, wagons and carts, as well as forage in the manner of hay, peas, corn, and oats. The price was $80,000, represented by 800 shares in the company, at a price of $100 each. Emanuel Samuels represented Oak Grove Planting for the transaction.

Only a year later, burdened by its indebtedness, Oak Grove Planting Company divested itself of its Bayou Lettsworth real estate, and the movable property on Oak Grove and McPhaul, selling it to brothers-in-law Sim H. Lowenburg and Emanuel Samuels in 1914. The conveyance was made through the brothers-in-law's assumption of the $18,205.37 debts of the company. Movables transferred included 29 mules, 20 horses, all corn and hay harvested, plows, harrows, machinery, wagons and gear. In 1915, Lowenburg and Samuels sold their properties on Bayou Lettsworth, plus 29 mules, 22 horses, all corn, hay and farming implements, for $80,000 to The Lettsworth Planting Company, represented by Max Rothschild, brother of Torras, Louisiana general merchant Isidore Rothschild, of the "Valley Mercantile Co."

According to the 1920 United States Federal Census, Sim H. Lowenburg, the president of a wholesale company, lived with his family on Amelia Street, just off St. Charles Avenue, in Uptown New Orleans. He died there on 17 June 1927. His widow, Medea Eiseman Lowenburg, died on 24 April 1941, in New Orleans. They were both interred at Metairie Cemetery in New Orleans.

Emanuel and Helen Lowenburg Samuels also moved to New Orleans, where he was a partner in a wholesale grocery company. Ill for almost five years with leukemia, Samuels sought treatment in New York, but died there on 11 November 1922. His remains were transported to Natchez, Mississippi, where he was interred on "Jewish Hill" in the Natchez City Cemetery.

Emanuel Samuels left an estate appraised at $132,557.49, which included a $10,000 promissory note from F.T. Hutson on Oak Grove Plantation; a number of stocks in I. Lowenburg Co. in Natchez and the Southern Yacht Club in New Orleans, government bonds from the City of Copenhagen, Denmark, the Republic of Cuba, and Russia; as well as household furnishings. The part-owner of four plantations on Bayou Lettsworth apparently died possessing a lot in Metairie Cemetery as his only real estate.

Whitney-Central Bank of New Orleans declared itself a creditor of Samuels' succession, in the amount of $144,876.46, for which the deceased had stood *in solido* for the Dunbar Dukate Company. Samuels' estate was authorized by the court to sell stocks left by the deceased to cover the debts of the succession.

Helen Lowenburg, widow of Emanuel Samuels, died on 15 January 1945, in Covington, St. Tammany Parish, Louisiana, and was interred with her husband on "Jewish Hill" in Natchez City Cemetery, Natchez, Mississippi.

THE LETTSWORTH PLANTNG COMPANY, INCORPORATED

In 1915, the Lettsworth Planting Company, Incorporated, represented by Max Rothschild, a resident of Concordia Parish, bought considerable real estate, livestock and other movables on Bayou Lettsworth from brothers-in-law Sim H. Lowenburg and Emanuel Samuels, wholesale grocers in Natchez, Adams County, Mississippi. The purchase price was $80,000, and consisted of: the Oak Grove Plantation, at Bienvenu Station on the west bank of the bayou, and comprising 1,359.52 acres; McPhaul Plantation, of 120 acres, on the east side and within a bend of the bayou; a one-third interest in a 392-acre tract (Hamilton Plantation), on the west bank of Bayou Lettsworth; 29 mules, 22 horses, and all farming "implements" belonging to the properties.

Max Rothschild was born on 13 August 1868, at Nordstetten, Kingdom of Württemberg (Germany), to Moses Marx Rothschild and Lea Hirsch. Max's brother, Isidore Rothschild, was the owner of the "Valley Mercantile Co." in the rebuilt town of Torras, Louisiana. According to his naturalization record, Max Rothschild arrived in the United States on 22 August 1885, and was admitted to citizenship on 18 March 1901, at Amite, Liberty County, Mississippi.

Leopold "Lee" Bohrman was engaged as the manager of Lettsworth Planting Company. He was born on 17 April 1853, at Hassloch, Rheinpfalz, Germany, to Jakob Bohrman, a native of Hassloch, and his wife, Franziska Kahn, born in Bubenheim, Rheinpfalz, Germany. Nineteen-year-old Leopold Bohrman immigrated to New York aboard the *SS. Rhein*, arriving on 4 November 1872. He was naturalized in New York City in 1879, where he worked as a merchant. Moving south, Bohrman was married on 22 June 1883, to Bertha Moses in Jacksonville, Duval County, Florida. She was born on 14 May 1866, in Chicago, Cook Co., Illinois, to Rabbi Marx Moses, born in Essingen, Rheinpfalz, Germany, and Caroline Buchbinder, a native of

Nuremberg, Rheinpfalz, Germany. Bertha Moses Bohrman's sister, Hattie Moses, was married to Torras, Louisiana, general merchant Isidore Rothschild, proprietor of the "Valley Mercantile Co." and Max Rothschild's brother.

Leopold and Bertha Moses Bohrman and their twenty-one-year-old daughter, Caroline "Carrie," were enumerated in the 1910 United Federal Census as residents of New York City where Leopold worked as a commercial traveler for a clothing company, and Carrie was employed as a vaudeville actress.

Bertha Moses Bohrman died at Lettsworth Station, Pointe Coupée Parish, Louisiana, on 31 March 1918, and was interred in Hebrew Rest Cemetery No. 1 in New Orleans. Shortly after Bertha Bohrman's death, the Lettsworth Planting Company was relocated to Vidalia, Concordia Parish, Louisiana.

The company entered an act of partition of Hamilton Plantation in 1918, with co-owners Henry P. Mounger, a Lettsworth Station planter, merchant and ginner, and his wife, Elizabeth Hamilton. The Moungers each owned a one-third interest in the property which measured 394.19 acres, less 50 acres which had already been sold. Lettsworth Planting was declared the owner of a 9/48 interest in Hamilton Plantation, and was put into full possession of 58.27 acres of cleared land and 46.90 acres woodland from the northwest portion of the plantation.

In 1920, the Lettsworth Planting Company, represented by its vice president, Max Rothschild, sold Oak Grove, McPhaul and its portion of the former Hamilton Plantation to Fulton H. Hutson, a merchant and planter of Isola, Humphreys, Co., Mississippi, for $107,500. Oak Grove was subsequently owned by Dr. Wiley Ross Buffington, who married Rowena Virginia Morrison, the widow of building contractor Joseph Wade Bouanchaud.

Max Rothschild was married ca. 1922 to Henrietta "Rhetta" Hough, the widow of Stanford Watson Scott. Henrietta had been born on 3 October 1882, in Mississippi, to Philip Hough and Rosie Miller. Working as a wholesale grocer, Max Rothschild died on 4 December 1930, in Vidalia, Concordia Parish, Louisiana, and was survived by his widow, née Henrietta Hough. She died on 20 December 1953. They were both interred in Zurhellen Plot No. 1 in Natchez City Cemetery in Natchez, Adams Co., Mississippi.

Leopold "Lee" Bohrman died on 25 October 1925, at (Dr. Henry William) Lloyd's Sanitarium at Nos. 6-8 St. Nicholas Place, corner of 150th Street, in Manhattan, New York. His death record (extract) states that he was buried at Holy Sepulchre Cemetery in New Rochelle, Westchester Co., New York, where his daughter, Caroline B. Forbes, was interred when she died in 1971.

MAX LOEB (ORIGINALLY SRULOVITZ)

As "Max Loeb," originally Max Srulovitz, born on 15 April 1880, in Romania, the former Bayou Latenache merchant resumed business after the 1912 flood, to the north at Lettsworth, Louisiana. The 16 January 1915 issue of the *Pointe Coupée Banner* included Max Loeb's notice to sell liquor at Lettsworth. In addition, the 1916 Pointe Coupée Tax Roll assessed his merchandise there at $175.

According to 1920 United States Federal Census, Max Loeb, his wife, Helena Kahn, and their children were living in Choctaw, Oklahoma Co., Oklahoma, where Max was identified as a merchant and pool hall operator. Leaving the Sooner State, the Loebs made Alabama their final home, settling there before the 1920 United States Federal Census. They took up residence at Toulminville-Prichard, in Mobile County, Alabama, where Max was the proprietor of a general merchandise store. Ten years later, Max and Helena Kahn Loeb were enumerated as grocery store keepers, assisted by their son, Samuel, in Plateau also known as Africatown, Mobile County, Alabama, where enslaved captives from the last slave ship, the *Clotilda*, arrived in July 1860, and after emancipation, founded the town, only several miles from the city of Mobile.

Max Srulovitz/Loeb died on 10 December 1965, in Mobile, Mobile Co., Alabama, and was interred there in the Ahavas Chesed Cemetery. His widow, née Helena Kahn, died on 3 February 1965, in Prichard, Mobile Co., Alabama, and was buried with her husband.

MORITZ HOFFMAN

Among the Jewish businessmen who operated briefly in Pointe Coupée Parish and moved on to "bigger things" in New York City was Moritz "Morris" Hoffman. According to the 1900 United States Federal Census, he was born in April 1866, in the Kingdom of Hungary, had immigrated in 1882, and was naturalized. His later marriage record identified his parents as Israël Hoffman and Latte Leindorfer. The death certificate of Moritz's younger brother, Emil Hoffman, who died in Manhattan, at age 72, on 12 August 1942, indicated that he, his parents, and likely Mortiz as well, had all been born in Turzovka, in present-day Slovakia.

Morris Hoffman was enumerated in the 1900 United States Federal Census as a merchant at Lettsworth, Louisiana, near the residence of Upper Pointe Coupée physician Dr. S.W. Turner and his family who resided on Idlewild Plantation. In its recapitulation of parish business for 1900-1901, the 23 March 1902 edition of the *Pointe Coupée Banner* listed M. Hoffman with sales of $400 in 1900 but delinquent in payment of his $10 operating license for 1901. By that time, he had moved to Manhattan, where he was married on 11 August 1901, to Katie Kling, born ca. 1877, in Hungary, to Jacob Kling and Nellie Ziegler.

The 1905 and 1915 New York State Censuses, as well as the 1910 and 1920 United States Federal Censuses indicated that Morris was a furrier. He and Kate moved from St. Mark's Place, to E. 11th Street, to Stuyvesant Place with their surviving children: Irene (b. ca. 1905), Morris, Jr. (b. ca. 1907), and Alice (b. ca. 1912).

Two unmarried boarders: Charles Hoffman (relationship to Morris, if any, not stated), age 30, a collector for the "fur house," and Frank Romm, 28, a collector for the "cloak house," both natives of Germany were included in the enumeration of the 1910 household. Morris's sister, Lena Hoffman, age 34, a seamstress from Hungary, made her first appearance in the household in the 1915 New York State Census.

Kate Kling Hoffman died on 3 June 1924, and was buried in Montefiore Cemetery in Springfield Gardens, Queens Co., New York. Morris Hoffman, a retired merchant, died on 1 April 1930, and was interred the following day in Beth David Cemetery in Elmont, Nassau Co., New York.

CHAPTER 15

RED RIVER LANDING – TORRAS – THREE RIVERS

> Here, at the mouth of Red River, is the site of a future city of some importance. It is the lowest conveniently accessible crossing place of travelers by land into the lower interior of Louisiana, and through to Texas. It is a great place of transhipment [*sic*] of goods, which are landed here by steamers coming down and going up the Mississippi, to be taken off by the Atchafalaya and Red River boats. Vast quantities of freight are thus deposited here, and the wharf-boat (the hull of the *Laurel Hill* steamer) is one of the largest and most admirably conducted on the river. (Dorr, J.W. "Louisiana in Slices," New Orleans *Crescent*, 17 May 1860.)

Although located more than five miles east of the mouth of the Red River, the principal Mississippi River port for northern Pointe Coupée Parish was called Red River Landing. Midway between the two places Three Rivers was located, so named because it was the juncture of the Red flowing from the north, the Atchafalaya flowing south, and Lower Old River, a remnant of a sharp bend cut off by Captain Shreve in 1831 which connected the two with the Mississippi River.

Miguel and Joseph Torras, natives of Barcelona, Spain, established a business at Red River Landing in 1845 and operated there for decades. A wharf boat, which rose and fell with the stages of the Mississippi, was also another early feature of the community. On it were two structures: a warehouse for the storage of freight in transit and a hotel operated by L.G. Picou & Co., for travelers. An old French plate glass mirror, treasured in the nearby store of George W. Reagan well into the 20th century, was a relic of and attested to the lavish appointments of the floating hotel.

The island formed by Shreve's cutoff to the north, called Turnbull Island, continued to be legally part of West Feliciana Parish, although the bulk of the neighboring parish was east of the Mississippi. The island was populated, cultivated, had a sugar mill, and was connected socially and commercially with Pointe Coupée Parish. The sharp peninsula which was part of Concordia Parish to the northeast of Turnbull was officially known as Carr Point, but nicknamed Monkey Point by local residents for the wheeled monkey cage of the renowned W.W. Cole Circus which accidentally slipped off a barge during an 1880s tour, necessitating the monkeys' rescue.

Many serious river accidents occurred in the vicinity, including the collision of the *DeSoto* and the *Buckeye* in 1844, in which as many as 80 passengers, including many enslaved people were drowned. Fire consumed French's *New Sensation* showboat at Elmwood Landing on the Atchafalaya in 1900, in which all the scenery, properties and wardrobe were also destroyed. Four days after the 1 May 1912 breach of the Lower Old River levee at Torras, the Louisville & Nashville Railroad transfer boat *William Edenborn* sank and remained pinned against the piers of the Texas & Pacific railroad bridge in front of the town. Three days before the Atchafalaya levee broke at McCrea on 24 May 1927, the relief boat *Thomas Buckingham*, transporting laborers and materials to the doomed site, struck the combination rail and vehicular bridge then under construction between Legonier in Pointe Coupée Parish with Simmesport in Avoyelles Parish, further delaying completion of the bridge.

Before the 1912 flood, northeastern Pointe Coupée Parish suffered an unprecedented number of levee failures along Lower Old River and the Mississippi in March 1882, the most severe of which was the loss of one mile of levee at Smithland, near the upper juncture of Raccourci-Old River. The Kingsbury & Cornwell warehouse in that river landing community was swept far inland by the onrush of water.

Tropical storms have often maintained hurricane force winds and caused considerable damage and destruction as far as northernmost Pointe Coupée. During the August 1888 hurricane, winds estimated at seventy-five miles per hour blew down several buildings on the Joseph Torras property near Red River Landing. More severe was the notorious "Grand Isle Hurricane" of September 1909, in which Pointe Coupée Parish suffered fifteen hours of wind, maxing out at eighty-five miles per hour. In addition to heavy damage in New Roads, Morganza, and Lottie, the Red River Landing-Torras community sustained considerable destruction at that time. George W. Reagan's landmark store near Red River Landing was downed, and the Sommer and Herzog stores in Torras were significantly damaged. Telephone and telegraph poles were toppled and lines cut by the winds as far north as Lettsworth. Parish crops suffered enormously, with sugar cane flattened and cotton bolls whipped from their stalks in the storm.

To the northwest of Red River Landing, at the place, where the newly-opened Texas & Pacific branch railroad crossed Lower Old River, Nathanial P. Phillips, the grandson of Joseph Torras, established the town of Torras in 1902. General and grocery stores, operated principally by Jewish merchants, as well as pharmacies, saloons and hotels opened in rapid succession. The Union Oil Co., a processor of cottonseed oil, was a major employer. Hundreds of persons lived in the area: in Torras proper, on the remainder of Lafayette Plantation where the town had been developed, and on surrounding plantations, including Tanglewood to the west and Pike's Peak to the south. St. Joseph Catholic Church and Cemetery and St. Cecilia Hall were located near the juncture of Lower Old River and the Mississippi, on property that had been donated by Joseph Torras. A ferry crossed the Mississippi between that neighborhood and Angola in West Feliciana Parish where the Louisiana State Penitentiary is located.

MARX MEYER

Marx Meyer, a native of Bavaria and former member of the mercantile and planting partnership of Meyer & Strauss on Pointe Coupée Road, was identified in the 1870 United States Federal Census as a dry goods merchant with $1,000 personal property next to planter William C. Gay near Red River Landing on the Mississippi River. Three doors from Meyer in the opposite direction was twenty-six-year-old David F. Horton, identified as clerking in a retail store, likely Meyer's employee. Meyer apparently discontinued business there within the next few years, because he was not listed amongst the holders of Parish Licenses for the year 1872 as recorded in the Minutes of the Pointe Coupée Parish Police Jury.

LEON MOÏSE/MOYSE

Leon Moyse was born Léon Moïse on 15 August 1841, at Condé-Northen, Moselle, France, to Joseph Moïse and his wife, Henriette Levy. Leon indicated in the 1900 United States Federal Census that he had immigrated in 1866 and had since been naturalized. By 1870 he was enumerated at Black Hawk Point in Concordia Parish, Louisiana, where he was working as a merchant.

Moyse served as Postmaster of Black Hawk, Louisiana, from 6 February 1871 until 27 August 1872. During that time, Moise was married on 7 March 1872, in New Orleans by Rabbi J.L. Leucht to Caroline "Carrie" Levy, who had been born in 1854, in the Kingdom of Bavaria. According to Carrie's obituary, she and her brother Leopold H. Levy immigrated to America in their youth, following the deaths of their parents, Feistel Levy and his wife, Caroline Langfeld (probably Lengsfeld intended). The Moise-Levy pre-nuptial contract stipulated that Caroline brought the sum of $3,000 cash into the marriage. A copy of the instrument was filed in the conveyance records of the Pointe Coupée Parish Clerk of Court in New Roads in 1874.

Soon after marriage, Leon and Carrie moved downriver to Red River Landing in Upper Pointe Coupée. The Police Jury minutes indicate that "Moïse Levy" (*sic*) received two licenses during the period 1 April -1 July 1872, in the amounts of $30 and $25, to operate a retail store and sell liquor. A person of that name did have a business interest in the area, as a partner in Sandman-Gunst & Co. at Merrick, Louisiana, but some three decades after the above license was issued. We believe that it is possible that the name "Léon Moïse" was intended for the license but entered in error in the Police Jury record.

In 1873, Leon Moyse acted as agent and attorney for his brother-in-law Leopold H. Levy of New Orleans in the sale from Levy to Mrs. M. Bell Bunch, widow of Suprez W. Bunch, of a 140-acre tract on the west bank of Bayou Lettsworth, for $2,500 cash.

New Orleans wholesale grocers Lehman, Goudchaux & Co. filed suit against Leon Moyse in the 7th Judicial District Court in New Roads in 1875. This file, No.1733, which cannot be located in the Pointe Coupée Parish Clerk of Court's holdings at this time, might have given us some illustration of Moyse's retail career at the important Southern port of Red River Landing.

Moyse took Charles J. Batchelor, a local planter, to court, (Late Parish Court, No. 683), in 1875 over an unpaid promissory note for $170.26, at eight percent interest from 1 January 1874. The suit record includes an itemized statement, totaling $8.15 for goods sold by Moyse to Batchelor in March-April 1874, which included two violin strings, a barrel of (corn) meal, a box of G.D. (gun) caps, two pint-bottles and two gallons of whiskey.

Léon and Carrie Moyse were the parents of seven children: Julius Leon (b. 1874), Ferdinand (b. 1878), Helen (b. 1879), Sidney Lloyd (b. 1883) Milton Myer (b. 1885), Irene (b. 1889), and Isadore (b. 1892). Only Jules was born in Louisiana, just prior to the suit filed against Moyse by Lehman, Godchaux & Co., after which the family relocated to Greenville, Washington Co., Mississippi. Léon Moyse, his wife Carrie, and children: Julius, Ferdinand and Helen were enumerated in the 1880 United States Federal Census for Greenville, where Leon was working as a dry goods merchant. Branching out into agriculture in the rich Mississippi Delta outside the city, Leon was enumerated as a planter in the 1900 United States Federal Census. He died in Greenville on 22 January 1906, and was buried in the city's Jewish Cemetery.

Outliving her husband by more than 40 years, and surviving the great flood of 1927 which proved disastrous for Greenville, Caroline "Carrie" Levy Moyse died there on 13 August 1948, and was interred with Leon. The Greenville *Delta Times-Democrat* dated 15 August 1948, described Mrs. Levy as "one of the city's most beloved residents," who had been active in many civic welfare projects as well as an organizer and the oldest member of the Temple Sisterhood of Hebrew Union Congregation.

ISRAËL and ISIDORE LOWENTHAL

Israël Lowenthal was born on 14 August 1837, in the Free City of Hamburg, German Confederation, to Meyer Lowenthal and a mother whose identity we could not locate. Israël, who immigrated to America ca. 1857, was a well-known dry goods merchant in Vicksburg, Warren Co., Mississippi. Lowenthal's wife, née Celia Marx/Marks, had been born on 18 October 1843, in Hamburg, Germany, to Reuben Marks and Rebecca Dresdner. Israël and Celia took out a license to be married at New Orleans on 1 April 1864, with her father, Reuben Marx as a witness. (Note: Sixty-year-old Reuben Marks died at Vicksburg on 23 August 1878, from yellow fever and was interred there at Anshe Chesed Cemetery.)

Israël, Celia, and their children: Rebecca (b. 1865), Joseph (b. 1867), Annie (b. 1869), Isidore (b. 1870), Lillie (b. 1872), Meyer (b. 1875), and Moses (b. 1876), lived near Red River Landing on the Mississippi River in Pointe Coupée Parish during the 1870s, where they operated a general store. The 1876-1877 edition of Bouchereau's *Statement of the Sugar Crops Made in Louisiana* featured an advertisement for I. Lowenthal's store near Red River Landing. His merchandise included dry goods, notions, hats, boots, shoes, groceries, wines, liquors, crockery, hardware, and saddlery.

The Lowenthal family eventually moved to Memphis, Shelby Co., Tennessee, where Israël died on 7 December 1920. His widow, Celia Marks Lowenthal, followed him in death on 18 September 1925. They were both interred in Anshe Chesed Cemetery in Vicksburg, Mississippi.

Their son, Isidore Lowenthal, who was born on 23 September 1870, in Vicksburg, succeeded his father as a merchant in northernmost Pointe Coupée Parish, but died on 3 September 1892, and was also interred in Anshe Chesed Cemetery at Vicksburg.

ALEX MANN & CO., "MERRICK STORE"

Alexander "Alex" Mann was formerly a merchant in Baton Rouge, after which he opened numerous stores in Pointe Coupée Parish including, the "Red Store" on Pointe Coupée Road, and the "New Orleans Cheap Store" in Waterloo. The firm of Alex Mann & Co. operated the "Merrick Store" on the plantation and in the community of that name on Lower Old River during the 1880s. The 1 January 1881 *Pointe Coupée Banner* identified Alex Mann in the list of Parish License holders. Mann paid $60 to operate as a retail merchant and $20 to sell bottled liquors. Mann & Co.'s merchandise rose in assessed value in the Pointe Coupée Parish Tax Roll from $2,250 in 1882 to $2,500 in 1884. Mann also had a retail presence in nearby West Feliciana Parish, where his employees staffed a general mercantile establishment. Alex Mann's sons, Dave S. and Daniel E. Mann, followed in the family retail tradition, and by 1903 had interests in three stores in the Merrick area.

WEINBERG & MANN

Weinberg & Mann was the partnership of general merchants and patent medicine proprietors Harry A. Weinberg and his Mann in-laws at Merrick, Louisiana, on Lower Old River in the 1890s. Harry Abraham Weinberg was born in May 1862, at Baltimore City, Maryland, to Abraham Weinberg and his wife, only identified as Rachel, natives of Poland, Kingdom of Prussia.

Harry Weinberg was married on 25 June 1888, in West Feliciana Parish, Louisiana, to Fanny Mann, who had been born ca. 1862 in New Orleans, to prominent South Louisiana merchant Alexander "Alex" Mann and his wife, Theresa Hausmann. Fannie's siblings included merchants Benjamin, David, Daniel and, Max Mann, and Sena Mann Lehman.

An 1891 *Pointe Coupée Banner* advertisement for Weinberg & Mann, at Merrick, Louisiana, proclaimed:

> Sole proprietors of Mann's Cream Liniment, For External and Internal Use, "a certain cure" for sprains, burns, sores, toothache, headache, neuralgia, sore throat, also for colic and botts in horses and mules, and "a dead shot" on screw worms, sold at stores and druggists, 50 cents and 25 cents.

Harry and Fannie were the parents of two children born in Louisiana: Joseph Lionel (b. 1889), and Julius Abram (b. 1893). Harry and Fannie Mann Weinberg moved to his native Baltimore, Maryland, before the birth of their third child, Hilda Theresa (b. 1895), where he was manufacturing umbrellas. Harry died in Baltimore on 24 February 1932, and was interred there in the Hebrew Friendship Cemetery. Fannie died in the city on 6 May 1949, and was buried with her husband.

DANIEL E. and DAVID S. MANN

D.E. & D.S. Mann, general merchants headquartered on Lower Old River at Merrick, Louisiana, had interests in three stores by 1903. Their first store had gross sales of $19,000 in 1900, and D.E. Mann paid $110 for a Parish License to operate in the following year. Another store, Mann & Carpenter, opened in 1901 with a $165 Parish License, according to the 23 March 1902 issue of the *Pointe Coupée Banner*.

Brothers Daniel E. and David S. Mann were sons of prominent Pointe Coupée and West Feliciana Parish merchant Alexander "Alex" Mann and Theresa Hausmann. David was born on 22 March 1866 (1 April 1865 on gravestone), and Daniel on 11 November 1870, both in New Orleans, Louisiana. Popularly known as "Dave" and "Dan," the Mann brothers employed their twenty-year-old nephew Joseph Levy, son of Maurice Cerf Levy and their sister Henriette Mann, as a clerk who boarded with them according to the 1900 United States Federal Census.

In a 1904 *Pointe Coupée Banner* notice, D.E. Mann called for customers to settle their accounts, as he and brother were moving their business and residences to Alexandria, Rapides Parish, Louisiana. In Alexandria, they operated as the Mann Bros., at the intersection of Third and Murray Streets, and continued in business, offering their own brand of clothing, until the 1920s (*Daily Town Talk*, Alexandria, Louisiana, various issues). Ben Mann came up from Bayou Sara to join Dan Mann in business after their brother Dave's death in 1914.

Both brothers married in Alexandria in 1905. Daniel was wed on 7 June to Bertha Rosenthal, born at Alexandria on 6 January 1876, to pioneer grocer Moses Rosenthal, a native of Oberlauterbach, Bas-Rhin, France, and his wife, Regina Bloom, born in Ingenheim, Rheinpfalz, Germany. David Mann was married on 26 November 1905, to Julia Malachowsky, born in Alexandria on 25 February 1887, to Joseph Malachowsky, a native of Poland, and his wife, Cecilia Weil. Julia's mother, Cecilia, a native of Louisiana, born either at Alexandria, Rapides Parish, or at Marksville, Avoyelles Parish, ca. 1860, was the daughter of longtime Alexandria merchant Edward Weil and his wife, Fannie Beer, both immigrants from Ingenheim, Rheinpfalz, Germany.

David S. "Dave" Mann was a member of the Knights of Pythias, Benevolent & Protective Order of Elks, and the Alexandria Retail Merchants' Association. He died on 6 April 1914, in Alexandria, and was interred in the Jewish Cemetery across the Red River in Pineville, Rapides Parish, Louisiana. Dave and Julia never had children. His widow, née Julia Malachowsky, styled herself as Julia Malcoskey Mann, the thirty-year-old widow of David Stuart Mann of Warrenton, Virginia, in order to marry again to John Weedman Brodix, personal secretary of New York City financial mogul Cornelius Vanderbilt, whom the Weedman family described as more of a "companion" than an employee, on 16 October 1923, in Manhattan, New York. The couple sailed on 10 November of the same year, for an extensive tour of Europe and the British Isles.

According to the 1930 and 1940 United States Federal Censuses for Manhattan, New York, Julia Mann, a widow, was living with her two sisters, Rita and Edna Walker-Malcoskey, neither of whom ever married, at the posh Stanhope Hotel located at No. 995 Fifth Avenue. Edna was a famous poet, novelist and lyricist who made her fortune writing "racy" (for the time) novels that appealed to the "liberated" women during the "roaring twenties. Both Julia, whose date of death we could not locate, and Edna, who died on 4 Jan 1969, in Manhattan, were interred in the Catholic Cemetery at Natchitoches, Natchitoches Parish, Louisiana.

Daniel E. "Dan" Mann's first wife, Bertha Rosenthal, was gunned down in Alexandria on 29 January 1916. Their seven-year-old daughter, Regina, who answered the door to the intruder and was shot first, survived the attack. Bertha Mann was interred in the Jewish Cemetery in Pineville, Rapides Parish. Daniel was married to his late wife's half-first cousin, Essie Rosenthal, on 25 October 1925, at the bride's home in Alexandria. Essie was born on 27 September 1883, to pioneer Alexandria grocer, Jonas Rosenthal, a native of Oberlauterbach, Bas-Rhin, France, and his wife, Jeanette Weil, born in Ingenheim, Rheinpfalz, Germany.

Daniel Mann died on 7 May 1949, in Lafayette, Lafayette Parish, Louisiana, and was buried in the Jewish Cemetery in Pineville. Essie Rosenthal Mann died in Alexandria on 16 April 1974, and was interred with her husband. Dan's daughter, Regina Mann died on 18 May 2004, in Galveston, Galveston Co., Texas, at the age of 95. The widow of Alex Kottwitz, the couple never had children.

SANDMAN-GUNST & CO.

Sandman-Gunst & Co., Limited were general retail merchants at Merrick, Louisiana, on Lower Old River, chartered on 2 February 1897, for a term of five years. Having an initial capital of $5,000, the company was represented by its organizers and shareholders: Alexander Henry

Sandman of Woodville, Mississippi, Préciosa G. Gunst of Pointe Coupée Parish, wife separate in property from Israël Gunst; and Moïse Levy of New Orleans. A copy of the charter was published in the 20 March 1897 issue of the *Pointe Coupée Banner*.

The identity of Moïse Levy, the New Orleans partner of Sandman-Gunst & Co., remains unclear at present. An individual of that name was indicated in the Pointe Coupée Parish Police Jury Minutes as receiving two licenses during the period 1 April -1 July 1872, in the amounts of $30 and $25, to operate a retail store and sell liquor. It is more likely that the name Léon Moïse was intended, as the latter commenced business near Red River Landing in that year.

Alexander Henry Sandman was born on 5 June 1851, in the District of Columbia, to Alexander Henry Sandman, Sr. and Rachel Roeschen, natives of Poland, Prussian Empire. Moving south, Alexander was married on 1 October 1890, in Woodville, Wilkinson County, Mississippi, to Tressa Gunst, the daughter of merchant Jakov Gunst, born ca. 4 October 1806, in the Kingdom of Hanover, and Miriam "Mary" Silverman, born in the Rheinpfalz, Germany, ca. 3 July 1820. Tressa was born in Bangor, Penobscot Co., Maine, on 27 March 1853.

Alexander, Tressa and their son, Percy, age three, were enumerated in Woodville, Wilkinson Co., Mississippi, in the 1900 United States Federal Census, where Sandman worked as a "barkeep" to support his family as well as his wife's widowed sister Hannah Gunst, the widow of Percy T. Joseph, and her three children. Ten years later, he was still supporting his wife, their son Percy, his sister-in-law, Hannah Gunst Joseph, and her daughter, Percye, as a produce buyer.

Préciosa Gonzalvo Henriqués was born on 31 October 1868, in Philadelphia, Philadelphia Co., Pennsylvania, to retail grocer Isaac Henriqués, a native of Jamaica, British West Indies, and Elisabeth Hickey, born in Pennsylvania. Préciosa was married on 23 February 1886, in New Orleans, Louisiana, to Israël Gunst, the son of Miriam Silverman and her husband, Jakov Gunst, the brother of Tressa Gunst Sandman. Israël was born on 19 April 1848, at Bangor, Penobscot Co., Maine, and had operated stores in Atlanta, Georgia, and in Woodville, Mississippi, before he and Préciosa moved to Pointe Coupée Parish, Louisiana in the 1890s.

Gross sales for Sandman-Gunst & Co. in 1900 amounted to $9,536.40. The firm paid $110 for the Parish License to operate in 1901, according to the 23 March 1902 *Pointe Coupée Banner*. Company letterhead and statements found in the few civil suits to which the firm was a party indicate that the merchandise carried included dry goods, clothing, hats, boots, shoes, staple and fancy groceries, liquors, harness, and burlap bagging. As did other firms of the time, Sandman-Gunst & Co. offered the "Highest Market Price" for cotton.

Sandman-Gunst & Co. also invested in real estate. In 1900, the firm purchased Section 34-T2S-R7E, containing 213.70 acres from J.W. Courège. The company sold the property to Isaac H. Hagan two years later, in 1902, as part of Sandman-Gunst & Co.'s liquidation of debts and liabilities.

Israël Gunst was afforded a biographical note and photograph in the July 1903 edition of *Men and Matters* magazine devoted to Pointe Coupée Parish, Louisiana. Although his wife, Préciosa, was the "Gunst" member of the firm of Sandman-Gunst & Co. at Merrick, Israël was described as a merchant. However, the article mentioned that his "pleasant home" was presided over by "a wife who is one of the handsomest women in the parish and a most charming lady."

Two years after the expiration of the corporation of Sandman-Gunst & Co., Israël Gunst, still living at Merrick, Louisiana, filed for personal bankruptcy in United States District Court. A copy of the District Court's 5 April 1904 ruling on behalf of Gunst's petition was published in the 20 April edition of the *Pointe Coupée Banner*.

Préciosa and Israël Gunst and their only child, Maude Henrietta, born on 6 June 1887, in Woodville, Wilkinson Co., Mississippi, moved to New Orleans, where they were enumerated in the 1910 United States Federal Census. Israël was said to be living on his own income. A decade later, however, he was operating a rooming house.

Israël Gunst died in New Orleans on 17 October 1929, and was interred in Beth Israël Cemetery in Woodville, Mississippi. His widow, Préciosa Gonzalvo Henriqués, died on 5 May 1951, also in New Orleans, and was interred with Israël in Woodville, Mississippi. Her widowed mother, Elisabeth Hickey Henriqués, had lived with Préciosa and family in New Orleans according to both the 1920 and 1930 United States Federal Censuses.

Alexander Henry Sandman, the former senior partner of Sandman-Gunst & Co., died on 28 April 1919, in Woodville, Wilkinson Co., Mississippi, and was interred there in Beth Israël Cemetery. His widow, née Tressa Gunst, died on 12 January 1928, also in Woodville, and was interred with Alexander.

L. & S. SOMMER, "THE LEADER STORE"

BOUGHT OF L. & S. SOMMER,
—DEALERS IN—
Dry Goods, Clothing, Notions, Hats, Boots and Shoes,
GROCERIES, LIQUORS, TOBACCO, CIGARS, ETC., ETC.

Beloved Louisiana dry goods and clothing merchants Leopold "Lep" and Sylvan "Syl" Sommer, were born at Schirrhoffen, Bas-Rhin, France: Leopold on 20 November 1874, and Sylvain on 9 September 1876, to Adolph Sommer and Valerie Braun, both natives of the town. Sylvan "Syl" Sommer arrived at New York, on 21 November 1892, from Le Havre, France, aboard the *SS La Champagne*, He lived for six years in Mississippi where he was naturalized in Fayette, Jefferson Co. He moved to Louisiana in 1898, and settled at Kahns, West Baton Rouge Parish, Louisiana, to work for the Kahn Brothers, who were also Schirrhoffen natives.

Syl Sommer was enumerated in the 1900 United States Federal Census as a clerk for enterprising merchants Jacques Welsch and Emanuel Levy, likewise natives of Schirrhoffen, in Ward 3, West Baton Rouge Parish. In 1915, the latter firm bought the three-story Fisher Building, formerly the S. I. Raymond department store, at the southwest corner of Main and Third Streets in Baton Rouge from regional businessman and financier Joseph Gottlieb, where they prospered for generations as Welsh & Levy men's and boys' wear.

In the meantime, Sylvan Sommer joined his brother Leopold "Lep" Sommer in 1903 to open "The Leader" store, L. & S. Sommer, props., in the year-old community of Torras, Pointe Coupée Parish, Louisiana. While specializing in the sale of quality dry goods and notions, clothing, hats, boots and shoes, the Sommers' company letterhead indicates that they also carried groceries, liquors, tobacco and cigars. The 1906 promotional publication *Beautiful Pointe*

Coupée and Its Prominent Citizens stated that the brothers "do a large advancing business and are heavy buyers of cotton."

Interior of the Leader Store, Leopold and Sylvain Sommer, proprietors. Original photo in *Beautiful Pointe Coupée and Her Prominent Citizens* (J.I. Sanford, 1906).

Sylvain Sommer returned to France in 1905 where he married his second cousin, Marguerite Kahn. The bride was born Marie Kahn on 16 December 1886, at Schirrhoffen, Bas-Rhin, France, to Heymann Kahn, a native of the town, and his second wife, Rachel Dreyfuss, born at Osthoffen, Bas-Rhin. Marguerite was the half-sister of Charles, Gus, and Seligman "Sol" Kahn, of Kahns, West Baton Rouge Parish, for whom Sylvain had previously worked. Sylvain, his mother, Valerie Braun Sommer, and his nineteen-year-old bride Marguerite, arrived in New York on 22 November 1905, aboard the *SS Kaiser Wilhelm der Grosse.* They returned to Torras, Pointe Coupée Parish, where their only child, Adolph N. Sommer, was born on 12 August 1906.

Marguerite Kahn, later Mrs. Sylvain Sommer. Original photo in *Beautiful Pointe Coupée and Her Prominent Citizens* (J.I. Sanford, 1906).

Leopold "Lep" Sommer, preceding his brother by one year, arrived in New York from Antwerp, Belgium, on 20 August 1891, aboard the *SS Westernland*. Leopold started his Louisiana career in 1900 as a clerk for Abraham Klotz, a native of Uhrwiller, Bas-Rhin, France, at Klotzville, Assumption Parish, Louisiana. Shortly thereafter, Lep moved to Hohen Solms, Ascension Parish, Louisiana, where he met Henrietta "Hattie" Moyse, a native of Donaldsonville, Ascension Parish. They were wed on 18 June 1902, at St. Gabriel, Iberville Parish. Hattie had been born at Donaldsonville on 7 November 1880, to merchant Simon Moyse, a native of Nancy, Meurthe-et-Moselle, France and his wife, Flora Joseph, born Fleurette Joseph on 5 March 1854, at Grosbliederstroff, Moselle, France, to Isaac Joseph and his wife Zippert (Caroline) Gottschott. (Note: Flora Joseph Moyse was the sister of Joseph Jules Joseph, whose son Léon Joseph was a prominent insurance agent who worked at New Roads, Pointe Coupée Parish, at the turn of the twentieth century.) A successful Ascension Parish general merchant, Simon Moyse owned stores simultaneously in Donaldsonville and its upriver suburb of Smoke Bend in the 1880s. He established his Donaldsonville business with merchandise surrendered at a sheriff's sale by Gottschalk "Cheap Charley" Feitel. The latter was an uncle of New Roads insurance agent Leon Joseph, son of Gottschalk's sister Bertha Feitel and her second husband, Joseph Jules Joseph.

Leopold "Lep" Sommer

Original photo in *Beautiful Pointe Coupée and Her Prominent Citizens* (J.I. Sanford, 1906).

Lep and Hattie's first child, Lydie, was born at St. Gabriel on 6 May 1903. Their second child, Rachel "Ray" Sommer, was born at Torras on 8 January 1906.

In addition to the store, L. & S. Sommer operated a saloon in another of their buildings. This enterprise ended in December 1908, however, when an early-morning fire beginning in Thomas Goldman's adjacent general store, resulted in the total destruction of Goldman's store and the Sommers's saloon.

With the continued economic distress begun with the arrival of the boll weevil in Pointe Coupée Parish, Louisiana, and the net value of company down to about $4,000, the Sommer mercantile business was reorganized in 1910, with Leopold Sommer acquiring full interest. Sylvain, Marguerite and their son Adolph, left Torras in 1911, to return to Kahns, West Baton Rouge Parish, to work with Marguerite's half-brothers.

Seriously hampered again by the epic flood occasioned by the levee breach nearby in 1912, Leopold Sommer stuck it out for a year or so at Torras, but finally moved his family to Baton Rouge, Louisiana, where he opened the "Lep Sommer" men's clothing store in the former Andrew Jackson hardware building in the 500 block of Main Street. Rapidly increasing in scope, Lep Sommer moved to the 300 block of Main, a few doors east of the city's largest department store, Rosenfield's, in 1916. He added a ladies' ready-to-wear department in 1917, and a second-floor section for piece goods in 1918. One of the region's most popular department stores, whose clientele included many shoppers from Pointe Coupée, Sommer's was doubled in size in 1920. The ladies' ready-to-wear and millinery departments were moved to the second floor, and an elevator was installed.

Railroad collapse near Lep Sommer's "Leader Store" at Torras in 1912.

Within a few years, however, Leopold Sommer began to scale back his operations. In 1925, he closed out the men's and boys' clothing and furnishing departments as well as the entire shoe department, to concentrate his efforts in women's, misses' and children's ready-to-wear and millinery. The last advertisements for Sommer's on Main Street appeared in the 1926 Baton Rouge *State-Times*. A branch of the Handelman's regional chain department store headquartered on Dryades Street in New Orleans soon assumed Sommer's former location.

In 1927, Leopold Sommer opened "The Fashion" ladies' apparel store in the 1900 block of North Street. After placing only a few ads in the Baton Rouge papers, the store was closed, and his quarter-century retail career ended. Leopold "Lep" Sommer died on 11 December 1932, in Baton Rouge, and was interred there in the Jewish Cemetery. Hattie Moyse Sommer died on 6 November 1973, at Baton Rouge, and was interred with her husband.

Meanwhile, Leopold Sommer's brother and former business partner at Torras, Sylvan "Syl" Sommer had remained at Kahns, West Baton Rouge Parish, and was identified as a merchant at Kahns in his World War I Draft Registration filed in 1918. He served as Postmaster at Kahns, Louisiana, from 1911 until 1928. By the time of the 1930 United States Federal Census, "Syl" Sommer had moved his family to Rayne, Acadia Parish, Louisiana, where he joined Sol and Charles Kahn in the "Sol Kahn Company" department store, which had been established in 1916. Following the deaths of the Kahns, Sommer sold the business to Julius Weill, Leonard Levy and Phillip Barbier of White Castle, Iberville Parish, Louisiana, who reorganized it into a unit of their popular Weill's Department Store chain.

Sylvan "Syl" Sommer died 6 March 1962, in Rayne, and was interred in the Jewish Cemetery in Baton Rouge. His widow, Marguérite Kahn, died in Rayne on 23 July 1976, and was interred with her husband in Baton Rouge.

SOMMER & TAYLOR PLANTING COMPANY, LTD.

Torras, Louisiana merchant Leopold "Lep" Sommer branched out into local agriculture through the establishment of the Sommer & Taylor Planting Company, Limited. Although documentation of this enterprise is sparse, it is known that Sommer was president of the firm, and his partner was likely James J. Taylor, who was enumerated as a farmer nearby in Ward 1 in the 1900 United States Federal Census.

Based on the dates in which Sommer and Taylor were defendants in civil suits, it is highly probable that they engaged in the cultivation of cotton, and suffered from the boll weevil infestation. Postlethwaite and Chase Co., of Natchez, Mississippi, were awarded a judgment (21st Judicial District Court, No. 1906) against Sommer and Taylor in the amount of $491.48, with eight percent interest from 15 November 1906, for an unpaid promissory note. Pointe Coupée Parish Deputy Sheriff J. Lamartine Langlois served a copy of the citation and petition on S.P. Ginn (Stanhope P. Ginn, Williamsport Postmaster, appointed in 1905), who was, at that time, in the "domicile of Sommer and Taylor."

In another judgment, (21st Judicial District Court, No. 1141), Raccourci Company Limited, headquartered in West Feliciana Parish, was awarded amounts owed them by Sommer and Taylor as follows: $1,242.66, at eight percent interest from 1905, less a credit of $585; and $5,120.99, at eight percent interest from 1906. Owing to Sommer and Taylor's inability to pay those amounts, a writ of *fieri facias* was entered on 21 October 1908. No further evidence of the existence of Sommer and Taylor Planting Company has been located.

THOMAS GOLDMAN

General merchant Thomas Goldman, his wife, Celia Friedberg, and their children moved from Bayou Lettsworth, Pointe Coupée Parish, to the promising but ill-fated nearby community of Torras, ca. 1904. Their last child, Sarah was born there on 3 April 1907. Between August and October 1908, Goldman advertised frequently in the *Pointe Coupée Banner* touting his line of wallpaper. He claimed that $10 worth of paper was enough to cover one room. As a sales incentive, he declared he would give one roll of wallpaper for each $1 that a customer spent in his store.

OFFICE OF
T. GOLDMAN,
GENERAL MERCHANDISE
AND PLANTER

CARLES PLANTATION
CLEMENCE PLANTATION
COURTNEY PLANTATION
OGLETHORPE PLANTATION
JAMES PLANTATION
COLE PLANTATION
DELOACHE PLANTATION
ST PAUL PLANTATION

Torras, La., 2/18 190 8

December 1908 was to be a fateful month for Thomas Goldman, and Upper Pointe Coupée, as three destructive fires occurred within a few days. The 12 December issue of the *Pointe Coupée Banner* reported that a 5 a.m. blaze broke out in the Goldman store resulting in its complete destruction, at a loss of more than $15,000 worth of property, as well as the adjacent saloon owned and operated by L. & S. Sommer.

By 1910, Goldman, his wife, Celia, and their children had providentially moved, in light of the destruction to come to Torras in 1912, to Houston, Harris Co., Texas, where he was enumerated as a restaurant owner in the United States Federal Census of that year. Ten years later, the family had relocated to New Orleans, Louisiana, where Goldman worked as a junk dealer.

Thomas Goldman died on the anniversary of the 1815 American victory at the Battle of New Orleans on 8 January 1927, in New Orleans. He was buried there in Gates of Prayer Cemetery. His widow, née Celie Friedberg, died on 1 November 1943, in Rodessa, Caddo Parish, Louisiana, where she had lived with her daughter Sarah Goldman, the wife of Arthur Scheff. Celia Goldman was laid to rest with her husband, Thomas, in Gates of Prayer Cemetery in New Orleans.

ABRAHAM HERZOG AND HERZOG BROS. & CO.

In the wake of the 1903 failure of the Lettsworth Station firm of L. Fishman & Co., in which Louis Fishman and Abraham Joel Herzog had been partners, Herzog and his family moved a few miles northeast to the growing community of Torras. Abraham opened a store there as sole proprietor, but had to close in 1908 due to a judgment rendered against him in a suit filed by Henry Lochte Co., Ltd. (21st Judicial District Court, No. 1492; suit file missing). Soon afterward, Charles Eli, Samuel, and Miss Mattie Herzog, three of Abraham Herzog's children by his first wife, Sarah Yetta Goldman, opened a new store as "Herzog Bros. & Co." in a building owned by Torras community founder Nathanial P. Phillips. It was located next to the J. Feduccia store and only 400 to 500 feet from the Herzog residence.

Mattie Herzog was born on 2 July 1883, Samuel on 14 October 1887, and Charles Eli on 24 August 1888, all in Vilna, Lithuania, Russian Empire. Samuel Herzog was identified as a clerk for his maternal uncle Thomas Goldman when the latter operated a store on Bayou Lettsworth, according to the 1900 United States Federal Census.

After a brief period of operation, Herzog Bros. & Co. were taken to court by the Bank of New Roads (21st Judicial District Court, No. 1461) at which time Eli and Samuel Herzog were identified as residents of Avoyelles Parish, Louisiana, and Mattie of Pointe Coupée. Two years later, in 1910, the court ruled in favor of the bank's petition for judgment against the three siblings in the amounts of $800 at eight percent interest from 14 September, less a credit of $107.30, and $300 at eight percent interest from 9 August 1908; and ten percent of the aggregate, for notes assigned the bank by Herzog Bros. & Co. under said terms.

Abraham Herzog, his second wife, Mary Sneike, and children moved to Oakdale, Allen Parish, Louisiana, where he was identified in the 1920 United States Federal Census as the owner of a retail store and "rust" (i.e., salvaged metal) shop. Living with them were Abraham's son by his first marriage, Louis, age 18, employed as clerk in a fruit stand, and Abraham and Mary's four and one-half-year-old daughter, Celie Herzog.

Louis Herzog died on 23 October 1924, unmarried, and was interred in Ahavas Sholem Cemetery in New Orleans. His father, Abraham Joel Herzog, died on 23 May 1929, and was interred in New Orleans in the Ahavas Sholem Cemetery with his first wife. Mary Sneike Herzog died on 3 February 1954, in Escambia Co., Florida, and was interred there at B'nai Israël Cemetery in Pensacola.

Celie "Cindy" Herzog, the only child of Abraham Herzog by his second wife, Mary Sneike, was born on 3 June 1915, probably at Oakdale, Allen Parish. She was married to Sheldon "Joshua Isaac" Chassin, who was born on 17 February 1906, in Birmingham, England, to Simon Chassin and his wife, Ryfka Gordon. Celie and Sheldon Chassin lived in Pensacola, Florida, and owned and operated a number of businesses, including the Imperial Shoe Store and Cindy's Shoe Salon. They later moved to Atlanta, Fulton Co., Georgia, where both died: Sheldon on 15 March 2000, and Celie on 11 June 2004. They were both interred in Ahavas Sholem Cemetery in Pensacola, Escambia Co., Florida.

Samuel Herzog moved to New Orleans, Louisiana, where he was identified in his 1917 World War I Draft Registration as a salesman for Pan American Coffee Co.; in the 1920 United States Federal Census as an insurance agent; and ten years later as a shoe salesman. He was married on 10 June 1923, in New Orleans to Ida Sweig, who had been born on 10 September 1900, in the Russian Empire to Samuel Sweig and Rachel Ingelman. Ida died on 31 August 1966, and Samuel followed 13 December 1971, both in New Orleans, Louisiana. They were interred there in Ahavas Sholem Cemetery.

Charles Eli Herzog was married to Gertrude Sneike-Kling, a native of Louisville, Jefferson Co., Kentucky, the daughter of Moishe Leib Sneike and Chia Smeade-Kling, both natives of Lithuania, Russian Empire, on 26 June 1921, in New Orleans. (Note: The New Orleans marriage record shows her parents as Henry Kling and Sarah Smith, but the 1900 U.S. Federal Census shows Morris and Henrietta Kling. Gertrude was the sister of Mary Sneike, the second wife of Abraham Herzog, Charles Eli's father.) Eli and Gertrude Herzog and their children: Morris (b. 1923), Leon Henry (b. 1925), and Madge (b. 1928), were enumerated in both the 1930 and 1940 United States Federal Censuses in El Dorado, Union Co., Arkansas. Originally a retail grocery owner, the later census recorded that Charles Eli Herzog owned a café.

They eventually moved to Houston, Harris Co., Texas, where Eli operated a restaurant. He died there on 13 April 1962, as a result of an auto accident, and was buried in Houston's Beth Jacob Cemetery. Gertrude died on 13 November 1986, in New Jersey and was interred in the Menorah Cemetery in Clifton, Passaic Co., New Jersey.

M. (MISS MATTIE) HERZOG

In 1908, Eli Herzog, former member of the commercial firm of Herzog Bros. & Co., was granted a license by the Pointe Coupée Parish Police Jury to sell alcoholic beverages at Torras. Subsequent lawsuits filed against his sister, Mattie, and their father, Abraham Herzog, however, called into question the ownership of the Herzog saloon. Frost Bros. a Louisville, Kentucky liquor distiller and wholesaler, received a judgment (21st Judicial District Court, No. 1481) against Miss Mattie Herzog in 1909 in the amount of $143.13 at eight percent interest from 6 July 1908 for liquor purchased.

Later in the year of 1909, Edwin Schiele Distilling Co. of St. Louis, Missouri, lost its case (21st Judicial District Court, No. 1623) against Abraham Herzog for payment of a merchandise account of $637.50, less a credit of $269.70. Witnesses contended that following Abraham's closing of his store at Torras in 1908, his children Eli, Samuel and Mattie Herzog, opened a new store, i.e., Herzog Bros. & Co.

Walter Smith of Baton Rouge, a traveling salesman for Henry Lochte Co., Ltd., stated the Herzog business was a combination store and saloon, and the saloon therein was conducted in the name of Miss M. Herzog. Deputy Sheriff E. B. Genin, a Torras resident who stated he had known Mattie Herzog since before she and her family moved from Bayou Lettsworth to Torras some four to six years prior, contended the saloon was for "colored and white" patrons. Genin continued that he saw Abraham Herzog and sons in the saloon, but never saw Mattie there, let alone operating it.

J. Allie Smith of New Roads, Abraham Herzog's defense attorney, stated that checks made on the saloon's account were made and signed "M. Herzog" by brother Eli Herzog, and Smith added that for a long time he thought "M. Herzog" and Eli were one and the same person. N.P. Phillips, founder of the town of Torras and owner of the building occupied by the Herzogs, testified that he had rented it for about two years to Mattie, but that business transactions were made on her behalf by her father, Abraham Herzog. The court ruled in favor of Abraham Herzog and against the plaintiff, Edwin Schiele Distilling Co., and ordered the suit dismissed at plaintiff's cost.

Just weeks before the levee breach at Torras and destructive flood which ensued, twenty-five-year-old Mattie Herzog married Benjamin Gold, age 24, on 16 April 1912, in New Orleans, Louisiana. Gold, also a native of the Russian Empire, was the son of Aaron Gold and Fannie (no last name available). Mattie died on 29 November 1918, in New Orleans, likely during the influenza pandemic. Benjamin Gold died on 18 February 1946, in New Orleans. Mattie and Benjamin were both interred there in Ahavas Sholem Cemetery.

SELIGMAN "SOL" KAHN

Seligman "Sol" Kahn, was born on 24 August 1875, at Schirrhoffen, Bas-Rhin, France, to Heymann Kahn and his wife, Marie née Kahn, both natives of the town. He followed his brothers, Gustave and Charles Kahn, to Louisiana, arriving at New York on 2 March 1891, aboard the *SS La Champagne*. He worked for several years at Kahns, West Baton Rouge Parish, Louisiana, at his brothers' general store as their clerk.

By 1905, "Sol" Kahn had settled in Torras, Louisiana, where he was a clerk for fellow natives of Schirrhoffen, Lep and Syl Sommer, in "The Leader" store. Sol was Syl Sommer's wife's second cousin. The *Pointe Coupée Banner,* dated 29 July 1905, mentioned that Kahn spent a week at Cooper's Well, near Raymond, Hinds Co., Mississippi, a favorite summertime resort for generations of Pointe Coupéeans during the second half of the 19th and early 20th centuries.

Sol Kahn went into business for himself in 1910 operating a saloon in Torras. The 4 December 1909 *Pointe Coupée Banner* published a notice of his application to sell "spiritous, vinous, malt and alcoholic beverage and liquors generally." The 1912 flood likely spelled the end of this venture.

In 1916, he opened what was to be one of the most successful contemporary department stores in Southwest Louisiana, the Sol Kahn Co. in Rayne, Acadia Parish. His brother Charles Kahn joined Sol in business there, and by the time of the 1930 United States Federal Census, Sylvan "Syl" Sommer, formerly of "The Leader" store in Torras, had become a third partner in the Sol Kahn Co. The Sol Kahn store occupied the northeast corner of East Louisiana and North Adams Avenues in Rayne, while a few doors down, the mammoth Mervine Kahn Co. department store encompassed the eastern half of the block of Louisiana, all the way to the intersection of North Polk Street. No relation to Sol and Charles Kahn, Mervine was born at Plaquemine, Iberville Parish, Louisiana, on 17 February 1855, to Lippman Kahn, a native of Riedseltz, Bas-Rhin, France, and his wife, Fleurette Goudchaux, born at Brumath, Bas-Rhin, France. Fleurette was one of the twenty-three children of Jacques Goudchaux, many of whom were Louisiana residents.

Seligman "Sol" Kahn married Suzanne Kahn/Cohn, the widow of Jacob/Jacques Welsch on 17 August 1927, at Baton Rouge, East Baton Rouge Parish. Suzanne, born on 22 September 1883, at Bischwiller, Bas-Rhin, France, had immigrated with her parents, Heymann Kahn, a native of Herrlisheim, Bas-Rhin, and his wife Palmyre Sommer, born at Schirrhoffen, Bas-Rhin, when she was six years old. Sol and Suzanne had no children. (Note: Suzanne's first husband, Jacob/Jacques Welsch, was also a native of Schirrhoffen, Bas-Rhin, born there on 23 August 1874, to Isaak Welsch and Henriette Levy, both natives of the town. Palmyre Sommer was Leopold and Sylvain Sommer's aunt.)

Sol's brother Charles died on 24 February 1933, at Rayne, and was interred in the Jewish Cemetery at Baton Rouge. Sol died at Natchez, Adams Co., Mississippi, on 7 March 1942, and was interred in the same cemetery. Sol's wife, Suzanne, died on 8 February 1966, in Vicksburg, Warren Co., Mississippi, and was interred with her first husband, Jacques Welsch, also in the Jewish Cemetery at Baton Rouge.

The sole remaining partner of the Sol Kahn Department Store, Sylvan Sommer, sold the business to Julius Weill, Leonard Levy and Phillip Barbier, who integrated the store into their popular Weill's Department Store chain.

BERNARD and HERMAN TEUTSCH

Brothers Bernard and Herman Teutsch, previously merchants in New Roads, on Pointe Coupée Road, and at New Texas above Morganza, were ultimately enumerated in the 1910 United States Federal Census as general merchants at Keller, Louisiana, west of Torras on Lower Old River.

Attesting to Bernard's frequent moves, the Teutsch letterhead, according to exhibits filed in 21st Judicial District Court suits against delinquent credit customers, was that of Bernard's former livery stable in the parish seat, with "New Roads" lined out and "Moreau Plantation" written above in ink. It is likely that the Teutsch brothers' operations on Moreau at Keller ceased as a result of the 1912 flood.

TATAR (ORIGINALLY TATARSKY) BROS. STORES

See all information on the Tatarsky Brothers, including their store located at Torras, in the "Atchafalaya River" section of this book.

I. ROTHSCHILD, "VALLEY MERCANTILE CO."

Isidore Rothschild was born on 1 October 1866, at Nordstetten, Kingdom of Wurttemberg, Germany, to Moses Marx Rothschild and Lea Hirsch. Isidore immigrated to America ca. 16 May 1883, and was naturalized at Woodville, Wilkinson Co., Mississippi, on 18 July 1892. He was married there on 12 February 1895, to Hattie Moses. The bride was born on 26 February 1871, in Peoria, Peoria Co., Illinois, to Rabbi Marx Moses, a native of Essingen, Rheinpfalz, Germany, and Caroline Buchbinder, born at Nuremberg, Rheinpfalz, Germany.

In the first two decades of the twentieth century, Isidore Rothschild and his family lived at Woodville where he worked as a bookkeeper. The Rothschilds moved to the rebuilt community of Torras, Pointe Coupée Parish, Louisiana, ca. 1917, where Isidore established the "Valley Mercantile Co." The Rothschilds were enumerated in the 1920 United States Federal Census at Torras, with Isidore identified as a retail dry goods merchant. Their eldest son, Morris, born on 23 August 1896 in Woodville, was employed as a dry goods salesman. According to his 1917 World War Draft Registration, Morris Rothschild's employer was the famous southern retailer D.H. Holmes Co. department store on Canal Street in New Orleans. Morris listed his father as next-of-kin, and recorded his father's address as Naples, Avoyelles Parish, Louisiana: a now-vanished port a few miles down and across the Atchafalaya River from Torras. Isidore and Hattie Rothschild had two other younger sons: Samuel (b. 1900), and Martin (b. 1905).

By 1921, Isidore had taken Morris in as a partner at the Torras store, and the firm was officially known as I. Rothschild & Son. In the several civil suits in which the Rothschilds were defendants, it is evident that their stock included dry goods, staple and fancy groceries, canned goods, candy, furniture, livestock and poultry feed. Their clientele extended well beyond Upper Pointe Coupée. Mrs. Fannie Scroggs, who filed suit against the Valley Mercantile Co. in 1919 (21st Judicial District Court, No. 2906) after the firm repossessed furniture that she had bought from them, lived at New Era, approximately 50 miles north in Concordia Parish.

The Rothschild family ultimately moved to New Orleans, Louisiana, where the 1930 United States Federal Census canvassers recorded that Isidore worked as a bookkeeper for a hat and shoe store. His son Morris was selling real estate. Isidore Rothschild died on 11 September 1932, and his widow, Hattie, died on 6 November 1940. They were both interred in New Orleans in Hebrew Rest Cemetery No. 2.

Morris Rothschild, became a New Orleans contractor and real estate broker. He died in New Orleans on 31 July 1972, and was interred in the Duncan family plot at Lafayette Cemetery No.

1 in Uptown New Orleans, with his wife, Ethel Duncan, who died on 22 November 1976. We could find no New Orleans record for their marriage.

ALFRED JOSEPH "JOE" DREYFUS

Alfred Joseph Dreyfus was among the several merchants who set up shop in and around Torras, Louisiana, in the wake of the 1912 flood which devastated the region. A native of Livonia, he was the son of prominent merchant, planter, and civic leader Theodore Dreyfus and his wife, Blondina Wolff. He became a general merchant in Torras following his World War I service with the United States Navy.

According to his son, Sidney Dreyfus, his father, Joe Dreyfus, kept tabs on major construction projects, particularly bridges, and opened commissaries in such places as Coushatta, Red River Parish. He ultimately opened a store specializing in clothing in Melville, and, later a large general merchandise business in Krotz Springs, both located in St. Landry Parish.

David S and Daniel E Mann.

CHAPTER 16

ATCHAFALAYA RIVER

A Choctaw-based term for "long river," the Atchafalaya, over the course of less than two centuries, was enlarged from a bayou to a deep waterway with a quick and dangerous current, while the Mississippi River continues its attempt to adopt the shorter, more vertically sloping route to the Gulf of Mexico. Since the construction of the Old River Control Structure in Concordia Parish to the north, some forty percent of the volume of the Mississippi has been diverted down the Atchafalaya, while the remaining sixty percent still flows down the Mississippi, past Pointe Coupée Parish, Baton Rouge and New Orleans and on to the Gulf of Mexico.

The leveeing of the east bank of the Atchafalaya proceeded only according to the spread of human settlement down from its head. At the time of the 1897 high water, the river was leveed only as far at the Texas & Pacific main line rail crossing at Red Cross – Melville. By the time of the 1912 high water, the levee extended to the boundary of Pointe Coupée and Iberville Parishes.

Along the Atchafalaya River in Pointe Coupée were, and are, to be found some of the most colorful plantation names. Unlike the French, who did not adopt the custom of naming their landholdings on a large scale until the later 19th century, Anglo-Saxon property owners were far more likely to assign a name to their plantations and farms, however small. Hailing from other Southern states and the Atlantic Seaboard, they undoubtedly were continuing the custom begun in Europe.

Plantations such as China Grove, Lucky Hit, Gum Stump, Ivanhoe, and Tidal Wave were founded in the area. The name "Tidal Wave" was sadly prophetic, as residents suffered from numerous levee breaks in times of high water, which inundated much of the low-lying area along thickly-settled Bayou Latenache and in the New Texas, Black Bayou, and French settlements around its juncture with the New Texas or State Road connecting the Atchafalaya with the Mississippi.

The McCrea community on the Atchafalaya gained notoriety for two 20th century events: The first was the last levee failure of the great flood of 1927 which occurred on 24 May of that year at McCrea. The second was the June 1971 "Festival of Life" which drew the largest crowd in Pointe Coupée Parish up to that time, estimated at more than 60,000 people from across the nation and abroad, for a multi-day rock festival featuring some top musicians. The event was marred by several of the billed performers failing to perform, excessive heat, rainstorms, drug overdoses, violence by the motorcycle "security" hired to police the site, and at least a few deaths by drowning.

MAX JACOBY

Max Jacoby, a native of Posen, Poland, Prussian Empire, born there, ca. August 1836, was said to have immigrated to America in 1850, and was naturalized. According to his burial record he served as a member of Hood's 2nd Texas Regiment, C.S.A. during the Civil War. His Civil War service record available at *www.fold3.com* indicates that he enlisted in Jefferson, Texas, on 26 April 1861, was severely "wounded in ankle and leg" in the engagement at Gaines's Farm (Mill intended), Coal (*sic* Cold) Harbor, near Mechanicsville, Virginia, on 27 June 1862. This hard-fought Confederate victory saved Richmond from the advancing Union Army. Max Jacoby was treated at Richmond, Virginia, where his right leg was amputated. He was discharged due to disability on 14 February 1863, at which time he was described as twenty-six-years-old, born in Poland, 5 ft. 4 in. tall, light complexion, grey eyes, black hair, employed as a merchant. Max Jacoby was followed to America by his brother Solomon, born ca. January 1847, in Poland, who immigrated in 1868, and was also naturalized.

Max Jacoby took out a license to marry Léonie Benedick on 19 February 1869 in New Orleans, Louisiana. Léonie was born ca. 1837, in France, perhaps at Paris, as some records suggest, although this information, due to lack of Parisian records before 1860, cannot be verified.

Seven-year-old Léonie had immigrated with her mother, Mathilde Dreyfous Benedick, arriving on 24 October 1844 at New Orleans from Le Havre, France, aboard the ship *Taglioni*. Accompanying them were two other children: Petrie (later "Betsey"), age five, and Laure, age three.

According to his immigration record, Jacob Benedick, Léonie's father, a native of "Bavaria," arrived in America in 1842, and was naturalized on 27 November 1848, at St. Tammany Parish, Louisiana. His tombstone located at the Hebrew Rest Cemetery in Corpus Christi, Nueces Co., Texas, indicates that he was born on 16 April 1810, at Albersheim (probably Albisheim, Rheinpfalz intended), Germany. His brother or cousin, Nathan Benedick, who arrived in Louisiana in 1839, filed for American citizenship also at St. Tammany Parish, in 1849. Both Jacob and Nathan relocated to New Orleans, and ultimately both moved to Texas, Jacob to Corpus Christi, and Nathan to Galveston. The latter's tombstone located there in the Hebrew Benevolent Society Cemetery shows a birth date of 1811 at Albisheim, Bavaria. According to both her Corpus Christi tombstone, as well as her obituary, Jacob's wife, Mathilde Dreyfous, was born at Paris, Île-de-France, France, on 16 June 1810, and married there in 1835, where Léonie, "Betsey," and Laure were said to have been born.

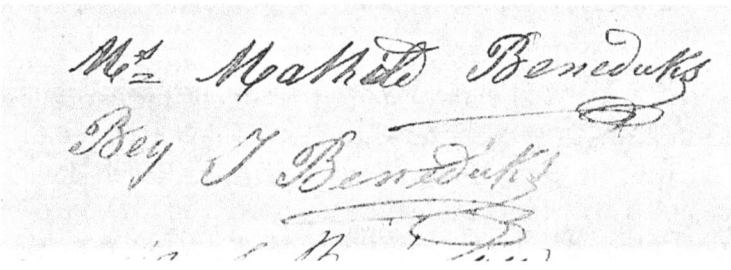

St. Tammany Parish Courthouse Records (Covington, St. Tammany Parish, LA), Conveyance Record # 426, "Sale of slaves of Richard Brenan to Mrs. Mathilde Benedicks," dated 5 November 1853.

Jacob and Mathilde had two more children born in Louisiana: Olivia, on 17 September 1849, at Covington, St. Tammany Parish, Louisiana, and Cecilia, on 14 April 1855, probably at New Orleans, although both girls had New Orleans birth certificates (surname spelled "Benedicks.") Again, according to Mathilde's obituary published in the New Orleans *Daily Picayune* on 8 October 1886, the family went back to France in 1856, where they stayed until returning to New Orleans in "1863," although they probably only arrived after the end of the Civil War in 1865.

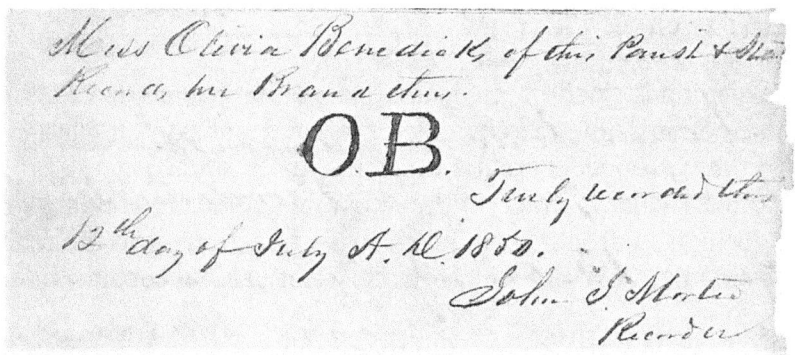

St. Tammany Parish Courthouse Records (Covington, St. Tammany Parish, LA), Mark and Brand Book A, p. 79 – Brand of Miss Olivia Benedick, dated 12 July 1850.

In two acts in 1877, Max Jacoby purchased 322.14 acres on the Atchafalaya River in Pointe Coupée Parish, Louisiana, the first acquisition being for the ½ interest therein of William J. Thrasher, payable in three notes of $450 each, and the second acquisition being for the ½ interest belonging to Miss Elizabeth McCraine Wren, for $1,000 cash. The tract was described as Lots of Sections 14 and 15 -T2S -R7E. Max and Léonie Jacoby sold the tract four years later, in 1881, to H.S. Van Eaton for the price of $2,000 cash.

Max and Léonie Jacoby were enumerated in both the 1880 and 1900 United States Federal Censuses, at Woodville, Wilkinson Co., Mississippi, where for more than twenty years Max was a merchant. Although they never had children, they shared their lives with Max's brother Solomon, also a merchant, and clerk in the Jacoby general store. In 1880, the three were enumerated living two doors away from Rabbi Simon L. Weil, who performed several marriages in 19th century Pointe Coupée Parish.

Max Jacoby left Woodville on 10 October 1901, to "have his leg treated" according to the 12 October 1901 *Woodville Republican*, but died in New Orleans on 14 November 1901, at Touro Infirmary. He was interred in the old Gates of Mercy Cemetery at Jackson and Saratoga Streets. His widow, Léonie Jacoby, died in New Orleans on 7 July 1919. She had been living with her sister, Laura Benedick Layman (d. 1916), and brother-in-law, Leopold Layman. Léonie's funeral was conducted from the Prytania Street home of Leopold Layman, according to her 8 July 1919 obituary in the *Times-Picayune*. She was interred in Hebrew Rest Cemetery No. 2.

Despite Max and Leonie Jacoby's relatively brief period as landowners in Pointe Coupée Parish, the area of their tract on the Atchafalaya is still referred to by their name. In 1892, Robert Lee Lindsey purchased the Jacoby Plantation and opened a general store. In 1895, the Jacoby Post Office was established in the store, with Lindsey as its first postmaster. In 1905, the "first modern school house" built in Pointe Coupée Parish by the school board was called the Jacoby High School which was located adjacent to the Lindsey store and post office, another remembrance of the brief tenure of Max and Leonie Jacoby in Pointe Coupée Parish.

Christ the King Chapel and Cemetery, established in the community by Sicilian immigrant and landowner Dominic Sparacino in the early 1900s, came to be popularly known as the "Jacoby" church and cemetery. It was a mission of the Seven Sorrows Church at New Texas Landing and later of St. Ann Church of Morganza. Although the little house of worship was dismantled later in the 20th century, the cemetery is still in use.

SIMON BLOCH, "RICHARDS TRACT"

Simon Bloch, born Sigismond Bloch in Riedseltz, Bas-Rhin, France, later a New Orleans sugar and cotton factor and commission merchant, planter and substantial landholder, owned two major properties in Pointe Coupée Parish Louisiana: the 1,586.01-acre Taylor Plantation on Bayou Latenache, and the Richards Tract on the Atchafalaya River. The latter encompassed 893 acres, being Lots 11 through 15 fronting on the river, and Section 44 to the rear, all in T3S-R7E, as well as the corresponding 150-acre *batture* between the levee and river bank, south of McCrea.

In 1896, Bloch acquired all interest in the property, less a ½ interest in Lot 15, at the sheriff's sale resulting from his suit against landowner William P. Stephens (14th Judicial District Court, No. 1122) for $7,789.96 in promissory notes and a $300 judgment due Bloch from Stephens. Bloch was the highest bidder, at $1,070. The other ½ interest in Lot 15 had been donated by William P. Stephens to William Hughes in 1885. In 1900, Bloch initiated two legal proceedings in the 21st Judicial District Court: the first, Suit No. 30, to receive judgment for promissory notes still due Bloch by Stephens, and the second, Suit No. 69, to obtain possession of the ½-interest in Lot 15 donated by Stevens to Hughes, the latter a resident of Montana.

The court passed monetary judgment, with interest, in Bloch's favor in Suit No. 30. In Suit No. 69, it declared that Hughes was a minor at the time of the donation, the terms of which were imprecise, and Stephens was indebted to Bloch at the time. The ½ interest in Lot 15 was seized, and adjudicated to Bloch at public sale through his high bid of $375.

Cécile Bloch Mayer was sole heir of Simon and Fanny Kaufman Bloch, who died in 1908 and 1905 respectively. She was put into possession of their estates, which included the former Richards Tract, subsequently known as the Bloch Property, on the Atchafalaya River in Pointe Coupée Parish, as well as real estate and movables in Calcasieu, Natchitoches, St. Landry, Orleans, St. Bernard, and Plaquemines Parishes, and $6,371.69 in the Commercial Germania Trust & Savings Bank of New Orleans.

A communication dated 14 December 1908, entered by Cécile in her father's succession proceedings in Orleans Parish (Civil District Court, No. 87478), established for the record that taxes had been paid on property in all parishes but Pointe Coupée, as she had been unable to "hear from Sheriff Ernest G. Beuker," although she expected them to be paid by 1 January 1909. The Bloch property was appraised for the succession at $5,000. In 1909, Cécile sold it to Miss Elizabeth B. Hoey of Chicago for $11,500. Passing through a number of owners, it was acquired in mid-20th-century by farmer and Rural Electrification Administration pioneer Alfred A. "Bubber" Robinson, a native of Jackson, Hinds Co., Mississippi. Befitting its former ownership by one of the south's leading cotton brokers, Simon Bloch, the plantation was the site of the first operation of a mechanical cotton picker in Pointe Coupée Parish, in July 1953, during Robinson's tenure.

The neighborhood of the Bloch Property has long and affectionately been known as "Coon" for the large number of raccoons encountered there. A post office named Coon, Louisiana, was established in 1920, but discontinued later in the 20th century.

Simon Bloch's daughter, Cécile Bloch's husband, Nathanial A. Mayer, died on 28 December 1924, in Chicago. Cecile Bloch Mayer survived him by nearly three decades. She died on 26 May 1954. They were both interred in Chicago's Rosehill Cemetery.

L.W. FRIEDBERG

One of the South's most familiar retail clothiers, L. W. Friedberg was, for several years, owner of historic White Hall Plantation on the Atchafalaya River, in Pointe Coupée Parish, Louisiana. Louis Wolf Friedberg was born on 27 February 1864, in Linow, Poland, Russian Empire, to Samuel Friedberg and his wife, Sarah Yawitz. He was said to have immigrated to America in 1889.

In 1898, Louis Friedberg relocated to Upper Pointe Coupée, where his brother-in-law Thomas Goldman, husband of Friedberg's sister Celia, owned and operated general stores on Bayou Lettsworth and in the nearby town of Torras, Louisiana. Friedberg bought White Hall Plantation at Legonier on the Atchafalaya River from the heirs of the late Samuel J. Norwood. He paid $5,000 in cash and assigned them notes for the balance of the $28,000 price for the 1,515-acre plantation, complete with the mansion and other improvements.

The main residence on White Hall, admired in the 21st century as one of the most beautifully preserved Southern antebellum homes, was built for Elias Norwood between 1848 and 1849, supposedly according to designs of renowned architect Henry Howard. At the time of the Civil War, the mansion and plantation were owned by Bennett Barton Simmes, a planter, riverboat captain, and Confederate Army officer for whom the town of Simmesport, across the Atchafalaya River in Avoyelles Parish, was named. This area was the site of considerable activity during the Civil War, including the retreat of Union General Nathanial Banks's forces after the disastrous Red River Campaign of 1864. For generations, cannonballs fired by Federal gunboats at White Hall remained lodged in the walls of the house, plastered over, and only removed when the rambling structure was moved to accommodate construction of a new levee after the disastrous 1912 flood.

The 27 May 1899 issue of the *Pointe Coupée Banner* published two news items concerning Louis W. Friedberg: the first, the announcement of his wedding five days earlier in New Orleans to Miss Annie Ginsburg, and the second, a notice of the impending sale of his White Hall Plantation for unpaid State of Louisiana and Atchafalaya Levee Board taxes for 1898.

Anna "Annie" Ginsberg was born in Vilna, Lithuania, Russian Empire, on 20 April 1879, to Miller Ginsberg and Eva whose maiden name, has as yet to be found. Louis Friedberg and Anna "Annie" Ginsberg were married on 21 May 1899, in New Orleans, with the Rev. L. Silverstein officiating. Thomas Goldman, Friedberg's brother-in-law and a merchant on Bayou Lettsworth in Pointe Coupée Parish, was a witness to the ceremony.

At the Tax Sale held shortly thereafter in New Roads, the Norwood heirs paid the taxes and costs and were adjudicated the plantation. In December of 1899, Louis Friedberg reacquired the property by reimbursing them for the taxes and costs they paid at the sale, plus an additional $20 in costs.

In 1902, Friedberg sold White Hall Plantation, with its 30 mules, two horses, and all farming implements to Philomène Manuel, the widow of Marcelin Chiquelin, represented by her son,

Denis Chiquelin. The price was $33,500, towards which she paid $3,000 in cash. Philomène, whose store was next to that of Aaron Loeb, was one of the few Gentile retailers on the Lower Chenal of False River, another being her nephew Auguste Manuel of the "Lake Store" fronting Petit Baie. Her son Denis Chiquelin was later a dry goods and clothing merchant on North Peters Street in New Orleans. White Hall Plantation passed through a succession of owners, including Martin Glynn of Glynn, Louisiana, on the Lower Chenal, one of several properties owned by him in Pointe Coupée and West Baton Rouge Parishes. The White Hall mansion was restored and entered on the National Register of Historic Places in the early 21st century.

After Louis Friedberg and Nathan Finkelstein's difficulties with the law over selling liquor without a license, both men relocated permanently to New Orleans. Friedberg and his wife, Anna, were enumerated in the 1910 United States Federal Census living on Hospital (subsequently Ursulines) Street in New Orleans with their children: Eva (b. 1900), Sarah (b. 1901), Samuel (b. 1903), Harry (b. 1905), and Deana (b. 1908). Friedberg, identified in that census as the proprietor of a clothing store, was also a partner in two New Orleans dry goods and notions companies: one, with brothers Nathan and Harry Finkelstein as Finkelstein Bros. & Friedberg; and the other with Harry Finkelstein as Finkelstein & Friedberg. Both companies suffered great losses due to fire which destroyed much of the merchandise and sundries in 1905. Finkelstein & Friedberg, located at 939 Decatur Street, advertised "spot cash" loan services in the 1906 New Orleans *Daily Picayune*.

Louis Friedberg later established a popular men's clothing and furnishings store at 517 Canal Street, flanked by two familiar landmarks: the old Leon Godchaux Clothing Co. and Stauffer-Eshleman & Co., a hardware store. While Louis operated these two stores simultaneously, his son Samuel "Sam" Friedberg opened a store of his own in 1928 called "Friedberg's Men's Bargain Center," at Nos. 521-23 Canal. Louis transferred his business to his son's location two years later. This "Friedberg's," in which Sam succeeded his father, retailed men's dress and casual civilian clothing, military uniforms, and shoes. It was in business until the close of the 20th century, and was one of the last of the old downtown clothiers in the nation.

Louis Wolf Friedberg died on 17 September 1935, in New Orleans, and was followed in death by his widow, née Anna Ginsberg, on 11 December 1938. They were both interred there in Gates of Prayer Cemetery.

TATAR (ORIGINALLY TATARSKY) BROS. STORES

Brothers Ben, Sam, Saul and Harry Tatarsky/Tatar were natives of Lithuania, Russian Empire. Ben was born on 12 January 1880, Saul on 15 March 1881, Samuel on 9 October 1886, and Harry on 14 January 1889, to Joel Tatarsky/Joseph Tatar and Mary Katz, who later immigrated to Louisiana as well. The Tatar Bros. were general merchants specializing in groceries at the "China Grove Store" on the Atchafalaya River Road, midway between Three Rivers and Legonier by 1910.

Saul Tatar also owned a saloon on Moreau Plantation, just east of Three Rivers on Lower Old River. The 18 December 1909 issue of the *Pointe Coupée Banner* included his notice of application for a license to sell liquors on Moreau for the year 1910.

Within the span of a few years, Tatar Bros. owned and operated two stores. According to information in their 1917-18 World War I Draft Registration files, Ben and Saul Tatar opened one store in the rebuilt-community of Torras, while Sam and Harry Tatar established another at Oakdale, Allen Parish, Louisiana. Their parents, Joseph and Mary Tatar, lived at the latter location. The Torras store was listed in the 1916 Pointe Coupée Parish Tax Roll as having merchandise assessed at $1,100, two horses at $60, and a vehicle at $15.

Samuel "Sam" Tatarsky/Tatar immigrated to America ca. July 1904, and was naturalized at New Roads, Louisiana on 13 December 1911. Sam, who never married, was living on the Atchafalaya River Road in Legonier, two doors down from his brother Ben Tatar and the latter's wife, Rachel, in China Grove, according to the 1910 United States Federal Census.

Sam Tatar filled out an application for a United States Passport on 30 October 1924 to return to Europe to visit relatives. He listed his address as 524 Common Street in New Orleans. Sam spent the rest of his life as a dry goods merchant, usually in conjunction with his brothers. According to the 1940 United States Federal Census, he was living with his brother Harry and the latter's family at Plaquemine, Iberville Parish, where they both worked as dry good merchants. In the 1942 World War II Draft Registration he filled out, Sam Tatar stated he was employed by Abe Hellman, Inc., a department store at Plaquemine. Sam died on 6 March 1969, in New Orleans, and was interred with other family members in Beth Israël Cemetery No. 2.

Benjamin "Ben" Tatarsky/Tatar immigrated to America, ca. 1905, and was also naturalized at New Roads in 1911. He was married on 10 January 1909 at New Orleans to Rachel "Ray" Fellman, born on 10 July 1887 to Samuel Fellman and his wife, Ziril Kleinstein. As of 1910, Ben and Rachel, who immigrated from Poland in 1895, were living on the Atchafalaya River Road in China Grove, near Ben's brother Sam Tatar. Ben and Rachel had one child, Sarah, born in 1908. Rachel Fellman Tatar died on 22 November 1912, and was interred at the Gates of Prayer Cemetery in New Orleans.

Ben was married a second time to twenty-eight-year-old Annie Bronik on 1 April 1917, at Alexandria, Rapides Parish, Louisiana. Annie had been born on 10 September 1888, at Vilna, Lithuania, Russian Empire. According to the 1920 United States Federal Census, Ben, working as a dry goods merchant, his wife Annie and daughter, Sarah, were living with his brother, Saul Tatar, a grocery merchant, Saul's wife, Mollie, and their five children, in the rebuilt Torras community.

According to the 1930 United States Federal Census, Ben, Annie, and Sarah were renting a house at Bogalusa, Washington Parish, Louisiana, where he was enumerated as the operator of a "Louisiana Chain Store." Ten years later, Ben, Annie and Sarah were the proprietors of a retail clothing store at White Castle, Iberville Parish, Louisiana. Ben died on 16 December 1942, at White Castle, and was interred at Beth Israël Cemetery No. 2 in New Orleans. Annie Bronik Tatar died on 5 November 1980, at Baton Rouge, and was interred there in the Liberal Synagogue Cemetery.

Solomon "Saul" Tatarsky/Tatar immigrated in 1904, and was naturalized at New Roads in 1911. He was married to Mollie Shemel, the daughter of David and Musa Shemel, on 10 February 1907. Mollie had been born on 14 June 1888, in Poland, and had come to America in 1905. By 1910, Saul and Mollie were living next door to his brother Ben and his wife, Rachel, on the Atchafalaya River Road in China Grove, with their first two children: David (b. 1909), and Thomas (b. 1910). The brothers were co-owners of a general store. According to the 1920 United States Federal Census, the two couples were living together in Torras, Pointe Coupée Parish, where Ben sold dry goods and Saul was a retail grocer. Saul and Mollie had had three more children: Sarah/Yetta (b. 1911), Rachel (b. 1914), and Morris/Mervin (b. 1919).

According to the 1930 United States Federal Census, Saul, his wife and five children were enumerated living on Penniston Street in New Orleans. Saul worked as a traveling dry goods salesman, David sold insurance, Thomas sold dry goods, and Sarah was a nurse in a hospital. Saul died on 23 September 1939, in New Orleans, and was interred there in Beth Israël Cemetery No. 2. Mollie died on 18 May 1962, at Pasadena, Harris Co., Texas, and was interred with her husband.

Harry Tatarsky/Tatar immigrated to America in 1905 and was naturalized at New Roads, Louisiana, in 1912. His 1917 World War I Draft Registration card identified him as a merchant with his brother Sam at Tatar Bros. store, in Oakdale, Allen Parish, Louisiana, where they were living with their parents. Harry was married on 27 September 1926, to Gertrude Rose Margolis. The bride was born on 2 October 1901, in New York City, to Joseph Margolis and his wife Hannah Rebecca Glick. Harry was enumerated in the 1930 United States Federal Census with his wife, Gertrude, and their first child, Helene (b. 1928) at New Orleans, living on Palmer Avenue and working as a retail merchant.

Ten years later, Harry Tatar, his wife, Gertrude, daughter, Helene, and twin sons Allan and Joel, born on 9 November 1930, were living in Fortville, a suburb of Plaquemine, Iberville Parish, along with his brother Sam, where they owned a retail dry goods store. Harry died on 10 August 1959, and was interred in Beth Israël Cemetery No. 2 with other family members. Gertrude Margolis Tatar died on 26 February 1984, at Plaquemine, and was interred with her husband.

ADVERTISERS' CORNER

AUGUST A. LEVY.

WATCHMAKER & REPAIRER.

Can be found at Mrs C. Wolff's

ALMA STORE.

Pointe Coupée Banner – July 23, 1887

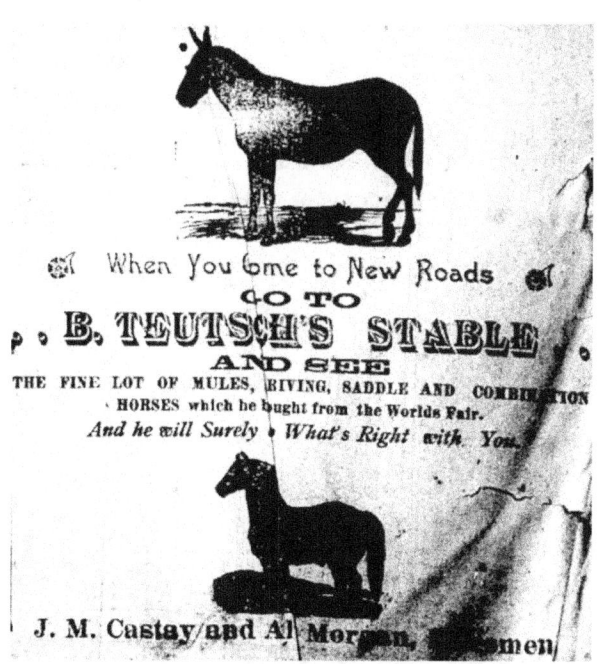

Pointe Coupée Banner – October 29, 1904

Chenal Poultry Farm

S. BAUM, Proprietor,

Chenal P. O., La.

Breeders of High-Class Poultry: W. Wyandottes, Barred Plymouth Rocks, S. C. W. Leghorns and Partridge Cochins. Eggs and Stock in season. Agents for Cypress Incubators and Brooders.

Correspondence Solicited.

Pointe Coupée Banner – December 12, 1904

WANTED — A young man as clerk in store, must speak French and exempt from draft. Good salary. Give reference and apply to

THEO. DREYFUS,

Livonia, La.

Pointe Coupée Banner – August 10, 1918

J. MOONSHINE

Jeweler & Optician,

Watch-Work A Specialty.

New Roads, La.

Pointe Coupée Banner – September 5, 1908

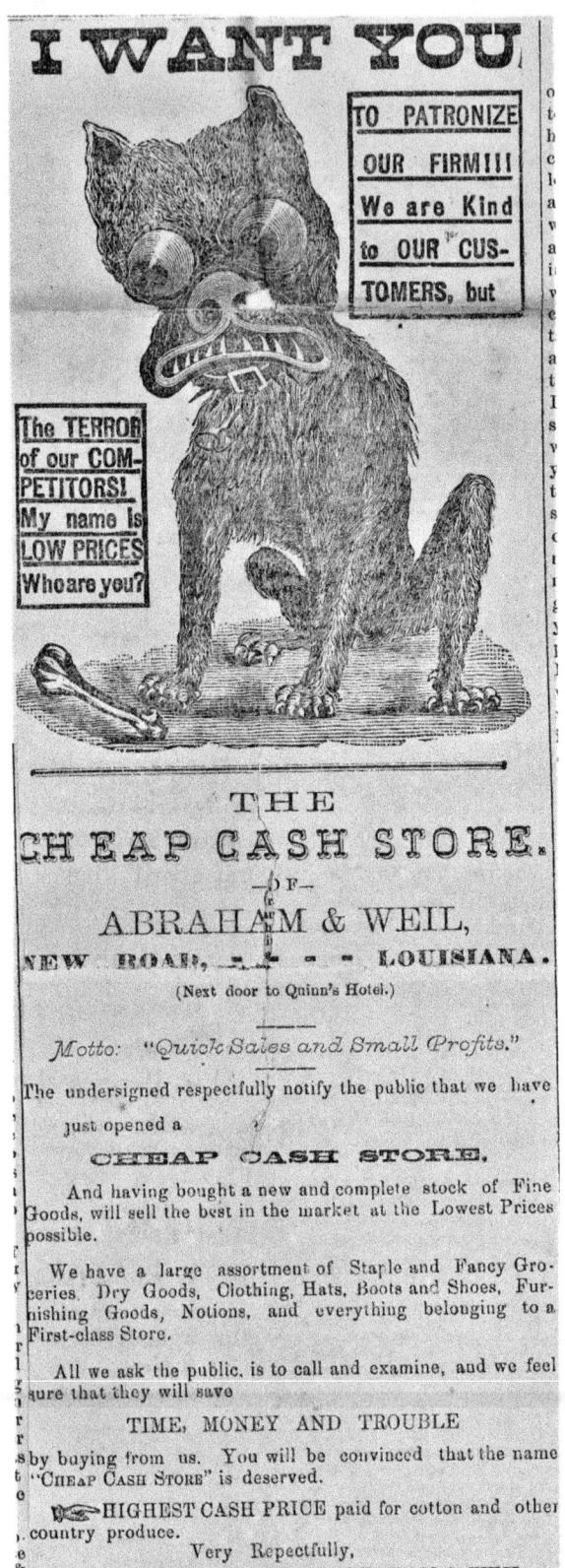

I WANT YOU

TO PATRONIZE OUR FIRM!!! We are Kind to OUR CUSTOMERS, but

The TERROR of our COMPETITORS! My name is LOW PRICES Who are you?

THE
CHEAP CASH STORE.
—OF—
ABRAHAM & WEIL,
NEW ROADS, - - LOUISIANA.
(Next door to Quinn's Hotel.)

Motto: "*Quick Sales and Small Profits.*"

The undersigned respectfully notify the public that we have just opened a

CHEAP CASH STORE.

And having bought a new and complete stock of Fine Goods, will sell the best in the market at the Lowest Prices possible.

We have a large assortment of Staple and Fancy Groceries, Dry Goods, Clothing, Hats, Boots and Shoes, Furnishing Goods, Notions, and everything belonging to a First-class Store.

All we ask the public, is to call and examine, and we feel sure that they will save

TIME, MONEY AND TROUBLE

by buying from us. You will be convinced that the name "CHEAP CASH STORE" is deserved.

☞HIGHEST CASH PRICE paid for cotton and other country produce.

Very Respectfully,
sept.5 85. ABRAHAM & WEIL.

Pointe Coupée Banner – October 17, 1885

Creole Store,

On the Lower Chenal of False River

Mrs. E. J. MEYER...Proprietress.

A FULL STOCK OF GENERAL Merchandise. Family and Plantation Supplies constantly kept on hand.

Sale of Horses and Mules a specialty.

Liberal Advances made on Cotton and all kinds of Country Produce.
tojan-1-'82.

Pointe Coupée Banner – April 1, 1882

CALL UP
MAYER CAHEN
Successor to
Bondy & Cahen,
New Roads Fancy Grocers
For Anything in the
Fancy Grocery Line.
Fresh Goods Arriving Daily.

From the *False River Telephone Book* – 1908

COFFINS, CASKETS, Etc.

A. Baum, Dealer in General Merchandise on the Lower Chenal of False River, announces to the public that he also deals in

Coffins, Caskets and Metallic Burial Cases.   mh 6.97

Pointe Coupée Banner - June 25, 1898

A CARD.

I desire to inform the public that by a judgment of the Honorable the 21st Judicial District Court, in and for the Parish of Pointe Coupée, my name has been changed from Isidore Srulovitz to Isidore Loeb; and that henceforth I shall conduct my affairs under the name of Isidore Loeb.

ISIDORE LOEB, formerly SRULOVITZ.

Morganza, April 2, 1909.

Pointe Coupée Banner – April 10, 1909

This Sailor 40c   This Sailor 40c

The Wholesale House That Sells Retail at Wholesale Prices. Branch of the Largest Wholesale Milly House in New Orleans.

Only a Block and a Half From Canal Street. Save Money by buying your Millinery Here.

40C   40C

SATURDAY SPECIAL.

This beautiful rough braid Sailor trimmed with grosgraine ribbon, assorted colors. Others would ask 98c.

On Sale SATURDAY, Our Price 40c

GROSSMAN-WEINFIELD MILLINERY CO., Ltd.,
NEW ORLEANS MILLY STORE, in building formerly occupied by New Roads Drug Store.
UP TO THE MINUTE MILLINERS
RETAIL DEPARTMENT   WHOLESALE DEPARTMENT
206 to 208 Magazine St.   210 to 212 Magazine St.

Pointe Coupée Banner – March 25, 1911

POINTE COUPEE DRUG STORE!

MR. JULES LEVY has just opened a NEW STORE on the plantation of Mr. F. O. Bouis, where he will keep constantly a complete assortment of
MEDICINES,
   FRESH DRUGS,
      PATENT MEDICINES,
         PERFUMERY, &c., &c.
DEPOT OF HUNGARIAN LEECHES.

☞ The Prescriptions of Physicians will be filled with care and dispatch, at all hours of the day or night.

☞ Drugs and Medicines for plantations in quantities to suit purchasers.   o1-1m

Pointe Coupée Democrat – November 5, 1859

A. LOEB,

LOWER CHENAL NEAR HERMITAGE

Dealer in

DRY GOODS,
  FANCY GOODS,
    NOTIONS,
      HATS AND CAPS,
        BOOTS & SHOES

GROCERIES,
  HARDWARE,
    TINWARE,
      CROCKERY,
        TRUNKS &c. &c.

Cigars, Tobacco, Wines & Liquors.

Competition defied, for price and qualities a20.

Pointe Coupée Banner – April 1, 1882

Pointe Coupée Banner – September 5, 1908

UMBRELLAS AND PARASOLS COVERED.

The undersigned is prepared to do all sorts of repairing and covering of umbrellas. Clothing cleaned, dyed or repaired. Pressing a specialty. Hats cleaned and re-blocked. Shoes repaired on short notice.

SAM FRANK.
Near Postoffice, New Roads.

Pointe Coupée Banner – April 10, 1909

Vee's 5 & 10 Store
Main St.   New Roads

CLOSING OUT SALE

All childrens' clothes 30% OFF
sizes 6 months to size 14
All Magnalite pots reduced
All threads (knitting, crochet & sewing) ½ OFF
All greeting cards ½ OFF

Zippers 10¢ each	All Sewing Books ½ price
Buttons 10¢ each	All Candy ½ price
Curtains ½ price	20% OFF gift wares
Ribbon ½ price	Ladies & Girls Panties ½ price
Lace & Trim ½ price	Panty Hose & Bras ½ price
Lamps $4⁰⁰ reg $16⁰⁰	All Jewelry 30% OFF

Our Final Sale--All Sales Final
Supply is Limited   (no Lay-A-Ways)

"Doors will be closed at 5:00 p.m. Saturday."

Vee's 5 & 10 Store

Pointe Coupée Banner – June 8, 1978

Pointe Coupée Banner – May 10, 1956

Pointe Coupée Banner – December 17, 1987

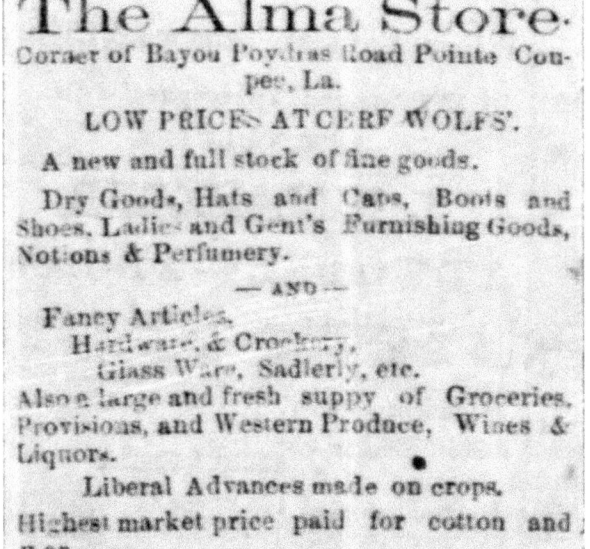

Pointe Coupée Banner - January 1, 1881

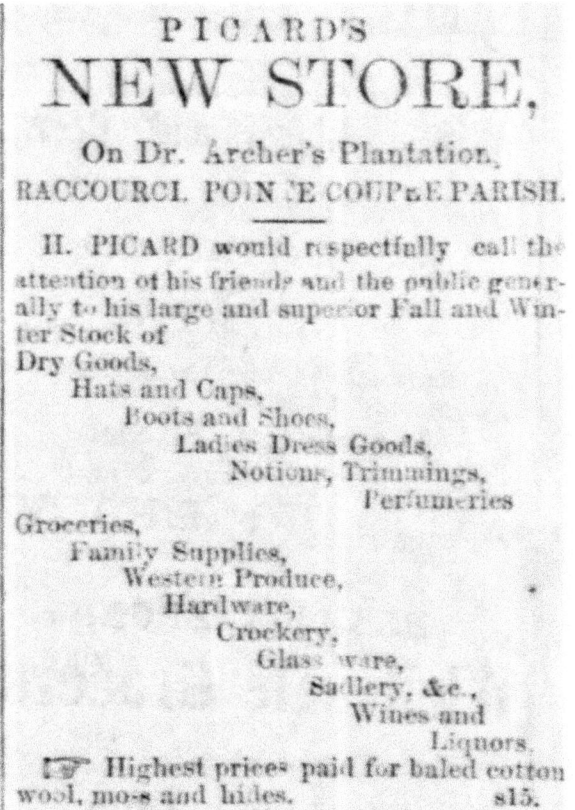

Pointe Coupée Banner – January 1, 1881

EVENING STAR STORE
—KEPT BY—

MEYER MICHEL,

AT

WATERLOO,

POINTE COUPEE PARISH

Keeps constantly on hand a full assortment of

Dry Goods,

Groceries

WETERN PRODUCE

CROCKERY & TINWARE

In fact all that is generally kept in a well supplied

COUNTRY STORE

Mr. Michel would remind his patrons that he is a great connoisseur in ready made

CLOTHING,

and suit's the most fastidious.

He has now on hand a full and fresh supply of FALL AND WINTER CLOTHING, all goods and merchandise sold at New Orleans prices for cash.

☞ Highest market prices paid for Cotton, Wool, Moss and hides.

Pointe Coupée Banner – May 16, 1885

MRS. C. WOLFF,

Lakeland - - - La.

DEALER IN

DRY GOODS

—AND—

General Merchandise

Ladies' Dress-Goods
Trimmings and Laces,
Gents' Furnishing Goods,
Sheetings, Domestics,
Kerseys, Flannels,
Drillings, Blankets,
Tickings, Jeans
Fancy Articles and Notions
BOOTS, SHOES, HATS, &c

Hardware
Crockery
Glassware,
Tinware,
Wooden and Willow ware,
Lamps and Fixtures.

Has and keeps constantly on hand a full supply of

STAPLE AND FANCY

Groceries,

Wines, Liquors, Tobacco,
Cigars, etc.

Pointe Coupée Banner – January 30, 1892

Livonia Saw Mill.

We have started the Livonia Saw Mill, with a first-class sawyer, and can deliver First-class Lumber, Cypress or Cottonwood to all points on False River and Mississippi river at the lowest figures.

For further information call on our clerk, Mr. Edward Joffrion, at the mill.

ap10'97   DREYFUS & VALLET.

Pointe Coupée Banner – June 5, 1897

H. TEUSTCH.
NEW STORE.

At Watson's Ld'g.,
POINTE COUPEE.

A Complete Stock of

GROCERIES, DRY GOODS,

FAMILY SUPPLIES.

AND

General Merchandise

Just Received

EVERYTHING NEW AND FRESH.

Boots and Shoes, Hats and Caps

TRUNKS AND VALISES.

TOBACCO AND CIGARS,

WINES AND LIQUORS,

ALL AT ROCK BOTTOM PRICES.

Give him a call at his New Store.

Pointe Coupée Banner – July 26, 1890

ABE MICHEL'S
CHEAP STORE,

WATERLOO, LA.,

DEALER IN

General Merchandise,

FANCY AND STAPLE

DRY GOODS,

Groceries,
Hardware,
Crockery,

QUEENSWARE,

GLASSWARE.

A full supply of fresh canned fruits, canned vegetables, canned fish, and other canned goods.
Fresh mackerel in kits, Soap and starch.

WESTERN PRODUCE.

Ready-Made Clothing,

BOOTS AND SHOES,

Trimmings, &c.

Tobacco, Whisky, Beer and other Liquors.

Stock Entirely New---Prices Bottom Rates---Can't be Undersold.

Pointe Coupée Banner – January 1, 1881

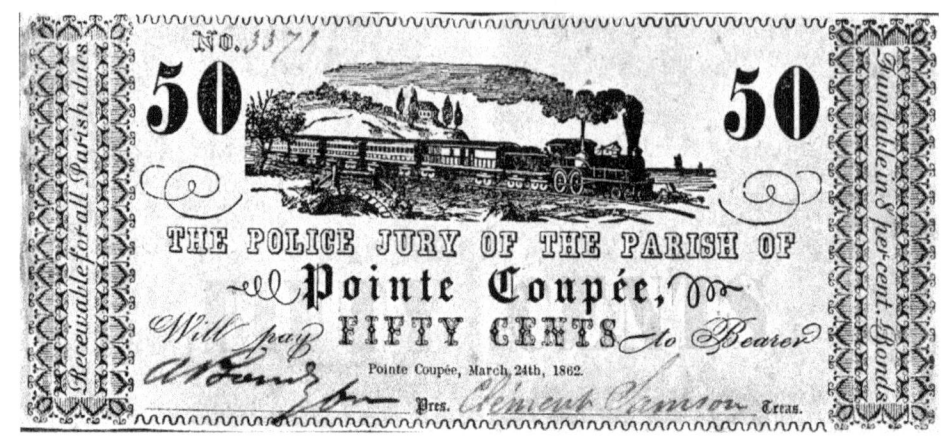

Parish of Pointe Coupée 50 cent bill issued March 24, 1862.

1970s photo of New Roads Hardware Store with Vee's 5 & 10 in background.

BIBLIOGRAPHY

NEWSPAPERS

Baton Rouge Capitolian-Advocate, Baton Rouge, East Baton Rouge Parish, Louisiana, 1880-1882

Chief, Donaldsonville, Louisiana, 1879-1883

Colfax Chronicle, Colfax, Grant Parish, Louisiana, 1878, 1880

Daily Advocate, Baton Rouge, Louisiana, 1888-1898

Daily Picayune, New Orleans, Louisiana, 1886-1909

Daily Signal, Crowley, Acadia Parish, Louisiana 1885

Daily State-Times, Baton Rouge, Louisiana, 1906-1909

Daily Town Talk, Alexandria, Rapides Parish, Louisiana, 1886, 1903, 1920

Delta Times-Democrat, Greenville, Mississippi, 1948

Démocrate de la Pointe Coupée/Pointe Coupée Democrat, False River [New Roads], Louisiana, 1858-1861

Feliciana Sentinel, Bayou Sara, Louisiana, 1882

Herald, Algiers, Louisiana, 1919

Jewish Outlook, Denver, Colorado, 1905

L'Abeille de la Nouvelle Orléans/New Orleans "Bee", New Orleans, Louisiana, 1835

Lafayette Advertiser, Lafayette, Louisiana, 1909

Leadville Daily Herald, Leadville, Colorado, 1881

Leadville Weekly Herald, Leadville, Colorado 1879

L'Echo de la Pointe Coupée/The Pointe Coupée Echo, Pointe Coupée [Post Office], Louisiana, 1869-1872

Le Meschacébé, Lucy, Louisiana, 1900

Le Sentinelle de Thibodaux, Thibodaux, Louisiana, 1896

Le Villagéois/The Villager, Marksville Louisiana, 1843

Morning Advocate, Baton Rouge, Louisiana, 1927

Natchez Democrat, Natchez, Adams Co., Mississippi, 1913

New Advocate, Baton Rouge, Louisiana, 1912

New Orleans Crescent, New Orleans, Louisiana, 1860

New Orleans Democrat, New Orleans, Louisiana, 1881

New Orleans Item, New Orleans, Louisiana, 1893-1939

New Orleans States, New Orleans, Louisiana, 1917-1946

New York Times, New York, New York, 1890-1927

Opelousas Courier, Opelousas, Louisiana, 1882

Opelousas Journal, Opelousas, Louisiana, 1872

Pointe Coupée Banner, New Roads, Louisiana, 1880-2020

Reveille, Port Gibson, Mississippi, 1902

St. Landry Clarion Herald, Opelousas, Louisiana, 1908

St. Louis Post Dispatch, St. Louis, Missouri, 1920

State-Times, Baton Rouge, Louisiana, 1928-1933

The Assumption Pioneer, Napoleonville, Louisiana, 1886

The Messenger, New Roads, Louisiana, 1893

The Pelican, New Roads, Louisiana, 1879-1880

Times-Picayune, New Orleans, Louisiana, 1917-1929

Weekly Iberville South, Plaquemine, Louisiana, 1895

Woodville Republican, Woodville, Mississippi, 1888-1902

BOOKS AND PERIODICALS

Bouchereau, A[lcée]. *Statement of the Sugar Crops Made in Louisiana in 1880-1881*. New Orleans, LA: Pelican Book and Job Printing Office, 1881.

Bouchereau, L[ouis]. *Statement of the Sugar and Rice Crops Made in Louisiana in 1876-1877, with an Appendix. Also, A Country Directory or Guide, for Businessmen*. New Orleans, LA: Pelican Book and Job Printing Office, 1877.

Costello, Brian J. *A History of Pointe Coupée Parish, Louisiana*, The Murray G. LeBeau Memorial Edition. New Orleans, LA: Margaret Media, Inc., 2010.

Costello, Brian J. *Canal Street and Beyond: Louisiana's 20th Century Department Stores*. New Roads, LA: Ewing's, 2003.

Costello, Brian J. *Carnival in Louisiana: Celebrating Mardi Gras from the French Quarter to the Red River*. Baton Rouge, LA: Louisiana State University Press, 2010.

Costello, Brian J. *C'est ca yé dit: Créole Folk Tales, Superstitions, Remedies, Customs, Nicknames and Linguistic Peculiarities of Pointe Coupée Parish, Louisiana*. New Roads, LA: New Roads Printing, 2004.

Costello, Brian J. *Desolation Unmeasured: The Tragic History of Floods in Pointe Coupée Parish, Louisiana*. New Roads, LA: New Roads Printing, 2007.

Costello, Brian J. *From Porche to Labatut: Two Centuries on the Pointe Coupée Coast*. Baton Rouge, LA: Franklin Press, 2002.

Costello, Brian J. *From Ternant to Parlange: A Créole Plantation Through Seven Generations*. New Roads, LA: Ewing's, 2002.

Costello, Brian J. *Quintessential Créoles: The Tounoir Family of Pointe Coupée*. New Roads, LA: Ewing's, 2003.

Costello, Brian J. *The Catholic Church in Pointe Coupée, A Faith Journey*. Marksville, LA: Randy DeCuir and Associates, Inc., 1996.

Costello, Brian J. *The Life, Family and Legacy of Julien Poydras*. New Roads, LA: Ewing's, 2001.

Denson and Nelson's New Orleans and Mississippi Valley Business Directory and River Guide for 1866 and '67. St. Louis, MO: P. M. Pinckard Printer: 1866.

Diocese of Baton Rouge. *Diocese of Baton Rouge Catholic Church Records, Volumes 2-22, 1770-1900*. Baton Rouge, LA: 1980-2007.

Diocese of Baton Rouge. *Diocese of Baton Rouge Catholic Church Records – Pointe Coupée Records 1770-1900 – Individuals without Surnames*. Baton Rouge, LA, 2007.

Directory of the False River Telephone Line, New Roads, Louisiana, July 1st 1908. N.p., Pointe Coupée Parish Library Historic Materials Collection, New Roads, Louisiana.

Dorr, J.W. "Louisiana in Slices," *New Orleans Crescent*, 14 May 1860.

DuFour LaCour, Jeraldine. *Avoyelleans of Yesteryear*. Bunkie, LA: Self-published, 1983.

Dun, R.G & Company, compilers. *Dun's Mercantile Agency Reference Book,* July 1889, (Vol 85), Image reprint (CD-ROM), PA-Genealogy.net, 2009.

Eshelman-Lee, Julie. *Our Family History: A Louisiana Homecoming*. Self-published, 1996.

Evans, M., ed. *Men and Matters, A Monthly Magazine of Fact, Fancy and Fiction*, "Point [sic] Coupee Parish, LA." edition, Vol. 9, No. 8, July 1903. New Orleans, LA.

Field, Martha R. "Catharine Cole's Letter" column in the New Orleans *Daily Picayune,* 22 November 1891 & 29 November 1891.

Harris, Wm. H., Louisiana State Commissioners of Agriculture and Immigration. *Louisiana Products, Resources and Attractions, With a Sketch of the Parishes.* New Orleans, LA: *Times-Democrat,* 1881.

Hébert, Rev. Donald G, compiler. *Southwest Louisiana Records (1750-1900) CD #101,* CD-ROM, database, Rayne, LA: Hébert Publications, 2001.

Hinchin, Rabbi Martin I., D.D. *Fourscore and Eleven, A History of the Jews of Rapides Parish 1828-1919.* Alexandria, LA: McCormick Graphics, 1984.

Klingler, Thomas A. *If I Could Turn My Tongue Like That: The Creole Language of Pointe Coupée Parish, Louisiana.* Baton Rouge, LA: Louisiana State University Press, 2003.

Korn, Bertram Wallace. *The Early Jews of New Orleans.* Waltham, MA: American Jewish Historical Society, 1969.

Mills-Nichol, Carol. *A Guide to the French and American Claims Commission 1880-1885: Our French Immigrant Ancestors and the American Civil War.* Santa Maria, CA: Janaway Publishing, Inc., 2017.

Mills-Nichol, Carol. *Louisiana's Jewish Immigrants from the Bas-Rhin, Alsace, France.* Santa Maria, CA: Janaway Publishing, Inc., 2014.

Mills-Nichol, Carol. *The Aubrys: Free People of Color in Early New Orleans.* Santa Maria, CA: Janaway Publishing, Inc., 2021.

Mills-Nichol, Carol. *The Forgotten Jews of Avoyelles Parish, Louisiana.* Santa Maria CA: Janaway Publishing, Inc., 2012.

Nitske, W. Robert, trans. Savoie Lottinville, ed. *Paul William Duke of Wurttemberg. Travels in North America 1822-1824.* Norman, OK: University of Oklahoma Press, n.d.

Ricaud, J.A. *Étude Commerciale, Industrielle, Économique, Constitutionelle, Etc. de la Grande République Amércaine, 17 Années Chez Les Yankees.* Paris, France: Bibliothèque Universelle, A.-M. Beaudelot, 1889.

Riffel, Judy, ed. *A History of Pointe Coupée Parish and its Families.* Baton Rouge, LA : Le Comité des Archives de la Louisiane, 1982.

Sanford, J.I. *Beautiful Pointe Coupée and Her Prominent Citizens.* New Orleans, LA: American Printing Co., Ltd., 1906.

Stubbs, W.C., W.W. Puch, W.J. Thompson, and John Dymond, eds. *Louisiana Planter and Sugar Manufacturer*, 22 September 1894. New Orleans, LA: Louisiana Planter and Sugar Manufacturer Co.

Simmons' Spice Mill, Vol. XXXVII, No. 4., April 1914. New York, p. 431. (available at https://www.googlebooks.com).

The New Era Druggists Directory of the United States, Canada, Cuba, Porto [sic], *Manila and Hawaiian Islands*, Vol. 11. New York City: D.O. Haynes, & Co., 1905.

United States War Dept. *The War of the Rebellion: A Compilation of the Official Records of the Union and Confederate Armies*. Washington, D.C.: Govt. Print. Off., 1800-1901.

Woods, Rev. Earl C. and Dr. Charles E. Nolan, eds. *Sacramental Records of the Roman Catholic Church of the Archdiocese of New Orleans*, Volumes 1-19, 1718-1831. New Orleans, LA: Archdiocese of New Orleans, 1989-2004.

GOVERNMENTAL RECORDS

Bureau of Refugees, Freedmen, and Abandoned Lands, Louisiana Freedmen's Bureau, New Roads, Louisiana Field Office, Library of Congress, Washington, D.C.

Normoyle, James Edward, USA. *Flood Sufferers in the Mississippi and Ohio Valleys*. Washington, D.C.: Government Printing Office, 1912.

Pointe Coupée Parish Clerk of Court, New Roads, Louisiana.

Pointe Coupée Parish Police Jury Minute Books, Pointe Coupée Parish Government, New Roads, Louisiana.

Pointe Coupée Parish Assessment Rolls, Pointe Coupée Parish Sheriff and Ex-Officio Tax Collector, New Roads, Louisiana.

Louisiana Supreme Court, New Orleans, Louisiana.

United States District Court, New Orleans, Louisiana.

United States Federal District Bankruptcy Court, New Orleans, Louisiana.

INTERVIEWS AND PERSONAL COMMUNICTIONS

Boatner, III, Mark M., Capt., USA (Ret), New Roads, Louisiana, 1987.

Bondy, Arthur A., Jr., New Roads, Louisiana, 2021.

Bueche, J.A., Jr., Lakeland, Louisiana, 2021.

Bueche, Melanie L., Lakeland, Louisiana, 1993.

Dreyfus, Sidney, Krotz Springs, Louisiana, 2021.

Chustz, Charles L., Lakeland, Louisiana, 1987.

Costello, Inez A., New Roads, Louisiana, 1987.

Eshelman-Lee, Julie, Fort Collins, Colorado, 1995.

Ewing, Dalton, Innis, Louisiana, 2009.

Gaspard, Mae B., Blanks, Louisiana, 2021.

Hill, Alice B., New Roads, Louisiana, 2021.

Hirsch, Rachelle D., Metairie, Louisiana, 2021.

Hoffman, Kenneth, New Orleans, Louisiana, 2021.

Jewell, J.P., Jr., New Roads, Louisiana, 1987.

King, Emily M., New Roads, Louisiana, 1993.

Langlois, Patricia L., Lakeland, Louisiana, 2021.

LeBeau, Murray G., New Roads, Louisiana, 1987, 1990.

Major, Marie L., Oscar, Louisiana, 1994.

Mann, Dr. Rob, Baton Rouge, Louisiana, 2001.

Melancon, Norris A., Jr., New Roads, Louisiana, 2021.

Weil, Dinah E., Livonia, Louisiana, 2021.

Weil, Jonathan, Livonia, Louisiana, 2021.

Weil, Ray Weill, Livonia, Louisiana, 1988.

Weil, Simon D., Livonia, Louisiana, 1988.

West, Geraldine P., Seal Beach, California, 1993.

Wooddy, Stuart W., Jarreau (Chenal), Louisiana, 1993.

INTERNET WEBSITES

Ancestry.com. https://www.ancestry.com/

Archives de Paris. http://archives.paris.fr/r/124/etat-civil-de-paris/

Archives départementales du Bas-Rhin. https://archives.bas-rhin.fr/

Archives départementales de la Gironde. https://archives.gironde.fr/

Archives départementales du Haut-Rhin. https://archives.haut-rhin.fr/search/home

Archives départementales de la Moselle. http://www.archives57.com/index.php/recherches/archives-en-ligne

Archives départementales de Meurthe-et-Moselle. https://archives.meurthe-et-moselle.fr/archives-en-ligne

Archives municipales de Bordeaux. https://archives.bordeaux-metropole.fr/

Archives municipales de Nancy. https://archives.nancy.fr/archives-numerisees/

Archives nationales d'outre-mer. http://anom.archivesnationales.culture.gouv.fr/caomec2/

Colorado Historic Newspapers. www.coloradohistoricnewspapers.org

FamilySearch.org. https://www.familysearch.org/en/

*Filae.com. https://www.filae.com/v4/genealogie/homepage.mvc/homepageconnected

FindAGrave.com. https://www.findagrave.com/

*Fold3.com. https://www.fold3.com/

*GenealogyBank.com. https://www.genealogybank.com/

*Geneanet.org. https://en.geneanet.org/

LAGenWeb. http://www.lagenweb.org/

Louisiana.hometown locator.com. https://louisiana.hometownlocator.com/la/pointe-coupee

*MyHeritage.com. https://www.myheritage.com/

*Newspapers.com. https://www.newspapers.com/

Rootsweb.com. https://home.rootsweb.com/

Note: Websites marked with an asterisk (*) are subscription only.

MAPS

Louisiana Highway Department Baton, Pointe Coupée Parish, Louisiana, 1955, Pointe Coupée Parish Historic Materials Collection, New Roads, Louisiana.

Sanborn Fire Insurance Maps, Morganza, Louisiana, 1921, Pointe Coupée Parish Library Historic Materials Collection, New Roads, Louisiana.

Sanborn Fire Insurance Maps, New Roads, Louisiana, 1905, 1907, 1909, 1920, 1930, Pointe Coupée Parish Library Historic Materials Collection, New Roads, Louisiana.

UNPUBLISHED SOURCES

Bergeron, Elida V. to Thomas Heard Campbell, Morganza, Louisiana, letter dated October 23, 1945. T.H. Campbell Collection, Louisiana State Archives, Baton Rouge, Louisiana.

Hewes, Thomas H. *Thomas H. Hewes Civil War Scraps, Etc., February 1st 1862.* Pointe Coupée Library Historic Materials Collection, New Roads, Louisiana.

LeJeune, Lelia Decuir, "The Story of My Life as Far as I Can Remember," edited by Julie Eshelman-Lee, 2010, Pointe Coupée Parish Library Historic Materials Collection, New Roads, Louisiana.

Lorio, Elaine C. "The Place-Names of Pointe Coupée Parish." Louisiana State University Master's Thesis, 1932.

Weil, Alphonse and Rosina Dreyfus, "Wedding Book," Simon D. Weil and Ray Weill Weil Family Collection, Livonia, Louisiana.

1895 Rand-McNally map of Pointe Coupée and surrounding parishes. Bayou Maringouin area is at lower center. Note the absence of Morganza in this map, which was near New Texas, shown middle center of this map. The Morganza Post Office had been discontinued between 1886 and 1899, hence the town's absence from the map.

INDEX

Aarons, Moses, 169
Aarons, Sarah, 169
Abbeville, Vermillion Parish, 227
Abe Michel's Cheap Store, 59, 60, 343
A.B. Mitchell & Co., 284
Abraham, Heinrich, 91
Abraham, Jacob B., 91, 92
Abraham, Julia, 222
Abraham, Pauline, 214, 222
Abraham, Simon, 101
Abraham & Weil, 90-92, 259, 274, 275, 304,
....338
Abraham Klotz Planting & Mercantile Co., Ltd.,
....222
Abrams, Henrietta, 61
Abramson, Abe, 178
Abramson, Annie/Hanchen, 151, 178, 179
Abramson, Hannah/Ann, 221
Abramson, Hyman, 178
Abramson, Samuel, 162, 178
Achée, Sampère, 126
Adler, Abraham, 215
Adler, Leonard Emil, 216
Adler, Solomon, 215, 216
A. Frank & Co., 111
Aguillard, Adèle, 72
Aguillard, Charles Swain, 72, 194
Aguillard, José/Joseph, 72
Aguillard, Paulin, 72
Aguillard, Paul Lucien, 72, 194
Aguillard, Séverine Inez, 212, 213
Albersweiler, Rheinpfalz, Germany, 189
Albisheim, Rheinpfalz, Germany, 49, 52, 145,
....170, 203, 330
Aldenhoven, Westphalia, Germany, 175
Alex Mann & Co., 314
Alex Mann's New Orleans Cheap Cash Store,
....57, 59, 314
Alexandria, Rapides Parish, 134, 135, 206,
...217,218, 241, 284, 315, 316, 335
Allain, François/Francisco, 3, 22, 245
Allain, Hyacinthe/Jacintha, 243, 245, 246
Allen, Frank, 147
Alma Plantation, 14, 15, 22,127, 131, 133,
....137,138, 156-158, 170, 172, 178
Alma Store, 14, 48, 77, 156-158, 178, 179, 341
Alsace Place, 44
Alsace Store, 44, 341
Altdorf, Rheinpfalz, Germany 73

Altkirch, Haut-Rhin, France, 141
Amar, Amélie, 110, 161, 198, 200, 232
Amar, Arnaud, 198
Amar, Céleste, 161
Amar, Joseph, 198
Amar, Palmyre, 198
Amar, René, 13
American Department Stores, 116, 117
American Legion of Honor, 7, 112
Amsterdam, Netherlands, 87
Anchor, PCP, 40, 41
Angola, WFP, 9, 16, 312
Angst, Maria Ursula, 292
Applebaum, Nathan, 156
Applebaum, Solon, 156
Arabi, St. Bernard Parish, 213, 221
Archer, Dr. William, 9, 268
Archer, Laura, 261
Archer's (Dr. John G.), Plantation, 275, 276, 341
Arent, Clara, 216
Argyle Store, 198, 231, 232
Arzheim, Rheinpfalz, Germany, 91
Ashbach bei Kusel, Rheinpfalz, Germany, 141
Asheville, NC, 234, 242
Ashkenazi Jews, xi, xii, xiv, 3
Asswiller, Bas-Rhin, France, 85
Atchafalaya River, 1-3, 17-19, 71, 139, 197,
    204, 231, 233, 237, 243, 244, 257, 258, 278,
    286, 288, 295, 297, 298, 301, 305, 311, 327,
    329, 331-336
Athlone, Concordia Parish, 305
Atlanta, GA, 181, 317, 324
Auerbach, Mina/Minette, 69
Augny, Moselle, France, 75
Austin, TX, 237
Avoyelles Parish, 69-72, 107, 113, 119, 120,
....139,192, 257, 262, 292, 311, 315, 323, 327,
…333
Bacau, Romania, 251
Baer, Marie, 179, 23
Baer, Mathilde (aka Mathilde Beer), 241
Bach, Schoenel, 263
Baginsky, Herman M. 60
Baginsky, Meyer (aka Louis), 57, 59, 60
Baginsky, Nathan, 58, 60
Baginsky, Rose Beatrice, 60
Baginsky, Victoria, See Victoria Singer
Balitz, Amelia, 260
Ball, Samuel, 190

Baltimore, MD, 98 103, 104, 314, 315
Banyliv, Ukraine, 251
Baptiste, Alida, 149
Barataria Canning Co., 219
Barbier, Philip, 118, 132
Barbin, Marceline Florence, 113
Bareigno, Pauline, 146
Barrier, Marie Anne, 109
Barthe, Lucille, 184, 185
Bart-Well, Inc. 118
Batchelor, PCP, 8, 18, 137, 234, 257, 272, 283,
....289, 290, 300, 301, 313
Baton Rouge, EBR, 1, 4, 5, 16-20, 22, 23, 27,
....32, 41, 48, 56, 58, 90, 96-99, 102, 110-113,
....118, 119, 132, 134, 135, 145, 149, 151, 158,
....159, 161, 162, 172, 173, 175, 178, 179, 182,
....187, 188, 191, 194, 195, 199, 201, 207, 214,
....215, 218, 223, 225-227, 232, 250, 251, 266,
....267,.271, 280, 289, 314, 318, 321, 322, 325,
....326, 329, 336
Baton Rouge, Grosse Tête & Opelousas
....Railway, 204, 237
Baum, Aaron, 5, 8 ,9, 13, 19, 97, 101, 138, 140,
....142-145, 151, 161, 173, 175, 181, 182, 187,
....188, 194, 195, 199, 200, 338
Baum, Dorothy Amelia, 145, 187
Baum, Isaac, 173, 174
Baum, Joseph Abraham (aka Abram J.), 194,
....195
Baum, Max, 173, 194
Baum, Sarah, 181
Baum, Simon, 5, 132, 133, 143, 145, 187, 188,
....337
Baum, Solomon, 8, 56, 144, 173, 194, 195
Baum & Patin Wholesale Grocery, 187
Baum's Hall, 8
Bayou Black, 197
Bayou Cholpe, 130
Bayou Cirier, 145, 146, 150, 158, 166, 201
Bayou Cirier Plantation, 157, 158, 176, 177,
....181
Bayou Fordoche, PCP, 2, 197, 198, 200, 213,
...231-234, 237, 243, 246, 258, 270, 289
Bayou George, 197
Bayou Goula, Iberville Parish, 220 266
Bayou Grosse Tête, PCP, 2, 3, 7, 11, 18, 130,
....145,150, 188, 197, 198, 201, 203, 204, 207,
...208, 209, 211, 213, 215, 220, 231, 232, 237,
...239, 244, 246

Bayou Latenache, PCP, 2, 44, 61, 251, 257, 258,
....268, 286, 289, 295, 297-302, 306, 309, 329,
....332,
Bayou Lettsworth, PCP, 2, 46, 177, 259, 262,
....263, 279, 288, 303, 304, 305-308, 313, 322,
....323, 325, 333
Bayou Maringouin, PCP, 3, 50, 123, 151, 152,
....173, 190, 197, 201, 204, 207, 208, 211, 214,
....233, 237, 239, 242, 352
Bayou Portage, PCP, 197, 198, 202
Bayou Poydras, PCP, 84, 85, 141, 148, 157, 158,
....172,176, 188
Bayou Sara, WFP, 10, 21, 33, 36, 37, 48, 52, 56-
....58, 72, 91, 92, 207, 233, 249, 263, 274-276,
....315
Bayou Tommy Plantation, 125, 130, 131-133
Beer, Fannie, 316
Behr, Sarah, 92
Beiner, Frederick, 76
Belfort, Haut-Rhin, France, 48
Belheim, Rheinpfalz, Germany 110
Belle Alliance, Assumption Parish. See
....Valenzuela
Belozi, Barthelemi, 69, 70
Bendel, Henry Willis, 227
Bendel, William Louis, 227
Bendel Gardens, 227
Benedick, Betsey, 330
Benedick, Cecilia, 330
Benedick, Jacob, 330
Benedick, Laure, 330, 331
Benedick, Léonie, 330, 331
Benedick, Nathan, 330
Benedick, Olivia, 330, 331
Ben Gerson & Son, 123, 155, 277
Benjamin, Leah, 291
Ben R. Mayer Grocery Co., 96, 97, 99
Bensadon, Joseph, 171
Bensadon, Josephine, 171
Bergeron, Adélon, 81
Bergeron, Eudora, 81
Bergeron, Hypolite, 81
Bergeron, Jean-Baptiste Sosthène, 171
Bergeron, Joséphine, 220
Bergeron, Julie, 81
Bergeron, Leon Paul, 220
Bergeron, Marie, 171
Bergeron, Olivia, 220
Bergeron, Paul, 220
Bergeron, Polite, 81

Berlichingen, Baden-Württemberg, Germany, ...215
Berlin, Germany, 106, 277
Bernard, Ida, 63, 65
Bernard, Jeanne, 63
Bernard, Mathilde, 63
Bernard, Oury, 63
Bernasky, S, 3
Bernheim, Clémence, 89
Bernheim, Moïse, 89
Bernstein, Samuel Nathan, 195
Bernstein, Solomon "Sol," 18, 97, 156, 185-....187, 190, 195
Bertha Lumber Co., 219
Berthet, Fr. Pierre, 6
Bertonière, Évariste, 50
Bertonière, Marie Angélique, 50
Bertonière, Napoléon, 50
Bertrand Landing, 41
Best, James Jewell, 26
Besthoff, Bertha "Birdie," 171
Besthoff, Simon, 171
Betz, Alethia, 90
Betz, Ferdinand, 90
Betz, Howard Rubin, 89, 90
Betz, Louis, 90
Betz, Robert, 90
Betz, William Frederick, 89
Beuker, Ernest G., 144, 162, 166, 169, 177, ...282, 299, 301, 332
Bialostowki, Jejza, 300
Bialystok, Poland, 221
Bickart, Adam, 273-275
Bickart, Esther, 273, 274
Bickart, Hirtz, 273, 274
Bickart, Isaac, See Henry Picard
Bickart, Isaac Jacques, 275
Bickart, Raphaël, 273, 275
Bickart, Samuel, See Samuel Picard
Biedesheim, Rheinpfalz, Germany, 58
Bierman, Bertha, 35
Bigman, Clara Rosalie, 125
Bigman, Dennis/Dennie, 125-127
Bigman, Isaac, 6, 15, 93, 95, 97, 125-136, 165, ...187, 189, 190, 215, 235
Bigman, Joseph, 125
Bigman, Joseph H. 125, 126
Bigman, Lillian, 125-127
Bigman, Miriam Fannie, 125, 126
Bigman Lane, 130, 220

Bigman & Hewes Ginnery, 97, 126, 128, 133, ...165
Bigman's Quality Shop, 127
Bigman vs. Lorio, 131-133
Billigheim, Rheinpfalz, Germany, 155
Bischheim, Bas-Rhin, France, 274
Bischwiller, Bas-Rhin, France, 326
Blanks, PCP, 18, 175, 197, 231, 235
Bloch, Adolph, 141
Bloch, Auguste, 284
Bloch, Beyen, 50, 297
Bloch /Block, Ephraim, 88, 89
Bloch, Caroline, 209
Bloch, Cécile Julia, 296, 297, 332, 333
Bloch, Charles, 296-298
Bloch, David, 286
Bloch, Ernest, 284
Bloch, Esther (aka Estelle Block), 284-286
Bloch, Gaston, 89
Bloch, Gertrude, 141
Bloch, Henry, 295
Bloch, Herman Ferdinand, 141
Bloch, Isaac, 141
Bloch, Isaac Lion, 88
Bloch, Jeanne/Jeannette, 180
Bloch, Jeannette/Henriette, 297
Bloch/Block, Joseph, 141, 142
Bloch, Joseph (s/o Henry), 295, 296
Bloch, Joseph (f/o Charles), 297
Bloch, Lazare, 205, 208-210
Bloch, Lazare (f/o Samson), 209
Bloch, Leon Frank, 141, 142
Bloch, Lucy, 89
Bloch, Malena, 141
Bloch, Marx, 209, 210
Bloch, Nathan, 141
Bloch, Pierre, 89
Bloch, Robert, 89
Bloch, Samson, 209
Bloch, Sarah (aka Sarah Block), 284-286
Bloch, Serette, 89
Bloch, Sigismond "Simon", 15, 285, 295-298, ...332, 333
Bloom, Regina, 315
Blue Store, 14, 29, 33-36, 80
Blum, Abraham, 266
Blum, Anne (aka Minette Jacob), 170
Blum, Aron, 266
Blum, Bernard, 251
Blum, Callie, 267
Blum, Clarence, 7, 267

Blum, Henriette, 266
Blum, Henry M., 266
Blum, Isidore, 7, 10, 262, 266, 267, 271, 272, ...287
Blum, Jack, 250
Blum, Joseph, 266
Blum, Lazare, 266
Blum, Lena, 266
Blum, Leopold Jacob, 267
Blum, Mina, 266
Blum, Minette, 267
Blum, Philip, 266
Blum, Rosalie, 266
Blum, Rosalie (sister of Isidore Blum) 266
Blum, Samuel, 266
Blum, Samuel dit Simon, 284
Blum, Thérèse, 266
Blumenthal, Rosa, 217
Böchingen, Rheinpfalz, Germany, 43, 210, 214, ...280
Bohrman, Caroline, 309
Bohrman, Jacob, 308
Bohrman, Leopold/Lee, 308, 309
Bois-le-Duc ('s-Hertogenbosch), Netherlands, ...181
Boll weevil, 14, 16, 18, 97, 106, 134, 186, 189, ...320, 322
Boiteux, Marie Lodoïska, 27
Bombet, Jules, 27
Bomer-Blanks Lumber Company, 220, 231
Bondy, Alcide, 6, 8, 27, 46, 100, 103
Bondy, Anna Elmire, 5, 27, 103, 104, 105
Bondy, Jean-Baptiste Alcide, 5, 103
Bondy & Cahen, 103
Bordeaux, Gironde, France, 22, 23, 75-77, 147, ...190, 216, 243, 293
Borowsky, Anna, (aka Chaja Feije Borowsky), ...299, 300
Borowsky, Stanislas, 299
Boudreau, Dorothée, 232
Boudreaux, Blanche, 7, 107
Boudreaux, James M., 7
Boudreaux, John, 107
Bouis Plantation, 28, 265
Bouligny, François Gabriel, 32
Bouligny, François Gabriel Florville, 32
Bouligny, George Claude, 32, 33
Bouligny, Joseph François, 32
Bouligny, Rose Emma (aka Ernestine), 32
Bourgeois, Pierre Félicien, 86, 244, 249, 270
Bouxwiller, Bas-Rhin, France, 208, 218

Bowlzer, Alfred H. 145
Bowman, Albert G. 58
Braun, Valerie, 318, 319
Breaux, Marie Viviane, 107
Breddo, David, 55
Britto, Manuel de, 14, 22, 123
Britto, Manuel, 122, 123
Bronik, Annie, 335, 336
Brooklyn, NY, 34, 35, 74, 107, 111, 125, 190, ...287, 300
Brownsville, TX, 88, 89
Brumath, Bas-Rhin, France, 27, 54, 150, 209, ...273, 326
Brun, Marie, 32
Brunschwig, Rifke/Rebecca, 141
Bubenheim, Rheinpfalz, Germany, 308
Buchanan, Martha/Mattie, 289
Buchbinder, Caroline, 308, 327
Bucholtz, Dora, 249
Buford, Robert McCoy, 162
Bunkie, Avoyelles Parish, 118, 292
Burnt Bridge Store, 6, 29, 48, 77, 157, 158, 176, ...177,181-183, 279, 304
Buswiller, Bas-Rhin, France, 174
Butoslovsky, Marla/Mollie, 233, 289
Bzurovski, Sarah, 116
Cadoré, Jules, 143
Cahen, Frahen, 75
Cahen, Israël, 101, 102
Cahen, Mayer, 6, 8, 27, 90, 93, 97, 101-105, ...111,.112, 338
Cahen, Thérèse, 101
Cahn, Abraham, 51
Cahn, Bertha, 51
Cakeland/Kateland, Grant Parish, 206, 207
Canebrake, PCP, (now Lottie), 231
Capital Billiard, Hall, 159
Cardoza, David Nunez, 291
Cardoza, Sara Nunez, 291
Carmouche, Louis, 194
Carrollton, Jefferson Parish, 246
Carvalho, Adelaïde, 169
Cazayoux, Br. Clair, S.J., 27
Cazayoux, Br. Cosmas, S.C., 27
Celina Plantation, 155, 156, 162-168, 173, 191
Cerf, Henri, 81, 83-85
Cerf, Reine, 83
Cerf, Simon, 83
Cerf, Sophie, 92
Charamel, Angélique, 107, 146, 147, 149, 150
Charamel, Jean, 146

Charamel, Joseph, 146, 147
Charamel, Numa, 146, 147
Charleston, SC, 25, 26, 61, 171, 291
Charlot, Josephine, 260
Chassin, Sheldon/Joshua Isaac, 324
Chassin, Simon, 324
Chattanooga, TN, 304
Chemin Neuf, PCP, 2, 18, 25, 67, 85, 127
Chenal, 8, 137, 187
Chenal-Glynn Farmers' Association, 7
Chenal Inférieur de la Fausse Rivière. See
....Lower Chenal of False River
Chenal Poultry Farm, 187, 337
Chenal Store, 150-152, 201, 271
Chenal Supérieur de la Fausse Rivière, PCP. See
…Upper Chenal of False River
Chicago, IL, 14, 33, 65, 80, 109, 125, 150, 260,
....264, 286, 297, 298, 303, 308, 332, 333
Childs, Nathan, 219, 220
Childs, Solomon Ned, 219
China Grove, PCP, 257, 329, 334-336
China Grove Store, 334
Chiquelin, Denis, 333, 334
Chiquelin, Marcelin, 193, 333
Cholpe, PCP, 17, 130, 197
Christopha, Eugénie, 198
Christophe, Marie Aspasie, 82
Chustz, Aglaé Colombe, 56, 194
Chustz, Gertrude Caroline, 50
Chustz, Reine Ordalie, 8, 56, 194
Cline, Albert, 156
Cincinnati, OH, 110, 111
Claiborne, Louis Bingaman, 9, 10, 129, 162
Clinton, EFP, 52, 54, 139, 141, 142
Cochran, John, 297
Cochran, Lillie B., 297
Cohen, Gustav M. 101, 143
Cohen, Sarah, 291
Cohen, Sidonia "Dearie," 101
Cohen & Loeb, 242
Cohn, Coralie, 180
Cohn, Henry (aka Guillaume Kahn), 180
Cohn, Joseph, Jr., 218
Cohn, Lena, 89, 90, 97, 100, 103, 111
Cohn, Suzanne, 326
Cole, Catharine, See Martha Field
Collins, Rosa, 148
Cologne, Germany, 241
Condé-Northen, Moselle, France, 312
Cooke, John, 41
Cook's Landing, PCP, 2, 14, 41, 49-52, 55, 56
.....61, 163, 164, 191, 194, 307
Cooley, Anna E., See Anna Elmire **Bondy**
Coon, PCP, 257, 332
Costello, Joseph, 213
Cotton, Annis, 289
Cotton, Jere Brown, 289
C.M. Eiseman & Co., 14, 60-62
Courtis, Pierre, 79, 80
Covington, St. Tammany Parish, 117, 308, 330,
.....331
Créole Landing, 203, 234, 257, 267-269, 279,
.....280, 282, 283, 289, 297, 299
Creole Store, 160, 161
Crescent Park Plantation, 231
Crowley, Acadia Parish, 284, 286, 289
Curaçao, 14, 22, 23, 123
Dahn, Rheinpfalz, Germany, 226
Dallas, TX, 88, 141, 274, 296-298
Dalsheimer, David, 265
Dampf, Max, 174
Dannheiser, Babette/Barbe, 209
Darensbourg, Albertine Livie, 199
Darensbourg, Eugénie Berthe, 149
Dauendorf, Bas-Rhin, France, 185
David, Alice, 223
David, Louis, 153, 163, 166-168, 191
Daÿ, Davit/David, (aka Daniel Weil), 57, 58
Daÿ, Dorès, 57
Dayton, OH, 199
deBlainville, Félix Eugène Ernest Edmond, 45
Decuir, Adoréa, 270
Decuir, Angella/Angelina, 149
Decuir, Antoinette, 60, 124
Decuir, Babet, 260, 261
Decuir, Jean-Baptiste Dorsin, II, 261
Decuir, Lélia, 161, 199
Decuir, Léon, 138, 139, 199
Decuir, Léonce, 149
Decuir, Marguérite Cléontine, 9, 28, 179, 259, 261
Decuir, Marie Angela, 161, 199, 200
Decuir, Palmyre, 199
Dehlingen, Bas-Rhin, France, 28
De Jumilhac, Armand, 294
De Jumilhac, Marie Odet Armand Aimable
....Chapelle, 294
De Jumilhac, Odile, 294
Delmonico Store, 14, 155, 156, 185
De Marigny, Marie Odile, 293
Demouy, Eugenia, 89
Demouy, Harry, Jr. 89

Demouy, Henri, 89
Demouy, Henry Adrien Joseph (aka Harry), 89, ...90, 100, 103, 112
Demouy, Leona, 89
Demouy Building, 90, 100, 103, 112
Dennis, Sarah, 94
Denver, CO., 10, 255, 256
Depau, Marie Catherine (aka la fille Gougis), ...67, 70
Des Armas, Honorine, 171
Detroit, MI, 107, 108, 273
De Ulloa, Antonio, 4
Deusterwaldt, Rosalie, 287
Diamond W Store, 29, 158, 176, 182
Diedelsheim, Baden, Germany, 206
Diefenthal, Adolph, 181-184
Diefenthal, Edward, 181, 183, 266
Diefenthal, Fannie, 183
Diefenthal, Matilda, 181-183
Diefenthal, Stanley Martin, 183, 184
Doll, Catharina, 175
Donaldsonville, Ascension Parish, 16, 69, ...91,102, 117-119, 156, 226, 227, 320
Dorfeuille, Marie Céleste Léda, 293
Dorr, J.W., 15, 39, 243, 246, 311, 347
Downing Plantation, 231
Dragusenii, Bessarabia, 249
Dresdner, Rebecca, 314
Dreyfous, Daniel, 70
Dreyfous, Mathilde, 330
Dreyfus, Alfred Joseph, 211, 220, 221, 228, 328
Dreyfus, Babette/Breundel, 195
Dreyfus, Daniel, 209
Dreyfus, David Stanley, 56
Dreyfus, Emma, 208, 209
Dreyfus, H. Artie, 56
Dreyfus, Henriette, 54, 55
Dreyfus, Henry Leon, 211, 213, 221, 228
Dreyfus, Hugo Clifton, 56
Dreyfus, Isaac, 55,
Dreyfus, Isaac, the younger, 52, 56
Dreyfus, Isaac (not identified), 234, 235
Dreyfus, Jacob/Jacques, 209
Dreyfus, Jerome Milford, 56
Dreyfus, Joseph, 150, 238, 328
Dreyfus, Mabel Sarah, 211, 214
Dreyfus, Marian Rose, 221
Dreyfus, Max Meyer, 211, 214, 220, 228
Dreyfus, Meyer, 210
Dreyfus, Rachelle, 213, 221
Dreyfus, Rosa, 145, 150
Dreyfus, Rosalie, 54, 55
Dreyfus, Rosina, 211, 213, 222-225, 228, 230
Dreyfus, Ruth, 56
Dreyfus, Sara, 273, 275
Dreyfus, Sidney, 212, 213, 220, 221, 225, 226, ...328
Dreyfus, Theodore "Theo," 1, 13-15, 18, 20, ...201, 204, 205, 210-214, 216-218, 222, 223, ...225,.228, 229, 235, 328, 337
Dreyfus, Theodore (s/o Alfred Joseph), 221
Dreyfus & Vallet, 216, 343
Dreyfus & Wolff, 211, 214
Dreyfus Department Store, 212, 225, 226, 228, ...250
Dreyfuss, Hortense, 232,233, 266
Dreyfuss, Jeannette, 284
Dreyfuss, Palmyre, 232, 266
Dreyfuss, Rachel, 319
Dreyfuss, Raphaël, 232
Druckman, Regina, 253
Duncan, Ethel, 328
Duportail, Marie, 75, 80
Duppigheim, Bas-Rhin, France, 195, 284
Durmenach, Haut-Rhin, France, 141
Duttlenheim, Bas-Rhin, France, 209, 284
Edward Loeb Frères & Co., 139, 142, 152
Eich, Rheinpfalz, Germany, 113
Eidensheim, Fannie, 140
Eiseman, Abraham, 60
Eiseman, Adolph, 61
Eiseman, Cassius Meyer 15, 60-64, 307
Eiseman, Harold, 61
Eiseman, Medea, 307
Eiseman, Rita Joseph, 61
El Dorado Plantation, 14, 207, 237-240, 242
El Dorado Station, 239, 241
El Dorado Store, 14, 207, 233, 237, 239, 240, ...242
Eliska Plantation, 200, 231
Eliska Store, 198, 231, 232
Elliot City, 197, 231
Emmich, Ellen, 160, 161
Emmich, Zacharias, 160
Engel, Fannie, 170
Enterprise Store, 277
Erlenbach, Rheinpfalz, Germany, 63
Erstein, Bas-Rhin, France, 292
Erwinville, WBR, 18, 131, 138, 244
Essingen, Baden-Württemberg, Germany, 92
Essingen, Rheinpfalz, Germany, 61, 308, 327
Estate of Theodore Dreyfus, Inc., 228

Eudel, Amelia, 85, 87
Eudora, AR, 253, 255
Evening Star Store, 14, 43, 44, 342
Everston, Maria, 245
Fabre, Madeleine, 122, 123
Fabre-Britto Plantation, 122, 123
Falk, Henrietta, 202, 264
Falk, Heymann, 284
Falk, Jeannette, 284
Falk, Johanna, 284
Falk, Julia, 80
Falk, Sara, 284
False River Store, 137, 145, 146, 150, 151, 158,
....201
False River Reporter, 227
Fan Plantation, 153, 155, 156
Fan Store, 153, 154, 156, 185
Fastio, Isaac Henriqués, 3, 21, 22-24, 123
Fayette, MS, 60, 61, 307, 318
Feder, Leon, 247, 248
Feder, Moses/Morris, 247, 248
Feibelman, Clara, 216
Feibelman, Frances/Fanny, 92
Feibelman, Moses, 216
Feibelman, Moyses, 92
Feist, Isaac, 259, 271-273
Feist, Marcus/Isaac (aka Félix Feist), 272, 273
Feist, Moÿse, 272
Feitel, Arthur, 53
Feitel, Daniel, 113
Feitel, Bertha, 313, 320
Feitel, Euphemia, 53, 201206
Feitel, Gottschalk (aka Cheap Charley), 320
Feitel, Josephine, 203, 205, 206
Feitel, Melanie, 206, 241, 242
Feitel, Nathan, 53, 203, 206
Feitel, Selma, 11, 53
Felix Loeb & Bros. 208
Fellman, Rachel/Ray, 335, 336
Fellman, Samuel, 335
Ferdinand Gumbel school, 11
Ferrier, Féroline, 109
Ferry Row Dry Goods Store, 111
Fey, Johanna, 173, 194
Field, Martha R., 6, 21, 67, 121
Finkelstein (aka Finkielsztejn), Abraham, 299,
....300
Finkelstein, Bettie, 306
Finkelstein, Dorothy, 306
Finkelstein, Eli, 286
Finkelstein, Esther, 299
Finkelstein, Florence, 306
Finkelstein, Gussie, 299
Finkelstein, Harry, 286, 287, 299, 300, 334
Finkelstein, Ida, 299
Finkelstein, Ida (d/o Israël), 300
Finkelstein, Israël Hercko, 287, 299, 300
Finkelstein, Joseph, 306
Finkelstein, Josiel Tavia, 286, 287, 299, 300
Finkelstein, Julia, 287
Finkelstein, Kate, 300
Finkelstein, Lena, 287
Finkelstein, Lily, 287
Finkelstein, Marx, 299
Finkelstein, Nathan, 287, 299, 300, 334
Finkelstein, Rashe Ethel, 300
Finkelstein, Rose, 287
Finkelstein, Reuben, 299, 306
Finkelstein, Ruby, 306
Finkelstein, Samuel, 287
Finkelstein, Solomon, 299, 300
Finkelstein & Friedberg, 286, 334
Finkelstein Bros. & Friedberg, 286, 300, 334
Finkelstein Dry Goods & Notions Co., 300
Firnberg, Helena, 295, 296
Firnberg, Solomon, 295, 296
Fisher-Srulovitz/Loeb Building, 249
Fishman, Lazar/Louis, 304, 323
Fishman, Rebecca, 305
F. J. Guérin, vs. Louis David, 163
Flood of 1912, 16-18, 20, 41, 126, 132, 186,
....215, 248, 256, 290, 301, 309, 312, 326-328,
....333
Flood of 1927, 16, 19, 313, 329
F. Munzesheimer & Co., 140
Fongravier, Elizabeth, 292
Fontaine, Arthur, 304
Fontaine, Mary, 260
Fordoche, PCP, 7, 17, 18, 197, 204, 221, 231,
....233, 234, 236, 243, 266, 289
Fordoche Lodge 292 – F. & A.M., 7, 215, 218,
....221, 233
Forstall, Emma Marie, 62
Fort Adams, MS, 143, 276
Fort-Louis, Bas-Rhin, France, 69
Fortlouis, Geneviève Stéphanie, 70, 192, 194
Fortlouis, Hélène Josephine, 27
Fortlouis, Jean Maurice, 27, 69-72, 120, 139,
....192
Fortlouis, John/Jean M. the younger, 70, 192-
....194
Fortlouis, Jules, 70

Fortlouis, Leopold, 71, 192, 193, 194
Fortlouis, Madele, 70, 72, 119, 120
Fortlouis, Mathilde, 70, 192
Fortlouis, Maurice, 27, 70, 193
Fortlouis, Michel, 70, 139, 192
Fortlouis, Philomène, 194
Fortlouis, Rosalie, 70, 72
Fortlouis, Théophile, 70, 192, 194
Fort Smith, AR, 218, 219
Fort Worth, TX, 145, 187, 241, 242
Fraenckel, Félix, 232
Fraenckel, Judith, 266
Fraenkel, Moses, 35.
Franck, Esther, 54
Frank, Abraham, 70, 72, 119
Frank, Abraham (h/o Barbara Silbernagel), 110
Frank, Adolph/Aron, 70, 119, 120, 262
Frank, Carrie, 110
Frank, Charles/Judah, 70, 262
Frank, Isidore, 72, 262
Frank, Jeannette, 241
Frank, Louis, 72, 262
Frank, Louis (s/o Sam Frank), 110
Frank, Matilda, 110
Frank, Myrtle, 111
Frank, Rebecca, 119
Frank, Sadie, 111
Frank, Samuel, 110, 111, 340
Frank, Samuel, Jr., 110
Frank, Sophie, 110
Frankfurt, Germany, 64, 217
Franklin, St. Mary Parish, 209
François, Hélène, 27
French and American Claims Commission, 9, ...262, 294
French Hotel, 14, 94, 249
Freyhan, Julius, 89, 92, 182
Freund, Sara, 28
Friedberg, Celia, 305, 306, 322, 323, 333
Friedberg, Deana, 334
Friedberg, Eva, 334
Friedberg, Harry, 334
Friedberg, Louis Wolf, 286, 288, 299, 300, 305, ...333, 334
Friedberg, Samuel, 305, 333
Friedberg, Samuel (s/o Louis), 334
Friedberg, Sarah, 334
Friedenberg, Baden, Germany, 160
Friedman, Etta, 184
Friedman, Eva, 184
Friedman, Harry, 184

Friedman, Joseph B., 184
Friedman, Leah, 184
Friedman, Lloyd Kling, 185
Friedman, Miriam, 184
Friedman, Rosa, 184
Friedman, Tillie, 184
Friedman, Tillie Gertrude, 185
Friedman, William L. "Willie," 184, 185
Frisco, PCP, 2, 11, 197, 198, 202, 204
Frisco Railway, PCP, 17, 19, 126, 130-132
Frishman, Abraham, 217
Frishman, Samuel, 217
Frogmore Plantation, 197, 215, 239
Galatz/Galati, Romania, 248, 254
Galveston, TX, 145, 187, 208, 256, 263, 316, ...330
Gamburg, Daniel/Gdal, 134
Gamburg, Dorothy Mae, 135
Gamburg, Harry/Gersh Joseph, 134
Gamburg, Joseph, 133-135
Gamburg, Mina/Minnie, 134
Gamburg, Nathan/Nechemia, 133, 190
Gamburg, Rosalie, 135
Garcia, Tony, 107
Garrot, Leon, 113
Garrot, Louise, 113, 114
Gaudschau, Caroline, 30
Gebhart, Meinard M., 47, 48, 198
Gebhart, Zénon, 78
Generes, Louisa, 210
George, Zulma, 107
Gerolsheim, Rheinpfalz, Germany, 58
Gerschel, Mathias, 30
Gerson, Benjamin, 123, 124, 152, 277, 278
Gerson, George, 15, 122, 123, 277-279
Gerson, Henry, 122
Gerson, Laura, 122
Gerson, Josephine, 122
Gerson, Julius, 122, 125
Gerson, Nathan, 122, 123, 277-279
Gerson, Reuben, 122
Gibbs, Rosa W. 53
Ginn, James M. 152, 153
Ginn & Keim, 152
Ginsberg, Anna/Annie, 333, 334
Ginsberg, Miller, 333
Glapion, Stephanie, 260
Glapion, Télésphore, 260
Glasser, Julia, 287
Glick, Hannah Rebecca, 336
Glotz, Salomon, 214

Glynn, PCP, 16, 19, 137, 162, 186, 187, 195, ...199, 200, 201
Glynn, Alphonse J., 65
Glynn, Martin, 65, 334
Glynnwood Plantation, 162
Godchaux/Godchot, Caroline/Zippert, 313
Godchaux/Godchot, Julie, 63
Goersdorf, Bas-Rhin, France, 209
Gold, Aaron, 325
Gold, Benjamin, 325
Golden Rule Department Store, 254, 255
Goldenberg, Bertha, 301
Goldenberg, Charles, 301
Goldman, Abraham F., 110, 111
Goldman, Esther, 306
Goldman, Hannah, 306
Goldman, Joseph, 37
Goldman, Mattie, 306
Goldman, Samuel, 306
Goldman, Sarah/Yetta, 305, 306, 323
Goldman, Solomon, 306
Goldman, Thomas, 288, 305, 306, 320, 322, 323, 333
Goldschmidt, David, 181
Goldsmith, Felice, 181
Goldsmith/Goldschmidt, Leopold, 144, 181
Goldsmith, Louis, 55
Goldsmith, Shirley Sarah, 181
Goldsmith, Haber & Co., 43, 44, 46, 55
Goldstein, Flora, 155
Goldstein, Moses, 155
Gomez, Francis, Jr., 268, 269
Gommersheim, Rheinpfalz, Germany, 188, 219
Gonzales, TX, 218
Gonzalvo-Henriqués, Préciosa, 317, 318
Gordon, Ryfka, 324
Gosselin, Octavie, 119
Gosserand, Adèle, 107
Gosserand, Joseph Philibert, 99, 127
Gosserand, Louise, 107, 171, 172
Gosserand, Séverin, 171
Gosserand, Villeneuve, 83
Gottlieb, Caroline, 98
Gottlieb, Charles, 98, 159
Gottlieb, Emanuel, 98
Gottlieb, Ike Hahn, 99
Gottlieb, Joseph, 98, 99, 159, 318
Gottlieb, Lewis, 99
Gottlieb, Moses, 98, 159
Gottlieb, Rosalie, 99
Gottlieb, Solomon, 98, 159

Gottlieb, Solomon J., 99
Goudchaux, Babette, 150
Goudchaux, Clément, 81, 82
Goudchaux, Jacques, 30, 31, 79, 81-84, 150, ...216, 261, 326
Goudchaux, Jacques (h/o Rosette Kahn), 150
Goudchaux, Maximilien/Max, 81, 82
Goudchaux/Gaudchau, Pauline, 30, 82
Goudchaux, Julie, 82
Goudchaux, Oralie, 82
Goudchaux, Séverine, 82
Goudchaux, Ursilia, 82
Gougis, Joséphine, 172
Grabenheimer, Edwin, 206
Grabenheimer, Henry/Herz, 201, 206
Grabenheimer, Hilda, 206
Grabenheimer, Lucille Ruth, 206
Grabenheimer, Norman, 206
Grabenheimer, Sadie, 206
Grabenheimer, Sidney H., 206
Grady, Joseph Glenna, 53
Grand Bay Plantation, 63, 65
Grand Bayou Plantation (later Alma), 22
Grand Leader Store, 215
Grand Levee, 28, 29, 243, 244, 265, 293
Grandpierre, Cecilia, 107
Grasioni/Grasiany, Esther, 247, 248
Grasioni/Grasiany, Sabetay, 247
Grathwohl, Fanny, 85
Graugnard-Richy Bldg., 79, 99, 116, 188, 239
Greenville, MS, 253, 255, 289, 313
Greisen, Germany, 288
Grimaldi. Albert Honoré Charles (aka Albert I ....of Monaco), 294, 295
Grosbliederstroff, Moselle, France, 113, 320
Grossman, Adolph, 115, 162
Grossman, Celina, 115, 162
Grossman, Isidore, 115, 162
Grossman, Jacob, 15, 51, 115, 155, 156, 162-....167, 169, 173, 178, 188, 191
Grossman, Louis, 162
Grossman's Landing, WBR, 162
Grossman vs. Kern & Kern, 164
Grossman vs. Rosine Kern, 153, 154
Grossman-Weinfeld Millinery Co., Ltd., 115, ...116, 162, 339
Grünstadt, Rheinpfalz, Germany, 73, 89, 102, ...117, 227
Guérin, Amelina, 26, 27
Guérin, Émile, Jr., 176
Gukenheim, Magdalena, 140

Gumbel, Beulah Louise, 202
Gumbel, Bryant, 147
Gumbel, Clara, 49, 53, 145, 170, 179, 198
Gumbel, Clara (d/o Richard Gumbel), 149
Gumbel, Charles Adalbert, "C.A," 110, 161, ...170, 198-200, 231, 232
Gumbel, Cora, 202
Gumbel, Cornélie, 107, 147, 150
Gumbel, Cornelius Jacob/Carl, 49, 52, 53, 107, ...142, 145-150, 197, 203, 205
Gumbel, Cornelius J. (b. 1895), 53
Gumbel, Elise, 202
Gumbel, Eugénie Virginie, 147, 149
Gumbel, Felicie, 53
Gumbel, Félicie Anastasie, 200
Gumbel, Ferdinand, 11, 27, 49, 52, 53, 74, 145, ...198, 203, 205, 206, 241, 242, 260
Gumbel, Florence, 201
Gumbel, Henry Elias, 11, 201
Gumbel, Herbert, 53
Gumbel, Horace Simon, 201
Gumbel, Jeannette, 49, 53, 145, 198, 203, 206
Gumbel, Joseph, 202
Gumbel, Joseph Cornelius "Jack," 147-149
Gumbel, Joseph Dunbar (aka Richard Dunbar), ...147, 149
Gumbel, Joseph Hildévert, "J.H.,"13, 110, 172, ...198, 200, 201, 232
Gumbel, Julia, 202
Gumbel, Leona, (aka Leona Ker), 27, 53
Gumbel, Léonce, 149
Gumbel, Lester, 202
Gumbel, Lucien Joseph, (aka Lucien Joseph ....Ker), 27, 53
Gumbel, Lucille, 202
Gumbel, Moses Hirsch, 49, 52, 145, 197
Gumbel, Neville, 53
Gumbel, Ophelia Rosalind, 202
Gumbel, Rosa, 198
Gumbel, Sarah "Settie," 41, 49, 145, 203, 267, ...269, 290, 298
Gumbel, Simon, 11, 35, 49, 52, 53, 110, 143, ...145, 146, 161, 191, 196, 197, 198, 200-203, ...232, 238, 239, 241, 264, 270
Gumbel, Mayer & Co., 146, 158, 204, 214
Gumbel, Mayer & Loeb, 137, 145, 146, 150-....152, 158, 197, 201, 203
Gumbel & Richy, 202, 203
Gumbel & Richy Mill, 203
Gundershoffen, Bas-Rhin, France, 170, 266, 295
Gunst, Hannah, 317

Gunst, Israel, 173, 317, 318
Gunst, Jacov, 317
Gunst, Maude Henrietta, 318
Gunst, Tressa, 317, 318
Gutton, Rev. Joseph Philibert, 127-128
Haas, Eliza, 263
Haber, Abraham, 55, 266
Haber, Caroline/Kindle, 266
Haber, Florence, 170, 171
Haber, Joseph, 266
Haber, Simon, 171
Haber, Valentin, 266
Haber & Blum, 10, 12, 266, 267, 291
Haguenau, Bas-Rhin, France, 49, 69, 75, 83, 303
Hahn, Rebecca, 99
Hall, George Otis, 293
Hamburg, Germany, 270, 277, 314
Hamilton Plantation, 308, 309
Hanover, Niedersachsen, Germany, 25, 174, 317
Harris, Mary, 107
Harskirchen, Bas-Rhin, France, 241
Hart, Anna Ruth, 254
Hart, Bertha, 218
Hart, Gabriel, 255 (See also Gabriel Srulovitz)
Hart, Gus, 34
Hart, Harold Irwin, 254
Hart, Max H., (See Max Srulovitz, the younger)
Hart, Noah Leon, 254
Hartstein, Chana/Anna, 306
Hartstein, Israël, 306
Hassloch, Rheinpfalz, Germany, 308
Hatten, Bas-Rhin, France, 48
Hattiesburg, MS, 76
Hausmann, Theresa, 36, 56-58, 233, 315
Hausser, Sara, 274
Hautviller, Michel, 75
Hautviller, Nanette, 75
Havard, Benjamin James, 108
Havard, Leonard, 108
Havard, Margie, 108
Hayem, Abraham, 179, 180
Hayem, Isaac, 74
Hayem, Lazard, 179
Hayem, Mamie Clémence, 179, 180
Hébert, Marie Zulma, 53
Hegenheim, Haut-Rhin, France, 141
Heidenheim, Rheinpfalz, Germany, 189
Heillecourt, Meurthe-et-Moselle, France, 202
Heine, Armand/Heyman, 293, 294
Heine, Heinrich, 293
Heine, Isaac, 293

Heine, Isaac Georges, 293
Heine, Marie Alice, 292-294
Heine, Michel, 293
Heine, Paul Henri, 293
Heine, Salomon, 293
Heller, Rabbi Max, 222, 297
Hellman & Stadeker, 44, 46
Henriqués, Isaac, 317
Herbéviller, Meurthe-et-Moselle, France, 63
Hermann, Jacques Simon, 50
Hermann, Joseph Jefferson, 51
Hermann, Louis, 51
Hermann, Louisa, 50
Hermann, Simon, 41, 50, 51, 55, 163, 164, 166,
....191, 192
Hermann & Grossman, 51, 163, 164, 166
Hermitage, PCP, 2, 8, 51, 121, 137, 140, 151,
....152, 163, 173, 176-178, 195, 244.
Hermitage Landing, PCP, 2, 51, 137, 163
Hernandez, Adilie, 217
Hernandez, Jerome Emanuel, 217
Herndon, George, 76
Herrlisheim, Bas-Rhin, France, 326
Herrlisheim-près-Colmar, Haut-Rhin, France,
....175
Herskovitz, Rebecca, 247, 248, 300
Herskovitz/Harris, David, 96
Herskovitz/Harris, Fannie, 95
Herskovitz/Harris, Henry, 95
Herskovitz/Harris, Isadore, 95
Herskovitz/Harris, Joseph, 95, 96
Herskovitz/Harris, Solomon, 96
Herxheim, Rheinpfalz, Germany, 55, 74, 178
Herzog, Abraham Joel, 304, 305, 306, 323-325
Herzog, Celia, 305, 324, 325
Herzog, Charles Eli, 305, 323-325
Herzog, Harry, 305
Herzog, Louis, 305, 324
Herzog, Mattie, 305, 323, 325
Herzog, Samuel, 305, 323, 324
Herzog, Samuel (s/o Abraham Herzog), 306
Herzog Bros. & Co., 323, 324
Hess, Jacob, 280-282
Hess, Regina, 58, 60
Hess, Rosina, 43, 60, 280
Heuchelheim, Rheinpfalz, Germany, 29, 41, 51,
.....55, 61
Hewes, Miguel T., 125, 128, 133
Hewes, Thomas H., 97, 122, 125, 133, 287
Heyman, Julia, 142
Hickey, Elizabeth, 317, 318

Hildesheim, Rhine-Hesse, Germany, 33
Hirsch, Abraham, 52
Hirsch, Amelia, 52
Hirsch, David, 29, 33, 51, 52, 55, 56
Hirsch, Fannie, 33, 52
Hirsch, Fanny, 218
Hirsch, Lea, 308, 327
Hirsch, Regina, 52
Hirsch, Sarah, 52
Hirschberger, Abraham, 44, 46
Hirschberger, Joseph, 31, 42, 44-46
Hochfelder, Bernard, 287
Hochfelder, Berthold, 287
Hochfelder, Joseph K., 287
Hochfelder, Julia, 287
Hochfelder, Max, 287, 288
Hoffenheim, Baden, Germany, 49
Hoffman, Emil, 310
Hoffman, Israël, 310
Hoffman, Lena, 310
Hoffman, Moritz/Morris, 310
Hollander, David Charles, 174, 175
Hollander, Gustavus, 174
Honoré, Émile, 270
Hope Plantation, 259-261
Horbourg-Wihr, Haut-Rhin, France, 273, 274
Hough, Henrietta/Retta, 309
Hough, Philip, 309
Houston, TX, 59, 160, 185, 206, 284, 286, 306,
....323, 324
Hubert & Spiro, 277
Husi, Western Moldovia, 95
Hydropolis, Avoyelles Parish, 71
Hyman, Bernard Harold, 170
Hyman, Flora, 158, 175, 208
Hyman, George, 158, 169, 170
Hyman, Henry 158, 158, 169, 175, 208
Hyman, Henry Joseph, 170
Hypolite, Françoise, 27
Icaza, Ida Isabel, 217
Idlewild Plantation, 310
I. Levi & Co., 198, 200, 231, 232
I. Lowenburg Co., 308
Illereichen, Rheinpfalz, Germany, 202
Immaculate Conception Church, 5, 6, 82, 137,
....144, 149, 150, 156, 163, 171, 172, 191, 195,
....199
Influenza Pandemic, 13, 99, 325
Ingelman, Rachel, 324
Ingenheim, Bas-Rhin, France, 261

Ingenheim, Rheinpfalz, Germany, 51, 217, 295, ...315, 316
Ingleside Plantation, 131-133, 138, 158
Ingwiller, Bas-Rhin, France, 50, 179, 233, 237, ...271, 303
Innis, PCP, 18, 262, 272, 286, 289, 290, 292, ...297
Innis, James, 262, 267
Innis Plantation, 267, 271
Innis Store, 271
Island of False River, PCP, 5, 11, 15, 26, 27, 40. ....41, 50, 56, 68, 76, 81, 82, 85, 97, 122, 148, ...150, 153, 171, 191-194, 244
Isaac, Alexandre, 56
Isaac, Reine Ordalie, 194
Isaac, Stratiote M., 56, 194
Isaacs, Sarah, 25, 26
Israël, Augustine, 210
Israël, Babette, 209
Israël, Ernestine, 210
Israël, Joseph, 210
Israël, Josephine, 210
Israël, Mamie, 210
Israël, Samuel, 209, 210
Israël, Samuel George, 210
I. Rothschild & Son., 327
I. Wolff, The Fancy Grocer, 100, 103, 115, 178
Jackson, Althea Ann, 90
Jackson, EFP, 82, 250, 251, 263
Jackson, MS, 108, 150, 332
Jacob Grossman vs. Abraham Kern and Rosine ....Kern, 155, 156, 178
Jacobs, Charlotte, 246
Jacobs, Janet, 221
Jacobs, Wolf, 221
Jacoby, Max, 329-330
Jacoby, Solomon, 330, 331
Jacoby, PCP, 257, 258
Jacoby Plantation, 331
James, Samuel L. 9
Jarreau, Carmelia, 150
Jarreau, Clarence, 150
Jarreau, Clément, 167, 169
Jarreau, Cornelius Alphonse, 150
Jarreau, Jean, 243
Jarreau, Jean Ursin, 61
Jarreau, Joseph Estelle/Steve, 150
Jarreau, Joseph Monford, 150
Jarreau, Joseph Neuville, 150
Jarreau, Lawrence, 150
Jarreau, Léonard, 107
Jarreau, Lillian, 150,
Jarreau, Marie Cecilia, 107
Jarreau, Marie Laurenza, 150
Jarreau, Neville, 150
Jarreau, Rose Delia, 150
Jarreau, Valérien, 107, 150
Jaworkowski, Chaja Rachel, 300
Jaworkowski, Girsz, 300
Jeanerette, Iberia Parish, 193, 194
Jérémie, Saint-Domingue, 146, 147
Jewell, Agnes, C.S.J., 26
Jewell, Alphonse Lamartine, 26, 27, 97
Jewell, Benjamin, 5, 8, 16, 25-27, 53, 97, 100, ...103, 232, 304
Jewell, Benjamin, II, 26, 27, 97
Jewell, Benjamin III, 27
Jewell, Edwin Lewis, 27
Jewell, Frederick Lewis, 27
Jewell, Isabella Virginia, 26
Jewell, Jane Marie, 26
Jewell, Joseph E., 27
Jewell, Joseph Émile, 27
Jewell, Joseph Philibert, Sr., 26
Jewell, Joseph Philibert, Jr., 26
Jewell, Joshua Joseph, 27
Jewell, Juliana "Hannah," 27, 53, 103
Jewell, Octave, 27
Jewell, Pierre Marius, 27
Jewell's Crescent City Illustrated, 27
Joe, Augustin, 82
Joe, Marie Madeleine, 82
Joffrion, Edward, 216
Joffrion, Oscar, 95, 126
Joffrion, Paul, 86
Joffrion, Sidney, 190
Jonas, Abraham Henry, 61
Jonas, Rosalie Swift, 61
Joseph, Agnes Miriam Joyce, 113
Joseph, Barbara Ann, 113
Joseph, Cecilia Meyer, 61
Joseph, Dorothy Ruth, 113
Joseph, Flora/Fleurette, 320
Joseph, Gordon Louis, 113
Joseph, Isaac, 313
Joseph, Jacob Judah, 61
Joseph, Joseph Jules, 113, 320
Joseph, Katie, 61, 63
Joseph, Leon, 113, 114, 320
Joseph, Leon Jules, 113
Joseph, Lisar/Elias H., 61
Joseph, Moïse, 113

Joseph, Percy T., 317
Joseph, Percye, 317
Judas, Jeanne, 284
Junger, Miriam, 266
Kahn, Blanche, 185
Kahn, Charles, 205, 208, 209, 319, 322, 325, ...326
Kahn, Daniel, 218
Kahn, Emilie, 117, 227
Kahn, Esther, 73, 74
Kahn, Franziska, 308
Kahn, Gilbert, 208
Kahn, Guillaume, See Henry Cohn
Kahn, Gustave/Gus, 325
Kahn, Harold Abraham, 208
Kahn, Helena, 301, 309, 310
Kahn, Henriette/Harriet, 273
Kahn, Hermann, 180
Kahn, Heymann, 319, 325
Kahn, Heymann (h/o Palmyre Sommer), 326
Kahn, Joseph, 301
Kahn, Lehman, 218, 219
Kahn, Lester James, 208
Kahn, Lucien, 218
Kahn, Magdalena, 93
Kahn, Marie, 325
Kahn, Marguerite/Marie, 319, 320, 322
Kahn, Mathias, 185
Kahn, Mathilde, 185
Kahn, Rosa, 119
Kahn, Rosette, 150
Kahn, Sarah, 91
Kahn, Seligmann/Sol, 319, 322, 325, 326
Kahn, Serette Emanuel, 47
Kahn, Serin (aka Serette) 57
Kahn, Théodore, 273
Kahns, WBR, 388-320, 322, 325
Kaiserslautern, Rheinpfalz, Germany, 52, 58, ...140, 189, 233
Kamil, Miriam Rebecca, 255
Karlsruhe, Baden, Germany, 69, 119
Kassel, Alfred, 107
Kassel, Louis, 105
Kassel, Martin, Jr., 107
Kassel, Meyer Louis, 107
Kassel, Moses/Martin, 105
Kassel, Myrtle, 107
Kassel & Stern, 105-109
Kateland, Grant Parish, See Cakeland
Katz, Alexander, 287
Katz, Daniel Simon, 226

Katz, Dora, 64
Katz, Doris Rose, 226
Katz, Jennie, 287, 288
Katz, Joseph, 226
Katz, Joseph Alphonse, 226
Katz, Mary, 334
Katz, Nellie, 287, 288
Katz, William Ruprecht, 214, 226
Katzenstein, David Salomon, 75
Katzenstein, Eugène, 74-76
Katzenstein, Marie Harriett, 76
Katzenstein, Nathan/Adrien, 74
Kauffmann, Abraham, 170
Kauffmann, Julie, 208
Kauffmann, Sarah, 170
Kaufman, Aaron, 151, 152, 178, 179
Kaufman, Abraham, 107, 170-172, 178, 180, ...239
Kaufman, Abe Hayem, 180
Kaufman, Abram (s/o Abraham), 171
Kaufman, Adrien, 180
Kaufman, Albert, 170, 171
Kaufman, Carrie, 176
Kaufman, Charlotte, 141
Kaufman, Deborah, 178
Kaufman, Ella, 172, 173
Kaufman, Ernest, 170
Kaufman, Ernest "To To," 171, 172
Kaufman, Ernest (s/o Samuel), 172
Kaufman, Emanuel, 162, 188, 189
Kaufman, Fanny, 295-298, 332
Kaufman, Ferdinand, 5, 170, 179, 180
Kaufman, Gertrude Theresa, 172
Kaufman, Henrietta/Harriett, 74, 151, 152, 176, ...271
Kaufman, Jacob (aka Jean), 170, 179
Kaufman, Jonathan, 295
Kaufman, Henry, 74, 170, 175, 178
Kaufman, Leola, 172
Kaufman, Léon Alfred, 171
Kaufman, Leopold, 143, 152, 170, 175, 208
Kaufman, Leslie, 180
Kaufman, Louis, 178
Kaufman, Marx, 188
Kaufman, Mathilda "Tillie," 188, 219
Kaufman, Melvin, 172
Kaufman, Melvin (s/o Emanuel Kaufman), 189
Kaufman, Miriam, 176
Kaufman, Otto, 170
Kaufman, Rosina, 172
Kaufman, Ruth, 176

Kaufman, Samuel, 172
Kaufmann, Lazar, 249
Kaufmann, Rebecca, 249
Keim, Isaac, 15, 42, 49, 50, 122, 123, 139, 142,
....152, 153, 168, 191, 233, 238, 239, 297
Keim, Zacharie, 50, 297
Keller, August, 15, 50, 152, 206, 207, 233, 237-
....239, 241, 242
Keller, Leib, 241
Keller, Zoë, 206, 241, 242
Keller, PCP, 37, 38, 50, 93, 257, 326, 327
Kellum, Leroy William, 195
Kenmore Plantation, 204, 237, 239, 242
Ker, Anatole E. 53
Kern, Abraham, 47, 79, 153-156, 163-169, 173,
....178, 185
Kern, Agathyne, 155, 156
Kern, Albert Herman, 80
Kern, Beijen, 79
Kern, Blanche, 92
Kern, Cyprien Léonce, 235
Kern, Daniel, 85
Kern, David, 47
Kern, Gerschel, 79
Kern, Henry, 92
Kern, Isaac Léonard, 155
Kern, Lazard, 47, 154
Kern, Lazare/Lazarus, 85, 154
Kern, Léonard, 47, 77, 78, 153
Kern, Léonard the younger, 47, 78
Kern, Leopold, 47
Kern, Meyer, 47, 154-156, 166
Kern, Nathan, 31, 40, 42, 46, 47, 75, 77-79, 85,
....152, 153, 162
Kern, Nathan (s/o Abraham Kern)155
Kern, Nathan, the younger, 75, 78-80
Kern, Regina, 211, 214
Kern, Rosebud, 155, 156
Kern, Rosina (aka Mrs. R. Kern), 47, 153, 155,
....165, 169, 178
Kern, Sadie, 155
Kern, Solomon, 47
Kiev, Ukraine, 304
Kirchheimbolanden, Rheinpfalz, Germany, 52,
....197
Kirrweiler, Rheinpfalz, Germany, 185, 201, 264
Kishinev, Bessarabia, 125
Kleborn, Christophe, 70, 77
Kleborn, Dr. Joseph Ildévert, 78, 110, 198
Klein, Caroline, 63
Klein, Frédéric, 48

Klein, Rabbi Marx, 48,
Kleinenbroich, Germany, 36
Kleinstein, Ziril, 335
Kling, Amelia, 185
Kling, David, 185
Kling, Jacob, 310
Kling, Katie, 310
Klinger, Rifke, 116
Klinger, Thomas A., 4, 5
Klotz/Glotz, Abraham, 214, 222, 320
Klotz/Glotz, Edmond David, 214
Klotzville, Assumption Parish, 214, 222, 320
Koenig, Alexander, 112, 113
Koenig, Dora, 112
Koenig, Judah Touro/Joseph, 112
Koenig & Brown, 113
Kohlman, Clara, 73, 74
Kohlman, Henry, 73
Kohn, Carl, 61
Kohn, Marie Amélie, 294
Kohn, Sarah Evelina, 61
Koritzky, Abram, 187
Koritzky, Herbert, 187
Kosminsky, Abraham, 286
Kosminsky, Charlotte/Lotta, 286, 287
Kottwitz, Alex, 316
Kovno, Lithuania, 253
Krakow, Poland, 85
Krotz Springs, St. Landry Parish, 221, 226, 328
Kujawsko-Pomorskie, Poland, 218
Kutzenhausen, Bas-Rhin, France, 30
Labatut, Euphémie, 293
Labatut, Jules, 293
Labatut Store, 29, 36, 37, 93
Labry, Eliska, 231
Lacour, Cécile, 31, 32
Lacour, Constance, 39
Lacour, Léon O., 277
Lacour, Marguérite, 261
Lacour, Ovide, 276, 298
Lacour (formerly Planchette), PCP, 257, 299
Ladmirault, Dr. Ludovic, 28, 83
Lafargue, Inez, 108
Lafayette, Jefferson Parish, 52, 55,
Lafayette, Lafayette Parish, 17, 118, 119, 221,
....225, 227, 228, 237, 316
Lakeland, PCP, 5-8, 15, 18, 22, 29, 47, 48, 77,
....94, 97, 100, 127, 131, 133, 137, 138, 146,
....149, 152, 156-159, 162-164, 166, 167, 169-
....173, 175-181, 183, 185-187, 189-191, 195,
....204, 208, 239, 279, 304, 342

Lakeside Cotton Oil Co., Ltd., 283
Lambsheim, Rheinpfalz, Germany 74, 178
Lanclos, Marie Celestine, 216
Landau, Arthur, 279
Landau, Arthur Peyser, 290
Landau, Dora/Babs, 290
Landau, Hubert G., 234
Landau, Jacob, 175
Landau, Julius, 174, 175
Landau, Julius Meyer, 234
Landau, Kurt, 175
Landau, Levy Leopold, 175
Landau, Marcus, 268, 279-283, 289, 299
Landau, Marie, 290
Landau, Martha, 175
Landau, Maurice David, 9, 18, 234, 279, 283,
....289, 290
Landau, Rosa, 290
Landau & Hess, 239, 268, 280-282
Landau, Rheinpfalz, Germany, 183, 307
Landau-Way Incident, 8, 290
Landis, Elizabeth, 291
Landry, Achille, 260
Landry, Auguste, 260
Landry, Auguste, Jr. 260
Langeais, Indre-et-Loire, France, 109
Langenfeld, Rheinpfalz, Germany, 182, 186,
....265
Langfeld, Caroline, 264, 313
Langlois, Dolorite, 41
Langlois, Jean-Baptiste, 77
Langlois, Julie, 70, 192
Langlois, Pierre, 76, 77
Langlois, Rosalie, 72
Langlois & Wolff, 48, 76, 77, 157
Lauchly, Sylvia Reed, 255
Laudanum, 13, 157, 240
Lauferti, Freda/Fanny, 233
Lautenberg, Poland, 115, 162
Lautersheim, Rheinpfalz, Germany, 142, 160,
....173, 181, 187, 194
La Walck, Bas-Rhin, France, 222
Layman, Leopold, 331
Lazard, Charlotte, 200, 201
Lazarus, Leopold, 138, 139, 142
Lazarus & Loeb, 138-140, 142
Leathers, Capt. Thomas P., 193, 246
LeBeau, Louella, 172
LeBeau, Murray, 13, 14, 122
Lecompte, Rapides Parish, 58
LeCoq, Auguste, 77

Ledoux, Amaron, 293
Ledoux, Miltenberger & Hall, 268, 292, 293
Lefebvre, Luce, 145
Legonier, PCP, 257, 286, 288, 311, 333-335
Lehman, Adèle, 233
Lehman, Alphonse, 237
Lehman, Bertha, 155
Lehman, Isidore, 50, 233, 237
Lehman, Israël, 179, 233
Lehman, Leon, 237
Lehman, Leona, 237
Lehman, Mabel, 237
Lehman, Maude, 237
Lehman, Sophie, 179, 233
Lehman, Theresa, 237
Lehmann, Judith/Jetta, 272
Leindorfer, Latte, 310
Lejeune, Ovide, 260, 261, 278
Lemle, Bertha 34
Lemmel, Leon, 185
Lengsfeld, Jacob H. 202, 264
Lengsfeld, Regina Eugenia, 264
Lengsfeld, Sophie Virginia, 201, 202
Lengsfeld, William H., 238
Leopold, Amelia, 58
Leopold, Rosine, 301
Leopold, Solomon, 58
Leopold Weil Building & Improvement Co., 304
Lesser, Amy Paul "Toot," 6, 108-110, 198
Lesser, William, 10, 109
Lettsworth, PCP, 8, 18, 19, 23, 44, 137, 257,
....302, 303, 306, 310, 312
Lettsworth Planting Company, PCP, 307-309
Lettsworth Station, PCP, 304, 309, 323
Leufroy, Ashley Joseph, 172
Levee, Edward Boudinot, Sr., 291, 292
Levee, Edward Boudinot, Jr., 291
Levee, Frank Landis, 291
Levee, Frederick Ransom, 291
Levee, Lillian, 292
Levee, Lionel Cardoza, 291
Levee, Lucius Place, 291, 292
Levee, Lucius Place, Jr., 292
Levee, William Aubrey, 291
Levi, Aaron, 232
Levi, Esther, 22
Levi, Emanuel, 263
Levi, Isaac (h/o Hortense Dreyfuss), 198, 231-
....233, 266
Levin, Isaac, 85
Levin, Jacob, 241

Levy, Aaron, 183
Levy, Abraham, 28, 258, 261, 265
Levy, Abraham Gaston, 265
Levy, Achille, 7, 28, 29, 176, 235, 259, 262, ...271-273,.288
Levy, Ada, 272
Levy, Adelaide, 31
Levy, Adele, 48
Levy, Alfred (aka. Alfred A.), 260
Levy, Amelia, 64, 65
Levy, Arthur, 9, 28, 176, 179, 259, 260-262, ...265, 272
Levy, Auguste Abraham., 9, 179, 260, 261, 262, ...337
Levy, Barbe, 227
Levy, Bella, 265
Levy, Beryl Estelle, 235
Levy, Beulah, 177
Levy, Caroline, 49
Levy, Caroline/Carrie (w/o Leon Moyse), 313
Levy, Carrie Leah, 272
Levy, Cécile (aka Henriette), 48
Levy, Cerf Wolf, 177
Levy, Charles Frank, 264
Levy, Dahlia, 208
Levy, Daniel, 263
Levy, David, 195
Levy, David (s/o Daniel), 263
Levy, David Cardoza, 291
Levy, Doris Amelia, 119
Levy, Édouard, 217
Levy, Edward, 203
Levy, Edward Boudinot, Sr. (later Levee), 291, ...292
Levy, Emanuel, 263, 318
Levy, Ernestine, 181
Levy, Ethel Mary, 260
Levy, Feistel, 264, 313
Levy, Frances (d/o David), 195
Levy, Frances/Fannie/Hattie (d/o Simon, Jr.), ...203
Levy, Gotton, 179
Levy, Hannah Jeannette, 284
Levy, Harriet/Hattie, 175, 235
Levy, Helen, 49
Levy, Henrietta, 272
Levy, Henrietta Müller, 177
Levy, Henriette, 312
Levy, Henry, 49
Levy, Henry Muller, 272
Levy, Irma, 49

Levy, Isaac, (b. Riedseltz, Bas-Rhin), 12, 41-43, ...49, 84, 203, 267- 269, 279-283, 290, 297
Levy, Isaac (unidentified), 290, 291
Levy, Jacob, 49
Levy, Jacob (s/o Moses), 175
Levy, Jeannette, 180
Levy, Jeannette (w/o Solomon Levy), 181
Levy, Joseph, 315
Levy, Josephine, 215
Levy, Josephine (w/o Simon Weil), 217
Levy, Jules, 28, 258-261, 265, 339
Levy, Julia Rose, 235, 265-267, 271, 272
Levy, Julie, 175
Levy, Julie (w/o Moïse Weill), 195
Levy, Leon "Mannie," 18, 175, 235, 272
Levy, Leona, 260
Levy, Leonard, 118, 322, 326
Levy, Leopold (s/o Abraham Levy), 28, 186, ...260, 265, 267, 271
Levy, Leopold (aka Leopold H. Levy), 201, 264, ...265, 313
Levy, Lion, 291
Levy, Lionel Cardoza, 291
Levy, Louise, 177
Levy, Malgy, 209, 210
Levy, Marcus, 264
Levy, Marx, 180
Levy, Mathilde "Tillie B.," 265-267, 271
Levy, Maurice (h/o of Esther Picard), 48
Levy, Maurice (h/o Rachel Wolff), 29, 49, 176, ...177, 182, 259, 279, 304
Levy, Maurice Cerf, 315
Levy, Mayer, 272
Levy, Merla, 177
Levy, Meyer, 12, 28, 29, 40, 158, 176, 177, 182, ...235, 258-259, 265, 271, 273, 279, 304
Levy, Meyer Arthur, 177
Levy, Mildred Lucy, 177, 272
Levy, Mina, 101, 102
Levy, Morris, 119
Levy, Moses/Moïse, 175, 235
Levy, Nancy, 123, 124, 277
Levy, Nanette/Jeannette, 232
Levy, Nellie, 264
Levy, Nephtali, 195
Levy, Oswald Jules, 260
Levy, Rose, 87-88
Levy, Rosine, 41-43, 49, 58, 279
Levy, Ruth, 272
Levy, Samson, 41, 49
Levy, Samuel (s/o Isaac Levy), 49

Levy, Samuel (s/o Moses), 175
Levy, Samuel B., 265
Levy, Sarah, 175, 176
Levy, Sarah (d/o Josephine Charlot), 260
Levy, Sarah (d/o Achille Levy), 272
Levy, Sarah/Sallie, 263
Levy, Simon, Jr., 203
Levy, Simon Weil, 177
Levy, Solomon, 181
Levy, Thérèse, 9, 260-262
Levy, Thérèse Albertine, 265
Levy, Tilden Arthur, 272
Levy, Vivian, 177
Levy & Feist, 259, 271, 273
Levy & Fontaine, 279, 304
Levy Rice Mill, 49, 268
Lewis, Lillian Helen, 145, 187, 188
Lewis, Moses, 187
L. Fishman & Co., 304, 305, 323
Lichtenau, Baden, Germany, 30
Lieber, Bessye, 108
Lieber, Leopold, 108
Littauer, Hannah, 87
Little Italy, PCP, 17, 130, 132, 197
Livaudais, Bertha, 125
Livonia, PCP, 4, 7, 8, 13, 14, 18, 20, 117, 125,
....145, 150, 151, 197, 198, 201, 202-206, 208-
....218, 220-229, 231, 233, 237, 238, 241, 242,
....246, 249, 250, 328
Livonia High School, 11, 204, 213, 214, 227
Livonia Lodge, 6, 7, 158, 177, 283
Livonia Saw Mill, 216, 343
Livonia Station, 237
Livonia Store, 150, 151, 201, 205
Ljubijana, Slovenia, 181
Lobdell's Store, WBR, 162
Lobstein, Joseph, 170
Lobstein, Menorah, 170
Loeb, Aaron, 73, 74, 79, 121, 122, 142, 145,
...150-152, 175, 176, 178, 201, 271, 334, 339
Loeb, Aaron, (h/o Fannie Eidensheim), 140
Loeb, Charles, 208
Loeb, Edward/Édouard, 138, 138-140, 142, 152
Loeb, Emanuel, 52, 73, 74, 138, 139
Loeb, Félix, 208
Loeb, Gerald Martin, 208
Loeb, Heinrich, 73, 74
Loeb, Henrietta/Hattie, 74, 271
Loeb, Isaac, 208
Loeb, Isidore, See Isidore Srulovitz
Loeb, Jeannette, 73

Loeb, Lazarus, 74
Loeb, Max, See Max Srulovitz the elder
Loeb, Mr. P., See Pincus/Philip Srulovitz
Loeb, Pauline, 170
Loeb, Pincus/Philip, See Pincus Srulovitz
Loeb, Rachel, 250, 251
Loeb, Rosette, 41, 49
Loeb, Sarah (w/o Jos. Simon, Jr.), 73, 74
Loeb, Sarah, (w/o Isaac Weil), 117
Loeb, Sarah (w/o Frederick Munzesheimer), ...140, 141
Loeb, Sarah (d/o Pincus Srulovitz), 250, 251
Loeb, Sidney, 208
Loeb, Solomon, 205, 208, 209, 242
Loeb, Tillie, 250, 251
Loeb, Gumbel & Co., 142, 152
Loeb, Gumbel & Simon, 52, 74, 139
Loeb's Department Store, 249, 250
Loeffel, Eduard Ernst, 220
Loeffel, Gustave Peter, 188, 219, 220
Lorio, Antoine Albéric, 131-133, 138, 158
Lorio, Edward Cadbert, 156
Lottie, PCP, 11, 17, 19, 197, 231, 312
Lottie School, See Simon Gumbel School
Louis Frank & Co., 110
Louisville, KY, 105, 106, 245, 311, 324, 325
Loupe Store, 36, 37, 93
Lowenburg, Dorothy, 307
Lowenburg, Isaac, 306-308
Lowenburg, Isaac (s/o Sim Hill), 307
Lowenburg, Helen, 307, 308
Lowenburg, Henrietta Ophelia, 307
Lowenburg, Sim Hill, 306-308
Lowenburg, Nettie, 187
Lowenstein, Henry, 42, 44, 46
Lowenthal, Annie, 314
Lowenthal, Isidore, 314
Lowenthal, Israël, 314
Lowenthal, Joseph, 314
Lowenthal, Lillie, 314
Lowenthal, Meyer, 314
Lowenthal, Meyer (s/o Israël Lowenthal), 314
Lowenthal, Moses, 314
Lowenthal, Rebecca, 314
Lower Chenal of False River, PCP, 2, 8, 22, 31,
....39, 47, 48, 50, 51, 74, 79, 121, 137-139, 142,
....147, 150, 164, 173, 174, 192, 194, 195, 199-
....201, 334, 338, 339
L. Strauss & Co., 33, 34
Lundi Gras, 7
Lunéville, Meurthe-et-Moselle, France, 63

Lviv, Ukraine, 306
Maas & Bloch, 209
Maasbommel, Netherlands, 181
Mackenheim, Bas-Rhin, France, 7
Macon, GA, 233, 234, 267, 288
Magot, Rachel, 125, 134, 135, 190
Mahoudeau, Amica Maria, 109, 110, 198
Mahoudeau, Amy Landry, 109, 110
Mahoudeau, Gilles, 109
Maier, Bena, 303
Mains, PCP, 251, 297, 299, 300
Major, Chérie Eugène, 190
Major, Joseph Duncan, 41
Major, Lubin, 126, 190
Major, Pervis Chérie, 99, 155, 163, 166, 176, …177, 182
Major, Philomène Adèle, 26
Major, Philomène Victoria, 194
Major, Virginie, 26
Major & Guérin, 176, 177, 182
Major-Bigman Station, 126, 131, 132
Malachowsky, Edna (aka Edna Walker ….Malcoskey), 316
Malachowsky, Joseph, 315
Malachowsky, Julia (aka Julia Malcoskey), 315, ….316
Malachowsky, Rita, 316
Mandler, Henrietta, 113
Mann, Abraham, 56
Mann, Abraham Louis, 36
Mann, Alexander, 12, 33, 36, 56, 57, 59, 60, ….233, 283, 314, 315
Mann, Benjamin, 36, 57, 233, 315
Mann, Daniel E., 56, 57, 233, 314-316, 328
Mann, David S., 56, 57, 233, 314-316, 328
Mann, Fanny, 56, 57, 233, 315
Mann, Henriette, 56, 57, 315
Mann, Jennie, 241
Mann, Joseph, 241
Mann, Lawrence Isaac, 58
Mann, Lottie, 36
Mann, Louis Marks, 36
Mann, Mathilde, 36
Mann, Max, 56-58, 233, 315
Mann, Mena, 56-58
Mann, Moses, 33, 52, 56, 92, 191
Mann, Regina/Sena, 56, 57, 233, 237, 315
Mann, Rose, 33
Mann, Theresa, 58
Mann, Vivian Claire, 58
Mann, Virginia, 56

Mann & Weinberg, 13, 315
Mannheim, Baden, Germany, 210, 295
Mansberg, Joseph, 186, 266
Mansberg, Julia, 186, 187
Manuel, François Bernard, 55
Marco, Natchitoches Parish, 217
Marcus McCausland Plantation, 152, 153
Mardi Gras, 7, 8, 89, 174
Margolis, Gertrude Rose, 336
Margolis, Joseph, 336
Marköbel (now Hammersbach), Hesse, ….Germany, 188, 219
Maringouin, Iberville Parish, 172, 173, 189, 201
Marks, Celia, 314
Marks, Reuben, 314
Marks, Sarah, 34, 35
Markstein, Jane (aka Jane Picard), 274-276
Markstein, Nathan, 274
Marksville, Avoyelles Parish, 71, 107, 113, 119, ….120, 315
Mars, Adelaïde, 75, 76
Mars, Gabriel, 75, 76
Mars, Jeanne Anaïs, 75
Mars, Marie, 75, 76
Mars, Théodore, 75
Mars, Théophile, 75, 76
Marshall, Joe, 172
Marshall, Louisa, 172
Marshall, Mary A., 201
Martin, Alma, 183, 184
Martin, Elizabeth, 183, 184
Martinique, 5, 103, 147
Marx, Augusta, 183
Marx, Jacob Lion, See Jacques Goudchaux
Marx, Mathias (aka Jacob Gotschot), 30
Marx, Samuel, 183
Mayer, Benjamin Raphael, 96-98
Mayer, Benjamin, Jr., 98
Mayer, Buffington Simon, 98
Mayer, Edwin, 298
Mayer, Eugene, 204
Mayer, Helen, 298
Mayer, John (aka Jacob Meyer Levi), 96, 307
Mayer, Julia, 204
Mayer, Leopold, 297
Mayer, Max, 145, 146, 150, 151, 201, 203-206, ….208-212, 214, 238, 239, 242
Mayer, Nathaniel A., 297, 298, 333
Mayer, Norman, 203, 204
Mayer, Ophelia, 306, 307

Mayer, Grabenheimer & Rose, 146, 150, 151, ...201, 206
McAlister, Robert/Bob, 289
McCrea, PCP, 19, 20, 257, 298, 301, 311, 329, ...332
McKinney, Scholastie, 149
McPhaul Plantation, 307-309
M. D. Landau & Co., 290
Mehlingen, Rheinpfalz, Germany, 60, 307
Memphis, TN, 99, 123, 171, 175, 314
Mendelsohn, Mathilde, 178
Mendelsohn, Simon Judas, 96, 178
Mendelsohn, Zerlina, 96, 97
Mendez Meyer, Joseph, 241
Merrick, PCP, 13, 257, 258, 313, 315-318
Merrick Store, 314
Mersier, Antoine, 292
Mersier, Marie Aimée, 292
Mertzwiller, Bas-Rhin, France, 175, 214
Mesritz, Albert, 87
Mesritz, Bernard Oriel "Banny", 86-88
Mesritz, Emma, 87
Mesritz, Frances, 87
Mesritz, Henry, 87
Mesritz, Isabella, 87
Mesritz, Jeannette, 87
Mesritz, Jefferson Davis, 87
Mesritz, Laura, 87
Mesritz, Maurice, 87
Mesritz, Richard, 87
Mesritz, Rosina, 87
Messner, Gaspar, 99
Messner, Rachel, 99, 100
Mettler/Mettlar, Anna Sophy, 111
Metz/Mertz, Francis, 158, 159, 169, 175
Metz, Moselle, France, 47, 48
Meyer, Abraham, 51
Meyer, Adolph, 61
Meyer, Caroline, 29, 33, 51, 55
Meyer, Caroline/Madeleine, 209
Meyer, Cassius Isaac (aka C.J. Meyer), 61, 62
Meyer, Edward, 29
Meyer, Esther, 160
Meyer, Fanette, 61
Meyer, Florette, 58
Meyer, Frederika, 140, 141
Meyer, Henrietta, 307
Meyer, Jacob S., 9, 33, 160, 161
Meyer, Jonathan, 141
Meyer, Joseph, 52, 55
Meyer, Louis, 160

Meyer, Manasses, 57
Meyer, Marx, 29, 312
Meyer, Miriam (aka Mina, Martha), 29, 33, 51, ...52, 55
Meyer, Rosine/Rosina, 29, 55
Meyer, Rosina (w/o Meyer Dreyfus), 210
Meyer, Sarah, 57, 58
Meyer, Simon, 209
Meyer, Solomon, 61
Meyer, Theodore David, 160
Meyer, Victor, 61
Meyer, Zacharias Emmich, 161
Meyer & Strauss, 29, 246, 312
Michael, Jacob, 207
Michael, Julia, 263
Michael, Louis Casper, 263
Michael, Maurice, 263
Michael, Michaelus, 207
Michael, Pauline, 207
Michael, Pierre Louis, 263
Michael, Victoria, 207
Michel, Abraham, 41, 42
Michel, Abraham J. (aka A. J.), 57-60, 343
Michel, Armand Simon, 48
Michel, Estelle, 43
Michel, Harriet, 48
Michel, Henriette, 42
Michel, Henry, 43
Michel, Herman, 43
Michel, Jacob (aka Jacques Michel), 42, 47, 54
Michel, Jacob (s/o Meyer Michel), 43
Michel, Judithe, 293
Michel, Lazard, 43
Michel, Marie Rosa, Widow Olinde, 95
Michel, Maurice Albert, 48
Michel, Melanie, 15, 42, 234, 268, 279-283, 289
Michel, Meyer Levi, 41-47, 49, 50, 54, 58, 60, ...279, 280, 290, 297, 342
Michel, Rachel, 43, 44, 60
Michel, Ralph, 48
Michel, Rose, 48
Michel, Rosine, 15, 31, 42, 46, 47, 54, 75, 77- ....80, 85,151-156, 162-169, 173, 185.
Michele, Rose, aka Michelé Wolf or Michelé ....Rose, 30
Michel Hotel (aka "The Michel"), 59, 60
Midonik, Rebecca, 252
Miller, Frieda, 116, 117
Miller, Rosie, 309
Miller, Gatzel, 116
Miltenberger, Aristide, 292

Miltenberger, Francisci Josephi, 292
Miltenberger, Georges Prosper, 293
Miltenberger, Gustave, 292
Miltenberger, Louis Christian, 292
Miltenberger, Louis Joseph Alphonse, 268, ...292, .293
Miltenberger, Marie Céleste Amélie, 293
Miltenberger, Odile, 293
Minville, Jacob, 242
Mitchell, Abraham B., 283-286
Mitchell, Beulah, 285
Mitchell, Hannah, 285
Mitchell, Julia, 285
Mitchell, Lazard, 285, 286
Mitchell, Willard, 285
M. L. Hellman Co., 44, 46
Mobile, Al, 59, 60, 81, 88, 114, 248, 250, 251, ...255, 274, 286, 287, 310
Moïse, Aaron, 291
Moïse, Abraham, 291
Moïse, Eleanor, 291
Moïse, Ferdinand, 313
Moïse, Helen, 313
Moïse, Irene, 313
Moïse, Isidore, 313
Moïse, Joseph, 312
Moïse, Julius Leon, 313
Moïse, Léon, 312, 313
Moïse, Milton, Myer
Moïse, Sidney Lloyd, 313
Mohr, Bertha, 181, 182, 266
Mohr, Caroline, 186, 265-267, 271
Mohr, Joseph, 182, 265
Mohr, Rebecca, 186, 187, 266
Monaco, Principality of, 165, 292-294
Monroe, Ouachita Parish, 108
Monsanto, Angelica, 22
Monsanto, Benjamin, 22, 23, 123
Monsanto, Eleanora, 22
Monsanto, Gracia, 22, 23
Monsanto, Isaac, 3, 22, 23, 123
Monsanto, Jacob, 22, 123
Monsanto, Manuel, 22, 24, 123
Monsanto, Pedro David Rodriquez, 22
Monsheim, Rhine-Hesse, Germany, 33, 56
Montgomery, AL, 234, 238, 248, 276, 289, 290
Montgomery, Anna, 276
Montgomery, Ben, 276
Montgomery, Celeste, 276
Montiache, Madeleine, 76
Montigny-lès-Metz, Moselle, France, 179

Moock, Babette, 272
Moock, Rosine 48
Moock, Zadock, 272
Moonshine, Israël, 94
Moonshine, Jacob, 94, 110, 198, 337
Morais, Adrien Joshua, 235
Morais, Irene Esther, 175, 235
Moran/Maurin, Emma, 260
Moreau Plantation, 37, 327, 334
Morel, Clairfait, 95, 239
Morgan, Adele, 246
Morgan, Blanche Mertel, 246
Morgan, Charles/Carlos, 243, 245
Morgan, Charles, Jr., 243, 245-247
Morgan, Charles III, 246
Morgan, Corinne, 246
Morgan, Elizabeth/Eliza, 200
Morgan, Julia Hyacinthe, 246
Morgan, Medora, 246
Morgan, Raphaël Clifton, 246
Morgan, Victoria/Victorine, 200
Morganza, PCP, 2, 6, 8, 9, 18, 19, 21, 28, 40, 44, ...87, 93, 130, 137, 139, 172, 173, 200, 204, ...231, 232, 238, 243-252, 254-259, 262, 265, ...270, 276, 295, 300, 312, 326, 331, 339
Morganza Theatre, 254, 255
Morhange, Thérèse, 48
Morningstar, Alexander, 248
Morningstar, Amelia, 248
Moses, Anna Marie, 291
Moses, Bertha, 308, 309
Moses, Hattie, 309, 327
Moses, Rabbi, Marx, 308, 327
Mötky, Marie Auguste Helene, 106
Mount, Alfred Isaac, 289
Mount, Bernard, 289
Mount, Bertha, 289, 290
Mount, Celia, 289
Mount, Dora, 7, 289
Mount, Harry David, 234, 289
Mount, Isidor Berg, 233, 234, 288-290
Mount, Martha, 289
Mount & Landau, 234
Moyse, Henrietta/Hattie, 320, 321
Moyse, Simon, 320
Mrs. H. Loeb & Co., 151, 178
Mulder, Everdina, 182
Mulhausen, Bas-Rhin, France, 266
Müller, Hevven "Henriette", 28, 176, 235, 259, ...271, 279, 304
Müller, Jacques, 28

Munster, Gottschalk, 220
Munster, Ray, See Rachel Seidenbach
Munzesheimer, Aaron, 141
Munzesheimer, Adolph, 141
Munzesheimer, Alexander, 141
Munzesheimer, Emma, 141
Munzesheimer, Florette, 141
Munzesheimer, Frederick, 140, 141
Munzesheimer, Frances, 140
Munzesheimer, Gustave, 141
Munzesheimer, Hardy, 141
Munzesheimer, Isidore Frederick, 141
Munzesheimer, Lawrence, 141
Munzesheimer, Lewis, 141
Munzesheimer, Marcus, 141
Munzesheimer, Moses, 141
Munzesheimer, Rita, 141
Munzesheimer, Sidonia, 141
Mur Goslin (near Poznan), Prussia, 87
Muscatine, IA, 270
Muse, Eliska Tircuit, 247, 249
Muse, James Fort, 34, 249
Musson, Iberville Parish, 8, 151, 201, 211, 214,
....215, 237
Myers, Alfred, 218
Myers, Hyman, 218
Myers, Joseph, 218
Myers, Louis, 218
Myers, Mary, 218
Myers, Robert, 218
Myers & Mann, 33
Nachman, Charles, 207
Nachman, Judah Benjamin "J. B.," 207, 208
Nachman, William B., 207
Nancy, Meurthe-et-Moselle, France, 28, 57,
....101, 179, 258, 259, 261, 265, 267, 320
Napoleonville, Assumption Parish, 91, 102, 119,
....179, 185, 214, 222, 235, 292
Natchez, MS, 15, 22, 23, 28, 34, 60, 61, 62, 96,
.....140, 193, 194, 217, 245, 246, 255, 256, 292,
.....302, 305-309, 322, 326, 345
Neuburger, Jeannette (aka Christine), 41, 46,
....47, 54
Neuburger, Margarethe (aka Anne Marie or
....Michelet), 54
Neuburger, Meyer, 54
Neuleiningen, Rheinpfalz, Germany, 73
Neumond/Newman, Annette, 189
Neumond/Newman, Carl, 189
Neustadt, Rheinpfalz, Germany, 74, 121, 151
Neustadt-Schirwindt, Poland, 185, 195

Neuwiller-lès-Saverne, Bas-Rhin, France, 48, 76
New Iberia, Iberia Parish, 208, 209, 216, 284,
....285, 289
New Orleans and San Francisco Railway. See
.....Frisco Railway.
New Orleans Cheap Store, 56-58, 283, 314,
New Roads, PCP, 1, 4-14, 16-24, 27-32, 34, 36-
....52, 54, 59, 60, 62, 65, 67-97. 99, 100, 103,
....104, 106-122, 127-129, 137, 142-144, 146,
....147, 149, 150, 153, 157, 159, 162, 168, 172,
....173, 176-178, 186, 188, 189, 191-195, 198,
....200, 202-204, 208, 210-212, 214-216, 219,
....226-228, 237-239, 241, 244, 246-250, 252,
....253, 258, 259, 261, 262, 264, 266-269, 271,
....274, 275, 279, 281, 283, 286, 288-290, 300,
....304, 305, 312, 313, 320, 323, 325-327, 333,
....335, 336-341, 344
New Roads Cheap Cash Store, 90, 91, 274, 275,
.....338
New Roads Fancy Grocery, 14, 27, 90, 103, 111,
...112, 338
New Roads Oil Mill, 16, 68
New Roads Opera House, 6, 110
New Roads Steam Cleaning & Dye Works, 111,
......340
New Texas Landing, PCP, 9, 36, 93, 172, 258,
....268, 331
Nicollet, Jean-Baptiste, 3, 21
Niederroedern, Bas-Rhin, France, 30
Nina Landing, 40, 61, 191, 307
Nina Plantation, formerly Pecan Grove, 14, 41,
......61-65, 307
Nina Store, 14, 60- 62, 307
Nolasco de Porcuna, Marie Agathe 217
Nordstetten, Württemberg, Germany, 64, 71,
.....119, 308, 327
Normandy Plantation, 268, 269, 297
Nowak, Daniel, 190
Nowak, Henry, 189, 190
Nowak, Jacob, 190
Nugent, J.M., 241
Nuremberg, Rheinpfalz, Germany, 277, 309,
...327
Oakdale, Allen Parish, 324, 335, 336
Oak Grove Plantation, 306-308
Oakland Plantation, 137
Oancea, Romania, 251
Oberlauterbach, Bas-Rhin, France, 315, 316
Oberlustadt, Rheinpfalz, Germany, 266
Obernai, Bas-Rhin, France, 96, 180, 307
Obernbreit, Rheinpfalz, Germany, 96, 178

Odessa, Ukraine, 125, 135, 255
Odratzheim, Bas-Rhin, France, 209
Oldenburg, Lower Saxony, Germany, 122, 277
Old Hickory Plantation, 258, 277-279
Olensky, Leila, 248
Olinde, Beauregard, 95
Olinde, Michel, 95
Olivier de Vézin, Olivia, 62
Olivo, Claire, 216
Olivo, Henri, 81
Olivo, Madeleine, 81-83, 216
Opelousas, St. Landry Parish, 83,119, 120, 135,
....141, 204, 216, 221, 295-297
Oppenheim, Caroline, 303
Oppenheim, Lena/Helena, 175, 235
Oscar, PCP, 6, 11, 17, 93, 95, 97, 125-132, 134,
....135, 165, 171, 187, 190, 195, 215, 287
Oscar Crossing, PCP, See Torbert
Ostermann, Frances, 87
Osthoffen, Bas-Rhin, France, 185, 319
Ostrowo, Poland, 276
Paincourtville, Assumption Parish, 213, 223
Palermo, Nicholas, 145
Pamias, Ernestine, 172
Pamias, Pierre, 172
Panama Canal Zone, 217
Parent, Délima, 38
Parent, Henry, 38
Paris, Île-de-France, France, 75, 84, 101, 209,
...223, 252, 293, 294, 330
Parlange Plantation, 39, 121, 122, 271
Parlange School, See Ferdinand Gumbel
....School
Patin, Alida, 149
Patin, Célima, 142
Patin, Cléoville, 143, 175
Patin, Dauphine, 149
Patin, Elevina, 149
Patin, Joseph, 74
Patin, Joseph Leonidas, 149
Patin, Joseph Spiridonia, 149
Patin, Justin, 128
Patin, Marie Angélique, 149
Patin, Marie Apolina, 149
Patin, Marie Cornelia, 149
Patin, Marie Laurelia, 149
Patin, Paul, 149
Patin, Valérien, 149
Patin, Valérien, Jr., 149
Patin, Virkison, 149
Patin & Baum, 142-145

Paul Bergeron Plantation, 220
Pechersky, Norman/Nathan (aka Nathan
....Chester), 255
Pedarré, Roch, 29, 34-36
Peiser, Tillie, 184
Pélichet, Annie, 173
Pélichet, Donnie, 173
Pélichet, Doris, 173
Pélichet, Edward, 173
Pélichet, Henry E., 173
Pélichet, Henry, Jr., 173
Pélichet, Leona, 173
Pélichet, Louis, 173
Pélichet, Mattie, 173
Pélichet, Torris, 173
Pensacola, Escambia Co., FL, 8, 22, 101, 324
Perrault, Eliza, 297
Peyser, Celia, 233, 288-290
Peyser, Gussie, 233, 234, 289
Peyser, Maurice/Morris, 233, 288
Phalsbourg, Moselle, France, 83
Philadelphia, PA, 134, 245, 246, 317
Phillips, Nathaniel P., 258, 312, 325
Picard, Esther, 48
Picard, Henry, 12, 245, 273-276, 341
Picard, Julius, 275, 276
Picard, Samuel, 274
Picard & Weil, 91, 92, 249, 274
Picayune Store, 163, 191
Pick, Barbetta/Bertha, 115
Pigott, John A., 59
Pigott, Lillian, See Lillian Slocum
Pineville, Rapides Parish, 119, 135, 209, 316
Pirmasens, Rheinpfalz, Germany, 50, 152, 297
Place, Alice Landis, 291
Place, Lucius Holmes, 291
Plaquemine, Iberville Parish, 35, 46, 69, 97, 118,
....156, 179, 209, 238, 326, 332, 335, 336
Pleasant View Plantation, 122, 125, 126, 287
Pleisweiler, Rheinpfalz, Germany, 41
Plonsky, Mary, 227
Pock/Poke, Celestine, 146, 147
Pointe à la Hâche, Plaquemines Parish, 46
Pointe Coupée Banner fire of 1921, 114
Pointe Coupée Democrat, 28, 73, 140, 202, 339
Pointe Coupée Drugstore, 28
Pointe Coupée Planting & Manufacturing Co.,
.......62-64
Pointe Coupée Road, 2, 14, 21, 25, 27, 29-33,
....37, 72, 79-81, 93, 173, 176, 191, 216, 258,
... 271, 293, 294, 312, 314, 326

Ponchatoula, Tangipahoa Parish, 186, 187, 190
Porche, Alexis, 42, 44, 46
Porche, Eulalie, 81
Porche, Julie Aurore, 70, 72, 192
Porche, Julienne, 148
Porche, Leon, 148
Porche, Michel, 70
Porche, Pierre, 148
Porche, Pierre Évariste, 148
Porche, Rosa, 148
Porche, Rosa (w/o Jack Gumbel), 149
Porche, Zénon, 29, 258, 271, 293
Port Gibson, MS, 174, 217
Port Hudson, EBR, 2, 17, 40, 51
Portsmouth, OH, 219
Portugal, xiii, 22, 123, 208
Posen, Poland, 107, 160, 233, 263, 289, 329
Poulailler, PCP, 2, 68, 81
Pourciau, Cyrille, 193, 194
Pourciau, Marie (Widow Robillard), 23
Pourciau, Victorin, 169
Poydras de la Lande, Benjamin, 22
Poydras, Eugène, 78
Poydras, Julien, 21, 24, 33, 122, 278
Poydras Funds, 278
Prag, Henrietta/Yetta, 274, 276
Prag, Isaac, 274
Prévost, Marie Sophie, 147
Prévost, (aka Prévost-Allen) Marie Valentine
....147, 149
Prévost, Sophie, 5, 8, 16, 25-27, 53, 100,
....103, 147, 232, 304
Prince, Harold, 186
Prince, Jacob, 186
Prince, Joseph, 186
Prince, Meyer, 185-187
Prince, Selina, 187
Provosty, Albin, 132, 133, 281, 282
Provosty, Olivier Otis, 294
Puttelange-aux-Lacs, Moselle, France, 96, 178
Quintana, Marie, 171
Raccourci Cotton Seed Oil Co., 15, 16
Raccourci-Old River, PCP, 2, 8, 9, 13, 28, 29,
....49, 72, 74, 121, 176, 203, 211, 233-235, 239,
....245, 257, 258, 262, 263, 266-269, 277-279,
....281, 283, 284, 289, 290, 292, 293, 295, 297-
....299, 301, 303, 312, 341
Rădăuți, Romania, 254
Ranson, Clélie, 293
Raphaël, Isaac, 245
Raphaël, Solomon, 245, 246

Raphaël, Virginia, 243, 245-247
Ravenswood Station, PCP, 231, 233, 237, 303,
....337
Rayne, Acadia Parish, 118, 237, 271, 322, 326,
....337
Red Cross, PCP, 19, 257, 329
Red River, 206, 241, 243, 316
Red River Campaign, 139, 333
Red River Landing, PCP, 2, 9, 29, 97, 173, 245,
....257, 258, 265, 303, 311-314, 317
Red River Parish, 220, 328
Red Store, 14, 21, 33, 36, 191, 244, 314
Red Store Plantation, 33
Reichenberg, Amalie/Malche, 188
Reichenberg, Bertha, 184
Reichshoffen, Bas-Rhin, France, 101, 208, 214,
....222, 223, 225
Reinach, Solomon, 220
Rey, Clovina, 108
Rey, Octave, 108
Richard, Maria Francisca/Françoise, 245
Richards Tract, 297, 332
Riché, Fannie, 243, 244
Richmond, VA, 25, 245, 304, 330
Richy, Auguste, 202
Richy, Hélène, 202
Richy, Joseph, 79, 83, 85, 99, 202, 239
Riedseltz, Bas-Rhin, France, 41, 49, 203, 267,
....290, 295, 297, 326, 332
Ries, Benjamin, 96
Ries, Caroline, 74, 170, 175, 308
Ries, Edward, 48
Ries, Jeannette, 96, 307
Ries, Minette, 96
Ries, Moses, 96
Ries, Nanette, 96
Ries, Pauline/Sibille, 96
Riga, Latvia, 184, 207
River Lake Plantation, 124, 155
Rixheim, Haut-Rhin, France, 31
Robillard, Anastasie, 107
Roeschen, Rachel, 315
Romanswiller, Bas-Rhin, France, 209, 210
Rose, Lena, 304
Rosedale, Iberville Parish, 170, 180, 231
Rosenfeld, Sophie, 96, 178
Rosensweig, Dora Streit, 98, 159
Rosenthal, Bertha, 315, 316
Rosenthal, Essie, 316
Rosenthal, Jonas, 316
Rosenthal, Moses, 315

Rosenthal, Regina, 316
Rosenwald, Julius, 11
Rosenwald Schools, 11
Rothbach, Bas-Rhin, France, 232, 266
Rothschild, Isidore, 307, 309, 327
Rothschild, Martin, 327
Rothschild, Max. 15, 307-309
Rothschild, Morris, 327, 328
Rothschild, Moses Marx, 308, 327
Rothschild, Samuel, 327
Rougon, PCP, 8, 13, 68, 97, 125, 137, 142, 144, ...158, 169, 171, 181, 187, 188. See also Chenal.
Rougon, Jean-Baptiste, 192
Rougon, Pierre Viléor, 192
Rudsztein, Fejga (aka Fejga Rotsztejn), 286, ...299, 300
Rülzheim, Rheinpfalz, Germany, 92, 216
Saint-Avold, Moselle, France, 51, 101
Saint-Domingue, 22, 23, 25, 123, 146, 147, 291, ...292
Saizan, Celina, 75
Saizan, Emma, 75
Salomon, Babette/Buna (aka Barbe Moyses), 75
Salomon, Bertha, 162, 178
Salomon, Lena, 115, 162
Samuel, Sarah, 117
Samuel, Sophie, 175
Samuels, Emanuel, 306-306
Samuels, Frank Lowenburg, 307
Samuels, Marguerite, 307
Sandman, Alexander Henry, 316-318
Sandman, Alexander Henry, Sr., 317
Sandman, Gunst & Co., 316-318
San Francisco, CA, 28, 149, 208
Sankt Pölten, Austria, 279
Santa Cruz, Blanche, 108
Santa Cruz, Harold, 108
Santa Cruz, Harold, Jr., 108
Santa Cruz, Olga Marguerite, 108
Sarrasin, André, 24
Sarre-Union, Bas-Rhin, France, 37
Satoraljaujhely, Hungary, 249
Sausenheim, Rheinpfalz, Germany, 73
Savannah, GA, 25, 26, 53
Saverne, Bas-Rhin, France, 209
Savignol, Casimir, 14, 94, 249
Savouré, Rev. Louis, 6, 126, 156
Scheyen, Ester, 180
Schirrhoffen, Bas-Rhin, France, 117, 174, 180, ...215, 218, 225, 227, 318, 319, 325, 326

Schlenker, David, 140
Schlenker, Moses, 140
Schlenker, Simon, 140
Schlesinger, Hattie/Henrietta, 58
Schlesinger, Jacob, 58
Schloss, Clara, 171
Schloss, Rosa, 221
Schneider, Margarethe, 119
Schulherr/Scooler, Louis, 44, 45
Schulherr/Scooler, Maurice, 44, 46
Schulsinger, Aaron, 85-88, 269, 270
Schultz, Regine, 297
Schwartz, Edith Jeanne, 65
Schwartz, Elsa, 65
Schwartz, Fannie, 101
Schwartz, Louis, 64, 65
Schwartz, Moses, 62-65
Schwartz, Philip, 101
Schwartz, Philippa Amelia, 101, 142
Schwartz, Simon, 63
Schwartzenburg, Eldridge John, 119, 120
Schwartzenburg, Ellis, 119, 120
Schwartzenburg, George Washington Xavier, ...119
Schwartzenburg, Ivy, 119
Schwartzenburg, John, 119
Schwartzenburg, Vernon, 119
Seckbach, Adolph, 15, 62-65
Seckbach, Arthur, 65
Seckbach, Doretta, 65
Seckbach, Effie Adele, 65
Seckbach, Herbert, 65
Seckbach, Markus, 64
Seckbach, Mathilde, 65
Seckbach, Myrtle, 65
Seckbach & Eiseman, 62
Seibersbach, Rhine-Hesse, Germany, 35
Seidenbach, Cecilia, 219
Seidenbach, Joseph, 219
Seidenbach, Judah, 188, 219, 220
Seidenbach, Lehmann, 219
Seidenbach, Meyer, 219
Seidenbach, Rachel (aka. Ray Munster), 219, ...220
Seidenbach, Samuel, 219
Seidenbach & Loeffel, 219, 220
Seidenbach & Loeffel Plantation, 188
Seiferth, Jonathan, 305
Sélestat, Bas-Rhin, France, 232
Seligman/Seeleman, Baruch, 140
Seligman/Seeleman, Caroline, 140

Sen, Sarah, 291
Sennfeld, Rheinpfalz, Germany, 80
Sephardic Jews, xiii, xiv, 3, 22, 123, 171, 235,
....243, 246, 291
Seren, Bertha, 256
S. Gumbel & Co., 65, 201, 202
Shay, Fannie Löb, 189
Shemel, David, 336
Shemel, Mollie, 335, 336
Shepherd, Lillian Sarah, 292
Showboat *Golden Rod*, 38, 41
Shreveport, Caddo Parish, 96, 135, 201, 264
Shymanski/Sherman, Jan Nepomuck/Nathan
....106
Sicard, Henrietta, 220
Sicard, Ursin, 39, 50, 191, 192
Sicard vs. Chustz, 39
Sichel, Friederika, 222
Siegel, Caroline, 219
Siess, Auger, 241
Silberman, Sarah Clara, 251
Silbernagel, Barbara, 110
Silverman, Miriam, 317
Simon Gumbel & Co., 35, 191, 238
Simon Gumbel School, 11
Simon, Loeb & Co., 28, 52, 73, 74, 121, 139,
....238, 239, 246
Simon, Bertha (w/o Isaac Dreyfus), 56
Simon, Bertha, 73
Simon, Elias (h/o Amelia Schwartz), 101, 143
Simon, Elias, 140
Simon, Henry, 73
Simon, Jacob, 140
Simon, Joseph, Jr., 72-74
Simon, Joséphine Valérien, 150
Simon, Julia, 5, 8, 101, 143, 145, 187, 188
Simon, Lazarus, 140, 142
Simon, Leo, 140
Simon, Louise, 101, 142
Simon, Maurice, 73
Simon, Rosa, 73
Simon, Reuben, 140
Simon, Simon, 73
Singer, Abraham, 58
Singer, J., 3
Singer, Victoria, 57-60
Singerman, Charles, 116
Singerman, Gustave, 116, 117
Singerman, Herman, 116
Singerman, Herman A. 116
Singerman, Jacob, 116, 117

Singerman, Max, 117
Sisters of St. Joseph, 7, 17, 19
Slocum, Lillian (aka Lillian Pigott), 59
Slocum, Samuel, 59
Slosower/Sloss, Erika, 253
Slosower/Sloss, Marie Dora (aka Mariem
....Zloczower), 252-254
Slosower/Sloss, Herbert, 253
Slosower/Sloss, Otto, 253
Slosower/Sloss, Yudel/Earl, 252
Smeade-Kling, Chia, 305, 324
Smithland, PCP, 257, 258, 284, 285, 287, 289,
.....292, 312
Sneike, Mary, 305, 324
Sneike, Moishe Leib, 305, 324
Sneike-Kling, Gertrude, 324
Sol Kahn Co., 326
Solomon, Jacob, 233
Solomon, John Z. 233
Sommelvitz/Schmuloff, Rachel/Rose, 105
Sommer, Adolph, 318
Sommer, Adolph N., 319, 320
Sommer, Leopold "Lep," 18, 318-322, 323, 326
Sommer, Lydie, 320
Sommer, Palmyre, 326
Sommer, Rachel/Ray, 320
Sommer, Sylvain "Syl", 318-320, 322, 323, 326
Sommer & Taylor Planting Co., Ltd.
Southern Scrap Material Co., 183, 184, 219
Speyer, Rheinpfalz, Germany, 110, 271
Spiro, Gustav, 276, 277
Spiro, Sarah, 270
Spitz, Anna Sophia Hubertina, 36
Srulovitz, Ersky, 254
Srulovitz, Fanny, 247
Srulovitz, Fanny Clara, 254-256
Srulovitz, Gabriel/Gavriel (aka Gabriel Hart), 8,
....247, 254-256
Srulovitz, Isidore (aka Isidore Loeb), 247, 248,
.....251, 252, 254, 300, 339
Srulovitz, Lazar, 247, 248, 300
Srulovitz, Max, the elder (aka Max Loeb),18
.....251, 254, 300, 301, 302, 309, 310
Srulovitz, Max, the younger (aka Max H.
.....Hart), 18, 19, 251-253, 301
Srulovitz, Pincus (aka Philip Loeb), 18, 248-
......251, 252, 254, 300
Srulovitz, Samuel, 310
Steamer *Natchez*, 193, 194
Stein, Catherine/Kate, 286
Steiner, Arthur, 288

Steiner, Edgar, 288
Steiner, Robert, 288
Stern, Audrey, 108
Stern, Benjamin Floyd, 107, 108
Stern, Benjamin Joseph, 7, 105-109
Stern, Benjamin, Jr., 108
Stern, Blanche Cécile, 107, 108
Stern, Charles, 105, 108
Stern, Charles Joseph, 108
Stern, Esther, 219
Stern, Esther/Fanny, 49, 52, 145, 197, 203
Stern, Ethel Rosalie, 107, 108
Stern, Henrietta/Yetta, 219, 220
Stern, Henry, 189
Stern, John D., 107
Stern, Joseph, 107
Stern, Juliette, 189
Stern, Leonard L., 189
Stern, Lois, 108
Stern, Marie, 108
Stern, Norman, 107, 108
Stern, Rita Mae, 108
Stern & Lesser, 6, 109
Stern Brothers, 105, 106, 108
Stich, Amelia, 207, 208
St. Amant, Joseph Charles, 149
St. Amant, Valentine Irène, 149
St. Claude Landing, 41
St. Claude Plantation 61
St. Francis of Pointe Coupée Church, 24
St. Francisville, WFP, 4, 16, 23, 25, 36, 38, 48,
....56-58, 89, 92, 93, 108. 120, 182, 274.
St. Germain, Joseph Aristide, 198, 231, 232
St. Germain, Jules, 232
St. Joseph Catholic Cemetery, Baton Rouge, 32,
....312
St. Louis, MO, 87, 101, 175, 184, 264, 265, 284,
....307, 325
St. Mary Cemetery, 13, 24, 32, 72, 83, 85, 89,
....104, 127, 150, 172, 194
St. Mary Church, 5, 31, 67, 68, 70, 71, 75, 77,
....79, 95, 103, 107, 125, 127, 149, 194
St. Maurice Plantation, 34
St. Maurice Landing, 29, 35, 36
St. Maurice Oak, 35
St. Maurice Plantation, 29, 34-36, 270
St. Paul, MN, 277
Ste. Marie, PCP., 2, 67.
Strasbourg, Bas-Rhin, France, 30, 81-84, 92,
....274, 291
Strassburg, Poland, 115, 162, 178

Strauss, Bertha/Birdie, 34
Strauss, Esther, 34
Strauss, Judas, 34
Strauss, Julie, 295
Strauss, Julius, 34, 35
Strauss, Louis/Lazarus, 15, 33-35, 270
Strauss, Marcus, 29
Strauss, Regina, 52, 55
Struth, Bas-Rhin, France, 41, 46, 47, 49, 50, 54,
....77, 79, 85, 185, 297
Stuttgart, Württemberg, Germany, 58
Sudlikov, Ukraine, 189
Sugar Land Plantation, 34, 35, 270
Sulzdorf, Rheinpfalz, Germany, 307
Surbourg, Bas-Rhin, France, 48
Sussman, Annie Leavett, 256
Suwalki, Poland, 286, 299, 300
Sweig, Ida, 324
Sweig, Samuel, 324
Tassin, Joseph Alfred, 107
Tassin, Rose Aureline, 107
Tatar/Tatarsky Bros., 18, 327, 334, 335
Tatarsky/Tatar, Allan, 336
Tatarsky/Tatar, Ben, 334-336
Tatarsky/Tatar, David, 336
Tatarsky/Tatar, Harry, 334, 335, 336
Tatarsky/Tatar, Helene, 336
Tatarsky/Tatar, Joel (s/o Harry), 336
Tatarsky/Tatar, Joel/Joseph, 334
Tatarsky/Tatar, Morris/Melvin, 336
Tatarsky/Tatar, Rachel, 336
Tatarsky/Tatar, Sam, 334-336
Tatarsky/Tatar, Sarah, 335, 336
Tatarsky/Tatar, Sarah/Yetta, 336
Tatarsky/Tatar, Saul, 334, 335
Tatarsky/Tatar, Thomas, 336
Taylor, James J. 322
Taylor Plantation, 295, 297, 298, 332
Teningen, Baden, Germany, 220
Ternant, Vincent Claude, 39
Teutsch, Bernard, 29, 36, 37, 93, 128, 129, 136,
....326, 327, 337
Teutsch, Hannah, 37
Teutsch, Herman, 36-38, 93, 128, 129, 326, 343
Teutsch, Jacob, 93
Teutsch, Ludwig/Louis, 36, 37, 93
Teutsch, Morris/Moritz, 36
Teutsch, Regina, 36, 93
Teutsch, Thekla, 226
Teutch, Bernard vs. Isaac Bigman, 128, 129

Texas & Pacific Railroad, 17, 19, 40, 68, 90,
....100,.109, 137, 186, 206, 215, 231, 239, 244,
....245, 252, 291, 301, 303-305, 311, 312, 329
The Gum Store, 247, 252, 254
The Hague, Netherlands, 22
The Leader Store (Kassel & Stern), 14, 24, 105-
....109, 111
The Leader Store (L & S. Sommer), 14, 318,
....319, 326
The Lettsworth Planting Company, Inc., 308,
....309
The Oak Grove Planting Company, 306-308
Thibodaux, Lafourche Parish, 102, 113, 118,
....142, 185, 292
Thompson, Angeline, 108
Thompson, Dorothy, 108
Thompson, Earl, 108
Thompson, Eunice, 108
Thompson, Jackie Leroy, 108
Three Rivers, PCP, 173, 257, 311, 334
Tichenor, George, 12, 13, 278
Tobias, Jasmin, 227
Tobias, Maas, 227
Torbert, PCP, 11, 17, 121, 125, 130, 131, 133,
...197
Torras, Joseph, 311
Torras, Miguel, 311
Torras, PCP, 16-18, 90, 132, 134, 137, 173, 203,
....299, 220, 257, 295, 299, 301, 303, 305, 306,
...309, 311, 312, 318-323, 325-328, 333, 335,
...336
Toulminville-Prichard, AL, 310
Tounoir, Hélène, 32
Tounoir, Jean-Baptiste, 21
Touro Infirmary, 53, 171, 173, 190, 202, 206,
...298, 331
Trager, Louis, 9, 10
Trévoux, Ain, France, 31
Trimbach, Bas-Rhin, France, 75, 117, 272, 273
Trois Chênes (Three Oaks), 85, 87, 269
Turpin, Dr. James A, 278
Turzovka, Slovakia, 310
Typhoid Fever, 13, 45, 132, 264, 284
Tyrian Lodge, 7
Uhrwiller, Bas-Rhin, France, 214, 222
Union Oil Mill Co., 16
Unique Plantation, 268, 269, 279, 281, 283, 290,
....297
Upper Chenal of False River, PCP, 2, 39, 40, 44,
...51, 68, 192, 193
Uttenheim, Bas-Rhin, France, 57

Valenzuela, Assumption Parish, 102, 103
Vallet/Vallette, DéDé, 216
Vallet/Vallette, Désiré, 216
Vallet/Vallette, Eulalie, 216
Vallet/Vallette, Louis Désiré, 216
Valley Mercantile Co., 307-309, 327
Valverda, PCP, 8, 197, 213
V. & A. Meyer & Co., 61, 62
Van Mesritz, Oriel Heyman, 87
Van Os, Doris, 221
Van Os, Joseph, 221
Vee's 5 & 10 Cent Stores, 119, 120, 340, 344
Venningen, Rheinpfalz, Germany, 36-38, 93
Ventress, PCP, 11, 26, 41, 148
Vernoux/Vernous, August Joseph, 32
Vernoux/Vernous, Catherine Léonard, 32
Vernoux/Vernous, Joseph, 32
Vernoux/Vernous, Marius, 31, 32
Vichy, Allier, France, 110
Vicksburg, MS, 49, 73, 143, 159, 169, 273, 314,
....326
Vidalia, Concordia Parish, 272, 309
Vignes, Adolphe, 27, 53
Vignes, Albert, 87
Vignes, Anna Mathilda, 232
Vignes, Delphin Vergès, 27, 53, 103, 245
Vignes, Edward, 27, 53, 90
Vignes, Edwin, 27
Vignes, Evelina, 5, 103
Vignes, John L., 87
Vignes, Marie Eudora, 27, 53
Vignes, Marie Philomène Élida, 245
Vignes, Mathilde, 27
Vignes, Raymond, 86
Vignes, Raoul, 97
Vignes-Bombet Wholesale Grocery, 27
Villéret, Charles W., 72
Villéret, Jean Baptiste Abraham, 72
Vilna, Lithuania, 304, 305, 323, 333, 335
Vogel, Braunle, aka Babette, 30, 82
Vogel, Kaufman Gotchel, 30
Vogel, Rosine, 266
Wachenheim, Albert, 203
Waco, TX, 291
Waldhilbersheim, Rheinpfalz, Germany, 140
Waldman, Bertha/Bonnie, 134, 190
Waldman, Daniel, 125, 134, 135, 190
Waldman, Fannie, 216, 135
Waldman, Golda/Goldie, 134, 135, 190
Waldman, Joseph W., 126, 127, 135

Waldman, Rosa, 125, 127, 128, 134, 135, 190, ...235
Wallfisch, Harry, 190
Wallfisch, Mordche/Morris, 190
Wallfisch, Nathan, 185, 190
Warsaw, Poland, 195
Washington, St. Landry Parish, 94
Wassman, Isaac, 304
Wassman, Stella, 304
Waterloo, PCP, 2, 14, 27, 39-53, 55-61, 70, 77, ...79, 84, 103, 107, 110, 124, 139, 152, 153, ...157,.158, 193, 198, 203, 232, 244, 261, 266, ...267,.277, 279, 283, 297, 314, 342, 343
Watson, George, 38
Watson's Landing, 38
Way, Augustus Boatner, 111, 290
Way, Blanche Amanda, 290, 111
Webre, Auguste, 133
Weedman-Brodix, John, 316
Weidinger, Rizha/Rosa, 306
Weil, Alfred M. (aka Manassé Meyer), 56-59
Weil, Alphonse, 4, 8, 196, 211, 213, 222, 223-....225, 230
Weil, Amalie, 303
Weil, Amelia, 57
Weil, Amélie, 153
Weil, Arthur, 217, 218
Weil, Arthur, Jr., 217
Weil, Benjamin, 30, 31, 46, 47, 77-83, 151, 153, ...173, 276
Weil, Benjamin Alfred, 58
Weil, Caroline/Carrie, 274
Weil, Catherine, 89
Weil, Cécile, 58
Weil, Cecilia, 315
Weil, Clara, 303
Weil, Daniel, (See Davit Daÿ.)
Weil, Daniel Alfred, 58
Weil, David Leopold, 303
Weil, David T., 57
Weil, Dinah Emilie, 4, 11, 225, 228, 350
Weil, Edward, 90, 91
Weil, Edward (h/o Fannie Beer), 316
Weil, Edward Simon, 217
Weil, Émile Wolf, 303
Weil, Ernest M. 7
Weil, Félix, 196, 222
Weil, Flora Mabel, 214, 223, 226-228
Weil, Hermina, 117, 119, 227
Weil, Isaac, 31
Weil, Isaac (h/o Sarah Loeb), 117

Weil, Jacob, 303
Weil, Jacob (aka Isaac), 54
Weil, Jacques, 223
Weil, Jonathan, 221
Weil, Josephine, 217
Weil, Leah, 58
Weil, Leopold, 302
Weil, Lion, 57
Weil, Marie Manouthe, 31-33
Weil, Marx, 303
Weil, Mathilde, 49
Weil, Meyer, 51, 55
Weil, Michel, (aka Michel Veil), 29, 33, 45, 46, ...51, 52, 54-56
Weil, Robert Simon, 223
Weil, Samuel, 303
Weil, Samuel/Seligmann, 57
Weil, Sarah, 271
Weil, Simon, 217
Weil, Simon (h/o Jane Markstein), 274, 275
Weil, Simon (f/o Alphonse Weil), 222
Weil, Simon Dreyfus, 8, 11, 211, 213, 214, 223, ...225-228
Weil, Simon Jonathan, 225, 228
Weil, Simon L., 4, 175, 177, 208, 267, 331
Weil, Simone Ray, 225
Weil, Thérèse, 28, 265
Weil, William Leopold, 303, 304
Weil Plantation, 217
Weill, Abraham, 227
Weill, Arthur Gaston, 92
Weill, Bernice, 117, 225, 227
Weill, Charles, 117, 227
Weill, David, 92
Weill, Emelie Leslie, 227
Weill, Gus Solomon, 227, 228
Weill, Gustave/Godchaux, 117, 119, 227
Weill, Joseph, 117
Weill, Julius, 117-119, 322, 326
Weill, Leopold, 4, 117, 118, 225, 227
Weill, Leopold (s/o David Weil), 303
Weill, Leopold (f/o Simon Weil), 274
Weill, Leopold, Jr., 227
Weill, Lester Isaac, 117
Weill, Marie Anne, 227
Weill, Moïse, 195
Weill, Ray, 117
Weill, Ray Sarah, 117, 214, 225, 226-228
Weill, Sophie, 195
Weill(er), Jeannette, 273, 274
Weill's Department Stores, 116-119, 322, 341

Weill's Wholesale Dry Goods Co., 118
Weinberg, Abraham, 314
Weill, Harry Abraham, 233, 314, 315
Weill, Hilda Theresa, 315
Weill, Jette, 274
Weill, Joseph Lionel, 315
Weill, Julius Abram, 315
Weill, Pearl, 241
Weinberg & Mann, 314, 315
Weinfeld, Alexander, 115, 162
Weinfeld, Jacob, 115
Weinstein, Unknown, 49
Weis, Emma, 51
Weiser, Rebecca, 95
Weiterswiller, Bas-Rhin, France, 232
Welsch, Isaak, 326
Welsch, Jacques, 318, 326
Welsch, Josephine, 174
Werner, Golda, 112, 113
Westheim, Bertha, 34
Westheimer, Caroline, 183
Westhouse, Bas-Rhin, France, 150
White Castle, Iberville Parish, 225, 227, 336
White Hall Plantation, 286, 288, 305, 333, 334
White Store, 14, 85-88, 112, 269
Widow Cerf Wolff vs. Lazard Wolff, 177, 178,
....182
Wildenfeld, Mollie/Mali, 190
Wiley Barrow Plantation, 233, 237
Williamsport, PCP, 7, 8, 10, 29, 158, 176, 177,
....201, 235, 257, 259, 263, 264, 266, 267, 271-
....273, 278, 279, 283, 284, 286-292, 299, 303,
....304, 322
Winder, Sarah, 99
Wingersheim, Bas-Rhin, France, 273
Winnweiler, Rheinpfalz, Germany, 159
Wintzenheim, Haut-Rhin, France, 89
Wohl, Alvina, 186
Wolf, Aaron, 271, 272
Wolf, Bena, 303
Wolf, Gustav, 173, 245, 276
Wolf, Kathchen, 175
Wolf, Lisette, 271
Wolfe, Clarissa Ann, 245
Wolff, Abraham, 211, 214
Wolff, Bertha, 182
Wolff, Blondina, 210, 211, 214, 220, 221, 222,
....328
Wolff, Cerf Isaac, 6, 29, 48, 49, 76-78, 83, 86,
....100, 146, 157, 158, 166, 167, 176-179, 181,
....182, 184, 341

Wolff, Cornelia, 49
Wolff, David, 174
Wolff, Fannie/Jeannette, 174
Wolff, Helen, 101
Wolff, Helen (w/o Simon Meyer), 209
Wolff, Helen Madeleine, 182, 183
Wolff, Helena, 49
Wolff, Isaac, 48
Wolff, Isidore, 49, 100, 101, 103, 115, 167, 168,
....171, 176-178, 182
Wolff, Joseph, 211, 214, 215
Wolff, Lazard, 49, 176-179, 181-183, 304
Wolff, Leman/Lazare, 174
Wolff, Leopold, 49
Wolff, Lois, 101
Wolff, Lucille, 101
Wolff, Maurice, 49
Wolff, Norma, 101
Wolff, Rachel, 49, 176, 177, 182, 279, 304
Wolff, Samuel, 174
Wolff, Sara, 101
Wolff, Thérésine, 49
Woodmen of the World, 7, 89, 107, 304
Woodville, MS, 4, 48, 58, 173-175, 177, 208,
....265, 267, 317, 318, 327, 331
Würzburg, Rheinpfalz, Germany, 203
Yatter, Esther, 99
Yatter, Joseph, 99, 100
Yatter, Julius, 99
Yatter, Sarah, 99
Yawitz, Sarah, 305, 333
Yellow Fever, 3, 13, 43, 73, 282, 314
Yoist, John, 28, 128, 130, 144, 157, 161
Young America Store, 29
Youngsville, Lafayette Parish, 216
Zacharias, Nathan, 49
Zacharias, Sarah, 49, 100, 157, 158, 166, 167,
....169, 176, 177, 181, 182, 342
Zadik, Joseph, 85, 87
Zadik, Roseta/Rosette, 85, 86
Zadik, William, 85-88
Ziegler, Nellie, 310
Zillisheim, Haut-Rhin, France, 175
Zloczower, Bruine, 252
Zloczower, Leo, 253
Zloczower, Mariem, 252
Zloczower, Motel, 252
Zolynia, Galicia, 190
Zurawie, Poland, 178
Zweibrücken, Rheinpfalz, Germany, 101, 140,
....143, 187

www.ingramcontent.com/pod-product-compliance
Lightning Source LLC
Chambersburg PA
CBHW080533300426
44111CB00017B/2709